Executive Functions and the Frontal Lobes

A Lifespan Perspective

Edited by

Vicki Anderson • Rani Jacobs • Peter J. Anderson

Taylor & Francis
Taylor & Francis Group
New York   London

Taylor & Francis is an imprint of the
Taylor & Francis Group, an informa business

Psychology Press　　　　　　　　　　Psychology Press
Taylor & Francis Group　　　　　　　　Taylor & Francis Group
270 Madison Avenue　　　　　　　　　27 Church Road
New York, NY 10016　　　　　　　　　Hove, East Sussex BN3 2FA

© 2008 by Taylor & Francis Group, LLC

Printed in the United States of America on acid-free paper
10 9 8 7 6 5 4 3 2 1

International Standard Book Number-13: 978-1-84169-490-0 (Hardcover)

Library of Congress Cataloging-in-Publication Data

Executive functions and the frontal lobes : a lifespan perspective / editors, Vicki
　　Anderson, Rani Jacobs.
　　　　p. ; cm. -- (Studies on neuropsychology, neurology, and
　　cognition)
　　Includes bibliographical references and index.
　　ISBN 978-1-84169-490-0 (hardback : alk. paper)
　　1. Clinical neuropsychology. 2. Frontal lobes. 3. Developmental psychobiology.
　　4. Higher nervous activity. I. Anderson, Vicki, 1958- II. Jacobs, Rani. III. Series.
　　　　[DNLM: 1. Frontal Lobe--injuries. 2. Frontal Lobe--physiology. 3. Brain
　　Injuries--rehabilitation. 4. Cognition--physiology. 5. Models, Neurological. WL
　　307 E9512 2007]

　　QP360.E94 2007
　　616.8--dc22　　　　　　　　　　　　　　　　　　　　　　2007048863

Visit the Taylor & Francis Web site at
http://www.taylorandfrancis.com

and the Psychology Press Web site at
http://www.psypress.com

Contents

**SECTION I   A Developmental–Theoretical Framework
for Executive Function**

SECTION II   Assessment of Executive Function across the Lifespan

List of Figures

from the injured hemisphere to the intact one after injury at either age. In addition, there is reduced density of corticospinal connections bilaterally in the day 1 operates and unilaterally (on the lesion side) in the day 10 operates. The relative density of the projections is indicated by the darkness of the lines.

Figure 4.4 Cycling cells and neuroblasts migrate to the site of injury in lesion rats that receive FGF-2. Lesion rats that did not receive FGF-2 (a and b) have a prominent lesion cavity, and do not show cells migrating to the site of injury. In comparison, in the lesion rats that received FGF-2 (c, d, and e), the lesion cavity shows a number of migrating neuroblasts (doublecortin positive DCx+) as well as cycling (ki67+) cells at the site of injury at P14 as well as P21 (P21 shown here). In adulthood, the cells from the filled cavity do not show clear laminar distribution (g) compared to no lesion rats (f). The lesion rats that did not receive FGF-2 all showed a lesion cavity in adulthood (h). Multiunit recordings performed in adulthood from the filled region revealed that cells from that region spontaneously fire action potentials. Shown in (i) is an example of spontaneous activity recorded from the filled region, and the isolation of a single spike in the gray rectangle. Analyses (shown in the bar graph) revealed that the mean firing rate was greater in the cells from motor cortex (controls) than in the cells from the regrown area (lesion rats that received FGF-2). Intracortical microstimulation of the regrown region (j) elicited electromyographic activity in the wrist extensors (k) that was comparable to no lesion rats (l), suggesting that FGF-2 treatment following bilateral motor cortex injury inflicted at P10 induced a functional reconnection of the previously lesioned region to the periphery. Shown in (k) and (l) are representative EMG traces from activity recorded in the wrist extensors of a lesion FGF-2-treated rat (k) and a no lesion control rat (l), respectively.

Chapter 6

Chapter 15

Figure 15.1 Magnetic resonance (MR) scan (coronal view) of a frontotemporal dementia (FTD) patient showing atrophy in the anterior cerebral hemispheres. The arrows draw attention to the frontal lobe atrophy, which is present in both hemispheres.

Figure 15.2 Single-photon emission computed tomography (SPECT) scan (sagittal view) of a frontotemporal dementia (FTD) patient showing reduced uptake of tracer in the fronto-temporal regions. (Normal perfusion is light (parietal and occipital regions). The dark areas (frontal and temporal) indicate underperfusion, reflecting loss of function.)

Figure 15.3 Design fluency performance in a frontotemporal dementia (FTD) patient. (a) The initial items produced during the course of the test show violation of the 4-line rule and response perseveration. (b) and (c) The later items show, in addition, an increased concrete tendency. The patient draws concrete objects rather than abstract, nonrepresentational designs as instructed.

Figure 15.4 Example of test material used in a study of social cognition/theory of mind.

Chapter 16

Figure 16.1 Simplified diagram of frontostriatal circuitry underlying executive impairment in PD. Panel (a) shows disrupted connectivity postulated by the nigrostriatal hypothesis of executive dysfunction in PD. The broken line represents the nigrostriatal dopaminergic pathway, and the stippled areas indicate the structures directly affected by dopamine depletion. The heavy solid lines show the bottom-up effect of a dopamine-depleted dorsolateral caudate nucleus on an intact dorsolateral prefrontal cortex. The mesocortical hypothesis (panel b) attributes the executive dysfunction in PD to a direct dopaminergic effect on frontal cortex mediated by the mesocortical pathway (broken line). A dysfunctional or damaged dorsolateral prefrontal cortex, in turn, exerts a top-down effect on other parts of the brain. (DLPFC = dorsolateral prefrontal cortex; DL CAUD = dorsolateral head of caudate nucleus; GPN = globus pallidus; SN = substantia nigra.)

Chapter 17

Figure 17.1 A model to help plan the rehabilitation needs of patients.

Figure 17.2 Goal Management Training (GMT).

Figure 17.3 Goal Management (Problem Solving) Framework.

Figure 17.4 Planning and Problem-Solving Template.

Figure 17.5 Oliver Zangwill Centre self-monitoring sheet.

Figure 17.6 A provisional model of cognitive rehabilitation.

Chapter 18

Figure 18.1 Simple graphic organizer for narrative structure (story grammar) representing the components: Setting (characters, place, and time), initiating event, characters' reactions, plan, carrying out of the action, resolution.

Chapter 19

List of Tables

Chapter 2

Table 2.1 Structural and functional development across infancy.

Table 2.2 Structural and functional development across the preschool and early school years.

Table 2.3 Structural and functional development across late childhood.

Table 2.4 Structural and functional development across adolescence.

Table 2.5 Structural and functional changes across adulthood and older age.

Chapter 4

Table 4.1 Rules governing recovery from prefrontal injury during development in rats.

Table 4.2 Factors modulating recovery.

Chapter 5

Table 5.1 Test–retest reliability for preschool experimental executive control tasks.

Table 5.2 Task performance at the first and second administrations.

Table 5.3 Mean performance by test group.

Table 5.4 Comparison of relations of criterion measure to A-not-B and Delayed Response task indexes.

Chapter 6

Table 6.1 Commonly used executive tests in child practice.

Table 6.2 Rey Complex Figure process scoring criteria (RCF-OSS): general information and instruction.

Chapter 7

Table 7.1 Inclusion criteria.

Table 7.2 Exclusion criteria.

Table 7.3 Age, gender, and education characteristics of the sample by age group.

Table 7.4 Results of performance on the trail making test.

Chapter 19

Editors

Vicki Anderson is a pediatric neuropsychologist with 20 years experience. She started her career working at the Royal Children's Hospital in Melbourne, Australia, where she worked as a clinician, and then as Coordinator of Neuropsychology Services, until taking up a lectureship at the University of Melbourne. She has recently been appointed Professor/Director of psychology at the Royal Children's Hospital. Her interests are disorders of childhood that impact on the central nervous system, including both developmental and acquired disorders. She has published over 70 papers in this field, and has obtained competitive research grants totaling over $2,000,000. Her research group has recently established the Centre for Child Neuropsychological Studies (CNS), at the Royal Children's Hospital, Melbourne, Australia. She serves as a consulting editor on a number of prestigious international neuropsychology journals, including the *Journal of the Neuropsychological Society*, *Child Neuropsychology*, and *Pediatric Rehabilitation*, and is associate editor of *Neuropsychology*. She has co-authored two books in the field: *Developmental Neuropsychology: A Clinical Approach* and *Attention Deficit Hyperactivity Disorder: A Disease for Our Time*.

Rani Jacobs is a psychologist and research fellow at the Murdoch Childrens Research Institute, where she has been a researcher for the past 11 years. She is a fellow of the Australian Centre for Child Neuropsychological Studies and also has a private practice. Her PhD (completed 2003) focused on the development of executive skills in children with focal brain lesions and her postdoctoral research stems from this with her main focus on neurobehavioral outcome in children with developmental and acquired brain lesions. Her other research projects include the impact of various central nervous system disorders (stroke, ADEM, MS, neurofibromatosis, congenital brain lesions) on neurobehavioral outcome in children.

Peter J. Anderson is a psychologist and senior research fellow at the University of Melbourne and Murdoch Childrens Research Institute. He is codirector of the Victorian Infant Brain Studies (VIBeS) team, as well as the Australian Centre for Child Neuropsychological Studies (AC-CNS), which is the leading center for pediatric neuropsychological research in Australia. Dr. Anderson's research focuses on improving the long-term outcome for children born very preterm, and he is involved in observational outcome studies, longitudinal neuroimaging studies, and randomized controlled trials. Dr. Anderson has written over 40 peer-reviewed journal articles and book chapters, and has published in high-ranking medical and psychological journals.

Contributors

Peter J. Anderson
School of Behavioural Science
University of Melbourne
Melbourne, Australia

Vicki Anderson
Department of Psychology
Royal Children's Hospital
School of Behavioural Science
University of Melbourne
Melbourne, Australia

Megan Banet
Southern Illinois University
Carbondale, Illinois, U.S.A.

Kathleen R. Biddle
Department of Education
Juniata College
Huntingdon, Pennsylvania, U.S.A.

Jennifer Bradshaw
School of Behavioural Science
University of Melbourne
Melbourne, Australia

Rebecca Bull
University of Aberdeen
Aberdeen, Scotland, U.K.

Cathy Catroppa
Department of Psychology
Royal Children's Hospital
School of Behavioural Science
University of Melbourne
Melbourne, Australia

Cinzia R. De Luca
Department of Psychology
Melbourne Neuropsychiatry Centre
Royal Children's Hospital
School of Behavioural Science
University of Melbourne
Melbourne, Australia

Paul J. Eslinger
Department of Neurology, Behavioural
  Sciences, Pediatrics and Radiology
College of Medicine
Pennsylvania State University and
  Hershey Medical Center
Hershey, Pennsylvania, U.S.A.

Kimberly Andrews Espy
University of Nebraska
Lincoln, Nebraska, U.S.A.

Jonathan Evans
Department of Psychological Medicine
University of Glasgow
Glasgow, Scotland, U.K.

Timothy Feeney
School of Community Support
  Services
Schenectady, New York, U.S.A.

Gerard A. Gioia
Children's National Medical Center
Washington, D.C., U.S.A.

A. Simon Harvey
Children's Neurosciences Centre
Royal Children's Hospital
University of Melbourne
Melbourne, Australia

Julie D. Henry
School of Psychology
University of New South Wales
Sydney, Australia

Kelly Howard
Department of Psychology
Royal Children's Hospital
School of Behavioural Science
University of Melbourne
Melbourne, Australia

Peter K. Isquith
Dartmouth Medical School
Hanover, New Hampshire, U.S.A.

Rani Jacobs
Department of Psychology
Royal Children's Hospital
School of Psychology
University of Melbourne
Melbourne, Australia

Heather Kaiser
Southern Illinois University
Carbondale, Illinois, U.S.A.

Laura E. Kenealy
Children's National Medical Center
Washington, D.C., U.S.A.

Bryan Kolb
Canadian Centre for Behavioural
  Neuroscience
University of Lethbridge
Lethbridge, Alberta, Canada

Richard J. Leventer
Children's Neuroscience Centre
Murdoch Children's Research
  Institute
University of Melbourne
Melbourne, Australia

Jessica Martin
Southern Illinois University
Carbondale, Illinois, U.S.A.

Skye McDonald
School of Psychology
University of New South Wales
Sydney, Australia

Marie Monfils
Canadian Centre for Behavioural
  Neuroscience
University of Lethbridge
Lethbridge, Alberta, Canada

Louise H. Phillips
School of Psychology
University of Aberdeen
Aberdeen, Scotland, U.K.

Michael M. Saling
School of Behavioural Science
University of Melbourne
Melbourne, Australia

Nicole Sherren
Canadian Centre for Behavioural
  Neuroscience
University of Lethbridge
Lethbridge, Alberta, Canada

Elizabeth Smith
Murdoch Children's Research
   Institute
La Trobe University
Melbourne, Australia

Julie Snowden
Cerebral Function Unit
Greater Manchester Neuroscience
   Centre
Salford Royal Hospitals Trust
Manchester, U.K.

Megan Spencer Smith
Department of Psychology
Royal Children's Hospital
School of Behavioural Science
University of Melbourne
Melbourne, Australia

H. Gerry Taylor
Case Western Reserve University
Rainbow Babies and Children's
   Hospital
Cleveland, Ohio, U.S.A.

Tracey Wardill
Melbourne Neuropsychology Services
School of Behavioural Science
University of Melbourne
Melbourne, Australia

Barbara A. Wilson
Medical Research Centre
Cognitive and Brain Sciences Unit
Cambridge

and

The Oliver Zangwill Centre
   for Neuropsychological
   Rehabilitation
Ely, Cambridge, U.K.

Amanda G. Wood
Department of Medicine
   (Neurosciences)
Monash University
Melbourne, Australia

Keith Owen Yeates
Department of Pediatrics
Ohio State University

and

Department of Psychology
Nationwide Children's Hospital
Columbus, Ohio, U.S.A.

Mark Ylvisaker
School of Education
College of Saint Rose
Albany, New York, U.S.A.

Note from the Series Editor

"Executive functioning" is an often cited but often misused term, both as a clinical concept and as a clinical descriptor for the functional contributions of the frontal cortex to behavior. This impressive volume, edited by Vicki Anderson, Rani Jacobs, and Peter Anderson, presents a unique understanding of executive functioning and how its components relate to anatomical subdivisions of the frontal lobes and their role as components in broad brain–behavior systems. The frontal lobes have also long been understood to have a clear developmental aspect in their participation in overall brain function, ranging from the regulation of attention and the acquisition of knowledge to the development of systems of behavioral control, to the impact of decreasing participation of brain–behavior systems in normal aging and in various dementing conditions.

The editors have gathered an impressive array of renowned experts as contributors, whose contributions to the understanding of executive functions and their relationship to the frontal lobes are well known. How developmental changes affect frontal cortical influence on behavior, how injury can disrupt it, and how the impact can be measured are all addressed here. Most importantly, the book also addresses what is known about potential interventions for executive dysfunction, all within the context of state-of-the-art and evidence-based approaches. The most recent evidence from animal and human experiments, behavioral descriptions, functional neuroimaging, and clinical experience is incorporated in achieving what is very likely one of the finest texts to address this topic. *Executive Functions and the Frontal Lobes: A Lifespan Perspective* deserves a prominent place in the library of all students, researchers, and practitioners who seek a contemporary understanding of this topic. This will include psychologists, neuropsychologists, neurologists, and psychiatrists among many others who focus their clinical skills on patients affected with brain–behavior syndromes and seek further understanding of behavioral organization through their research endeavors. After reading this book, it is safe to say the global term "frontal lobe syndrome" will transform from common use as a catchall phrase to a sophisticated construct for complex brain–behavior interactions, which this text elucidates. It is a proud addition to our series.

Linas Bieliauskas
Ann Arbor

Preface

Executive Functions and the Frontal Lobes: A Lifespan Perspective, or, as we first conceptualized it, "the rise and fall of the frontal lobes," was conceived over many lively discussions and debates among clinicians, researchers, and inquiring students, bemoaning the complexities of grappling with the notion of executive function and its cerebral underpinnings, and marveling at the striking observation that there are indeed many similarities between pediatric and geriatric populations and practice, most particularly with respect to the frontal lobes and executive function. The dilemma is exacerbated by the relative dearth of research and theory relating directly to children and older people and the developing/degenerating brain. At every turn we meet obstacles—there are no established and agreed definitions or models of this abstract construct; the measures available are often unable to quantify the often striking clinical observations of executive dysfunction or to detect the debilitating problems described by children and older people in their daily lives; the traditional clinical assessment context is frequently inadequate to capture presenting complaints; and rehabilitation approaches often avoid addressing these problems due to pessimistic reports of executive dysfunction incorporating lack of insight, and inability to generalize and make use of therapeutic interventions.

With this book, we address some of these limitations within the field, in an attempt to assist us, and our readers, in gaining a better understanding of these unresolved issues. The book and its philosophy derive from our clinical and research practices with children and older adults. We sought to include contributions from clinicians and researchers, with a fundamental requirement being an evidence-based approach to understanding executive skills. We have taken some steps toward developing a more cohesive definition of executive skills and to exploring the possibility of a model of executive function, which incorporated the processes that take place across the lifespan. However, being a clinical research team, it was also critical to include work that contributed to our knowledge and practice in the area of assessment and diagnosis of executive function. We endeavor to encompass the varying models of assessment, including traditional psychometric and hypothesis-based approaches, together with more recently emerging genetic and neuroimaging techniques, as we believe each of these methods is critical not only for the reliable assessment of executive abilities but also for accurate diagnosis in age groups where these skills might be maturing or degenerating. Finally, we look to complete the picture by including a range of contemporary perspectives for the treatment of executive dysfunction, in order to provide readers with ideas about how these complex problems can be managed and treated to ensure maximal quality of life for our patients and their families. Again we focus on intervention models, which are founded on theoretical principles and whose effectiveness has been supported by empirical data.

A brief history of executive functions: Definitions and models

Over the last few decades the notion of executive function has received increasing attention; however, reports of executive type deficits can be found in the literature more than a century ago. Phineas Gage is the earliest and best cited example of the impact of frontal lobe pathology on executive function. After having a tamping iron penetrate his skull and damage his frontal cortex, his erratic behavior and debilitating personality change were well documented (Harlow, 1948). More recent interest in these abilities emerged in the context of a small number of fascinating case reports and case series, which described similar abnormal cognition and behavior following war injuries (Luria, 1966, 1973) and frontal lobectomy for psychiatric conditions (Walsh, 1978). From these clinical data, early theories emerged (Fuster, 1989; Mesulem, 2002; Shallice, 1990; Stuss & Benson, 1986), although these were almost universally limited to the cognitive domain. Initial models of executive function opted to explain these cognitive abilities using a unitary, homogenous framework, where specific components of executive function were not identified and where the biological basis was simply allocated to the frontal lobes. While superficially appealing, the limitations of such an "umbrella" concept were soon realized, as those working in the field observed different patterns of deficit across individual patients and patient groups and noted that varying pathology sites within the frontal lobes did not necessarily produce the same behavioral profiles. Today, executive functions are acknowledged to represent a highly complex, interrelated set of cognitive abilities, which are critical for adaptive function.

Debate remains about the characteristics that define a process as "executive," and about which abilities should be considered when conceptualizing the construct. We have chosen to adopt an inclusive approach, which incorporates a wide range of skills and functions that are important to "enable a person to engage successfully in purposeful, self-serving behaviors" (Lezak, 1995, p. 42), and which are activated in novel or unfamiliar circumstances, where no previously established routines for responding exist (Shallice, 1990; Walsh, 1978). In taking this approach we acknowledge the lessons learnt from Phineas Gage, as well as contemporary developments in the field that distinguish between the traditional "cold" or cognitive aspects of executive function, as well as the more recently described "hot" or social/affective dimension. This extension of the executive construct provides an exciting opportunity not only to understand social/affective functions and their biological underpinnings but also to link them with cognitive functions, to provide a more holistic perspective on executive dysfunction. The following chapters reflect this approach, incorporating elements that are not necessarily encompassed by all, or even the most established, executive models, such as attention, information processing, working memory, and social skills.

The frontal lobes and executive function: Are they synonymous?

It is probably fair to say, from the current vantage point of technological change and theoretical development, that early views of the cerebral underpinning of executive function were as unsophisticated as the psychological construct itself. Initially, in the context of human lesion studies, it was accepted that executive functions were subsumed by frontal structures. Later, as localization models became more refined, the prefrontal cortex was identified as the seat of these functions. This approach made many assumptions about the links between the frontal lobes and executive functions, leading to terminology such as "frontal lobe syndrome," which confused anatomical and behavioral dimensions, and provoked much debate in neuropsychological circles between those who viewed executive functions as a psychometric construct and those who believed that standardized multidimensional psychological tests could provide a direct measure of the activity occurring within the frontal lobes.

A number of lines of research have assisted the field in moving this debate forward. Using well-controlled experiments, animal work has examined normal developmental trajectories as well as the impact of injury within the frontal lobes, demonstrating that at least some specific components of executive function can be localized to these regions (e.g., inhibitory control, working memory, and social processing) (Fuster, 2002; Pellis et al., 2006; Robbins, 2000). Recent advances in neuroimaging, particularly functional imaging, have supported these findings, documenting a range of functional networks that incorporate frontal regions and allocate them particular tasks (D'Esposito et al., 1995; Goldman-Rakic & Leung, 2002; Moll et al., 2002; Tulving et al., 1996). Finally, moving forward from case descriptions, human lesion work has become more sophisticated, and there are now numerous rigorous empirical reports, primarily focused on adult samples that provide evidence for links between specific elements of executive function and focal regions within the prefrontal cortex (Bouquet, Bonnaud, & Gil, 2003; Lough, Gregory, & Hodges, 2001; Stuss, 1992).

Despite the building evidence base supporting a key role for the frontal lobes, and prefrontal cortex in particular, in mediating executive function, each of these research endeavors has also documented findings consistent with the argument that executive functions and frontal lobes are not synonymous. Rather, while the prefrontal cortex clearly plays a critical role in executive function, it appears to be increasingly accepted that this region does not act in isolation, but is part of a broader functional system, which involves other brain regions. Further, it may be that for children and older adults, where brain structure and function are more fluid, the role of the prefrontal cortex is further diminished, with executive abilities requiring the integrity of the entire brain for effective function (Anderson, Jacobs, & Harvey, 2005; Grady, McIntosh, & Craik, 2005; Jacobs & Anderson, 2002). The extension of empirical research into these age groups has the potential to further determine the limits of the frontal lobe-executive function relationship, across the lifespan. To this end, the following chapters will discuss this issue, in the context of both theoretical and clinical debate.

Developmental perspectives

Examining both ends of the age spectrum, it appears that there is a sequence for the maturation of the frontal lobes, which parallels the emergence of aspects of executive function, and the possibility that degenerative processes in old age may mirror this sequence. Imaging studies also identify parallels across these age groups, with both the young and the old demonstrating more distributed brain activation patterns than those of healthy adults (Grady et al., 2005; Wood et al., 2004), suggesting that a number of cerebral regions may be necessary for the efficient execution of more demanding aspects of executive tasks in these age groups. Several chapters will comment on the similarities and differences in developmental trajectories and clinical characteristics, which are observed when comparing children and the elderly in the executive domain.

With these fundamental developmental issues in mind, it is clearly important for any framework of executive function to have relevance across the lifespan it needs to take account of developmental processes. Until recently, few attempts had been made to include the full lifespan when conceptualizing executive abilities; however, recently a number of impressive attempts have been made to rectify this limitation. For example, Andres and Van der Linden (2000) have reported on age effects for the supervisory attentional system, as have Baddeley et al. (1991) for working memory, while others have put forward broader models, specific for particular age groups (Albert & Kaplan, 1980; Anderson, 2002; Salthouse, 1999; Zelazo, Qu, & Muller, 2004). A number of the following chapters will discuss, evaluate, and extend these models, with a view to achieving a single "lifespan" perspective.

Assessment issues

A final, though integral, challenge within the field of executive function is that of valid and reliable assessment. Dilemmas exist at multiple levels: Are our standard measures sensitive to subtle executive deficits? Which test variables tap into executive abilities specifically, and how can we ensure their integrity? What developmental factors do we need to take into account when conducting an assessment? Does the structure of the clinic environment mask executive dysfunction? What is the role of qualitative observation in the detection of executive dysfunction? Should we use multiple contexts and informants for accurate assessment and diagnosis of these difficulties? What is the role of neuroimaging in clinical practice?

It has become clear in recent times that executive deficits are often difficult to identify within the clinical context, using traditional psychometrically sound measures. There are a number of explanations for these limitations. First, the typical clinic environment provides artificial structure and order, and does not simulate the more demanding day-to-day situations experienced by the individual. To facilitate more ecologically valid assessment, it is important to incorporate data from multiple settings (e.g., school, home) and informants (e.g., school, home), and to include more functional measures of executive skills (e.g., parents, peers, self-ratings). Second, the use of psychometrically supportable, but multifactorial summary scores are necessarily limited in detecting specific executive abilities, as they necessarily tap into a range of other, nonexecutive cognitive skills. As a consequence, quantitative test data may need to be supplemented with qualitative observations and by employing "microanalytic" techniques in an attempt to distinguish specific executive elements within test performances. Finally, consideration of age-related factors is crucial for accurate diagnosis in pediatric and geriatric populations. In children, where executive skills are emerging, routine adult test paradigms, such as copying complex geometric designs or generating words under specific conditions, may reflect impairments in lower order skills such as motor coordination or articulation, respectively, rather than in higher order executive domains. Within the elderly, issues such as deteriorating sight and hearing may lead to performances that could be misinterpreted as indicating executive impairments.

These issues are all canvassed in the text and will provide the reader with important insights into appropriate clinical practice across the lifespan and the additional steps required to meeting these standards when working with children and the older people.

Approaches to the management and intervention of executive impairments

Early unitary views of executive impairment or "frontal lobe syndrome" painted a pessimistic picture of the potential for rehabilitation and recovery. The assumption was that, where such impairments were present, they would be characterized by a lack of insight, unmanageable behavior, and problems generalizing therapeutic training to daily life, which would interfere with the goals of treatment and its long-term efficacy. Thus, patients presenting with frontal lobe pathology were frequently considered untreatable. Along with the maturation of the concept of executive function comes the notion that not all victims of frontal lobe injury and executive impairment necessarily experience these problems. Further, depending on the nature of the insult, cognitive and affective deficits may be quite circumscribed, leaving the potential for compensation via intact abilities.

The final section of this book addresses evidence-based models of treating executive impairments. Each provides a theoretical framework for its treatment philosophy, and all argue that interventions need to be context specific to have maximal benefit. Specific techniques and outcomes from these approaches are discussed, based on case study and group data, providing the reader with a practical guide to effective intervention for executive problems.

Concluding comments and acknowledgments

We hope that this work appeals to a range of readers interested in the area of executive functions, from clinical, research, educative, and treatment perspectives. We believe that it represents one of the few attempts in the field to provide an overview of executive functions across the lifespan and to highlight some of the similarities and differences that may be present from childhood to old age.

We would like to thank the many people who contributed to the final product. First to those who provided the content: we thank you for your generosity in joining us in this venture, and your patience and timeliness in bringing the book to completion. In addition, a number of individuals have tirelessly worked to provide chapter reviews: Cathy Catroppa, Linda Gonzalez, Anna Mandalis, Lis Northam, and Robyn Stargatt, while others, including our many curious and questioning postgraduate students, who have challenged us to seek a better understanding of the concepts we are encouraging them to study. We would also like to acknowledge the administrative support of our team: Mary Iliadis, Nicholas Anderson, Inge Timmerman, and Lee-Ann Jones.

Finally, we want to thank our families and acknowledge their patience and support in this project.

Vicki Anderson
Rani Jacobs
Peter J. Anderson

References

Albert, M. S., & Kaplan, E. (1980). Organic implications of neuropsychological deficits in the elderly. In L. W. Poon, J. L. Fozard, L. S. Cermak, D. Arenberg, & L. W. Thompson (Eds.), *New directions in memory and aging* (pp. 403–432). Hillsdale, NJ: Erlbaum.

Anderson, P. (2002). Assessment and development of executive function (EF) during childhood. *Child Neuropsychology, 8*(2), 71–82.

Anderson, V., Jacobs, R., & Harvey, A. H. (2005). Prefrontal lesions and attentional skills in childhood. *Journal of the International Neuropsychological Society, 11*, 817–831.

Andres, P., & Van der Linden, M. (2000). Age-related differences in supervisory attentional system functions. *Journal of Gerontology: Psychological Sciences, 55*, 373–380.

Baddeley, A., Della Sala, S., Logie, R., & Spinnler, H. (1991). The decline of working memory in Alzheimer's disease: A longitudinal study. *Brain, 114*, 2521–2542.

Bouquet, C. A., Bonnaud, V., & Gil, R. (2003). Investigation of supervisory attentional system functions in patients with Parkinson's disease using the Hayling task. *Journal of Clinical and Experimental Neuropsychology, 25*(6), 751–760.

D'Esposito, M., Detre, J. A., Alsop, D. C., Shin, R. K., Atlas, S., & Grossman, M. (1995). The neural basis of the central executive system of working memory. *Nature, 378* (6554), 279–281.

Fuster, J. (2002). Physiology of executive functions: The perception-action cycle. In D. Stuss & R. Knight (Eds.), *Principles of frontal lobe function* (pp. 96–108). New York: Oxford University Press.

Fuster, J. M. (1989). *The prefrontal cortex*. New York: Raven Press.

Goldman-Rakic, P., & Leung, H. (2002). Functional architecture of the dorsolateral prefrontal cortex in monkeys and humans. In D. Stuss & R. Knight (Eds.), *Principles of frontal lobe function* (pp. 85–95). New York: Oxford University Press.

Grady, C. L., McIntosh, A. R., & Craik, F. I. M. (2005). Task-related activity in prefrontal cortex and its relation to recognition memory performance in young and old adults. *Neuropsychologia, 43*, 1466–1481.

Harlow, J. (1948). Passage of an iron rod through the head. *Boston Medical and Surgical Journal, 39*, 389–393.

Jacobs, R., & Anderson, V. (2002). Planning and problem solving skills following focal frontal brain lesions in childhood: Analysis using the Tower of London. *Child Neuropsychology, 8,* 93–106.

Lezak, M. D. (1995). *Neuropsychological assessment.* New York: Oxford University Press.

Lough, S., Gregory, C., & Hodges, J. R. (2001). Dissociation of social cognition and executive function in frontal variant frontotemporal dementia. *Neurocase, 7,* 123–130.

Luria, A. (1973). *The working brain.* New York: Basic Books.

Luria, A. R. (1966). *Higher cortical functions in man.* New York: Basic Books.

Mesulem, M. (2002). The human frontal lobes: Transcending the default mode through contingent encoding. In D. Stuss & R. Knight (Eds.), *Principles of frontal lobe function* (pp. 8–31). New York: Oxford University Press.

Moll, J., Oliveira-Souza, R., Eslinger, P. J., Bramati, I. E., Mourao-Miranda, J., Andreiuolo, P. A., & Pessoa, L. (2002). The neural correlates of moral sensitivity: A functional magnetic resonance imaging investigation of basic and moral emotions. *Journal of Neuroscience, 22,* 2730–2736.

Pellis, S. M., Hastings, E., Takeshi, T., Kamitakahara, H., Komorowska, J., Forgie, M. L., & Kolb, B. (2006). The effects of orbital frontal cortex damage on the modulation of defensive responses by rats in playful and non-playful social contexts. *Behavioral Neuroscience, 120*(1), 72–84.

Robbins, T. (2000). Dissociating executive functions of the prefrontal cortex. In A. Roberts, T. Robbins, & L. Weiskrantz (Eds.), *The prefrontal cortex* (pp. 117–130). New York: Oxford University Press.

Salthouse, T. A. (1999). Theories of cognition. In K. W. Schaie (Ed.), *Handbook of theories of aging* (pp. 196–208). New York: Springer.

Shallice, T. (1990). *From neuropsychology to mental structure.* New York: Oxford University Press.

Stuss, D. T. (1992). Biological and psychological development of executive functions. *Brain and Cognition, 20*(1), 8–23.

Stuss, D. T., & Benson, D. F. (1986). *The Frontal Lobes.* New York: Ravens Press.

Tulving, E., Marvowitsch, H., Craik, F., Habib, R., & Houle, S. (1996). Novelty and familiarity activations in PET studies of memory encoding and retrieval. *Cortex, 6,* 71–79.

Walsh, K. (1978). *Neuropsychology: A clinical approach.* New York: Churchill Livingston.

Wood, A., Harvey, A. S., Wellard, M., Abbott, D., Anderson, V., Kean, M., Saling, M., & Jackson, G. (2004). Language cortex activation in normal children. *Neurology, 63,* 1035–1044.

Zelazo, P. D., Qu, L., & Muller, U. (2004). Hot and cool aspects of executive function: Relations in early development. In W. Schneider, R. Schumann-Hengsteler, & B. Sodian (Eds.), *Young children's cognitive development: Interrelationships among executive functioning, working memory, verbal ability, and theory of mind* (pp. 71–93). Mahwah, NJ: Lawrence Eribaum.

Section I

A developmental–theoretical framework for executive function

1   Towards a developmental model of executive function

Peter J. Anderson

Contents

Executive function is not a unitary cognitive process, but instead is a psychological construct that is composed of multiple interrelated high-level cognitive skills. A plethora of definitions for this construct have been proposed, and while these definitions are general and broad due to the construct's multiplicity, common themes are clearly present. There is also some agreement with regards to the skill set that falls under the umbrella of executive function. Various theoretical models of executive function have been developed, and these models have influenced research and clinical practices. Operational, or clinically relevant, frameworks for this construct are important as they provide the basis for assessment tools, interpreting test performance and everyday behavior, and understanding executive function development. The aim of this chapter is to review relevant conceptual models and frameworks of executive function in order to provide a more thorough understanding of the conceptual and clinical issues associated with this psychological construct.

Executive function

Before discussing conceptual models or clinical frameworks it is necessary to define executive function. Descriptions of executive function indicate that it encompasses the highest levels of human functioning such as intellect, thought, self-control, and social interaction (David, 1992). Not only is executive function responsible for the synthesis of external stimuli, preparation for action and formation of programs, but it is also critical for allowing action to take place and for verifying that it has taken the proper course (Luria, 1973). Lezak (1982) describes executive processes as those mental capacities necessary for formulating goals, planning how to achieve them, and carrying out these plans effectively. She suggests that they are the heart of all socially useful, personally enhancing, constructive, and creative activities. Similarly, Welsh and Pennington (1988) define executive function as "the ability to maintain an appropriate problem-solving set for attainment of a future goal," comprising the capacity to inhibit or defer a response, to strategically plan future actions, and to maintain a mental representation of the desired goal stated and the information presented. Thus, executive function is a collection of interrelated functions, or processes, which are responsible for goal-directed or future-oriented behavior, and has been referred to as the "conductor" which controls, organizes, and directs cognitive activity, emotional responses and behavior (Gioia, Isquith, & Guy, 2001). The key elements of executive function include (a) anticipation and deployment of attention; (b) impulse control and self-regulation; (c) initiation of activity; (d) working memory; (e) mental flexibility and utilization of feedback; (f) planning ability and organization; and (g) selection of efficient problem-solving strategies. Executive function is not exclusive to cognitive processes, but is also characterized in emotional responses and behavioral actions (Gioia, Isquith, Guy, & Kenworthy, 2000). As such, it has been recently proposed that the processes that constitute executive function could be dichotomized as "cool" executive processes or "hot" executive processes (Zelazo, Qu, & Muller, 2004). "Cool" executive processes are considered purely cognitive, and tapped during abstract, decontextualized problems. In contrast, "hot" executive processes refer to affective aspects of executive functioning and are required when a situation is meaningful and involves the regulation of affect and motivation.

Impaired executive functioning, sometimes referred to as executive dysfunction, is not a unitary disorder. A variety of presentations can describe executive dysfunction including an inability to focus or maintain attention, impulsivity, disinhibition, reduced working memory, difficulties monitoring or regulating performance, inability to plan actions in advance, disorganization, poor reasoning ability, difficulties generating and/or implementing strategies, perseverative behavior, a resistance to change activities, difficulties shifting between conflicting demands, and a failure to learn from mistakes. Not surprisingly, executive dysfunction is usually associated with academic or workplace concerns. Executive dysfunction may also be associated with maladaptive affect, energy level, initiative, and moral and social behavior (Anderson, Bechara, Damasio, Tranel, & Damasio, 1999; Eslinger, Grattan, Damasio, & Damasio, 1992; Grattan & Eslinger, 1991). For example, patients with executive dysfunction may present as apathetic, unmotivated, and unresponsive, or impulsive and argumentative. They may ask embarrassing or socially inappropriate questions, make hurtful statements, struggle to appreciate humor, or tell distasteful jokes. These patients commonly disregard the consequences of actions and ignore social rules and conventions. As a consequence, many patients exhibiting executive dysfunction display poor interpersonal skills and experience difficulties maintaining meaningful social relationships. In a developmental context, some of these behaviors may not be considered 'deviant,' as in the case of an infant or young child. Therefore, it is critical that developmental expectations of executive processes are well understood.

From this description of executive function it is obvious that attention processes are either essential subordinate skills of this construct, or can in themselves, be considered executive processes. For example, selective and sustained attention, inhibition, and shifting attention are cognitive processes that are often tapped during goal-directed future-oriented behaviors. In fact Barkley (1996) argues that the executive system could be considered a general form of attention. He argues that attention relates to the individual's response to an event to achieve an immediate change in the environment, while executive function is "attention to the self."

Some individuals with significant executive deficits score within normal ranges on tests of intelligence, which has been used as evidence to the claim that executive functioning is unrelated to general intelligence (Friedman et al., 2006). Duncan, Burgess, and Emslie (1995) proposed that the poor agreement between performance on executive and standard intelligence measures could be explained by the relative dependence of standard intelligence tests on crystallized intelligence (i.e., acquired knowledge) rather than fluid intelligence (i.e., reasoning and problem solving). However, a number of studies have reported an association between specific executive domains and intelligence (Luciano et al., 2001; Miyake, Friedman, Emerson, Witzki, & Howerter, 2000; Miyake, Friedman, Rettinger, Shah, & Hegarty, 2001), and a recent study by Friedman et al. (2006) suggests that executive processes are differentially related to general intelligence. For example, working memory appears to be most strongly associated with intelligence, while other executive domains such as inhibition and flexibility correlate weakly with intelligence measures. Interestingly, Friedman et al. (2006) also found that these relationships were consistent regardless of intelligence measure (crystallized, fluid, or general intelligence).

Traditionally it has been argued that executive skills are only activated in novel or complex activities, such as when the individual is required to inhibit behavior, formulate new plans and strategies, and monitor performance. In contrast, simple or routinized tasks were thought to be performed instinctively, and therefore, without the activation of executive processes (Shallice, 1990). Consistent with this premise, Walsh (1978) states that in order to assess executive functioning a test needs to be novel, complex, and involve the integration of information. However, defining a task as routine, overlearned, complex, or novel is not always straightforward as what may be complex or novel for one person may be simple or routine for another (Alexander & Stuss, 2000; Gioia et al., 2001; Stuss & Alexander, 2000). In other words, the level of executive control needed to complete a specific task is likely to vary across individuals. Furthermore, some theorists claim that all cognitive tests involve executive functioning to some extent (Alexander & Stuss, 2000; Della Sala, Gray, Spinnler, & Trivelli, 1998; Denckla, 1994). For example, Barkley (1997a) claims that any activity that involves verbal instructions, especially when the instructions compete with environmental stimuli, is drawing on executive processes.

It is well accepted that anterior regions of the brain mediate executive functioning, at least to some extent (Lezak, 1995; Stuss et al., 2002). This conclusion has been derived from research that shows executive deficits often follow damage to the prefrontal cortex (Grattan & Eslinger, 1991; Stuss et al., 2002; Stuss & Benson, 1984), as well as functional neuroimaging studies that report significant activation within the prefrontal cortex while performing executive function measures

(Baker et al., 1996; Morris, Ahmed, Syed, & Toone, 1993; Rezai et al., 1993). Executive processes are associated with numerous, complex, and interrelated frontal neural systems, which is not surprising given that the prefrontal cortex is dependent on efferent and afferent connections with virtually all other brain regions including the brain stem, occipital, temporal, and parietal lobes, as well as limbic and subcortical regions (Fuster, 1993; Stuss & Benson, 1984). Damage or loss of function at any level of one these neural systems is expected to result in executive deficits (Lezak, 1995). Thus, executive dysfunction is not always associated with prefrontal pathology directly, but may be related to network disconnections such as white matter damage or impairment to other brain regions (Alexander & Stuss, 2000; Andres, 2003; Eslinger & Grattan, 1993; Stuss et al., 2002). In summary, it may be argued that the integrity of the prefrontal cortex is a necessary, but not a sufficient, condition for intact executive functioning (Della Sala et al., 1998).

Given that the anterior regions of the brain play an important role in higher-order cognitive functioning (Fuster, 1993; Luria, 1973; Stuss & Benson, 1984; Walsh, 1978), "executive function" and "frontal lobe function" have sometimes been used interchangeably (Stuss & Alexander, 2000). However, "frontal lobe functioning" and "executive functioning" are now considered separate but related concepts (Stuss, 1992, 2006), as damage to the frontal lobes does not always result in executive dysfunction (Roberts, Robbins, & Weiskrantz, 1998; Stuss & Benson, 1984), and diffuse brain injury can lead to impairment of various executive processes even without frontal involvement (Stuss, 2006). Thus, executive processes may be subsumed by the prefrontal cortex, but they are also dependent on posterior and subcortical regions of the brain. In summary, executive function is a psychological construct, but the concomitant neural systems (i.e., prefrontal cortex and related systems) provide important information about specific processes and the integration of these functions.

Models of executive function

Neuropsychological models clearly provide a theoretical framework for the assessment of cognitive domains. To be useful, a model should be theoretically valid, integrate all aspects of the construct, account for different patterns of impairment, propose specific brain–behavior relations, and translate to assessment methodologies (Gioia et al., 2001). While a number of conceptual models of executive function have been proposed, no model has been uniformly accepted. The underlying assumptions and rationale for devising these models differ, which explains to a large extent why the various models are so disparate. For example, some of these models focus on a specific executive domain such as working memory (Baddeley, 1996, 2000, 2002) or self-regulation (Barkley, 1997b), while other theories are developmentally oriented (Anderson, 2002; Dennis, 1991). Further, while some are based primarily on clinical perspectives, other theorists have employed statistical approaches to derive their models.

Early attempts to conceptualize executive function resulted in unitary models such as the "central executive"(Baddeley, 1986) or "supervisory activating system" (Norman & Shallice, 1986), however subsequent research has demonstrated that a modular unit is too simplistic and that the construct is more likely to be composed of distinct but interrelated components (Baddeley, 1998; Parkin, 1998). Evidence for the fractionation of executive function derives from several key findings: patients rarely exhibit global executive dysfunction (Bigler, 1988; Grattan & Eslinger, 1991; Pennington & Ozonoff, 1996); executive processes can be localized within the prefrontal cortex (Courtney, Petit, Maisong, Ungerleider, & Haxby, 1998; Rezai et al., 1993; Stuss et al., 2002); measures of executive processes correlate poorly (Cripe, 1996; Della Sala et al., 1998); factor analytic studies identify multiple factors (Lehto, Juujarvi, Kooistra, & Pulkkinen, 2003; Miyake et al., 2000); and the developmental trajectories of specific executive processes vary (Anderson, 2002; Welsh, Pennington, & Groisser, 1991). As a consequence, concepts such as the "central executive" and "supervisory system" have been modified including an attempt to fractionate subcomponents of the various control systems (Baddeley, 1996; Shallice & Burgess, 1996). However, while the executive function may comprise several distinct processes, they are interrelated and could still be conceptualized, and referred to, as an integrated supervisory or control system (Alexander & Stuss, 2000; Stuss & Alexander, 2000). Following is a brief review of prominent contemporary executive function models and frameworks.

Supervisory attentional system

The "supervisory attentional system" (SAS) is a widely adopted conceptualization of executive function. It was first introduced by Norman and Shallice (1986) in a broad model regarding the role of attention in active behaviors. This model differentiates actions that are automatic and those that require "deliberate attentional resources." Automatic responses are those that are performed without awareness of their performance, can be initiated without deliberate attention, and are performed without interfering with other actions. In contrast, situations that require deliberate attention include those that involve planning or decision making, troubleshooting, a novel sequence of actions, overcoming a strong habitual response or resisting temptation, or situations that are dangerous or technically difficult. To deal with these two levels of action, Norman and Shallice proposed a model that included two complementary processes: contention scheduling and SAS.

Contention scheduling is for responses that are implemented automatically. This process schedules well-formed schemata for completing an automatic action, but it also inhibits conflicting schemata. Schemata are essentially behavioral programs for completing routine tasks or skills. Given a number of competing schemata may be available and share common structures and operations, contention scheduling resolves conflicts on the basis of activation values, which are determined by a combination of factors such as how well matched the schema is to the required action and environmental factors. The selected schema continues to operate until it has achieved its goal, it has been blocked or actively switched off, or conditions alter such that some other more highly activated schema is utilized. However, schemata are unlikely to exist when the task is novel or complex, such as those involving executive functioning. According to Norman and Shallice (1986), in these situations additional attentional control is required, which is the role of the supervisory attentional system.

Shallice and Burgess (1996) expanded on this initial model, specifically focussing on the supervisory system. While they argued that the supervisory system is a globally integrated system, they acknowledged that it performs a variety of processes that are carried out by different "subsystems." The model proposed by Shallice and Burgess (1996) argues that the supervisory system comprise three stages and multiple processes, all of which involve the prefrontal cortex.

- *Stage 1* involves constructing new "temporary" schemata for the novel situation, and this stage may be referred to as strategy generation. Problem solving is a common approach of generating new strategies. This involves problem orientation, goal setting (what needs to be achieved), and subsequent phases of "deepening of a solving attempt," and the assessment of the solution attempt. Alternatively, temporary new schemata can occur spontaneously, that is, devised to tackle a specific situation without an explicit attempt to solve a problem. Strategy generation can also take place in advance, such that a strategy is prepared for a specific situation that might arise in the future.
- *Stage 2* is the implementation of the new temporary schema for the novel situation. Shallice and Burgess (1996) state that this will involve working memory for the specific purpose of holding online the "temporally active schema."
- *Stage 3* is the process whereby the implementation of schema is monitored, and can result in schema being rejected or modified if deemed ineffective.

The supervisory system may perform a range of processes and involve a variety of subsystems differentially localized within the prefrontal cortex, however Shallice and Burgess (1996) believe it represents a single system as these subsystems are operating interactively within an overall processing system in order to achieve a common overall function.

The supervisory system has also been adopted by Stuss and colleagues for the specific role of characterizing anterior attentional functions (Stuss, Shallice, Alexander, & Picton, 1995). In this model, the supervisory system is utilized when there is no established solution to the task, when the selection between schemata is necessary, when the inhibition of inappropriate schemata is required, and when weakly activated schemata are evoked. In this model, five independent supervisory processes are proposed: energization of schemata, inhibition of schemata, adjustment of contention scheduling, monitoring schemata activity, and control of "if-then" logical processes.

1. *Energizing schemata* refers to the activation of target schemata and the reenergizing of the schemata as they become inactive, such as in situations that require the maintenance of attention.
2. *Inhibition of schemata* is important so that the system ensures that inappropriate schemata are not activated and capture behavior.
3. Tasks often require the activation of similar target schemata and *adjusting of contention scheduling* is necessary to ensure that one schema is not more active and inhibiting the behavior of other less activated schemata.

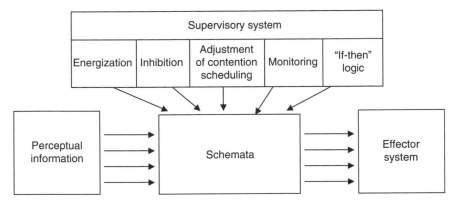

Figure 1.1   Supervisory systems in human attention. Adapted from "A multidisciplinary approach to anterior attentional functions," by D. T. Stuss, T. Shallice, M. P. Alexander, & T. W. Picton, 1995, *Annals of the New York Academy of Sciences, 769*, p. 191.

4. Role of the *monitoring* system is to ensure that behavior is appropriate and that there are few errors, to ensure that other competing schemata do not influence behavior, and ensure that the target schemata do not become inactive.
5. *If-then logic analysis* utilizes monitored feedback to maintain and alter processes by reenergizing schemata, inhibiting schemata, or adjusting contention scheduling.

Stuss and associates (1995) applied this model (Figure 1.1) for characterizing the processes involved in the control of attention across a range of tasks (sustaining, concentrating, sharing, suppressing, switching, preparing, and setting of attention) and postulated attentional subprocesses required during these tasks. They argue that there is no central executive, and that their proposed supervisory system incorporates a number of processes that involve multiple brain regions.

While the supervisory system was initially described as a homunculus, this model has been modified to take into account that executive functioning; in particular attentional control, involves a variety of independent subprocesses, and is associated with complex prefrontal neural systems with extensive reciprocal connections with most brain regions. This model accounts for high-level attentional control and most processes associated with executive functioning, it accounts for impairments in various attentional control tasks, and attempts have been made to determine the specific neural networks underlying the supervisory system (Shallice & Burgess, 1996; Stuss et al., 2002, 1995). However, given the theoretical nature of the model, it does not easily translate to clinical practice, such as assessment methodologies.

Working memory model

Working memory plays a significant role in complex activities (Baddeley, 1996, 2002) and is considered an integral component of executive functioning. Accordingly, when reviewing influential models of executive function it is appropriate to consider Baddeley's model of working memory (Baddeley, 2000). In this model working memory is defined as "a limited capacity system allowing the temporary storage and manipulation of information necessary for such complex tasks as comprehension, learning and reasoning" (Baddeley, 2000).

Baddeley's working memory model (Figure 1.2) was originally designed to replace the concept of a unitary short-term memory capacity, and comprised three components: the phonological loop, the visuo-spatial sketch-pad, and the central executive (Baddeley & Hitch, 1974). More recently this model has been modified to deal with shortcomings and the episodic buffer has been included as a fourth component (Baddeley, 2000, 2002). According to this model, working memory consists of a limited capacity attentional system (central executive) and two subsidiary slave systems (phonological loop, visuo-spatial sketch-pad). Briefly, the functions of the central executive include selective attention, coordinating two or more concurrent activities, switching attention, and retrieval of information from long-term memory (Baddeley, 1996, 2002). The phonological loop temporarily maintains and manipulates speech-based information, while the visuo-spatial sketch-pad holds and manipulates visuo-spatial information. The episodic buffer, which is controlled by the central executive, provides a workspace for the temporary storage of information and is capable of integrating information from the slave systems and long-term memory in order to create a unitary episodic event or representation (Baddeley, 2000).

More specifically, the central executive offers a conceptual framework within which to describe executive processes. While the central executive serves various functions, Baddeley believes further research is required to determine whether these multiple functions are components of a single coordinated system (i.e., unitary controller) or are a cluster of independent processes (Baddeley, 1996). According

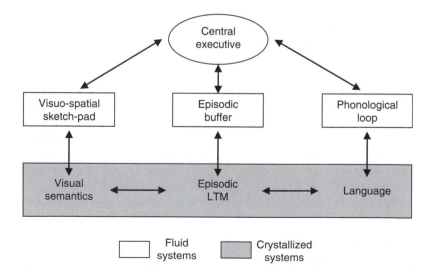

Figure 1.2   Working memory model. Adapted from "The episodic buffer: A new component of working memory?" by A. Baddeley, 2000, *Trends in cognitive sciences*, *4*, p. 417.

to Baddeley's model, the central executive has four primary functions (Baddeley, 1996, 2002). Firstly, the central executive selectively attends to one stream of information while ignoring irrelevant information and distractions. Selective attention impairment results in an inability to attend to targeted stimuli and maintain goal-directed behavior due to actions being strongly influenced by distractions and intruding thoughts. Secondly, the central executive enables multiple tasks to be completed concurrently by coordinating adequate working memory resources across the various tasks. The third component of the central executive is the capacity to switch attention and response set within a task or situation that requires mental flexibility. This function is important for overriding habitual or stereotyped behaviors, and impairment will result in rigid performance and perseverative behavior. The final function of the central executive is the selective and temporary activation of representations from long-term memory which is important to be able to respond to the demands of the environment.

While many of the central executive processes are associated with the prefrontal cortex (Baddeley, 2000; D'Esposito et al., 1995), Baddeley argues that his working memory model "is principally a functional model that would exist and be useful even if there proved to be no simple mapping on to underlying neuroanatomy" (Baddeley, 1996). He suggests that concepts such as the "central executive" should not be defined in terms of a specific anatomical location or network, as many parts of the brain are involved and one is in danger of excluding processes that are not located within the prefrontal cortex but are obviously executive in nature (Baddeley, 1996, 1998). The working memory model has been studied extensively and is considered a well-validated theoretical model. While the model accounts for some specific patterns of executive impairments, it is not inclusive of all executive impairments. For example, this model neglects elements of executive functioning such as goal setting, volition, reasoning, and planning.

Model of executive (self-regulatory) functions

Self-regulation is a major element of executive functioning and a principle component of the model proposed by Barkley (1997b). According to Barkley (1997b), self-regulation is any response set designed "to alter the probability of the individual's subsequent response to an event, and, in so doing, functions to alter the probability of a later consequence related to that event." On the basis of this definition (Figure 1.3), he suggests that self-regulation incorporates the majority of the key components of executive function including goal-directed behavior; devising plans to achieve future-oriented goals; utilization of self-directed (private) speech, rules and plans; and impulse control. In this model a prerequisite for executive, or self-regulatory, processes is intact behavioral inhibition. Barkley argues that behavioral inhibition provides a delay period necessary for executive processes to occur. Behavioral inhibition is multidimensional and comprises three interrelated processes: (1) inhibition of a prepotent response, which is a response that has been previously associated with immediate reinforcement; (2) discontinuation of a specific response pattern in order to allow time to react; and (3) interference control which protects this delay period and executive processes from distracting events and responses. As well as

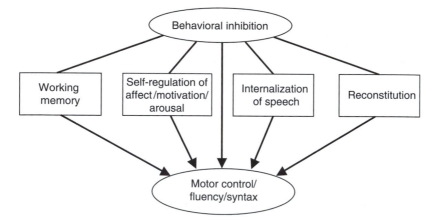

Figure 1.3   Neuropsychological model of self-regulation. Adapted from "Behavioral inhibition, sustained attention, and executive functions: Constructing a unifying theory of ADHD," by R. A. Barkley, 1997b, *Psychological Bulletin, 121*(1), p. 65.

being essential for executive processes, behavioral inhibition has a controlling influence over the motor system such as motor control, fluency, and syntax. Thus, an inhibitory deficit will result in impaired executive and motor functioning. Unlike other executive function models, Barkley's considers behavioral inhibition as a system that is distinct and hierarchically higher than the systems controlling executive processes.

Barkley's self-regulatory model is based on earlier theories (Bronowski, 1977; Fuster, 1989, 1995) and includes four primary executive domains which he has labelled working memory, self-regulation of affect/motivation/arousal, internalization of speech, and reconstitution.

1. Working memory domain comprises a number of elements. It involves the capacity to refer the present situation to previous events as well as the retention of information derived from this analysis in order to generate and retain future-oriented goals. The action plan (anticipatory set) is temporarily represented, allowing the appropriate responses to be executed in sequence, until the future-oriented goal has been achieved. In other words, working memory is required for the temporary storage of goals and intentions, the generation of response plans, and the execution of goal-directed behaviors. Further, given that working memory enables the temporary representation of events in a temporal sequence, it is important for the sense of time, which has implications for complex motor and behavioral programs. As already implied, working memory is dependent on behavioral inhibition as it provides protection from internal and external sources of interference that can disrupt this phase of goal formulation and planning.

2. Second executive domain in Barkley's model is *self-regulation of affect/ motivation/arousal*. In order to execute goal-directed behavior, self-regulation of emotion is clearly important, and at times emotions may need to be induced.

Specific events and situations can provoke highly emotional thoughts, which if not well regulated will impair one's capacity to formulate appropriate goals, generate response sets, and execute goal-directed behavior. Further, to achieve future-oriented goals, the regulation of motivation and arousal levels is vital.

3. *Internalization of speech* is thought to have considerable impact on behavior. Self-directed (private) speech is a method for self-reflection, description of events and emotions, self-questioning and monitoring, and formulating rules and plans. Therefore, internalization of speech can help to guide problem solving, and in conjunction with working memory, may contribute to moral reasoning. Further, internalization of speech is considered to have the capacity to significantly influence self-control.

4. *Reconstitution* comprises two parts: analysis and synthesis. Analysis involves breaking down the situation or behavior into its component parts. These parts can then be modified or reordered to construct a new approach or response set, which is referred to as synthesis. This process enables more complex and novel response sets to be devised.

The self-regulatory model was essentially developed to explain the cognitive and behavioral deficits associated with attention deficit hyperactivity disorder (ADHD), and validation of the model has principally involved this population. As Barkley argues that most of the deficits associated with ADHD are executive, and given that this model was based on earlier models of language (Bronowski, 1977) and prefrontal functions (Fuster, 1989, 1995), it is quite possible that the self-regulatory model may be applicable to other populations which exhibit frontal pathology or executive dysfunction. Barkley (1997b) acknowledges that the model needs further validation and that a number of issues remain unresolved, such as the degree of dependency behavioral inhibition has on each executive domain, whether there is a hierarchical organization within the executive domains, whether the executive domains can be further reduced or need to be subdivided, and whether the four executive domains are distinct and independent or represent a general executive system. Further, in most other conceptualizations of executive function, behavioral inhibition is regarded as an executive process, not a precondition as proposed by Barkley (1997b).

Components of executive functions

Lezak (1995) conceptualized executive function as consisting of four broad domains that she labelled (1) volition; (2) planning; (3) purposive action; and (4) effective performance. She proposes that while each of these executive processes comprises a distinct set of behaviors, it is rare for a patient to exhibit impairments in only one executive domain. Lezak also acknowledges that executive dysfunction could be due to impairment in any of these domains. Rather than representing a theoretical model, this conceptualization of executive function is essentially a framework for the assessment of executive function and has been influential in determining how clinicians and researchers define and assess executive functioning.

Volition refers to the conscious decision to perform some action, or an intention to carry out goal-directed or future-oriented behavior (Lezak, 1995). Lezak proposes that volition requires the capacity to generate goals and form future-oriented intentions, but motivation and self awareness are necessary preconditions. Impairments in this domain tend to be characterized by an inability to initiate activities, and an inability to think of things to do. Individuals who lack volitional capacity may have the ability to solve abstract problems and complete complex tasks, but lack the initiative to do so without prompting.

Once a future-oriented intention or goal is formulated, a plan is needed to achieve the intended end-state. Planning refers to the capacity to identify a sequence of steps necessary to solve a problem or accomplish the goal. Thus, the ability to perceive future actions and appreciate how future actions might alter circumstances are prerequisites for devising effective plans. Impulse control, working memory and sustained attention are other cognitive processes that are necessary for planning future actions. Good planning is associated with the capacity to think of alternative approaches, and apply the approach that is most effective.

Following the formulation of a future-oriented intention or goal and the development of a plan to achieve this goal, the planned sequence of steps needs to be performed. The behaviors and processes that comprise this executive domain are referred to as "purposive action." Purposive action is the initiation and maintenance of the steps involved in the plan, as well as the capacity to modify or discontinue the planned actions as needed. Severe programing difficulties are characterized by an inability to perform the sequence of actions necessary to achieve a goal despite being able to formulate a goal and develop a plan. More subtle programming impairments are reflected in difficulties in self-regulation and task-modification. Individuals need to regulate their behavior, alter plans, and shift to a new response set according to the demands of the situation. An inability to modify behavior and shift to an alternative approach is a feature of perseverative behavior. Thus, mental flexibility is often needed for solving problems and achieving goals.

The final level of Lezak's framework is "effective performance," which refers to the capacity to monitor, self-correct, and regulate behavior. A failure to self-correct errors usually occurs as a result of inadequate monitoring, and as such mistakes are not identified.

Lezak's framework is useful, especially for providing a structure for the assessment of specific executive processes; however, it neglects, to a certain degree, some important executive skills, which have been more clearly delineated recently. For example, Lezak acknowledges the role of intact memory; however working memory is clearly understated in her framework of executive function. In addition, while impulse control is inherent in planning, it is not explicitly stated or discussed. Further, while Lezak's work has been critical in moving towards better models of assessment of executive function, the approach remains largely conceptually and clinically based, and there have been few attempts to validate this framework.

Problem-solving framework

Rather than conceptualizing executive function as a group of sub functions, Zelazo and colleagues (Zelazo, Carter, Reznick, & Frye, 1997) proposed a problem-solving framework that describes the "distinct phases" of executive functioning. They refer to this problem-solving framework as a "macroconstruct," which illustrates the way in which distinct executive processes operate in an integrative manner in order to solve a problem or achieve the goal state. Zelazo et al. (1997) suggest that defining executive function as a series of basic processes (e.g., inhibition) fails to acknowledge the "complex strategic and metacognitive processes involved in executive function."

This problem-solving framework comprises four phases that are temporally and functionally distinct: (1) problem representation; (2) planning; (3) execution; and (4) evaluation. The first stage of the problem-solving process is problem representation. One must acknowledge the problem and have an understanding of the problem prior to developing a plan for solving it. Once a representation of the problem has been constructed, a plan is devised. Planning involves the selection of actions in a specific sequence, and an important aspect is selecting the most efficient sequence of steps from many alternatives. Following the development of a plan the execution phase is implemented. To execute a plan it is essential that the sequence of steps can be maintained in memory for a sufficient period to guide the appropriate actions and behaviors (referred to as "intending"), and then the individual must be prepared to perform the steps prescribed in the plan (referred to as "rule use"). In this framework these two components of the execution phase, "intending" and "rule use" are differentiated and classified as subphases. The final phase of problem solving occurs if the three previous steps have occurred, and relates to the evaluation of the individual's behavior as well as monitoring the final solution. Thus, evaluation comprises both error detection and error correction.

This executive function framework emphasizes an integrative functional approach, in that it focuses on how various executive processes, or subfunctions, work together to achieve a goal such as solving a problem. According to Zelazo et al. (1997), higher-order functions are clearly composed of various subprocesses and subsystems, "but it is counterproductive to consider them outside of the larger systems of which they are part."

Executive control system

The executive control system (Anderson, 2002) is a conceptual framework principally derived from the developmental neuropsychology literature, and is largely influenced by factor analytic and developmental studies. Factor analytic studies using purported tests of executive function (Kelly, 2000; Levin et al., 1991; Welsh et al., 1991) have tended to identify three to four factors, suggesting the existence of independent domains. Interestingly, similar executive factors have been reported across studies despite variations in test batteries and small samples across a wide age range. Factors that are commonly described include planning (Kelly, 2000; Levin et al., 1991; Welsh et al., 1991), selective attention (Mirsky, Anthony, Duncan, Ahearn, & Kellam, 1991; O'Donnell, MacGregor, Dabrowski, Oestreicher, & Romero, 1994), impulse control (Brocki & Bohlin, 2004; Lehto et al., 2003; Levin et al., 1991; Miyake et al., 2000; Welsh et al., 1991), concept reasoning (Kelly, 2000; Levin et al., 1991; O'Donnell et al., 1994), flexibility (Lehto et al., 2003; Mirsky et al., 1991; Miyake et al., 2000), working memory (Brocki & Bohlin, 2004; Lehto et al., 2003; Miyake et al., 2000) and fluency/response speed (Brocki & Bohlin, 2004; Kelly, 2000; Welsh et al., 1991).

This model conceptualizes executive function as an overall control system which comprises four distinct domains: attentional control, cognitive flexibility, goal setting, and information processing. These domains are considered independent in that they have been shown to exhibit different developmental trajectories (Anderson, 2002). They are assumed to be associated with selective prefrontal networks, although research is required to validate this claim. According to the executive control system model (Figure 1.4), while these domains are independent and comprise discrete functions, in order to operate in a functional manner, they must interact and have bidirectional relationships. Therefore, these domains are interrelated, and together they function as an overall control system. The mechanisms operating the executive control system are task-dependent, that is, the nature of the task determines the level of input from each. Each domain involves highly integrated cognitive processes, and each receives and processes stimuli from various sources including subcortical, motor, and posterior brain regions.

The *attentional control* domain includes the capacity to selectively attend to specific stimuli and the ability to focus attention for a prolonged period. This domain also involves the regulation and monitoring of actions, so that plans are executed in the correct order, errors are identified, and goals are achieved. Impulse control, such as the capacity to delay gratification, is also an integral component of this domain. Individuals with impairments in this domain are likely to be impulsive, lack self-control, fail to complete tasks, commit procedural mistakes which they fail to correct, display lapses in attention, misunderstand or forget instructions, and respond inappropriately.

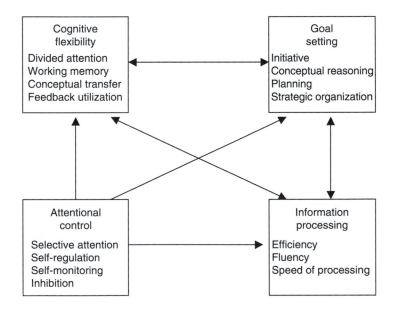

Figure 1.4   The executive control system. Adapted from "Assessment and development of executive function (EF) during childhood," by P. Anderson, 2002, *Child Neuropsychology*, *8*(2), p. 71.

Cognitive flexibility is considered a principal component of executive function in this model. This domain includes the ability to shift between response sets, learn from mistakes, devise alternative strategies, divide attention, and process multiple sources of information concurrently. Working memory, defined as the process whereby information is temporarily stored and manipulated, is also integral to this domain. Inflexible individuals are generally considered rigid and ritualistic, struggling when activities or procedures are changed and failing to adapt to new demands. They will generally struggle to mentally manipulate information (e.g., mental arithmetic) or recall previously presented information. Impairment in this domain is also often associated with perseverative behavior, in which individuals continue to make the same mistake or break the same rule. In severe cases, dissociation between knowledge and action may occur, in which an individual is able to describe the correct procedure but then fails to execute the appropriate action.

The third executive domain is goal setting. This domain includes the ability to initiate, or the capacity to start an activity and devise a plan to complete the activity. It also comprises the ability to plan. Planning ability involves anticipating future events, formulating a goal or endpoint, and devising a sequence of steps or actions that will achieve the goal or end-state. Goals can be achieved in numerous ways and good planning ability generally refers to a sequence of actions that is strategic and efficient. Related to planning ability is organization. Organization in this model refers to the ability to arrange complex information or a sequence of steps in a logical, systematic, and strategic manner. Organization has important consequences as to how efficiently and effectively goals are attained, and is associated with how well information or plans are remembered and retrieved. Impairments in this domain will result in poor problem-solving ability characterized by inadequate planning, disorganization, difficulties developing efficient strategies, reliance on previously learned strategies, and poor conceptual reasoning.

In contrast to other models of executive function, the executive control system includes information processing as a distinct executive domain rather than classifying it as an "ingredient" function. The inclusion of information processing as a separate domain is supported by factor analytic studies that have found that fluency/response speed variables from executive function tasks load on a separate factor (Kelly, 2000; Welsh et al., 1991). It is reasoned that aspects of executive functioning, in particular cognitive flexibility and goal setting, can not be assessed without taking into account issues of fluency, efficiency and speed of output. This relationship between information processing and other executive domains is bidirectional. For example, performance on executive tasks can be significantly compromised in those individuals with slow information processing, however fluency and efficiency can also be enhanced when efficient organizational strategies are utilized. This bidirectional relationship may partly explain why speed of processing is task-specific (Kail, 1991). The functionality of this domain is assumed to be related to the efficiency of prefrontal neural networks, and evaluated in terms of the speed, quantity, and quality of output. Impairments in this domain may be reflected by reduced output, delayed responses, hesitancy, and slow reaction times.

Rather than being a theoretical model of executive function, the executive control system can be more accurately described as a conceptual framework. It accounts for the various patterns of impairment considered "executive," tentatively proposes the neurological networks underlying the model, and provides a structure or template for the assessment of executive function. The model is yet to be validated and research is required to test the structure of the model and investigate the neural correlates of these broad executive domains.

Conclusions

Neuropsychological models have a number of functional applications. For example, they can guide and motivate the development of sensitive and specific measures, provide insight into impaired functioning and aberrant behavior, implicate brain structures for specific impairments, and provide a structure for studying the differential development of specific cognitive processes. Given that executive function is a psychological construct, universal agreement as to the structure of this broad multidimensional construct is unlikely to be achieved. This is illustrated in the vast discrepancies between the models presented in this chapter. Differences across theoretical models can be partly explained by the motivation for the model's development such as understanding attention control, working memory, ADHD, or cognitive development. However, executive function is clearly an important human cognitive domain and further attempts are needed to devise new alternative models as well as to validate and modify existing models.

References

Alexander, M. P., & Stuss, D. T. (2000). Disorders of frontal lobe functioning. *Seminars in Neurology, 20*(4), 427–437.

Anderson, P. (2002). Assessment and development of executive function (EF) during childhood. *Child Neuropsychology, 8*(2), 71–82.

Anderson, S., Bechara, A., Damasio, H., Tranel, D., & Damasio, A. (1999). Impairment in social and moral behavior related to early damage in human prefrontal cortex. *Nature Neuroscience, 2*(11), 1032–1037.

Andres, P. (2003). Frontal cortex as the central executive of working memory: Time to revise our view. *Cortex, 39*(4–5), 871–895.

Baddeley, A. (1996). Exploring the central executive. *Quarterly Journal of Experimental Psychology, 49A*, 5–28.

Baddeley, A. (1998). The central executive: A concept and some misconceptions. *Journal of the International Neuropsychological Society, 4*(5), 523–526.

Baddeley, A. (2000). The episodic buffer: A new component of working memory? *Trends in Cognitive Sciences, 4*, 417–423.

Baddeley, A. (2002). Fractionating the central executive. In D. T. Stuss & R. T. Knight (Eds.), *Principles of frontal lobe function* (pp. 246–260). New York: Oxford University Press.

Baddeley, A. D. (1986). *Working memory*. Oxford: Oxford University Press.

Baddeley, A. D., & Hitch, G. J. (1974). Working memory. In G. A. Bower (Ed.), *Psychology of learning and motivation* (Vol. 8). New York: Academic Press.

Baker, S., Rogers, R., Owen, A., Frith, C., Dolan, R., Frackowiak, R., et al. (1996). Neural systems engaged by planning: A PET study of the tower of London task. *Neuropsychologia, 34*(6), 515–526.

Barkley, R. A. (1996). Linkages between attention and executive functions. In G. R. Lyon & N. A. Krasnegor (Eds.), *Attention, memory, and executive function* (pp. 307–325). Baltimore: Paul H. Brookes Publishing.

Barkley, R. A. (1997a). Additional evidence supporting the existence of the executive functions. In R. A. Barkley (Ed.), *ADHD and the nature of self-control*. New York: The Guildford Press.

Barkley, R. A. (1997b). Behavioral inhibition, sustained attention, and executive functions: Constructing a unifying theory of ADHD. *Psychological Bulletin, 121*(1), 65–94.

Bigler, E. (1988). Frontal lobe damage and neuropsychological assessment. *Archives of Clinical Neuropsychology, 3,* 279–297.

Brocki, K. C., & Bohlin, G. (2004). Executive functions in children aged 6 to 13: A dimensional and developmental study. *Developmental Neuropsychology, 26*(2), 571–593.

Bronowski, J. (1977). Human and animal languages. In J. Bronowski (Ed.), *A sense of the future* (pp. 104–131). Cambridge, MA: MIT Press.

Courtney, S., Petit, L., Maisong, J., Ungerleider, L., & Haxby, J. (1998). An area specialized for spatial working memory in human frontal cortex. *Science, 279,* 1347–1350.

Cripe, L. I. (1996). The ecological validity of executive function testing. In R. J. Sbordone & J. Long (Eds.), *Ecological validity of neuropsychological testing* (pp. 171–202). FL, England: Gr Press/St Lucie Press, Inc.

David, A. (1992). Frontal lobology—Psychiatry's new pseudoscience. *British Journal of Psychiatry, 161,* 244–248.

Della Sala, S., Gray, C., Spinnler, H., & Trivelli, C. (1998). Frontal lobe functioning in man: The riddle revisited. *Archives of Clinical Neuropsychology, 13*(8), 663–682.

Denckla, M. B. (1994). Measurement of executive function. In G. R. Lyon (Ed.), *Frames of reference for the assessment of learning disabilities: New views on measurement issues* (pp. 117–142). Baltimore: Paul H Brookes Publishing.

Dennis, M. (1991). Frontal lobe function in childhood and adolescence: A heuristic for assessing attention regulation, executive control, and the intentional states important for social discourse. *Developmental Neuropsychology, 7*(3), 327–358.

D'Esposito, M., Detre, J. A., Alsop, D. C., Shin, R. K., Atlas, S., & Grossman, M. (1995). The neural basis of the central executive system of working memory. *Nature, 378*(6554), 279–281.

Duncan, J., Burgess, P., & Emslie, H. (1995). Fluid intelligence after frontal lobe lesions. *Neuropsychologia, 33,* 261–268.

Eslinger, P. J., & Grattan, L. (1993). Frontal lobe and frontal-striatal substrates for different forms of human cognitive flexibility. *Neuropsychologia, 31*(1), 17–28.

Eslinger, P. J., Grattan, L., Damasio, H., & Damasio, A. (1992). Developmental consequences of childhood frontal lobe damage. *Archives of Neurology, 49,* 764–769.

Friedman, N. P., Miyake, A., Corley, R. P., Young, S. E., DeFries, J. C., & Hewitt, J. K. (2006). Not all executive functions are related to intelligence. *Psychological Science, 17* (2), 172–179.

Fuster, J. M. (1989). *The prefrontal cortex*. New York: Raven Press.

Fuster, J. M. (1993). Frontal lobes. *Current Opinion in Neurobiology, 3,* 160–165.

Fuster, J. M. (1995). Memory and planning: Two temporal perspectives of frontal lobe function. In H. H. Jasper, S. Riggio, & P. S. Goldman-Rakic (Eds.), *Epilepsy and the functional anatomy of the frontal lobe*. New York: Raven Press.

Gioia, G. A., Isquith, P. K., & Guy, S. C. (2001). Assessment of executive functions in children with neurological impairment. In R. J. Simeonsson & L. Rosenthal (Eds.), *Psychological and developmental assessment: Children with disabilities and chronic conditions* (pp. 317–356). New York: Guilford Press.

Gioia, G. A., Isquith, P. K., Guy, S. C., & Kenworthy, L. (2000). Behavior rating inventory of executive function. *Child Neuropsychology, 6*(3), 235–238.

Grattan, L., & Eslinger, P. J. (1991). Frontal lobe damage in children and adults: A comparative review. *Developmental Neuropsychology, 7*(3), 283–326.

Kail, R. (1991). Developmental change in speed of processing during childhood and adolescence. *Psychological Bulletin, 109*(3), 490–501.

Kelly, T. (2000). The development of executive function in school-aged children. *Clinical Neuropsychological Assessment, 1*, 38–55.

Lehto, J. E., Juujarvi, P., Kooistra, L., & Pulkkinen, L. (2003). Dimensions of executive functioning: Evidence from children. *British Journal of Developmental Psychology, 21*(1), 59–80.

Levin, H. S., Culhane, K. A., Hartmann, J., Evankovich, K., Mattson, A. J., Harward, H., et al. (1991). Developmental changes in performance on tests of purported frontal lobe functioning. *Developmental Neuropsychology, 7*(3), 377–395.

Lezak, M. D. (1982). The problem of assessing executive functions. *International Journal of Psychology, 17*(2–3), 281–297.

Lezak, M. D. (1995). *Neuropsychological Assessment*. New York: Oxford University Press.

Luciano, M., Wright, M., Smith, G., Geffen, G., Geffen, L., & Martin, N. (2001). Genetic covariance among measures of information processing speed, working memory, and IQ. *Behavior Genetics, 31*, 581–592.

Luria, A. (1973). *The working brain*. New York: Basic Books.

Mirsky, A. F., Anthony, B. J., Duncan, C. C., Ahearn, M. B., & Kellam, S. G. (1991). Analysis of the elements of attention: A neuropsychological approach. *Neuropsychology Review, 2*(2), 109–145.

Miyake, A., Friedman, N. P., Emerson, M. J., Witzki, A. H., & Howerter, A. (2000). The unity and diversity of executive functions and their contributions to complex "frontal lobe" tasks: A latent variable analysis. *Cognitive Psychology, 41*(1), 49–100.

Miyake, A., Friedman, N. P., Rettinger, D. A., Shah, P., & Hegarty, M. (2001). How are visuospatial working memory, executive functioning, and spatial abilities related? A latent-variable analysis. *Journal of Experimental Psychology: General, 130*(4), 621–640.

Morris, R., Ahmed, S., Syed, G., & Toone, B. (1993). Neural correlates of planning ability: Frontal lobe activation during the Tower of London test. *Neuropsychologia, 31*(12), 1367–1378.

Norman, D. A., & Shallice, T. (1986). Attention to action: Willed and automatic control of behaviour. In R. J. Davidson, G. E. Schwartz, & D. E. Shapiro (Eds.), *Consciousness and self-regulation* (Vol. 4, pp. 1–14). New York: Plenum Press.

O'Donnell, J. P., MacGregor, L. A., Dabrowski, J. J., Oestreicher, J. M., & Romero, J. J. (1994). Construct validity of neuropsychological tests of conceptual and attentional abilities. *Journal of Clinical Psychology, 50*(4), 596–600.

Parkin, A. J. (1998). The central executive does not exist. *Journal of the International Neuropsychological Society, 4*(5), 518–522.

Pennington, B. F., & Ozonoff, S. (1996). Executive functions and developmental psychopathology. *Journal of Child Psychology and Psychiatry, 37*(1), 51–87.

Rezai, K., Andreasen, N., Alliger, R., Cohen, G., Swayze, V., & O'Leary, D. (1993). The neuropsychology of the prefrontal cortex. *Archives of Neurology, 50*, 636–642.

Roberts, A. C., Robbins, T. W., & Weiskrantz, L. (1998). *The prefrontal cortex: Executive and cognitive functions*. New York: Oxford University Press.

Shallice, T. (1990). *From neuropsychology to mental structure*. New York: Oxford University Press.

Shallice, T., & Burgess, P. W. (1996). The domain of supervisory processes and temporal organisation of behaviour. *Philosophical Transactions of the Royal Society of London B: Biological Sciences, 351*, 1405–1412.

Stuss, D. T. (1992). Biological and psychological development of executive functions. *Brain and Cognition, 20*(1), 8–23.

Stuss, D. T. (2006). Frontal lobes and attention: Processes and networks, fractionation and integration. *Journal of the International Neuropsychological Society, 12*, 261–271.

Stuss, D. T., & Alexander, M. P. (2000). Executive functions and the frontal lobes: A conceptual view. *Psychological Research, 63*(3–4), 289–298.

Stuss, D. T., Alexander, M. P., Floden, D., Binns, M. A., Levine, B., McIntosh, A. R., et al. (2002). Fractionation and localization of distinct frontal lobe processes: Evidence from focal lesions in humans. In D. T. Stuss & R. T. Knight (Eds.), *Principles of frontal lobe function.* New York: Oxford University Press.

Stuss, D. T., & Benson, D. (1984). Neuropsychological studies of the frontal lobes. *Psychological Bulletin, 95*, 3–28.

Stuss, D. T., Shallice, T., Alexander, M. P., & Picton, T. W. (1995). A multidisciplinary approach to anterior attentional functions. *Annals of the New York Academy of Sciences, 769*, 191–211.

Walsh, K. (1978). *Neuropsychology: A clinical approach.* New York: Churchill Livingston.

Welsh, M. C., & Pennington, B. F. (1988). Assessing frontal lobe functioning in children: Views from developmental psychology. *Developmental Neuropsychology, 4*(3), 199–230.

Welsh, M. C., Pennington, B. F., & Groisser, D. B. (1991). A normative-developmental study of executive function: A window on prefrontal function in children. *Developmental Neuropsychology, 7*(2), 131–149.

Zelazo, P. D., Carter, A., Reznick, J., & Frye, D. (1997). Early development of executive function: A problem-solving framework. *Review of General Psychology, 1*(2), 198–226.

Zelazo, P. D., Qu, L., & Muller, U. (2004). Hot and cool aspects of executive function: Relations in early development. In W. Schneider, R. Schumann-Hengsteler, & B. Sodian (Eds.), *Young children's cognitive development: Interrelationships among executive functioning, working memory, verbal ability, and theory of mind* (pp. 71–93). Mahwah, NJ: Lawrence Erlbaum Associates Publishers.

2 Developmental trajectories of executive functions across the lifespan

Cinzia R. De Luca and Richard J. Leventer

Contents

Executive function (EF) is an umbrella term traditionally used to represent higher-order abilities involved in goal-oriented behavior (Lezak, 1995). Refinement of this notion has seen the inclusion of novelty, or unfamiliarity, as an essential component in activation of the executive system (Shallice, 1990); however, some researchers continue to argue that most daily activities require at least some minimal employment of executive control (Stuss & Alexander, 2000). Cognitive skills commonly ascribed to this domain are sometimes referred to as 'cold' executive abilities and include strategic planning, organization, goal setting, behavior monitoring, problem solving, inhibition, working memory, and cognitive flexibility (Anderson, 1998; Fuster, 2002; Hughes, 1998; Temple, 1997; Weyandt & Willis, 1994). Recently it has been acknowledged that empathy, theory of mind, emotional regulation, and affective decision making are essential components to our organization and execution of purposeful behavior, and have been labeled by some as 'hot' executive skills (Happaney, Zelazo, & Stuss, 2004; Kerr & Zelazo, 2004).

Despite their theoretical distinction, cold and hot EFs are considered intimately connected and are almost always utilized in combination for daily functions. Indeed, these combined executive skills are thought to provide humankind with the unique capacity for reflection and guilt, and establish our autonomy from the environment. Without these higher level abilities we would be reduced to reflexive creatures, responding, but not truly interacting with our surroundings in a meaningful and constructive way. Given that EFs are central to our ability to purposely mediate our actions, it is easy to appreciate that their developmental trajectory covers childhood and potentially the lifespan. From the primitive reflexes of the immature and helpless newborn, to the development of imaginative play and self-autonomy of the young child, on to the planning and organization of a career and family in adulthood, and finally to the decline of one's self-sufficiency in later life. When executive development follows its projected route we see the creation of unique individuals, but when disrupted, either through biological or environmental insults, havoc is wreaked on cognitive, social, academic, and vocational growth. As one would expect, the timing, extent, and location of this disruption is important in defining the type and severity of the deficits suffered.

This chapter attempts to provide a brief outline of current views of EFs and their development over the lifespan. First, the neural circuitry, involving prefrontal areas, that has been proposed to support these functions will be described followed by a discussion of the notion that the 'central executive' represents a fractionated but intimately connected set of higher level skills. The developmental trajectory of these unique abilities is then discussed, highlighting when they first come 'online' in childhood and reach mature levels. This includes an emphasis on key structural and cognitive milestones that occur at each developmental phase from infancy to old age, as well as an exploration of parallels in advances in both these areas. Finally, comparison of the deficits that underlie executive dysfunction in children as compared to the elderly is included to highlight the complexity of this system and how changes in different aspects can masquerade as equivalent deficits in performance on formal testing.

Localization and fractionation

The psychological understanding of what constitutes an executive function is notoriously ill-defined. Traditionally EF has been seen as a unitary concept with the 'central executive' or 'supervisory system' discretely localized to the frontal lobes of the brain (Baddeley & Della Sala, 1998; Parkin, 1996; Stuss & Alexander, 2000). The prefrontal cortex (PFC) in particular has been implicated as the neural seat of one's executive capabilities (Fletcher, 1996). This interchangeable use of the terms "executive" and "frontal," arose from adult lesion studies that reported consistent findings of a debilitating dysexecutive disorder in patients with large, acquired frontal lobe injuries (Luria, 1973). While compelling, the *frontal metaphor* began to falter as a more elaborate understanding of the intricate network of areas involved in higher-order thinking evolved (Stuss, 1992). This paradigm shift was driven by clinical research describing patients with a frontal syndrome pattern of dysfunction in the absence of a frontal lesion (Baddeley & Della Sala, 1998), and has been strengthened by more recent functional imaging studies which highlight the activation of widely distributed systems in dealing with novel information (Luna & Sweeney, 2004; Rubia et al., 2000; Tamm, Menon, & Reiss, 2002).

Evidence of fractionated executive abilities following damage to the PFC has also led to their acceptance as a group of heterogeneous and dissociable functions that rely on the integrity of the whole brain for effective implementation (Anderson, 1998; Garth, Anderson, & Wrennall, 1997). The search for a frontal homunculus has been replaced with the broader psychological concept of a frontal system that highlights the monitoring capacity of the PFC, while emphasizing the importance of this larger system (Stuss & Alexander, 2000). The PFC is certainly uniquely positioned to coordinate executive skills as they share associated circuitry with all other major functional systems of the brain including: the hypothalamus, hippocampus, and other limbic structures; association areas of the parietal, temporal, and occipital cortices; and the anterior and dorsal thalamus (Cummings, 1993; Fuster, 2002). Disruption, mis-wiring, or impaired development of the numerous pathways and feedback loops of this frontal system are considered the likely cause of many of the executive deficits characteristic of both acquired and developmental disorders (Luna et al., 2002; Pantelis et al., 1997; Tramontana & Hooper, 1989).

There is increasing focus on the parallels between the functional emergence of executive capabilities and the structural maturation of the frontal lobes. Both are known to be present in an immature state in the young child, with protracted development through adolescence into early adulthood (Casey, Giedd, & Thomas, 2000; Steinberg, 2005). The PFC begins its development in utero, but its complex connections both within the frontal lobes and to other brain areas continue to remodel and mature well into adulthood. The human frontal lobes are the last regions of the brain to mature, both from a developmental and an evolutionary perspective, and are the major feature that helps differentiate the human brain from those of other species. While not the largest in the animal kingdom, the human brain is advanced in the higher number of cortical neurons and greater information processing capacity it has in comparison to other primates and mammals (Roth & Dicke, 2005). More importantly, the neurons of the PFC have been shown to have a greater density of spines and dendrites relative to other cortical areas (Elston, Benavides-Piccione, & DeFelipe, 2001). This allows for the greater capacity to integrate highly complex and diverse information, and execute intricate plans. The frontal lobes are also one of the first areas of the brain to degenerate, both in the normal ageing process and as part of pathological dementias such as Alzheimer's disease that are becoming more prevalent as our lifespan increases.

Maturation of the frontal lobes involves a number of dynamic processes which are controlled by both genetic coding and in response to environmental stimuli. These include "positive" mechanisms of gray (neuronal proliferation and differentiation) and white matter development (axonal and dendritic arborization), and "negative" mechanisms of neuronal cellular apoptosis (or programmed cell death) and "pruning" of synaptic connections (Huttenlocher, 1979; Kuan, Roth, Flavell, & Rakic, 2000). In addition, as with white matter circuitry in the rest of the brain, axons in the frontal lobes undergo a prolonged process of insulation (called myelination), which ensures rapid transmission of electrical signals (Yakovlev & Lecours, 1967). The prefrontal regions are the last areas of the brain to complete this process of myelination which continues well into the third decade (Klingberg, Vaidya, Gabrieli, Moseley, & Hedehus, 1999; Sowell, Thompson, Holmes, Jernigan, & Toga, 1999; Sowell et al., 2004; Yakovlev & Lecours, 1967). This balance of positive and negative influences on neuronal growth and connectivity, and the protracted process of white matter myelination in the anterior frontal lobes is necessary for the optimal development of the complex circuitry needed for healthy cognitive and EFs appropriate to the individual's developmental stage.

Due to the delayed maturation of the PFC, EFs are among the last functions to reach maturity. Differences in the neural sophistication of specific areas within the frontal cortices are reflected in the unique timing of when these skills come 'online' and reach adult levels (Anderson, 2002; Casey et al., 2000; Espy, 2004; Luciana, Conklin, Hooper, & Yargar, 2005; Luciana & Nelson, 1998). In keeping with the hierarchical pattern of brain development, acquisition of executive skills also appears to follow a sequence from more fundamental abilities to more complex and multi-factorial skills. In particular, attentional control and working memory are considered by some researchers as essential to success on all executive tasks (Senn, Espy, & Kaufmann, 2004). These skills are therefore thought to come online earlier in life, and contribute to the development of more specialized EFs, such as planning and organization, by progressively expanding the processing capacity of the brain during adolescence and early adulthood (Smidts, Jacobs, & Anderson, 2004).

Whether discrete EFs follow a stagelike or linear developmental trajectory remains a point of contention. Piaget (1965) claimed that children progressed through invariant and universal stages that could not be expedited or reorganized in any way. Much literature supports this early argument through evidence of 'spurts' in skills at various ages that appear to herald the development of a new awareness or strategy which was not previously available to the child (Anderson, Anderson, Northam, Jacobs, & Catroppa, 2001; Klimkeit, Mattingley, Sheppard, Farrow, & Bradshaw, 2004). This stepwise improvement in cognitive ability is thought to reflect maturational events in frontal areas (Casey et al., 2000). Anderson (2002) proposed a model with four distinct cognitive domains: attentional control, informa-tion processing, cognitive flexibility, and goal setting, to represent this fractionated by highly interrelated executive system. Importantly, the model views development in each domain as distinct, not necessarily linear, and highly dependent on the other domains for efficient performance, thus providing a useful framework to explore milestones in acquisition of executive competence. In support of this model, studies taking a lifespan perspective on executive development have consistently reported a bell-shaped curve in acquisition and later loss of these skills, highlighting the existence of nonlinear trajectories (Cepeda, Kramer, & Gonzalez de Sather, 2001; De Luca et al., 2003; Kray, Eber, & Lindenberger, 2004; Zelazo, Craik, & Booth, 2004).

There is also emerging evidence disputing the invariability of these stages which shows that young children can be taught how to think "beyond the square" with appropriate training (Dowsett & Livesey, 2000), and that their executive competency can be influenced by family and social factors, thus negating the idea that develop-mental stages are time-locked or neurally restricted (Perner, Ruffman, & Leekam, 1994; Walker, Hennig, & Krettenauer, 2000). This highlights the important role of environmental stimulation in driving brain development, as well as the potential for children to accelerate their learning. Not surprisingly, the environment and our exposure to experience are often overlooked when seeking parallels between struc-ture and function. In discussing the maturation of executive abilities it is necessary to acknowledge that the diversity and intricacy of our experiences with the world typically increases as we age, and that these signals, both from our external and internal environment, will have a major impact on the connections that our brains will establish, reinforce, and maintain (Gottlieb & Halpern, 2002; Pennington, 2002;

Rutter, 2002). This helps us explain why a child raised in a nomadic sub-Sahara community is likely to display very different sensibilities to an apartment-dwelling child in Manhattan, while at the same time showing similar gains in their ability to process, manipulate, monitor, update, shift, and inhibit information.

Early frontal lobe development: First steps toward the executive summit

The human nervous system begins to develop at 18 days gestation. Neurons destined to form the frontal cortex are born as neuroblasts in the anterior periventricular region at approximately 6 weeks gestation (Dobbing & Sands, 1973). These neuroblasts proliferate and differentiate in the periventricular zone before beginning sequential and overlapping waves of radial migration along specialized radial glial cells toward the developing cortical plate (Rakic, 1988). Neuronal migration is largely complete by 24 weeks. Cortical development during the remaining months of fetal development is largely comprised of cortical organization. During this time neurons arrange themselves in the supporting structures of the cortex, sending out axons and arborizing with both nearby and distant neurons forming the foundations for the frontal lobe circuitry required for survival at birth and continued development in the neonatal period (Volpe, 1995).

At birth the brain is largely unmyelinated and the majority of its development has been programmed and controlled by genetic factors. The basic anatomical structure of the frontal lobes is developed, and the cerebral surface shows the typical convoluted gyral pattern that it will maintain throughout life (Welker, 1990). The neurons are already wired into a network which includes connections between different cortical layers and to and from more distant structures such as other cortical areas in the ipsilateral and contralateral hemispheres and subcortical structures including the thalamus, basal ganglia, cerebellum, brainstem, and spinal cord. Despite the foundations of the frontal lobes being present at birth, this region of the human brain is still relatively immature, particularly the anterior frontal lobes, traditionally divided into the dorsolateral and ventromedial PFC. In contrast to in utero development, the postnatal development of the cortex relies upon both genetic programs and environmental stimuli through activity-dependent mechanisms (Katz & Shatz, 1996; Shatz, 1992).

During the first two years of life, two important processes of cortical development are most active, leading to a brain at the age of 2 years that is approximately 80% the weight of an adult brain (Kretschmann, Kammradt, Krauthausen, Sauer, & Wingert, 1986). The first of these processes is a period of rapid synapse formation, thought by some to be an overproduction of synapses relative to those needed in the adult state (Casey et al., 2000). The peaks of synaptogenesis differ between different cortical regions, with the peak occurring relatively late in the PFC (Huttenlocher, 1979; Huttenlocher & Dabholkar, 1997). This has been confirmed by ultrastructural studies of synaptic density (Huttenlocher & Dabholkar, 1997), and positron emission tomography (PET) studies of cerebral glucose metabolism which have mirrored changes in synaptic density by showing a rapid rise in glucose metabolism in infancy and early childhood (Chugani & Phelps, 1991). The second process that is most active during this period is myelination (Dobbing & Sands, 1973). Although myelination continues well into adult life, it is during the first 2 years that the majority of brain myelination occurs (Brody, Kinney, Kloman, & Gilles, 1987; Kinney, Brody, Kloman, & Gilles, 1988). This process takes place in an orderly and predictable pattern and proceeds from caudal to anterior and from dorsal to ventral regions, with sensory before motor regions and central before peripheral areas myelinating first (Brody et al., 1987; Kinney et al., 1988). By the end of the second year, the majority of pathways in the human brain have completed myelination. The PFC, particularly the dorsolateral regions, however, are the last regions of the brain to myelinate, with myelination in these areas continuing into the third decade (Klingberg et al., 1999; Yakovlev & Lecours, 1967).

The first two years of life are acknowledged for the huge developmental gains made in motor and language skills. They are not typically associated with the types of functions housed under the executive umbrella. In fact early adult models of cerebral organization and cognitive development suggested that EF was an adult capacity that only appeared around the time of puberty (Golden, 1981). This claim corresponded well with Piaget's stage transition from concrete operational to formal operational thinking, around 12 years of age (Stuss, 1992; Travis, 1998). However, these findings were based on flawed studies that utilized adult tests which did not account for the qualitative and quantitative differences in children's understanding and processing of information, and therefore masked children's executive capabilities (Anderson, 1998; Espy, 2004; Kempton, Vance, Luk, Costin, & Pantelis, 1999). By adjusting the motor, language, and memory requirements of tasks and carefully modelling how children approach executive activities, it has now come to light that the first steps in executive development occur in the very young child (Smidts et al., 2004; Zelazo et al., 2004).

As newborns we are completely dependent on our parents, and show only primitive reflexes in our interaction with the world. Despite the relative immaturity of the brain at this stage, it is certainly not a *tabula rasa*, nor the child a completely passive recipient. Infants are active participants in their environment, and display signs of self-exploration and an emerging understanding of their own agency by 2 months of age (Rochat & Striano, 1999). At 12 weeks they are able to detect the goal structure of an event after personal experience in trying to acquire a desired object (Sommerville, Woodward, & Needham, 2005). The first signs of working memory and inhibitory control arise between 7 and 8 months of age, aspects of which are considered to be under the management of the dorsolateral and orbital prefrontal cortices (Dias, Robbins, & Roberts, 1997; Tsujimoto, Yamamoto, Kawaguchi, Koizumi, & Sawaguchi, 2004; Weinberger et al., 2001). Diamond (1985) found that infants of 7.5 months could correctly retrieve objects on a delayed response task when the delay was limited to 1 or 2 seconds. By 12 months of age a delay of 10 seconds was necessary to elicit perseverative errors suggestive of a failure to maintain the current hiding place of an object in mind and inhibit a previously rewarded response. Major gains in performance of this task are then seen between 3 and 4 years of age, with perfect performance at 10–30 second delays seen by the time a child reaches 5 (Espy, Kaufmann, Glisky, & McDiarmid, 2001; Espy, Kaufmann, McDiarmid, & Glisky, 1999).

The delayed non-matching-to-sample task is considered a robust measure of recognition memory in adults, but appears to tap working memory processes in children. Traditionally children were found to fail on this task before the age of 2 years, arguably because of an inability to deduce the abstract rule governing performance (Zelazo et al., 2004). Diamond refuted this argument by showing that children of 12 months of age were capable of representing and using this information provided that the stimulus and reward were physically connected (Diamond, Lee, & Hayden, 2003). Other factors, such as an inability to resist the interference from the reward that is presented after each correct search, were found to be impacting on children's performance (Diamond, Towle, & Boyer, 1994). Once the reward was removed, children of 12–15 months were performing at a 21-month-old level, demonstrating that a lack of inhibition is able to account for the failure of young child on this task.

Studies on the development of 'hot' executive skills are clearly lacking in this age range. This is despite the perception in the field that these affective skills, which rely more heavily on the orbitofrontal (or ventromedial) cortices, may emerge prior to the more laterally based 'cold' executive abilities (Orzhekhovskaya, 1981). The paucity of information on early 'hot' executive milestones reflects the relative immaturity of the theories driving this research. Concepts, such as theory of mind, affective decision making, and moral reasoning are ill-defined and their relationship to theories of social cognition and emotional intelligence varied, much like the tools used to assess them. As a result, they are rarely found to correlate with each other, and do not appear to maintain stability over time (Hongwanishkul, Happaney, Lee, & Zelazo, 2005). The intimate relationship between 'hot' executive abilities and language acquisition presents another confound which makes it extremely difficult to target these functions in very young children given the available tests (e.g., false-belief, appearance-reality) (Meltzoff, 1999). Indeed, there even appears to be a dissociation between the social knowledge children can infer with their eyes and with their words at difference ages, making developmental trajectories particularly difficult to define (Leslie, 2005).

Intuitively, we know that infants are notoriously bad at regulating their emotions, delaying rewards and view the world from an 'egocentric' pedestal. It would therefore seem that 'hot' executive skills are absent at this age and that infants do not make the significant jump to a more mature, and inclusive, understanding of emotions and intentions until the development of empathy and perspective taking, the so-called theory of mind skills (the ability to represent and interpret the mental states and actions of oneself and others) around the age of 4 years (Perner & Lang, 1999). However, it is now evident that some of the precursors to theory of mind emerge much earlier, with the ability to distinguish between inanimate and animate objects established by 6 months of age (Woodward, 1998). At 12 months children begin to show joint attention skills which allow them to represent the perception of a shared object by another person (Sabbagh, 2003), and from 14 to 18 months of age they start to actively follow a person's gaze to an object, which later allows for correct object naming to occur (Saxe, Carey, & Kanwisher, 2004). Social referencing, the ability to utilize information about objects from the emotional reactions of others, also comes online around this time, as represented in the ability of infants to

Table 2.1   Structural and functional development across infancy.

Age	Brain development	Cold EF	Hot EF
Prenatal	CNS development begins at 18 days gestation 6 weeks neuroblasts for frontal regions develop 24 weeks migration complete 24+ cortical organization		
Birth	Gyri formed Neurons wired into networks Brain largely unmyelinated		
12 weeks		Able to detect goal structure of events	
7–8 months	Synaptogenesis Myelination	First signs of working memory and inhibition systems	Able to distinguish animate and inanimate objects
12 months	Synaptogenesis Myelination		Joint attention
14 months	Synaptogenesis Myelination		Social referencing
2 years	Brain 80% weight of adult brain	Improvements in inhibition and working memory	Understanding of pretense

distinguish what food another person desires by their facial responses (Repacholi & Gopnik, 1997).

While these important milestones occur on the journey to 'hot' executive functioning, researchers in this field are skeptical that a true awareness of mental states exists in a child of 1-year-old (Flavell, 1999). In contrast, by the end of the second year of life, a robust, albeit very simple understanding of emotions, intentions, desires, and their relationship to goals emerges (Bartsch & Wellman, 1989; Brune & Brune-Cohrs, 2006; Flavell, 1999), along with the ability to distinguish between reality and pretense (Leslie, 1987). This understanding of a pretend thought results in the commencement of imaginary play, a skill which is notably absent in children with autism (Table 2.1).

Preschool development: The "why" years

In preschool children, the frontal lobes continue to increase steadily in size, due to increases in both gray and white matter. Pathological and neuroimaging studies confirm a steady increase in both cortical gray matter and white matter volumes of up to 1-mm per year in early childhood (Dobbing & Sands, 1973; Huttenlocher & Dabholkar, 1997; Matsuzawa et al., 2001; Sowell et al., 2004), although from age

5 years, there is no significant increase in cerebral volume (Reiss, Abrams, Singer, Ross, & Denckla, 1996). Studies of cerebral metabolism using PET scanning show high rates of metabolism until approximately age 9 years, followed by a mild decline over the next decade to adult levels (Chugani & Phelps, 1991).

Preschoolers are renowned for their thirst for knowledge and unwavering determination to find out how the world works. This is a reflection of the substantial improvement in their processing capacity and ability to form meaningful connections between temporally separated events that results from increases in gray and white matter. However, a lack of inhibitory control and susceptibility to interference continue to be the main factors limiting children's performance at this age. The day/night task is a measure of inhibitory control which requires children to hold two rules in mind, while inhibiting a prepotent response (Gerstadt, Hong, & Diamond, 1994). It is this latter skill which results in young children's errors, for when the semantic loading of responses (and therefore the inhibitory demands of the task) is reduced, 4-year-old children can easily perform the task despite still having to remember an embedded rule system (Diamond, Kirkham, & Amso, 2002), and simply forcing children to take longer to think about their answer also improves their performance considerably (Diamond et al., 2002). Five-year-olds show superior inhibitory skills to 3- and 4-year-olds on go/no-go tasks of inhibition (Dowsett & Livesey, 2000), while 7- to 9-year-olds show a spurt in success on more complex continuous performance tasks (Brocki & Bohlin, 2004). Luria's tapping task has similar requirements for the inhibition of a prepotent response, and young children are found to improve in their accuracy and speed of performance on this task from 3.5 to 6 years of age (Diamond & Taylor, 1996). In summary, major gains in executive control (i.e., inhibition and sustained attention) are seen from 3 to 5 years of age, with the 4-year-old child showing a spurt in performance on such tasks. Further, what is striking from this research is that, while children as young as 3 years of age can regularly state the rules of the game, demonstrating that they obviously know what they have to do, they have difficulty resisting their automatic response to an environmental stimulus.

Greater mental flexibility and improved concept formation can also be seen during the preschool years. From 4 to 8 years of age, children's memory spans increase providing a base for them to develop more elaborate strategies and shift more efficiently between ideas (Luciana & Nelson, 1998). This is seen in children's improved performance on a modified version of the object classification task from 3 to 7 years, with major gains from 4 to 5 years of age in the ability to formulate sorting rules on the basis of abstract characteristics, and inhibit a previously rewarded response (Smidts et al., 2004). Set-shifting requires disengagement from one task and the reestablishment of focus on other activities. As inhibition improves from 4 to 5 years, so too does the child's cognitive flexibility (Luciana & Nelson, 1998).

By 5 years of age children begin to show an increased ability to hold and manipulate complex information online. Verbal and visuospatial working memory systems are thought to be fractionated from this early age, with children's performance on working memory tasks said to be consistent with Baddeley's modular model which incorporates a separate phonological loop and visuospatial sketchpad that both feed into a central executive (Alloway, Gathercole, Willis, & Adams, 2004). This structure is thought to be in place by the age of 4–6 years. The development of nonverbal working memory has been probed through use of the Spatial Working Memory Task from the Cambridge Neuropsychological Test Automated Battery (CANTAB: CeNes Plc, Cambridge, UK). Luciana and Nelson (1998) observed a steady increase over the period of 5–8 years of age in the number of boxes children could successfully search through to find rewards. This improved performance was found to reflect both development of working memory ability and strategic planning. In fact, by 7 years of age, children had reached adult levels of performance on the simpler 2- and 4-item searches (Luciana & Nelson, 2002).

Goal-directed behaviors and planning begin to mature in the preschool period. Many researchers argue that these advances are only possible because of the major gains described above in inhibition and working memory skills (Brocki & Bohlin, 2004). In support of this view, a recent path analysis study looking at the composition of EF in preschool children found that a model which included only inhibition and working memory provided the best fit for the data and was able to predict 29% of the variance in complex problem solving in children from 2 to 6 years of age (Senn et al., 2004). Tower tasks are classic measures of planning and organization which has been linked to prefrontal functioning in adults and used quite extensively in children. Espy et al. (2001) found that 4- to 5-year-old children could correctly complete more items on the 3-disc Tower of Hanoi (TOH) Task than 2- to 3-year-old children. Importantly, Luciana and Nelson found that while some 4-year-old children could complete the easier 2-move trials on the Tower of London (a variant of the TOH) as well as older children (5–8 years of age), their performance steadily decreased as the number of moves required increased (Luciana & Nelson, 1998). The main difficulty for young children on Tower tasks is thought to be moving balls in a direction which is counterintuitive to the final solution. Performance on the task is moderated by task difficulty, which distinguishes the performance of children from 5 to 8 years of age, to that of young adults (Luciana & Nelson, 1998).

Theory of mind undergoes its most significant development in the phase from 3 to 5 years of age, with children around 4 beginning to pass false-belief and deception tasks (Sodian, Taylor, Harris, & Perner, 1991). There are generally three camps of thought on the processes underlying success on theory of mind tasks at this age. Some researchers argue that it is due to a fundamental developmental advance in the representation of mental states through maturation of a specific theory of mind mechanism (Gallagher & Frith, 2003; Leslie, Friedman, & German, 2004). Others speak of the interdependence of mental state reasoning on improved executive control (Flynn, O'Malley, & Wood, 2004; Prencipe & Zelazo, 2005), in particular inhibitory skills which at 24 months of age have been found to predict theory of mind success at 39 months (Carlson, Mandell, & Williams, 2004). The role of working memory and planning skills is also acknowledged in this model, but their contribution is less understood (Hughes, 2002; Perner, Lang, & Kloo, 2002). Another interpretation is that children younger than 4 years are limited in their performance of such tasks because of 'the curse of knowledge,' that is, a difficulty appreciating a more naïve perspective as the result of being biased by one's own knowledge (Birch, 2005). The strength of this bias is thought to diminish with age, perhaps as a consequence of the improvements in inhibitory control discussed above. Finally, other researchers hold that development of more general factors, such as language acquisition, simply allows for children of this age to adequately represent their understanding of mental states (Meltzoff, 1999).

When thinking about others' thoughts, children of 3 years are only able to understand another person's unitary desire (Choe, Keil, & Bloom, 2005), and it is not until the age of 5–6 years that they become aware that a person can hold beliefs about another person's beliefs (Wimmer & Perner, 1983), or understand mistaken beliefs (Perner & Wimmer, 1985). Furthermore, an appreciation of the possible existence of conflicting mental states in an individual (i.e., the ability to experience both happiness and sadness about an event, or the desire to eat a sweet and not to eat a sweet at the same time) is not robustly seen until around 7 years of age (Wimmer & Perner, 1983).

'Hot' executive skills, such as affective decision making, an ability under the control of the orbitofrontal cortex, have also been studied in preschool children using the children's version of the Iowa Gambling Task. Kerr and Zelazo (2004) provide evidence of significant development in affective decision making from the age of 3–4 years. They found that the performance of 3-year-old children was governed by immediate rewards, while the older group was more likely to alter their choices to favor the decisions which were more advantageous in the long run. In contrast, Garon and Moore (2004) found no significant difference in the decisions made by 3- to 6-year-old children on this task, but observed that older children had a greater awareness of the game which increased their likelihood of choosing from the more advantageous decks.

Despite these advancements, preschool children are still a long way from the peak of the executive mountain and their ascent is beset by ongoing failures in many domains. Their frontal lobes are still increasing in size, with the processes of refinement, particularly of gray matter, still in the formative stages. As Espy (2004) comments in a recent review, "preschoolers do not suffer a lack of abilities, but rather from the ability to deploy these abilities in particular contexts, that is, they lack basic metacognitive awareness of when, and how, to apply their knowledge and to deploy particular strategies effectively" (p. 380). Therefore, while young children display executive abilities, they are often gross and notoriously error prone at this stage (Table 2.2).

Preadolescence period

The preadolescent years mark a time of significant change in cortical gray matter development in the frontal lobes. While white matter development and myelination continue to progress steadily, there is a preadolescent spurt or second wave of cortical gray matter development, peaking at age 11 in girls and 12 in boys (Rapoport et al., 1999). This acceleration in frontal lobe gray matter volume will be the last during the individual's lifetime. From early adolescence onwards, gray matter volume slowly declines, firstly as part of a pruning process, thought to optimize and mature frontal lobe circuitry, and later in adulthood, as part of the normal ageing process (Ge et al., 2002; Scahill et al., 2003).

By late childhood many executive skills enter a mature phase of development. In particular, the ability to shift attentional set, classically measured by the Wisconsin Card Sorting Task, is thought to reach adult levels by 10 years of age (Chelune &

Table 2.2   Structural and functional development across the preschool and early school years.

Age	Brain development	Cold EF	Hot EF
3 years	Increased gray and white matter volumes Increased metabolism	Improvement in inhibitory control and sustained attention until age 5	Improvement in affective decision making over this year
4 years	Increased gray and white matter volumes Increased metabolism	Improved cognitive flexibility	Success at false-belief tasks
5 years	Increased gray and white matter volumes Increased metabolism	Gains in working memory and strategy formation Beginnings of planning and goal-directed behavior	Awareness that a belief can be held about another's beliefs
6 years	Increased metabolism		Sophisticated adult-like theory of mind
7 years	Increased metabolism		Understanding of conflicting mental states

Baer, 1986; Welsh & Pennington, 1988). Our own study investigated the trajectory of executive development in 194 participants ranging in age from 8 to 64 years using the CANTAB (De Luca et al., 2003). We focused on various executive domains including cognitive flexibility, working memory, strategic planning and goal setting. Progression was witnessed in all areas except for set-shifting ability which was mature in even the youngest children tested (8- to 10-year-olds) (Figure 2.1). Luciana and Nelson (2002) looked at a younger group of children using the Wisconsin task and found their performance to be at ceiling level by 7 years of age. Brocki and Bohlin (2004) also found a decrease in disinhibited behavior from 9 to 11 years, with

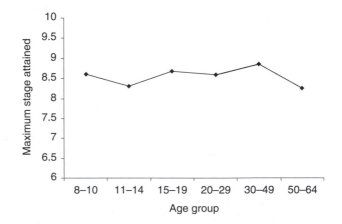

Figure 2.1   Intradimensional/extradimensional set-shifting task. Highest level achieved as a function of age.

little further improvement after that time, while Lehto, Juujarvi, Kooistra, and Pulkkinen (2003) found only a weak correlation between age and inhibitory control in children aged 8–13 years. Klimkeit et al. (2004) observed major gains in vigilance, set-shifting, response inhibition, selective attention, and impulsive responding between 8 and 10 years of age. These findings provide support for the relatively early maturation of cognitive flexibility in comparison to other executive skills, such as working memory and strategic planning which continue to develop well into the teens.

Not surprisingly, greater flexibility of thought can also be a hindrance when the older child and teenager become aware of multiple dimensions on which information can be analyzed. This can at times mask the obvious solution to a problem, and lead to overanalysis of the material. Children at this developmental stage can therefore show significant fluctuation in their ability to perform tasks, and make more errors as a result of their naivety in how to implement and constrain their new found skills (Anderson, 2002; De Luca et al., 2003, p. 313).

All other EFs demonstrate a spurt during the period of 9–12 years. Working memory undergoes a significant jump in capacity and efficiency (Brocki & Bohlin, 2004). They also become less sensitive to interference (Leon-Carrion, Garcia-Orza, & Perez-Santamaria, 2004). Strategic thinking improves (Luciana & Nelson, 2002) and fluency shows steady increases to age 12 years and above (Korkman, Kemp, & Kirk, 2001; Welsh & Pennington, 1988). Goal-directed behavior increases, with a possible spurt at 12 years of age (Anderson et al., 2001; Levin et al., 1991), particularly in the ability of children to monitor and flexibly alter their behavior in the face of changing environmental demands.

Research on 'hot' EF development in this age group is scarce. It appears certain that there is continued maturation and refinement of one's understanding of emotions, intentions, beliefs, desires, etc., and that children become aware of more subtle and complex issues in this area over time. Some late developing theory of mind skills, such as the ability to decipher metaphors (Ackerman, 1981), and forms of social deception including white lies (Happe, 1994) are seen to come online in the school age child. An example of this is the development of an understanding of faux pas which is not reliably established until at least 9–11 years of age (Baron-Cohen, O'Riordan, Stone, Jones, & Plaisted, 1999). Faux pas (i.e., a social blunder when a person says or behaves in a way in which they should not have, but are unaware of their error) is an advanced aspect of theory of mind as it requires the representation of two mental states simultaneously, and as discussed in the previous section, the precursors to this are only beginning to develop around age 7. Hughes and Leekam (2004) argue that while these enhancements in 'hot' executive capability should lead to increased social harmony, they also allow for manipulation of social situations, bullying and heightening sensitivity to criticism, which take precedence during adolescence (Table 2.3).

Adolescence: Testing the executive boundaries

Adolescence is a poorly defined developmental phase. While its onset is usually thought to be heralded by puberty, these two events do not necessarily co-occur (Dubas, 1991). Generally adolescence is considered to cover teenagers from 13 to 19 years of age. Adolescents, much like their younger counterparts, demonstrate an

Table 2.3   Structural and functional development across late childhood.

Age	Brain development	Cold EF	Hot EF
8 years	Increased white matter in frontal areas	Mature cognitive flexibility skills Improvements in inhibition, vigilance and sustained attention seen until 11	Understanding of metaphors and social deception
9 years	Increased white matter in frontal areas	Gains in working memory and strategic planning	Understanding of faux pas develops until age 11
10 years	Increased white matter in frontal areas		
11 years	Second wave of cortical development seen for girls		
12 years	Second wave of cortical development seen for boys	Spurt in goal-directed behavior	

astounding contradiction in their ability to "know" but not "do", or at least not apply, their knowledge consistently (Steinberg, 2005). They are notorious for engaging in risk-taking behaviors, experimenting with drugs, exploring their sexuality, rebelling against authority figures, and focusing on peer interactions. However, adolescence is also a time of increased independence, responsibility, and social awareness. Context may explain these diverse and often conflicting aspects of development. Adolescents are under unique social and emotional pressures, including peer expectations and heightened desires and motivations (Steinberg, 2005). Their reasoning and decision-making processes are therefore not only a simple reflection of their cognitive abilities but also their emotional, social, and physical situation. Importantly, adolescence needs to be viewed as another step on the road to executive mastery, rather than the end point of executive development.

While we may expect teenagers to behave in similar ways to adults, their frontal circuitry is not yet up to the challenge. Adolescence heralds major changes in frontal lobe development. White matter continues to increase in volume in a steady fashion; yet gray matter volume begins to decrease. Much of the work to support this reduction in gray matter volume comes from early pathological studies showing a decrease in synaptic density with adolescence (Huttenlocher, 1990; Huttenlocher & Dabholkar, 1997; Rakic, Bourgeois, & Goldman-Rakic, 1994). This work has been supported more recently by *in vivo* imaging studies including various morphometric examinations of changing gray matter volume across time (Giedd, 1999; Giedd et al., 1996; Gogtay et al., 2004; Sowell et al., 2003, 2004; Sowell, Thompson, Tessner, & Toga, 2001; Sowell, Thompson, & Toga, 2004), combined with PET scan techniques (Chugani & Phelps, 1991; Chugani, Phelps, & Mazziotta, 1987), functional magnetic resonance imaging (fMRI) (Olesen, Nagy, Westerberg, & Klingberg, 2003), and electroencephalography (Segalowitz & Davis, 2004). For example, Gogtay et al. (2004) mapped cortical gray matter development in 13 healthy children using serial brain MR imaging over 8–10 years. Gray matter development was extrapolated from a model of gray matter density derived using cortical surface and sulcal landmarks. A loss in gray matter density was thought to reflect the synaptic pruning observed in pathological studies, and thus reflect cortical maturation. The authors were able to produce time lapse movies of the sequence of changes in gray matter density over time. They showed that higher-order association cortices (such as the PFC) mature only after the maturation of lower-order cortical areas such as visual cortex, and primary motor and sensory cortex. Association cortex was found to mature in adolescence and early childhood.

It is uncertain whether the apparent decrease in gray matter density from puberty measured by these and other MRI studies represents a pruning of synapses, a loss of neurons, an increase in intracortical myelination, or a combination of all three (Paus, 2005). What is clear is that the human cerebral cortex undergoes significant maturational changes during adolescence, particularly in the frontal lobes, with the orbitofrontal cortex thought to be the last area of the brain to complete maturation (Gogtay et al., 2004). The pattern of decrease in gray matter during the second decade of life closely follows the milestones in human development, with primary motor and sensory areas maturing first, followed only later by the prefrontal areas required for cognitive development and EFs. This pattern of cortical development also follows the same time course as the evolution of the cerebral cortex, with more primitive areas maturing first, followed later by more advanced areas in the anterior frontal lobes which are unique to humans.

In addition to changes in gray matter and white matter volumes, fMRI studies have also suggested a 'switch' in the utilization of pathways for cognition, language, and emotion during adolescence from more instinctual circuits to circuits utilizing prefrontal regions as they come on line with maturation. An example is the switch from childhood to adulthood in using more primitive amygdala-based circuits to more advanced frontal lobe circuits as measured using fMRI during paradigms thought to utilize emotional functions (Killgore, Oki, & Yurgelun-Todd, 2001).

Luna and Sweeney (2004) describe adolescence as a period of "transition to efficient brain collaboration", which occurs as executive circuits become more refined and better connected, and therefore more efficient and effective in organizing and monitoring behavior. As evidence that attentional brain systems become better integrated, they report the stabilization of response suppression errors on an antisaccade task by 15 years of age and highlight that even though young children can inhibit a response, their efficiency in applying this knowledge consistently is what improves into adolescence (Luna, Garver, Urban, Lazar, & Sweeney, 2004). Other executive domains also mature during this developmental stage. Inhibitory control, as measured on the Stroop task is seen to improve steadily during adolescence, and possibly beyond (Leon-Carrion et al., 2004). Attentional control and processing speed undergo steady development over this period, with a possible spurt at 15 years of age (Anderson et al., 2001).

Working memory begins to take on adult form late in adolescence, with studies reporting mature levels of performance by 19 years of age (Luna et al., 2004). These authors found that the distinguishing factor in success on an oculomotor delayed response task was the accuracy of the information encoded, rather than the length of time for which the information could be held online. Luciana et al. (2005) observed improvement in both the mnemonic abilities recruited by a Spatial Working Memory Task and the ability to strategically plan behavior over the age range from 9 to 20 years. Specifically, they found strategic development to reach mature levels at 16–17 years of age.

The multidimensional nature of executive abilities and the considerable inter-dependence of the neural circuits which subserve them mean that although their maturation can be differentiated to some extent, progress in one part of the system will necessarily impact on the development of other related skills. This appears to be the case in the association between gains in strategic planning and organization of goal-directed behavior and the maturation of working memory capability. Our sample of 15- to 19-year-olds were able to devise and apply more efficient self-ordered search strategies in looking for items on the Spatial Working Memory Task (De Luca et al., 2003) (Figure 2.2). Strategic planning for the more difficult items of the task had reached adult levels, and was thought to contribute significantly to reduction in the type of working memory errors seen in younger children whose poor search strategy placed greater pressure on their ability to maintain and manipulate information to direct their actions. The ability to undertake complex problem solving with minimal errors was also demonstrated by 15- to 19-year-olds on a Tower of London Task. As discussed earlier, this discrepancy in performance between younger children and adolescents was seen only on more difficult levels which required greater forward planning and self-monitoring for successful problem solving.

Affective decision-making skills continue to develop throughout adolescence and possibly into adulthood. Hooper, Luciana, Conklin, and Yargar (2004) looked at performance on the Iowa Gambling Task from 13 to 17 years and found that 14- to 17-year-olds shifted their preferences to the advantageous decks earlier than the

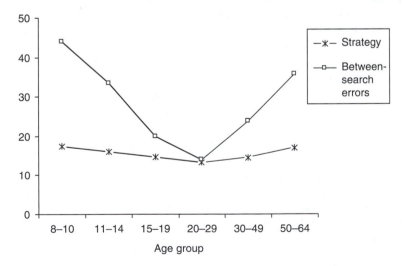

Figure 2.2   Spatial working memory task. Search strategy employed at the most difficult levels of the task, and the number of between-search errors incurred by each age group. *Note*: Lower scores indicate better performance.

Table 2.4 Structural and functional development across adolescence.

Age	Brain development	Cold EF	Hot EF
13 years	Increased white matter in frontal areas Decreased gray matter seen—reduced synaptic density		
14 years	Increased white matter in frontal areas Decreased gray matter seen—reduced synaptic density		Improvements in affective decision making until 17
15 years	Increased white matter in frontal areas Decreased gray matter seen—reduced synaptic density	Improved attentional control Increased processing speed Mature inhibition	
16–19 years	Increased white matter in frontal areas Decreased gray matter seen—reduced synaptic density	Gains in working memory, strategic planning, and problem solving until 19	

younger groups. They also found that this improvement in 'hot' executive functioning was independent from the advances in working memory and inhibitory control that also occur around this time. Importantly, even the 17-year-old teenagers were taking longer than adults to shift their response pattern, suggesting that the ventromedial PFC and orbitofrontal cortex which underlie performance on this task are still undergoing development through late adolescence (Table 2.4).

Adulthood and normal aging: Brief plateau and then the slow decline to older age

Most people would expect that once a person reaches early adulthood they are fully equipped with all the thinking abilities necessary to successfully cope with the demands of higher education, work, and relationships. However, the timing of mature adulthood has been questioned in light of recent data from studies which suggest continued changes in both gray and white matter development well into the third decade, particularly in the frontal and temporal lobes (Benes, Turtle, & Farol, 1994; Sowell et al., 2001). From a person's mid-20s until the latter half of the third decade of life the major change taking place in the PFC is the continued steady increase in myelination (Paus et al., 2001). This is not to say that cortical gray matter remains stable during this period, but perhaps a balance is struck between synaptogenesis and synaptic pruning during early adulthood, such that major changes using structural or functional measures do not detect an alteration in gray matter volume or function. This continued brain maturation was reflected in results from our lifespan study (De Luca et al., 2003), with 20- to 29-year-olds exhibiting peak level executive skills (Figure 2.3). With the final refinement of the frontal system, working memory,

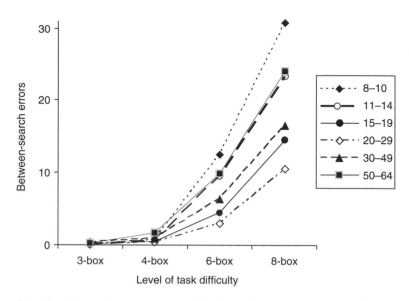

Figure 2.3 Spatial working memory task. Number of "Between-search errors" for each age group at each level of task difficulty. *Note*: Lower scores indicate better performance.

strategic planning, goal setting, and problem solving all reach superior levels. Consistent with this neural maturation, the 20- to 29-year-old group displayed a capacity to take on the most complex and demanding challenges. This level of efficiency and effectiveness appears to last only a few decades before these skills begin to deteriorate in later adulthood. In fact, research on theory of mind skills in adults suggests that mental state reasoning is never truly mastered in the human, which may highlight its recent phylogenetic past. It appears that adults continue to mistakenly predict their own and others' behavior when they are knowledgeable about outcomes, as is proposed by theories of "the curse of knowledge" (Birch & Bloom, 2004; Birch, 2005; Keysar, Lin, & Barr, 2003).

With normal ageing there is a mild deterioration in certain cognitive skills, such as slowed performance of complex tasks, reduction in language complexity, increased time to grasp new activities, and forgetfulness in noncritical areas (Storandt, Grant, Miller, & Morris, 2006). Most of these changes are not obvious until after age 80, although 'degenerative' brain changes may begin as early as the third decade (Yang, Ang, & Strong, 2005). Brain weight begins to decline from age 30, dropping by 10% to age 90 (Brickman et al., 2006). The cause of this weight loss is uncertain, and it is not clear if it reflects loss of neurons or reduction in synaptic connectivity, although there is preferential white matter loss in the prefrontal regions (Salat et al., 2005). While imaging studies are unable to tell us about the underlying histological/ neuropathological changes underlying this reduction in cortical matter, it is suspected that the process of pruning that is occurring at this stage of life is distinct from that involved in refinement of the circuitry during the period from childhood to early adulthood (Sowell et al., 2004). Other changes taking place in older age include the deposition of lipofuscin pigment in nerve cells, the appearance of senile plaques and neurofibrillary tangles (Braak & Braak, 1997), reduction in certain neurotransmitters, and a decrease in cerebral blood flow (de Leon, 2001). These are all considered part of normal ageing of the human brain. Degenerative diseases on the other hand, such as Alzheimers disease, frontotemporal dementia, and Parkinson's disease show acceleration in some of these processes with a propensity to target certain areas such as the frontal and temporal lobes in Alzheimer's disease and the dopaminergic system in Parkinson's disease.

Consistent with findings of neural degeneration beginning from as early as 30 years of age, the developmental literature is now suggesting that declines in executive abilities may begin much earlier than previously thought, with deficient performance on complex tasks occurring well before the original benchmark age of 65 years. From as early as 30–49 years spatial span is reported to decrease significantly, suggesting that these individuals may be considerably less proficient in holding and sequencing information (De Luca et al., 2003). While this does not appear to impact on working memory performance for this group it highlights that processing resources are beginning to diminish, therefore affecting the type and quality of information being delivered to the frontal lobes.

Indeed it has been argued that standard EF tests may be too structured and supportive to elicit subtle deficits in middle-aged individuals. However, Garden, Phillips, and MacPherson (2001) utilized more ecologically valid, open-ended planning tasks to explore whether declines were evident in the age range from 53 to 64 years. They found no difference in performance on the Six Elements Test and Multiple Errands Task for this group when compared to a group of 31- to 46-year-olds. They then contrasted this outcome to performance on a number of formal EF tests, and found that the older group made significantly more errors on two out of the three tasks, with some decline in their concept generation, organization, planning, and attentional set-shifting abilities. These authors concluded that this discrepancy in performance on ecologically valid as compared to clinical tests may reflect the greater opportunity to effectively apply compensatory strategies and knowledge to successfully perform everyday type tasks as opposed to the more abstract formal tests.

In keeping with this argument, we have reported a pronounced reduction in the performance of 50- to 64-year-old adults on aspects of EF (De Luca et al., 2003), with this group performing at levels comparable to our 8- to 10-year-olds on most CANTAB tasks. By 64 years of age spatial span had been reduced to five locations, most likely as a function of forgetting, or an inability to access or retrieve this information once in memory (Cabeza, McIntosh, Tulving, Nyberg, & Grady, 1997; Grady et al., 1995). Working memory had become inefficient with poor strategic planning and a greater number of errors observed on the more difficult trials of the Spatial Working Memory Task. Goal setting and organization had also declined, with older adults requiring significantly more moves to complete the most difficult trials of the Tower task.

While compelling, we must acknowledge the possibility of confounding factors that may have distorted the magnitude of deficits observed in this group. For example, the computer-based medium utilized may have disadvantaged the less-experienced adults. In contrast to the majority of studies in older adults, our tasks were nonverbal, thereby tapping more fluid cognitive functions than the commonly used verbal-based hold tasks. The stimuli presented in some CANTAB tasks are time-limited, potentially restricting the processing and storage of material in the aged population. Our age range was also quite broad, and may have masked the true age at which significant executive decline begins. Finally, our older sample was not screened for medical and psychological disorders such as heart disease, diabetes, chronic illness, and depression, which may have contributed unique variation to performance on these tasks. Such limitations may also be responsible for the inconsistent findings found in the literature on loss of executive ability in the elderly.

Studies supporting our findings include those of Brennan, Welsh, and Fisher (1997) and Raz, Gunning-Dixon, Head, Dupuis, and Acker (1998) who have reported reduced performance on Tower tasks and high perseverative errors in elderly groups. Cognitive flexibility and monitoring skills have been suggested to experience a late onset of impairment past the age of 70 years, although some groups report much earlier deterioration (Boone, 1999; Robbins et al., 1998). One task which has proved sensitive to this decline in set-shifting ability is the Conditional Associative Learning Task (Petrides, 1985). Studies utilizing this test have shown that the basis of the rigid responding made by elderly individuals is attributable to deficits in strategic planning, rather than a function of general cognitive slowing (Levine, Stuss, & Milberg, 1997; Robbins et al., 1998). Older adults also show greater interference on the Stroop task which could be accounted for by decreased working memory function (McCabe, Robertson, & Smith, 2005).

Findings from the literature on cognitive decline raise an important issue; whether all areas of the brain are affected equally, or if specific areas such as the PFC are in fact more vulnerable to age-related processes. Salthouse (2000) provides the main impetus for the 'global-speed hypothesis,' which contests that most age-related discrepancy in task performance can be accounted for by a general decline in processing speed. He has recently adjusted the focus of this argument to suggest that while decline in the elderly is due to a common variable, the nature of this remains questionable (Salthouse, 2000, 2002), and may actually represent a change in information processing capacity rather than simply slowed performance speed (Salthouse, 2001).

There is considerable support for the global-speed hypothesis in the literature. Fisk and Sharp (2004) have described age-related declines in performance for their oldest participants (above 51 years of age) on tasks of inhibition, updating and shifting components of EF. However, once processing speed effects were controlled, this effect was significantly attenuated, raising speculation as to whether executive skills per se are more susceptible to age decline or if general cognitive slowing was responsible for the older adults' difficulties (Fisk & Warr, 1996). Some have argued that findings of an age-related decline in executive functioning in adults over the age of 81 years are spurious as they are simply a reflection of an association with subclinical signs of neurodegenerative disorders which are more frequent in this population (Piguet et al., 2002). However, Wardill and Anderson (chapter 7) demonstrate that this late decline in EF is evident, even when elderly participants are rigorously screened for medical, sensory, or psychiatric conditions.

Span, Ridderinkof, and van der Molen (2004) performed one of the only studies that attempted to solve the puzzle of whether age-related declines in performance on executive tasks, and for that matter, improvement in the performance of children, can be better accounted for by the 'frontal lobe hypothesis' or the 'global-speed hypothesis'. They found that neither model could fully account for the age changes seen over the lifespan from 8 to 79 years of age. However, they did observe that the 60- to 79-year-old group took a disproportionate amount of time to perform executive, as compared to nonexecutive tasks, suggesting that a general slowing in response speed could not account for this discrepancy. Similarly, Verhaeghen and Cerella (2002), in a review of age-related deficits in attentional processes, concluded that a "one-parameter" slowing theory is insufficient to explain all age-related decline.

The general argument against a global-speed hypothesis is that even when provided with no time constraints, elderly people tend to fail on complex executive tasks, although they are still able to perform these activities in their simpler form. While this may represent some aspect of cognitive slowing in that the more time it takes to process information the more susceptible that information becomes to interference, distortion, or loss, it appears more plausible that their performance is a reflection of the brain changes occurring in the PFC and a loss of effectiveness on top of efficiency. This multidimensional model is supported by Schretlen et al.'s (2000) study of 112 participants ranging in age from 20 to 92 years, which explored the contribution of speed, executive skills, and frontal integrity to performance on tests of fluid intelligence. The results showed that each of these factors made a significant contribution to the variance in cognitive ability, suggesting that the 'global-processing' and 'frontal lobe' hypotheses are complementary rather than distinct theories.

It may well be that the inconsistency in findings from the older adult literature result from a number of interacting processes including a reduction in processing speed, which is overlaid on more distinct impairments in other cognitive areas. Arguing for a uniform decline across executive skills may therefore not be appropriate as it would appear that discrete abilities show impairment at different phases of the age spectrum as unique areas of the frontal lobes are more sensitive to age-related atrophy than others. This is not a new idea and has been proposed by other researchers who have found unique age-related deficits in particular executive domains. Not surprisingly though, different studies have found support for earlier decline in opposing areas of the PFC (Garden et al., 2001; Maylor, Moulson, Muncer, & Taylor, 2002).

Lamar and Resnick (2004) set out to specifically compare performance of older adults from 65 to 75 years of age on tasks known to elicit the support of orbitofrontal cortex with those that require the dorsolateral PFC. They found that older individuals were only impaired in performance on orbitofrontal tasks (Iowa Gambling Task and Delayed Matching to Sample Task) when compared to their group of young adults, suggesting that this area may be more vulnerable to age-related changes. Maylor et al. (2002) also found a group of older adults aged 75–89 years performed worse on classic theory of mind tasks when compared to young adults (16–29 years old); however, the errors made by the 60- to 74-year-old group were related to memory decline rather than a breakdown in mental state representation. In contrast,

Garden et al. (2001) and MacPherson, Phillips, & Della Sala (2002) argued that the dorsolateral PFC may undergo earlier decline as they witnessed impairment in the performance of older adults (53–64 years) on formal executive tests purported to involve dorsolateral activation, while they effectively completed complex socially oriented everyday tasks without any difficulty. On a practical level, impaired executive performance on formal assessment has been found to be the best predictor of functional decline in the elderly (Cahn-Weiner, Malloy, Boyle, Marran, & Salloway, 2000).

This confusion in what aspects of cognition decline with age is not surprising considering that the findings are just as inconsistent at the other end of the age spectrum. Certainly in everyday life it would seem that older adults begin to falter in many areas including how quickly they can accomplish things, how well they can solve problems, how long they can maintain focus on a task, and how much they can remember. Contribution from the executive system is necessary for the successful application of all these processes, just as the integrity of all these skills is vital to successful executive performance. Disentangling the primacy or magnitude of such deficits is a necessarily complex task, and will require further study to tip the scales in favor of either aging hypothesis (Table 2.5).

Table 2.5   Structural and functional changes across adulthood and older age.

Age	Brain development	Cold EF	Hot EF
20–29 years	Completion of myelination	Mature working memory, strategic planning	Mature affective decision making ToM deficits still evident under specific circumstances
30–49 years	Brain weight begins to decline, drops by 10% to age 90		
50–64 years	Preferential white matter loss in prefrontal cortex	Sees the beginning of decreased concept generation, organization, planning, set-shifting, working memory, and goal setting Slowed processing speed	
65–74 years	Senile plaques and neurofibrillary tangles Decreased cerebral blood flow		Reduced performance in affective decision making
75+ years	Senile plaques and neurofibrillary tangles Decreased cerebral blood flow		Theory of mind deficits become evident

Do young children and older adults fail executive tasks for the same reasons?

As we have seen, young children are generally immature in their performance on executive tasks, lacking the capacity to plan, monitor, update, and shift their goal-directed actions. Their higher-order skills are prone to perturbation under increased task demands and they have limited ability to utilize other strategies or knowledge to circumvent deficits in a particular area. Older adults on the other hand are often able to complete tasks but are slower and often need to utilize compensatory strategies. In contrast to children, older persons' perseverative errors are due to forgetting, limited capacity for temporal ordering, poor object location, and deficient retrieval of information (Brennan et al., 1997; Cabeza et al., 1997; Raz et al., 1998).

Functional MRI studies comparing activation patterns between children and young adults on executive tests have been helpful in informing knowledge in this area. Studies looking at the development of response inhibition skills show a steady increase in activation of frontal, parietal, cingulate, striatal, and thalamic areas from childhood to adulthood (Luna & Sweeney, 2001; Rubia et al., 2000). An increase in activation of lateral PFC with age has also been described on tasks of working memory (Klingberg, Forssberg, & Westerberg, 2002), along with resistance to interference (Schroeter, Zysset, Wahl, & Yves von Cramon, 2004). These studies suggest that the power of activation corresponds to the extent of functional maturation, and therefore, voluntary control over ones actions (Kwon, Reiss, & Menon, 2002; Rubia et al., 2000).

In contrast, other functional imaging studies hold that essentially the same circuits are activated in children and adults, although the activation is greater in children, both for the volume of cortex engaged to perform the task and the percent signal change (Casey et al., 2000; Gaillard et al., 2000; Tsujimoto et al., 2004). Selective activation of PFC areas involved in inhibitory control with increasing age has also been shown, with adults recruiting fewer and more specific areas than children (Tamm et al., 2002). Interestingly the same pattern of hyperactivation has also been found with tasks of 'hot' EF (Levesque et al., 2004). These studies suggest that the extra neural areas recruited by children are necessary because of the immaturity of the areas primarily subserving these functions, and that the different activation pattern is probably a reflection of the use of distinct strategies to approach the task.

Similar findings of hypo- and hyperactivation of executive circuits have also been reported in the older adult literature (Tisserand & Jolles, 2003). The arguments for decreased activation of PFC areas as corresponding to deficits in executive performance, and increased activation demonstrating the need for more neural resources to perform a task successfully, also pertain to this population. Less strongly lateralized activation is also seen in older adults and young children suggesting that comparable areas in both hemispheres are necessary to deal with novel, complex material, with less specialization resulting in decreased effectiveness of the circuitry involved (Cabeza, 2002; Tsujimoto et al., 2004).

Concluding remarks

The human brain is in a constant state of change from 3 weeks into gestation until death. This dynamic process is most marked in the cerebral cortex and follows an orderly, nonlinear pattern of overlapping stages of new development, remodelling, and ultimate degeneration. Each of these stages is under the control of both genetic factors and environmental influences including the experiences we are exposed to throughout out lives and the patterns of actions and behavior that we repeat and reinforce. The human cortex is unique in size and complexity, no doubt giving humans the capacity for intellectual and cognitive functions far beyond those of our nearest evolutionary species, in particular, executive functioning. Humans have the most protracted childhood and adolescence of all species, and it is during this time that development of the frontal lobes, and particularly the prefrontal cortex, is most active. These areas have been identified as vital contributors to the executive system, and their prolonged maturation parallels the protracted development of these higher-order skills into early adulthood, and their later decline in old age. As these skills come online, behavior becomes more independent, self-directed, and purposeful. Individuals are able to cope with more complex material, and strike a harmony between their emotional and cognitive life. Refinement of this system occurs in stages, with children differing quantitatively and qualitatively from adults in the skills available to them. The developmental trajectory of executive skills follows the childhood gains and older age declines of the frontal lobes, with superior performance reached during one's twenties (Figure 2.4). This system not only provides humans with unique abilities and skills, but also places us at risk of unique diseases, cognitive disabilities, and psychological symptoms related to dysfunction of our volitional, goal-directed actions.

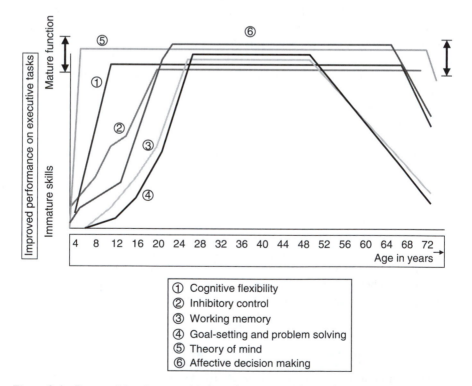

Figure 2.4   Proposed developmental trajectories over the lifespan for selected 'cold' and 'hot' executive functions.

References

Ackerman, B. (1981). Young children's understanding of a false utterance. *Developmental Psychology, 31*, 472–480.

Alloway, T. P., Gathercole, S. E., Willis, C., & Adams, A. -M. (2004). A structural analysis of working memory and related cognitive skills in young children. *Journal of Experimental Child Psychology, 87*, 85–106.

Anderson, P. (2002). Assessment and development of executive function (EF) during childhood. *Child Neuropsychology, 8*(2), 71–82.

Anderson, V. (1998). Assessing executive function in children: Biological, psychological and developmental considerations. *Neuropsychological Rehabilitation, 8*(3), 319–349.

Anderson, V., Anderson, P., Northam, E., Jacobs, R., & Catroppa, C. (2001). Development of executive functions through late childhood and adolescence: An Australian sample. *Developmental Neuropsychology, 20*, 385–406.

Baddeley, A., & Della Sala, S. (1998). Working memory and executive control. In A. C. Roberts, T. W. Robbins, & L. Weiskrantz (Eds.), *The prefrontal cortex: Executive and cognitive functions* (pp. 9–22). Oxford: Oxford University Press.

Baron-Cohen, S., O'Riordan, M., Stone, V., Jones, R., & Plaisted, K. (1999). Recognition of faux pas by normally developing children and children with Asperger syndrome or high-functioning autism. *Journal of Child Psychology and Psychiatry, 38*, 813–822.

Bartsch, K., & Wellman, H. M. (1989). Young children's attribution of action to beliefs and desires. *Child Development, 60*, 946–964.

Benes, F. M., Turtle, M., & Farol, P. (1994). Myelination of a key relay zone in the hippocampal formation occurs in the human brain during childhood, adolescence, and adulthood. *Archives of General Psychiatry, 51*, 477–484.

Birch, S. A. J. (2005). When knowledge is a curse. Children's and adults' reasoning about mental states. *Current Directions in Psychological Science, 14*(1), 25–29.

Birch, S. A. J., & Bloom, P. (2004). Understanding children's and adults' limitations in mental state reasoning. *Trends in Cognitive Sciences, 8*(6), 256–260.

Boone, K. B. (1999). Neuropsychological assessment of executive functions: Impact of age, education, gender, intellectual level and vascular status on executive test scores. In B. L. Miller, & J. L. Cummings (Eds.), *The human frontal lobes: Function and disorders* (pp. 247–261). New York: The Guilford Press.

Braak, H., & Braak, E. (1997). Frequency of stages of Alzheimer-related lesions in different age categories. *Neurobiology of Aging, 18*(4), 351–357.

Brennan, M., Welsh, M. C., & Fisher, C. B. (1997). Aging and executive function skills: An examination of a community-dwelling older adult population. *Perceptual and Motor Skills, 84*, 1187–1197.

Brickman, A. M., Zimmerman, M. E., Paul, R. H., Grieve, S. M., Tate, D. F., Cohen, R. A., et al. (2006). Regional white matter and neuropsychological functioning across the adult lifespan. *Biological Psychiatry, 69*(5), 444–453.

Brocki, K. C., & Bohlin, G. (2004). Executive functions in children aged 6 to 13: A dimensional and developmental study. *Developmental Neuropsychology, 26*(2), 571–593.

Brody, B. A., Kinney, H. C., Kloman, A. S., & Gilles, F. H. (1987). Sequence of central nervous system myelination in human infancy. I: An autopsy study of myelination. *Journal of Neuropathology and Experimental Neurology, 46*, 283–301.

Brune, M., & Brune-Cohrs, U. (2006). Theory of mind-evolution, ontogeny, brain mechanisms and psychopathology. *Neuroscience and Biobehavioral Reviews, 30*, 437–455.

Cabeza, R. (2002). Hemispheric asymmetry reduction in older adults: The HAROLD model. *Psychology and Aging, 17*, 85–100.

Cabeza, R., McIntosh, A. F., Tulving, E., Nyberg, L., & Grady, C. L. (1997). Age-related differences in effective neural connectivity during encoding and recall. *NeuroReport, 8*(16), 3479–3483.

Cahn-Weiner, D. A., Malloy, P. F., Boyle, P. A., Marran, M., & Salloway, S. (2000). Prediction of functional status from neuropsychological tests in community-dwelling elderly individuals. *Clinical Neuropsychology, 14*(2), 187–195.

Carlson, S. M., Mandell, D. J., & Williams, L. (2004). Executive function and theory of mind: Stability and prediction from ages 2 to 3. *Developmental Psychology, 40*(6), 1105–1122.

Casey, B. J., Giedd, J. N., & Thomas, K. M. (2000). Structural and functional brain development and its relation to cognitive development. *Biological Psychiatry, 54*, 241–257.

Cepeda, N. J., Kramer, A. F., & Gonzalez de Sather, J. C. (2001). Changes in executive control across the lifespan: Examination of task-switching performance. *Developmental Psychology, 37*(5), 715–730.

Chelune, G. J., & Baer, R. A. (1986). Developmental norms of the Wisconsin Card Sorting Test. *Journal of Clinical and Experimental Neuropsychology, 8*(3), 219–228.

Choe, K. S., Keil, F. C., & Bloom, P. (2005). Children's understanding of the Ulysses conflict. *Developmental Science, 8*(5), 387–392.

Chugani, H. T., & Phelps, M. E. (1991). Imaging human brain development with positron emission tomography. *Journal of Nuclear Medicine, 32*, 23–26.

Chugani, H. T., Phelps, M. E., & Mazziotta, J. C. (1987). Positron emission tomography study of human brain functional development. *Annals of Neurology, 22*, 487–497.

Cummings, J. L. (1993). Frontal-subcortical circuits and human behaviour. *Archives of Neurology, 50*, 873–880.

de Leon, M. J. (2001). Prediction of cognitive decline in normal elderly subjects with 2-[(18)F] fluoro-2-deoxy-D-glucose/positron-emission tomography (FDG/PET). *Proceedings of the National Academy of Science USA, 98*(19), 10966–10971.

De Luca, C. R., Wood, S. J., Anderson, V., Buchanan, J. -A., Proffitt, T., Mahony, K., et al. (2003). Normative data from the CANTAB. I: Development of executive function over the lifespan. *Journal of Clinical and Experimental Neuropsychology, 25*(2), 242–254.

Diamond, A. (1985). Development of the ability to use recall to guide action, as indicated by infants' performance on AB. *Child Development, 56*(4), 868–883.

Diamond, A., Kirkham, N., & Amso, D. (2002). Conditions under which young children can hold two rules in mind and inhibit a prepotent response. *Developmental Psychology, 38*(3), 352–362.

Diamond, A., Lee, E., & Hayden, M. (2003). Early success in using the relation between stimuli and rewards to deduce an abstract rule: Perceived physical connection is key. *Developmental Psychology, 39*(5), 825–847.

Diamond, A., & Taylor, C. (1996). Development of an aspect of executive control: Development of the abilities to remember what I said and to "Do as I say, not as I do". *Developmental Psychobiology, 29*(4), 312–334.

Diamond, A., Towle, C., & Boyer, K. (1994). Young children's performance on a task sensitive to the memory functions of the medial temporal lobe in adults—the delayed nonmatching-to-sample task—reveals problems that are due to non-memory-related task demands. *Behavioural Neuroscience, 108*(4), 659–680.

Dias, R., Robbins, T. W., & Roberts, A. C. (1997). Dissociable forms of inhibitory control within prefrontal cortex with an analog of the Wisconsin Card Sort Test: Restriction to novel situations and independence from "on-line" processing. *Journal of Neuroscience, 17*(23), 9285–9297.

Dobbing, J., & Sands, J. (1973). Quantitative growth and development of human brain. *Archives of Disease in Childhood, 48,* 757–767.

Dowsett, S. M., & Livesey, D. J. (2000). The development of inhibitory control in preschool children: Effects of "executive skills" training. *Developmental Psychobiology, 36*(2), 161–174.

Dubas, J. (1991). Cognitive abilities and physical maturation. In R. Lerner, et al. (Eds.), *Encyclopedia of adolescence* (Vol. 1, pp. 133–138). New York: Garland Publishing.

Elston, G. N., Benavides-Piccione, R., & DeFelipe, J. (2001). The pyramidal cell in cognition: A comparative study in human and monkey. *The Journal of Neuroscience, 21,* RC163.

Espy, K. A. (2004). Using developmental, cognitive, and neuroscience approaches to understand executive control in young children. *Developmental Neuropsychology, 26*(1), 379–384.

Espy, K. A., Kaufmann, P. M., Glisky, M. L., & McDiarmid, M. D. (2001). New procedures to access executive functions in preschool children. *The Clinical Neuropsychologist, 15*(1), 46–58.

Espy, K. A., Kaufmann, P. M., McDiarmid, M. D., & Glisky, M. L. (1999). Executive functioning in preschool children: Performance on A-Not-B and other delayed response format tasks. *Brain and Cognition, 41,* 178–199.

Fisk, J. E., & Sharp, C. A. (2004). Age-related impairment in executive functioning: Updating, inhibition, shifting, and access. *Journal of Clinical and Experimental Neuropsychology, 26*(7), 874–890.

Fisk, J. E., & Warr, P. (1996). Age and working memory: The role of perceptual speed, the central executive, and the phonological loop. *Psychological Aging, 11*(2), 316–323.

Flavell, J. H. (1999). Cognitive development: Children's knowledge about the mind. *Annual Review of Psychology, 50,* 21–45.

Fletcher, J. M. (1996). Executive functions in children: Introduction to the special series. *Developmental Neuropsychology, 12*(1), 1–3.

Flynn, E., O'Malley, C. O., & Wood, D. (2004). A longitudinal, microgenetic study of the emergence of false belief understanding and inhibition skills. *Developmental Science, 7*(1), 103–115.

Fuster, J. M. (2002). Frontal lobe and cognitive development. *Journal of Neurocytology, 31,* 373–385.

Gaillard, W. D., Hertz-Pannier, L., Mott, S. H., Barnett, A. S., LeBihan, D., & Theodore, W. H. (2000). Functional anatomy of cognitive development: fMRI of verbal fluency in children and adults. *Neurology, 54*(1), 180–189.

Gallagher, H. L., & Frith, C. D. (2003). Functional imaging of 'theory of mind'. *Trends in Cognitive Sciences, 7*(2), 77–83.

Garden, S. E., Phillips, L. H., & MacPherson, S. E. (2001). Midlife aging, open-ended planning, and laboratory measures of executive function. *Neuropsychology, 15*(4), 472–482.

Garon, N., & Moore, C. (2004). Complex decision-making in early childhood. *Brain and Cognition, 55,* 158–170.

Garth, J., Anderson, V., & Wrennall, J. (1997). Executive functions following moderate to severe frontal lobe injury: Impact of injury and age at injury. *Pediatric Rehabilitation, 1*(2), 99–108.

Ge, Y., Grossman, R. I., Babb, J. S., Rabin, M. L., Mannon, L. J., & Kolson, D. (2002). Age-related total gray matter and white matter changes in normal adult brain. Part I: Volumetric MR imaging analysis. *AJNR American Journal of Neuroradiology, 23*(8), 1327–1333.

Gerstadt, C. L., Hong, Y. J., & Diamond, A. (1994). The relationship between cognition and action: Performance of children $3\frac{1}{2}$–7 years old on a stroop-like day–night test. *Cognition, 53*(2), 129–153.

Giedd, J. N. (1999). Brain development during childhood and adolescence: A longitudinal MRI study. *Nature Neuroscience, 2*(10), 861–863.

Giedd, J. N., Vaituzis, A. C., Hamburger, S., Lange, N., Rajapakse, J. C., Kaysen, D., et al. (1996). Quantitative MRI of the temporal lobe, amygdala, and hippocampus in normal development: Ages 4–18 Years. *The Journal of Comparative Neurology, 366*, 223–230.

Gogtay, N., Giedd, J. N., Lusk, L., Hayashi, K. M., Greenstein, D., Vaituzis, A. C., et al. (2004). Dynamic mapping of human cortical development during childhood through early adulthood. *Proceedings of the National Academy of Science USA, 101*, 8174–8179.

Golden, C. J. (1981). Luria Nebraska children's battery: Theory and formulation. In G. W. Hynd & J. E. Obzut (Eds.), *Neuropsychological assessment of the school-aged child* (pp. 277–302). NT: Grune and Stratton.

Gottlieb, G., & Halpern, C. (2002). A relational view of causality in normal and abnormal development. *Developmental Psychopathology, 14*(3), 421–435.

Grady, C. L., McIntosh, A. R., Horwitz, B., Maisog, J. M., Ungerleider, L. G., Mentis, P. P., et al. (1995). Age-related reductions in human recognition memory due to impaired encoding. *Science, 269*, 218–221.

Happaney, K., Zelazo, P. D., & Stuss, D. T. (2004). Development of orbitofrontal function: Current themes and future directions. *Brain and Cognition, 55*, 1–10.

Happe, F. (1994). An advanced test of theory of mind: Understanding of story characters' thoughts and feelings by able autistic, mentally handicapped, and normal children and adults. *Journal of Autism and Developmental Disorders, 24*, 129–154.

Hongwanishkul, D., Happaney, K., Lee, W. S. C., & Zelazo, P. D. (2005). Assessment of hot and cold executive function in young children: Age-related changes and individual differences. *Developmental Neuropsychology, 28*(2), 617–644.

Hooper, C. J., Luciana, M., Conklin, H. M., & Yargar, R. S. (2004). Adolescents' performance on the Iowa gambling task: Implications for the development of decision making and ventromedial prefrontal cortex. *Developmental Psychology, 40*(6), 1148–1158.

Hughes, C. (1998). Executive function in preschoolers: Links with theory of mind and verbal ability. *British Journal of Developmental Psychology, 16*, 233–253.

Hughes, C. (2002). Executive functions and development: Emerging themes. *Infant and Child Development, 11*, 201–209.

Hughes, C., & Leekam, S. R. (2004). What are the links between theory of mind and social relations? Review, reflections and new directions for studies of typical and atypical development. *Social Development, 13*(4), 590–619.

Huttenlocher, P. R. (1979). Synaptic density in human frontal cortex—developmental changes and effects of aging. *Brain Research, 163*, 195–205.

Huttenlocher, P. R. (1990). Morphometric study of human cerebral cortex development. *Neuropsychologia, 28*, 517–527.

Huttenlocher, P. R., & Dabholkar, A. S. (1997). Regional differences in synaptogenesis in human cerebral cortex. *Journal of Comparative Neurology, 387*, 167–178.

Katz, L. C., & Shatz, C. J. (1996). Synaptic activity and the construction of cortical circuits. *Science, 274*, 1133–1138.

Kempton, S., Vance, A., Luk, M. E., Costin, J., & Pantelis, C. (1999). Executive function and attention deficit hyperactivity disorder: Stimulant medication and better executive function performance in children. *Psychological Medicine, 29*, 527–538.

Kerr, A., & Zelazo, P. D. (2004). Development of "hot" executive function: The children's gambling task. *Brain and Cognition, 55*, 148–157.

Keysar, B., Lin, S., & Barr, D. J. (2003). Limits on theory of mind use in adults. *Cognition, 89*, 25–41.

Killgore, W. D., Oki, M., & Yurgelun-Todd, D. A. (2001). Sex-specific developmental changes in amygdala responses to affective faces. *NeuroReport, 12,* 427–433.

Kinney, H. C., Brody, B. A., Kloman, A. S., & Gilles, F. H. (1988). Sequence of central nervous system myelination in human infancy. II. Patterns of myelination in autopsied infants. *Journal of Neuropathology and Experimental Neurology, 47,* 217–234.

Klimkeit, E. I., Mattingley, J. B., Sheppard, D. M., Farrow, M., & Bradshaw, J. L. (2004). Examining the development of attention and executive functions in children with a novel paradigm. *Child Neuropsychology, 10*(3), 201–211.

Klingberg, T., Forssberg, H., & Westerberg, H. (2002). Increased brain activity in frontal and parietal cortex underlies the development of visuospatial working memory capacity during childhood. *Journal of Cognitive Neuroscience, 14*(1), 1–10.

Klingberg, T., Vaidya, C. J., Gabrieli, J. D. E., Moseley, M. E., & Hedehus, M. (1999). Myelination and organization of the frontal white matter in children: A diffusion tensor MRI study. *NeuroReport, 10,* 2817–2821.

Korkman, M., Kemp, S. L., & Kirk, U. (2001). Effects of age on neurocognitive measures of children ages 5 to 12: A cross-sectional study on 800 children from the United States. *Developmental Neuropsychology, 20*(1), 331–354.

Kray, J., Eber, J., & Lindenberger, U. (2004). Age differences in executive functioning across the lifespan: The role of verbalization in task preparation. *Acta Psychologica, 115,* 143–165.

Kretschmann, H. J., Kammradt, G., Krauthausen, I., Sauer, B., & Wingert, F. (1986). Brain growth in man. *Bibliotheca Anatomica, 28,* 1–26.

Kuan, C. Y., Roth, K. A., Flavell, R. A., & Rakic, P. (2000). Mechanisms of programmed cell death in the developing brain. *Trends in Neuroscience, 23*(7), 291–297.

Kwon, H., Reiss, A. L., & Menon, V. (2002). Neural basis of protracted developmental changes in visuo-spatial working memory. *Proceedings of the National Academy of Science USA, 99*(22), 13336–13341.

Lamar, M., & Resnick, S. M. (2004). Aging and prefrontal functions: Dissociating orbito-frontal and dorsolateral abilities. *Neurobiology of Aging, 25*(4), 553–558.

Lehto, J. E., Juujarvi, P., Kooistra, L., & Pulkkinen, L. (2003). Dimensions of executive functioning: Evidence from children. *British Journal of Developmental Psychology, 21,* 59–80.

Leon-Carrion, J., Garcia-Orza, J., & Perez-Santamaria, F. J. (2004). Development of the inhibitory component of the executive functions in children and adolescents. *International Journal of Neuroscience, 114,* 1291–1311.

Leslie, A. (2005). Developmental parallels in understanding minds and bodies. *Trends in Cognitive Sciences, 9*(10), 459–462.

Leslie, A. M. (1987). Pretense and representation: The origins of "theory of mind". *Psychological Review, 51,* 412–426.

Leslie, A. M., Friedman, O., & German, T. P. (2004). Core mechanisms in "theory of mind". *Trends in Cognitive Sciences, 8*(12), 528–533.

Levesque, J., Joanette, Y., Mensour, B., Beaudoin, G., Leroux, J. -M., Bourgouin, P., et al. (2004). Neural basis of emotional self-regulation in childhood. *Neuroscience, 129,* 361–369.

Levin, H. S., Culhane, K. A., Hartmann, J., Evankovich, K., Mattson, A. J., Harward, H., et al. (1991). Developmental changes in performance on tests of purported frontal lobe functioning. *Developmental Neuropsychology, 7,* 377–395.

Levine, B., Stuss, D. T., & Milberg, W. P. (1997). Effects of aging on conditional associative learning: Process analysis and comparison with focal frontal lesions. *Neuropsychology, 11*(3), 367–381.

Lezak, M. (1995). *Neuropsychological assessment*. New York: Oxford.

Luciana, M., Conklin, H. M., Hooper, C. J., & Yargar, R. S. (2005). The development of nonverbal working memory and executive control processes in adolescents. *Child Development, 76*(3), 697–712.

Luciana, M., & Nelson, C. A. (1998). The functional emergence of prefrontally-guided working memory systems in four- to eight-year-old children. *Neuropsychologia, 36*(3), 273–293.

Luciana, M., & Nelson, C. A. (2002). Assessment of neuropsychological function through use of the Cambridge Neuropsychological Testing Automated Battery: Performance in 4- to 12-year-old children. *Developmental Neuropsychology, 22*(3), 595–624.

Luna, B., Garver, K. E., Urban, T. A., Lazar, N. A., & Sweeney, J. A. (2004). Maturation of cognitive processes from late childhood to adulthood. *Child Development, 75*(5), 1357–1372.

Luna, B., Minshew, N. J., Garver, K. E., Lazar, N. A., Thulborn, K. R., Eddy, W. F., et al. (2002). Neocortical system abnormalities in autism: An fMRI study of spatial working memory. *Neurology, 59*, 834–840.

Luna, B., & Sweeney, J. A. (2001). Studies of brain and cognitive maturation through childhood and adolescence: A strategy for testing neurodevelopmental hypotheses. *Schizophrenia Bulletin, 27*(3), 443–455.

Luna, B., & Sweeney, J. A. (2004). The emergence of collaborative brain function: fMRI studies of the development of response inhibition. *Annals New York Academy of Sciences, 1021*, 296–309.

Luria, A.R. (1973). *The working brain: An introduction to neuropsychology*. Great Britain: Penguin Books.

MacPherson, S. E., Phillips, L. H., & Della Sala, S. (2002). Age, executive function, and social decision making: A dorsolateral prefrontal theory of cognitive aging. *Psychological Aging, 17*(4), 598–609.

Matsuzawa, J., Matsui, M., Konishi, T., Noguchi, K., Gur, R. C., Bilker, W., et al. (2001). Age-related changes of brain gray and white matter in healthy infants and children. *Cerebral Cortex, 11*, 335–342.

Maylor, E. A., Moulson, J. M., Muncer, A. -M., & Taylor, L. A. (2002). Does performance on theory of mind tasks decline in old age? *British Journal of Psychology, 93*, 465–485.

McCabe, D. P., Robertson, C. L., & Smith, A. D. (2005). Age differences in stroop interference in working memory. *Journal of Clinical and Experimental Neuropsychology, 27*(5), 633–644.

Meltzoff, A. N. (1999). Origins of theory of mind, cognition and communication. *Journal of Communication Disorders, 32*(4), 251–269.

Olesen, P. J., Nagy, Z., Westerberg, H., & Klingberg, T. (2003). Combined analysis of DTI and fMRI data reveals a joint maturation of white and grey matter in a fronto-parietal network. *Brain Research, Cognitive Brain Research, 18*, 48–57.

Orzhekhovskaya, N.S. (1981). Fronto-striatal relationships in primate ontogeny. *Neuroscience and Behavioural Physiology, 11*, 379–385.

Pantelis, C., Barnes, T. R., Nelson, H. E., Tanner, S., Weatherley, L., Owen, A. M., et al. (1997). Fronto-striatal cognitive deficits in patients with chronic schizophrenia. *Brain, 120*, 1823–1843.

Parkin, A. J. (1996). *Explorations in cognitive psychology*. Oxford: Blackwell.

Paus, T. (2005). Mapping brain maturation and cognitive development during adolescence. *Trends in Cognitive Sciences, 9*, 60–68.

Paus, T., Collins, D. L., Evans, A. C., Leonard, G., Pike, B., & Zijdenbos, A. (2001). Maturation of white matter in the human brain: A review of magnetic resonance studies. *Brain Research Bulletin, 54*(3), 255–266.

Pennington, B. F. (2002). *The development of psychopathology: Nature and nurture.* New York: The Guilford Press.

Perner, J., & Lang, B. (1999). Development of theory of mind and executive control. *Trends in Neuroscience, 3*(9), 337–344.

Perner, J., Lang, B., & Kloo, D. (2002). Theory of mind and self-control: More than a common problem of inhibition. *Child Development, 73*, 752–767.

Perner, J., Ruffman, T., & Leekam, S. R. (1994). Theory of mind is contagious: You catch it from your sibs. *Child Development, 65*, 1228–1238.

Perner, J., & Wimmer, H. (1985). 'John thinks that Mary thinks that...': Attribution of second-order beliefs by 5- to 10-year old children. *Journal of Experimental Child Psychology, 39*, 437–471.

Petrides, M. (1985). Deficits on conditional associative-learning tasks after frontal- and temporal-lobe lesions in man. *Neuropsychologia, 23*, 601–614.

Piaget, J. (1965). *Moral judgment of the child.* New York: Free Press.

Piguet, O., Grayson, D. A., Broe, G. A., Tate, R. L., Bennett, H. P., Lye, T. C., et al. (2002). Normal aging and executive function in "old–old" community dwellers poor performance is not an inevitable outcome. *International Psychogeriatrics, 14*(2), 139–159.

Prencipe, A., & Zelazo, P. D. (2005). Development of affective decision making for self and other. Evidence for the integration of first- and third-person perspectives. *Psychological Science, 16*(7), 501–505.

Rakic, P. (1988). Specification of cerebral cortical areas. *Science, 241*, 170–176.

Rakic, P., Bourgeois, J. A., & Goldman-Rakic, P. S. (1994). Synaptic development of the cerebral cortex: Implications for learning, memory, and mental illness. *Progress in Brain Research, 102*, 227–243.

Rapoport, J. L., Giedd, J. N., Blumenthal, J., Hamburger, S., Jeffries, N., Fernandez, T., et al. (1999). Progressive cortical change during adolescence in childhood-onset schizophrenia. A longitudinal magnetic resonance imaging study. *Archives of General Psychiatry, 56*(7), 649–654.

Raz, N., Gunning-Dixon, F. M., Head, D., Dupuis, J. H., & Acker, J. D. (1998). Neuroanatomical correlates of cognitive aging: Evidence from structural magnetic resonance imaging. *Neuropsychology, 12*(1), 95–114.

Reiss, A. L., Abrams, M. T., Singer, H. S., Ross, J. L., & Denckla, M. B. (1996). Brain development, gender and IQ in children. A volumetric imaging study. *Brain, 119*(Pt 5), 1763–1774.

Repacholi, B. M., & Gopnik, A. (1997). Early reasoning about desires: Evident from 14- and 18-month-olds. *Developmental Psychology, 33*, 12–21.

Robbins, T. W., James, M., Owen, A. M., Sahakian, B. J., Lawrence, A. D., McInnes, L., et al. (1998). A study of performance on tests from the CANTAB battery sensitive to frontal lobe dysfunction in a large sample of normal volunteers implications for theories of executive functioning and cognitive aging. *Journal of the International Neuropsychological Society, 4*(5), 474–490.

Rochat, P., & Striano, T. (1999). Emerging self-exploration by 2-month-old infants. *Developmental Science, 2*(2), 206–218.

Roth, G., & Dicke, U. (2005). Evolution of the brain and intelligence. *Trends in Cognitive Sciences, 9*(5), 250–257.

Rubia, K., Overmeyer, S., Taylor, E., Brammer, M., Williams, S. C., Simmons, A., et al. (2000). Functional frontalisation with age: Mapping neurodevelopmental trajectories with fMRI. *Neuroscience Biobehavioural Review, 24*(1), 13–19.

Rutter, M. (2002). The interplay of nature, nurture, and developmental influences. *Archives of General Psychiatry, 59*, 996–1000.

Sabbagh, M. A. (2003). Understanding orbitofrontal contributions to theory-of-mind reasoning: Implications for autism. *Brain and Cognition, 55,* 209–219.

Salat, D. H., Tuch, D. S., Greve, D. N., van der Kouwe, A. J. W., Hevelone, N. D., Zaleta, A. K., et al. (2005). Age-related alternations in white matter microstructure measured by diffusion tensor imaging. *Neurobiology of Aging, 26*(8), 1215–1227.

Salthouse, T. A. (2000). Aging and measures of processing speed. *Biological Psychiatry, 54,* 35–54.

Salthouse, T. A. (2001). Attempted decomposition of age-related influences on two tests of reasoning. *Psychology and Aging, 16*(2), 251–263.

Salthouse, T. A. (2002) Age-related effects on memory in the context of age-related effects on cognition. In P. Graf, & N. Ohta (Eds.), *Lifespan development of human memory* (pp. 139–158). Massachusetts: The MIT Press.

Saxe, R., Carey, S., & Kanwisher, N. (2004). Understanding other minds: Linking developmental psychology and functional neuroimaging. *Annual Review of Psychology, 55,* 87–124.

Scahill, R. I., Frost, C., Jenkins, R., Whitwell, J. L., Rossor, M. N., & Fox, N. C. (2003). A longitudinal study of brain volume changes in normal aging using serial registered magnetic resonance imaging. *Archives of Neurology, 60*(7), 989–994.

Schretlen, D., Pearlson, G. D., Anthony, J. C., Aylward, E. H., Augustine, A. M., Davis, A., et al. (2000). Elucidating the contributions of processing speed, executive ability, and frontal lobe volume to normal age-related differences in fluid intelligence. *Journal of the International Neuropsychological Society, 6*(1), 52–61.

Schroeter, M. L., Zysset, S., Wahl, M., & Yves von Cramon, D. (2004). Prefrontal activation due to Stroop interference increases during development—An event-related fNIRS study. *NeuroImage, 23,* 1317–1325.

Segalowitz, S. J., & Davis, P. L. (2004). Charting the maturation of the frontal lobe: An electrophysiological strategy. *Brain and Cognition, 55,* 116–133.

Senn, T. E., Espy, K. A., & Kaufmann, P. M. (2004). Using path analysis to understand executive function organisation in preschool children. *Developmental Neuropsychology, 26*(1), 445–464.

Shallice, T. (1990). *From neuropsychology to mental structure.* New York: Cambridge University Press.

Shatz, C. J. (1992). The developing brain. *Scientific American, 267,* 35–41.

Smidts, D. P., Jacobs, R., & Anderson, V. (2004). The object classification task for children (OCTC): A measure of concept generation and mental flexibility in early childhood. *Developmental Neuropsychology, 26*(1), 385–401.

Sodian, B., Taylor, C., Harris, P. L., & Perner, J. (1991). Early deception and the child's theory of mind: False trails and genuine markers. *Child Development, 62,* 468–483.

Sommerville, J. A., Woodward, A. L., & Needham, A. (2005). Action experience alters 3-month-old infants' perception of others' actions. *Cognition, 96*(1), B1–B11.

Sowell, E. R., Peterson, P. B., Thompson, P. M., Welcome, S. E., Henkenius, A. L., & Toga, A. W. (2003). Mapping cortical change across the human lifespan. *Nature Neuroscience, 6,* 309–315.

Sowell, E. R., Thompson, P. M., Holmes, C. J., Jernigan, T. L., & Toga, A. W. (1999). *In vivo* evidence for post-adolecent brain maturation in frontal and striatal regions. *Nature Neuroscience, 2*(10), 859–861.

Sowell, E. R., Thompson, P. M., Leonard, C. M., Welcome, S. E., Kan, E., & Toga, A. W. (2004). Longitudinal mapping of cortical thickness and brain growth in normal children. *Journal of Neuroscience, 24,* 8223–8231.

Sowell, E. R., Thompson, P. M., Tessner, K. D., & Toga, A. W. (2001). Mapping continued brain growth and gray matter density reduction in dorsal frontal cortex: Inverse relationships during postadolescent brain maturation. *The Journal of Neuroscience*, *21*(22), 8819–8829.

Sowell, E. R., Thompson, P. M., & Toga, A. W. (2004). Mapping changes in the human cortex throughout the span of life. *Neuroscientist*, *10*, 372–392.

Span, M. M., Ridderinkhof, K. R., & van der Molen, M. W. (2004). Age-related changes in the efficiency of cognitive processing across the lifespan. *Acta Psychologica*, *117*, 155–183.

Steinberg, L. (2005). Cognitive and affective development in adolescence. *Trends in Cognitive Sciences*, *9*(2), 69–74.

Storandt, M., Grant, E. A., Miller, J. P., & Morris, J. C. (2006). Longitudinal course and neuropathologic outcomes in original vs revised MCI and in pre-MCI. *Neurology*, *67*(3), 467–473.

Stuss, D. T. (1992). Biological and psychological development of executive functions. *Brain and Cognition*, *20*, 8–23.

Stuss, D. T., & Alexander, M. P. (2000). Executive functions and the frontal lobes: A conceptual view. *Psychological Research*, *63*(3–4), 289–298.

Tamm, L., Menon, V., & Reiss, A. L. (2002). Maturation of brain function associated with response inhibition. *Journal of the American Academy of Child and Adolescent Psychiatry*, *41*(10), 1231–1238.

Temple, C. (1997). *Developmental Cognitive Neuropsychology*. London: Psychology Press.

Tisserand, D. J., & Jolles, J. (2003). On the involvement of prefrontal networks in cognitive aging. *Cortex*, *39*, 1107–1128.

Tramontana, M. G., & Hooper, S. R. (1989). Neuropsychology of child psychopathology. In C. R. Reynolds & E. Fletcher-Janzen (Eds.), *Handbook of clinical child neuropsychology* (pp. 87–106). New York: Plenum Press.

Travis, F. (1998). Cortical and cognitive development in 4th, 8th and 12th grade students: The contribution of speed of processing and executive function to cognitive development. *Biological Psychiatry*, *48*, 37–56.

Tsujimoto, S., Yamamoto, T., Kawaguchi, H., Koizumi, H., & Sawaguchi, T. (2004). Prefrontal cortical activation associated with working memory in adults and preschool children: An event-related optical topography study. *Cerebral Cortex*, *14*(7), 703–712.

Verhaeghen, P., & Cerella, J. (2002). Aging, executive control, and attention: A review of meta-analyses. *Neuroscience and Biobehavioral Reviews*, *26*, 849–857.

Volpe, J. J. (1995). Neuronal proliferation, migration, organization and myelination. In J. J. Volpe (Ed.), *Neurology of the newborn* (3rd ed., pp. 43–92). Philadelphia: Saunders.

Walker, L. J., Hennig, K. H., & Krettenauer, T. (2000). Parent and peer contexts for children's moral reasoning development. *Child Development*, *71*(4), 1033–1048.

Weinberger, D. R., Egan, M. F., Bertolino, A., Callicott, J. H., Mattay, V. S., Lipska, B. K., et al. (2001). Prefrontal neurons and the genetics of schizophrenia. *Biological Psychiatry*, *50*(11), 825–844.

Welker, W. (1990). Why does the cerebral cortex fold? A review of determinants of Gyri and Sulci. In E. G. Jones, & A. Peters (Eds.), *Cerebral cortex* (Vol. 1, pp. 3–136). New York: Plenium Press.

Welsh, M. C., & Pennington, B. F. (1988). Assessing frontal lobe functioning in children: Views from developmental psychology. *Developmental Psychology*, *4*, 199–230.

Weyandt, L. L., & Willis, W. G. (1994). Executive functions in school-aged children: Potential efficacy of tasks in discriminating clinical groups. *Developmental Neuropsychology*, *10*(1), 27–38.

Wimmer, H., & Perner, J. (1983). Beliefs about beliefs: Representation and constraining function of wrong beliefs in young children's understanding of deception. *Cognition, 13*, 103–128.

Woodward, A. L. (1998). Infants selectively encode the goal object of an actor's reach. *Cognition, 69*, 1–34.

Yakovlev, P. I., & Lecours, A. R. (1967). The myelogenetic cycles of regional maturation of the brain. In A. Minokowski (Ed.), *Regional development of the brain in early life* (pp. 3–70). Philadelphia: Blackwell.

Yang, W., Ang, L. C., & Strong, M. J. (2005). Tau protein aggregation in the frontal and entorhinal cortices as a function of aging. *Developmental Brain Research, 156*(2), 127–138.

Zelazo, P. D., Craik, F. I. M., & Booth, L. (2004). Executive function across the lifespan. *Acta Psychologica, 115*, 167–183.

3   Adult aging and executive functioning

Louise H. Phillips and Julie D. Henry

Contents

Prior to the mid-1990s, the dominant theory of cognitive aging explained deficits in memory and reasoning in terms of general information processing parameters such as processing speed (Cerella, 1985; Salthouse, 1985). Such theories arose to explain the fact that age differences in apparently simple tasks such as choice reaction time often have overlapping variance with age differences in much more complex tasks such as episodic memory or visuospatial reasoning. In the past decade, the main explanatory variables within cognitive aging research have changed from general resource measures to more specific cognitive control or executive functions. This has arisen largely from the influence of structural neuroimaging studies, which have indicated localized and early age-related deterioration in the frontal lobes of the brain. Because the frontal lobes have been so closely linked with executive functioning, this has led to the *frontal-executive theory of aging* (see also chapter 7, this volume), which proposes that age changes in the structure and function of the frontal lobes cause impaired executive functioning, which in turn leads to the well-documented changes in a range of cognitive processes such as episodic memory and fluid intelligence (Moscovitch & Winocur, 1992; West, 1996). In neurophysiological terms, the frontal-executive theory of aging proposes that age-related changes in cognition are explained by early, localized changes found in the frontal lobes of the brain. In cognitive terms, age changes in a variety of memory and reasoning tasks are attributed to poorer executive functions, i.e., less efficient operation of cognitive control processes such as inhibition, switching, and planning.

In this chapter, we outline the effects of aging across a range of these executive functions, and the advantages and disadvantages of various approaches to measurement in this domain. We describe some of the problems inherent in attributing these effect, specifically to the frontal lobes, and we consider the implications that these changes have for cognition and behavior in old age. Here we focus solely on normal aging, that is, the effects of increasing age in the absence of identifiable dementia or other serious brain disease. Aging is clearly a continuum, but following tradition in the field we define "old age" to roughly correspond with retirement age (i.e., beginning at 60–65). The majority of research studies on cognitive aging usually compare performance of a younger group of people aged below 40 with an older group aged above 60; so this comparison is the focus of the current chapter. Relatively little is known about potentially interesting change in executive functions in middle age (Garden, Phillips, & MacPherson, 2001). There is also evidence that in the latter stages of old age (e.g., above the age of 80, chapter 7, this volume), cognitive and neural changes may accelerate. Executive functions include multiple skills such as planning, inhibition, task switching, memory updating, cognitive flexibility, and performance monitoring. Each function involves a complex network of brain areas and multiple cognitive processes. It is unlikely that aging will influence each of these functions in exactly the same way, and so different types of executive function need to be considered independently.

Frontal-executive theory of aging

The frontal-executive theory of aging proposes that early, localized age changes in the frontal lobes of the brain are associated with deficits in executive control processes (Daigneault, Braun, & Whitaker, 1992; Mittenberg, Seidenberg, O'Leary, & DiGiulio, 1989; Moscovitch & Winocur, 1992; Troyer, Graves, & Cullum, 1994; West, 1996). Recently a number of studies have investigated age-related changes in *functional* activation during cognitive performance, with a focus on the levels of frontal activation. A mixed pattern has emerged. Older adults tend to show lower levels of frontal lobe activation when at rest than younger adults (Petit Taboué, Landeau, Desson, Desgranges, & Baron, 1998). There is evidence of lower frontal activation in older adults during tasks such as memory encoding (Grady, 2002) and attentional control (Milham et al., 2002) and this may be interpreted as older adults engaging in less effortful processing during complex cognitive tasks (Madden et al., 2002).

However, most research has produced a different pattern. Older adults tend to show more widespread and higher levels of activation in frontal lobe regions than younger adults during cognitive task performance (Grady, 2002; Reuter-Lorenz, 2002). In tasks such as episodic memory, younger adults tend to show a well-replicated pattern of left lateralized prefrontal activation during encoding but right prefrontal activation during retrieval (Nyberg, Cabeza, & Tulving, 1996). This neat asymmetry is not replicated in older adults, where bilateral frontal activation is generally seen at both encoding and retrieval (for a review see Cabeza, 2002).

The most common explanation for increased prefrontal activation with age during cognitive tasks proposes that compensatory mechanisms are responsible. A range of different compensatory mechanisms have been proposed. The prefrontal effort hypothesis suggests that tasks which are relatively easy for young participants are more difficult for older participants, and thus require more widespread neural recruitment (Tisserand & Jolles, 2003). The strategic recruitment hypothesis suggests that additional neural circuits are recruited as a result of age differences in the cognitive strategies used to carry out tasks, in response to changes in processing fidelity. Finally, the reorganization hypothesis proposes that the neural circuitry left intact by the aging process shows changes in organizational pattern to compensate for lost networks. Cabeza (2002) argues that neural reorganization is a more likely explanation than strategic recruitment because similar patterns of increased frontal lobe activation are seen in older adults in simple sensory discrimination tasks as well as more complex tasks.

The frontal-executive theory of aging predominantly derives from evidence that there are greater age-related changes in both the neuroanatomy and neurochemistry of the frontal lobes than in other cortical areas (Fuster, 1989; Woodruff-Pak, 1997). These neural changes are thought to cause disturbances in affect, cognition, and behavior that parallel the dysfunction associated with localized damage to the frontal cortex (Daigneault et al., 1992; Moscovitch & Winocur, 1992). Thus, it has been explicitly proposed that in order to better understand the process of cognitive aging, we need to look to the functions associated with the frontal lobes (Parkin, 1997; West, 1996) and in particular, to try to map the deficits seen in older adults to those shown by patients with focal frontal lobe lesions (Moscovitch & Winocur, 1992).

The frontal lobes of the brain are associated with many different cognitive, social, and emotional functions, and it has been specifically proposed that adult aging is likely to impact on the cognitive control functions associated with the dorsolateral prefrontal regions (MacPherson, Phillips, & Della Sala, 2002; Phillips & Della Sala, 1998). There is a great deal of evidence that the neural substrates of executive processes lie at least partially in dorsolateral prefrontal regions (see Stuss & Benson, 1986). Patients who sustain damage to this cortical region often experience difficulty with tasks that require the integration and synthesis of information, and may exhibit impaired self-regulation and planning, perseveration with cognitive rigidity and stimulus boundedness, and a lack of spontaneity (Eslinger, Grattan, & Geder, 1995). This deficit profile is consistent with most definitions of executive impairment (Crawford & Henry, 2005; Lezak, 1993; Moscovitch & Melo, 1997; Perret, 1974; Phillips, 1997; Shallice, 1988; Stuss & Benson, 1986).

The majority of research into the frontal-executive hypothesis of aging has been based on the so-called *frontal lobe* tests, which are purported to tap into functions that are specifically subsumed by frontal lobe structures and prefrontal cortex in particular. Unfortunately, such terminology reflects a lack of understanding of the complexity of this area. Stuss (1992) addressed this issue, distinguishing the frontal lobes, a neuroanatomical term, from executive function, a psychological construct.

Stuss emphasized the problems of confusing these two dimensions when considering brain–behavior relationships. Despite this compelling argument, the neuropsychological literature remains littered with examples of confusion regarding this distinction. In an attempt to address this issue, throughout the following discussion we define frontal lobe tests as those that have traditionally been purported to have some sensitivity to frontal lobe dysfunction, but due to their multidetermined nature, they are likely to be mediated by a complex set of cognitive skills. Following the argument made by Stuss (1992), we distinguish these measures from those that have emerged within the tradition of cognitive psychology, and which explicitly attempt to delineate measures of individual executive functions (e.g., inhibition, planning). In this review, we refer to such tasks as *executive function tasks* because they have been developed to test particular cognitive control processes without reference to associated brain regions. In particular, we review and contrast available findings with respect to the effects of aging for each of these approaches.

One of the key issues to be considered is whether age changes in executive function are best interpreted as reflecting specific deficits of cognitive control processes, are symptoms of the more general age changes in information processing efficiency. Where age declines in frontal or executive task performance are found in an individual study, these may reflect changes in other parameters, such as speed, memory, attention, or motivation, rather than indicating a specific executive deficit (Rabbitt, 2002). In other words, assumptions cannot be made about the nature of age-related cognitive deficits seen on frontal and executive tasks without detailed task analysis. Aging causes deficits in multiple domains of cognition, and it is not appropriate to assume that a poor score on a test for an older adult reflects a specific type of cognitive deficit, as opposed to a more global impairment, without further information about why that score arises (Phillips, 1997). For each task discussed below, we provide evidence based on experimental manipulations, or relative task performance, as to where the locus of any age effects might lie.

Age differences in frontal lobe tests

Most of the literature investigating age differences in executive functioning have concentrated on frontal lobe tests. It is a curious aberration in neuropsychological assessment that in all other domains, tasks have historically been named according to the cognitive function assessed (e.g., neglect or episodic memory), while tasks aimed to assess executive functions are often called frontal lobe tests. A number of frontal lobe tests have frequently been employed in aging research. Here we outline the effects of aging on two most commonly used frontal lobe tests in research studies: verbal fluency (Delis, Kaplan, & Kramer, 2001) and the Wisconsin Card Sorting Test (WCST) (Heaton, 1981), with reference to the difficulties inherent in this method, which assumes a direct relationship between a psychometric test and a specific brain region. Although there is a wide range of such frontal lobe tests, which have been investigated in relation to adult aging, it is beyond the scope of this chapter to review all of that literature in detail (for more detail, see Phillips, MacPherson, & Della Sala, 2002; Salthouse, in press; West, 1996).

Verbal fluency

Tests of verbal fluency are among the most widely used measures of executive dysfunction, and have traditionally been assumed to provide a good index of frontal lobe function. These measures require time-restricted generation of multiple response alternatives under constrained search conditions, and involve associative exploration and retrieval of words based on phonemic criteria (phonemic or initial letter fluency, e.g., words beginning with A) or semantic criteria (semantic or category fluency, e.g., types of animal). Most fluency tasks require verbal generation but written versions have also been used. Use of standard clinical versions of these fluency measures in combination with structural and functional brain imaging methods supports the assumption of frontal lobe involvement in the tasks. For example, Stuss et al. (1998) report that pathology in left dorsolateral, and left or right medial frontal regions impaired aspects of verbal fluency performance, along with other regions in the parietal lobes and left striatum. In contrast, pathology in the right dorsolateral frontal cortical or the medial inferior lobe of either hemisphere was not associated with impaired phonemic fluency. Converging results from functional imaging paradigms show activation within left prefrontal cortex, and most commonly the left medial frontal gyrus in letter fluency (Wood, Saling, Abbott, & Jackson, 2001).

In relation to the validity of fluency tasks as indicators of frontal lobe dysfunction, a meta-analytic integration of the research literature found that relative to healthy controls, patients with focal frontal lesions presented with large and comparable deficits on measures of phonemic and semantic fluency (Henry & Crawford, 2004). When compared to frontal lesions, temporal lobe lesions were associated with smaller deficits in phonemic fluency, but a substantially larger semantic fluency deficit. Thus, if it could be demonstrated that aging is associated with comparable deficits across tests of phonemic and semantic fluency this would be consistent with the pattern associated with frontal dysfunction.

However, the existing literature that has investigated age effects on fluency is inconsistent. A number of researchers have documented age deficits in fluency (Capitani, Laiacona, & Barbarotto, 1999; Kempler, Teng, Dick, Taussig, & Davis, 1998; Parkin & Lawrence, 1994; Phillips, 1999; Prinz et al., 1999; Schaie & Parham, 1977; Tombaugh, Kozak, & Rees, 1999), while in other studies, no such age effects has been described (Bolla, Lindgren, Bonaccorsy, & Bleecker, 1990; Crawford, Bryan, Luszcz, Obonsawin, & Stewart, 2000). Further, some studies describe greater word production among older adults compared to young adults (Henry & Phillips, 2006; Parkin & Walter, 1991; Veroff, 1980; Yeudall, Fromm, Reddon, & Stefanyk, 1986). While the presence and direction of the age effects has proven inconsistent, individual studies have only rarely demonstrated the presence of large age effects, and in the few studies that have done so, this has often been attributed to nonexecutive deficits. Phillips (1999), for instance, found that older adults produced considerably fewer words than a middle-aged group on a written fluency task, but this was attributable to a reduction in motor speed, indicating the importance of considering nonexecutive contributions to test performance.

Where studies have investigated the relative prominence of phonemic and semantic fluency deficits in healthy aging, most have demonstrated disproportionate semantic fluency impairment, with older participants performing relatively worse on semantic than phonemic fluency relative to their younger counterparts (Crawford et al., 2000; Keys & White, 2000; Kozora & Cullum, 1995; Libon et al., 1994; Parkin, Hunkin, & Walter, 1995). This pattern in normal aging of poorer performance on semantic relative to phonemic fluency is also observed in Alzheimer's disease (Henry, Crawford, & Phillips, 2004) and, as noted earlier, in patients with focal temporal lobe lesions (Henry & Crawford, 2004). Relative performance on tests of phonemic and semantic fluency therefore does not suggest that the major factor underlying fluency performance in old age is frontal lobe change, but rather implicates age-related temporal lobe atrophy (Raz, Rodrigue, Head, Kennedy, & Acker, 2004; Scahill et al., 2003).

Henry and Phillips (2006) have suggested that age deficits in fluency may only reflect distinctive executive dysfunction where fluency paradigms that load more heavily on retrieval switching are used. Alternating fluency tasks require the generation of one word from a specific category (e.g., words beginning with A), then a word from a second category (e.g., type of animal). These two category prompts are then alternated (e.g., for the example noted, participants would be required to alternate between A and animal). Henry and Phillips found that while performance on a standard measure of semantic fluency did not differentiate younger and older adults, the capacity to alternate between semantic dimensions was particularly impaired with age. Since standard tests of semantic fluency and semantic alternating fluency tasks presumably impose comparable demands upon semantic memory (for both tasks, participants are requested to find words belonging to a specified semantic category), and are equally constrained by speed, the larger deficit for the alternating fluency measure suggests that retrieval switching may be particularly impaired in aging. Such manipulations of standardized clinical measures assist in focusing on specific executive elements of performance.

Verbal fluency tasks involve a range of cognitive skills, in addition to executive skills. There are demands on vocabulary and semantic knowledge, which are aspects of cognition that are often unimpaired in old age. Older adults seem able to retrieve knowledge relatively effectively, even if the criteria for retrieval are unusual (i.e., producing words beginning with a specified letter). The contradictory findings in the literature on age changes in fluency suggest that it would be unwise to use standard fluency measures as an indicator of executive deficits in relation to age changes in cognition.

Wisconsin card sorting test

Along with tests of verbal fluency, the WCST (Heaton, 1981) is one of the most commonly used measures of "frontal lobe functioning" employed in neuropsychological research (Anderson, 1998). In the WCST, participants are presented with four stimulus cards with symbols that differ in shape, number, and color, and a pack of 128 response cards. Instructions are given to place each response card under one of the four stimulus cards. Only one of the dimensions is correct, color in the first instance. However, the participant is not told which dimension is correct and therefore must identify the matching card through trial and error, using the feedback provided. After 10 correct responses with color, the criterion is changed to shape without the participant's knowledge. When the sorting dimension is changed the participant must shift cognitive set to identify and attend to the new dimension. The main measure of executive function from the task is the number of perseverative errors made, that is, how many times participants continue to categorize cards that belong to a previously relevant, but now irrelevant dimension. The WCST involves concept formation, cognitive set switching, and ability to inhibit previously incorrect responses (Sanz, Molina, & Calcedo, 2001).

There are many studies which have demonstrated that performance on the WCST declines in older adulthood. For example, Daigneault et al. (1992) found significant age declines from 40 years onward, while Fristoe, Salthouse, and Woodard (1997) found that older adults were impaired on all performance measures from the WCST, even when years of education and health variables were partialled out. A recent meta-analysis also indicated substantial age-related deficits in the number of perseverative errors made on the WCST (Rhodes, 2004). Experimental studies suggest that age differences on the WCST are due partially to less efficient use of feedback to determine future choices, as well as to differences in working memory and processing speed (Fristoe et al., 1997). However, using complex tests such as the WCST does not shed much light on the cognitive nature of age changes in executive functions. Like verbal fluency, the WCST is a complex multidimensional task which is cognitively opaque, that is, many different cognitive operations are involved, and there are many reasons for obtaining poor scores. Thus, as well as imposing substantial demands on executive functions, such as switching, working memory, and inhibition, it is likely that the WCST will place substantial demands on nonexecutive functions, such as attentional capacity and cognitive speed.

It is also of concern that the WCST is not selectively sensitive to frontal lobe dysfunction. For instance, in a very large sample of patients with brain injury, Axelrod, Goldman, Heaton, Curtiss, et al. (1996) reported that the WCST achieved a modest degree of overall discrimination between patients and controls but did not discriminate between the different patient samples, that is, the frontal lobe lesions had no greater effect on performance than more posterior damage. Indeed, in a review of the WCST literature Mountain and Snow (1993) stated that "the evidence that frontal patients perform more poorly than non-frontal patients is weak. There is insubstantial evidence to conclude that the WCST is a measure of dorsolateral-frontal dysfunction. The clinical utility of the test as a measure of frontal lobe dysfunction is not supported" (p. 108). Stuss and colleagues (2000) have further investigated this premise in their sample of patients with frontal lobe pathology. They found that patients with superior medial damage, regardless of lesion laterality, were the most impaired on all WCST measures (categories achieved, perseverations) except for loss of set. Lateral damage was also related to impaired performance, with deficits somewhat less severe.

Thus, although there is substantial evidence of age-related decline in WCST performance, it remains unclear whether this is attributable to executive impairment (Rhodes, 2004). Indeed, it has been argued that age changes in WCST performance might instead reflect declines in working memory (Hartman, Bolton, & Fehnel, 2001), or processing speed (Fristoe et al., 1997). The WCST is therefore a task, which is sensitive to many types of cognitive impairment, but it does not provide information as to the processes that underlie an observed deficit for a given individual.

Summary of age changes in frontal lobe tests

Much previous research on the cognitive neuropsychology of aging has focused on complex tasks such as letter fluency or the WCST, which involve many different cognitive functions. The available evidence does not support the use of these tasks to assess executive functions in older populations. Standard fluency tests do not stretch the executive functions of older adults, and adaptations which have explicit demands to switch between retrieval categories may prove more informative. Older adults do tend to show impaired performance on the WCST, but the complex cognitive and neural processes involved in this task mean that it is unwise to interpret such deficits in terms of specific executive functions. These lessons also apply to other neuro-psychological tasks as discussed below in relation to the Stroop Test (Perret, 1974) and Tower of London (TOL) Test (Shallice, 1982). Only careful manipulations of tasks and detailed analysis of performance can provide useful information about the nature of any executive deficits with age.

Aging effects on specific executive functions

Another means by which executive functions can be researched in aging is through the use of paradigms that have been developed in the cognitive psychology literature to investigate specific control functions. Although these types of executive function tasks are not generally standardized tests that have been studied in large normative samples, they are useful in that they allow manipulations of executive load and therefore better understanding of the cognitive nature of age-related deficits. Below we outline the effects of aging on three such executive control processes: inhibition, switching, and planning.

There is some consensus that there are numerous types of cognitive control process, which are likely to rely on overlapping neuroanatomical and cognitive mechanisms, but also have separable components (Miyake, Friedman, Emerson, Witzki, & Howerter, 2000). The types of executive control mechanisms identified in this way include inhibition, switching, updating in working memory, planning, monitoring, and strategy generation. Recent aging studies have investigated the nature of changes in executive functioning using cognitive paradigms, which are designed to more carefully pull apart the specific executive functions involved. Rather than using the more traditional, clinical frontal lobe tests where task validity is determined by rather dubious evidence of neuroanatomical localization, this approach takes advantage of research into the nature of cognitive control mechanisms to produce more specific executive measures.

Within the aging context one problem that can immediately be identified with these cognitive techniques is that they often depend on reaction time as the major performance variable. It is well established that processing speed declines with age (Salthouse, 1985) and so this factor will need to be controlled in some manner if accurate interpretations are to be made. In many executive function paradigms, the critical dependent variable is an executive *cost*, that is, the difference in latency between a high and a low executive load baseline condition. This gives rise to a range of measurement problems. First, latency measures tend to be negatively skewed; although this is sometimes corrected through exclusion of outlying reaction times and data transformation, it can lead to difficulty in understanding findings. Second, calculating difference scores tends to result in relatively unreliable data (Cohen & Cohen, 1983), particularly where the difference in reaction time between control and executive conditions is small. The issues of skew, unreliability, and small magnitude effects are exacerbated in aging, because older adults, like young children, tend to produce reaction time distributions that are more variable and more negatively skewed than those seen in healthy young adults. Finally, calculating such difference scores is also often fraught with theoretical difficulties of interpretation (Perfect & Maylor, 2000), as well as psychometric difficulties.

With these limitations in mind, we now outline the evidence for age differences in three specific components of executive functions on which a reasonable quantity of evidence is available: inhibition, switching, and planning. While employing some traditional neuropsychological measures, the following approach uses a more conceptual framework based around specific cognitive processes, rather than following the test-based model described in the previous section. Adoption of this more theoretically driven method may provide a better understanding of the under-pinnings of executive impairments associated with the aging process, if indeed they exist.

Inhibition

Before the current interest in the frontal-executive theory of cognitive aging, Hasher and Zacks (1988) proposed that a decline in the efficiency of inhibitory processes was an important cause of age changes in a wide range of cognitive tasks. Aging results in poorer performance in a variety of well-established paradigms dependent on inhibitory processing, e.g., the stop signal task (Kramer, Humphrey, Larish, Logan, & Strayer, 1994), Stroop task (Houx, Jolles, & Vreeling, 1993), antisaccade task (Butler, Zacks, & Henderson, 1999), and the directed forgetting task (Andres, Van der Linden, & Parmentier, 2004). However, other studies report no age effects on tasks dependent on inhibition, e.g., on inhibition of return (Connelly & Hasher, 1993).

The most widely used measure of inhibition is the Stroop task (Perret, 1974), in which the inhibitory condition requires participants to name the color of ink in which a color word is printed (for example, the word RED is written in green ink)—requiring the suppression of the tendency to read the color word. A review of aging studies on the Stroop task makes clear how difficult it can be to interpret age differences in performance on even this relatively simple task of executive function-ing. There are many studies that indicate greater age-related slowing on the inhibition condition of the Stroop task (name the color in which a color word is printed) compared to a baseline conditions (name the color of rows of X's). However, the inhibitory condition of this task takes considerably longer than baseline conditions for young adults as well as older adults, and so the aging effect may simply reflect a scalar factor of slowing (Rabbitt, Lowe, & Shilling, 2001). Verhaegen and De Meersman (1998) show through meta-analysis of mean response times on the Stroop task that a single function can explain age differences in both baseline and interference conditions of the Stroop task, unlike in Alzheimer's disease where the effects of dementia on baseline and interference conditions need to be explained by separate functions (Amieva, Phillips, Della Sala, & Henry, 2004). Verhaegen and De Meersman (1998) argue that their results indicate that Stroop effects can be explained in terms of slowed information processing with age. However, Rabbitt (2002) argues that the conclusions drawn by Verhaegen and De Meersman from their scalar analysis are inappropriate since only mean reaction times for older adults and young were considered, and the mean does not constitute an adequate summary of the complex effects of age on reaction time distributions.

Other evidence contradicts the theory that age differences in Stroop task performance are due to general slowing. Evoked potential studies of brain activity during Stroop tasks indicate selective age-related attenuation of frontal activation reflecting parameters of inhibition but provide no evidence that general age-related slowing influenced inhibition (West & Alain, 2000). Despite a considerable number of studies investigating this issue, there is still debate in the literature as to whether age-related variance in the critical interference condition of the Stroop task reflects a specific inhibitory deficit or instead is better interpreted within a framework of slowed information processing. Factors such as task-specific practice and the exact type of stimuli used may influence the results obtained (Lowe & Rabbitt, 1997; Rabbitt, 2002; Shilling, Chetwynd, & Rabbitt, 2002). Shilling et al. (2002) argue that the lack of correlation between different versions of the Stroop task indicates that individual differences in Stroop performance are due to other factors than a common inhibitory component. Rabbitt (2002) proposes that in order to demonstrate age differences in inhibitory function using the Stroop task, it is necessary to look at the proportionate age-related slowing on both inhibitory and baseline task conditions that are matched for complexity; however, no published studies have matched this stringent condition to date.

As suggested above, there is consistent evidence for age differences on tasks that require controlled and conscious inhibition, such as the Stroop task where participants must actively try to stop themselves from carrying out the prepotent process of word-reading. There is also evidence that age does not cause poorer performance on paradigms in which the inhibitory processing is more automatic and not subject to conscious control. For example, in the *inhibition of return* task, a cue is presented in the visual field, followed by a delay of one to two s. Subsequent presentations of targets in the area of the initial cue are responded to more slowly than targets in another area of visual field. This effect is thought to reflect a bias of attention toward novel events. Numerous studies report no age differences in this type of automatic inhibitory process (Connelly & Hasher, 1993; Faust & Balota, 1997; Hartley & Kieley, 1995; Langley, Fuentes, Hochhalter, Brandt, & Overmier, 2001; Langley, Vivas, Fuentes, & Bagne, 2005; McCrae & Abrams, 2001). A similar pattern of preserved automatic inhibition, but impaired controlled inhibition, has also been reported in Alzheimer's disease (see Amieva et al., 2004 for a review). Andres,

Guerrini, Phillips, and Perfect (in press) addressed the issue of differential age effects on automatic and controlled inhibition directly by combining inhibitory paradigms requiring automatic and controlled processing within the same experiment. The controlled and automatic inhibition tasks were designed to be as similar as possible, except for the nature of the inhibitory demands in the task. Results indicated that older adults showed problems in controlled inhibition tasks (Stroop and stop signal responsiveness), but there were no age differences on automatic inhibition tasks (two versions of negative priming). The consistency of findings provides strong support that controlled inhibition is more vulnerable to aging processes than automatic inhibition, and cannot be explained by age differences in processing speed.

Switching

A large number of studies have investigated the effects of aging on the ability to switch attention. Shifting attention between either different task sets or stimulus–response mappings is a key element of executive functioning (Miyake et al., 2000). A very technical literature has developed around the field of task switching, which delineates local and global switches, task and response-set switches, predictable and unpredictable switches, and other task demands. In the task-switching paradigms typically used in the aging literature, the main measure of interest is the contrast in performance between conditions in which task sets need to be changed across successive trials and ones in which task sets are invariant.

Kray and Lindenberger (2000) investigated the issue of age differences in global versus local switching costs. Global switch costs are those associated with maintaining two different task–response sets (A and B) in mind, while local switch costs are measured at the point of switching from one mental set to another, see Figure 3.1. In the Kray and Lindenberger study, global switching costs were calculated by comparing the time taken to respond to single task set conditions (e.g., a series of only AAAAAA trials) compared to dual task set (e.g., a series of AABBAABB), whereas local switch costs were measured by comparing latencies of switch trials to those of non-switch trials within the AABBAABB condition. Aging resulted in increased

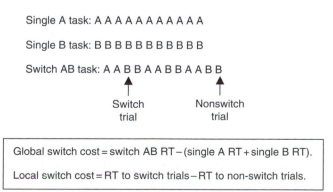

Figure 3.1   Local and global costs associated with switching tasks.

global switch costs, but had no effect on local switch costs, suggesting that age is associated with difficulty in maintaining two competing mental sets in mind, rather than difficulty in the specific execution of the mental switch. This result was supported by a meta-analysis carried out by Verhaeghen and Cerella (2002) in which they concluded that age effects were larger in the global cost of having to carry out any switch during a task as compared to the local cost in actually carrying out a switch.

This finding of greater age differences in global compared to local switch costs may be moderated by the number of task sets to be maintained and the predictability of switching trials. Kray, Li, and Lindenberger (2002) report that age differences in local task switch costs were much higher when the number of mental sets was increased from two to four, indicating again the importance of maintaining information simultaneously in working memory. There is evidence (Van Asselen & Ridderinkhof, 2000) that older adults are particularly impaired in task switching where the switches must be made at unpredictable intervals (e.g., AABBBBAAABB...) as compared to predictable intervals (e.g., AABBAAB-BAA...). Kray et al. (2002) suggest that, when switching is unpredictable, local switch costs are likely to be much higher for older adults, because multiple stimulus–response mental sets are not being actively maintained across the entire sequence of switches.

There is some evidence that impairments in task-switching overlap in variance with measures of processing speed (Salthouse, Fristoe, McGuthry, & Hambrick, 1998), although the switching measure taken in the Salthouse study was a local switch cost, which is generally subject to smaller age effects than more global switch measures. Using meta-analytic techniques Verhaeghen and Cerella (2002) found that the age deficits in global task switching exceed the magnitude predicted by changes in general cognitive changes such as processing speed. This suggests that the ability to juggle multiple task sets is impaired in aging, and this deficit is independent of more general cognitive changes with age.

Many aspects of task demands influence the magnitude of age effects in switching. Where multiple task demands load on working memory heavily, or the timing of switches cannot be predicted, older adults perform particularly poorly. Reliable findings of age differences in global switch costs indicate that older people may have difficulty in maintaining multiple action sets in mind. This has implications for everyday functioning in complex settings where attention-focus and action-sets must often be changed online. However, so far the literature on age and switching has concentrated on laboratory settings so there is little empirical evidence available to evaluate the everyday importance of any deficit in task switching.

Planning

The ability to efficiently formulate and execute plans is a central aspect of executive functioning in everyday life. A widely used measure of planning ability is the TOL task (Shallice, 1982). In this task, colored disks must be moved one-by-one from an initial state to match a goal state, and instructions are generally given to mentally plan the sequence of moves prior to executing that plan. Older adults tend to be slower than younger adults to complete the TOL, and need more moves to solve specific TOL trials. Both of these findings suggest that aging may be associated with less efficient planning (Andres & Van der Linden, 2000; Gilhooly, Phillips, Wynn, Logie, & Della Sala, 1999; Robbins et al., 1998). Planning tasks are at their most difficult where *goal conflict* arises. This is where one or more activated goals require conflicting actions, and so a decision must be made as to which goal to prioritise. In the TOL task, goal conflict occurs where a disk must be moved to a place other than its final position to allow another disk to be moved. Patients with frontal lobe injuries tend to have particular problems in their first encounter with goal conflict (Morris, Miotto, Feigenbaum, Bullock, & Polkey, 1997). In contrast, older adults do not show particular difficulty in dealing with goal conflict (Gilhooly et al., 1999), suggesting that age differences do not reflect difficulties in deciding which move to prioritise.

Gilhooly et al. (1999) investigated the nature of mental planning in the TOL task through the use of verbal protocols, where participants were asked to "think-aloud" during the task. The plans articulated by older adults were shorter and more error-prone relative to the plans made by young adults. A measure of correspondence was obtained between the verbal plans and the actual moves that were subsequently executed, and this indicated that older participants showed a particularly poor match between planned and executed moves. There was no evidence of age differences in the strategies used to carry out planning on the TOL, and Gilhooly et al. instead argue that the age deficits in mental planning were attributable to declines in working memory capacity. In support of this interpretation, analysis of partial correlations suggests that some of the age variance in accuracy of solving TOL trials can be explained by differences in visuospatial working memory capacity (Phillips & Forshaw, 1998).

Although older adults perform reliably poorly on abstract planning tasks, such as the TOL, they often perform relatively well on more familiar planning tasks, such as scheduling shopping errands (Phillips, MacLeod, & Kliegel, 2005). Garden et al. (2001) examined performance on a complex shopping task in younger and middle-aged adults. There was no evidence of age differences in planning ability in terms of the route taken, or the scheduling of the errands, and the two groups did not differ on the number of errands that were completed. Phillips, Kliegel, and Martin (2006) compared abstract and more familiar planning in a sample of younger and older adults, and found clear age deficits in the abstract task (TOL), but no age effects on the familiar task (a work schedule planning paradigm). In a further attempt to investigate this issue, Kliegel, Martin, McDaniel, and Phillips (in press) investigated parallel planning tasks that differed only in whether the material was abstract or contextually meaningful. In the case of the contextual task, there was no age deficit in planning, but in the abstract task (which had exactly the same structure and number of planning elements), there was a significant decline in planning performance with age. Applying multiple regression analyses, Kliegel et al. demonstrated that in the contextual planning task, older adults were able to compensate for resource-related deficits in planning performance by using the selective strategy of focusing on relevant task features. This indicates that, despite declining cognitive resources, older adults may be able to perform well on executive tasks if they can use their knowledge or experience to focus their attention on the most salient task features. Unlike patients with frontal lobe lesions (Shallice & Burgess, 1991), older adults may perform relatively well on executive-demanding tasks when set in realistic situations or with familiar materials (Phillips et al., 2005).

Thus, overall the literature on planning suggests that forward planning is impaired in aging, particularly where heavy demands are placed on working memory. However, the deficits in planning seen in laboratory settings do not extend to more naturalistic tasks, where age differences are either smaller or nonexistent.

Issues involved in researching executive function change with age

Complexities in determining whether age differences in executive functions are specific or if they reflect global cognitive change

It is clear from the above review that there are age differences in many aspects of executive function, particularly where the task demands are novel (e.g., laboratory-based planning), the process requires conscious, effortful control as opposed to more automatic executive functions (e.g., controlled inhibition such as in the Stroop task), and where there are extensive demands placed on working memory (e.g., the global cost of having to switch between task sets). In all cases, as the executive task becomes more demanding, the age differences increase. This means that many of the results outlined above are compatible with more general theories of cognitive changes with age, which propose that as tasks become more complex, they involve more cognitive components, and thus tend to show greater age effects. There are a number of methods which have been employed in an attempt to disentangle whether cognitive changes with age might best be explained in terms of general processing parameters, or with reference to more specific cognitive control processes.

One approach has been to use analysis of variance techniques to investigate interactions between age and cognitive tasks that differ in their executive load. It might be assumed that larger age effects on more executively loaded tasks indicate greater age declines in executive compared to baseline conditions. However, there are problems with this assumption, because even theories which rely on relatively primitive cognitive parameters, such as processing speed, to explain age changes in complex cognitive tasks predict proportionately greater age effects on complex conditions which require more processing steps. This means that age x complexity interactions cannot be unequivocally interpreted to support specific executive deficits with age.

Another way of addressing this issue is through the use of correlational techniques such as partial correlations or hierarchical regression. Most of the research described above, which investigates the role of processing speed or working memory in age differences in executive function takes this approach. There is often overlap in age variance between measures of executive function and apparently simpler measures of processing speed (Salthouse et al., 1998). Such data are sometimes interpreted as indicating that processing speed is a more primitive variable which underlies age differences in executive tasks. However, apparently simple speed-of-processing tasks, such as choice reaction time or the Digit Symbol subtest from the Wechsler

Adult Intelligence Scales, may not be as straightforward as often assumed (Rabbitt, 2002). Such tasks are dependent on control of speed-accuracy trade-off functions (Phillips & Rabbitt, 1995), error monitoring and correction (Rabbitt & Vyas, 1970), and learning curves (Piccinin & Rabbitt, 1999). This means that it may be premature to conclude that age differences in tasks such as Digit Symbol or choice reaction time are attributable to slowed processing speed. Indeed, age differences on these tasks could be argued to reflect poorer strategic control, working memory capacity, or inefficient inhibition, that is, impaired executive functioning. There are theoretical difficulties in interpreting age-related change in multiple overlapping cognitive variables in terms of causal pathways (Lindenberger & Potter, 1998; Perfect & Maylor, 2000). Also, there are statistical problems in apportioning age-related variance in numerous variables in an attempt to determine what underlies age differences in a particular task (Lindenberger & Potter, 1998).

While the issue of whether age-related variance in executive functions might be attributable to more primitive and general cognitive resources might be of theoretical interest, there is no straightforward methodological way to address this question. Any technique that could be used has inherent problems that limit interpretation of the results. It therefore seems prudent to conclude that there has been adequate demonstration of age declines in executive functions such as inhibition and switching, and to accept that we cannot with current techniques determine whether this reflects a specific set of deficits or more general cognitive changes with age.

Do age differences in executive function result from changes in the frontal lobes of the brain?

It is ironic that the main impetus for studying executive functioning in older adults has been the evidence of localized structural age changes in the frontal lobes of the brain, yet there is relatively scant evidence to evaluate whether there is actually any relationship between structural neural change with age and poor executive function. For example Tisserand and Jolles (2003, p1107) argue that "At present, there is no direct evidence for a relationship between regional neuronal number and cognitive performance in non-pathological aging . . .".

Several studies (Gunning-Dixon & Raz, 2003; Head, Raz, Gunning-Dixon, Williamson, & Acker, 2002; Raz, Gunning-Dixon, Head, Dupuis, & Acker, 1998; Schretlen et al., 2000) have shown that performance on the WCST is correlated with frontal lobe volume. Three of these studies (Head et al., 2002; Gunning-Dixon & Raz, 2003; Raz et al., 1998) have provided direct evidence, through path analysis, that the relationship between age and perseverative errors on the WCST may be mediated by the decline in prefrontal volume. Schretlen et al. (2000) investigated the contribution of speed, executive function, and frontal lobe volume variance to age differences in fluid intelligence. Using regression analysis, they found that cognitive speed, executive functioning (as indexed by the WCST), and frontal lobe volume made separate and significant contributions to explaining age variance in fluid ability. They conclude that processing speed and frontal-executive accounts of age differences in cognition are both partially correct.

Although there are other demonstrations of correlations between indices of frontal integrity and performance on tests purported to measure executive functions, such as fluency (Deary et al., 2006), there are no studies which directly test whether age differences in a range of executive functions can be explained in terms of the size and integrity of the frontal lobes. It would be very useful to have more studies which directly address whether anatomical changes within the frontal lobes have an effect on the performance of executive function tests.

What might age declines in executive functioning mean for the quality of life of older adults?

It has often been argued that the most devastating cognitive deficits encountered by patients suffering brain injury are those involving executive functions. This is because functions like inhibition, switching, and planning are important in so many everyday tasks but relatively difficult to measure and rehabilitate (Wilson, Evans, Alderman, Burgess, & Emslie, 1997). It therefore seems plausible that changes in executive function might negatively impact on older adults' quality of life, given the importance of these functions in household tasks, such as cooking and shopping, work, and social interaction. However, in contrast to patients with brain injury who regularly show impairments in these everyday tasks (Shallice & Burgess, 1991), older adults seem to perform relatively well on more everyday measures of executive functioning (Garden et al., 2001). As outlined above, the age declines seen in laboratory-based measures of planning are sometimes not replicated in more naturalistic measures of these abilities. This suggests that, given the slow deterioration across the age range in executive functions, and the well-practiced and familiar nature of everyday tasks such as shopping, older adults are able to compensate for cognitive declines through practiced strategies and neural recruitment (Grady, McIntosh, & Craik, 2005). This is an important conclusion as it suggests that we must be very wary in extrapolating clear evidence of declines in basic processes of executive function in the lab to draw conclusions about the effects in everyday life.

It would also be useful to carry out research into the role of executive functions in situations where older people must adapt to new environments, or learn to use new technology. The difficulties outlined above for older adults in dealing with new situations emphasize the importance of familiar environments in maximizing functioning. Constant changes to shop layout and methods of banking may be inevitable in current culture but they are likely to cause greatest difficulty to older people. Changes of environment (e.g., to a new town or home) often have a deleterious impact on the cognitive and behavioral functioning of older adults, and this may arise because of impairments in executive functioning to cope with novel situations.

The frontal aging hypothesis has so far concentrated almost exclusively on laboratory-based abstract tasks. This may give a very misleading picture of the impact of frontal lobe changes with age on real-world functioning. From the vast evidence of age-related declines in performing novel executive tasks, it would seem logical to predict that this could have a deleterious effect on older adults' ability to cope with activities essential in everyday life. It is imperative that future research investigating frontal lobe changes with age explores not just artificial but also well-practiced or socially relevant executive tasks. This would permit a better understanding of the relationship between age, neural changes, and the behavioral functions actually utilized in everyday life.

Conclusions

Summary scores from complex neuropsychological tests of frontal lobe function have not shed much light on the causes or nature or cognitive decline with age. Evidence from more specific paradigms designed to measure individual executive functions such as inhibition, switching, and planning indicates that older adults perform worse than younger adults on most of these cognitive control functions. In some cases, these age-related declines may overlap with more general cognitive changes such as slowed processing, but there is also evidence suggesting that some aspects of executive function may show specific decline with age. There is very little direct evidence to date that supports the main tenet of the frontal-executive theory of aging: that age changes in executive function directly relate to atrophy in the frontal lobes of the brain. The frontal-executive theory of aging needs to be replaced by a more sophisticated model of neuropsychological changes with age which takes into account subregions within the frontal lobes and cortical and subcortical frontal networks. The impact of impairments in executive functioning on the everyday life of older adults has not been adequately addressed in research to date, and should be an important topic for future research.

References

Amieva, H., Phillips, L. H., Della Sala, S., & Henry, J. D. (2004). Inhibitory functioning in Alzheimer's Disease. *Brain*, *127*, 949–964.

Anderson, V. (1998). Assessment of executive function in children. *Neuropsychological Rehabilitation*, *8*, 319–349.

Andres, P., Guerini, C., Phillips, L. H., & Perfect, T. (in press). Aging effects on automatic and controlled inhibition. Developmental Neuropsychology.

Andres, P., & Van der Linden, M. (2000). Age-related differences in supervisory attentional system functions. *Journal of Gerontology: Psychological Sciences*, *55*, 373–380.

Andres, P., Van der Linden, M., & Parmentier, F. B. R. (2004). Directed forgetting in working memory: Age-related differences. *Memory*, *12*, 248–256.

Axelrod, B. H., Goldman, R. S., Heaton, R. K., Curtiss, G., et al. (1996). Discriminability of the Wisconisn Card Sorting Test using the standardization sample. *Journal of Clinical and Experimental Neuropsychology*, *18*, 338–342.

Bolla, K. I., Lindgren, K. N., Bonaccorsy, C., & Bleecker, M. L. (1990). Predictors of verbal fluency (FAS) in the healthy elderly. *Journal of Clinical Psychology*, *46*, 623–628.

Butler, K. M., Zacks, R. T., & Henderson, J. M. (1999). Suppression of reflexive saccades in younger and older adults: Age comparisons on an antisaccade task. *Memory and Cognition*, *27*, 584–591.

Cabeza, R. (2002). Hemispheric asymmetry reduction in older adults: The HAROLD model. *Psychology and Aging*, *17*, 85–100.

Capitani, E., Laiacona, M., & Barbarotto, R. (1999). Gender affects word retrieval of certain categories in semantic fluency tasks. *Cortex*, *35*, 273–278.

Cerella, J. (1985). Information processing rates in the elderly. *Psychological Bulletin, 98,* 67–83.

Cohen, J., & Cohen, P. (1983) *Multiple Regression/Correlation for the Behavioral Sciences* (2nd ed.): Hillsdale, NJ: Erlbaum Associates.

Connelly, S. L., & Hasher, L. (1993). Aging and the inhibition of spatial location. *Journal of Experimental Psychology: Human Perception and Performance, 19,* 1238–1250.

Crawford, J. R., Bryan, J., Luszcz, M. A., Obonsawin, M. C., & Stewart, L. (2000). The executive decline hypothesis of cognitive aging: Do executive deficits qualify as differential deficits and do they mediate age-related memory decline? *Aging, Neuropsychology and Cognition, 7,* 9–31.

Crawford, J. R., & Henry, J. D. (2005). Assessment of executive deficits. In P.W. Halligan & N. Wade (Eds.), *The effectiveness of rehabilitation for cognitive deficits* (pp. 233–246). London: Oxford University Press.

Daigneault, S., Braun, C. M. J., & Whitaker, H. A. (1992). Early effects of normal aging on perseverative and non-perseverative prefrontal measures. *Developmental Neuropsychology, 8,* 99–114.

Deary, I. J., Bastin, M. E., Pattie, A., Clayden, J. D., Whalley, L. J., Starr, J. M., et al. (2006). White matter integrity and cognition in childhood and old age. *Neurology, 66,* 505–512.

Delis, D., Kaplan, E., & Kramer, J. (2001). *Delis–Kaplan Executive Function System.* San Antonio, TX: Psychological Corporation.

Eslinger, P. J., Grattan, L. M., & Geder, L. (1995). Impact of frontal lobe lesions on rehabilitation and recovery from acute brain injury. *Neurorehabilitation, 5,* 161–182.

Faust, M.E., & Balota, D.A. (1997). Inhibition of return and visuospatial attention in healthy older adults and individuals with dementia of the Alzheimer type. *Neuropsychology, 11,* 13–29.

Fristoe, N. M., Salthouse, T. A., & Woodard, J.L. (1997). Examination of age-related deficits on the Wisconsin Card Sorting Test. *Neuropsychology, 11,* 428–436.

Fuster, J. M. (1989). *The Prefrontal Cortex* (2nd ed.). New York: Raven Press.

Garden, S., Phillips, L. H., & MacPherson, S. E. (2001). Mid-life aging, open-ended planning and laboratory measures of executive function. *Neuropsychology, 15,* 472–482.

Gilhooly, K. J., Phillips, L. H., Wynn, V. E., Logie, R. H., & Della Sala, S. (1999). Planning processes and age in the 5 disc Tower of London task. *Thinking and Reasoning, 5,* 339–361.

Grady, C. L. (2002). Age-related differences in face processing: A meta-analysis of three functional neuroimaging experiments. *Canadian Journal of Experimental Psychology, 56,* 208–220.

Grady, C. L., McIntosh, A. R., & Craik, F. I. M. (2005). Task-related activity in prefrontal cortex and its relation to recognition memory performance in young and old adults. *Neuropsychologia, 43,* 1466–1481.

Gunning-Dixon, F., & Raz, N. (2003). Neuroanatomical correlates of selected executive functions in middle-aged and older adults: A prospective MRI study. *Neuropsychologia, 41,* 1929–1941.

Hartman, M., Bolton, E., & Fehnel, S. E. (2001). Accounting for age differences on the Wisconsin Card Sorting Test: Decreased working memory, not inflexibility. *Psychology and Aging, 16,* 385–399.

Hartley, A. A., & Kieley, J. M. (1995). Adult age differences in the inhibition of return of visual attention. *Psychology and Aging, 10,* 670–683.

Hasher, L., & Zacks, R. T. (1988). Working memory, comprehension, and aging: A review and a new view. In G. H. Bower (Ed.), *The psychology of learning and motivation, 22* (pp. 193–225). Orlando, FL: Academic Press.

Head, D., Raz, N., Gunning-Dixon, F., Williamson, A., & Acker, J. D. (2002). Age-related differences in the course of cognitive skill acquisition: The role of regional cortical shrinkage and cognitive resources. *Psychology and Aging, 17*, 72–84.

Heaton, R. K. (1981). *A Manual for the Wisconsin Card Sorting Test*. Odessa, FL: Psychological Assessment Resources.

Henry, J. D., & Crawford, J. R. (2004). A meta-analytic review of verbal fluency performance following focal cortical lesions. *Neuropsychology, 18*, 284–295.

Henry, J. D., Crawford, J. R., & Phillips, L. H. (2004). Verbal fluency performance in dementia of the Alzheimer's type: A meta-analysis. *Neuropsychologia, 42*, 1212–1222.

Henry, J. D., & Phillips, L. H. (2006). Covariates of production and perseveration on tests of phonemic, semantic and alternating fluency in normal aging. *Aging, Neuropsychology and Cognition, 13*, 1–23.

Houx, P. J., Jolles, J., & Vreeling, F. W. (1993). Stroop interference: Aging effects assessed with the Stroop Color-Word Test. *Experimental Aging Research, 19*, 209–224.

Kempler, D., Teng, E. L., Dick, M., Taussig, I. M., & Davis, D. S. (1998). The effects of age, education, and ethnicity on verbal fluency. *Journal of the International Neuropsychological Society, 4*, 531–538.

Keys, B. A., & White, D. A. (2000). Exploring the relationship between age, executive abilities, and psychomotor speed. *Journal of the International Neuropsychological Society, 6*, 76–82.

Kliegel, M., Martin, M., McDaniel, M., & Phillips, L. H. (in press). Older adults' planning: Familiarity can compensate for cognitive decline. *Experimental Aging Research*.

Kozora, E., & Cullum, C. M. (1995). Generative naming in normal aging: Total output and qualitative changes using phonemic and semantic constraints. *Clinical Neuropsychologist, 9*, 313–320.

Kramer, A. F., Humphrey, D. G., Larish, J. F., Logan, G., & Strayer, D. (1994). Aging and inhibition: Beyond a unitary view of inhibitory processing in attention. *Psychology and Aging, 9*, 491–512.

Kray, J., Li, K. Z. H., & Lindenberger, U. (2002). Age-related changes in task-switching components: The role of task uncertainty. *Brain and Cognition, 49*, 363–381.

Kray, J., & Lindenberger, U. (2000). Adult age differences in task switching. *Psychology and Aging, 15*, 126–147.

Langley, L., Fuentes, L., Hochhalter, A., Brandt, J., & Overmier, J. (2001). Inhibition of return in aging and Alzheimer's disease: Performance as a function of task demands and stimulus timing. *Journal of Clinical and Experimental Neuropsychology, 23*, 431–446.

Langley, L., Vivas, A., Fuentes, L., & Bagne, A. G. (2005). Differential age effects on attention-based inhibition: Inhibitory tagging and inhibition of return. *Psychology and Aging, 20*, 356–360.

Lezak, M. D. (1993). Newer contributions to the neuropsychological assessment of executive functions. *Journal of Head Trauma Rehabilitation, 8*, 24–31.

Libon, D. J., Glosser, G., Malamut, B. L., Kaplan, E., Goldberg, E., Swenson, R., et al. (1994). Age, executive functions, and visuospatial functioning in healthy older adults. *Neuropsychology, 8*, 38–43.

Lindenberger, U., & Potter, U. (1998). The complex nature of unique and shared effects in hierarchical linear regression: Implications for developmental psychology. *Psychological Methods, 3*, 218–230.

Lowe, C., & Rabbitt, P. (1997). Cognitive models of aging and frontal lobe deficits. In P. Rabbitt (Ed.), *Methodology of frontal and executive functions* (pp. 39–59). Hove, UK: Psychology Press.

MacPherson, S. E., Phillips, L. H., & Della Sala, S. (2002). Age, executive function, and social decision making: A dorsolateral prefrontal theory of cognitive aging. *Psychology and Aging, 17*, 598–609.

Madden, D. J., Turkington, T. G., Provenzale, J. M., Denny, L. L., Langley, L. K., Hawk, T. C., et al. (2002). Aging and attentional guidance during visual search: Functional neuro-anatomy by Positron Emission Tomography. *Psychology and Aging, 17*, 24–43.

McCrae, C., & Abrams, R. (2001). Age-related differences in object- and location-based inhibition of return of attention. *Psychology and Aging, 16*, 437–449.

Milham, M. P., Erickson, K. I., Banich, M. T., Kramer, A. F., Webb, A., Wszalek, T., et al. (2002). Attentional control in the aging brain: Insights from an fMRI study of the Stroop task. *Brain and Cognition, 49*, 277–296.

Mittenberg, W., Seidenberg, M., O'leary, D. S., & DiGiulio, D. V. (1989). Changes in cerebral functioning associated with normal aging. *Journal of Clinical and Experimental Neuropsychology, 11*, 918–932.

Miyake, A., Friedman, N. P., Emerson, M. J., Witzki, A. H., & Howerter, A. (2000). The unity and diversity of executive functions and their contributions to complex "frontal lobe" tasks: A latent variable analysis. *Cognitive Psychology, 41*, 49–100.

Morris, R. G., Miotto, E. C., Feigenbaum, J. D., Bullock, P., & Polkey, C. E. (1997). The effect of goal-subgoal conflict on planning ability after frontal- and temporal-lobe lesions in humans. *Neuropsychologia, 35*, 1147–1157.

Moscovitch, M., & Melo, B. (1997). Strategic retrieval and the frontal lobes: Evidence from confabulation and amnesia. *Neuropsychologia, 35*, 1017–1034.

Moscovitch, M., & Winocur, G. (1992). The neuropsychology of memory and aging. In F. I. M. Craik & T. A. Salthouse (Eds.), *The handbook of aging and cognition* (pp. 315–372). Hillsdale, NJ: Lawrence Erlbaum Associates.

Mountain, M. A., & Snow, W. G. (1993). Wisconsin Card Sorting Test as a measure of frontal pathology: A review. *The Clinical Neuropsychologist, 7*, 108–118.

Nyberg, L., Cabeza, R., & Tulving, E. (1996). PET studies of encoding and retrieval: The HERA model. *Psychonomic Bulletin and Review, 3*, 135–148.

Parkin, A. J. (1997). Normal age-related memory loss and its relation to frontal lobe dysfunction. In P. M. A. Rabbitt (Ed.), *Methodology of frontal and executive function* (pp. 177–190). Hove, UK: Psychology Press.

Parkin, A. J., Hunkin, N. M., & Walter, B. M. (1995). Relationships between normal aging, frontal lobe function, and memory for temporal and spatial information. *Neuropsychology, 9*, 304–312.

Parkin, A. J., & Lawrence, A. (1994). A dissociation in the relation between memory tasks and frontal lobe tests in the normal elderly. *Neuropsychologia, 32*, 1523–1532.

Parkin, A. J., & Walter, B. M. (1991). Aging, short-term memory, and frontal dysfunction. *Psychobiology, 19*, 175–179.

Perfect, T. J., & Maylor, E. A. (2000). Rejecting the dull hypothesis: The relation between method and theory in cognitive aging research. In T. J. Perfect & E. A. Maylor (Eds.), *Models of cognitive aging* (pp. 1–18). Oxford University Press.

Perret, E. (1974). The left frontal lobe of man and the suppression of habitual responses in verbal categorical behavior. *Neuropsychologia, 12*, 323–330.

Petit Taboué, M. C., Landeau, B., Desson, J. F., Desgranges, B., & Baron, J. C. (1998). Effects of healthy aging on the regional cerebral metabolic rate of glucose assessed with statistical parametric mapping. *Neuroimage, 7*, 176–184.

Phillips, L. H. (1997). Do 'frontal tests' measure executive function? Issues of assessment and evidence from fluency tests. In P. M. A. Rabbitt (Ed.), *Methodology of frontal and executive function* (pp. 191–213). Hove, UK: Psychology Press.

Phillips, L. H. (1999). Age and individual differences in letter fluency. *Developmental Neuropsychology, 15,* 249–267.

Phillips, L. H., & Della Sala, S. (1998). Aging, intelligence and anatomical segregation in the frontal lobes. *Learning and Individual Differences, 10,* 217–243.

Phillips, L. H., & Forshaw, M. J. (1998). The role of working memory in age differences in reasoning. In R. H. Logie & K. J. Gilhooly (Eds.), *Working memory and thinking* (pp. 23–43). Hove, UK: Psychology Press.

Phillips, L. H., Kliegel, M., & Martin, M. (2006). Age and planning tasks: The influence of ecological validity. *International Journal of Aging and Human Development, 62,* 175–184.

Phillips, L. H., MacLeod, M., & Kliegel, M. (2005). Adult aging and cognitive planning. In G. Ward & R. Morris (Eds.), *The cognitive psychology of planning* (pp. 111–134). Hove, UK: Psychology Press.

Phillips, L. H., MacPherson, S., & Della Sala, S. (2002). Age, cognition and emotion: The role of anatomical segregation in the frontal lobes. In J. Grafman (Ed.), *Handbook of neuropsychology,* 2nd ed., Vol. 7: *The frontal lobes* (pp. 73–97). Amsterdam: Elsevier Science B.V.

Phillips, L. H., & Rabbitt, P. M. A. (1995). Impulsivity and speed-accuracy strategies in intelligence test performance. *Intelligence, 21,* 13–29.

Piccinin, A. M., & Rabbitt, P. M. A. (1999). Contribution of cognitive abilities to performance and improvement on a substitution coding task. *Psychology and Aging, 14,* 539–551.

Prinz, P. N., Scanlan, J. M., Vitaliano, P. P., Moe, K. E., Borson, S., Toivola, B., et al. (1999). Thyroid hormones: Positive relationships with cognition in healthy, euthyroid older men. *Journals of Gerontology A: Biological Sciences and Medical Sciences, 54,* 111–116.

Rabbitt, P. M. A. (2002). Aging and cognition. In H. Pashler & J. Wixted (Eds.), *Steven's handbook of experimental psychology,* Vol. 4: *Methodology in experimental psychology* (pp. 793–860). New York: Wiley.

Rabbitt, P. M. A., Lowe, C., & Shilling, V. (2001). Frontal tests and models for cognitive ageing. *European Journal of Cognitive Psychology, 13,* 5–28.

Rabbitt, P. M. A., & Vyas, S. M. (1970). An elementary preliminary taxonomy for some errors in laboratory choice RT tasks. In A. F. Sanders (Ed.), *Attention and performance III* (pp. 56–76). Amsterdam: North-Holland.

Raz, N., Gunning-Dixon, F. M., Head, D., Dupuis, J. H., & Acker, J. D. (1998). Neuroanatomical correlates of cognitive aging: Evidence from structural magnetic resonance imaging. *Neuropsychology, 12,* 95–114.

Raz, N., Rodrigue, K. M., Head, D., Kennedy, K. M., & Acker, J. D. (2004). Differential aging of the medial temporal lobe—a study of a five-year change. *Neurology, 62,* 433–438.

Reuter-Lorenz, P. A. (2002). New visions of the aging mind and brain. *Trends in Cognitive Sciences, 6,* 394–400.

Rhodes, M. G. (2004). Age-related differences in performance on the Wisconsin Card Sorting Test: A meta-analytic review. *Psychology and Aging, 19,* 482–494.

Robbins, T. W., James, M., Owen, A. M., Sahakian, B. J., Lawrence, A. D., McInnes, L., et al. (1998). A study of performance on tests from the CANTAB battery sensitive to frontal lobe dysfunction in a large sample of normal volunteers: Implications for theories of executive functioning and cognitive aging. *Journal of the International Neuropsychological Society, 4,* 474–490.

Salthouse, T. A. (1985). *A Theory of Cognitive Aging.* Amsterdam: North-Holland.

Salthouse, T. A. (in press). Executive functioning. In D. C. Park & N. Schwarz (Eds.), *Cognitive aging: A primer.* New York: Psychology Press.

Salthouse, T. A., Fristoe, N. M., McGuthry, K. E., & Hambrick, D. Z. (1998). Relation of task switching to speed, age, and fluid intelligence. *Psychology and Aging, 13,* 445–461.

Sanz, M., Molina, V., & Calcedo., A. (2001). The Wisconsin Card Sorting Test and the assessment of frontal function in obsessive-compulsive patients: An event-related potential study. *Cognitive Neuropsychiatry, 6,* 109–129.

Scahill, R. I., Frost, C., Jenkins, R., Whitwell, J. L., Rossor, M. N., & Fox, N. C. (2003). A longitudinal study of brain volume changes in normal aging using serial registered magnetic resonance imaging. *Archives of Neurology, 60,* 989–994.

Schaie, K. W., & Parham, I. A. (1977). Cohort-sequential analyses of adult intellectual development. *Developmental Psychology, 13,* 649–653.

Shallice, T. (1982). Specific impairments of planning. *Philosophical Transactions of the Royal Society of London, 298,* 199–209.

Shallice, T. (1988). *From Neuropsychology to Mental Structure.* Cambridge: Cambridge University Press.

Shallice, T., & Burgess, P. W. (1991). Deficits in strategy application following frontal-lobe damage in man. *Brain, 114,* 727–741.

Shilling, V. M., Chetwynd, A., & Rabbitt, P. M. A. (2002). Individual inconsistency across measures of inhibition: An investigation of the construct validity of inhibition in older adults. *Neuropsychologia, 40,* 605–619.

Stuss, D. T. (1992). Biological and psychological development of executive functions. *Brain and Cognition, 20,* 8–23.

Stuss, D. T., Alexander, M. P., Hamer, L., Palumbo, C., Dempster, R., Binns, M., et al. (1998). The effects of focal anterior and posterior brain lesions on verbal fluency. *Journal of the International Neuropsychological Society, 4,* 265–278.

Stuss, D. T., & Benson, D. F. (1986). *The Frontal Lobes.* New York: Raven Press.

Stuss, D. T., Levine, B., Alexander, M. P., Hong, J., Palumbo, C., Hamer, L., et al. (2000). Card Sorting Test performance in patients with focal frontal and posterior brain damage: Effects of lesion location and test structure on separable cognitive processes. *Neuropsychologia, 38,* 388–402.

Tisserand, D. J., & Jolles, J. (2003). On the involvement of prefrontal networks in cognitive ageing. *Cortex, 39,* 1107–1128.

Tombaugh, T. N., Kozak, J., & Rees, L. (1999). Normative data stratified by age and education for two measures of verbal fluency: FAS and animal naming. *Archives of Clinical Neuropsychology, 14,* 167–177.

Troyer, A. K., Graves, R. E., & Cullum, C. M. (1994). Executive functioning as a mediator of the relationship between age and episodic memory in healthy aging. *Aging and Cognition, 1,* 45–53.

Van Asselen, M., & Ridderinkhof, K. R. (2000). Shift costs of predictable and unexpected set shifting in young and older adults. *Psychologica Belgica, 40,* 259–273.

Verhaeghen, P., & Cerella, J. (2002). Aging, executive control, and attention: A review of meta-analyses. *Neuroscience and Biobehavioral Reviews, 26,* 849–857.

Verhaeghen, P., & De Meersman, L. (1998). Aging and the Stroop effect: A meta-analysis. *Psychology and Aging, 13,* 120–126.

Veroff, A. E. (1980). The neuropsychology of aging: Qualitative analysis of visual reproductions. *Psychological Research, 41,* 259–268.

West, R., & Alain, C. (2000). Effects of task context and fluctuations of attention on neural activity supporting performance of the Stroop task. *Brain Research, 873,* 102–111.

West, R. L. (1996). An application of prefrontal cortex function theory to cognitive aging. *Psychological Bulletin, 120,* 272–292.

Wilson, B. A., Evans, J. J., Alderman, N., Burgess, P. W., & Emslie, H. (1997). Behavioral assessment of the dysexecutive syndrome. In P. M. A. Rabbitt (Ed.), *Methodology of frontal and executive function* (pp. 239–250). Hove, UK: Psychology Press.

Wood, A. G., Saling, M. M., Abbott, D. F., & Jackson, G.D. (2001). A neurocognitive account of frontal lobe involvement in orthographic lexical retrieval: An fMRI study. *Neuro-image*, *14*, 162–169.

Woodruff-Pak, D. D. (1997). *The neuropsychology of aging*. Oxford: Blackwell.

Yeudall, L. R., Fromm, D., Reddon, J. R., & Stefanyk, W. O. (1986). Normative data stratified by age and sex for 12 neuropsychological tests. *Journal of Clinical Psychology*, *42*, 918–946.

4 Recovery from frontal cortical injury during development

Bryan Kolb, Marie Monfils, and Nicole Sherren

Contents

One of the major accomplishments of neuropsychological studies in the 1970s and 1980s was a new understanding of the functions of the frontal lobe of mammals. Once seen as the seat of human intelligence, the frontal lobe has come to be understood as a region that exerts "executive control" of cognitive functions both in human and nonhuman mammals. Although the detail of exactly what the frontal lobe is doing is still a matter of serious debate, there is a general consensus that the frontal lobe functions to organize behavior in space and time (Fuster, 1998; Kolb, 2007). Damage to the frontal lobe in adulthood thus produces significant disturbance of executive functions (EF) (for a review, see Kolb & Whishaw, 2003). The effects of damage to the frontal lobe during development are less well-understood but there is considerable evidence that the chronic behavioral effects of frontal injury vary with the age-at-injury. The goal of this chapter is to review studies on laboratory animals, and especially rats, in which precise developmental age has been manipulated and both functional and anatomical outcome has been examined. In addition, we shall consider treatments that can modify the age-dependent effects of early cortical injuries. We begin, however, with a brief overview of the effects of frontal injury in children (see Anderson, Jacobs, & Harvey, this volume).

Effects of frontal lobe injury in children

One of the first references to the effects of early frontal lobe injury in children was given by Broca in the late 1800s as he wrote "I am convinced that a lesion of the left third frontal convolution, apt to produce lasting aphemia (aphasia) in an adult, will not prevent a small child from learning to talk" (Finger & Almli, 1988, p. 122). Because language ought to have been affected by the injuries, it was reasonable to presume that there had been a fundamental change in the cortical organization of these children. Studies after a century showed this to be a correct assumption. For example, Rasmussen and Milner (1977) showed that depending upon the precise age-at-injury, the language zones of the left frontal lobe could move either to the right hemisphere or to an alternate region of the damaged left hemisphere. Damage to frontal language zones in the first 2 years of life leads to a shift of the affected zone to the right hemisphere whereas damage after 2 years leads to a shift within the left hemisphere. Damage after about 10 years of age does not permit language zones to move. Thus, it is clear that developmental age is important neurologically. What is less clear, however, is exactly why it is so important and whether it is true of other frontal lobe functions.

Studies by Hebb in the 1940s (Hebb, 1949) suggested that other frontal lobe functions might also show age-dependent effects of injury but rather than emphasizing the resilience of these functions to early injury, he emphasized just the opposite. Based on his studies of children with frontal lobe injuries, Hebb concluded that an early injury may prevent the development of some intellectual capacities that an equally extensive injury, at maturity, would not have destroyed. Hebb believed that this outcome resulted from a failure of initial organization of the brain, thus making it difficult for the child to develop many behaviors, especially socioaffective behaviors and what we now refer to as "executive" functions. Although there have not been extensive studies following Hebb's early observations, there are some data supporting his proposal. For example, Kolb (1995) found that epileptic children with perinatal brain injuries had deficits in both executive and socio-affective behaviors that were larger than would be expected from adults with similar injuries (see chapter 11, this volume).

We are thus left with a conundrum. There appear to be age-dependent effects of frontal injuries in children but it appears that under some circumstances there is a better outcome from early injury whereas under other circumstances there is a poorer outcome. Studies on laboratory monkeys in the 1960s and 1970s only added to this confusion. Although sample sizes were small, behavioral outcome from early frontal injury in monkeys appeared to vary depending upon the exact age-at-injury, the location of the injury, the nature of the behavioral tests, and the age-at-behavioral testing (Goldman, 1974). One disadvantage of using the rhesus monkey as a subject in these studies is that they are born more mature than humans and it is thus difficult to mimic perinatal injury in humans except by rather difficult prenatal surgeries (Goldman & Galkin, 1978). In addition, monkeys normally have only one infant, which is relatively slow growing, so it is difficult to do studies with large sample sizes. Two other common laboratory animals, rats and cats, provide an advantage on both these problems as they are born younger than humans, and thus it is possible to do *ex utero* studies that try to mimic a wide range of human-equivalent postnatal ages, and they typically have litters of young, which allows studies on a larger subject sample.

Rat as a model for mammalian frontal function

Although once believed to have a primitive cortex with little functional relevance to the human cortex, it is now clear that mammals in general have a strikingly similar cortical organization (Kaas, 1987; Kolb & Tees, 1990). Although the frontal cortex of most nonprimate mammals was essentially not studied until the last 25 years, there is now an extensive literature on the frontal cortex of many species, the rat in particular (Kolb, 1984, 1990; Uylings, Groenewegen, & Kolb, 2003). Although the details of this literature are beyond the scope of this chapter, it is worth briefly reviewing the anatomical organization and behavioral functions of the frontal cortex of rats.

Like primates, the frontal cortex of rats is characterized by having several distinct cytoarchitectonic regions (Figure 4.1) that can be grossly seen as a medial prefrontal (mPFC), lateral orbital prefrontal (OFC), and motor region. The prefrontal regions have distinct patterns of connections with the dorsomedial thalamic nucleus, amygdala, striatum, and brainstem, and these connections are remarkably similar to those seen in the dorsolateral and orbital prefrontal regions of the monkey (Uylings et al., 2003).

Injury to the medial and lateral orbital regions in rats produces very different behavioral syndromes, and these changes are strikingly similar to those observed in primates with lesions to the dorsolateral and orbitofrontal regions, respectively (for reviews see Kolb, 1984, 1990). For example, damage to the mPFC area produces severe deficits in acquisition and retention of working memory tasks such as delayed response (Kolb, Nonneman, & Singh, 1974), delayed alternation (Wikmark, Divac, & Weiss, 1973), different types of delayed nonmatching-to-sample tasks (Dunnett, 1990; Kolb, Buhrmann, McDonald, & Sutherland, 1994; Otto & Eichenbaum, 1992), and related tasks (Kesner & Holbrook, 1987). Recently, deficits have been shown in various types of attentional tasks (Muir, Everitt, & Robbins, 1996) and in a task requiring a shift of attention from one set of cues to another (Birrel & Brown, 2000). Medial frontal lesions also produce disruptions to the production of various motor- and species-typical behaviors that require the ordering of motor sequences, such as in nest building, food hoarding, or latch opening (Kolb & Whishaw, 1983; Shipley & Kolb, 1977).

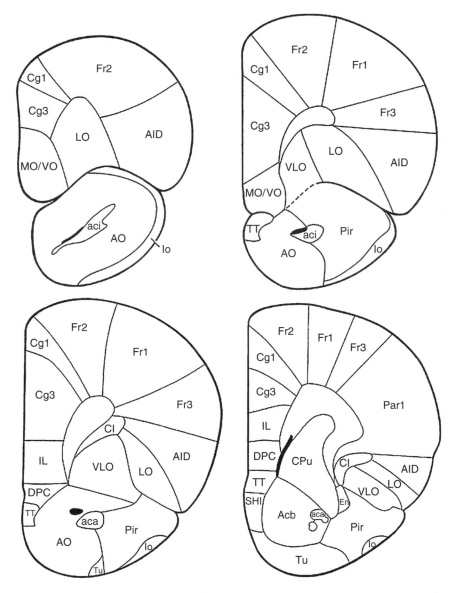

Figure 4.1   Schematic representation of coronal sections through the prefrontal cortex of the rat. The medial prefrontal regions (mPFC) include the shoulder cortex (Fr2), dorsal anterior cingulate cortex (Cg1,2), prelimbic cortex (Cg3), infralimbic cortex (IL), and medial orbital cortex (MO). The orbital frontal cortex (OFC) includes the ventral and lateral orbital regions (VO, VLO, LO), and agranular insular cortex (AI). (After Zilles, 1985.)

The lateral orbital region receives significant olfactory and taste input and although OFC lesions do not produce deficits in olfactory or taste discriminations, they do produce deficits in tasks requiring working memory for odor or taste information (DeCoteau, Kesner, & Williams, 1997; Otto & Eichenbaum, 1992;

Ragozzino & Kesner, 1999). Furthermore, lesions to the lateral orbital region disrupt the learning of cross-modal associations that involve odor or taste cues (Whishaw, Tomie, & Kolb, 1992). More recently, studies by Schoenbaum and his colleagues (Gallagher, McMahan, & Schoenbaum, 1999; Schoenbaum & Setlow, 2002) have emphasized a role of the orbital cortex in the encoding of the acquired incentive value of cues. For example, both rats and primates can show intact performance on discriminations that require responding to neutral cues (such as a light) that predicts reward, while at the same time showing marked deficits when the incentive value of the stimulus is reduced. Such deficits can be seen during extinction when the incentive value of a stimulus is reduced to zero, yet animals continue to respond to the cue as though reward is expected (Baxter, Parker, Lindner, Izquierdo, & Murray, 2000; Gallagher et al., 1999). The role of the orbitofrontal cortex in stimulus-reward associations is further seen in studies measuring the tuning characteristics of neurons in the orbital region of both rats and monkeys (see review by Schoenbaum & Setlow, 2002). Finally, damage to the orbitofrontal cortex produces deficits in social and play behavior in rats (de Bruin, 1990; Kolb, 1974).

Development of the cortex of rats

There are several stages to the development of cortex in any species. These include cell proliferation, cell migration, cell differentiation, dendritic and axonal growth, synaptogenesis, gliogenesis, and cell and synaptic death. In the rat most cell proliferation is complete at birth but migration continues for an another week, especially in the posterior cortex (for details see Bayer & Altman, 1991). Dendritic arborization, synaptic formation, and gliogenesis are intense in the second and third weeks (Figure 4.2) (see Kolb & Whishaw, 1989 for detailed references). As dendrites and

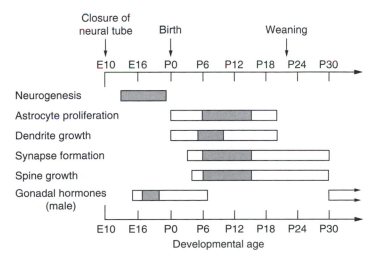

Figure 4.2   Schematic summary of the time course of cerebral development in the rat. The shaded regions indicate the time of maximum activity.

synapses develop they are influenced by afferent input: enhanced input increases synaptic formation whereas reduced input attenuates synaptic formation and may lead to atrophy (Fifkova, 1970). The effects of stimulation vary with precise age, however. We have shown, for example, that placing animals in complex environments at different developmental ages has qualitatively different effects on synaptic formation (see below for more details). The key point here is that brain injury at different stages in development will have different effects on the brain because the brain is different at different ages and its response to injury is different as well.

An important issue in the study of cortical development in rats is in defining the equivalent ages in other species and particularly humans. This is not an easy task largely because different measures of nervous system development lead us to different conclusions. For example, although neuronal migration is complete and synaptogenesis is active at the beginning of the second postnatal week, the rats' eyes do not open until day 15, which is rather late when compared to the developmental state of the cortex, or when we consider that the animals are weaned at about day 21. The general consensus in the behavioral literature is that postnatal day 7 is roughly equivalent to birth in humans although this date is not universally accepted in the anatomical literature (Bayer & Altman, 1991). Nonetheless, for the current review we shall take postnatal day 7 in rats to be roughly equivalent to birth in humans. On the basis of the rate of dendritic growth, which is most intense in rats around day 12 and in human infants around 8 months, we can use these ages as rough equivalents. Similarly, maximum synaptic density in the cortex of rats is about day 35 compared to about 12 months in humans. Finally, puberty is at about 60 days in rats and about 12 years in humans. It is obvious that the developmental rates are not moving at the same pace in the two species and the long development before puberty in humans likely attests to the much larger effect of a wide range of experiences on cortical development in humans.

Recovery from prefrontal injury during development

Over the past 30 years we have come a long way in understanding some of the rules that describe the outcome of frontal injury during different stages of development. We shall briefly summarize our progress to date.

Recovery is age-dependent

There is a qualitative change in the effects of prefrontal injury over the first few weeks. Damage to the prefrontal or motor cortex during the first week has severe behavioral consequences that are worse than after similar injuries in adulthood whereas prefrontal injury in the second week allows remarkable functional recovery (Kolb, 1987; Kolb, Cioe, & Whishaw, 2000; Kolb, Petrie, & Cioe, 1996). This latter age-at-injury advantage continues until at least weaning although the extent of recovery is maximal around day 10–12. The effects of injury from weaning through adolescence and into adulthood have not been systematically studied although there appears to be a functional advantage of injuries as late as puberty (Kolb & Nonneman, 1976).

Recovery varies with behavioral measure

As a rule of thumb recovery of cognitive/EFs is much greater than recovery of species-typical and motor behaviors. Thus, animals with early prefrontal injuries in the second week show almost complete recovery of cognitive/EFs (working memory, strategy formation), partial recovery of motor behaviors, and no recovery of social/affective behaviors (Kolb & Whishaw, 1981). This behavioral difference may be similar to the difference between the recoveries of at least certain cognitive functions (such as language) in human infants who at the same time have severe chronic deficits in social/affective behavior (see above).

Recovery varies with age-at-behavioral analysis

As noted above, rats with prefrontal injury in the second week show good functional recovery of cognitive abilities when tested in adulthood. To our surprise, however, there is virtually no recovery when the animals are tested as juveniles (Kolb & Gibb, 1993). That is, the animals appear to "grow out of their deficits." This time course of recovery must reflect changes in brain organization and structure that follow the injury and it seems likely that these changes must mature before behavior can recover and, as we shall see shortly, this is the case. But, it is not only that animals with early lesions grow out of their deficits, but they also grow into deficits. It is very difficult to detect any motor deficits in young rats with either prefrontal or motor cortex injury but as normal rats develop the ability to make skilled forelimb movements needed for behaviors such as nest building or reaching and grasping food items, the deficits begin to emerge in the frontal-injured animals (Kolb & Whishaw, 1985a).

Effects of bilateral lesions are much more severe than unilateral lesions

Most studies of early brain injury in the prefrontal cortex are done in laboratory animals with bilateral injuries because the cognitive effects of unilateral injuries are small and difficult to study. Nonetheless, rats with perinatal, unilateral, prefrontal, or motor cortex lesions do show both cognitive and motor deficits (Kolb & Cioe, 2000; Kolb, Zabrowski, & Whishaw, 1989; Sherren, Akins, & Kolb, 2005). Although the age-dependent effects of bilateral injuries are not dependent upon the size of injury, this is not the case with unilateral injuries. Rats with small unilateral mPFC lesions in the first versus second week show only small cognitive deficits and these are equivalent whether the injuries are on day 1, 5, or 10 (Sherren et al., 2005). In contrast, there is still an age effect on motor behaviors as the animals with earlier injuries have more severe deficits than those with injuries on day 10. Curiously, damage at any of the ages produces a bilateral motor deficit when animals are tested on measures of skilled reaching. It thus appears that animals with small unilateral mPFC lesions must compensate with morphological/organizational changes that can support cognitive functions but not motor functions. Furthermore, there must be some difference in the compensatory response of large versus small lesions. The nature of these differences is not yet known.

Motor cortex injury allows less functional recovery than prefrontal injury

When the motor cortex adjacent to the prefrontal cortex is removed at different ages in development there is still a clear age-at-injury effect but the recovery is less extensive than after prefrontal injuries. One other difference is that rats with either unilateral or bilateral motor cortex lesions in the first week show cognitive deficits typical of rats with mPFC lesions in adulthood (Kolb & Cioe, 2000; Kolb et al., 2000). Rats with injuries at day 10 do not show these cognitive deficits. One explanation for the reduced recovery in animals with motor cortex lesions is that the compensatory response of the brain must be different after the two injuries. Given the unexpected cognitive deficits it also seems likely that the early motor cortex injuries somehow interfere with the normal development of the mPFC.

There are morphological changes that correlate with functional outcome of early prefrontal injury

Perhaps the most striking difference in the effects of even small prefrontal lesions at different ages in development is the effect on brain weight in adulthood: the earlier the injury, the smaller the brain. For example, rats with bilateral mPFC lesions on day 1–5 have adult brains that are only 80–85% of normal size whereas rats with day 7–12 lesions have adult brains that are about 90% of normal size. The simple conclusion from this observation is that there is a difference in the response of the brain to prefrontal injury in the first versus second week. There is, however, one puzzling conundrum. When we look at the effects of similar lesions in adulthood, the brains of the adult operates are even larger. The only way to reconcile the fact that day 10 animals have better recovery than the adults, yet have smaller brains, is to conclude that there is some fundamental difference in the way the brain of the day 10 operates is organized, that is, the neural networks that develop after the day 10 injuries must convey some advantage that is independent of size.

The simplest way to study neural networks is to examine the dendritic morphology. Changes in the structure of the dendritic fields must reflect changes in connectivity because we know that virtually all dendritic space is occupied by synapses. Thus, if there is an increase in dendritic space, there must be more synapses whereas if there is a decrease, there must be an increase. Our first clue to what the differences in neural organization might be came when we analyzed the dendritic arborization of rats with day 1 versus day 10 lesions. Whereas rats with the early lesions had a marked atrophy of dendritic arborization in pyramidal cells throughout the remaining cortex relative to normal littermates, rats with day 10 lesions showed a dramatic hypertrophy not only of dendritic length but also of spine density (Kolb, Gibb, & van der Kooy, 1994). Rats with adult lesions showed only a small, although significant, increase in dendritic fields. Thus, it appears that the animals with the best outcomes had the most complex cells whereas those with the worst outcomes had the simplest cells.

Recall that we had found that rats with day 10 injuries "grew out of their deficits." We thus wondered if the behavioral changes would correlate with anatomical changes. They did. Both day 1 and day 10 operates had simpler than normal dendritic fields when examined on day 25, at which time they both showed cognitive deficits, but when a similar study was done at day 60, when the cognitive deficits were gone, the day 10 animals had hypertrophied dendrites and spine density in cortical pyramidal neurons (Kolb & Gibb, 1993). Thus, there was a parallel between the complexity of the neural circuits in the remaining cortex and the functional outcome.

Our second clue to age-related differences in the response to prefrontal injury came from our serendipitous observation that there was spontaneous neurogenesis occurring after day 7–12 but not after day 1–5 mPFC or adult mPFC lesions (Kolb, Gibb, Gorny, & Whishaw, 1998). Thus, when the mPFC is removed around day 10 there is mobilization of cells from the subventricular zone and these cells migrate to the lesion site and differentiate into neurons that form at least some of the original connections of the mPFC region. We hasten to point out that the regenerated tissue is only about 60% of normal volume and thus we would anticipate residual behavioral effects of the lesions and of course this is the case. Either removal of the regenerated tissue or prevention of regeneration by interfering with the stem cells in the subventricular zone completely block the functional recovery (Dallison & Kolb, 1993; Kolb, Pederson, & Gibb, 2005). The neurogenesis after mPFC lesions appears to be unique as it is not seen after OFC or motor cortex lesions at the same age. This difference is curious given that these latter lesions are adjacent to the mPFC. In fact, it appears that there is something special about the midline telencephalon. Removal of the olfactory bulb at day 10 also allows for regeneration as does removal of the entire midline cortex (Gonzalez, Gibb, & Kolb, 2002; Gonzalez, Whishaw, & Kolb, 2003). The latter result is interesting because removal of the posterior cingulate cortex alone does not allow regeneration whereas removal of the mPFC in addition to the remaining cingulate cortex leads to at least partial regeneration of the cingulate cortex.

Our final clue to how the brain is compensating from the early injuries came from an analysis of the changes in the expression of certain growth factors after early mPFC injury at different ages. In particular, basic fibroblast growth factor (FGF-2), a neurotrophic factor that plays a key role in neurogenesis during brain development, is upregulated after day 10 but not day 1–3 mPFC lesions. It seems likely that this upregulation of FGF-2 is important in the neurogenesis seen after day 10 lesions and may also play some role in the dendritic changes. We have also recently shown that there is a differential phenotypic distribution of FGF-2 expression throughout development that varies as a function of the brain region under investigation (Monfils, Driscoll, Melvin, & Kolb, 2006b), and proposed that this might explain the differential recovery observed following postnatal neocortical lesions inflicted at different time points after birth (Kolb et al., 1996, 2000). We return to the role of FGF-2 shortly.

There are differences in the morphological changes after bilateral and unilateral lesions

One obvious difference between the effects of unilateral and bilateral lesions is that there is an undamaged hemisphere in the former case. This may seem obvious but is important because an injured hemisphere will initiate reparative processes that will not be necessary in the undamaged hemisphere. Furthermore, the compensatory processes that begin after a unilateral injury may include directing projections from one hemisphere to the other (either to or from the injured hemisphere) whereas this is unlikely in the case of a bilateral injury. Analysis of changes in cortical–subcortical connectivity after bilateral injuries has shown that prefrontal injury on days 1–5 leads to a variety of anomalous projections including abnormal thalamocortical and brainstem-cortical connections whereas injury in the second week appears to have little effect on these connections (Kolb et al., 1994). In contrast, unilateral lesions on day 1–5 reduce corticostriatal connectivity on both sides of the brain, and produce abnormal thalamostriatal connections on the damaged side. There are also anomalous thalamic projections to the intact mPFC. When the injury occurs during the second week, changes in connectivity are largely confined to the damaged hemisphere and result in fewer, rather than abnormal, connections. At all ages there is an aberrant connection between the CA1 subfield of the hippocampus and the caudate in the damaged hemisphere, and both damaged and intact hemispheres show increases in intracortical connectivity. Unilateral prefrontal damage also produces a hemispheric shift in amygdalostriatal connectivity, resulting in an abnormally large crossed projection from the amygdala on the damaged side to the caudate on the intact side. Unilateral motor cortex lesions also produce a hemispheric shift in connectivity. Reorganization of the corticospinal tract results in an anomalous ipsilateral corticospinal projection from the normal hemisphere, allowing the intact cortex to control both sides of the body (Figure 4.3).

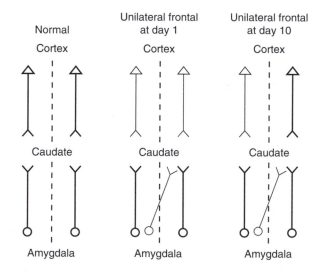

Figure 4.3 Schematic summary of the changes in cerebral circuitry after unilateral frontal injuries on postnatal day 1 or 10. There is an anomalous crossed amygdalostriatal connection from the injured hemisphere to the intact one after injury at either age. In addition, there is reduced density of corticospinal connections bilaterally in the day 1 operates and unilaterally (on the lesion side) in the day 10 operates. The relative density of the projections is indicated by the darkness of the lines.

Table 4.1   Rules governing recovery from prefrontal injury during development in rats.

Recovery is age-dependent
Recovery varies with behavioral measure
Recovery varies with age-at-behavioral analysis
The effects of bilateral lesions are much more severe than unilateral
  lesions
Motor cortex injury allows less functional recovery than prefrontal injury
There are morphological changes that correlate with functional outcome
  of early prefrontal injury
There are differences in the morphological changes after bilateral and
  unilateral lesions

Summary

We have identified several rules that describe the effects of early frontal injury in rats and appear to be applicable to other species as well (Table 4.1). Indeed, understanding the rules makes interpretation of the effects of early injuries in children simpler. In particular, recovery varies with precise developmental age, unilaterality versus bilaterality of the injury, and with the nature of the behavior in question. It is clear that cognitive behaviors such as language follow a different pattern of recovery than social behaviors. In addition, there are clear anatomical correlates of recovery in rodents and similar correlates are likely to be found in other species, including humans.

Broader picture

Although we have made considerable progress in understanding the effects of early cortical injuries, there are still large areas of ignorance, however. To date, most of our studies have been on the effects of either large prefrontal lesions, which include both mPFC and OFC, or on just mPFC lesions. We have begun to study focal OFC lesions and there is a clear age-at-injury effect that is parallel to that seen with mPFC lesions but there are some differences. In contrast to mPFC lesions, OFC lesions in the first week produce both cognitive and motor deficits that are not seen after similar lesions in adulthood (Kolb & Whishaw, 1985b; Kolb et al., 2007). These deficits are unexpected and not easily explained although one possibility is that the early OFC lesions are interfering with the development of the adjacent motor cortex or mPFC. Early OFC lesions produce large deficits in play behavior both during development and later in adulthood but we do not yet know if these deficits are reduced if the lesions are in the second week (Pellis et al., 2006). It is also not yet clear what the morphological/organizational sequelae of early OFC lesions might be but neurogenesis is not one of them.

One question that arises from our studies of frontal cortical injuries during development is whether these results are unique to the frontal cortex or generalize to posterior cortical regions. The general answer is that they are generally similar in the posterior cortex. We have done parallel studies in animals with posterior cingulate, posterior parietal, visual, and temporal cortex lesions and in all cases there is an age-dependent effect of the injuries that favors week two. In addition, with the exception of the posterior parietal injuries, the week two advantage is correlated with dendritic hypertrophy. As a general rule, however, we can say that recovery of cognitive functions is better after day 7–10 mPFC lesions than after similar age lesions in any posterior region. We also note that damage to the mPFC leads to the largest compensatory changes in dendritic arborization and there is no significant neurogenesis after lesions in any cortical area except the mPFC. The puzzle that remains is why and whether it is possible to stimulate neurogenesis after injury outside the mPFC. We shall see that it is.

A second question that arises is whether the observations on rats can be generalized to other species. A similar pattern of results can be seen in parallel studies of the effects of cortical lesions in kittens by Villablanca and his colleagues (Villablanca, Carlson-Kuhta, Schmanke, & Hovda, 1998; Villablanca, Hovda, Jackson, & Infante, 1993). If the kitten frontal cortex is damaged between embryonic day 55 (E55) and postnatal day 60 (P60), there is an excellent functional outcome. Injury prior to E55 days leads to a poor functional outcome and damage after P60 days leads to a progressive worsening of the lesion effects. Most studies done on monkeys are done much later in development than the rat and kitten studies because monkeys are born relatively mature, even in comparison to humans. The one monkey study by Goldman and Galkin (1978) that did show recovery after a prenatal frontal injury was, in fact, making lesions roughly equivalent to the age at which rats and kittens also show recovery. A key point here is that birth date is irrelevant. It is the developmental stage of the brain at injury that is critical. Thus, because rats and kittens are born at an embryologically younger age than primates, including humans, the time scale for functional outcome must be adjusted to match the neural events that are underway at the time of injury. If we extrapolate the findings from kittens and rat pups to humans, it appears that the worst time to have frontal injury in humans would be in the third trimester and likely for at least a couple of weeks postnatally. This would be followed by a period during which we should expect better functional recovery, likely lasting until at least 2 years of age although this is merely a guess at this point.

Factors modulating recovery from frontal injury in rats

It is known that intervention programs are effective in improving cognitive development in premature infants (Brooks-Gunn, Liaw, & Klebanov, 1992; Shonkoff & Hauser-Cram, 1987). What is not known, however, is why they work and what are the most effective treatments. Nonetheless, the general idea is that it should be possible to influence the endogenous processes of neural development by intervening behaviorally (sensory or motor experience) or chemically (diet, hormones, growth factors, and drugs). Thus in animals with early brain injury it might be possible to reinitiate neurogenesis or enhance synaptogenesis, which in turn might enhance functional outcome. Indeed, this appears to be the case, although there is still much ignorance about what treatments are most effective and why. We will review what is known to date (see Table 4.2).

Table 4.2 Factors modulating recovery.

Factors Enhancing Recovery
  Behavioural interventions (e.g., social stimulation, tactile stimulation,
    and complex housing)
  Growth factors (e.g., FGF-2)
  Diet (e.g., choline, vitamin, and mineral supplements)
Factors Interfering with Recovery
  SSRIs
  Catecholamine or gonadal hormone disruption
  Stress

Behavioral interventions are effective if begun early

There have been many studies of the effects of various types of experience on functional outcome after cerebral injury in adult laboratory animals, with the most studied and effective treatment being complex housing (Biernaskie & Corbett, 2001; Kolb & Gibb, 1991; Will & Kelche, 1992). The consistent finding in such studies is that placing animals in complex environments induces synaptogenesis throughout the cerebral cortex and this provides significant benefit to animals with cerebral injuries. One important question from these studies is just what the human equivalent might be. The general consensus is that complex housing provides continuous social and sensorimotor stimulation and thus a human equivalent might be a rehabilitation unit in which people were engaged in various therapeutic and social activities for several hours a day. This is likely not practical for infants but the general idea that sensorimotor and perhaps social stimulation might be beneficial seems reasonable. We thus placed animals with day 3 mPFC lesions in complex environments either at weaning or in adulthood and examined cognitive and motor functions after 3 months of this experience. The general result was that early housing stimulated functional recovery of both cognitive and motor behaviors whereas later experience provided little benefit. The fact that the earlier experience was better led us to try using even earlier experience. This was accomplished by tactilely stimulating the pups for 45 min a day (3 bouts of 15 min each) beginning the day after day 3 frontal surgery and continuing until weaning. The results showed a clear benefit of tactile stimulation on both motor and cognitive tasks (Gibb & Kolb, 2005; see also Chou et al., 2001). The tactile stimulation regime was chosen because a similar treatment had been shown to enhance development in premature human infants (Field et al., 1986) so it seems reasonable to suppose that tactile stimulation would benefit human infants with frontal injuries as well.

When we looked for morphological correlates of the behavioral interventions we found that both the complex housing and the tactile stimulation acted to reverse the dendritic atrophy seen after the day 3 lesions (Comeau, Gibb, Hastings, Cioe, & Kolb, 2007; Gibb, Gorny, & Kolb, 2005; Gibb & Kolb, 2005). In addition, we were able to show that tactile stimulation increased the expression of FGF-2 in both the skin and the brain (Gibb & Kolb, 2005). Recall that we had found previously that FGF-2 was enhanced after day 10 mPFC lesions but not after day 1 lesions, suggesting that FGF-2 may play an important role in stimulating recovery. Our tactile stimulation results suggest that it is possible to modify the endogenous production of growth factors by behavioral manipulations, which in turn modifies the brain development and leads to a functional benefit.

Growth factors can modify development and recovery from frontal injury

The increased expression of FGF-2 in response to tactile stimulation led us to administer FGF-2 as a postinjury treatment for animals with day 3 frontal mPFC or day 10 motor cortex lesions. (Recall that there was no spontaneous neurogenesis after either lesion and recovery was very poor in the day 3 mPFC animals and only partial after day 10 motor cortex lesions.) Animals received subcutaneous FGF-2 for a week following their cortical injuries and in both mPFC and motor cortex studies the treatment was effective in stimulating enhanced recovery although the mechanisms appear to be quite different in the two models.

When FGF-2-treated rats with day 3 mPFC lesions were tested on both cognitive and motor tests as adults they showed significant benefits and this was correlated with enhanced dendritic arborization in pyramidal cells throughout the remaining cortex (Comeau, Hastings, & Kolb, 2005). There was, however, neither obvious change in the size of the cortical injury nor evidence of neurogenesis. In contrast, when we administered bFGF after day 10 motor cortex injuries we found that not only do the animals show enhanced functional recovery but they also show partial regrowth of the lost cortex (Monfils et al., 2005; 2006a; in press). We note, however, that this tissue was not normal in appearance as there was little lamination typical of normal cortex (Figure 4.4). Electrophysiological analysis of this tissue revealed that although intra-cortical microstimulation induced a very limited number of forelimb movements (Monfils, et al., 2005), it produced detectable EMG responses in forelimb extensors, and tracing studies revealed corticospinal

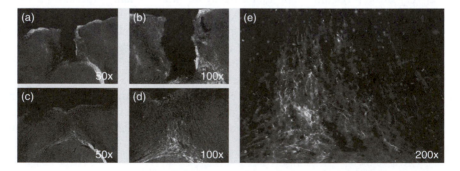

Figure 4.4   Cycling cells and neuroblasts migrate to the site of injury in lesion rats that receive FGF-2. Lesion rats that did not receive FGF-2 (a and b) have a prominent lesion cavity, and do not show cells migrating to the site of injury. In comparison, in the lesion rats that received FGF-2 (c, d, and e), the lesion cavity shows a number of migrating neuroblasts (doublecortin positive DCx+) as well as cycling (ki67+) cells at the site of injury at P14 as well as P21 (P21 shown here) (from Monfils et al., 2006).

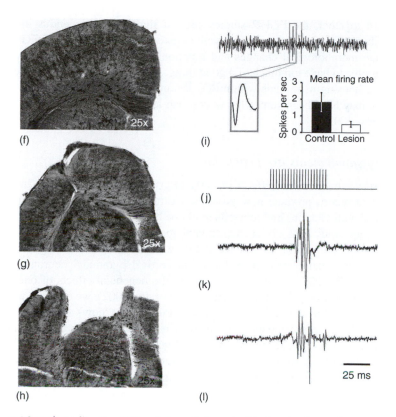

Figure 4.4 (continued)   In adulthood, the cells from the filled cavity do not show clear laminar distribution (g) compared to no lesion rats (f). The lesion rats that did not receive FGF-2 all showed a lesion cavity in adulthood (h) (from Monfils et al., 2005). Multiunit recordings performed in adulthood from the filled region revealed that cells from that region spontaneously fire action potentials. Shown in (i) is an example of spontaneous activity recorded from the filled region (from Monfils et al., 2006a), and the isolation of a single spike in the gray rectangle. Analyses (shown in the bar graph) revealed that the mean firing rate was greater in the cells from motor cortex (controls) than in the cells from the regrown area (lesion rats that received FGF-2). Intracortical microstimulation of the regrown region (j) elicited electromyographic activity in the wrist extensors (k) that was comparable to no lesion rats (l), suggesting that FGF-2 treatment following bilateral motor cortex injury inflicted at P10 induced a functional reconnection of the previously lesioned region to the periphery. Shown in (k) and (l) are representative EMG traces from activity recorded in the wrist extensors of a lesion FGF-2-treated rat (k) and a no lesion control rat (l), respectively. From "Differential Expression of Basic Fibroblast Growth Factor-2 in the Developing Rat Brain," by M. H. Monfils, I. Driscoll, N. R. Melvin, and B. Kolb, 2006b, *Neuroscience*, 141, pp. 213–221.

connections from the regrown tissue (Monfils et al., in press). As in our experiments showing spontaneous regeneration of the mPFC after day 10 lesions, we then blocked the growth of the new cortical tissue by prenatal suppression of the subventrical stem cells, and this, in turn, blocked the recovery of function (Monfils et al., 2006a).

Taken together, the FGF-2 studies suggest that both endogenous induction of bFGF by behavioral therapies as well as exogenous injections of FGF-2 act to stimulate morphological changes and functional recovery. We note, however, that it is possible to have too much of a good thing. When we added bFGF-2 treatment to complex housing in animals with mPFC lesions the animals showed no benefit and actually may have been somewhat worse than lesion animals without any treatment (Hastings, 2003).

Dietary supplements are beneficial

Because the regenerative effects of early injuries presumably require heavy meta-bolic demands to produce new proteins, we reasoned that feeding animals a diet enhanced with vitamins and minerals might be beneficial. Indeed, we had shown in a preliminary study that giving a postnatal diet enhanced with choline stimulated recovery from P4 frontal lesions and this was correlated with large increases in dendritic arborization and spine density in cortical pyramidal neurons (Halliwell, Tees, & Kolb, 2007). As we were aware of the beneficial effects of one particular supplement (Kaplan, Crawford, Gardner, & Farrelly, 2002), we chose to use this and simply added to the animal's usual base diet (Purina Rat Chow). Postnatal addition of vitamin/mineral supplements showed even better behavioral effects than choline alone and again the functional improvement was correlated with enhanced dendritic growth (Halliwell & Kolb, 2003). One question that arises from the dietary studies is what the mechanism might be and, in particular, how dietary manipulation might be related to the growth factors. To date, we have no answer.

Not all treatments are beneficial

In view of our findings that stimulating neurogenesis was beneficial after early frontal lesions we wondered if another mitogenic drug, namely fluoxetine (i.e., Prozac) might also be beneficial after day 3 mPFC lesions. Because fluoxetine is known to stimulate neurogenesis, at least in hippocampus, we wondered if fluoxetine treatment might have effects like FGF-2. Furthermore, postnatal treatment with fluoxetine is known to induce plasticity in the postnatal developing visual system (Bastos, Marcelino, Amaral, & Serfaty, 1999) so it seemed reasonable to expect a similar result after cortical perturbation. To our surprise, prenatal fluoxetine treat-ment (dose equivalent to human therapeutic dose) actually made animals worse after P3 mPFC lesions, and in fact, even sham-lesion animals had impairments on behavioral tasks relative to vehicle-treated rats (Day, Gibb, & Kolb, 2003). In addition, we also found that prenatal fluoxetine actually blocks the spontaneous recovery seen in rats with day 10 mPFC lesions. We are still looking at the effects of postinjury injections of fluoxetine but our preliminary results suggest that it has effects similar to those seen with prenatal injections.

The finding that certain treatments might interfere with normal recovery is not without precedent. We have found, for example, that neonatal removal of gonadal hormones (Kolb & Stewart, 1995) or cerebral noradrenalin (Kolb & Sutherland, 1992) blocks recovery from day 7 mPFC lesions. In both cases the failed recovery is correlated with an absence of compensatory dendritic and synaptic growth. Finally, although the data are not complete, there is reason to believe that prenatal events such as maternal stress may interfere with recovery (Gibb, Halliwell, & Kolb, unpublished).

Conclusions

One of the many intriguing questions about functioning of the frontal lobe concerns the manner in which the developing brain can modify its structure and ultimately its function after frontal injury early in life. As the preceding review has suggested, recovery from perinatal frontal cortical injury in lab animals is tightly tied to the precise ontogenetic stage of the brain at the time of injury. Thus, damage to the frontal cortex during the completion of neural migration and neuronal differentiation generally has a dismal outcome whereas damage during the peak time of dendritic growth and the emergence of cortical astrocytes allows remarkable functional recovery. It is possible to modify the outcome of early lesions, however, by manipulating a variety of postnatal factors including experience, growth factors, and diet.

Changes in behavior after brain injury during development are correlated with changes in cerebral morphology. For example, animals with good functional outcomes show enhanced dendritic arborization, increased spine density, altered protein expression, and in some cases, enhanced neurogenesis relative to animals with poor functional outcomes. Furthermore, injury-induced changes in cortical structure are modified by those factors that enhance functional outcome, although it is not yet known exactly what the mechanisms underlying these changes might be.

References

Bastos, E. F., Marcelino, J. L., Amaral, A. R., & Serfaty, C. A. (1999). Fluoxetine-induced plasticity in the rodent visual system. *Brain Research, 824*, 28–35.

Bayer, S. A., & Altman, J. (1991). *Neocortical development.* New York: Raven Press.

Baxter, M. G., Parker, A., Lindner, C. C. C., Izquierdo, A. D., & Murray, E. A. (2000). Control of response selection by reinforcer value requires interaction of amygdala and orbitofrontal cortex. *Journal of Neuroscience, 20*, 4311–4319.

Biernaskie, J., & Corbett, D. (2001). Enriched rehabilitative training promotes improved forelimb motor function and enhanced dendritic growth after focal ischemic injury. *Journal of Neuroscience, 21*(14), 5272–5280.

Birrel, J. M., & Brown, V. J. (2000). Medial frontal cortex mediates perceputal attentional set shifting in the rat. *Journal of Neuroscience, 20*, 4320–4324.

Brooks-Gunn, J., Liaw, F. R., & Klebanov, P. K. (1992). Effects of early intervention on cognitive function of low birth weight preterm infants. *Journal of Pediatrics, 120*, 350–359.

Chou, I. -C., Trakht, T., Signori, C., Smith, J., Felt, B. T., Vazquez, D. M., et al. (2001). Behavioral/environmental intervention improves learning after cerebral hypoxia-ischemia in rats. *Stroke, 32*, 2192–2197.

Comeau, W., Gibb, R., Hastings, E., Cioe, J., & Kolb, B. (2007). Therapeutic effects of complex rearing or bFGF after perinatal frontal lesions. Developmental Psychobiology, in press.

Comeau, W., Hastings, E., & Kolb, B. (2005). Differential effect of pre and postnatal FGF-2 following medical prefrontal cortical injury. *Behavioural brain research, 180*, 18–27.

Dallison, A., & Kolb, B. (1993). Recovery from infant frontal cortical lesions in rats can be reversed by cortical lesions in adulthood. *Behavioural Brain Research, 146,* 57–63.

Day, M., Gibb, R., & Kolb, B. (2003). Prenatal fluoxetine impairs functional recovery and neuroplasticity after perinatal frontal cortex lesions in rats. *Society for Neuroscience Abstracts, 29.* 459.10.

deBruin, J. P. C. (1990). Social behaviour and the prefrontal cortex. *Progress in Brain Research, 85,* 485–500.

DeCoteau, W. E., Kesner, R. P., & Williams, J. M. (1997). Short-term memory for food reward magnitude: The role of the prefrontal cortex. *Behavioural Brain Research, 88,* 239–249.

Dunnett, S. B. (1990). Role of the prefrontal cortex and striatal output systems in short-term memory deficits associated with ageing, basal forebrain lesions, and cholinergic-rich grafts. *Canadian Journal of Psychology, 44,* 210–232.

Field, T., Schanberg, S. M., Scafidi, F., Bauer, C. R., Vega-Lahr, N., Nystrom, G. R., et al. (1986). Effects of tactile-kinesthestic stimulation on preterm neonates. *Pediatrics, 77,* 654–658.

Fifkova, E. (1970). The effects of monocular deprivation on the synaptic contacts of the visual cortex. *Journal of Neurobiology, 1,* 285–294.

Finger, S., & Almli, C. R. (1988). Margaret Kennard and her "principle" in historical perspective. In S. Finger, T. E. Le Vere, C. R. Almli, & D. G. Stein (Eds.), *Brain injury and recovery: Theoretical and controversial issues* (pp. 117–132), New York: Plenum.

Fuster, J. M. (1998). *The prefrontal cortex: Anatomy, physiology, and neuropsychology of the frontal lobe* (3rd ed.) New York: Raven.

Gallagher, M., McMahan, R. W., & Schoenbaum, G. (1999). Orbitofrontal cortex and representations of incentive value in associative learning. *Journal of Neuroscience, 19,* 6610–6614.

Gibb, R., Gorny, G., & Kolb, B. (2005). Therapeutic effects of complex rearing after frontal lesions in infancy vary with sex. Manuscript in submission.

Gibb, R., & Kolb, B. (2005). Tactile stimulation stimulates recovery from perinatal frontal injury in rats by upregulation of FGF-2. Manuscript in submission.

Goldman, P. S. (1974). An alternative to developmental plasticity: Heterology of CNS structures in infants and adults. In D. G. Stein, J. J. Rosen, & N. Butters (Eds.), *Plasticity and recovery of function in the central nervous system* (pp. 149–174). New York: Academic Press.

Goldman, P. S., & Galkin, T. W. (1978). Prenatal removal of frontal association cortex in the fetal Rhesus monkey: Anatomical and functional consequences in postnatal life. *Brain Research, 152,* 451–485.

Gonzalez, C. L. R., Gibb, R., & Kolb, B. (2002). Functional recovery and dendritic hypertrophy after posterior and complete cingulate lesions on postnatal day 10. *Developmental Psychobiology, 40*(2), 138–146.

Gonzalez, C. L., Whishaw, I. Q., & Kolb, B. (2003). Complete sparing of spatial learning following posterior and posterior plus anterior cingulate cortex lesions at 10 days of age in the rat. *Neuroscience, 122,* 563–671.

Halliwell, C., & Kolb, B. (2003). Vitamin/mineral supplements enhance recovery from perinatal cortical lesions in rats. *Society for Neuroscience Abstracts, 29.*

Halliwell, C., Tees, R. C., & Kolb, B. (2007). Choline supplementation enhances recovery from neonatal cortical lesions in rats. Manuscript in submission.

Hastings, E. (2003). *Environmental and pharmacological intervention following cortical brain injury.* Unpublished M.Sc. thesis, University of Lethbridge.

Hebb, D. O. (1949). *The organization of behavior*. New York: Wiley.

Kaas, J. (1987). The organization of neocortex in mammals: Implications for theories of brain function. *Annual Review of Psychology, 38*, 129–151.

Kaplan, B. J., Crawford, S. G., Gardner, B., & Farrelly, G. (2002). Treatment of mood lability and explosive rage with minerals and vitamins: Two case studies in children. *Journal of Child Adolescent Psychopharmacology, 12*, 205–219.

Kesner, R. P., & Holbrook, T. (1987). Dissociation of item and order spatial memory in rats following medial prefrontal cortex lesions. *Neuropsychologia, 25*, 653–664.

Kolb, B. (1974). The social behavior of rats with chronic prefrontal lesions. *Journal of Comparative and Physiological Psychology, 87*, 466–474.

Kolb, B. (1984). Functions of the frontal cortex of the rat: A comparative review. *Brain Research Reviews, 8*, 65–98.

Kolb, B. (1987). Recovery from early cortical damage in rats. I. Differential behavioral and anatomical effects of frontal lesions at different ages of neural maturation. *Behavioural Brain Research, 25*, 205–220.

Kolb, B. (1990). Animal models for human PFC-related disorders. *Progress in Brain Research, 85*, 491–509.

Kolb, B. (1995). *Brain plasticity and behavior*. Mahwah, NJ: Lawrence Erlbaum.

Kolb, B. (2007). Do all mammals have a prefrontal cortex? In J. Kaas (Eds.), *Evolution of the nervous system*. New York: Elsevier, *3*, 443–450.

Kolb, B., Buhrmann, K., McDonald, R., & Sutherland, R. J. (1994). Dissociation of medial prefrontal, posterior and parietal, and posterior temporal cortex for spatial navigation and recognition memory in the rat. *Cerebral Cortex, 4*, 15–34.

Kolb, B., & Cioe, J. (2000). Is there an optimal age for recovery from unilateral motor cortex lesions? Behavioural and anatomical sequelae of unilateral motor cortex lesions in rats on postnatal days 1, 10, and in adulthood. *Restorative Neurology and Neuroscience, 17*, 61–70.

Kolb, B., Cioe, J., & Whishaw, I. Q. (2000). Is there an optimal age for recovery from motor cortex lesions? I. Behavioural and anatomical sequelae of bilateral motor cortex lesions in rats on postnatal days 1, 10, and in adulthood. *Brain Research, 882*, 62–74.

Kolb, B., & Gibb, R. (1991). Environmental enrichment and cortical injury: Behavioral and anatomical consequences of frontal cortex lesions in rats. *Cerebral Cortex, 1*, 189–198.

Kolb, B., & Gibb, R. (1993). Possible anatomical basis of recovery of function after neonatal frontal lesions in rats. *Behavioral Neuroscience, 107*, 799–811.

Kolb, B., Gibb, R., Gorny, G., & Whishaw, I. Q. (1998). Possible regeneration of rat medial frontal cortex following neonatal frontal lesions. *Behavioural Brain Research, 91*, 127–141.

Kolb, B., Gibb, R., & van der Kooy, D. (1994). Neonatal frontal cortical lesions in rats alter cortical structure and connectivity. *Brain Research, 645*, 85–97.

Kolb, B., & Nonneman, A. J. (1976). Functional development of the prefrontal cortex in rats continues into adolescence. *Science, 193*, 335–336.

Kolb, B., Nonneman, A. J., & Singh, R. (1974). Double dissociation of spatial impairment and perseveration following selective prefrontal lesions in the rat. *Journal of Comparative and Physiological Psychology, 87*, 772–780.

Kolb, B., Pedersen, B., & Gibb, R. (2007). Recovery from frontal cortex lesions in infancy is blocked by embryonic pretreatment with bromodeoxyuridine. In submission.

Kolb, B., Petrie, B., & Cioe, J. (1996). Recovery from early cortical damage in rats. VII. Comparison of the behavioural and anatomical effects of medial prefrontal lesions at different ages of neural maturation. *Behavioural Brain Research, 79*, 1–13.

Kolb, B., & Stewart, J. (1995). Changes in neonatal gonadal hormonal environment prevent behavioral sparing and alter cortical morphogenesis after early frontal cortex lesions in male and female rats. *Behavioral Neuroscience, 109*, 285–294.

Kolb, B., & Sutherland, R. (1992). Noradrenaline depletion blocks behavioral sparing and alters cortical morphogenesis after neonatal frontal cortex damage in rats. *Journal of Neuroscience, 12,* 2221–2330.

Kolb, B., & Tees, R. C. (Eds.) (1990). *The cerebral cortex of the rat.* Cambridge, MA: MIT Press.

Kolb, B., & Whishaw, I. Q. (1981). Neonatal frontal lesions in the rat: Sparing of learned but not species-typical behavior in the presence of reduced brain weight and cortical thickness. *Journal of Comparative and Physiological Psychology, 95,* 863–879.

Kolb, B., & Whishaw, I. Q. (1983). Dissociation of the contributions of the prefrontal, motor and parietal cortex to the control of movement in the rat. *Canadian Journal of Psychology, 37,* 211–232.

Kolb, B., & Whishaw, I. Q. (1985a). Earlier is not always better: Behavioral dysfunction and abnormal cerebral morphogenesis following neonatal cortical lesions in the rat. *Behavioural Brain Research, 17,* 25–43.

Kolb, B., & Whishaw, I. Q. (1985b). Neonatal frontal lesions in hamsters impair species-typical behaviors and reduce brain weight and cortical thickness. *Behavioral Neuroscience, 99,* 691–706.

Kolb, B., & Whishaw, I. Q. (1989). Plasticity in the neocortex: Mechanisms underlying recovery from early brain damage. *Progress in Neurobiology, 32,* 235–276.

Kolb, B., & Whishaw, I. Q. (2003). *Fundamentals of human neuropsychology* (5th ed.). New York: Worth.

Kolb, B., Zabrowski, J., & Whishaw, I. Q. (1989). Recovery from early cortical lesions in rats. V. Unilateral lesions have different behavioral and anatomical effects than bilateral lesions. *Psychobiology, 17,* 363–369.

Monfils, M. H., Driscoll, I., Kamitakahara, H., Wilson, B., Flynn, C., Teskey, G. C., et al. (2006a). FGF-2-induced cell proliferation stimulates anatomical, neurophysiological, and functional recovery from neonatal motor cortex injury. *European Journal of Neuroscience, 24,* 739–749.

Monfils, M. H., Driscoll, I., Melvin, N. R., & Kolb, B. (2006b). Differential expression of basic fibroblast growth factor-2 in the developing rat brain. *Neuroscience, 141,* 213–221.

Monfils, M. H., Driscoll, I., Vandenberg, P. M., Thomas, N. J., Danka, D., Kleim, J. A., et al. (2005). Basic fibroblast growth factor stimulates functional recovery after neonatal lesions of motor cortex in rats. *Neuroscience, 134,* 1–8.

Monfils, M. H., Driscoll, I., Vavrek, R., Kolb, B., & Fouad, K. (2007). FGF-2-induced functional improvement from neonatal motor cortex injury via corticospinal projections. *Experimental Brain Research,* in press.

Muir, J. L., Everitt, B. J., & Robbins, T. W. (1996). The cerebral cortex of the rat and visual attentional function: Dissociable effects of mediofrontal, cingulate, anterior dorsolateral and parietal cortex lesions on a five-choice serial reaction time task. *Cerebral Cortex, 6,* 470–481.

Otto, T., & Eichenbaum, H. (1992). Complementary roles of the orbital prefrontal cortex and the perirhinal-entorhinal cortices in an odor-guided delayed-nonmatching-to-sample task. *Behavioral Neuroscience, 106,* 762–775.

Pellis, S. M., Hastings, E., Takeshi, T., Kamitakahara, H., Komorowska, J., Forgie, M. L., et al. (2006). The effects of orbital frontal cortex damage on the modulation of defensive responses by rats in playful and non-playful social contexts. *Behavioral Neuroscience, 120*(1), 72–84.

Ragozzino, M. E., & Kesner, R. P. (1999). The role of the agranular insular cortex in working memory for food reward value and allocentric space in rats. *Behavioural Brain Research, 98,* 103–112.

Rasmussen, T., & Milner, B. (1977). The role of early left-brain injury in determining lateralization of cerebral speech functions. *Annals of the N.Y. Academy of Sciences, 299,* 355–369.

Schoenbaum, G., & Setlow, B. (2002). Integrating orbitofrontal cortex into prefrontal theory: Common processing themes across species and subdivisions. *Learning and Memory, 8,* 134–147.

Sherren, N., Akins, L., & Kolb, B. (2005). Functional outcome and anatomical correlates of focal unilateral medial frontal cortex lesions at different developmental ages in neonatal rats. *Society for Neuroscience Abstracts,* 835.11.

Shipley, J. E., & Kolb, B. (1977). Neural correlates of species typical behavior in the Syrian Golden hamster. *Journal of Comparative and Physiological Psychology, 91,* 1056–1073.

Shonkoff, J. P., & Hauser-Cram, P. (1987). Early intervention for disabled infants and their families: A quantitative analysis. *Pediatrics, 80,* 650–658.

Uylings, H., Groenewegen, H., & Kolb, B. (2003). Does the rat have a prefrontal cortex? *Behavioural Brain Research, 146,* 3–17.

Villablanca, J. R., Carlson-Kuhta, P., Schmanke, T. D., & Hovda, D. A. (1998). A critical maturational period of reduced brain vulnerability to developmental injury. I. Behavioral studies in cats. *Brain Research. Developmental Brain Research, 105,* 309–324.

Villablanca, J. R., Hovda, D. A., Jackson, G. F., & Infante, C. (1993). Neurological and behavioral effects of a unilateral frontal cortical lesion in fetal kittens. II. Visual system tests, and proposing a 'critical period' for lesion effects. *Behavioural Brain Research, 57,* 79–92.

Whishaw, I. Q., Tomie, J., & Kolb, B. (1992). Ventrolateral frontal cortex lesions in rats impair the acquisition and retention of a tactile–olfactory configural task. *Behavioral Neuroscience, 106,* 597–603.

Wikmark, R. G. E., Divac, I., & Weiss, R. (1973). Delayed alternation in rats with lesions of the frontal lobes: Implications for a comparative neuropsychology of the prefrontal system. *Brain, Behaviour, and Evolution, 8,* 329–339.

Will, B., & Kelche, C. (1992). Environmental approaches to recovery of function from brain damage: A review of animal studies (1981 to 1991). In F. D. Rose & D. A. Johnson (Eds.), *Recovery from brain damage: Reflections and directions* (pp. 79–104). New York: Plenum Press.

Zilles, K. (1985). The cerebral cortex of the rat: A stereotaxic atlas. New York: Springer-Verlag.

Section II

Assessment of executive function across the lifespan

5 Methodological and conceptual issues in understanding the development of executive control in the preschool period

Kimberly Andrews Espy, Rebecca Bull,
Heather Kaiser, Jessica Martin,
and Megan Banet

Contents

This purpose of this chapter is to highlight methodological issues that are not always considered when trying to understand how children come to regulate their cognition and behavior during the preschool period. To give some background, there has been a rapid increase in the number of papers addressing the development of executive control in very young, preschool children. This expansion has resulted from four primary issues. First, it is now widely recognized that executive dysfunction is a central feature, or a strong contributor to outcome, of many neurodevelopmental disorders that either emerge or are detectable during this age range (Anderson, Anderson, Grimwood, & Nolan, 2004; Espy, Kaufmann, & Glisky, 1999; Espy et al., 2002; Ewing-Cobbs, Prasad, Landry, Kramer, & DeLeon, 2004; Pennington & Ozonoff, 1996). Second and concomitantly, executive control plays a critical role in other cognitive processes, including memory, attention, consciousness/theory of mind, reading and mathematics, and social skills (Baddeley & Hitch, 1994; Bull & Scerif, 2001; Desimone & Duncan, 1995; Espy et al., 2004; Gathercole & Pickering, 2000; Hughes, 1998a; Hughes, White, Sharpen, & Dunn, 2000; Isquith, Gioia, & Espy, 2004; Perner, Lang, & Kloo, 2002; Posner & Petersen, 1990). Third, the application of cognitive neuroscience paradigms had enabled the examination of executive abilities in this age range in a novel and more accessible manner (Blair, Zelazo, & Greenberg, 2005; Diamond, Prevor, Callendar, & Druin, 1997; Espy, 2004). Finally, with the protracted course of prefrontal development (Benes, 2001; Giedd et al., 1999; Huttenlocher & Dabholkar, 1997; Sowell, Thompson, Holmes, Jernigan, & Toga, 1999), there is the potential to uncover the fundamental principles of executive control in its ontogeny at a period where cognition is less complicated, which should further illuminate the fundamental nature of executive control in humans (Espy, 2004; Hughes, 2002).

Although a substantial literature base has developed, the precise nature of executive control in children, or adults for that matter, is far from resolved. Differing accounts vary fundamentally according to (1) whether executive control is viewed as a unitary process (Allport & Wylie, 2000; Duncan & Owen, 2000; Miller & Cohen, 2001; Munakata, 1998) or composed of "fractionated," interdependent subprocesses (Carlson & Moses, 2001; Miyake, Friedman, Rettinger, Shah, & Hegarty, 2001; Pennington, 1997); (2) the relative weights or uniqueness that these executive constructs are ascribed (Bishop, Aamodt-Leaper, Creswell, McGurk, & Skuse, 2001; Friedman & Miyake, 2004; Nigg, 2000); (3) the differential localization within the brain (Casey et al., 2000; Durston et al., 2002); or (4) the manner or pattern of development during childhood (Kirkham, Cruess, & Diamond, 2003; Zelazo, Mueller, Frye, & Marcovitch, 2003). There remains a paucity of commercially available, norm-referenced, psychometric tests to measure executive function in this age, with the only specific individually administered battery including specific "executive" measures being the NEPSY (Korkman, Kirk, & Kemp, 1998). Therefore, executive control typically has been studied in preschool children with experimental tasks, where different stimuli or response requirements are varied systematically to reveal critical performance differences that shed light on the nature of the executive cognitive process. Such tasks include rule governed, attribute-based sorting tasks (Espy, Kaufmann, McDiarmid, & Glisky, 1999; Hughes, 1998b) such as the Dimensional Change Card Sorting (DCCS) task (Zelazo, Frye, & Rapus, 1996); tasks with manual selection or verbal naming of stimuli that conflict or interfere on the basis of natural associations (Carlson & Moses, 2001; Davidson, Amso, Anderson, & Diamond, 2006; Diamond, Briand, Fossella, & Gehlbach, 2004; Diamond, Kirkham, & Amso, 2002; Gerstadt, Hong, & Diamond, 1994; Prevor & Diamond, 2005; Wright, Waterman, Prescott, & Murdoch-Eaton, 2003); manual search tasks with working memory maintenance demands (Diamond et al., 1997; Espy, Kaufmann, Glisky, & McDiarmid, 2001; Hughes, 1998b) and with inhibiting prepotent or prohibited somatic motor responses (Carlson & Moses, 2001; Diamond & Taylor, 1996; Espy, Kaufmann, McDiarmid et al., 1999; Kochanska, Murray, Jacques, Koenig, & Vandegeest, 1996; Korkman et al., 1998; Reed, Pien, & Rothbart, 1984).

Although this study has revealed important insights, such as the critical role of conflict (Brooks, Hanauer, Padowska, & Rosman, 2003; Diamond et al., 2002; Perner & Lang, 2002; Rennie, Bull, & Diamond, 2004), interference/distraction (Espy & Bull, 2005; Espy & Cwik, 2004; Zelazo et al., 2003), and information maintenance (Alloway & Gathercole, 2005; Hughes, 1998b), we argue that further progress in understanding the nature of executive control in very young children has been hampered by a lack of attention to psychometric theory, the methodological tenets upon which all instruments rest. From a methodological standpoint, notice that the majority of work done to date has focused on characterizing performance in preschoolers by manipulating task conditions to better isolate important cognitive mechanisms that are/are not operative in these contrasting conditions. This type of design has a critical place in developmental cognitive neuroscience and has lead to the development of several important theories of executive control development (Kirkham et al., 2003; Munakata, 1998; Zelazo et al., 2003). The advantages of this design include the ability to make comparisons within subjects, thereby taking advantage of the reduced error variance and maximizing the likelihood of detecting condition-related differences. Furthermore, from a theoretical perspective, it is quite compelling when it can be demonstrated that children behave in one way in one condition but completely differently in another, when relatively small alterations to the tasks are made. These discrepancies can be extended further by the inclusion of a contrast group that performs in an alternative manner in response to this condition manipulation. Such findings reveal a "double-dissociation" that is considered the "gold standard" of behavioral neurology (Van Orden, Pennington, & Stone, 2001). This approach, for example, has been used productively to reveal differences in executive control among children with attention-deficit/hyperactivity disorder (ADHD) (Berwid et al., 2005), head injury (Ewing-Cobbs et al., 2004), preterm birth (Espy et al., 2004; Luciana, 2003), phenylketonuria (PKU) (Diamond et al., 1997), and autism (Ozonoff, South, & Provencal, 2005) to name just a few.

As compelling as these findings are, there are other considerations derived from clinical science in the application of this method that are often ignored. From the perspective of psychometric test theory, it is important to keep in mind that the experimental tasks and their various conditions do not differ from commercially available, psychometric tests. Like psychometric tests, experimental tasks also have demands that necessarily elicit specific cognitive processes that are necessary to perform the task. In like fashion, in both psychometric tests and experimental tasks, the demands of any test/task typically do not elicit only one cognitive process or construct, regardless how "discrete" the test/task is designed to be. For example, although one might be interested in assessing visual–spatial processing with the commercially available, psychometric test, Block Design (The Psychological Corporation, 2003), which has considerably more task demands than just visual–spatial processing. At a minimum, independent of the visual–spatial demands, the child must visually perceive the differential color that comprise the pictured stimulus, and manually place the blocks in the desired configuration, in temporally integrated and proficient manner. To reduce the extraneous motor task demands, one might select a visual matching task to assess visual–spatial processing. Even here, minimally, the child must visually perceive the pictured stimuli and formulate and select the appropriate verbal response.

In the cases of both experimental tasks and psychometric tests, the relation between task performance and task demands can be represented as "true score" variance according to classic test theory, that is, the portion of performance that is related reliably to the underlying cognitive process or latent construct of interest. The portion that is non-reliable is considered error. "Reliably" is important—in that it is the proportion of the variance that is reproducible across test items, administrations and participants. True score variance can be further decomposed into smaller portions of variance that are related to specific constructs, and into error variance that includes subject-specific factors, administration-specific factors, time-specific factors, and random chance. In most of the studies described earlier that have used experimental tasks, however, the task and its experimental conditions typically are treated as fully representing the latent cognitive construct of interest in a one-to-one fashion. When a performance difference is observed between a clinical and control group or between children of differing ages, this difference is attributed solely to the discrete cognitive processes that the authors are trying to study by experimental task administration. However, because the true relations between the latent cognitive construct and experimental task performance are unknown, it is equally plausible that performance differed on the second condition related to subject-specific factors that were not considered. Using the overly simple Block Design example, younger children might perform more poorly on Block Design because of less precise motor skills in manipulating the blocks, not related to fundamental differences in visual–spatial processing. Critically in the case of executive control, where the executive control of cognition inherently involves the regulation of other cognitive processes, such as language, visual–spatial ability, memory, etc., it is easy to conceive of experimental task manipulation that might results in performance differences that in fact are related to other differences in cognitive processes, rather than to the intended executive control itself. Without knowing the relation of observed task performance to the latent construct, even with experimentally manipulated conditions, there can be unexpected differences in demands that can yield differential results that are unrelated to the question of interest. This issue is particularly prominent when studying groups of very young children who exhibit substantial variation in language, motor, memory, and social skills, all of which can affect the obtained pattern of task performance results.

The differential attention to the reliable, "true score" portion of the variance in performance comes from the difference in intended purpose between psychometric tests and experimental tasks. Most psychometric tests initially were developed to be used in the clinical context where one needs to make inferences about individual children—inferences about whether a child's level of performance is so discrepant from age peers to warrant a clinical diagnosis or treatment. With such a "high-stakes" outcome, it is not surprising that reliability in the relation between latent cognitive construct and observed performance needs to be highly specific and reproducible. On the other hand, experimental tasks do not require such a burden, and are more commonly used to make inferences about groups of children in a general sense. Therefore, commonly, experimental task performance is treated to fully represent the cognitive process of interest, both in terms of its reliability and validity. This treatment can be justified to a degree in that there are no real "consequences" for mis-specification, as scientific knowledge is built through replication. Presumably, if observed differences were spuriously due to some cognitive process other than what was attributed, results from other studies over time would be discrepant from the original to challenge the erroneous inference.

In this "high-stakes" context, considerable efforts are made to reliably identify the cognitive processes that comprise a child's psychometric test performance at a given point in time. These efforts typically are composed to two basic approaches: (1) characterizing reliability by identifying the consistency in content and performance stability over time; and (2) examining the evidence for convergent and discriminative validity by characterizing the relations between the target test and other measures that are similar/discordant in demands. Because those using experimental tasks traditionally have not considered test theory or the resultant psychometric issues regarding reliability as is commonly done with commercially available psychometric tests, here, we apply these two approaches to reliability of experimental tasks that have been used to understand the development of executive control in both typically developing preschool children, as well as those with neurodevelopmental conditions, to elucidate the consequences of treating task performance to fully represent the latent executive cognitive process.

Reliability across administrations

We (Kaiser, Martin, Banet, & Espy, 2004) conducted a small study of the test–retest reliability of some experimental executive tasks commonly administered to preschool children. Thirty-five preschool children, aged from 2.5 to 6.0 years (*M* age = 4.6, SD = 0.9) years, were recruited from local preschools and health clinics in a rural, Midwestern community. Children were administered a battery of tasks individually by a trained examiner on two occasions. The mean interval between administrations was 2.3 weeks, ranging from 1 to 5.4 weeks. Because children under 3 years were not administered some tasks and some children did not complete all tasks, the sample size ranged from 19 to 33 children. Test–retest reliability was calculated for each of the tasks using Spearman Rho correlation coefficients, due to its robustness when the underlying variable distribution is abnormal. Then, analyses of variance were performed to determine whether executive task performance differed between the administrations to examine practice effects. The executive function battery included the following measures that are described briefly; for more specific information regarding the tasks, please see the primary reference.

- *Delayed response* (DR; Diamond, 1990). For this task, two inverted beige cups covered the drilled lateral wells of a gray testing board. The child watched while the examiner placed a reward in one well and covered the wells with the cups. After the 10-s delay, the child retrieved the reward by displacing the correct cup. The total number of correct responses over 17 trials was scored.
- *Delayed alternation* (DA) (Goldman, Rosvold, Vest, & Galkin, 1971). This task used the same testing board and delay as DR, but the reward was hidden out of the child's sight. In DA, the child uses the information from the previous trial to search correctly on the present trial, where the reward was hidden in the well opposite the last correct response. The number of consecutive correct alternations was scored.
- *Spatial reversal* (SR) (Kaufmann, Leckman, & Ort, 1989). Similar to DA, rewards were hidden out of the child's sight at the same location until the child correctly retrieved it for four consecutive trials. Then the opposite well was baited, until the 4-trial set was achieved, reversing the contingency again, etc., for 16 trials. The number of correct retrievals was scored.
- *Spatial reversal with irrelevant color cues* (SRC) (McDiarmid & Espy, 2003). This task was identical to SR, except that the cups used to cover the wells were painted different colors (blue and yellow) as an irrelevant distractor. The number of correct trials was scored.

- *Six Boxes* (Diamond et al., 1997). Six Boxes is modeled after the Hamilton Search Task (Hamilton, 1911) and involved two conditions: nonspatial (using color and shape cues) and spatial (using location cues). In each condition, rewards were hidden in each of six small boxes while the child watched. The child was asked to find a reward each time the boxes were presented. The boxes were presented until all rewards were found. An efficiency score (number of boxes opened divided by number of moves made) was calculated for each condition.
- *Children's continuous performance task* (C-CPT) (Kerns & Rondeau, 1998). In this computerized task, several common animals were displayed one at a time, with random animal noises, for a total duration of 3 min. The child pressed the response key whenever a target animal (sheep) was presented. The percent of commission errors of total responses was scored.
- *Self-control* (Lee, Vaughn, & Kopp, 1983). The child was presented with an attractive wrapped gift and told not to touch the gift until instructed. The latency to touch the gift (with a maximum of 150 s) was scored.
- *Whisper* (Kochansko, Murray, Jacques, Koenig, & Vandgeest, 1996). The child was shown pictures of 10 familiar cartoon characters and asked to whisper their names. A verbal prompt reminding the child to whisper is provided when presenting the fifth picture. The child receives higher scores for whispering names and a lower score for shouting or speaking at a normal decibel level. A nonresponse is prorated so that the child is not penalized for failure to respond. The child's total score was used for analyses.
- *TRAILS-P* (Espy & Cwik, 2004). Preschool children were presented with a book with colorful dog characters in order of size. The children were then provided an inked stamp with a child size handle for easy gripping. In Condition A, the baseline control, the children were instructed to stamp the dogs in order of size, starting from the "baby" to the "daddy". Condition B (attentional control) involved the introduction of like-sized bones, which the child had to "match" the dogs with their bones, that is, control attention and responding to flexibly shift among the like-sized stimuli in order. To assess the response suppression, in Condition C, using the given inked stamp, the child stamped the dogs in order of size, but now ignored the bones. Condition D assessed the effects of distraction. Here, cats were intermixed as distractors with the target dogs and bones, requiring the child again to alternate between the dogs and bones in size order, while ignoring the cats. For each condition, the latency to stamp all stimuli (with correction for wrong stamps as in the original Trail Making Test), and the number of errors were scored.
- *Shape School* (Espy, 1997; Espy, Bull, Martin, & Stroup, 2006). Using a storybook format depicting child-like figures in a school setting, there are four conditions: A-baseline control, B-response suppression, C-attentional control, and D-concurrent. The baseline control Condition A requires children to name the figures' color to set up a prepotent response. In Condition B, the figures are depicted with either happy or sad facial expressions, where the child has to name the color of the figures with happy faces only and suppress naming the sad-faced figures. In Condition C, figures are shown with either hats or without hats, where

the child must flexibly control attention to name the color of the figures without hats and the shape of the figures with hats. In Condition D, the previous conditions are crossed, containing figures with happy or sad faces and either with hats or without hats. An efficiency score (number correct divided by latency) was scored for each Shape School condition.

- *Tower of Hanoi* (Welsh, Pennington, & Groisser, 1991). In this problem-solving and planning task, the child moves three rings of varying size and color on three pegs of the same height to achieve specified configurations that vary in difficulty. Children are required to move one ring at a time, to put smaller rings on top of larger rings, and not to place the rings anywhere other than the apparatus. The total problems were solved, with a bonus for the number of moves, was scored.

The correlation results are shown in Table 5.1 and mean task performances across administrations is presented in Table 5.2. Spearman correlation coefficients varied substantially among the experimental executive tasks. Notice that the correlation coefficients of all tasks were below the recommended standard of .90 for application in clinical decision making. Tasks that demonstrate adequate reliability include the C-CPT, Shape School, TRAILS-P, and Tower of Hanoi. Other tasks had correlation

Table 5.1   Test–retest reliability for preschool experimental executive control tasks.

Variable	Spearman's P
Delayed response, # correct	.40*
Delayed alternation, # consecutive alternations	.44*
Spatial reversal, # correct	.33
Spatial reversal w/irrelevant color cues, # correct	.39*
Six Boxes, efficiency	
Nonspatial	.16
Spatial	.31
C-CPT, percent of commission errors	.73**
Self-control, latency	.54***
Whisper, # correct	.17
TRAILS-P, latency	
Condition A—baseline control	.64***
Condition B—attentional control	.45**
Condition C—response suppression	.77***
Condition D—distraction	.69***
Shape School, efficiency	
Condition A—baseline control	.60**
Condition B—response suppression	.71**
Condition C—attentional control	.57*
Condition D—concurrent	.68**
Tower of Hanoi, total problems solved with bonus	.59***

* $p < .05$.
** $p < .01$.
*** $p < .001$.

Table 5.2   Task performance at the first and second administrations.

Variable	M_1	SD_1	M_2	SD_2	
Delayed response, # correct	14.54	2.25	13.97	2.67	
Delayed alternation, # consecutive alternations	4.38	3.18	5.00	4.04	
Spatial reversal, # correct	10.97	1.85	11.62	1.60	
Spatial reversal w/irrelevant color cues, # correct	10.5	1.75	11.12	1.85	
Six Boxes					
Nonspatial	0.77	0.18	0.79	0.18	
Spatial	0.81	0.21	0.78	0.22	
C-CPT, percent of commission errors	0.96	1.43	0.67	1.26	
Self-control, latency	112.35	57.80	110.18	56.67	
Whisper, # correct	18.58	2.99	19.61	1.58	
TRIALS-P					
Condition A—baseline control	31.47	17.17	21.97	15.19	$p < .05$
Condition B—attentional control	23.6	10.84	18.73	9.84	
Condition C—response suppression	24.2	13.12	20.13	12.3	
Condition D—distraction	24.43	10.53	24.07	12.18	
Shape School					
Condition A—baseline control	0.70	0.34	0.72	0.33	
Condition B—response suppression	0.67	0.25	0.83	0.32	$p < .01$
Condition C—attentional control	0.28	0.10	0.34	0.17	
Condition D—concurrent	0.34	0.15	0.46	0.19	$p < .01$
Tower of Hanoi, total problems solved with bonus	11.91	10.22	15.88	10.41	$p < .05$

values that differed significantly from zero, but clearly need further reformulation to achieve reliabilities in the adequate range (DR, DA, self-control, SRC). Finally, the Six Boxes, SR, and Whisper tasks showed nonsignificant test–retest correlations, and therefore demonstrate low reliability and poor clinical utility, at least as currently designed. Interestingly, there was little evidence of significant differences in average performance on most executive tasks administered at an average of 2 weeks apart.

In sum, there was substantive evidence of stability in performance for some of the experimental executive tasks administered, an important platform upon which to base subsequent work aimed at determining the development of executive control or how it might go awry in preschool children with differing conditions. Given the variability in attention and concentration in young children, it might be difficult to achieve the high reliability for clinical standards on these experimental executive tasks that measure more fluid skills. In fact, the observed test–retest relations for C-CPT, TRIALS-P, Shape School, and Tower of Hanoi are consistent with those reported for the executive subtests from the commercially available, psychometric instrument, the NEPSY, designed for use in this age range (Korkman et al., 1998). For example, the NEPSY test–retest correlation in the 3- to 4-year-old range for the Visual Attention subtest was .62. For the Statue subtest, it was .48. For the 5- to 6-year-old range, these values were .54 and .75, respectively. The test–retest correl- ations obtained for the C-CPT, Shape School, TRIALS-P, and Tower of Hanoi also are somewhat lower than the core subtests of the WPPSI-III (The Psychological Corporation, 2002), particularly relative to subtests that measure more stable, crystallized abilities like vocabulary ($r = .87$), but are more consistent with reliability of those that assess fluid abilities like Block Design ($r = .69$) in this age range.

Importantly, for those tasks where the correlations between test and retest administrations was nonzero, it is clear that substantial redesign is required before adequate consistency in performance across administrations can be achieved. Note, however, the problem does not appear to be due to inordinate practice effects, as generally, there was little difference in performance at the group level between administrations. For Six Boxes, SR, and Whisper, mean task performance at administration 1 and 2 did not differ significantly. The obtained pattern means that although there was no net difference in mean performance at each administration, individual children varied markedly in where they fell relative to the overall distribution of performance across the two assessments. In clinical decision making, this fluctuation is a key, as an erroneous decision could be made based on the first task performance, where if the task were administered again only 2 weeks later, the same child could achieve a markedly different score. Although the impact in clinical decision making is straightforward, there are, however, implications even when task administration is only for group-based research. In Diamond et al. (2004), for example, Six Boxes performance was unrelated to a genotype that codes for a protein enzyme that metabolizes dopamine, co-methyl-transferase (COMT). The authors concluded that the COMT gene, therefore, must not be related to spatial working memory in children. In fact, when considered in light of this evidence of poor task reliability for this experimental task, it is equally plausible that Six Boxes performance is not an adequate indicator of spatial working memory, hence the lack of the observed relation to the COMT genotype.

Reliability in the construct representing the cognitive process

Now, we turn to consider the other aspect of reliability, the consistency that should reliably reflect the cognitive process or latent construct that the psychometric test or experimental task is designed to measure. As noted, experimental task performance typically is treated to fully represent the latent cognitive process that underlies observed performance. Here, we present an example to illustrate the consequences of this approach. In Diamond (1990), the author argues that A-not-B (AB), a task commonly used in the developmental literature popularized by Piaget (1954), and delayed response (DR), commonly used in the nonhuman primate literature, both measure executive control, in this case, working memory and inhibition. These simple, straightforward tasks indeed are very similar in administration method, as Diamond notes. In AB, the child is shown two covered wells, in which one well is placed a reward. The child successfully retrieves that reward at that location for a prespecified number of trials, and then the reward is placed in the well at the other location. Older infants and young children make a classic developmental error that Piaget noted—they continue to search at the previously rewarded location, despite the fact that reward was hidden at the new location in plain view of the child. Similarly, in DR, the monkey is trained to retrieve rewards from one of the two locations. Here, instead of the hiding location depending upon the monkey's performance on the last trial, the reward is hidden according to a randomized schedule between the two locations. Monkeys, like young children, make the classic perseverative error and continue to search at the previously rewarded location after the alternate location is baited. In fact, to further substantiate that these two very similar tasks, both measure executive control in the same fashion, Diamond (1990) graphically depicted that the mean performance is identical among the two tasks.

One might question whether in two tasks that are so similarly administered, how is it possible that they might draw upon differing latent cognitive processes? For the purposes here, we investigated this issue empirically using the same design we used previously (Bull, Espy, & Senn, 2004) to study differences in the two commonly used executive tasks, the Tower of London (Shallice, 1982) and Tower of Hanoi (Simon, 1975). Here, the design involved administering AB and DR to two separate groups of well-matched children, while also administering the same battery of comparison tasks to both child groups. Then, the respective relations between the target experimental tasks and the comparison tasks are examined between groups. If the target experimental tasks are similar in cognitive process demands, one expects the correlations to the comparison tasks to be similar among AB and DR. Briefly, the overall sample was composed of 94 preschool children (mean age = 4.76 years, SD = 0.38, range = 4.03 – 5.49), 40 boys, and 54 girls. The racial/ethnic composition of the sample was predominantly White, non-Hispanic, and participating children were from a range of socioeconomic backgrounds, with a mean maternal education of 14 years. Children were typically developing, free of any known medical, neurological, or developmental conditions known to affect cognition, consistent with the mean vocabulary score of the sample of 105 (SD = 14). There were no differences in any of the background demographic characteristics between the two testing groups (all $p > .60$).

Children were divided into two groups: half were administered AB and half were administered DR. Each of these tasks consisted of 10 trials, with a 10-s delay between hiding and retrieval. In both tasks, the rewards were hidden within plain view of the child and their attention was gained before hiding. Two dependent indexes were scored; the number of correct retrievals (CORR) and the maximal consecutive incorrect retrievals (perseverative run [PRUN]). Within each task, the correlation between CORR and PRUN indexes was 0.77.

In addition to the AB or DR, three other executive tasks were administered to both groups of children for comparative purposes. These comparison executive tasks were served as the reference criteria by which to compare the measurement properties of AB and DR. The criterion referenced tasks were a mix of commercially available, psychometric subtests, NEPSY Statue and Differential Abilities scale (Elliott, 1990) digit recall, and one of the experimental tasks included in the reliability study described earlier, Shape School (accuracy from conditions B—response suppression and C—attentional control).

The performance of the two groups on AB and DR are displayed in Table 5.3. Similar to Diamond (1990), there were no differences in mean performance on the number correct reward retrievals (CORR) on AB versus DR, $F(1,93) = .98$, $p > .32$, or on the respective maximal number of consecutive incorrect retrievals (PRUN),

Table 5.3 Mean performance by test group.

	AB Group (n = 47)		DR Group (n = 47)	
	MEAN	*SD*	*MEAN*	*SD*
Correct (%)	87.23	12.8	84.48	14.16
Perseverative runs (trials)	0.81	0.65	1.21	1.68
SS-B Accuracy	13.55	2.31	13.55	2.88
Statue	24.26	5.87	21.96	8.11
Digits*	3.55	0.75	4.10	0.98
SS-C Accuracy	7.99	6.05	8.96	6.14

* $p < .05$.

$F(1,93) = 2.27$, $p > .13$. Notice too, that there was no difference in mean performance on the criterion tasks between groups, with the exception of digit recall. On this task, the DR group obtained a mean that was approximately half a digit string higher than the AB group.

If these tasks draw upon similar cognitive processes and index constructs comparably, the correct retrieval index from AB and DR should be related to the criterion measures in a similar manner. That is, both ABCORR and DRCORR would be related significantly to performance on Statue, Shape School conditions, or Digit Recall. In like fashion, similar relations among the referenced criterion instruments and the respective ABPRUN and DRPRUN indexes would be expected. To investigate this possibility, a series of regression models were run. The first set of models was conducted where each index predicted the referenced criterion as the only predictor in the regression model. Then, age and child vocabulary were introduced into the model to investigate if the relation between the task and criterion were robust after accounting for these influences. Finally, we added the other executive tasks as covariates in addition to age and vocabulary, to determine whether the task and the referenced criterion were uniquely related. These results are shown in Table 5.4.

Despite the comparable means and tightly matched demographics between the testing groups, there were substantial differences in the patterns of respective relations between the AB and DR indices and the referenced criterion tasks. Starting with the correct retrieval indexes, DRCORR was strong related to accuracy on Shape School Condition C, where the child had to flexibly shift attention and responding when cued to appropriately name the stimuli. In contrast, ABCORR was related to NEPSY Statue performance, where the child had to suppress movements consistent with a rule.

A similar discrepancy was noted on the PRUN index. Here, the number of consecutive error responses on DR (DRPRUN) was related to accuracy in Shape School Condition C, similar to what was observed for DRCORR. However, ABPRUN was related to Shape School Condition B—response suppression, where the child has to inhibit a learned response when cued. Note that these differences among the relations between AB and DR and the key reference criterion were robust, regardless of whether age and vocabulary are controlled, or whether considered as a unique predictor holding the other criterion referenced tasks constant.

Table 5.4 Comparison of relations of criterion measure to A-not-B and Delayed Response task indexes.

	ABPRUN		DRPRUN		ABCORR		DRCORR	
	β	t	β	t	β	t	β	t
Single Predictor								
Statue	0.02	0.17	−0.20	0.17	0.28	1.90t	**0.35**	**2.50**
SS-B Accuracy	**−0.19**	**−2.13**	0.15	−1.39	0.03	0.23	−0.04	−0.25
Digits	0.00	0.01	−0.07	−0.43	−0.04	−0.28	−0.01	−0.03
SS-C Accuracy	−0.02	−0.14	**−0.38**	**−2.74**	0.21	1.41	**0.34**	**2.44**
Age and Child Vocabulary Controlled								
Statue	0.03	0.18	−0.13	−0.88	**0.38**	**2.23**	0.28	1.92t
SS-B Accuracy	**−0.31**	**−2.00**	0.19	1.25	0.11	0.72	−0.08	−0.56
Digits	0.09	0.15	−0.12	−0.79	−0.09	−0.50	0.04	0.24
SS-C Accuracy	0.04	0.23	**−0.35**	**−2.43**	0.22	1.38	0.28	1.89t
Age and Child Vocabulary Controlled, Unique Predictor								
Statue	0.01	0.05	−0.14	−0.97	**0.35**	**1.94**	**0.32**	**2.17**
SS-B Accuracy	**−0.32**	**−2.01**	0.26	1.76	0.11	0.67	−0.13	−0.83
Digits	0.10	0.54	−0.03	−0.18	−0.20	−1.12	−0.07	0.50
SS-C Accuracy	0.02	0.14	**−0.50**	**−3.19**	0.18	1.05	**0.44**	**2.78**

Note: Those values in bold differ significantly from zero at $p < .05$. AB = A-not-B task; DR = delayed response task; CORR = number of correct retrievals, PRUN = maximal number of consecutive perseverative errors.

These differential relations suggest that indeed small differences in task administration can lead to substantive differences in the relations to other referenced criterion indicators, and suggest that indeed the two very similar tasks might not measure precisely the same latent constructs or cognitive processes. Indeed, conceptually, the differential pattern of loadings makes sense if one considers the differences in surface task demands between AB and DR. In AB, the reversal of the reward to the alternate location depends directly on the subject's response required to establish a consistent set. Therefore, it might not be surprising that the AB indexes were related more strongly to other executive measures that require response suppression, that is, Shape School Condition B and NEPSY Statue. In contrast, for DR, the reward is hidden by a predetermined schedule, where the child flexibly must guide their search strategy according to the observed schema. Similarly then, the DR indexes were related more to the attentional control subtest of Shape School, Condition C, where the child has to select and implement their response differentially according to environmental cues. Note although the communalities across like indexes, where both DRPRUN and ABPRUN were related to NEPSY Statue subtest performance, perhaps indicating the shared requirement to inhibit motor response in order for the child to successfully minimize perseveration.

Conclusions

What can be concluded from these findings? Many elegant experimental tasks have been developed that have helped to shed light on precisely what preschool children can and cannot do to achieve goal-directed, well-regulated thought, namely executive control. These tasks also have yielded important insights into what processes are disturbed in children with differing medical disorders. Despite these advances, there remains fundamental disagreement regarding the nature of executive control in young children. Put more simply, there remains considerable disagreement about what "executive control" is. Clearly, such fundamental disagreement limits what further knowledge can be achieved. One approach to resolve this conundrum is to return to basic psychometric test theory to better elucidate the relations between observed performance, be it on experimental tasks or commercially available psychometric tests, and the underlying, determinant cognitive processes or latent construct. The two sets of results reviewed here suggest that stability of performance on experimental executive tasks varies dramatically, with some tasks achieving a level of stability that is at or near those of commercially available psychometric tests, whereas others have reliabilities that are indistinguishable from chance. Furthermore, these results highlight that face validity alone is not sufficient upon which to draw inferences regarding latent cognitive processes—even in the experimental context when one is making inferences at the level of groups of children. Considerably more attention needs to be paid to developing methodologically rigorous and robust instruments to more fully capture the executive processes that change so substantially in this age range. Without such work, there is a risk that the findings will continue to comprise a patchwork of knowledge, without the emergence of a coherent picture in this critical developmental period. These efforts become more important as the field moves to use the concept of executive control to understand higher stakes phenomena, such as school achievement and response to clinical interventions, where the distinction between individually based clinical decision making and group-based inference is less clear. Furthermore, if we ever hope to understand how the brain truly subserves cognitive function in this critical age period where there are such dramatic changes in brain organization, at the multiple genetic and physiological levels, fundamentally the cognitive phenomenon of interest, here executive control, must be characterized more precisely by utilizing known psychometric theory.

Acknowledgments

This research was supported in part by grants MH065668, DA014661, HD038051, HD050309 from the National Institutes of Health and from the Rita Rudel Foundation to Espy, and grants from the Carnegie Trust and British Academy to Bull. The authors thank the participating families, undergraduates, medical students, project staff, and graduate students who assisted in various laboratory tasks associated with this study.

References

Alloway, T., & Gathercole, S. (2005). Working memory and short-term sentence recall in young children. *European Journal of Cognitive Psychology, 17*, 207–220.
Allport, A., & Wylie, G. (2000). Task switching: Positive and negative priming of task set. In G. W. Humphreys, J. Duncan, & A. Triesman (Eds.), *Attention, space, and action: Studies in cognitive neuroscience* (pp. 273–296). London: Oxford University Press.

Anderson, V., Anderson, P., Grimwood, K., & Nolan, T. (2004). Cognitive and executive functions 12 years after childhood bacterial meningitis: Effect of acute neurologic complications and age of onset. *Journal of Pediatric Psychology, 29,* 67–82.

Baddeley, A. D., & Hitch, G. J. (1994). Developments in the concept of working memory. *Neuropsychology, 8*(4), 485–493.

Benes, F. M. (2001). The development of prefrontal cortex: The maturation of neurotransmitter systems and their interactions. In C. A. Nelson & M. Luciana (Eds.), *Handbook of developmental cognitive neuroscience* (pp. 79–105). Cambridge, MA: MIT Press.

Berwid, O., Curko Kera, E., Marks, D., Santra, A., Bender, H., & Halperin, J. (2005). Sustained attention and response inhibition in young children at risk for attention deficit hyperactivity disorder. *Journal of Child Psychology and Psychiatry, 46,* 1219–1229.

Bishop, D. V. M., Aamodt-Leaper, G., Creswell, C., McGurk, R., & Skuse, D. H. (2001). Individual differences in cognitive planning on the Tower of Hanoi task: Neuropsychological maturity or measurement error? *Journal of Child Psychology and Psychiatry, 42,* 551–556.

Blair, C., Zelazo, P. D., & Greenberg, M. (2005). The measurement of executive function in early childhood. *Developmental Neuropsychology, 28,* 561–571.

Brooks, P. J., Hanauer, J. B., Padowska, B., & Rosman, H. (2003). The role of selective attention in preschoolers' rule use in a novel dimensional card sort. *Cognitive Development, 18,* 195–215.

Bull, R., Espy, K. A., & Senn, T. E. (2004). A comparison of performance on the towers of London and Hanoi in young children. *Journal of Child Psychology and Psychiatry, 45,* 743–754.

Bull, R., & Scerif, G. (2001). Executive functioning as a predictor of children's mathematics ability: Inhibition, switching, and working memory. *Developmental Neuropsychology, 19,* 273–293.

Carlson, S. M., & Moses, L. J. (2001). Individual differences in inhibitory control and children's theory of the mind. *Child Development, 72,* 1032–1053.

Casey, B. J., Thomas, K. M., Welsh, T. F., Badgaiyan, R., Eccard, C. H., Jennings, J., et al. (2000). Dissociation of response conflict, attentional control, and expectancy with functional magnetic resonance imaging (fMRI). *Proceedings of the National Academy of Sciences, 97,* 8728–8733.

Davidson, M., Amso, D., Anderson, L., & Diamond, A. (2006). Development of cognitive control and executive functions from 4 to 13 years: Evidence from manipulations of memory, inhibition, and task switching. *Neuropsychologia, 44,* 2037–2078.

Desimone, R., & Duncan, J. (1995). Neural mechanisms of selective attention visual attention. *Annual Review of Neuroscience, 18,* 193–222.

Diamond, A. (1990). The development and neural bases of memory functions as indexed by AB and delayed response tasks in human infants and infant monkeys. *Annals of the New York Academy of Sciences, 608,* 267–317.

Diamond, A., Briand, L., Fossella, J., & Gehlbach, L. (2004). Genetic and neurochemical modulation of prefrontal cognitive functions in children. *American Journal of Psychiatry, 161,* 125–132.

Diamond, A., Kirkham, N., & Amso, D. (2002). Conditions under which young children can hold two rules in mind and inhibit a pre-potent response. *Developmental Psychology, 38,* 352–362.

Diamond, A., Prevor, M. B., Callender, G., & Druin, D. P. (1997). Prefrontal cortex cognitive deficits in children treated early and continuously for PKU. *Monographs of the Society for Research in Child Development, 62,* 1–208.

Diamond, A., & Taylor, C. (1996). Development of an aspect of executive control: Development of the abilities to remember what I said and to "Do as I say, not as I do". *Developmental Psychobiology*, *29*, 315–334.

Duncan, J., & Owen, A. M. (2000). Common regions of the human frontal lobe recruited by diverse cognitive demands. *Trends in Neuroscience*, *23*, 475–483.

Durston, S., Thomas, K., Yang, Y., Ulug, A., Zimmerman, R., & Casey, B. J. (2002). A neural basis for the development of inhibitory control. *Developmental Science*, *5*, F9–F16.

Elliott, C. D. (1990). *Differential abilities scale*. San Antonio, TX: Psychological Corporation.

Espy, K. A. (2004). Using developmental, cognitive and neurosciences approaches to understand executive control in young children. *Developmental Neuropsychology*, *26*, 379–384.

Espy, K. A. (1997). The Shape School: Assessing executive function in preschool children. *Developmental Neuropsychology*, *13*, 495–499.

Espy, K. A., Bull, R. B., Martin, J., & Stroup, W. (2006). Measuring the development of executive control with the Shape School. *Psychological Assessment*.

Espy, K. A., & Bull, R. B. (2005). Inhibitory processes in young children and individual variation in short-term memory. *Developmental Neuropsychology*, *28*, 669–688.

Espy, K. A., Kaufmann, P. M., & Glisky, M. L. (1999). Neuropsychological function in toddlers exposed to cocaine in utero: A preliminary study. *Developmental Neuropsychology*, *15*, 447–460.

Espy, K. A., Kaufmann, P. M., Glisky, M. L., & McDiarmid, M. D. (2001). New procedures to assess executive functions in preschool children. *Clinical Neuropsychologist*, *15*, 46–58.

Espy, K. A., Kaufmann, P. M., McDiarmid, M. D., & Glisky, M. L. (1999). Executive functioning in preschool children: Performance on A-not-B and other delayed response format tasks. *Brain and Cognition*, *41*, 178–199.

Espy, K. A., & Cwik, M. F. (2004). The development of a Trail Making Test in young children: The TRAILS-P. *The Clinical Neuropsychologist*, *18*, 1–12.

Espy, K. A., McDiarmid, M. D., Cwik, M. F., Senn, T. E., Hamby, A., & Stalets, M. M. (2004). The contributions of executive functions to emergent mathematic skills in preschool children. *Developmental Neuropsychology*, *26*, 465–486.

Espy, K. A., Stalets, M. M., McDiarmid, M. D., Senn, T. E., Cwik, M. F., & Hamby, A. (2002). Executive functions in preschool children born preterm: Application of cognitive neuroscience paradigms. *Child Neuropsychology*, *8*, 83–92.

Ewing-Cobbs, L., Prasad, M. R., Landry, S. H., Kramer, L., & DeLeon, R. (2004). Executive functions following traumatic brain injury in young children: A preliminary analysis. *Developmental Neuropsychology*, *26*, 487–512.

Friedman, N. P., & Miyake, A. (2004). The relations among inhibition and interference control functions: A latent-variable analysis. *Journal of Experimental Psychology: General*, *133*, 101–135.

Isquith, P. K., Gioia, G., & Espy, K. A. (2004). Executive functions preschool children: Examination through everyday behavior. *Developmental Neuropsychology*, *26*, 403–422.

Gathercole, S. E., & Pickering, S. J. (2000). Working memory deficits in children with low achievements in the national curriculum at 7 years of age. *British Journal of Educational Psychology*, *70*, 177–194.

Gerstadt, C. L., Hong, Y. J., & Diamond, A. (1994). The relationship between cognition and action: Performance of 3.5- to 7-year-olds on Stroop-like Day–Night Test. *Cognitiion*, *53*, 129–153.

Giedd, J. N., Blumenthal, J., Jeffries, N. O., Castellanos, F. X., Liu, H., Zijdenbos, A., et al. (1999). Brain development during childhood and adolescence: A longitudinal MRI study. *Nature Neuroscience*, *2*, 861–863.

Goldman, P. S., Rosvold, H. E., Vest, B., & Galkin, T. W. (1971). Analysis of the delayed-alternation deficit produced by dorsolateral prefrontal lesions in the rhesus monkey. *Journal of Comparative and Physiological Psychology, 77*, 212–220.

Hughes, C. (1998a). Finding your marbles: Does preschoolers' strategic behavior predict later understanding of mind. *Developmental Psychology, 34*, 1326–1339.

Hughes, C. (1998b). Executive function in preschoolers: Links with theory of mind and verbal ability. *British Journal of Developmental Psychology, 16*, 233–253.

Hughes, C. (2002). Executive functions and development: Why the interest? *Infant and Child Development, 11*, 69–71.

Hughes, C., White, A., Sharpen, J., & Dunn, J. (2000). "Hard-to-manage" preschoolers' peer problems and possible cognitive influences. *Journal of Child Psychology and Psychiatry, 41*, 169–179.

Huttenlocher, P. R., & Dabholkar, A. S. (1997). Developmental anatomy of prefrontal cortex. In N. A. Krasnegor, G. R. Lyon, & P. S. Goldman-Rakic (Eds.), *Development of the prefrontal cortex: Evolution, neurobiology, and behavior* (pp. 69–83). Baltimore: Paul H. Brookes.

Kaiser, H., Martin, J., Banet, M., & Espy, K. A. (2004). Test–retest reliability of executive function tasks for use with young children. *The Journal of the International Neuropsychological Society, S1*, 63.

Kaufmann, P., Leckman, J. M., & Ort, S. I. (1989). Delayed response performance in males with Fragile-X. *Journal of Clinical and Experimental Neuropsychology, 12*, 69.

Kerns, K. A., & Rondeau, L. A. (1998). Development of a continuous performance test for preschool children. *Journal of Attention Disorders, 2*, 229–238.

Kirkham, N. Z., Cruess, L., & Diamond, A. (2003). Helping children apply their knowledge to their behavior on a dimension-switching task. *Developmental Science, 6*, 449–467.

Kochanska, G., Murray, K., Jacques, T., Koenig, A., & Vandegeest, K. (1996). Inhibitory control in young children and its role in emerging internalization. *Child Development, 67*, 490–507.

Korkman, M., Kirk, U., & Kemp, S. (1998). *NEPSY: A Developmental Neuropsychological Assessment Manual.* San Antonio, TX: The Psychological Corporation.

Lee, M., Vaughn, B. E., & Kopp, C. B. (1983). The role of self-control in young children's performance on a delayed response memory for location task. *Developmental Psychology, 19*, 40–44.

Luciana, M. (2003). Cognitive development in children born preterm: Implications for theories of brain plasticity following early injury. *Development and Psychopathology, 15*, 1017–1047.

McDiarmid, M. D., & Espy, K. A. (2003). Relation between low-level lead exposure and attention in preschool children. *The Journal of the International Neuropsychological Society, 9*, 264.

Miller, E., & Cohen, J. (2001). An integrative theory of prefrontal cortex function. *Annual Reviews of Neuroscience, 24*, 167–202.

Miyake, A., Friedman, N. P., Rettinger, D. A., Shah, P., & Hegarty, M. (2001). How are visuospatial working memory, executive functioning, and spatial abilities related? A latent-variable analysis. *Journal of Experimental Psychology: General, 130*, 621–640.

Munakata, Y. (1998). Infant perseveration and implications for object permanence theories: A PDP Model of the A-not-B task. *Developmental Science, 1*, 161–184.

Nigg, J. T. (2000). On inhibition/disinhibition in developmental psychopathology: View from cognitive and personality psychology and a working inhibition taxonomy. *Psychological Bulletin, 126*, 220–246.

Ozonoff, S., South, M., & Provencal, S. (2005). Executive functions. In F.R. Volkmar, R. Paul, A. Klin, & D. Cohen (Eds.), *Handbook of autism and pervasive developmental disorders, Vol. 1: Diagnosis, development, neurobiology, and behavior* (3rd ed., pp. 606–627). Hoboken, NJ: John Wiley & Sons.

Pennington, B. F. (1997). Dimensions of executive functions in normal and abnormal development. In N. A. Krasnegor, G. R. Lyon, & P. S. Goldman-Rakic (Eds.), *Development of the prefrontal cortex: Evolution, neurobiology, and behavior* (pp. 265–281). Baltimore: Brookes.

Pennington, B. F., & Ozonoff, S. (1996). Executive functions and developmental psychopathology. *Journal of Child Psychology and Psychiatry and Allied Disciplines, 37*, 51–87.

Perner, J., & Lang, B. (2002). What causes 3-year-olds difficulty on the dimensional change card sorting task? *Infant and Child Development, 11*, 93–105.

Perner, J., Lang, B., & Kloo, D. (2002). Theory of mind and self-control: More than a common problem of inhibition. *Child Development, 73*, 752–767.

Piaget, J. (1954). *The construction of reality in the child.* New York: Basic Books.

Posner, M. I., & Petersen, S. E. (1990). The attention system of the human brain. *Annual Review of Neuroscience, 13*, 25–42.

Prevor, M., & Diamond, A. (2005). Color–object interference in young children: A stroop effect in children 31/2–61/2. *Cognitive Development, 20*, 256–278.

Reed, M. A., Pien, D. L., & Rothbart, M. K. (1984). Inhibitory self-control in pre-school children. *Merrill-Palmer Quarterly, 30*, 131–147.

Rennie, D., Bull, R., & Diamond, A. (2004). Executive functioning in preschoolers: Reducing the inhibitory demands of the Dimensional Change Card Sort task. *Developmental Neuropsychology, 26*, 423–443.

Shallice, T. (1982). Specific impairments of planning. *Philosophical Transactions of the Royal Society of London, B298*, 199–209.

Simon, H. A. (1975). The functional equivalence of problem solving skills. *Cognitive Psychology, 7*, 268–288.

Sowell, E. R., Thompson, P. M., Holmes, C. J., Jernigan, T. L., & Toga, A. W. (1999). *In vivo* evidence for post-adolescent brain maturation in frontal and striatal areas. *Nature Neuroscience, 2*, 859–861.

The Psychological Corporation (2002). *WPPSI-III.* San Antonio, TX: Harcourt.

The Psychological Corporation (2003). *WISC-IV.* San Antonio, TX: Harcourt.

Van Orden, G., Pennington, B., & Stone, G. (2001). What do double dissociations prove? *Cognitive Science, 25*, 111–172.

Welsh, M. C., Pennington, B. F., & Groisser, D. B. (1991). A normative-developmental study of executive function: A window on prefrontal function in children. *Developmental Neuropsychology, 7*, 131–149.

Wright, I., Waterman, M., Prescott, H., & Murdoch-Eaton, D. (2003). A new stroop-like measure of inhibitory function development: Typical developmental trends. *Journal of Child Psychology and Psychiatry, 44*, 561–575.

Zelazo, P. D., Frye, D., & Rapus, T. (1996). An age-related dissociation between knowing rules and using them. *Cognitive Development, 11*, 37–63.

Zelazo, P. D., Mueller, U., Frye, D., & Marcovitch, S. (2003). The development of executive function in childhood. *Monographs of the Society for Research in Child Development, 68*(3), Serial # 274.

6 Development and assessment of executive function: From preschool to adolescence

Vicki Anderson, Peter J. Anderson, Rani Jacobs, and Megan Spencer Smith

Contents

While no firm consensus has been achieved, it is generally agreed that the term executive function (EF) refers to a set of skills, which are necessary for independent, purposeful, goal-directed activity (Lezak, 1995; Stuss & Benson, 1986). Historically, frontal structures, and in particular prefrontal cortices, have been considered to play an integral role in subserving and coordinating executive abilities (Benton, 1991; Damasio, Grabowski, Frank, Galaburda, & Damasio, 1994: Stuss & Alexander, 2000). These cerebral regions are relatively immature during childhood, with development thought to be a protracted process, which continues into early adolescence at least (Barnea-Goraly et al., 2005; Giedd et al., 1999; Gogtay et al., 2004; Sowell et al., 2003; Yakovlev & Lecours, 1967). Parallels between ongoing maturation of the frontal lobes and the emergence of executive capacities have been reported in a number of studies. These results suggest that, where developmentally appropriate behavioral assessment tools are employed, evidence of EF can be reliably elicited in children as young as age three (Anderson & Lajoie, 1996; Diamond, 2002; Espy, 2004; Passler, Isaac, & Hynd, 1985; Smidt, Jacobs, & Anderson, 2004; Welsh, Pennington, & Groisser, 1991; Zelazo, Craik, & Booth, 2004).

It is now well established that children suffering from both developmental and acquired disorders, and disease of the central nervous system (CNS) are at risk of experiencing executive impairments, or dysexecutive syndrome. Such problems may interfere with the child's capacity to develop normally and interact effectively with the environment, thus leading to ongoing cognitive, academic, and social disturbances (Anderson & Catroppa, 2005; De Luca et al., 2003; Dennis, 1989; Levin & Hanten, 2005). Individual case studies provide anecdotal evidence of problems in planning, problem solving, and abstract thinking in the day-to-day lives of these children (Anderson, 1988; Eslinger, Flaherty-Craig, & Benton, 2004; Mateer & Williams, 1991), however such 'executive dysfunction' is often difficult to detect using traditional assessment tools. Further evidence comes from a handful of recent studies, which have examined EF following childhood brain injuries. Findings suggest that residual deficits in planning, problem solving, and adaptive behavior are associated with traumatic brain injury (Anderson & Catroppa, 2005; Asarnow, Satz, Light, Lewis, & Neumann, 1991; Ewing-Cobbs, Prasad, Landry, Kramer, & DeLeon, 2004; Levin & Hanten, 2005; Pentland, Todd, & Anderson, 1998), hydro-cephalus and spina bifida (Jacobs, Northam, & Anderson, 2001; Landry, Jordan, & Fletcher, 1994), and cranial irradiation for treatment of childhood cancers (Anderson, Godber, Smibert, Weiskop, & Ekert, 2004; Brouwers, Riccardi, Poplack, & Fedio, 1984; Stehbens et al., 1991). However, accurate and reliable identification of such deficits, both in clinical practice and research endeavors, continue to be a challenge due to a scarcity of developmentally appropriate assessment tools, and the common use of outcome parameters that are not uniquely specific to EF.

This chapter aims to review evidence on the development of EF. Consistent with contemporary developmental neuroscience approaches, three dimensions will be considered: psychological, biological, and developmental. A second objective is to consider methods of assessment of EF relevant to pediatric practice, and their strengths and weaknesses.

Theoretical models of executive function

Traditionally, EFs have been conceptualized as taking a managerial role within the neurobehavioral domain, directing attention, monitoring activity, coordinating, and integrating information and activity. Lezak states that EFs are "capacities that enable a person to engage successfully in independent, purposeful, self-serving behaviors" (Lezak, 1995, p. 42). She further distinguishes between cognitive abilities, which have domain-specific properties, and EFs, which she argues have a more global impact on thinking and behavior. She proposes that the integrity of these functions is essential for appropriate, socially responsible conduct. Shallice (1990) and Walsh (1978) have fine tuned this description further, arguing that EFs are activated under specific conditions: (a) novel or unfamiliar circumstances, where no previously established routines for responding exist; (b) where tasks are complex; and (c) where there is a need for integration of information. Other researchers include processes such as focussed and sustained attention, working memory, generation and implementation of strategies, monitoring and utilization of feedback under the umbrella term "EF" (Fuster, 2002; Glosser & Goodglass, 1990; Mateer & Williams, 1991; Mesulam, 2002; Stuss & Benson, 1986).

Contemporary views refute the notion of a unitary EF, opting for a multidimensional model, incorporating a number of separate, interacting components. In 1992,

Stuss argued for such an integrated model that emphasized cognitive aspects of EF and included separate but interrelated skills, which allow the individual to develop goals, hold them in active memory, put them into practice, monitor performance, and control interference in order to achieve them. However, as with many psychological constructs, there is no agreed definition of which specific skills should be included under this EF umbrella. Further, developmental factors have largely been ignored in attempts to conceptualize EF.

In recent years the concept of EF has been further extended, with some authors distinguishing between cold (cognitive) EF, as has been described above and hot (affective) EF, which refer to more socially and emotionally-based domains such as self-awareness, mood, affect, emotional control, moral behavior, and social information processing (Eslinger et al., 2004; Gioia, Isquith, Guy, & Kenworthy, 2000; Mesulam, 2002; Stuss & Anderson, 2004; Tranel, 2002). Deficits in the hot aspect of EF can result in a range of symptoms including apathy, reduced initiative, flat affect or conversely, aggression, socially inappropriate behaviors, and hyperactivity (Anderson, Bechara, Damasio, Tranel, & Damasio, 1999; Barrish, Tranel, & Anderson, 2000; Eslinger et al., 2004; Grattan & Eslinger, 1992). Some argue that it may be these hot EFs that uniquely define the function of frontal cortex (Stuss & Alexander, 2000), while others support a close interaction between the two sets of EFs. Certainly, there is evidence to suggest that these two executive domains may have different anatomical underpinnings, with cold EFs related to dorsolateral prefrontal cortex, and hot EFs subserved more by orbitofrontal and ventral regions (Stuss & Anderson, 2004; Tranel, 2002).

A developmental perspective

Until relatively recently the frontal lobes of the brain in children have been considered to be functionally silent, as they develop and network with other cerebral regions (Golden, 1981). Similarly, EFs have been thought to emerge only late in childhood, and thus have received relatively little attention in pediatric neuropsychology research. There is now an established literature describing activation within frontal cortex in infancy and early childhood (Chugani & Phelps, 1986; Chugani, Phelps, & Mazziotta, 1987), and the emergence of EF early in life, with empirical reports documenting evidence of these skills as early as 1 year (Diamond, 2002; Espy, 2004; Smidt et al., 2004; Zelazo et al., 2004). Despite these reports, our knowledge of the emergence and establishment of EF is limited, and theoretical approaches encompassing developmental principles are rare (P. Anderson, 2002; Zelazo et al., 2004). Coupled with findings of executive dysfunction following brain insults in childhood, there is a clear challenge for child-focussed researchers to address these gaps and provide a better basis for understanding these skills in instances of normal and disrupted development.

For the purposes of this chapter, we will employ the child-based framework described by Peter Anderson (2002, this volume), which focuses specifically on cognitive aspects of EF. Within the clinical and theoretical frameworks provided by adult literature, and using data obtained from normative studies of children and factor analytic techniques (Anderson, Anderson, Northam, Jacobs, & Catroppa, 2001;

Duncan, 1986; Lezak, 1995; Luria, 1973; Neisser, 1967; Shallice, 1990; Stuss & Alexander, 2000), Anderson has argued that at least three subcomponents of EF can be identified in children: (i) attentional control: selective attention, sustained attention, and response inhibition; (ii) goal setting: initiating, planning, problem solving, and strategic behavior; and (iii) cognitive flexibility: working memory, attentional shift and conceptual transfer. These domains are thought to represent discrete functions that, at least in the adult literature, can be linked to specific frontal systems. Anderson suggests that these executive subcomponents operate in an integrative manner and can be conceptualized as a functional system. Attentional control, the first executive process to emerge, greatly influences the efficient performance of the other two EF components, while cognitive flexibility and goal setting are more interrelated and interdependent, receiving and processing information from other components.

Dysfunction within this EF system may be characterized by difficulties generating and implementing strategies for problem solving, poor planning and organization, perseveration, inability to correct errors or use feedback, and mental inflexibility (Stuss & Benson, 1986; Walsh, 1978). Qualitative features of impairments in EF include disorganization, adynamia, reduced self-control, impulsivity, perseverative, erratic or careless response behaviors, and deficient high-level communication skills (Lezak, 1995). Such symptoms are readily identified as deviant in adults following frontal injury, however, in children, where such features may be developmentally appropriate, diagnosis of executive impairment is more complex.

Biological underpinnings of executive function

Knowledge of CNS maturation and related cognitive development is gradually increasing, with advances in technical methodologies. Cerebral development is ongoing during childhood, although human brain development has been shown to be a nonlinear process (Gogtay et al., 2004; Johnson, 2000; Luna et al., 2001; Thatcher, 1992). Brain weight increases from around 400 gm at birth to 1,500 gm at maturity in early adulthood, with most maturation occurring during the first decade of life (Caeser, 1993). While prenatal development is characterized by the most dynamic activity, it is primarily concerned with gross structural formation that remains incomplete at birth (Casey, Giedd, & Thomas, 2000; Orzhekhiovskaya, 1981), and only reaches maturity around puberty. Subtle qualitative and quantitative changes associated with elaboration of the CNS have been found to progress postnatally and into adolescence (Giedd et al., 1999; Klinberg et al., 1999; Orzhekhiovskaya, 1981; Sowell et al., 1999; Toga, Thompson, & Sowell, 2006; Yakovlev, 1962). Processes such as dendritic aborization, myelination, and synaptogenesis have all been reported to progress rapidly during infancy and early childhood, in a largely hierarchical manner, with anterior regions the last to reach maturity (Fuster, 1993; Gogtay et al., 2004; Jernigan & Tallal, 1990; Klinberg et al., 1999). Maturation appears to follow a set sequence, with primary sensorimotor cortices and frontal and occipital poles maturing first and the remainder of structures developing in a posterior–anterior direction (Gogtay et al., 2004).

Historically, based on adult literature from brain-damaged populations, frontal structures, and in particular prefrontal cortices, have been considered to play an integral role in subserving and coordinating executive abilities (Benton, 1991; Damasio et al., 1994; Luria, 1973; Stuss & Alexander, 2000; Toga et al., 2006). Recently this localizationist view has been questioned, with reports of adults demonstrating deficits in EF following cerebral pathology not confined to frontal cortex (Stuss et al., 1999). Now many researchers argue that while the frontal lobes may play a critical role in subserving EF, the integrity of the entire brain may be necessary for efficient EF (Stuss, 1992; Welsh & Pennington, 1988). During development, when the structure and connectivity of the brain are changing rapidly, and when functional organization is less rigid, this argument may be particularly relevant (Anderson, Levin, & Jacobs, 2002), with disruption to these processes likely to impact on both the hard wiring of the brain and its functional organization, creating a challenge for those working within the pediatric domain.

A number of neurophysiological studies refute the historical view that the frontal lobes were functionally silent in infancy and early childhood and executive skills not measurable until the second decade of life. For example, Chugani et al. (1987) measured local cerebral metabolic rates of glucose in infants and young children, and found evidence of frontal activation in infants as young as 6 months of age. Similarly, Bell and Fox (1992) have documented changes in scalp recorded EEGs in frontal regions during the first year of life, relating these to improvements in behavioral performances. Many researchers now support the notion that these biological growth markers may explain some of the age-related variation in non-biological development, such as cognition (Caeser, 1993; Thatcher, 1991, 1992). To date, new forms of functional neuroimaging have not been employed in these very young age groups, as the requirements of such approaches (e.g., positron emission tomography [PET], functional magnetic resonance imaging [fMRI]) are considered inappropriate for infants and very young children.

In keeping with the ongoing development of EF through infancy, childhood, and adolescence, prefrontal regions demonstrate protracted development, with evidence of continued maturation until early adulthood (Klinberg et al., 1999). The prefrontal cortex receives input from all areas of the frontal and posterior neocortex (Barbas, 1992; Fuster, 1993, 2002). Thus, sensory and perceptual data are processed by the frontal lobes where actions are organized and executed. This pattern of connectivity suggests that, while prefrontal regions may 'orchestrate' behavior, they are also dependent on all other cerebral areas for input, with efficient functioning reliant upon the quality of information received from other cerebral regions.

Diamond (2002) has provided a useful chronology of structural and metabolic development of the prefrontal cortex, categorizing the key developmental periods as follows: less than 1 year, 1–3 years, 3–7 years, and more than 7 years; based on the classification of increments in executive skills observed through childhood. Using this approach, Diamond notes that the first year of life is characterized by increases in dendritic length within prefrontal cortex to full extension by 12 months of age (Koenderink, Uylings, & Mrzljak, 1994), as well as increases in neuronal density to 55% above adults levels (Huttenlocher, 1990) and similar increases in levels of glucose metabolism (Chugani & Phelps, 1986; Chugani et al., 1987), neurotransmitters, and receptors (dopamine, acetylcholinesterase) (Lidow & Goldman-Rakic, 1991). In contrast to these multiple changes, the period between 1 and 3 years appears relatively uneventful. Consistent with major changes in EF capacity during the preschool period (Smidt et al., 2004; Zelazo et al., 2004), significant changes occur within prefrontal cortex between ages 3 and 7 years. Specifically, it appears that during this developmental period, prefrontal cortex takes on a more adult appearance, with neuronal and synaptic density now only 10% above adult levels, reflecting substantial pruning from infancy (Huttenlocher, 1990). There is also a marked expansion in dendritic trees in the dorsolateral prefrontal cortex during this period (Koenderink et al., 1994). Prefrontal cortex changes continue after age 7, and into adulthood. Some researchers have documented increases in gray matter within frontal cortex until age 12 followed by reductions after this age (Giedd et al., 1999), while others describe reductions in gray matter density (Reiss, Abrams, Singer, Rosss, & Denckla, 1996; Sowell, Delis, Stiles, & Jernigan, 2001) from 7 years, being most evident until age 16, and then continuing until adulthood.

Associated with these growth spurts is the concept of critical or sensitive periods. A critical period is a stage in the developmental sequence during which an aspect of behavioral function may experience a major progression. These critical periods have been conceptualized as a window of opportunity during which skills need to be consolidated so that the system involved can then establish interconnections with other systems (Anderson, Northam, Hendy, & Wrennall, 2001; Johnson, 2003). A disruption to the maturational process during a critical period may be particularly detrimental, causing a cessation of development or altering the course of future development. If this progression does not occur appropriately, then it may never occur (see Kolb et al., this volume). For example, within language and visual systems deprivation during such critical periods has been shown to have irreversible effects for ongoing maturation and ultimate mastery of particular processes (Blakemore, 1974; Lennenberg, 1967). A similar process may be predicted for other behavioral domains. Thus, if brain development is disrupted during a critical period for frontal lobe development, as described above, there may be a residual impact on skills subsumed by this region, such as self-awareness or executive abilities.

In summary, cortical development appears to be somewhat hierarchical, with tertiary association areas (including frontal) maturing last. Most indices of development suggest a staged maturation, with a level of completeness by puberty but some indices continue to mature until the late 20s, early 30s.

Parallels between the development of executive functions and frontal lobes

The terms 'EF' and 'frontal lobe function' have developed in parallel in the neuropsychological literature, and are often employed interchangeably, most likely due to early observations from the adult literature of executive dysfunction in patients with frontal lobe damage (Benton, 1968; Luria, 1973; Parker & Crawford, 1992; Walsh, 1978, 1985; Welsh & Pennington, 1988). However, as previously noted, the practice of localizing EF to the frontal lobes has been questioned recently, with similar patterns of behavioral disturbance identified in patients where pathology is not restricted to these regions (Albert & Kaplan, 1980; Anderson, Anderson, Northam, Jacobs, & Mikiewicz, 2002; Glosser & Goodglass, 1990; Walsh, 1985). It may be argued that, while the frontal regions play a vital role in their mediation, the integrity of the entire brain is necessary for intact EF. Alternatively, EF may be interpreted purely as a psychological concept, relating to a set of observable behaviors, without any reference to possible anatomical underpinnings (Stuss, 1992). Before rejecting the unique role of the frontal lobes for EF, it has been argued that it is important to clarify whether the lack of association may be more due to the insensitivity of standardized clinical measures purported to test EF, and their, necessarily, multidimensional nature, or perhaps due to the use of research samples where cerebral pathology is not sufficiently circumscribed. Stuss et al. (1999) have addressed these issues in their research, demonstrating that, with a carefully selected sample, and using discrete neuropsychological measures (for example, error measures), it is possible to differentiate not only frontal versus extra-frontal pathology, but also functional differences within the frontal lobes. These findings are supported by results from functional brain imaging studies (D'Esposito & Postle, 2002; Goldman-Rakic & Leung, 2002; Rolls, 2002), which identify specific activation within prefrontal cortex using cognitive activation tasks tapping executive skills.

Together, these findings suggest that, in adults at least, the frontal lobes have a special role for EF. The challenge is to determine whether this role is innate, or if it develops during childhood. There are two potential approaches to this challenge. The first is provided by the natural process of development, where development in frontal brain regions may be correlated with the emergence of EF through childhood, to identify any parallels. The second, discussed in later chapters, is to study children with focal frontal lesions and, in addition, to compare outcomes on frontal measures for children with focal frontal pathology to those with damage to extra-frontal regions.

A number of links may be hypothesized between patterns of neuroanatomic change and cognitive development. For example, paralleling ongoing cerebral maturation, children and adolescents acquire the capacity for more rapid information processing with increasing myelination of nerve tracts (Halford & Wilson, 1980; Klinberg et al., 1999; Sowell et al., 2001). The incomplete development of frontal lobes during childhood and adolescence implies a limited ability to apply effective executive skills. This suggestion has been supported by developmental research which has documented increases in EF through childhood and adolescence (V. Anderson et al., 2001; Anderson, Lajoie, & Bell, 1995; Bjorkland, 1989; Levin et al., 1991; Luciana & Nelson, 1998; Romine & Reynolds, 2005; Simon, 1975; Todd, Anderson, & Lawrence, 1996; Welsh et al., 1991). Historically, theoretical models of cognitive development have strongly supported such a hierarchical view. In particular, Piagetian theories (Piaget, 1963), while providing no reference to possible neural substrates, are compatible with current understandings of cerebral development. Piaget describes four sequential cognitive stages including sensorimotor (birth to 2 years), preoperational (2–7 years), concrete operational (7–9 years), and formal operational (early adolescence), with Piaget's hypothesized timing of transitions between his cognitive stages paralleling documented growth spurts within the CNS.

Development of executive functions

Cold (cognitive) executive functions

Empirical studies report progressive increments in EF, coinciding with growth spurts in frontal lobes (Anderson et al., 1995; P. Anderson, V. Anderson, & Garth, 2001; Bell & Fox, 1992; Levin et al., 1991; Luciana & Nelson, 1998; Sowell et al., 2001; Thatcher, 1991, 1992; Welsh & Pennington, 1988). Early studies employed Piagetian-type paradigms to examine the relationship between cerebral and cognitive development. In particular, Diamond and colleagues (Diamond, 2002; Diamond & Goldman-Rakic, 1985, 1989; Goldman-Rakic, 1987) report evidence that frontally mediated, goal-directed behavior can be detected as early as 12 months of age in human infants. Others document a stage-like progression of EF, with mastery not achieved at age 12 years or later in many areas (Becker, Isaac, & Hynd, 1987; Chelune & Baer, 1986; Passler et al., 1985; Welsh et al., 1991).

Recently, researchers have examined the possibility that specific aspects of EF may display varying developmental trajectories. Most research to date has focused on younger, school-aged children, with little information available regarding EF development for either the preschool period or adolescence. Welsh et al. (1991) were the first to implement such an approach. They studied a sample of normal children, aged 3–12 years, using a series of EF measures commonly employed in clinical practice. Their results are consistent with a stage-like process of EF development, with some components maturing earlier than others, thus supporting a multidimensional notion of EF. They described three specific developmental stages from 3 to 12 years. The first commenced around age 6, and is characterized by maturation of the ability to resist distraction. The second spurt occurred about age 10, with organized search, hypothesis testing, and impulse control emerging at this time. Finally, verbal fluency, motor sequencing, and planning skills were found to reach maturity in early adolescence. When they examined qualitative features of these patterns the authors identified three discrete factors: Factor 1, described as representing speeded responding; Factor 2, as an indicator of hypothesis testing and impulse control; and Factor 3, as reflecting planning ability.

Looking specifically within the preschool period, a number of studies have now established that EF can be measured in very young children, and that development of these skills is surprisingly rapid (Espy, Kaufmann, McDiarmid, & Glisky, 1999). For example, Espy investigated attentional control in preschoolers, using the Shape School Test, and documented emergence beginning between 4 and 5 years of age. Similarly, Jacques and Zelazo (2001), using a concept generation paradigm, found a significant growth spurt between 3 and 4 years in normally developing children. In contrast to 3-year-olds, 4-year-old children were able to identify a common dimension (e.g., color, shape) across two nonidentical stimuli, with further progress observed in a 5-year-old group. Smidt et al. (2004) compared 3- to 7-year-old children ($n = 99$), on tasks tapping a range of EFs, including working memory, planning, task switching, and attentional control. As illustrated in Figure 6.1, findings suggested different EF trajectories, across even this small age range. Attentional control (e.g., inhibition of responses) emerged first, and was relatively stable by

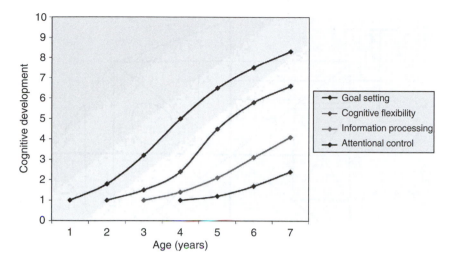

Figure 6.1 Schematic representation of executive function development through the pre-school years.

age 5. Consistent with the work of Espy (1997) and Jacques and Zelazo (2001), task switching developed rapidly from 3 to 5 years, but continued to mature across the age span under study. In contrast, working memory showed incremental progression from 3 to 7 years. Planning skills proved more difficult to assess, with traditional measures unable to elicit reliable findings in children under age 5. Gradual emergence of these skills was evident, however, from 5 to 7 years. These findings suggest that subcomponents of EF can be differentiated using developmentally appropriate techniques, and that these subcomponents have unique developmental trajectories that may be mapped to specific prefrontal networks in the future providing a better understanding of the links between frontal function and executive skills.

Focusing on later stages of development, Levin et al. (1991) replicated and extended the results of Welsh et al. (1991). These researchers evaluated 52 normal children and adolescents across three age bands: 7–8, 9–12, and 13–15 years. They administered a range of executive measures and identified developmental gains across all tasks, reflecting considerable progress in concept formation, mental flexibility, and goal-setting skills through middle childhood. They also identified three factors associated with specific aspects of EF, as well as unique developmental patterns. Factor 1 tapped semantic association/concept formation and Factor 3 was primarily concerned with problem solving, with each of these abilities showing a gradual progression over the three age ranges. Factor 2 was related to impulse control and mental flexibility and these skills were noted to reach adult levels by age 12.

Developmental timelines for EFs have also been investigated in our laboratory (P. Anderson, V. Anderson, & Lajoie, 1996; P. Anderson et al., 2001; V. Anderson

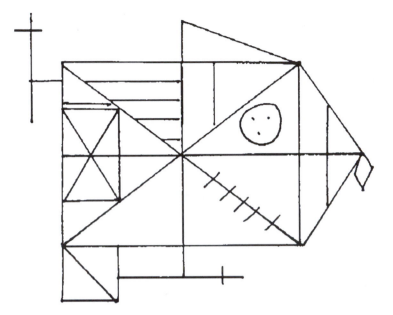

Figure 6.2   Rey Complex Figure. From *L'examen clinique en psychologie*, by A. Rey, 1964, Paris: Presses Universitaires de France.

et al., 2001; Jacobs, Anderson, & Harvey, 2001). We examined a sample of 250 healthy children, aged 7–13 years, using established clinical tests of EF: (a) goal setting: Complex Figure of Rey (Rey, 1964; Figure 6.2), Tower of London (Shallice, 1982; Figure 6.3); (b) attentional control: Digit Span (Backwards, Forwards: Wechsler, 1991), Trail Making Test (Reitan, 1969); and (c) cognitive flexibility: Controlled Oral Word Association Test (Gaddes & Crockett, 1975); Contingency Naming Test (Anderson, Anderson, Northam, & Taylor, 2000) (Figure 6.4). For further details on administration and scoring for these measures see Baron (2004). As illustrated in Figures 6.5–6.7, developmental increments were evident for each of these measures across the age range of the study. However, it may be that these developmental transitions are not only associated with increases in executive skills. For example, careful examination of these data detected developmental regression between 11 and 13 years, particularly in the areas of self-regulation and strategic decision-making (Anderson et al., 1996; 2001) and potentially linked to a transitional period between developmental phases (Kirk, 1985), resulting in conflicts between developing cognitive processes. During these periods the implementation of conceptual and holistic strategies clashes with the execution of self-regulatory processes, which requires close monitoring of performance and prefers the "de-construction" of tasks. Balancing and prioritizing these competing demands requires executive control, which may only be possible when each executive domain reaches a certain maturity level.

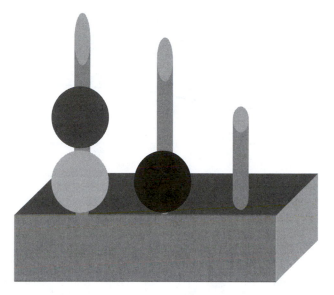

Figure 6.3 Tower of London. From "Specific impairments of planning," by T. Shallice, 1982, *Philosophical Transcripts of the Royal Society of London*, *298*, pp. 199–209.

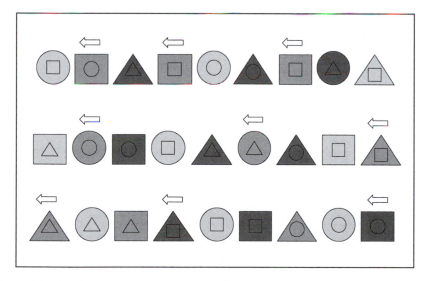

Figure 6.4 Contingency Naming Test. From "Standardization of the Contingency Naming Test (CNT) for school-aged children: A measure of reactive flexibility," by P. Anderson, V. Anderson, E. Northam, and H. G., 2000, *Clinical Neuropsychological Assessment*, *1*, pp. 247–273.

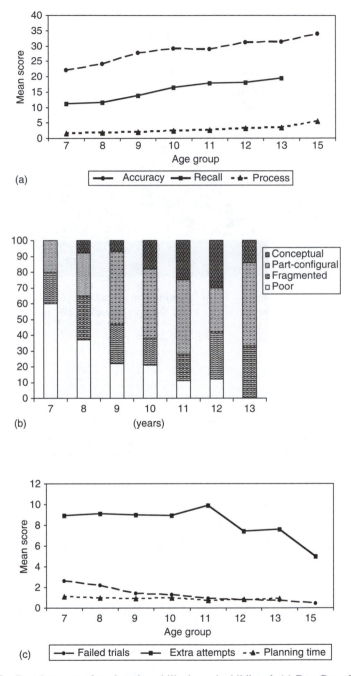

Figure 6.5 Development of goal-setting skills through childhood. (a) Rey Complex Figure: accuracy, recall, and process scores. (b) Rey Complex Figure: relationship between age and process scores. (c) Tower of London: strategy scores.

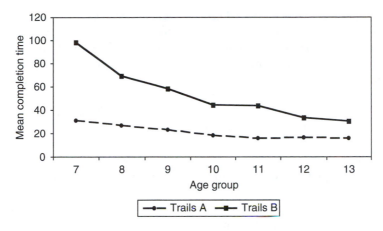

Figure 6.6 Development of attentional control skills through childhood (Trail Making Test).

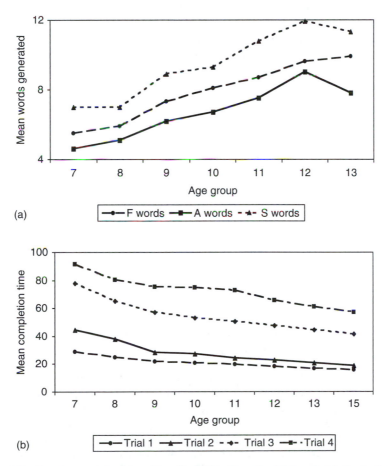

Figure 6.7 Developmental of cognitive flexibility through childhood. (a) Controlled Oral Word Association Test. (b) Contingency Naming Test.

Extension of this work into the adolescent and adult age ranges has identified ongoing, but more subtle, development in some executive domains (V. Anderson et al., 2001; De Luca et al., 2003). Cognitive flexibility remained most stable from age 7 to early adulthood, with only incremental improvements in goal setting during adolescence, and then a significant spurt after age 19. Working memory showed gradual improvement in childhood, but improved dramatically around age 11, and again between ages 15 and 19, being at its maximum in early adulthood. There was also evidence of improvements in attentional control around age 15 years, specifically for performances on more cognitively demanding tasks. It is debatable whether these continued increments reflect improved EF, or if they may be more related to better implementation and integration of these skills, in association with the final stages of brain maturation.

Of interest, and in contrast to the lack of gender differences described in younger samples, there was some evidence of gender-specific effects particularly in early adolescence. Specifically, before that time, girls tended to exhibit inferior performances, but after age 12 or 13, female performances were slightly superior across a range of tasks. These results parallel research describing gender-specific maturation changes in brain development in early adolescence (Giedd et al., 1996).

In reviewing the data from these studies, some trends emerge, and are summarized in Figure 6.8. Attentional control is the earliest executive skill to emerge, sometime between the ages of 7 and 12 months (Diamond, 2002). By age 3, children possess the capacity to inhibit instinctive behaviors (Diamond, 2002; Espy, 1997) and

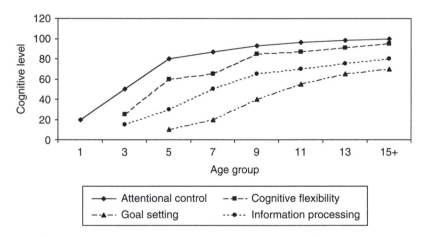

Figure 6.8   Schematic of developmental trajectories across childhood and adolescence. Adapted from *Neuropsychological Assessment of the School-Aged Child*, by V. Anderson, G. Lajoie, and R. Bell, 1995, Department of Psychology, University of Melbourne, Australia; *Developmental Neuropsychology: A Clinical Approach*, by V. Anderson, E. Northam, J. Hendy, and J. Wrennall, 2001, London: Psychology Press; "The Object Classification Task for Children (OCTC): A measure of concept generation and mental flexibility in early childhood," by D. Smidt, R. Jacobs, and V. Anderson, 2004, *Developmental Neuropsychology, 26*, pp. 385–402.

improvements in speed and accuracy continue until around age 9 (Anderson et al., 1996). Another spurt at around 15 can be seen on more cognitively demanding tasks (V. Anderson et al., 2001). Cognitive flexibility begins to emerge around age 3 (Espy, 1997; Jacques & Zelazo, 2001; Smidt et al., 2004) with the capacity for mental flexibility extending from two- to three-dimensional shifts at around age 7 (Anderson, 2002; P. Anderson et al., 2001; Jacobs et al., 2001), with relative stability from that time into adolescence (P. Anderson et al., 2001). Goal setting is difficult to elicit in the preschool years, but shows continued maturation from middle childhood through late adolescence (Anderson, 2002; V. Anderson et al., 2001; De Luca et al., 2003; Krikorian, Bartok, & Gay, 1994; Todd et al., 1996; Welsh et al., 1991). Working memory shows the most protracted developmental trajectory, emerging in the preschool period (Smidt et al., 2004), developing rapidly in middle child-hood (P. Anderson et al., 1996) and through to adolescence and early adulthood (V. Anderson et al., 2001; DeLuca et al., 2003).

Hot (socio-affective) executive functions

Research addressing the acquisition of aspects of hot EFs (e.g., self-awareness theory of mind, moral judgment) is less easy to interpret. Evidence indicates that these skills emerge, in a rudimentary state, quite early in childhood, with reports that children between 9 and 12 months of age have expectations about the actions of those around them, and by 18 months are able to understand intentions (Kain & Perner, 2001; Meltzoff, Gopnik, & Repacholi, 1997). Progress over the next few years is gradual, characterized by increasing understanding of desires and intentions and emergence of symbolic play (Bartsch & Wellman, 1989). At around age 4, there is a dramatic shift, with evidence of a capacity to understand false beliefs and deceptive ploys (Sodian, Taylor, Harris, & Perner, 1991), the basic requirements for mature theory of mind. The capacity to interpret affective or nonverbal cues (e.g., sarcasm, humor) from the environment develops slowly through childhood (Dennis, Purvis, Barnes, Wilkinson, & Winner, 2001), and it is only in mid- to late childhood that the capacity to recognize deliberate falsehoods and take into account and weigh up the facts of the situation and what they believe the speaker means begins to emerge. Similar patterns of maturation have been documented for the emergence of moral reasoning (Couper, Jacobs, & Anderson, 2002; Gibbs, Basinger, & Fuller, 1992). However, as with other cognitive and behavioral domains, while the foundations are laid down in early childhood, the subtleties of these skills are not mature until much later, with ongoing refinement into adolescence, as the individual begins to comprehend the complex-ities of social relationships and the thoughts and opinions of others.

The parallels between the emergence of EF and the stages described in anatomical reports of CNS development are striking, providing clear support for mediation of EF via anterior cerebral regions (Anderson, 1998; Casey et al., 2000). Further, the data suggest that EF, rather than being a unitary construct, may be divided into a number of subcomponents, demonstrating varying developmental trajectories, and reaching maturity at differential times. Potentially, these varying patterns may reflect mediation by specific areas within the frontal lobes, also maturing at different rates.

However, it is important to be mindful that these regions are dependent upon input from other brain areas, making it difficult to isolate frontal functions from those of other developing cerebral structures. It may be that the gradual emergence of EF demonstrated through childhood reflects the integrity of development throughout the brain. The development of EF may be intimately linked with the well-established progression of other cognitive capacities (Anderson & Lajoie, 1996; Baddeley, 1986; Case, 1985; Gaddes & Crockett, 1975; Hale, Bronik, & Fry, 1997; Halperin, Healey, Zeitchik, Ludman, & Weinstein, 1989; Howard & Polich, 1985; McKay, Halperin, Schwartz, & Sharma, 1994; Miller & Weiss, 1962; Simon, 1975), such as language, attention, speed of processing, and memory capacity.

In summary, recent multidisciplinary research has established tentative links between development of executive skills and frontal structures, but there is no way to define these relationships, or to determine developmental patterns of EF, divorced from lower-order cognitive capacities. Advancing functional brain imaging technology, utilizing more carefully designed cognitive measures, may provide the necessary tools for such investigations. Regardless, this convergence of evidence emphasizes the importance of close communication among disciplines involved in improving our understanding of brain–behavior relationships in the developing child.

Assessing executive functions in children

Early localizationist models identified single tests such as the Complex Figure of Rey (Rey, 1964) or the Wisconsin Card Sorting Test (Heaton, 1981) as indicators of frontal lobe function or EF. Contemporary neuropsychological theory would argue that such an approach is too simplistic. The efficiency of EF, and frontal lobe functioning, is clearly mediated by lower-order processes. Thus, EF must be considered in the context of these other functions, and assessment tools must be able to isolate, or at least identify, lower-order skills as well as the specific components of EF they purport to measure. Using an hypothesis-driven approach (Walsh, 1978, 1985), assessment and isolation of executive deficits may rely on administration of multiple tests, each focussing on specific aspects of function, and sequentially ruling out skills as intact or deficient, or utilization of test variables specific to the aspects of EF under consideration.

In addition to being accessible only through tests that include lower-order functions, executive skills may be difficult to detect within the clinical context, using standardized assessment tools. Typically the neuropsychological assessment is conducted in a well structured, quiet clinic setting, with the tester initiating and directing the patient's responses. Lezak (1995) emphasizes these problems, noting that deficits in EF are rarely reflected in test scores, due to the high level of structure of assessment tools. Parker and Crawford (1992), in a review of assessment procedures that claimed to measure EF, found "disappointingly few sensitive and reliable tests which the clinical neuropsychologist can depend upon" (p. 286). We have also identified surprising low associations between scores on clinical tests of EF and parent reports on the Behavioral Rating Inventory of EF (BRIEF: Gioia et al., 2000)

(Anderson et al., 2002), again questioning the validity of clinic-based assessment of EF in isolation.

Given the vulnerability of EF to early brain damage, their importance to ongoing cognitive development (Dennis, 1989), and to the success of treatment and rehabilitation programs, there is a need to devise valid and well-standardized assessment measures, specifically designed for children, and based on current understandings of the nature of both cerebral and cognitive development through childhood. To date, most tests of EF employed in pediatric practice have been developed for use with adults, are often of little interest or relevance to young children, and frequently lack normative information with respect to developmental expectations. Further, there exists an underlying assumption that such measures will detect similarly localized dysfunction in both adults and children. Such assumptions may be inappropriate, given the greater potential for functional reorganization in the young child, suggesting that caution is required when providing 'localizing' interpretations of test performance (Taylor & Fletcher, 1990). As previously noted, this problem is particularly evident for younger children where traditional, adult-derived tests are often inappropriate or too conceptually difficult to elicit meaningful responses (Smidt et al., 2004).

To establish valid measures, which overcome the problems described above, it is essential that they tap the various components of EF: attentional control, goal setting, and cognitive flexibility, as detailed above (V. Anderson et al., 2001; Lezak, 1995; Luria, 1973; Shallice, 1990; Welsh & Pennington, 1988). In order to effectively assess these skills, tasks require several characteristics: novelty, complexity, and the need to integrate information (Walsh, 1978). Based on Walsh's 'formula' for assessment of EF, Shallice (1990) states that routinized tasks can be performed almost automatically, without reference to executive skills. However, novel or complex tasks require the individual to develop new schema, formulate new strategies, and monitor their effectiveness, thus activating executive skills. The most widely accepted measures of EF have been designed or borrowed from cognitive psychology, with these basic requirements in mind. Table 6.1 provides a sample of measures commonly considered to evaluate EF. A number of more laboratory-based methods are frequently cited in research, but less commonly employed clinically, due to lack of child-based norms and standardized administration protocols (e.g., go/no go paradigms, A-not-B tasks, sorting tests). In addition, several test batteries have emerged recently, which incorporate examination of aspects of EF, or include a subset of tests addressing this domain: Delis–Kaplan EF system (Delis, Kaplan, & Kramer, 2001), NEPSY (Korkman, Kirk, & Kemp, 1998), and the Test of Everyday Attention for Children (Manly, Anderson, Robertson, & Nimmo-Smith, 1999), and the Behavioral Assessment of the Dysexecutive Syndrome for Children (BADS-C: Emslie, Wilson, Burden, Nimmo-Smith, & Wilson, 2003). A handful of age-normed parent- and teacher-rated behavior questionnaires have also been developed to tap into day-to-day aspects of EF. These include the BRIEF (Gioia et al., 2000) and the Dysexecutive-Child Questionnaire (BADS-C; Emslie et al., 2003).

Traditionally, EF tests are scored on the basis of a summary or end point score, which reflect an integration of all the cognitive skills (executive and nonexecutive) necessary to complete the task. Thus, poor overall performance, characterized by

Table 6.1 Commonly used executive tests in child practice.

Executive function	Test	Standard administration	Normative data	References
Attentional control	Matching Familiar Figures (MFF)	Yes	7–12	Kagan (1966)
	Contingency Naming Test (CNT: 1&2)	Yes	6–16	Anderson et al. (2000)
	Trail Making - A (TM)	Yes	6–13	Reitan (1969)
	Logan Stop Signal Task (SST)	Yes	—	Logan (1994)
Goal setting	Test of Everyday Attention for Children (TEA-Ch)	Yes	6–15	Manly et al. (1999)
	Complex Figure of Rey (CFR)	Multiple	6–16	Rey (1964)
	Porteus Mazes (PM)	Yes	5–13	Porteus (1950)
	Tower of London (TOL)	Multiple	6–16	Shallice (1982)
	Tower of Hanoi (TOH)	Multiple	3–12	Simon (1975)
Cognitive flexibility	Controlled Oral Word Association (COWAT)	Yes	6–16	Gaddes & Crockett (1975)
	Contingency Naming Test (CNT: 3&4)	Yes	6–16	Anderson et al. (2000)
	Concept Generation Test (CGT)	Yes	7–16	Jacobs et al. (2001)
	Wisconsin Card Sorting (WCST)	Yes	6–14	Heaton (1981)
	Stroop Test (STROOP)	Yes	6–12	Golden (1978)
	Category Test (CT)	Yes	5+	Reitan & Wolfson (1985)
Executive batteries	D-KEFS	Yes	8+	Delis et al. (2001)
	NEPSY	Yes	5–12	Korkman et al. (1998)
	BADS-C	Yes	5–12	Emslie et al. (2003)
	Preschool EF Battery (PEFB)	Yes	2–5	Espy (1997); Espy, Kaufmann, Glisky, & McDiarmid (2001)
	NASAC	Yes	7–13	Anderson et al. (1995)

below par end point scores, may sometimes reflect impairments in lower order (nonexecutive) skills rather than executive processes. To fully appreciate the role of executive processes in standard EF measures, techniques for isolating and quantifying the involvement of specific features of performance (e.g., planning, reasoning and attention) are needed (Anderson, 1998). It may be argued that qualitative aspects of performance or microanalysis of individual skills required for adequate performance provides a more valid picture of EF. In the adult literature such methods have been found to be sensitive to subtle deficits in EF not apparent on standard end point measures (e.g., Levine, Stuss, & Milberg, 1995). Discourse analysis procedures (Dennis & Barnes, 1990; Didus, Anderson, & Catroppa, 2000) have been employed to investigate subtle differences in conversation patterns between clinical and control groups, with some success. This real-life approach has also proved useful in evaluation of hot EFs such as social information processing and moral judgment (Couper et al., 2002).

Researchers investigating functional planning skills in normal children and adolescents (e.g., Todd et al., 1996) have documented procedures to record use of strategies, presence of purpose, and assistance gained by aids, to determine what constitutes good planning. Some researchers have begun to use these methods with clinical populations (P. Anderson et al., 1996, 2001; Condor, Anderson, & Saling, 1996; Jacobs et al., 2001; Pentland et al., 1998; Todd et al., 1996; Waber & Holmes, 1985; Wansart, 1990) to fractionate aspects of executive skills exhibited by children with disabilities. Information obtained from such qualitative analysis of behavior may be usefully employed in the design of rehabilitation programs and remedial interventions.

Garth, Anderson, and Wrennall (1997) outline one such model, utilizing process-oriented scores that enable discrimination of specific executive skills. They divided task performance as follows: (1) Mastery: a summary score, providing a general indicator of performance reflecting a range of cognitive skills, such as speed, accuracy, perception, and language; (2) Rate: a measure of processing speed; and (3) Strategy: a measure of adaptive or high-level aspects of performance, predicted to be specifically impaired in frontal injuries. The validity of this approach has been described and validated in a number of child-based studies (P. Anderson et al., 1996, 2000, 2001; Anderson, Fenwick, Robertson, & Manly, 1998; Anderson, Bond, Catroppa, Grimwood, Nolan, & Keir, 1997; Matthews, Anderson, & Anderson, 2001). For example, on the Complex Figure of Rey, the mastery score is indicated by the overall copy score, rate by the time taken to complete the task, and strategy by a process-oriented organizational score, which quantifies the organizational approach taken by the child (P. Anderson et al., 2001).

We have also employed this approach with brain-damaged groups, with results suggesting that strategy scores may tap into specific aspects of EF and their associations with the frontal lobes. For example, Matthews et al. (2001) employed this microanalytic approach with the Complex Figure of Rey, to compare performances across four groups of children: (1) frontal pathology; (2) temporal pathology; (3) generalized insults; and (4) healthy age-matched controls. Using the traditional summary measure of copy accuracy as well as an organizational (strategy) score (P. Anderson et al., 2001) (see Table 6.2), results showed that children with generalized insults performed poorly on all measures, reflecting the global nature

Table 6.2   Rey Complex Figure process scoring criteria (RCF-OSS): general information and instruction.

Rey Complex Figure process scoring criteria

General Information

Vertical and horizontal centerlines are pivotal to organization of the RCF-OSS

The accuracy of drawing is not being measured, consequently parts of figure may be missing or drawn incorrectly

The orientation of drawing may be incorrect

The examiner should carefully record sequence in which figure is completed

Retrospective scoring can often increase rating difficulty

Definitions

Rectangle: refers to large rectangle and is a configural component of figure

Centerlines: refers to vertical and horizontal bisectors of rectangle. Centerlines are also configural components of figure, and separately drawn portions must connect.

Contour: refers to outline of figure. This may (or may not) include total outline, such as cross, diamond, or triangle.

Diagonals: refers to diagonals of rectangle. Diagonals do not have to be completed as single whole lines and sections of each diagonal do not have to connect.

Outside attachments: refers to all sections of figure external to rectangle, includes left vertical cross; horizontal cross below rectangle; triangle on top of rectangle; triangle on right side of rectangle; and small box below rectangle.

Internal sections: refers to all internal sections of large rectangle, which could be divided into half, quarters, or eighths. This includes four parallel lines and small horizontal line in left upper quadrant; circle with three dots and small vertical line in right upper quadrant; rectangle with diagonals in left upper and lower quadrants; and five parallel lines along diagonal in right lower quadrant.

Alignment: refers to an "attempt" (i.e., perfect execution not necessary) to align or connect outside attachments and internal sections with centerlines. Alignment of diagonals refers to an "attempt" to connect sections of each diagonal at midpoint junction of vertical and horizontal centerlines.

RCF-OSS Instructions

Level 7	Excellent Organization: Configural elements, the rectangle and centerlines, are completed first
Criteria	(a) Rectangle is drawn first (may include the left hand cross)
	(b) Both vertical and horizontal centerlines are drawn directly after the rectangle
	(c) All of the internal sections, outside attachments and the diagonals aligned with centerlines
Level 6	Conceptual Organization: Vertical and horizontal centerlines are drawn early
Criteria	(a) Either rectangle, contour, an internal section or outside attachment is drawn first
	(b) Both centerlines are drawn as whole single lines and are completed before drawing diagonals and internals sections
	(c) Diagonals are aligned with centerlines (i.e., meet at the midpoint juction)
	(d) Majority of internal sections and outside attachments are aligned with centerlines

(*continued*)

Table 6.2 (continued)   Rey Complex Figure process scoring criteria (RCF-OSS): general information and instruction.

Rey Complex Figure process scoring criteria
Level 5   Part-Configural Organization: Vertical and horizontal centerlines are present
Criteria   (a) Either rectangle, contour, an internal section or outside attachment is drawn first
(b) Both centerlines are present
(c) At least one internal section or outside attachment is aligned with vertical centerline, and at least one internal section or outside attachment is aligned with horizontal centerline
(d) At least one centerline is drawn as a whole single line, while remaining centerline can be completed fragmentally (i.e., in segments), although portions must connect
(e) A piecemeal approach is not adopted
Level 4   Piecemeal/Fragmented Organization: Piecemeal, fragmented or part-whole approach (subunits/sections are drawn sequentially piece by piece)
Criteria   (a) Either rectangle, contour, an internal section, or outside attachment is drawn first
(b) Only one centerline is completed as a whole single line unless the contour or rectangle is completed first, in which case, neither centerline can be completed as a whole
(c) Remaining internal sections and outside attachments are completed one at a time in a piecemeal manner (subsequent sections of drawing can be aligned with segments of centerlines)
Level 3   Random Organization: Only one complete centerline is used for alignment
Criteria   (a) Either rectangle, contour, an inside section, or outside attachment is drawn first
(b) One complete centerline aligned with at least one internal section/outside attachment is present (centerline can be completed fragmentally, i.e., in segments, although segments must connect)
(c) Remaining centerline, if present, is not utilized for alignment of other components
(d) If present, segments of an incomplete centerline can be utilized to align sections of drawing
(e) Piecemeal approach is not adopted
Level 2   Poor Organization: Criteria for levels 3–7 have not been satisfied
Criteria   (a) Any attempt to draw figure
(b) Any part of figure is drawn first
(c) If present, centerlines are not aligned to any of internal sections or outside attachments
(d) Piecemeal approach is not adopted
Level 1   Unrecognizable or Substitution: No attempt is made to draw figure. Child may draw a substitution or an unrecognizable scrawl

of their brain pathology. In contrast, children with frontal lobe involvement scored most poorly on organization, with productions characterized as piecemeal, fragmented, and poorly planned. Children with temporal lobe lesions performed similarly to controls on both measures (see Figure 6.9).

Using a similar design, Jacobs, Anderson, and Harvey (2002) compared children with focal frontal and extra-frontal lesions, global pathology and healthy controls

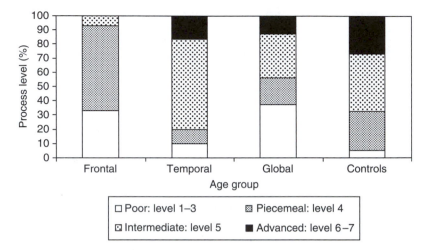

Figure 6.9   Rey Complex Figure process scores for children with frontal, extra-frontal, and global brain pathology, compared with healthy children. From "Assessing the validity of the Rey Complex Figure as a diagnostic tool: Accuracy, recall and organisational strategy scores in children with brain insult," by L. Matthews, V. Anderson, and P. Anderson, 2001, *Clinical Neuropsychological Assessment, 2*, pp. 85–100.

using a Tower of London paradigm. As with the Matthews study (2001), summary measures (total score, items correct) did not discriminate the groups. Rate scores (planning time, completion time) were also insensitive to group membership. In contrast, strategic problems, including rule breaks and perseverative errors, were higher for children with frontal lobe involvement (Figure 6.10). Using structural brain imaging, Levin et al. (1994) have also demonstrated the efficacy of this approach in children, showing correlations between errors and number of failed attempts on the Tower of London and frontal lobe pathology in their group of traumatically brain injured children, but no such association for the more multi-determined summary measures.

In summary, in order to establish valid and reliable assessment tools to tap EF in children, further research is essential. First, traditional tests need to be normed for children, to provide information with respect to age-appropriate test performances, thus enabling detection of deviant results. Second, rather than restricting interpretation to summary scores, maximum information should be obtained from these tests through a microanalysis of test performance, where individual test variables are considered and interpreted with respect to specific components of EF. Third, drawing on current knowledge from both adult neuropsychology and developmental psychology, new 'child friendly' procedures need to be designed and validated.

Future directions

Several lines of evidence now provide a picture of ongoing development of EF throughout childhood. Physiological research describes substantial CNS

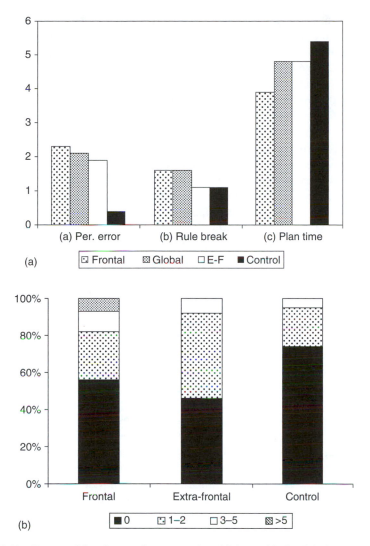

Figure 6.10   Tower of London performances for children with focal lesions and healthy controls. (a) Tower of London strategy scores for children with prefrontal pathology, global pathology, and healthy controls. (b) Tower of London failed attempts for children with focal or extra-frontal pathology and healthy controls. From "Planning and problem solving skills following focal frontal brain lesions in childhood: Analysis using the tower of London," by R. Jacobs, V. Anderson, and A. S. Harvey, 2002, *Child Neuropsychology, 8*, pp. 93–106.

development continuing, at least into early adulthood, with anterior cerebral regions maturing relatively late, and showing a series of growth spurts. Neuropsychological studies have also identified growth spurts represented by distinct improvements in performance on tests purported to measure EF. Further, there is a suggestion that these physiological and cognitive spurts may coincide, with transitions in cognitive development reflecting ongoing cerebral development.

The immaturity of EFs through childhood suggests that they may be vulnerable to the impact of early cerebral insult, where emerging and developing abilities have been noted to be particularly at risk (Dennis, 1989). The presence of dysexecutive syndrome early in life may have important implications for ongoing cognitive development. The lack of ability to attend, self-regulate, plan, reason, abstract, and think flexibly may impinge on a child's capacity to learn and benefit from the environment. Clinical observations of children with brain injury support this notion, with research also demonstrating the presence of residual executive dysfunction following early cerebral insult. To accurately describe the range of deficits associated with childhood brain insult, and provide appropriate treatment, neuropsychologists need to include measures tapping these skills in their assessment protocols. At present there are few useful tests of EF available for childhood populations. Of those currently employed, most have been designed for adult populations. Many lack standardized administration and scoring procedures. Few have adequate developmental norms, precluding accurate interpretation of developmentally appropriate levels of performance. Importantly, there have been few attempts to develop ecologically valid measures, which avoid the structure inherent in the clinical context and tap into day-to-day aspects of these complex skills. In consequence, clinicians are often required to base their analysis of EF on qualitative observation and contextual data.

In order to establish valid and reliable assessment of EF in children, further research is essential. First, traditional tests need to be normed for children, to provide information with respect to age-appropriate test performances, thus enabling detection of deviant results. Second, rather than restricting interpretation to summary scores, maximum information should be obtained from these tests through a micro-analysis of test performance, where individual test variables are considered and interpreted with respect to specific components of EF. Third, drawing on both adult tests and developmental psychology, new child friendly procedures need to be designed and validated. Further, current findings are largely based on cross-sectional studies. Longitudinal studies, mapping developmental trajectories for individual children, may provide additional insights into the pattern of development of EF through childhood.

References

Albert, M. S., & Kaplan, E. F. (1980). Organic implications of neuropsychological deficits in the elderly. In L. W. Poon, J. Fozard, L. Cermak, D. Arenberg, & L. W. Thompson (Eds.), *New directions in memory and aging: Proceedings of the George A. Talland Memorial Conference* (pp. 403–432). Hillsdale, NJ: Erlbaum.

Anderson, P. (2002). Assessment and development of executive function (EF) during childhood. *Child Neuropsychology, 8*(2), 71–82.

Anderson, P., Anderson, V., & Garth, J. (2001). Assessment and development of organisational ability: The Rey Complex Figure organisational strategy score (RCF-OSS). *The Clinical Neuropsychologist, 15*, 81–94.

Anderson, P., Anderson, V., & Lajoie, G. (1996). The Tower of London test: Validation and standardization for pediatric populations. *The Clinical Neuropsychologist, 10*, 54–65.

Anderson, P., Anderson, V., Northam, E., & Taylor, H. G. (2000). Standardization of the contingency Naming Test (CNT) for school-aged children: A measure of reactive flexibility. *Clinical Neuropsychological Assessment, 1*, 247–273.

Anderson, S. W., Bechara, A., Damasio, H., Tranel, D., & Damasio, A. R. (1999). Impairment of social and moral behavior related to early damage in human prefrontal cortex. *Nature Neuroscience, 2*, 1032–1037.

Anderson, V. (1988). Recovery of function in children: The myth of cerebral plasticity. In M. Matheson & H. Newman (Eds.), *Brain impairment* (pp. 223–247). Proceedings from the Thirteenth Annual Brain Impairment Conference, Sydney.

Anderson, V. (1998). Assessment of executive function in children. *Neuropsychological Rehabilitation, 8*, 319–349.

Anderson, V. (2002). Executive function in children: An introduction. *Child Neuropsychology, 8*, 69–70.

Anderson, V., Anderson, P., Northam, E., Jacobs, R., & Catroppa, C. (2001). Development of executive functions through late childhood and adolescence in an Australian sample. *Developmental Neuropsychology, 20*, 385–406.

Anderson, V., Anderson, P., Northam, E., Jacobs, R., & Mikiewicz, O. (2002). Relationships between cognitive and behavioral measures of executive function in children with brain disease. *Child Neuropsychology, 8*, 231–240.

Anderson, V., Bond, L., Catroppa, C., Grimwood, K., Nolan, T., & Keir, E. (1997). Childhood bacterial meningitis: Impact of age at illness and medical complications on long-term outcome. *Journal of the International Neuropsychological Society, 3*, 147–158.

Anderson, V., & Catroppa, C. (2005). Recovery of executive skills following pediatric traumatic brain injury (TBI): A two year follow-up. *Brain Injury, 19*(6), 459–470.

Anderson, V., Fenwick, T., Robertson, I., & Manly, T. (1998). Attentional skills following traumatic brain injury in children: A componential analysis. *Brain Injury, 12*, 937–949.

Anderson, V., Godber, T., Smibert, E., Weiskop, S., & Ekert, H. (2004). Impairments of attention following treatment with cranial irradiation and chemotherapy in children. *Journal of Clinical and Experimental Neuropsychology, 26*, 684–697.

Anderson, V., & Lajoie, G. (1996). Memory and information processing skills in children: A developmental neuropsychological model. *Applied Neuropsychology, 3/4*, 128–139.

Anderson, V., Lajoie, G., & Bell, R. (1995). *Neuropsychological assessment of the school-aged child*. Department of Psychology, University of Melbourne, Australia.

Anderson, V., Levin, H., & Jacobs, R. (2002). Developmental and acquired lesions of the frontal lobes in children: Neuropsychological implications. In D. Stuss & R. Knight (Eds.), *Principles of frontal lobe function*. Oxford University Press.

Anderson, V., Northam, E., Hendy, J., & Wrennall, J. (2001). *Developmental Neuropsychology: A Clinical Approach*. London: Psychology Press.

Asarnow, R. F., Satz, P., Light, R., Lewis, R., & Neumann, E. (1991). Behavior problems and adaptive functioning in children with mild and severe closed head injury. *Journal of Pediatric Psychology, 16*, 543–555.

Baddeley, A. (1986). *Working memory*. Oxford University Press.

Barbas, H. (1992). Architecture and cortical connections of the prefrontal cortex in the rhesus monkey. In P. Chauvel & A. Delgado-Esceuta (Eds.), *Advances in neurology* (pp. 91–115). New York: Raven Press.

Barnea-Goraly, N., Menon, V., Eckert, M., Tamm, L., Bammer, R., & Karchemskiy, A. (2005). White matter development during childhood and adolescence: A cross-sectional diffusion tensor imaging study. *Cerebral Cortex, 15*, 1848–1854.

Baron, I. (2004). *Neuropsychological evaluation of the child*. New York: Oxford University Press.

Bartsch, K., & Wellman, M. (1989). Young children's attribution of action to beliefs and desires. *Child Development, 60,* 946–964.

Barrish, J., Tranel, D., & Anderson, S. (2000). Acquired personality disturbances associated with bilateral damage to the ventromedial prefrontal region. *Developmental Neuropsychology, 18,* 355–381.

Becker, M. G., Isaac, W., & Hynd, G. (1987). Neuropsychological development of non-verbal behaviors attributed to the frontal lobes. *Developmental Neuropsychology, 3,* 275–298.

Bell, M. A., & Fox, N. A. (1992). The relations between frontal brain electrical activity and cognitive development during infancy. *Child Development, 63,* 1142–1163.

Benton, A. L. (1968). Differential behavioral effects of frontal lobe disease. *Neuropsychologia, 6,* 53–60.

Benton, A. L. (1991). Prefrontal injury and behavior in children. *Developmental Neuropsychology, 7,* 275–281.

Bjorkland, D. (1989). *Children's thinking: Developmental function and individual differences.* Pacific Cove, CA: Brooks/Cole.

Blakemore, C. (1974). Development of functional connections in the mammalian visual system. In R. Gaze & J. Keating (Eds.), *Development and regeneration in the nervous system. British Medical Bulletin, 30,* 152–157.

Brouwers, P., Riccardi, R., Poplack, D., & Fedio, P. (1984). Attentional deficits in long-term survivors of childhood acute lymphoblastic leukemia. *Journal of Clinical Neuropsychology, 6,* 325–336.

Caeser, P. (1993). Old and new facts about perinatal brain development. *Journal of Child Psychology and Psychiatry, 34,* 101–109.

Case, R. (1985). *Intellectual Development: Birth to Adulthood.* Orlando, FL: Academic Press.

Casey, B., Giedd, J., & Thomas, K. (2000). Structural and functional brain development and ots relation to cognitive development. *Biological Psychology, 54,* 241–257.

Chelune, G. J., & Baer, R. A. (1986). Developmental norms for the Wisconsin card sorting test. *Journal of Clinical and Experimental Neuropsychology, 8,* 219–228.

Chugani, H. T., & Phelps, M. E. (1986). Maturational changes in infants determined by 18FDG positron emission tomography. *Science, 231,* 840–843.

Chugani, H. T., Phelps, M. E., & Mazziotta, J. C. (1987). Positron emission tomography study of human brain functional development. *Annals of Neurology, 22,* 287–297.

Condor, A., Anderson, V., & Saling, M. (1996) Do reading disabled children have planning problems? *Developmental Neuropsychology, 11,* 485–502.

Couper, E., Jacobs, R., & Anderson, V. (2002). Adaptive behaviour and moral reasoning in children with frontal lobe lesions. *Brain Impairment, 3,* 105–113.

Damasio, A., Grabowski, T., Frank, R., Galaburda, A., & Damasio, H. (1994). The return of Phineas gage: Clues about the brain from the skull of a famous patient. *Science, 264,* 1102–1105.

Delis, D., Kaplan, I., & Kramer, J. (2001). *The Delis–Kaplan executive function system: Examiner's manual.* San Antonio, TX: Psychological Corporation.

De Luca, C., Wood, S., Anderson, V., Buchanan, J., Profitt, T., Mahoney, K., et al. (2003). Normative data from the CANTAB: Development of executive function over the lifespan. *Journal of Clinical and Experimental Neuropsychology, 25,* 242–254.

Dennis, M. (1989). Language and the young damaged brain. In T. Boll & B. K. Bryant (Eds.), *Clinical neuropsychology and brain function: Research, measurement and practice* (pp. 89–123). Washington: American Psychological Association.

Dennis, M., & Barnes, M. A. (1990). Knowing the meaning, getting the point, bridging the gap, and carrying the message: Aspects of discourse following closed head injury in childhood and adolescence. *Brain and Language, 39,* 428–446.

Dennis, M., Purvis, K., Barnes, M., Wilkinson, M., & Winner, E. (2001). Understanding of literal truth, ironic criticism and deceptive phrase following childhood head injury. *Brain and Language, 78*, 1–16.

D'Esposito, M., & Postle, B. (2002). The organization of working memory function in lateral prefrontal cortex: Evidence from event related functional MR. In D. Stuss & R. Knight (Eds.), *Principles of frontal lobe function* (pp. 168–187). New York: Oxford University Press.

Diamond, A. (2002). Normal development of prefrontal cortex from birth to young adulthood: Cognitive functions, anatomy, and biochemistry. In D. Stuss & R. Knight (Eds.), *Principles of frontal lobe function* (pp. 466–503). New York: Oxford University Press.

Diamond, A., & Goldman-Rakic, P. S. (1985). Evidence for involvement of prefrontal cortex in cognitive changes during the first year of life: Comparison of human infants and rhesus monkeys on a detour task with transparent barrier. *Neurosciences Abstracts (Pt. II), 11*, 832.

Diamond, A., & Goldman-Rakic, P. S. (1989). Comparison of human infants and rhesus monkeys on Piaget's AB task: Evidence for dependence on dorsolateral prefrontal cortex. *Experimental Brain Research, 74*, 24–40.

Didus, E., Anderson, V., & Catroppa, C. (2000). The development of pragmatic communication skills in head-injured children. *Pediatric Rehabilitation, 3*, 177–186.

Duncan, J. (1986). Disorganization of behavior after frontal lobe damage. *Cognitive Neuropsychology, 3*, 271–290.

Emslie, H., Wilson, F. C., Burden, V., Nimmo-Smith, I., & Wilson, B. (2003). *Behavioural assessment of dysexecutive syndrome for children*. Bury St Edmunds, UK: Thames Valley Test Company.

Eslinger, P., Flaherty-Craig, C., & Benton, A. (2004). Developmental outcomes after early prefrontal cortex damage. *Brain and Cognition, 55*, 84–103.

Espy, K. (2004). Using developmental, cognitive and neuroscience approaches to understand executive control in young children. *Developmental Neuropsychology, 26*, 379–384.

Espy, K. A. (1997). The Shape School: Assessing executive function in preschool children. *Developmental Neuropsychology, 13*(4), 495–499.

Espy, K., Kaufmann, P. M., Glisky, M., & McDiarmid, M. (2001). New procedures to assess executive functions in preschool children. *The Clinical Neuropsychologist, 15*, 46–58.

Espy, K., Kaufmann, P., McDiarmid, M., & Glisky, M. (1999). Executive functioning in preschool children: Performance on A-not-B and other delayed response format tasks. *Brain and Cognition, 41*, 178–199.

Ewing-Cobbs, L., Prasad, M., Landry, S., Kramer, L., & DeLeon, R. (2004). Executive functions following traumatic brain injury in young children: A preliminary analysis. *Developmental Neuropsychology, 26*, 487–512.

Fuster, J. (1993). Frontal lobes. *Current Opinion in Neurobiology, 3*, 160–165.

Fuster, J. (2002). Physiology of executive functions: The perception–action cycle. In D. Stuss & R. Knight (Eds.), *Principles of frontal lobe function* (pp. 96–108). New York: Oxford University Press.

Gaddes, W. H., & Crockett, D. J. (1975). The Spreen Benton Aphasia tests: Normative data as a measure of normal language development. *Brain and Language, 2*, 257–279.

Garth, J., Anderson, V., & Wrennall, J. (1997). Executive functions following moderate to severe frontal lobe injury: Impact of injury and age at injury. *Pediatric Rehabilitation, 1*, 99–108.

Gibbs, J. C., Basinger, K. S., & Fuller, D. (1992). *Moral maturity: Measuring the development of sociomoral reflection*. Hillsdale, NJ: Lawrence Erlbaum.

Giedd, J., Blumenthal, J., Jeffries, N., Castellanos, F., Lui, H., Zijdenbos, A., et al. (1999). Brain development during childhood and adolescence: A longitudinal MRI study. *Nature Neuroscience, 2,* 861–863.

Giedd, J., Snell, J., Lange, N., Rajapaske, J., Casey, B., Kozuch, P., et al. (1996). Quantitative magnetic resonance imaging of human brain development: Ages 4–18. *Cerebral Cortex, 6,* 551–560.

Gioia, G. A., Isquith, P. K., Guy, S. C., & Kenworthy, L. (2000). *Behavior rating inventory of executive function.* Odessa, FL: Psychological Assessment Resources.

Glosser, G., & Goodglass, H. (1990). Disorders in executive control functions among aphasic and other brain damaged patients. *Journal of Clinical and Experimental Neuropsychology, 12,* 485–501.

Gogtay, N., Giedd, J., Lusk, L., Hayashi, K., Greenstein, D., Vaituzis, C., et al. (2004). Dynamic mapping of human cortical development during childhood and early adulthood. *Proceedings of the National Academy of Science, 101,* 8174–8179.

Golden, C. (1981). The Luria-Nebraska children's battery: Theory and formulation. In G. W. Hynd & J. E. Obrzut (Eds.), *Neuropsychological assessment of the school-aged child* (pp. 277–302). New York: Grune & Stratton.

Goldman-Rakic, P. S. (1987). Development of cortical circuitry and cognitive function. *Child Development, 58,* 601–622.

Goldman-Rakic, P. S., & Leung, H. (2002). Functional architecture of the dorsolateral prefrontal cortex in monkeys and humans. In D. Stuss & R. Knight (Eds.), *Principles of frontal lobe function* (pp. 85–95). New York: Oxford University Press.

Grattan, L. M., & Eslinger, P. J. (1992). Long-term psychological consequences of childhood frontal lobe lesion in patient DT. *Brain and Cognition, 20,* 185–195.

Halford, G., & Wilson, W. (1980). A category theory approach to cognitive development. *Cognitive Psychology, 12,* 356–411.

Hale, S., Bronik, M., & Fry, A. (1997). Verbal and spatial working memory in school-aged children: Developmental differences in susceptibility to interference. *Developmental Psychology, 33,* 364–371.

Halperin, J. M., Healey, J. M., Zeitchik, E., Ludman, W. L., & Weinstein, L. (1989). Developmental aspects of linguistic and mnestic abilities in normal children. *Journal of Clinical and Experimental Neuropsychology, 11,* 518–528.

Heaton, R. K. (1981). *Wisconsin Card Sorting Test (WCST).* Odessa, FL: Psychological Assessment Resources.

Howard, L., & Polich, J. (1985). P300 latency and memory span development. *Developmental Psychology, 21,* 283–289.

Huttenlocher, P. (1990). Morphometric study of human cerebral cortex development. *Neuropsychologia, 28,* 517–522.

Jacobs, R., Anderson, V., & Harvey, A. S. (2001). Concept generation test: A measure of conceptual reasoning skills in children. Examination of developmental trends. *Clinical Neuropsychological Assessment, 2,* 101–117.

Jacobs, R., Anderson, V., & Harvey, A. S. (2002). Planning and problem solving skills following focal frontal brain lesions in childhood: Analysis using the tower of London. *Child Neuropsychology, 8,* 93–106.

Jacobs, R., Northam, E., & Anderson, V. (2001). Cognitive outcome in children with myelominingocele and perinatal hydrocephalus. *Journal of Developmental and Physical Disabilities, 13,* 389–405.

Jacques, S., & Zelazo, P. (2001). The Flexible Item Selection Task (FIST): A measure of executive function in preschoolers. *Developmental Neuropsychology, 20,* 573–591.

Jernigan, T. L., & Tallal, P. (1990). Late childhood changes in brain morphology observable with MRI. *Developmental Medicine and Child Neurology, 32*, 379–385.

Johnson, M. H. (2000). Functional brain development in infants: Elements of an interactive specialisation framework. *Child Development, 71*, 75–81.

Johnson, M. H. (2003). Development of human brain functions. *Biological Psychiatry, 54*, 1312–1316.

Kagan, J. (1966). Reflection-impulsivity: The generality and dynamics of conceptual tempo. *Journal of Abnormal Psychology, 71*, 17–24.

Kain, W., & Perner, J. (2001). Do children with ADHD not need their frontal lobes for theory of mind? A review of brain imaging and neuropsychological studies. In M. Brune, H. Ribbert, & W. Schiefenhovel (Eds.), *The social brain: Evolution and pathology* (pp. 197–230). Chicester, UK: John Wiley.

Kirk, U. (1985). Hemispheric contributions to the development of graphic skills. In C. Best (Ed.), *Hemispheric function and collaboration in the child* (pp. 193–228). New York: Academic Press.

Klinberg, T., Vaidya, C. J., Gabrieli, J. D., Moseley, M. E., & Hedehus, M. (1999). Myelination and organization of the frontal white matter in children: A diffusion tensor MRI study. *Neuroreport, 10*, 2817–2821.

Koenderink, M., Uylings, H., & Mrzljak, L. (1994). Post-natal maturation of the layer-III pyramidal neurons in the human prefrontal cortex: A quantitative golgi analysis. *Brain Research, 653*, 173–182.

Korkman, M., Kirk, U., & Kemp, S. (1998). *Manual for the NEPSY*. San Antonio, TX: Psychological Corporation.

Krikorian, R., Bartok, J., & Gay, N. (1994). Tower of London procedure: A standard method and developmental data. *Journal of Clinical and Experimental Neuropsychology, 16*, 840–850.

Landry, S. H., Jordan, T., & Fletcher, J. M. (1994). Developmental outcomes for children with spina bifida and hydrocephalus. In M. G. Tramontana & S. R. Hooper (Eds.), *Advances in child neuropsychology* (Vol. 2, pp. 85–118). New York: Springer-Verlag.

Lennenberg, E. (1967). *Biological foundations of language*. New York: Wiley.

Levin, H. S., Culhane, K. A., Hartmann, J., Evankovich, K., Mattson, A. J., Harward, H., et al. (1991). Developmental changes in performance on tests of purported frontal lobe functioning. *Developmental Neuropsychology, 7*, 377–395.

Levin, H. S., & Hanten, G. (2005). Executive functions after traumatic brain injury in children. *Pediatric Neurology, 33*, 79–93.

Levin, H. S., Mendelsohn, D., Lily, M. A., Fletcher, J. M., Culhane, K. A., Chapman, S. B., et al. (1994). Tower of London performance in relation to magnetic resonance imaging following closed head injury in children. *Neuropsychology, 8*, 171–179.

Levine, B., Stuss, D. T., & Milberg, W. P. (1995). Concept generation: Validation of a test of executive functioning in a normal aging population. *Journal of Clinical and Experimental Neuropsychology, 17*, 740–758.

Lezak, M. (1995). *Neuropsychological assessment*. New York: Oxford.

Lidow, M., & Goldman-Rakic, P. S. (1991). Synchronised overproduction of neurotransmitter receptors in diverse regions of the primate cerebral cortex. *Proceedings of the National Academy of Science, 88*, 10218–10221.

Logan, G. (1994). On the ability to inhibit thought and action. A user's guide to the stop signal paradigm. In D. Dagenbach & T. Carr (Eds.), *Inhibitory processes in attention, memory and language* (pp. 189–239). San Diego, CA: Academic Press.

Luciana, M., & Nelson, S. (1998). The functional emergence of frontally-guided working memory systems in four- to eight-year old children. *Neuropsychologia, 36*, 273–293.

Luna, B., Thulborn, R., Munoz, D., Merriam, E., Garver, K., & Minshew, N. (2001). Maturation of widely distributed brain function subserves cognitive development. *Neuroimage, 13*, 786–793.

Luria, A. R. (1973). *The working brain.* New York: Basic Books.

Manly, T., Anderson, V., Robertson, I., & Nimmo-Smith, I. (1999). *The test of everyday attention for children.* London: Thames Valley Test Company.

Mateer, C. A., & Williams, D. (1991). Effects of frontal lobe injury in childhood. *Developmental Neuropsychology, 7*, 69–86.

Matthews, L., Anderson, V., & Anderson, P. (2001). Assessing the validity of the Rey Complex Figure as a diagnostic tool: Accuracy, recall and organisational strategy scores in children with brain insult. *Clinical Neuropsychological Assessment, 2*, 85–100.

McKay, K. E., Halperin, J. M., Schwartz, S. T., & Sharma, V. (1994). Developmental analysis of three aspects of information processing: Sustained attention, selective attention, and response organization. *Developmental Neuropsychology, 10*, 121–132.

Meltzoff, A., Gopnik, A., & Repacholi, B. (1997). Toddlers' understanding of intentions, desires and emotions: Explorations of the dark ages. In P. Zelazo, J. Astington, & D. Olson (Eds.), *Developing theories of intention: Social understanding and self-control* (pp. 17–41). Mahwah, NJ: Erlbaum.

Mesulam, M. (2002). The human frontal lobes: Transcending the default mode through contingent encoding. In D. Stuss & R. Knight (Eds.), *Principles of frontal lobe function* (pp. 8–30). New York: Oxford University Press.

Miller, P. H., & Weiss, M. G. (1962). Children's attentional allocation, understanding of attention, and performance on the incidental learning task. *Child Development, 52*, 1183–1190.

Neisser, U. (1967). *Cognitive psychology.* New York: Appleton-Century-Crofts.

Orzhekhiovskaya, N. S. (1981). Fronto-striatal relationships in primate ontogeny. *Neuroscience and Behavioral Physiology, 11*, 379–385.

Parker, D. M., & Crawford, J. R. (1992). Assessment of frontal lobe dysfunction. In J. R. Crawford, D. M. Parker, & W. W. McKinlay (Eds.), *A handbook of neuropsychological assessment* (pp. 267–294). London: Lawrence Erlbaum Associates.

Passler, M. A., Isaac, W., & Hynd, G. W. (1985). Neuropsychological development of behavior attributed to frontal lobe functioning in children. *Developmental Neuropsychology, 1*, 349–370.

Pentland, L., Todd, J. A., & Anderson, V. (1998). The impact of head injury severity on planning ability in adolescence: A functional analysis. *Neuropsychological Rehabilitation, 8*, 301–317.

Piaget, J. (1963). *The origins of intelligence in children.* New York: W. W. Norton.

Porteus, S. (1950). *The Porteus Maze Test and intelligence.* Palo Alto, CA: Psychological Corporation.

Reiss, A., Abrams, M., Singer, H., Rosss, J., & Denckla, M. (1996). Brain development, gender and IQ in children. A volumetric imaging study. *Brain, 119*, 1763–1774.

Reitan, R. (1969). *Manual for administration of neuropsychological test batteries for adults and children.* Indianapolis, IN: Author.

Reitan, R., & Wolfson, D. (1985). *The Halstead–Reitan neuropsychological battery.* Tuscon, AR: Neuropsychological Press.

Rey, A. (1964). *L'examen clinique en psychologie.* Paris: Presses Universitaires de France.

Rolls, E. (2002). The function of the orbitofrontal cortesx. In D. Stuss & R. Knight (Eds.), *Principles of frontal lobe function* (pp. 354–375). New York: Oxford University Press.

Romine, C., & Reynolds, C. (2005). A model of the development of frontal lobe functioning: Findings from a meta-analysis. *Applied Neuropsychology, 12*, 190–201.

Shallice, T. (1982). Specific impairments of planning. *Philosophical Transcripts of the Royal Society of London, 298,* 199–209.

Shallice, T. (1990). *From neuropsychology to mental structure.* New York: Cambridge University Press.

Simon, H. A. (1975). The functional equivalence of problem solving skills. *Cognitive Psychology, 7,* 268–288.

Smidt, D., Jacobs, R., & Anderson, V. (2004). The Object Classification Task for Children (OCTC): A measure of concept generation and mental flexibility in early childhood. *Developmental Neuropsychology, 26,* 385–402.

Sodian, B., Taylor, C., Harris, P., & Perner, J. (1991). Early deception and the child's theory of mind: False trails and genuine markers. *Child Development, 62,* 468–483.

Sowell, E., Delis, D., Stiles, J., & Jernigan, T. (2001). Improved memory functioning and frontal lobe maturation between childhood and adolescence: A structural MR study. *Journal of the International Neuropsychological Society, 7,* 312–322.

Sowell, E., Thompson, P., Holmes, C., Batth, R., Jernigan, T., & Togaa, A. (1999). Localizing age-related change in brain structure between childhood and adolescence using statistical parametric mapping. *Neuroimage, 9,* 587–597.

Sowell, E., Thompson, P., Welcome, S., Henkenius, A., Toga, A., & Peteresen, B. (2003). Cortical abnormalities in children and adolescents with attention deficit/hyperactivity disorder. *Lancet, 362,* 1699–1707.

Stehbens, J. A., Kaleita, T. A., Noll, R. B., MacLean, W. E., O'Brien, R. T., Waskerwitz, M. J., et al. (1991). CNS prophylaxis of childhood leukemia: What are the long term neurological, neuropsychological and behavioral effects? *Neuropsychological Review, 2,* 147–177.

Stuss, D. T. (1992). Biological and psychological development of executive functions. *Brain and Cognition, 20,* 8–23.

Stuss, D., & Alexander, M. (2000). Executive functions and the frontal lobes: A conceptual view. *Psychological Research, 63,* 289–298.

Stuss, D., & Anderson, V. (2004). The frontal lobes and theory of mind: Developmental concepts from adult focal lesion research. *Brain and Cognition, 55,* 69–83.

Stuss, D. T., & Benson, D. F. (1986). *The frontal lobes.* New York: Raven Press.

Stuss, D., Toth, J., Franchi, D., Alexander, M., Tipper, S., & Craik, F. (1999). Dissociation of attentional processes in patients with focal frontal and posterior lesions. *Neuropsychologia, 37,* 1005–1027.

Taylor, H. G., & Fletcher, J. M. (1990). Neuropsychological assessment in children. In G. Goldstein & M. Herson (Eds.), *Handbook of psychological assessment* (2nd ed., pp. 228–255).

Thatcher, R. W. (1991). Maturation of the human frontal lobes. Physiological evidence for staging. *Developmental Neuropsychology, 7,* 397–419.

Thatcher, R. W. (1992). Cyclical cortical reorganization during early childhood. *Brain and Cognition, 20,* 24–50.

Todd, J. A., Anderson, V. A., & Lawrence, J. (1996). Planning skills in head injured adolescents and their peers. *Neuropsychological Rehabilitation, 6,* 81–89.

Toga, A. W., Thompson, P., & Sowell, E. (2006). Mapping brain maturation. *Trends in Neuroscience, 29,* 148–159.

Tranel, D. (2002). Emotion, decision making and the ventromedial prefrontal cortex. In D. Stuss & R. Knight (Eds.), *Principles of frontal lobe function* (pp 338–353). New York: Oxford University Press.

Waber, D. P., & Holmes, J. M. (1985). Assessing children's copy productions of the Rey-Osterreith Complex Figure. *Journal of Clinical and Experimental Neuropsychology*, *7*, 264–280.

Walsh, K. W. (1978). *Neuropsychology: A clinical approach*. New York: Churchill Livingston.

Walsh, K. W. (1985). *Understanding brain damage: A primer of neuropsychological evaluation*. New York: Churchill Livingston.

Wansart, W. (1990). Learning to solve a problem: A microanalysis of the solution strategies of children with learning disabilities. *Journal of Learning Disabilities*, *23*, 164–170.

Wechsler, D. (1991). *Manual for the Wechsler Scale of children's intelligence-III*. New York: Psychological Corporation.

Welsh, M. C., & Pennington, B. F. (1988). Assessing frontal lobe functioning in children: Views from developmental psychology. *Developmental Neuropsychology*, *4*, 199–230.

Welsh, M. C., Pennington, B. F., & Groisser, D. B. (1991). A normative-developmental study of executive function: A window on prefrontal function in children. *Developmental Neuropsychology*, *7*, 131–149.

Yakovlev, P. I. (1962). Morphological criteria of growth and maturation of the nervous system in man. *Research Publications Association for Research in Nervous and Mental Disease*, *39*, 3–46.

Yakovlev, P. I., & Lecours, A. R. (1967). The myelogenetic cycles of regional maturation of the brain. In A. Minkiniwski (Ed.), *Regional development of the brain in early life* (pp. 3–70). Oxford, England: Blackwell.

Zelazo, P., Craik, F., & Booth (2004). Executive function across the life span. *Acta Psychologia*, *115*, 167–183.

7 Assessment of executive functioning in older adults

Tracey Wardill and Vicki Anderson

Contents

As a consequence of the aging of our population, clinicians are increasingly being asked to assess the cognitive functioning of older people. This chapter addresses important issues in the assessment of cognition, and in particular, executive functioning, in older adults. More specifically, we describe the nature of our aging population, and discuss the relationship between health status and cognition. We also propose suitable approaches to the cognitive assessment of older people, in particular appropriate measures of executive function (EF) in the aged, and present the age-related changes in executive functioning that occur in older adults. Case studies will be presented to illustrate the issues raised in this chapter.

Critical to the assessment of executive functioning in older adults is an understanding of what constitutes a normal performance on measures of EF. To examine this question, data obtained from a recent study on normal cognitive performance in healthy older adults in the age range 65–94 (Wardill, 2003) will be presented. Not only can this normative data be used by clinicians to evaluate an individual's performance, but it also provides information on how the aging process impacts on executive functioning.

Aging, illness, and cognition

Although age 65 is an arbitrary cutoff point, it is commonly used to define the aged population. In the 1950s, just under 10% of the Australian population were aged 65 and over. By 1998 this figure had increased to 12%, and is projected to increase to 16% by 2016 (ABS, 1996). The annual rates of increase are higher for the aged than for the population as a whole, with rates of increase highest amongst the very old, those 80 years and over. In 1996, nearly half a million Australians were aged over 80, an increase of 5% since 1976. By 2016 over 800,000 Australians, representing

24% of the aged population, will be over 80 years of age (Gibson, Benham, & Racic, 1999). Similar trends with respect to the proportion of aged people within the population are found worldwide. Given the aged suffer from an increased incidence of illness, disease, and disability, this aging of the population, now a characteristic of all developed nations, has significant implications for health management and the provision of health services.

Many diseases that have a higher prevalence in the aged affect brain functioning and, as a consequence, impact on cognition and behavior. Thus, an increasing need to accurately assess the cognitive performance of the aged can be expected. If aged patients are to be appropriately treated and managed, accurate diagnosis of cognitive disorders is vital. An awareness of the range of conditions that can impact on the cognitive performance of older people is essential if those working with the aged are to diagnose cognitive dysfunction.

A principal feature of an aging population is an increase in dementia. Many disorders, including dementia of the Alzheimer's type, fronto-temporal dementia (see chapter 15, this volume), dementia with Lewy bodies and cortico-basal degeneration all impact directly on cognitive functioning. Other degenerative disorders, such as Parkinson's disease, can result in measurable changes in cognitive performance (see chapter 16, this volume). All these disorders can potentially impact on executive functioning. Clinicians working with the aged require a detailed knowledge of the various degenerative disorders and their different presentations.

Like the dementias, the incidence of vascular disease increases with age. Strokes can have a direct impact on cognitive performance, depending on the location and severity of the event. The aged, however, may also suffer from more subtle forms of vascular disease such as hypertension and cardiovascular disease, which have been associated with changes in cognitive performance (Hertzog, Schaie, & Gribbin, 1978; Spieth, 1964). For example, chronic hypertension has been reported to impact on performance of various measures, including cognitive screening measures and tests of psychomotor speed, memory, learning, and executive abilities (Starr, 1999; Viitanen & Guo, 1997). Although Elias (1998) stresses that hypertensive patients should not be characterized as cognitively impaired, he concludes that. "... there is an increased risk of lowered cognitive functioning and accelerated decline in cognitive ability associated with both untreated and chronic hypertension ..." (p. S52). Hypotension has also been associated with changes in cognitive performance (Guo, Viitanen, & Winblad, 1997; Keefover, 1998; Sands & Meredith, 1992).

In a similar vein, there are a number of systemic diseases that can impact on cognition. Non-insulin-dependent diabetes mellitus (NIDDM), for example, has the potential to alter central nervous system function (Mooradian, 1997). Difficulties in the learning and recall of new information, and disturbances of working memory have been described (Perlmutter et al., 1984; Tun, Nathan, & Perlmutter, 1990). Keefover (1998) notes that the deleterious effects of diabetes, including cognitive changes, may not become apparent for many years after the onset of the disease process. Consequently, the impact of NIDDM on cognition may be more apparent in older people.

Hyper- and hypothyroidism are more common in older people (Keefover, 1998) and both are thought to impact on cognitive functioning. Hypothyroidism can result in poor memory, cognitive slowing, and disturbances in attention, concentration, and mood. Hyperthyroidism can lead to anxiety, restlessness, tremor, emotional lability, and sleep disturbance (see Bäckman, Small, Wahlin, & Larsson, 2000). Similarly, vitamin B_{12} deficiency can result in impairments in attention and memory, and a slowing in mental processes (van Goor, Woiski, Lagaay, Meinders, & Tal, 1995). Sleep apnea has a higher incidence in the older population (Hayward et al., 1992), and can result in a range of cognitive difficulties, including changes in intellectual efficiency, attention and concentration, memory, and executive functioning (see Rourke & Adams, 1996).

Psychiatric conditions, such as major depression and anxiety, can be associated with cognitive abnormalities. Depressed people of any age group frequently complain of memory and concentration difficulties (King and Caine, 1996). For older people, grief associated with major life events, such as retirement, the death of a spouse, or the loss of friends of similar age, can also result in disturbances of cognitive functioning (Carman, 1997).

The impact of medication on cognitive performance also assumes particular importance in the elderly, given the increased utilization of medications with age (Berg & Dellasega, 1996; Gilbert, Luszcz, & Owen, 1993; Petersen, Whittington, & Payne, 1979). Psychotropic medications including anxiolytics, hypnotics, and antidepressants are reported to have a negative, cumulative effect on cognition (Berg & Dellasega, 1996). Some antidepressant medications can impair attention, concentration and aspects of memory (Knegtering, Eijck, & Huijsman, 1994), and the aging brain can be particularly sensitive to benzodiazepines (Closser, 1991). Such drugs may result in a decline in cognitive performance in the aged, especially on memory tasks (Foy et al., 1995).

Gray, Lai, and Larson (1999) note that in addition to higher rates of medication use, age-related alterations in pharmacokinetics and pharmacodynamics increase the likelihood that some medications will have a greater impact on cognition in the aged. Research suggests that the elderly may be more susceptible to the impact of medications because of the age-related changes that occur in liver and kidney functioning (Kayne, 1978). Given the higher use of medications in the aged, their greater sensitivity to medication effects, and the potential for various medications to impact on cognitive performance, it is important that current medications are considered when assessing the cognitive performance of older adults.

Finally, it is also important to consider that some illnesses impact differently on older people. As a result, what are relatively trivial disorders for younger patients can cause a major disturbance of cognition in the elderly. For example, a urinary tract infection is a common cause of acute confusion or delirium in the elderly (Rummans, Evans, Krahn, & Fleming, 1995). In general, the aged are more susceptible to developing a delirium (Keefover, 1998), and in this population, the acute cognitive disturbance associated with delirium can take some time to resolve.

In summary, the range of illnesses, conditions, and medications that can potentially impact on cognitive performance in the aged is broad and more extensive than that seen in younger people. This has important implications. In the clinical arena, cognitive changes that signify the onset of pathological brain changes, or reflect a potentially treatable illness, must be distinguished from those that occur as part of the normal aging process. In other words, clinicians working with the aged must be able to distinguish between normal and pathological aging. This requires an awareness of the range of disorders and conditions which can potentially cause cognitive change in this population, and an understanding of what constitutes a normal cognitive performance in the aged based on experience and reliable normative data.

Executive function and aging

While precise definitions may vary, executive functions are generally considered to encompass those skills required for purposeful, planned, goal-directed activity (Luria, 1966; Shallice, 1982; Stuss & Benson, 1986). Contemporary models acknowledge that EF is an umbrella term covering a number of separate but interacting components. The model of EF described by Anderson (2002) proposes four distinct domains of EF: information processing, attentional control, cognitive flexibility, and goal setting. These domains are considered to be discrete functions, related to specific frontal systems but which operate in an integrated manner.

The anatomical underpinnings of executive functions are complex. In simple terms, however, it is the anterior regions of the brain which are considered to mediate executive functioning. It is well documented that damage to the frontal lobes can lead to executive dysfunction (Stuss et al., 1994; Walsh, 1987). Complex neural connections, however, link the prefrontal cortex and other regions of the brain. Disconnection of these pathways due to white matter damage, or impairments in other brain regions, can also result in executive dysfunction.

Executive functions are often considered to be particularly vulnerable to the aging process. The frontal systems hypothesis proposes that executive functioning may decline as part of the normal aging process. This theory of age-related cognitive change has arisen, at least in part, as a result of neuroanatomical findings, which suggest that age-related brain changes appear to be selective, rather than global. The findings in many studies have focused attention on the frontal lobes as one possible area that may be particularly vulnerable to age-related changes. Changes in volume in the frontal lobes (Coffey et al., 1992; Pfefferbaum, Sullivan, Rosenbloom, Mathalon, & Lim, 1998), or in subcortical nuclei that are structurally and functionally associated with the prefrontal cortex (Jernigan et al., 1991) are reported. Shrinkage of cells in the frontal lobes has also been described (Haug & Eggers, 1991; Terry, DeTeresa, & Hansen, 1987).

Some authors have proposed that the major structural changes seen in the brain with age are white matter changes (Guttmann et al., 1998; Meier-Ruge, Ulrich, Bruhlmann, & Meier, 1992). Guttman et al. (1998) found a highly significant decrease in white matter with age, whereas gray matter showed only minimal age-related change. Salat, Kaye, and Janowsky (1999) also found an age-related decline in white matter volume, particularly in subjects over 85 years of age. At a microscopic level, a breakdown in myelin has been hypothesized (Peters, 1994). Age-related white matter loss will reduce the efficiency of neural networks, including frontal systems, leading to a disruption of EF in older adults.

The frontal systems hypothesis of aging has a long tradition. Over a quarter of a century ago, Albert and Kaplan (1980) proposed that age-related changes in the frontal lobes and their subcortical connections could explain a number of the cognitive changes observed in older adults. Support for this theory, however, has been mixed. In a review of the literature Kaszniak and Newman (2000) cite age-related changes on frontal lobe tests such as Verbal Fluency and the Wisconsin Card Sorting Test (WCST: Axelrod & Henry, 1992). Boone, Miller, Lesser, Hill, & D'Elia (1990), however, found few statistically significant differences between the perform-ance of subjects in their 50s, 60s, and 70s on four tests proposed to measure frontal lobe functioning: WCST, Stroop Test, Auditory Consonant Trigrams, and Verbal Fluency. Importantly, the subjects in the Boone study were carefully screened for evidence of neurological, medical, or psychiatric conditions that could affect central nervous system functioning. The screening included neurological examinations, electroencephalography (EEG), and magnetic resonance imaging (MRI). Boone et al. (1990) concluded that changes in performance on frontal lobe tests were a reflection of the poor health status of the subjects being examined. These findings are in keeping with even earlier proposals (Willis, Yeo, Thomas, & Garry, 1988) that, "changes in executive or frontal lobe skills may be more a reflection of the increasing prevalence of illness in the elderly than a reflection of age-related brain changes" (p. 27).

Mixed findings regarding the frontal systems hypothesis of aging may reflect methodological factors such as the inadequate screening of study samples, the use of different measures of EF, and the age of the subjects under investigations. Studies such as those of Boone et al. (1990) only examined subjects up to age 80. Some authors have found changes in performances on measures of executive functioning only when subjects reach their 80s (e.g., Haaland, Vranes, Goodwin, and Garry (1987) on WCST; Benton, Eslinger, and Damasio (1981) on a Verbal Fluency Test). This raises the possibility, addressed later in this chapter, that if changes in EF occur in the aged they only become evident in those over 80.

Approaches to the cognitive assessment of older adults

For clinicians, the assessment of executive functioning forms a central role in the cognitive assessment of older adults. As noted earlier, many of the conditions that can impact on cognitive performance in the aged can result in impairments in EF. Appropriate assessment of EF, therefore, can be crucial for the accurate *diagnosis* of a range of cognitive disorders. The assessment of executive functioning can also be central to the assessment of an older person's *capacity* to drive, and to make informed financial, legal, medical, and lifestyle decisions. It is often impaired executive functioning which proves the crucial factor in deciding that an older person lacks the capacity to make informed decisions.

If clinicians are to obtain reliable test results in the assessment of EF in older adults, their clinical practice must be based on a sound approach. In order to cater to the particular needs of this population, the assessment approach needs to be flexible and capable of adapting to the needs of the individual. Although it can be argued that this should be the case for all age groups, it takes on particular importance with older adults. Whereas many older patients present as robust and healthy, and have no difficulties applying themselves throughout the assessment, more common are issues of physical frailty, sensory loss, medical comorbidities, and negative or inappropriate attitudes toward testing.

Approaches to testing fall into two major traditions (Kaszniak, 1990). The first relies on the administration of a fixed battery of standard tests. Other information about the patient is incorporated after the test results have been obtained and analyzed (Mitrushina, Boone, & D'Elia, 1999). While the fixed-battery approach allows for the systematic acquisition of data on a wide range of tests, this approach is time consuming and does not allow for consideration of the individual needs of the patient (Mitrushina et al., 1999). Further, Palmer, Boone, Lesser, and Wohl (1998) cite a number of studies, which have shown that when cutoff scores from one well-known battery—Halstead–Reitan Neuropsychological Battery (HRNB)—are used to evaluate the performance of healthy elderly subjects, a high rate of false positives is seen. The fixed-battery approach, therefore, is unsuitable for use with this population because (1) it can be too arduous for the aged patient, and (2) it may result in the over diagnosis of pathology.

The over diagnosis of pathology in the aged can have particular ramifications. When older people demonstrate signs suggestive of cognitive dysfunction, there is a tendency to attribute these changes to a degenerative process, and a label of dementia may be inappropriately applied. This, in turn, can result in significant restrictions on an older person's independence. The ability to live alone, to make lifestyle or financial decisions, and even to drive, can all be brought into question following a diagnosis of dementia. Avoiding the over diagnosis of pathology in older people is important if we are to ensure that limitations to their independence and significant lifestyle changes are not made unnecessarily.

The second approach to the assessment of cognitive functioning adopts a qualitative, flexible, hypothesis testing model (LaRue, 1992; Lezak, 1995; Walsh, 1991). An extreme example of this approach is reflected in the work of Luria, which relies almost exclusively on qualitative observations of a patient's performances on various measures (Luria, 1966). The more contemporary approach to the hypothesis testing model, however, draws on both quantitative and qualitative information. Clinicians working within this model will tend to utilize a core group of tests and then draw on other measures as appropriate.

In the hypothesis testing model, the specific tests chosen for administration will be based on a priori hypotheses developed by the clinician. These hypotheses will be guided by the nature of the referral question, the circumstances surrounding the assessment, and the characteristics of the patient under consideration. The patient's medical and psychiatric history, a collaborative history obtained from family or carers, the results of medical investigations including brain imaging, the patient's occupational and educational background, and self-reports of cognitive difficulties, are all taken into consideration. Given the behavior changes which can result from executive dysfunction, observations of the patient's behavior during the assessment are also critical. Further decisions related to test selection will be made as a result of the patient's performance, and can occur during the assessment process. The cognitive assessment, therefore, is tailored to the individual.

From a clinician's perspective the more flexible hypothesis testing model is well suited for use with the geriatric population. This approach takes into account issues including physical frailty, fatigue, sensory and hearing impairments, medical comorbidities, and motivation toward the assessment process. Of importance with this population, the hypothesis testing approach ensures that unnecessarily long assessments are avoided. Consequently, poor performances on the tests administered are more likely to be the result of actual cognitive impairment, rather than the result of fatigue, or a reflection of the patient being overwhelmed by a lengthy battery of tests. Furthermore, this approach ensures that referral questions can be answered in a timely manner, so that important diagnostic information and practical implications of the findings can be quickly relayed to treating doctors and patients' families.

A wide range of tests is available, which can be used by clinicians working within the hypothesis testing model to obtain information on a patient's EF. In the geriatric setting, however, Bryan and Luszcz (2000) stress the need to employ tests of EF that are suitable for use with older adults. They advocate the use of measures which are not too tiring or overwhelming for this population. When choosing tests of EF for use with older adults, an additional consideration is the availability of normative data. Many EF measures that may be suitable for use with older adults lack appropriate normative data which have been obtained from well-screened samples.

Normative data are the means by which clinicians can determine the normality of a patient's cognitive performance. In obtaining such normative data, researchers must be vigilant in ensuring that research protocols distinguish between the impact of disease and the impact of age on cognitive performance. As Bäckman et al. (2000) note, "Given that health conditions increase in very old age, the failure to assess these conditions will inevitably overestimate the size of normal age-related change in late-life cognitive performance" (p. 521). The health status of older adults, therefore, must be considered when developing normative data for use with this population.

Our research on the cognitive performance of aged Australians (Wardill, 2003) was designed to obtain normative data on tests which were suitable for use with older adults. The tests utilized in our study, including measures of EF, were chosen after surveying experienced neuropsychologists working throughout Australia, where the flexible hypothesis testing model has a strong tradition. Clinicians currently working in the geriatric setting, or with past experience or particular interest in geriatric neuropsychology, were asked to nominate the tests they commonly used in the assessment of the aged. This allowed us to determine which measures of cognitive functioning were most commonly used in clinical practice with aged patients in Australia. The tests utilized in our study, therefore, were considered appropriate for use with the aged population and generated normative data which can be applied with confidence when assessing elderly Australians. Data from a number of the measures administered in the study also provide specific information on EF decline in older adults. Before presenting the findings from this study, it is important to discuss the crucial issue of sample selection.

Sample selection

Normative studies must give careful consideration to the health status of the subjects from which data are obtained, especially when it involves older adults. For our

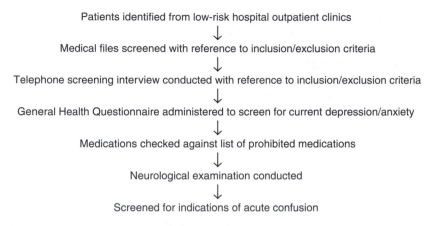

Figure 7.1   Subject selection process.

study the subjects were obtained using a rigorous selection process, as outlined in Figure 7.1. Medical files were examined and detailed screening interviews were conducted with reference to the study's inclusion and exclusion criteria (see Tables 7.1 and 7.2). These were developed with the assistance of a range of medical specialists and designed to exclude those with health conditions that could potentially impact on cognitive performance. This allowed us to examine the impact of the aging process on cognitive functioning independent from the effects of illnesses and diseases that can accompany aging.

Details of the sample utilized in our study are provided in Table 7.3. There were no statistically significant differences between the age groups in terms of their years of education. Education is often found to be a predictor of performance on cognitive tasks, and correlated with performance on all but one of the EF measures discussed in this chapter. Frequently, however, normative data are obtained from samples with educational backgrounds which do not reflect that of the general population. In this study, the sample was representative of the older Australian population in terms of educational background with the majority of Australians aged over 65 having 10 years or less of formal education. Although this may seem a relatively low level of education by modern standards, educational experiences may be influenced by, amongst other things, political crises, and societal expectations. For people in the age range from which our sample was drawn, the Great Depression and World War II resulted in many people leaving school at a relatively early age. In this cohort, a low educational level reflects a lack of opportunity rather than a low level of

Table 7.1   Inclusion criteria.

Age 65 years or older
Fluent in English
Adequate vision and hearing, with aids if necessary, to undertake testing
Physically well enough to cope with the demands of testing

Table 7.2 Exclusion criteria.

Exclusion criteria	Definition
1. Depression	Current depressive illness (General Health Questionnaire) or documented history of major depressive illness in the last 12 months. Treatment with ECT in the last 12 months.
2. Anxiety state	Current moderate or severe anxiety (General Health Questionnaire).
3. History of major psychotic illness	History or current evidence of psychotic illness, including a diagnosis of schizophrenia, bi-polar affective disorder, delusional disorder, schizoaffective disorder, and schizophreniform disorder.
4. Hypertension	Existing uncontrolled hypertension (systolic >180 mmHg or diastolic >95 mmHg). Previous controlled hypertension for more than 5 years duration.
5. Hypotension	Symptomatic postural hypotension with a drop of >20 mmHg on standing or asymptomatic postural drop in blood pressure of >50 mmHg in the systolic reading. Asymptomatic systolic blood pressure of 90 mmHg or less.
6. Cerebrovascular disease	Documented history of stroke. CT evidence of small or large vessel infarction whether asymptomatic or symptomatic. Symptomatic transient ischemic attack. Asymptomatic carotid stenosis of >80%. History of carotid endarterectomy. Unexplained true syncope (one in last 12 months or three in previous 5 years). Syncope secondary to postural hypotension (>20 mmHg) or cardiac disease. Diagnosis of vertebro-basilar insufficiency.
7. Cardiovascular disease	Poorly controlled (daily) angina. Documented myocardial infarction. Coronary artery bypass graft surgery. Valvular surgery. Angioplasty. Moderate congestive cardiac failure (SOB at <100 yards walking).
8. Dementia and major neurological disorders	Diagnosis of dementia. Documented cognitive impairment. Diagnosis of epilepsy. Peripheral or central neurological disorders that may be associated with cognitive impairment.
9. Substance abuse/ dependence	Current alcohol, drug, or other substance abuse/dependence or any history of substance abuse/dependence (DSM 111-R criteria). Any history of a 10-year period (or longer) when average daily intake of alcohol exceeded 40 g for men and 20 g for women.
10. Traumatic brain injury	History of head injury meeting one of following criteria: LOC > 20 min, PTA > 24 hr, Hospital admission >3 days because of traumatic brain injury (i.e., not only orthopedic). Mild head injury in last 5 years: LOC < 20 min, PTA < 24 hr, hospital admission <3 days.
11. Chronic uremia	Chronic renal impairment currently requiring dialysis, or being considered for dialysis. Any recent or sustained creatinine level of >.2 or urea level of >20.

(*continued*)

Table 7.2 (continued)   Exclusion criteria.

Exclusion criteria	Definition
12. Diabetes	Insulin-dependent diabetes or mature-onset diabetes requiring medication.
13. Thyroid dysfunction	Treated hypothyroidism or a history of hyperthyroidism in the last 5 years.
14. Endocrinology	Addison's disease, Cushing's disease, hyperlipodemia or hypercholesterolemia. Currently on steroid treatment. Prednisolone dose of ≤ 10 mg for arthritis is acceptable (must be at this dose for at least 4 weeks if previously on higher dose.) Exclude if prednisolone prescribed for neurological reasons.
15. Pernicious anemia	Well-documented B_{12} deficiency.
16. Sleep disorders	Diagnosis of sleep apnea.
17. Recent major surgery	Surgery requiring general anesthetic >1 hr within last 6 months.
18. Recent significant bereavement	Within last 6 months.
19. Delirium	History of delirium (according to DSM 111 – R criteria) within last 12 months.
20. Confusion/disorientation	Any indication at interview and utilizing orientation questions from the MMSE and WMS 1, of confusion/disorientation.
21. Prohibited medications	Antipsychotics, hypnotics, tricyclics, non-tricyclic antidepressants; benzodiazepines; mood stabilizers/anticonvulsants.

intellectual ability. For our sample, in which 70% of subjects obtained 10 years or less of education, the mean IQ score was 105 on the WAIS-R.

To determine the impact of gender on task performance, roughly equal numbers of men and women were included in the sample. Gender, however, did not correlate significantly with any of the measures discussed in this chapter.

Only 5% of the sample was working at the time of inclusion in the study. Socio-economic status (SES), therefore, was established by rating subjects' main previous occupations using the Daniel's Scale of Occupational Prestige (Daniel, 1983). This

Table 7.3   Age, gender, and education characteristics of the sample by age group.

Age (years)	N	Mean age (SD)	Men	Women	Education (years) M (SD)
65–69	50	67.14 (1.51)	26	24	10.48 (2.82)
70–74	51	72.22 (1.39)	30	21	9.71 (1.84)
75–79	51	77.02 (1.58)	27	24	10.49 (2.40)
80+	48	83.38 (3.17)	23	25	9.38 (2.39)
Total	200	74.85 (6.29)	106	94	10.02 (2.42)

scale rates occupations between 1 and 7, where a score of 1 reflects high SES, and a score of 7 refers to low status. This sample obtained a mean score of 4.94 (SD = 1.08), with no significant difference in the SES of the four age groups ($p = .58$).

Performance of older adults on measures of executive functioning

To understand the impact of the normal aging process on EF, we examine data obtained from this sample of 200 elderly Australians. The four domains proposed by Anderson (2002) in his model of EF will be used to examine performance across four age groups (65–69 years; 70–74 years; 75–79 years; and 80 years and older).

Information processing refers to "fluency, efficiency, and speed of output" (Anderson, 2002, p. 74). We used performance on the FAS test (Benton & Hamsher, 1978) and Part A of the Trail Making Test (TMT) (Reitan, 1979) to assess age-related changes in this aspect of EF.

On the FAS test, subjects in our study were required to generate as many words as possible, in 60 seconds, beginning with the letter F, A, and S. They were required to adhere to rules whereby proper nouns, repetitions, or providing the same stem word with different endings were not allowed. In our sample, age was not a significant predictor of performance on this test ($r = -.03$). This relative stability in performance with age is consistent with previous findings such as those of Bolla, Lindgren, Bonaccorsy, and Bleecker (1990), Crossley, D'Arcy, and Rawson (1997) and Troyer (2000).

TMT Part A is a timed paper and pencil test, which also provides data on the fluency, efficiency, and speed of subjects' output. In contrast to FAS, however, it involves a motor component. In our sample, there was a significant correlation between age and performance on Part A of the TMT ($r = .25$).

As can be seen in Table 7.4, a linear relationship was observed between age and time taken to complete Trails A, with a significant difference between the youngest (65–70 years) and oldest (80+ years) age groups. Taken together, these findings suggest that for adults aged 65 and over, the information processing aspect of EF remains stable but some motor slowing is seen in those 80 and over.

The domain of *attentional control* refers to the capacity to "selectively attend to specific stimuli and inhibit prepotent responses, and the ability to focus attention for a prolonged period" (Anderson, 2002, p. 73). Of those tests commonly used in the assessment of aged patients, errors made on the FAS test and the TMT Part A provide information about this aspect of EF in the normal aged.

Table 7.4   Results of performance on the trail making test.

Age group	65–69 (n = 49) M (SD)	70–74 (n = 48) M (SD)	75–79 (n = 49) M (SD)	80+ (n = 46) M (SD)	F
TMT: Part A	39.55 (12.14)	44.14 (12.75)	44.53 (14.76)	51.37 (16.00)	5.74
TMT: Part B	117.22 (63.55)	129.65 (63.55)	131.43 (61.59)	199.72 (91.80)	13.51
TMT: AB ratio	1.99 (1.05)	2.00 (1.12)	2.11 (1.49)	2.98 (1.70)	5.68

Note: All group differences <.001.

In our sample, the overall number of errors made by older adults on FAS was low and there was no association with age, education, or gender. The mean number of total errors made on this task was 2.14 (SD = 2.10) with a range of 0–8. Similarly, only five subjects made errors on Trails A. These data indicate that the attentional control aspect of EF is not impacted on by age in our sample of older adults.

A decline in performance on the FAS test is often cited as support for the frontal system hypothesis of aging (Kaszniak & Newman, 2000), and patients with frontal lobe dysfunction are reported to demonstrate reduced word retrieval and an increase in errors (Lezak, 1995; Walsh, 1987). This was not the pattern of performances seen in our normal aged sample.

The *cognitive flexibility* domain of EF encompasses "the ability to shift between response sets, learn from mistakes, devise alternative strategies, divide attention and process multiple sources of information" (Anderson, 2002, p. 74). Data from the TMT Part B, which requires the subject to shift between alternative sets of stimuli, provide information on this aspect of EF. Another useful measure of cognitive flexibility is the AB ratio on the TMT. This measure, where the time to complete Part B is expressed as a ratio of Part A, was developed by Stuss and Binns (2002) in an attempt to isolate the shifting demands of Part B from the visual search and rapid motor responses common to both parts of the test.

In our sample of older adults, there was a relationship between age and performance on both Part B and the AB ratio of the TMT. The mean scores obtained by the four age groups are presented in Table 7.4. Post hoc analyses revealed that the 80+ subgroup performed significantly slower than the three younger age groups. These data suggest that cognitive flexibility may remain stable up to 80 years of age after which time performance begins to decline. In support of these findings, previous normative data for this measure also fails to identify significant age-related decrements until age 80 (Stuss & Binns, 2002).

Results obtained from performance on the Color Form Sorting (CFS) Test (Goldstein & Scheerer, 1941; Weigl, 1941), also support the notion that cognitive flexibility may decline in those over 80 years of age. This test assesses the ability to identify the concepts of color and shape, and the ability to shift between these concepts. Administration of this task is a relatively easy way of examining cognitive flexibility in older adults, and unlike the measures discussed, this task is not timed.

Performance on the CFS was measured by allocating a subject's performance to one of six categories based on their ability to identify the concepts, name them, and shift between the two concepts. These six categories of sorting were then collapsed into two levels: "abstract" performance (categories 1 and 2); "concrete" performance (categories 3–6). Abstract performance refers to the capacity to recognize and verbalize both concepts and to shift between the concepts with either a single prompt or no prompting at all. Table 7.5 contains information on the percentage of subjects in each age group who produced an abstract and concrete performance. A significant difference is evident in the performance of those subjects 80 years and older.

On the CFS, over 80% subjects in the age range 65–79 performed the task without any difficulty, or required only minimal prompting to sort by both color and shape, and to verbalize the concepts involved. For subjects aged 80 years and over, however, a wider range of performances was evident. Half of the subjects in this

Table 7.5 Color form sorting: Percentage of subjects in each age group x performance group.

Age group	65–69	70–74	75–79	80+
Abstract performance (%)	84	92	88	49
Concrete performance (%)	16	8	12	51

Note: $p < .001$.

age group produced a concrete performance, that is, they required prompting to shift between concepts and were unable to verbalize both concepts. It appears, therefore, that even on a task that is not timed, many of our oldest adults, those aged 80 and over, experience age-related changes in their performance on tasks that require them to shift their attention between concepts. These findings are consistent with Levine, Stuss, and Milberg (1995), who identified age-based differences in the elderly on the Concept Generation Test.

The *goal setting* domain of EF involves the capacity to develop initiatives and concepts, to plan and organize, and the ability to approach tasks efficiently (Anderson, 2002). The data already presented on the CFS suggests that adults aged 80 and over have more difficulty forming concepts under conditions where they are required to shift mental set. Data on the ability to form concepts, where a shifting component was not required, were obtained by examining subjects' performances on the similarities subtest of the WAIS-R (Wechsler, 1981). As seen in Table 7.6, a slight linear relationship with age was observed on this measure, with those subjects aged 80 years and over performing at a significantly lower level than the other three age groups. These findings are consistent with previous studies that have also found a decline in these abilities for those over 80 (Haaland et al., 1987; Talland, 1961), and no age-related effects for those aged under 80 (Boone et al., 1990). Thus, concept formation appears to decline substantially in many of those aged 80 and over.

Older adults planning and organizing skills were examined using data from the Rey Complex Figure (RCF) test (Osterrieth, 1944; Rey, 1941). This is a complex copying task, commonly used in the assessment of aged patients. Relatively quick and easy to administer, it is a multifactorial task which, among other things, can provide information on a patient's planning and organizational abilities. Data on a patient's organizational skills can be obtained by examining the approach taken in copying the complex figure. The scoring method developed by Anderson, Anderson, and Garth (2001) was used to obtain an organizational or "process" score for our

Table 7.6 Performance on the WAIS-R: Scaled scores (uncorrected for age) for four age groups.

Age group	65–69 (n = 50)	70–74 (n = 51)	75–79 (n = 51)	80+ (n = 48)	F
Similarities M (SD)[a]	8.46 (2.15)	7.94 (2.34)	7.71 (2.15)	6.35 (2.32)	7.82
Block Design M (SD)[a]	8.46 (2.31)	7.73 (2.24)	6.96 (1.65)	6.02 (1.45)	14.07

[a] $p < .001$.

Table 7.7   Rey Complex Figure organization score–percentage
of each age group *x* organizational strategy.

Age group	65–69	70–74	75–79	80+
Poor (%)	20	31	31	54
Part-configural (%)	70	51	61	39
Conceptual (%)	10	18	8	7

Note: $p = .01$.

subjects, with performance rated from level 1 to 7. Following Anderson et al. (2001), we classified strategic organization of reproductions as "poor," "part-configural," or "conceptual." As illustrated in Table 7.7, subjects aged 75 and over were less likely to adopt a conceptual approach to the task and subjects in the oldest age group were more likely to adopt a poor strategy.

A similar pattern of results was obtained by our subjects on the Block Design subtest from the WAIS-R (see Table 7.6). This task requires subjects to utilize planning and organizing skills to manage novel problems and information, under timed conditions. Our data revealed a significantly lower level of performance for those over 80 compared to all other age groups, and for those aged 75 and over compared to the youngest age group. These data suggest that planning and organizational skills may begin to decline in the late 70s, with difficulties becoming more apparent for those aged over 80.

In summary, our data indicate that, for older adults who are free of diseases which could impact on their cognitive functioning, the attentional control and information processing aspects of EF, remain relatively stable in old age. For the other domains of EF there is evidence of change for many of those aged 80 and over. More of those aged 80 and over experience difficulties on tasks requiring cognitive flexibility and concept formation. For many in this age group, tasks requiring goal setting, planning, and organization, may also prove more difficult. While the data suggest that difficulties with this domain of EF may begin to become apparent for some in their late 70s, the problems become more evident in the ninth decade of life.

Case studies

Many of the issues which are important in the assessment of EF in older adults, can be illustrated by the case of AB, a 73-year-old man with moderate hearing impairment, who had been admitted to the medical ward of a major hospital with pneumonia. AB had responded well to treatment of his pneumonia and was keen to return home to live alone. Staff on the ward, however, were concerned by the fact that he appeared to be demonstrating memory difficulties. In what is a reasonably common scenario for those working with the aged, a cognitive assessment was requested to determine AB's ability to make informed lifestyle and financial decisions; issues crucial to his future.

The assessment of AB's cognition had to be tailored to his specific situation. First, consideration was given to the fact that his pneumonia could have caused an acute disturbance of his cognitive functioning. Initial contact with AB revealed no signs of acute confusion which would have suggested a delirium. A history obtained from his neighbors revealed evidence of difficulties managing at home dating back at least 12 months. For example, neighbors reported that he appeared to be losing weight and were concerned that he was not shopping or cooking for himself on a regular basis. He appeared more disheveled than he had been in the past, and they had found rotting food in his fridge. They were concerned that there appeared to be unpaid bills lying around his home, and he did not seem to reliably remember information they told him.

The tests administered to AB needed to take into account his sensory loss and the noisy testing environment of a hospital ward. An even moderately lengthy, fixed battery of tests would not be appropriate, nor would tests which relied solely on the accurate processing of verbal information. Impaired performances in these circumstances could easily be a reflection of AB's sensory difficulties and the testing environment rather than his actual cognitive capacity.

On interview, AB did not believe that he was experiencing any cognitive problems. He denied experiencing any difficulties managing in the home environment and was adamant that he would not need any assistance when he returned home. AB was alert and co-operative, his behavior was appropriate, and his mood appeared euthymic.

AB's test results are provided in Table 7.8. He was oriented for place, year, and month. He had difficulty recalling any details of major newsworthy events which

Table 7.8 AB's test results.

Test	AB's scores	Age norms M (SD)/ASS
Lhermitte SLT		
No. correct per trial	4,5,4,6,7,7,8,8,9,8	3.57* (1.73)
Delayed recall	5	7.79 (1.44)
Savings (%)	55%	87% (14.91)
FAS (total words)	18	PS 33
CFS	Category 4	4% of subjects in this age
	One sort, unable to shift	group obtained this score
RCF		
Copy	22	32.37 (3.21)
Recall	4	15.21 (6.25)
Organization	3	4.59 (1.12)
WAIS-R		
Information	RS 24	ASS 13
Block Design	RS 10	ASS 6
Similarities	RS 11	ASS 7

*   The score, 3.57 represents the mean number of trials to reach two errorless trials.

Note: SLT: Spatial Learning Test; FAS: Verbal Fluency Test; CFS: Color Form Sorting Test; RCF: Rey Complex Figure; WAIS-R: Wechsler Adult Intelligence Scale-Revised; PS: predicted score using regression-based norms, ASS: age-scaled scores; RS: raw score. The data in column 3 are from Wardill, T. D. (2003). Cognitive function in the Australian aged: A normative study. PhD thesis. University of Melbourne.

had occurred in recent months and weeks. Testing revealed that memory was impaired across a range of measures. Performance on the Lhermitte spatial learning task, where information was presented visually, and only a pointing response was required, was impaired for his age. He had difficulty learning new information and, of the material acquired, only 55% was retained after a delay.

Assessment of AB's executive functioning was crucial in determining his capacity to return home to live alone and to manage his own affairs. A range of measures designed to tap all four domains of EF were administered. AB produced a total of only 18 words on the FAS and made five rule breaking errors. He was only able to identify and verbalize a single concept on the CFS and was unable to shift to a second concept, even when prompted. Simple copying tasks were completed without difficulty; however, AB's copy of the Rey figure was disorganized (see Figure 7.2), and his copy and recall scores were both impaired for his age. His performances on the Block Design subtest from the WAIS-R fell in the "borderline" range on our age appropriate norms. His performance on the Similarities subtest also fell well below expected levels. In contrast, performance on the Information subtest fell in the "above average" range for age, in keeping with premorbid expectations for someone who had previously been a sales manager. AB's performances on all domains of EF, including information processing, attentional control, cognitive flexibility, and goal setting, were impaired when referenced to our age appropriate norms. AB's lack of insight also suggested executive dysfunction.

It could be concluded with confidence that AB was suffering from memory and executive difficulties which were not the result of age-related cognitive decline.

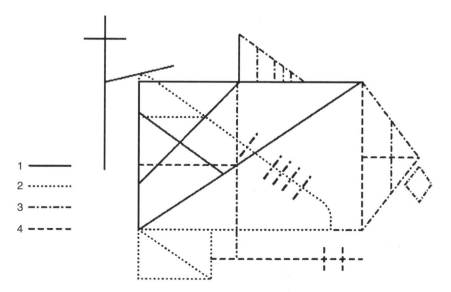

Figure 7.2   AB's copy of the Rey figure.

Subsequent investigations revealed evidence of widespread cerebrovascular disease. As a result of AB's executive dysfunction, including his impaired insight, he was considered to lack the ability to make informed lifestyle or financial decisions. A guardian and administrator were subsequently appointed.

The case of LD also illustrates the importance of the accurate assessment of executive functioning in the aged. LD was an 88-year-old woman referred to a memory clinic with a provisional diagnosis of dementia. Six months earlier she had presented to the Emergency Department of her local hospital complaining of "light-headedness". While at the hospital she was noted to be asking "odd questions," and appeared unable to recall relevant personal information. Around the same time she underwent two driving tests, both of which she failed, and her licence was cancelled. She subsequently had no recall of these assessments.

Following these events her local doctor believed she was suffering from dementia. He requested a formal diagnosis to assist in planning for her future. He expressed concerns about her ability to continue to live at home with her elderly husband and about her decision-making capacity.

When seen for assessment LD complained of some mild memory difficulties, but believed she was managing well at home. She confirmed that she had no recall of her driving assessments. There was no evidence to suggest depressed mood and LD readily engaged in the assessment process. Her family reported that over the last year or two she had appeared more rigid and inflexible in her thinking. She appeared to have some difficulties coping with more complex problems associated with the management of her financial affairs, and did not cope as well if there were changes to her routine. Her memory could be unreliable at times, particularly if required to remember a large amount of information, or when she was unwell. Based on her family's reports, she was not demonstrating rapid forgetting of new information.

On testing LD was well oriented and recalled some details of recent newsworthy events. Her performances on measures of her memory, visuospatial, and language functioning fell within normal limits on our age appropriate norms. Reports from the family had raised some concerns about LD's executive functioning. Her performances on a range of measures of EF, including FAS, Block Design, Similarities, and TMT Parts A and B, were evaluated using normative data obtained from our subjects aged 80 and over. All her performances fell within the average range for her age, in keeping with estimates of her premorbid level of functioning (Table 7.9). Her copy of the Rey figure stands in contrast to that of AB (see Figure 7.3), despite the fact that she was 15 years older. The difficulties with cognitive flexibility, goal setting, and planning, which had been observed by her family at a functional level were felt to be a result of age-related change rather than a degenerative process. The difficulties she had demonstrated 6 months earlier appeared to have been transient and were considered to have been related to a possible subacute delirium associated with moderate hyponatremia.

LD's local doctor and family could subsequently be reassured that her cognition was normal for her age and that she was not suffering from dementia. She retained decision-making capacity but her family provided support to assist her with the management of the more complex aspects of her financial affairs. She was able to remain living at home with her elderly husband.

Table 7.9   LD's test results.

Test	LD's scores	Age norms M (SD)/ASS
Lhermitte SLT		
No. correct per trial	6,8,9,9	3.57* (1.73)
Delayed recall	8	7.79 (1.44)
Savings (%)	88%	87% (14.91)
Hopkins VLT		
Total recall over 3 trials	18	19.33 (5.0)
Discrimination index	10	10.9 (1.12)
Savings (%)	75	81.76 (23.1)
RCF		
Copy	35	30.23 (3.50)
Recall	11	10.51 (4.97)
Organization	7	3.98 (1.11)
WAIS-R		
Information	RS 17	ASS 10
Block Design	RS 12	ASS 9
Similarities	RS 15	ASS 11
Trail Making Test (TMT)		
Part A (seconds)	47	51.37 (16.0)
Part B (seconds)	165	199.72 (91.80)
AB ratio	3.5	2.98 (1.70)
Boston Naming Test	55	50.3 (6.14)
FAS (total words)	32	PS 30

*   The score, 3.57 is the mean number of trials to reach two errorless trials.

Note: SLT: Spatial Learning Test; FAS: Verbal Fluency Test; VLT: Verbal Learning Test; RCF: Rey Complex Figure; WAIS-R: Wechsler Adult Intelligence Scale-Revised; PS: predicted score using regression-based norms, ASS: age-scaled scores; RS: raw score. The data in column 3 are from Wardill, T. D. (2003). Cognitive function in the Australian aged: A normative study. PhD thesis. University of Melbourne.

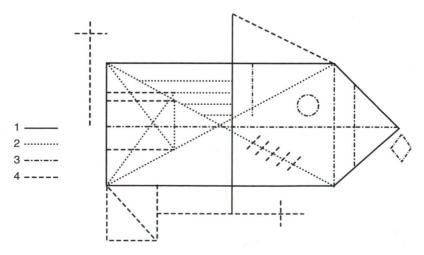

Figure 7.3   LD's copy of the Rey figure.

Conclusions

As a result of our aging population, the numbers of older people presenting for accurate diagnosis of cognitive disorders and assessment of cognitive capacity will continue to increase. If clinicians are to adequately meet the demands imposed by an aging population a number of issues need to be addressed. Consideration must be given to how we approach the assessment of cognitive functioning in older adults. The approach adopted when assessing the older members of our population needs to take into account the particular characteristics of many in this group. The flexible hypothesis testing model caters well to the demands of this population. It allows consideration of any sensory impairments, medical conditions or physical frailties the patient may suffer and can be adapted to potential time limitations imposed by the patient's condition or situation.

Executive functioning is a complex and multifaceted aspect of cognition. Consequently, many of the tests commonly used to measure EF are complex and lengthy. Some EF tests administered to older people may prove overwhelming due to the person's medical condition, general frailty, or sensory impairments. Thus, impaired performances may result due to the inappropriate nature of the task and not as the result of executive dysfunction. Poor performance by an older adult on a highly complex EF task, therefore, does not necessarily equate to executive dysfunction.

As with the assessment of any cognitive domain, reliance on a single measure of EF to detect impairment can lead to diagnostic errors. A pattern of difficulties on a range of measures of EF provides the best means of detecting the presence of cognitive difficulties of this nature. Further, while test selection is important, behavioral observations remain crucial in the diagnosis of executive difficulties. Of importance, the normal aged do not display the behavioral problems of apathy, disinhibition, or obvious personality changes, which can be the hallmarks of fronto-temporal dementia, as described by Snowden (chapter 15).

In order to accurately interpret the performance of older adults on EF tests, appropriate normative data are required. When selecting normative data, it is important to be aware of the health status of the sample from which the norms were obtained. A review of the exclusion criteria adopted in many normative data studies reveals a disturbing lack of detail and a clear failure to exclude many conditions that can potentially affect cognitive performance in older people. Of importance in our study, not all people with health problems were excluded. Health problems are more common in the aged. To avoid obtaining a pristinely healthy and, hence, unrepresentative sample, those with health conditions which would not impact on cognitive performance were included. As we have done, however, normative samples should exclude subjects with conditions that potentially impact on cognitive performance. The norms can then be used to distinguish between age and disease.

If clinicians are to adequately assess and diagnose cognitive disorders in the aged they must be aware of the pattern of age-related changes in cognition. A striking finding from our study was that a steady, progressive decline in functioning across our sample of older adults was not observed on any of the measures administered to our subjects, including measures of EF. A number of measures showed a subtle but insignificant decline in performance across the age groups. A significant decrement in performance, however, occurred only after age 80. While the results obtained from our age-restricted sample may show significant differences in performance if compared to younger samples, for those aged 65 years and over, the picture is not one of a steadily *progressive* cognitive decline with increasing age.

The data obtained in our study support previous findings which indicate that variability in performance is a feature of the aged population (Albert, Duffy, & Naeser, 1987; LaRue, 1992; Malec, Ivnik, & Smith, 1993; Salthouse, 1999; Schaie, 1990). Of importance, even when there was a significant decline in performance for those in the oldest age group, many of these older subjects continued to perform at a level comparable to subjects in the younger age groups. Our findings suggest that the spectrum of normality for those aged over 80 is wider than that observed in people in their late 60s and 70s. Consequently, it is crucial that the cognitive performances of patients over the age of 80 are compared to performances of people their own age. Our findings caution against merely extrapolating from data obtained on younger subjects, even from subjects in their 70s. Norms for aged people that combine data for all those 65 and older in the one data group are not appropriate.

Our findings do not support a simple hypothesis which proposes that frontal lobe changes account for age-related cognitive decline. Rather, our findings are consistent with previous research which identified changes in aspects of EF in those aged 80 and over. It is apparent that when considering evidence pertaining to the frontal hypothesis of aging, important factors to bear in mind are the health status and the age of the subjects being examined, and the measures of EF which are being utilized in the research.

Finally, our findings regarding the age-related changes in different domains of EF are interesting from a life span perspective. As outlined in Anderson's chapter on executive functioning in childhood and adolescence (chapter 6), recent theories propose that specific domains of EF may display varying developmental trajectories. Anderson documents findings which support the notion that the attentional control aspect of EF appears to be the earliest executive skill to emerge. Cognitive flexibility is thought to develop next, followed by the later development of goal setting skills. If we examine performances on measures of EF at the other end of the life span, our data also reveal varying trajectories of decline for different domains of EF. Attentional control remains the most stable in older adults; some changes in cognitive flexibility become apparent in those over 80; and the most obvious age-related changes in EF are apparent on goal setting tasks. It appears, therefore, that those EF skills which are acquired earliest remain the most resistant to the ageing process, while those developed last appear to show the most age-related change.

References

ABS. (1996). Population by age and sex: States and Territories of Australia (Cat.No.3201.0). Canberra: Australian Bureau of Statistics.

Albert, M. S., Duffy, F. H., & Naeser, M. (1987). Nonlinear changes in cognition with age and their neuropsychologic correlates. *Canadian Journal of Psychology, 41*(2), 141–157.

Albert, M. S., & Kaplan, E. (1980). Organic implications of neuropsychological deficits in the elderly. In L. W. Poon, J. L. Fozard, L. S. Cermak, D. Arenberg, & L. W. Thompson (Eds.), *New directions in memory and aging* (pp. 403–432). Hillsdale, NJ: Erlbaum.

Anderson, P. (2002). Assessment and development of executive function (EF) during childhood. *Child Neuropsychology*, *8*(2), 71–82.

Anderson, P., Anderson, V., & Garth, J. (2001). Assessment and development of organizational ability: The Rey Complex Figure organizational strategy score (RCF-OSS). *The Clinical Neuropsychologist*, *15*(1), 81–94.

Axelrod, B. N., & Henry, R. R. (1992). Age-related performance on the Wisconsin card sorting, similarities, and controlled oral word association tests. *Clinical Neuropsychologist*, *6*(1), 16–26.

Bäckman, L., Small, B. J., Wahlin, A., & Larsson, M. (2000). Cognitive functioning in very old age. In F. I. M. Craik, & T. A. Salthouse (Eds.), *The handbook of aging and cognition* (2nd ed., pp. 499–558). Hillsdale, NJ: Erlbaum.

Benton, A. L., Eslinger, P. J., & Damasio, A. R. (1981). Normative observations on neuropsychological test performances in old age. *Journal of Clinical Neuropsychology*, *3*(1), 33–42.

Benton, A. L., & Hamsher, K. (1978). *Multilingual Aphasia Examination Manual*. Iowa City, IA: AJA Associates.

Berg, S., & Dellasega, C. (1996). The use of psychoactive medications and cognitive function in older adults. *Journal of Aging & Health*, *8*(1 February), 136–149.

Bolla, K. I., Lindgren, K. N., Bonaccorsy, C., & Bleecker, M. L. (1990). Predictors of verbal fluency (FAS) in the healthy elderly. *Journal of Clinical Psychology*, *46*(5), 623–628.

Boone, K. B., Miller, B. L., Lesser, I. M., Hill, E., & D'Elia, L. (1990). Performance on frontal lobe tests in healthy, older individuals. *Developmental Neuropsychology*, *6*(3), 215–223.

Bryan, J., & Luszcz, M. (2000). Measurement of executive function: Considerations for detecting adult age differences. *Journal of Clinical and Experimental Neuropsychology*, *22*(1), 40–55.

Carman, M. B. (1997). The psychology of normal aging. *The Psychiatric Clinics of North America*, *20*(1 March), 15–24.

Closser, M. (1991). Benzodiazepines and the elderly: A review of potential problems. *Journal of Substance Abuse and Treatment*, *8*, 35–41.

Coffey, C. E., Wilkinson, W. E., Parashos, I. A., Soady, S. A., Sullivan, R. J., Patterson, L. J., et al. (1992). Quantitative cerebral anatomy of the aging human brain: A cross-sectional study using magnetic resonance imaging. *Neurology*, *42*(3, Pt. 1), 527–536.

Crossley, M., D'Arcy, C., & Rawson, N. S. B. (1997). Letter and category fluency in community-dwelling Canadian seniors: A comparison of normal participants to those with dementia of the Alzheimer or vascular type. *Journal of Clinical and Experimental Neuropsychology*, *19*(1), 52–62.

Daniel, A. (1983). *Power, privilege and prestige: Occupations in Australia*. Melbourne: Longman Cheshire.

Elias, M. F. (1998). Effects of chronic hypertension on cognitive functioning. *Geriatrics*, *53* (Suppl. 1), S49–S52.

Foy, A., O'Connell, D., Henry, D., Kelly, J., Cocking, S., & Halliday, J. (1995). Benzodiazepine use as a cause of cognitive impairment in elderly hospital inpatients. *Journals of Gerontology: Medical Sciences*, *50*, 99–106.

Gibson, D., Benham, C., & Racic, L. (1999). *Older Australia at a glance* (2nd ed.). Canberra: Australian Institute of Health and Welfare.

Gilbert, A., Luszcz, M., & Owen, N. (1993). Medication use and its correlates among the elderly. *Australian Journal of Public Health, 17*(1 March), 18–22.

Goldstein, K., & Scheerer, M. (1941). Abstract and concrete behavior: An experimental study with special tests. *Psychological Monographs, 53*(No. 2), Whole No. 239.

Gray, S. L., Lai, K. V., & Larson, E. B. (1999). Drug-induced cognition disorders in the elderly: Incidence, prevention and management. *Drug Safety, 21*(2 August), 101–122.

Guo, Z., Viitanen, M., & Winblad, B. (1997). Clinical correlates of low blood pressure in very old people: The importance of cognitive impairment. *Journal of the American Geriatrics Society, 45*, 701–705.

Guttmann, C. R. G., Jolesz, F. A., Kikinis, R., Killiany, R. J., Moss, M. B., Sandor, T., et al. (1998). White matter changes with normal aging. *Neurology, 50*(April), 972–978.

Haaland, K. Y., Vranes, L. F., Goodwin, J. S., & Garry, P. J. (1987). Wisconsin Card Sort Test performance in a healthy elderly population. *Journal of Gerontology, 42*(3), 345–346.

Haug, H., & Eggers, R. (1991). Morphometry of the human cortex cerebri and corpus striatum during aging [comment]. *Neurobiology of Aging, 12*(4), 336–338; discussion 352–355.

Hayward, L., Mant, A., Eyland, A., et al. (1992). Sleep disordered breathing and cognitive function in a retirement village population. *Age & Ageing, 21*, 121.

Hertzog, C., Schaie, K. W., & Gribbin, K. (1978). Cardiovascular disease and changes in intellectual functioning from middle to old age. *Journal of Gerontology, 33*(6), 872–883.

Jernigan, T. L., Archibald, S. L., Berhow, M. T., Sowell, E. R., Foster, D. S., & Hesselink, J. R. (1991). Cerebral structure on MRI, Part I: Localization of age-related changes. *Biological Psychiatry, 29*(1), 55–67.

Kaszniak, A. W. (1990). Psychological assessment of the aging individual. In J. E. Birren, & K. W. Schaie (Eds.), *Handbook of the psychology of aging* (3rd ed., pp. 427–445). San Diego, CA: Academic Press.

Kaszniak, A. W., & Newman, M. C. (2000). Toward a neuropsychology of cognitive aging. In S. H. Qualls, & N. Abeles (Eds.), *Psychology and the aging revolution* (pp. 43–67). Washington, DC: American Psychological Association.

Kayne, R. C. (1978). *Drugs and the elderly*. Los Angeles: University of Southern California Press.

Keefover, R. W. (1998). Aging and cognition. *Neurologic Clinics of North America, 16*(3 August), 635–648.

King, D. A., & Caine, E. D. (1996). Cognitive impairment and major depression: Beyond the pseudodementia syndrome. In I. Grant, & K. M. Adams (Eds.), *Neuropsychological assessment of neuropsychiatric disorders* (2nd ed., pp. 200–217). New York: Oxford University Press.

Knegtering, H., Eijck, M., & Huijsman, A. (1994). Effects of antidepressants on cognitive functioning of elderly patients. A review. *Drugs & Aging, 5*(3 September), 192–199.

LaRue, A. (1992). *Aging and neuropsychological assessment*. New York: Plenum Press.

Levine, B., Stuss, D. T., & Milberg, W. P. (1995). Concept generation: Validation of a test of executive functioning in a normal aging population. *Journal of Clinical and Experimental Neuropsychology, 17*(5), 740–758.

Lezak, M. D. (1995). *Neuropsychological assessment* (3rd ed.). New York: Oxford University Press.

Luria, A. R. (1966). *Higher cortical functions in man*. New York: Basic Books.

Malec, J. F., Ivnik, R. J., & Smith, G. E. (1993). Neuropsychology and normal aging. In R. W. Parks, R. F. Zec, & R. S. Wilson (Eds.), *Neuropsychology of Alzheimer's disease and other dementias*. New York: Oxford University Press.

Meier-Ruge, W., Ulrich, J., Bruhlmann, M., & Meier, E. (1992). Age-related white matter atrophy in the human brain. *Annals New York Academy of Science, 673*, 260–269.

Mitrushina, M. N., Boone, K. B., & D'Elia, L. F. (1999). *Handbook of Normative Data for Neuropsychological Assessment*. New York: Oxford University Press.

Mooradian, A. D. (1997). Pathophysiology of central nervous system complications in diabetes mellitus. *Clinical Neuroscience, 4*(6), 322–326.

Osterrieth, P. A. (1944). Le test de copie d'une figure complexe. *Archives de Psychologie, 30*, 206–356; translated by J. Corwin, & F. W. Bylsma (1993) *The Clinical Neuropsychologist, 1997*, 1999–1915.

Palmer, B. W., Boone, K. B., Lesser, I. M., & Wohl, M. A. (1998). Base rates of "impaired" neuropsychological test performance among healthy older adults. *Archives of Clinical Neuropsychology, 13*(6), 501–511.

Perlmutter, L. C., Hakami, M. K., Hodgson-Harrington, C., Ginsberg, J., Katz, J., Singer, D. E., et al. (1984). Decreased cognitive function in aging non-insulin-dependent diabetic patients. *American Journal of Medicine, 77*(6 December), 1043–1048.

Peters, A. (1994). Structural changes in the normally aging cerebral cortex of primates. *Progressive Brain Research, 136*, 455–465.

Petersen, D. M., Whittington, F. J., & Payne, B. P. (1979). *Drugs and the elderly: Social and pharmacological issues*. Springfield, IL: Charles C Thomas.

Pfefferbaum, A., Sullivan, E. V., Rosenbloom, M. J., Mathalon, D. H., & Lim, K. O. (1998). A controlled study of cortical gray matter and ventricular changes in alcoholic men over a 5-year interval. *Archives of General Psychiatry, 55*(10), 905–912.

Reitan, R. M. (1979). *Manual for Administration of Neuropsychological Test Batteries for Adults and Children*. Tuscon, AZ: Neuropsychology Laboratory.

Rey, A., 28, 286–340. (1941). L'examen psychologique dans les cas d'encephalopathie traumatique. *Archives de Psychologie, 28*, 286–340. Psychological examination in cases of traumatic encephalopathy. Sections translated by J. Corwin, & F. W. Bylsma, *The Clinical Neuropsychologist, 1993*, 1994–1999.

Rourke, S. B., & Adams, K. M. (1996). The neuropsychological correlates of acute and chronic hypoxemia. In I. Grant, & K. M. Adams (Eds.), *Neuropsychological assessment of neuropsychiatric disorders* (2nd ed., pp. 379–402). New York: Oxford University Press.

Rummans, T. A., Evans, J. M., Krahn, L. E., & Fleming, K. C. (1995). Delirium in elderly patients: Evaluation and management. *Mayo Clinic Procedures, 70*(October), 989–998.

Salat, D. H., Kaye, J. A., & Janowsky, J. S. (1999). Prefrontal gray and white matter volumes in healthy aging and Alzheimer disease. *Archives of Neurology, 56*(March), 338–344.

Salthouse, T. A. (1999). Theories of cognition. In K. W. Schaie (Ed.), *Handbook of theories of aging* (pp. 196–208). New York: Springer.

Sands, L., & Meredith, W. (1992). Blood pressure and intellectual functioning in late midlife. *Journals of Gerontology: Psychological Sciences, 47*, 81–84.

Schaie, K. W. (1990). Intellectual development in adulthood. In J. E. Birren, & K. W. Schaie (Eds.), *Handbook of the psychology of aging* (3rd ed., pp. 291–309). San Diego, CA: Academic Press.

Shallice, T. (1982). Specific impairments of planning. *Philosophical Transcripts of the Royal Society of London, 298*, 199–209.

Spieth, W. (1964). Cardiovascular health status, age, and psychological performance. *Journal of Gerontology, 19*, 277–284.

Starr, J. M. (1999). Blood pressure and cognitive decline in the elderly. *Current Opinion in Nephrology and Hypertension, 8*(3), 347–351.

Stuss, D. T., Alexander, M. P., Pulumbo, C. L., Buckle, L., Sayer, L., & Pogue, J. (1994). Organisational strategies of patients with unilateral or bilateral frontal lobe injury in word list learning tasks. *Neuropsychology, 8,* 355–373.

Stuss, D. T., & Benson, D. F. (1986). *The frontal lobes.* New York: Raven Press.

Stuss, D. T., & Binns, M. A. (2002). Aging: Not an escarpment but multiple slopes. In M. Naveh-Benjamin, M. Moscovitch, & H. L. Roediger (Eds.), *Perspectives on human memory and cognitive aging: Essays in honour of Fergus Craik* (pp. 334–347). East Sussex, UK: Psychology Press.

Talland, G. A. (1961). Effect of aging on the formation of sequential and spatial concepts. *Perceptual and Motor Skills, 13,* 210.

Terry, R. D., DeTeresa, R., & Hansen, L. A. (1987). Neocortical cell counts in normal human adult aging. *Annals of Neurology, 21*(6), 530–539.

Troyer, A. K. (2000). Normative data for clustering and switching on verbal fluency tasks. *Journal of Clinical and Experimental Neuropsychology, 22*(3), 370–378.

Tun, P. A., Nathan, D. M., & Perlmutter, L. C. (1990). Cognitive and affective disorders in elderly diabetics. *Clinics in Geriatric Medicine, 6*(4 November), 731–746.

van Goor, L. P., Woiski, M. D., Lagaay, A. M., Meinders, A. E., & Tal, P. P. (1995). Review: Cobalamin deficiency and mental impairment in elderly people. *Age and Ageing, 24,* 536–542.

Viitanen, M., & Guo, Z. (1997). Are cognitive function and blood pressure related? *Drugs and Aging, 11*(3 September), 165–169.

Walsh, K. W. (1987). *Neuropsychology: A clinical approach* (2nd ed.). Edinburgh, UK: Churchill Livingstone.

Walsh, K. W. (1991). *Understanding brain damage* (2nd ed.). Edinburgh, UK: Churchill Livingstone.

Wardill, T. D. (2003). Cognitive function in the Australian aged: A normative study. PhD thesis. University of Melbourne.

Wechsler, D. (1981). *Wechsler intelligence scale-revised.* New York: The Psychological Corporation.

Weigl, E. (1941). On the psychology of so-called processes of abstraction. *Journal of Normal and Social Psychology, 36,* 3–33.

Willis, L., Yeo, R. A., Thomas, P., & Garry, P. J. (1988). Differential declines in cognitive function with aging: The possible role of health status. *Developmental Neuropsychology, 4*(1), 23–28.

8 Assessment of behavioral aspects of executive function

Gerard A. Gioia, Peter K. Isquith, and Laura E. Kenealy

Contents

Assessment of executive function has historically been confined to laboratory-based performance tests. While such tests offer the advantages of strong internal validity, control over extraneous variables, and potential to fractionate and examine components of executive function separately such as planning versus working memory, they are necessarily limited in ecological validity, or predictive value of functioning in the everyday environment. Fundamentally, executive functions are necessary for organization of goal-directed behavior in this everyday, "real world," environment. Thus, in addition to assessing these functions with clinical performance measures, it is essential to also capture actual behavioral manifestation of executive function or dysfunction. This chapter focuses on measurement of executive function through assessment of individuals' behavior in their everyday environment. First, the concept of ecological validity is discussed in relationship to assessment of executive function. This is followed by descriptions of five measures that capture individuals' executive functioning via their everyday behavior. We review the Dysexecutive Questionnaire (DEX) (Wilson, Alderman, Burgess, Emslie, & Evans, 1996), Frontal Behavior Inventory (Kertesz, Davidson, & Fox, 1997), Behavior Rating Inventory of Executive Function (BRIEF) (Gioia, Isquith, Guy, & Kenworthy, 2000), Frontal Systems Behavior Scale (Grace & Malloy, 2001), and the Executive Function Index (EFI) (Spinella, 2005).

As articulated in previous chapters, the term "executive function" is an umbrella construct for a collection of interrelated functions that are responsible for purposeful, goal-directed, and problem-solving behavior. The executive functions may be defined as the control or self-regulatory functions that organize and direct all cognitive activity, emotional response, and overt behavior. We view executive function as a broad umbrella term within which a set of interrelated subdomains can be defined that manifest behaviorally. Although authors vary in which functions are viewed as executive function domains, they typically include: initiation of goal-directed behavior, inhibition of competing actions or stimuli, planning and selection of relevant task goals, organization of behavior to solve complex problems, flexible shifting of problem-solving strategies when necessary, and monitoring and evaluation of problem-solving behavior. In support of these behaviors, working memory capacity plays a fundamental role in holding information actively "on-line" in the service of problem solving (Pennington, Bennetto, McAleer, & Roberts, 1996). Importantly, the executive functions are not exclusive to cognition; emotional control is also relevant to effective problem-solving activity and should be considered in any definition.

Deficits in various subdomains of the executive functions are central characteristics of many developmental and acquired neurological disorders across the life span, yet their measurement can be complex and challenging. Given the central importance of the executive functions to the direction and control of dynamic "real world" behavior, reliance on clinic-based test performance measures potentially can yield a limited, incomplete assessment (Gioia & Isquith, 2004; Silver, 2000). While performance tests attempt to tap executive functions in explicit and specific ways, multiple confounds can limit their ecological validity and generalizability. Burgess (1997) argues that neuropsychological tests alone are inadequate for assessing executive function because they artificially and ambiguously fractionate an integrated system. Performance-based measures tap individual components of the executive function system over a short time frame and not the integrated, multidimensional, relativistic, priority-based decision making that is often demanded in real-world situations (Goldberg & Podell, 2000; Shallice & Burgess, 1991).

The structured and interactive nature of the typical assessment situation may reduce demands on the executive functions, and thereby reduce the opportunities to observe critical processes associated with the executive functions (Bernstein & Waber, 1990). That is, in many testing situations, the examiner provides the structure, planning, organization and guidance as well as the cueing and monitoring necessary for an individual's optimal performance. In this manner, executive control is provided by the examiner (Kaplan, 1988; Stuss & Benson, 1986). As a result, individuals with substantial executive dysfunction can often perform adequately on well-structured tests when the examiner is allowed to cue and probe for more information, relieving the individual of the need to be appropriately inhibited, flexible, strategic in planning, and goal directed.

Given the challenges of executive function assessment in the laboratory and the inherent limitations to applicability in the everyday environment, increasing attention is being given to alternative methods of evaluation that offer enhanced ecological validity (Silver, 2000). Assessment methods that reliably tap the individual's everyday executive problem-solving in natural settings offer a complementary approach to clinical performance-based assessment. The challenge in assessing executive dysfunction is not only to find appropriate performance measures (tests), as Lezak (1995) and others suggest, but also to evaluate the functional, real-world impact of executive dysfunction as expressed in everyday activities. In this chapter, we address behavioral assessment of executive functions as a time and cost efficient measurement method that complements traditional performance-based test methodology. We approach this problem from an ecological perspective, examining measures that capture the everyday behavior of the individual. We briefly discuss ecological validity in assessment of executive function, followed by a review of the assessment tools that use everyday behavior as the primary data source.

Ecological validity and assessment of executive function

Ecological validity in the psychological literature refers to the ability to generalize results of controlled experiments to naturally occurring events in the real world (Brunswick, 1955). With regard to neuropsychological assessment, ecological validity may be more narrowly defined as the "functional and predictive relationship between the patient's behavior on a set of neuropsychological tests and the patient's behavior in a variety of real-world settings..." (Sbordone, 1996, p. 16). Thus, an ecologically valid assessment tool is one that has characteristics similar to a naturally occurring behavior and has value in predicting everyday function (Franzen & Wilhelm, 1996). These concepts inherent in the notion of ecological validity serve as the foundation for the behavioral assessment of executive function.

When neuropsychological tests are developed and applied to identify or quantify deficits, traditional validity (e.g., construct validity) is often paramount and ecological validity may be of less concern. In practice, however, neuropsychologists are increasingly asked to not only identify functional strengths and weaknesses but also to translate such findings into implications and predictions for the individual in his or her everyday milieu (Manchester, Priestley, & Jackson, 2004). Implicit in definitions of ecological validity as the concept is applied to neuropsychological assessment are two requirements: first, that the demands of a test and the testing conditions resemble demands in the everyday world of the individual and, second, that performance on a test predicts some aspect of the individual's functioning on a day-to-day basis. The first requirement, that of *verisimilitude*, overlaps with face validity and describes the "topographical similarity" or theoretical relationship between the method of data collection and skills or behaviors required in the natural environment of the individual (Franzen & Wilhelm, 1996). Considerations of verisimilitude include not only the demands of a given test itself but also the conditions in which the test is administered. That is, in evaluating the degree of verisimilitude for a given test, both the required skills and the testing environment and methods need to be considered. The second requirement of ecological validity in neuropsychological assessment is *veridicality*, or the degree to which test performance predicts some aspect of the individual's everyday functioning. This aspect is both theoretical and empirical: Theoretically, is there reason to believe the test might predict real-world behavior; and empirically, does test performance correlate with some measure of real-world functioning (Franzen & Wilhelm, 1996; Rabin, 2001)?

Given the recent attention to the generalizability of assessment findings in general and executive functions in particular, several measures have been developed over the past decade that are specifically designed to capture individuals' executive functioning in the everyday environment. These measures attempt to respond not only to an increasing need to capture individuals' executive functioning in their everyday environments as an ecologically valid component of a comprehensive assessment that includes more internally valid performance tools, but also as a measure of real-world behavior against which the veridicality of performance tools can be measured. Whether completed by the individual or by knowledgeable informants, these measures follow in the well-established tradition of utilizing structured behavior rating systems in the assessment of psychological and neuro-psychological functions, including social, emotional, and behavioral functioning (e.g., Achenbach, 1991a,b; Reynolds & Kamphaus, 1992). Observation of the individual in the home, work or school provides an essential source of information in the assessment of executive functions.

It is important to appreciate those behavioral assessment methods that rely on self- and/or informant reports which also present their own limitations. First, while providing a more global or molar view of behavior, they necessarily provide less process-specific information. For example, while performance tests may attempt to fractionate and measure specific subdomains of executive function such as working memory versus planning or organization, specific components of the executive functions in the everyday context may be less separable. Indeed, much of everyday behavior may depend on the integration of executive function subdomains, such as the ability to inhibit distraction that facilitates or protects working memory which, in turn, may enable planning and organization of goal-directed behavior. As such, it may be more difficult to capture and parse deficits in specific executive functions via reported behaviors. Second, the evaluator has much more limited control of environmental influences or contingencies that may affect ratings on behavioral scales. One individual who describes their executive functions as inadequate to meet their daily needs may do so relative to a highly demanding, multi-tasking work environment that places extraordinary demands on the executive function system, while another individual may find their self-regulatory capacity up to the challenge of a simpler, more routine environment. Unlike the laboratory testing setting where such contingencies are controlled, the evaluator has little control over the individual's environment or how these environmental demands vary across individuals or over time. Third, rater perspective or bias must be considered when interpreting rating scales. An individual's emotional state or personality character-istics may influence their ratings, or simply whether or not they like or dislike the rated individual. For example, one teacher may dislike a child or, as is sometimes the case, simply dislike completing rating scales, while another teacher may enjoy the same child and appreciate the opportunity to provide input into the evaluation process.

In sum, rating scales designed to measure the impact of executive functions in the real world may offer enhanced ecological validity to the overall assessment process, or an understanding of how laboratory performance test findings may play out in the everyday environment. Like performance tests, however, they are not without inherent limitations. As a result, we advocate a model of executive function assess-ment that integrates findings from the more internally valid performance measures with the more ecologically valid behavioral measures.

Review of behavioral assessment instruments

Five published measures that assess everyday behavioral manifestation of executive function in individuals are reviewed and presented in Table 8.1. All five scales were developed to specifically measure executive function difficulties in adults while one also taps these behaviors in children and adolescents from 2 through 18 years. The measures differ along a number of dimensions including the rater (self-report versus informant report or both), the executive function domains assessed, and the clinical populations of interest (See Malloy & Grace, 2005, for a recent review). Generally, the primarily adult-oriented measures attempt to capture changes in frontal lobe functioning, such as might be seen following a brain injury, stroke or the onset of dementia. In contrast, the developmentally oriented measure was intended to be sensitive to variations in executive control abilities across the life span. Each of these measures is discussed below.

Dysexecutive questionnaire

The Dysexecutive Questionnaire is a 20-item self- and informant report questionnaire included within the Behavioural Assessment of the Dysexecutive Syndrome (BADS; Wilson et al., 1996), a battery of cognitive tasks tapping executive function problems that was designed with particular attention to strong verisimilitude and increased ecological validity. The DEX assesses four areas of functioning: emotions/ personality, motivation, behavior, and cognition, and asks raters to indicate the frequency of problems on a 5-point Likert scale. The item responses are summed to yield one overall score. Parallel forms are available for patient self-reports and for informant reports.

Norms: Normative data for the DEX are limited. The manual provides percentile equivalents of raw scores relative to a normative sample of 216 subjects. Chan (2001) tested a group of 93 normal participants with the BADS and reported that the non-clinical samples demonstrate some degree of the problem behaviors captured on the DEX. These findings point to the need to understand base rates of these behaviors in normative groups.

Reliability: Internal consistency and test–retest reliability for the DEX are not reported in the manual. Recent examination in a hospital population (Bennett, Ong, & Ponsford, 2005) found high internal consistency for family member informant reports (Cronbach's $\alpha = 0.93$). In addition, ratings from two "expert" informants (the neuro-psychologist and the occupational therapist working with the patient) were very strongly associated, suggesting reasonable inter-rater reliability.

Validity: Factor analysis based on a small number of patients reported in the DEX manual resulted in three factors: Behavior, Cognition, and Emotion. The first two factors correlated with various subtests of the larger BADS battery, and all three factors were correlated with the Total BADS score. A Varimax rotated factor analysis on the informant form of the DEX revealed five factors (Burgess, Alderman, Evans, Emslie, & Wilson, 1998). Three were cognitive factors (Inhibition, Intentionality, and Executive Memory), and two were small factors related to emotions. Chan (2001) also found five factors in his study of normal participants and

Table 8.1 Measures for behavioral assessment of executive function.

Measure	Executive function subdomains	Publisher/reference	Report form	Age range	Psychometric properties
Executive Function Index (EFI)	Empathy, strategic planning, organization, impulse control, and motivational drive	Spinella (2005a)	Self-report	Unspecified adults	Acceptable internal consistency Good correlation with other self-report executive measures Limited normative data
Dysexecutive Questionnaire (DEX)	Several different factor analyses reveal different subdomains. One example: inhibition, intentionality, executive memory, emotions	Thames Valley Test Company	Self-report Informant report	Unspecified adults	Appropriate internal consistency Variable evidence for convergent validity Limited normative data
Frontal Systems Behavior Scale (FrSBe)	Apathy, disinhibition, executive control	Psychological Assessment Resources, Inc.	Self-Rating Form Family Rating Form	18 to >60 years	Appropriate internal consistency and test–retest reliability Validity well studied Normative data are available
Frontal Behavioral Inventory (FBI)	Various symptoms of frontal lobe dementia	Kertesz et al., 1997	Clinician completed ratings via caregiver interview	Unspecified adults	Appropriate interrater reliability and internal consistency Distinguishes between frontal lobe dementia and other disorders
Behavior Rating Inventory of Executive Function (BRIEF)		Psychological Assessment Resources, Inc.			

Preschool	Inhibit, shift, emotional control, working memory, plan/organize	Parent form Teacher form	2–5 years	Appropriate internal consistency and test–retest reliability Validity well studied in multiple clinical populations Normative data are available
School Age	Inhibit, shift, emotional control, initiate, working memory, plan/organize, organization of materials, monitor	Parent form Teacher form	5–18 years	Appropriate internal consistency and test–retest reliability Validity well studied in multiple clinical populations Normative data are available
Adolescent Self-Report	Inhibit, shift, emotional control, working memory, plan/organize, organization of materials, monitor task completion	Self-report	11–18 years	Appropriate internal consistency and test–retest reliability Validity well studied in multiple clinical populations Normative data are available
Adult	Inhibit, shift, emotional control, self-monitor, initiate, working memory, plan/organize, organization of materials, task monitor	Self-report Informant report	18–90 years	Appropriate internal consistency and test–retest reliability Validity well studied in multiple clinical populations Normative data are available

78 patients with various diagnoses (traumatic brain injury, dementia, or stroke): inhibition, intentionality, knowing-doing dissociation, in-resistance, and social regulation.

Neuropsychologist and occupational therapist ratings on the DEX were moderately correlated with measures of severity of traumatic brain injury (length of post-traumatic amnesia and processing speed). Data from family members on the DEX did not, however, relate to these measures of injury severity. Wilson and colleagues (1996) found significant associations between informant ratings on the DEX and the BADS performance subtests in the standardization sample, although several subsequent studies have not replicated this finding (Bennett et al., 2005; Norris & Tate, 2000). While Evans, Chua, McKenna, and Wilson (1997) found significant correlations between BADS subtests and family members' DEX ratings in a brain-injured group, this relationship was not found for self-report on the DEX in the brain-injured group, nor for self- or family-report on the DEX in a group diagnosed with schizophrenia. Some studies have not found evidence of validity based on convergence between the DEX and other measures of executive function (Bogod, Mateer, & MacDonald, 2003; Norris & Tate, 2000), although Burgess and colleagues (1998) report associations between the informant DEX and standard neuropsychological measures in a mixed group of neurological patients. Recently, Odhuba, van den Broek, and Johns (2005) reported positive correlations with two tests of executive function tapping initiation and inhibition (The Hayling Test; Burgess & Shallice, 1997) and rule-following and response flexibility (The Brixton Test; Burgess & Shallice, 1997).

Numerous studies have employed the DEX with a range of clinical groups including individuals with traumatic brain injuries (Alderman, Dawson, Rutterford, & Reynolds, 2001; Allain et al., 2004; Azouvi et al., 2004; Bogod et al., 2003; Chan, Hoosain, Lee, Fan, & Fong, 2003; Chan & Manly, 2002; Hart, Whyte, Kim, & Vaccaro, 2005; Williams, Evans, Needham, & Wilson, 2002), stroke (Annoni, Devuyst, Carota, Bruggimann, & Bogousslavsky, 2005; Bellebaum et al., 2004), dementia (Kahokehr, Siegert, & Weatherall, 2004), frontal lesions (Beldarrain, Garcia-Monco, Astigarraga, Gonzalez, & Grafman, 2005), schizophrenia (Chan & Chen, 2004; Chan, Chen, Cheung, & Cheung, 2004), phenylketonuria (Channon, Mockler, & Lee, 2005), autism (García-Villamisar & Della Sala, 2002), alcohol abuse (Heffernan, Ling, & Bartholomew, 2004), multiple sclerosis (Kleeberg et al., 2004), Parkinson's disease (Mathias, 2003), Prader-Willi Syndrome (Walley & Donaldson, 2005), and normal aging (Amieva, Phillips, & Sala, 2003).

Frontal behavioral inventory

The Frontal Behavioral Inventory (FBI) was designed specifically for the diagnosis of frontal lobe dementia (Kertesz et al., 1997). The rating scale is completed by a clinical professional via structured interview with the patient's caregiver as the informant, and usually takes 15–30 min to complete. The FBI consists of 24 items covering behaviors including apathy, inflexibility, verbal apraxia, alien hand syndrome, impulsivity, and perseveration. Items are rated on a 4 point severity scale and were derived from the literature on frontotemporal dementia diagnosis. Scoring yields a global total score. Cut-off scores are provided for distinguishing between frontal lobe dementia and other conditions such as Alzheimer's disease.

Norms: There are no standardized norms reported for the FBI beyond suggested cut-off scores for diagnosis of frontal lobe dementia.

Reliability: Kertesz and colleagues (2000) administered the FBI to 108 caregivers of geriatric patients with Alzheimer's disease, frontal lobe dementia, primary progressive aphasia, vascular dementia, and depressive disorders. Interrater reliability (Cohen's $\kappa = 0.89$) and internal consistency (Cronbach's $\alpha = 0.89$) were both high.

Validity: The FBI has been shown to successfully distinguish frontal lobe dementia from several other dementing disorders (Kertesz, Nadkarni, Davidson, & Thomas, 2000). Some individuals with vascular dementia also achieved high scores on the FBI, but the authors indicate which items are particularly useful in discriminating between the groups. In a later study, Kertesz and colleagues (2003) found that the FBI was more effective than neuropsychological test scores in distinguishing between patients with frontal lobe dementia and those with Alzheimer's disease in a hierarchical discriminant function analysis. Sensitivity and specificity were found to be high (90% sensitive, 100% specific) when using the optimal cut-off score for diagnosis, but the authors note that the diagnostic yield will likely be lower in an unselected population.

Studies with the FBI have shown that frontal lobe dementia patients differ from comparison groups in age, gender, or both, yet these demographic variables were not included as covariates in analyses (Malloy & Grace, 2005). Thus, it is not entirely clear to what extent the FBI scores may be influenced by factors such as increasing age, although the inclusion of items that appear clearly abnormal at any age (e.g., alien hand syndrome) may make specific age and gender norms less relevant. Because the FBI focuses on specific symptoms of frontal lobe dementia, it is most useful in that population, and not across disorders or at different points in development. In keeping with the focus on dementia, the majority of studies examining the FBI in clinical populations have focused on groups with Mild Cognitive Impairment, Alzheimer's Dementia, and frontotemporal dementia (e.g., Bathgate, Snowden, Varma, Blackshaw, & Neary, 2001; Fernandez-Duque & Black, 2005; Kertesz, 2000; Kertesz, Davidson, McCabe, & Munoz, 2003; Marczinski, Davidson, & Kertesz, 2004; Skjerve & Brenne, 2003; Starkstein, Garau, & Cao, 2004; Vogel, Hasselbalch, Gade, Ziebell, & Waldemar, 2005).

Behavior rating inventory of executive function

The BRIEF was developed to capture the behavioral manifestations of executive dysfunction across the life span from the age of two to ninety years. Four different versions are available: the BRIEF-Preschool Version for ages 2–5 years with separate parent and teacher/caregiver report forms (Gioia, Espy, & Isquith, 2003; Isquith, Gioia, & Espy, 2004), the original BRIEF for ages 5–18 years with separate parent and teacher report forms (Gioia et al., 2000), the BRIEF-Self-Report Version for adolescents aged 11–18 years (Guy, Isquith, & Gioia, 2004), and the BRIEF-Adult

Version for ages 18–90 years with separate self- and informant report forms (Roth, Isquith, & Gioia, 2005). The BRIEF assesses multiple interrelated domains of executive function commonly discussed in the neuropsychological literature (e.g., Denckla, 1989; Stuss & Benson, 1986; Welsh, Pennington, & Grossier, 1991). The measure is a problem-oriented rating scale that asks the respondent to indicate if the specific behavior is never, sometimes, or often a problem. Although each version of the BRIEF varies in scale composition to some degree, the general domains assessed and scale names (in parentheses) include inhibitory control (Inhibit), cognitive and behavioral flexibility (Shift), emotional regulation (Emotional Control), self-monitoring in the social context (Self-Monitor), ability to initiate activity (Initiate), ability to sustain working memory (Working Memory), planning and organization of cognition and problem solving (Plan/Organize), organization of materials and environment (Organization of Materials), and monitoring of problem solving (Task Monitor). Initiation was not included in the BRIEF-Self-Report for adolescents but a Task Completion scale emerged. There was insufficient resolution of the metacognitive scales (Plan/Organize, Initiate, and Monitor) for the BRIEF-Preschool Version resulting in retention of the Inhibit, Shift, Emotional Control, and Working Memory scales but collapsing of the remaining scales into a Plan/Organize scale. Each of the BRIEF versions summarizes individual scales within indices based on factor structure of the measures.

Norms: Each of the four versions of the BRIEF has large representative standardization samples that approximate US Census statistics for sex, education, and race/ethnicity. Developmental age and sex effects have been examined and norms developed accordingly when significant effects were identified. All versions offer norms for separate age bands and all but the BRIEF-Adult Version offer separate norms for males and females, as there were no sex differences in the standardization sample for the latter version. T-scores and percentiles are available for each of the individual scales as well as the broader indexes and an overall Global Executive Composite.

Reliability: Each version of the BRIEF demonstrates appropriate internal consistency per scale and Index (BRIEF-Preschool $\alpha = 0.80$ to 0.97; school-age BRIEF $\alpha = 0.80$ to 0.98; Adolescent BRIEF-Self-Report $\alpha = 0.75$ to 0.96; BRIEF Adult Version $\alpha = 0.73$ to 0.98) and stability over time (Preschool Version mean parent/teacher test–retest: $r = 0.86$; school-age parent: $r = 0.82$; school-age teacher: $r = 0.88$; adolescent self-report: $r = 0.77$; adult self-report: $r = 0.90$; adult informant report $r = 0.92$).

Validity: Evidence for validity of the BRIEF has been investigated based on content, internal structure via exploratory and confirmatory factor analytic methods, convergence and divergence with other measures, and concurrence with diagnostic groups. Each version shows appropriate correlations with other measures used with the same age group. For example, the BRIEF-Adult Version has been examined with other measures of executive functions such as the FrSBe, DEX, and Cognitive Failures Questionnaire (Broadbent, Cooper, Fitzgerald, & Parkes, 1982) as well as measures of emotional functioning such as the Clinical Assessment of Depression (Bracken & Keith, 2004), the Beck Depression Inventory II (Beck, Steer, & Brown, 1996) and the State-Trait Anxiety Inventory (Spielberger, 1983), while measures of behavioral functioning such as the Child Behavior Checklist (Achenbach, 1991a,b) and Behavior Assessment System for Children (Reynolds & Kamphaus, 1992) have been correlated with the School Age version.

Multiple principal factor analytic studies have been conducted with clinical and normative samples, resulting in consistent two factor solutions that define the indexes on the original BRIEF, BRIEF-SR, and BRIEF-A. Each analysis revealed a Behavioral Regulation factor that included the Inhibit, Shift and Emotional Control Scales, and a Metacognition factor that included the Initiate, Working Memory, Plan/Organize, and Organization of Materials scale. The Monitor scale from the original BRIEF fell within the Metacognition factor on that form of the BRIEF but the scale was divided into a Task Monitor and Self-Monitor scale on the BRIEF-A and separated on the factors, with Task Monitor falling within the Metacognition factor and Self-Monitor falling within the Behavioral Regulation factor. Factor analysis of the BRIEF-Preschool Version resulted in three overlapping factors: Inhibitory Control with Inhibit and Emotional Control, Flexibility with Shift and Emotional Control, and Emergent Metacognition with Working Memory and Plan/Organize (Gioia, Isquith, Retzlaff, & Espy, 2002).

Executive function deficits using the BRIEF have been demonstrated in a variety of populations such as Attention-Deficit/Hyperactivity Disorder (Gioia & Isquith, 2001; Gioia, Isquith, Kenworthy, & Barton, 2002; Jarratt, Riccio, & Siekierski, 2005; Kenealy, 2002; Lawrence et al., 2004; Mahone et al., 2002), TBI (Brookshire, Levin, Song, & Zhang, 2004; Gioia & Isquith, 2004; Landry, Swank, Stuebing, Prasad, & Ewing-Cobbs, 2004; Mangeot, Armstrong, Colvin, Yeates, & Taylor, 2002; Vriezen & Pigott, 2002), frontal lesions (Anderson, Anderson, Northam, Jacobs, & Mikiewicz, 2002; Jacobs & Anderson, 2002), Type 1 Diabetes Mellitus (Detzer, Whitaker, Isquith, Christiano, & Casella, 2004; Whitaker, Detzer, Isquith, Christiano, & Casella, 2004), autism spectrum disorders (Gilotty, Kenworthy, Sirian, Black, & Wagner, 2002; Gioia et al., 2002), learning disabilities (Gioia et al., 2002), myelomeningocele and hydrocephalus (Burmeister et al., 2005; Mahone, Zabel, Levey, Verda, & Kinsman, 2002), Tourette's syndrome (Cummings, Singer, Krieger, Miller, & Mahone, 2002; Mahone et al., 2002), phenylketonuria (Antshel & Waisbren, 2003), bipolar disorder (Shear, DelBello, Rosenberg, & Strakowski, 2002), obstructive sleep apnea (Beebe & Gozal, 2002; Beebe et al., 2004), 22q11 deletion syndrome (Antshel, Conchelos, Lanzetta, Fremont, & Kates, 2005; Kiley-Brabeck, 2004), galactosemia (Antshel, Epstein, & Waisbren, 2004), sickle cell disease (Kral & Brown, 2004), and early focal frontal lesions (Anderson et al., 2002; Jacobs & Anderson, 2002). The BRIEF-Adult Version has been examined in individuals with Mild Cognitive Impairment (Rabin et al., 2006) and the manual includes clinical group studies with patients with ADHD, Multiple Sclerosis, Alzheimer's disease, and Traumatic Brain Injury (Roth et al., 2005).

Frontal systems behavior scale

Formerly known as the Frontal Lobe Personality Scale (FLOPS; Grace, Stout, & Malloy, 1999), the Frontal Systems Behavior Scale (FrSBe) (Grace & Malloy, 2001) is a 46-item questionnaire based on Cummings' (1993) behavioral neurology model and was designed to measure behaviors associated with lesions in the frontal system (Grace & Malloy, 2001). The FrSBe has self-report and family member report forms, and offers the option of capturing each item twice: Once, retrospectively, to reflect premorbid functioning, and again to describe current (post-injury or illness) behavior. Items are placed within three scales consistent with the model of Cummings (1993, Mega & Cummings, 1994): Apathy, Disinhibition, and Executive Dysfunction. Items are rated in terms of frequency on a five-point scale, and scoring results in a Total score as well as separate scores for the three scales.

Norms: Normative data are provided for self-report ratings and the ratings of family members. Norms are based on 436 individuals between the ages of 18–95 years of age, with T-scores stratified for age, gender, and education.

Reliability: The FrSBe demonstrates high overall internal consistency (Cronbach's α for Total Score: 0.94 on the family form, 0.92 on the self-report form; Grace & Malloy, 2001) with similar coefficients reported in additional studies (Stout, Ready, Grace, Malloy, & Paulsen, 2003; Velligan, Ritch, Sui, DiCocco, & Huntzinger, 2002). Test–retest reliability was reported as 0.78 for the Total scale with a range of 0.65–0.68 for subscales in a sample of psychiatric patients (Velligan et al., 2002).

Validity: Construct validity has been demonstrated in several ways. Exploratory factor analysis (Stout et al., 2003) of the FrSBe-Family Version with 324 neurological patients showed a three-factor solution accounting for 41% of the variance. Eighty-three percent of individual items loaded on factors corresponding to the three scales (Apathy, Disinhibition, Executive Control). A five-factor solution was found by Azzara (2005), with 85% of items loading saliently. Grace and colleagues (1999) demonstrated that the scale captures significant change in the behavior of frontal lesion patients from baseline to post-lesion. The author's further report expected differences between frontal lobe patients and normal controls, as well as differences between patients with frontal and non-frontal brain injuries.

Convergent and discriminant validity have been documented for the FrSBe. Meaningful correlations have been found between the FrSBe and other scales and behavioral ratings of frontal behaviors including the Neuropsychiatric Inventory in dementia patients (NPI; Norton, Malloy, & Salloway, 2001), relevant symptoms from the Brief Psychiatric Rating Scale in patients with schizophrenia (Velligan et al., 2002), and measures of disinhibited eating in an eating disordered population (Spinella & Lyke, 2004). Relationships between the FrSBe scales and executive function performance tasks such as the Trailmaking Test and Verbal Fluency have also been reported (e.g., Velligan et al.; Chiaravalloti & DeLuca, 2003).

Several clinical group studies report findings with the FrSBe, primarily in individuals with dementias (Benke et al., 2004; Boyle & Malloy, 2003; Boyle et al., 2003; Cahn-Weiner, Grace, Ott, Fernandez, & Friedman, 2002; Ready, Ott, Grace, & Cahn-Weiner, 2003; Stout, Wyman, Johnson, Peavy, & Salmon, 2003; Zawacki et al., 2002) but also with schizophrenia (Velligan et al., 2002) and multiple sclerosis (Chiaravalloti & DeLuca, 2003).

Executive function index

The Executive Function Index is a recently developed self-report rating scale of executive function (Spinella, 2005a) that was developed exclusively using a community sample of 188 adults without known cognitive or psychiatric risks. Items were generated conceptually based on domains of executive function found through literature review and tap motivation, impulse control, empathy, planning, and social conduct. Factor analysis was used to reduce the scale to 27 items within five scales: Empathy, Strategic Planning, Organization, Impulse Control, and Motivational Drive.

Norms: Formal representative norms have not yet been reported for this measure, although means and standard deviations for each scale and the total score are now available for a sample of 701 participants (Spinella, 2005b). Given that scores differ as a function of age, gender, and education, the development of more specific stratified norms will be useful for future work with the EFI.

Reliability: Cronbach's α ranged from 0.69 to 0.76 for the five subscales with an overall of .82 for the total score. Test–retest reliability was not reported.

Validity: Evidence of validity for the EFI comes from exploratory principal components factor analysis with orthogonal rotation. The five factors, Empathy, Strategic Planning, Organization, Impulse Control, and Motivational Drive, collectively accounted for 49.7% of the variance. Evidence of validity based on convergence with other measures was demonstrated via correlations with other self-report measures of executive control including the Frontal Systems Behavior Scale, Barratt Impulsiveness Scale (Patton, Stanford, & Barratt, 1995), and the Interpersonal Reactivity Index (Davis, 1980). Further work is underway examining relationships between the EFI and obsessive-compulsive symptoms, alcohol use, sexual behavior, attitudes toward exercise and eating behavior (Spinella, personal communication, 2005). Clinical utility of the EFI has not yet been demonstrated in clinical groups. Absence of an informant report form may limit applicability of the measure in clinical populations given the oft-cited lack of awareness shown by patients with frontal lobe dysfunction (Anderson & Tranel, 1989).

Clinical implications

While all measures reviewed in this chapter are similar in that they capture aspects of everyday executive function using rating scale methodology, there are important fundamental distinctions between the various measures in how they were developed and for what purposes. As a result, these differences impact their ecological validity. For example, the FBI was developed solely as a tool for diagnosing frontal dementia and helping differentiate this patient group from other patients with various types of dementia. Thus, its use with other populations or to capture self-regulation in a non-demented population is limited. The FrSBe was designed from a behavioral neurology model based on the work of Cummings (1993) that defines three behavioral syndromes: executive cognitive dysfunction associated with dorsolateral prefrontal circuitry, disinhibition associated with orbital prefrontal circuitry, and apathy/akinesia associated with anterior cingulated circuitry. The FrSBe assists in identifying patients with various characteristics of these behavioral syndromes ascribed to frontal systems, and provides useful information toward helping detect and discriminate between various forms of dementias such as Alzheimer's disease, Parkinson's disease, Huntington's disease, frontotemporal dementia, Lewy Body dementia, vascular dementia and traumatic brain injury. Further, the FrSBe includes explicit ratings of pre- and post-injury or event, facilitating pre–post comparisons.

In contrast, measures such as the DEX and the BRIEF were developed not with diagnosis or predicting underlying neuropathophysiology as a primary focus but instead to capture individuals' everyday functioning in the real world to enhance the ecological validity of performance testing. The DEX, as part of the BADS, was included explicitly in order to evaluate the ecological validity of the performance tests included in the BADS. It is a concise measure that offers a global executive function score without further attempt to differentiate subdomains. While all reviewed measures are appropriate for adults, the BRIEF was originally conceptualized and developed from a developmental neuropsychological framework and covers a broad age range from 2 to 90 years. It also does not attempt to measure or predict underlying neuropathophysiology, but instead follows a functional neuropsychological framework to assess multiple domains of executive function simultaneously.

In considering the ecological validity of these five measures, recall that there are two considerations, verisimilitude and veridicality. To achieve verisimilitude, the demands of a test must be similar to demands in the everyday world of the individual. To achieve veridicality, the test performance must predict some aspect of the individual's daily functioning. With respect to verisimilitude, each of the measures was explicitly designed to capture everyday executive control behaviors while balancing the demands for reliability and construct validity. The items in these clinical scales reflect everyday manifestations of executive dysfunction, focusing on behaviors related to working memory, inhibition, flexible problem solving and perseveration, abstract thinking, apathy, motivation, judgment, and decision making. Such behaviors were selected to be a direct reflection of real-world difficulties encountered by individuals with difficulties in their executive function and thus inherently possess strong verisimilitude.

The measures also show promise for veridicality, i.e., predicting behavior in the natural environment. While data to date are limited, the measures are increasingly being examined in relationship to other indications of everyday functioning. Correlational analyses with some of the measures, particularly the BRIEF and FrSBe, suggest strong, logical relationships between executive function and everyday behaviors such as impulsivity with aggression and working memory with attention problems. There is some indication that scores from these scales may correlate with other real-world functioning such as adaptive functioning in individuals with developmental disabilities (Gilotty et al., 2002; Janusz, Ahluvalia, & Gioia, 2002) and scholastic achievement (Mahone, Koth, Cutting, Singer, & Denckla, 2001; Waber, Gerber, Turcios, Wagner, & Forbes, 2006). Indeed, Waber et al. (2006) recently reported that teacher ratings of executive function on the BRIEF were the strongest predictor of student performance on high-stakes testing. Finally, certain profiles of executive function in the everyday environment may be related to specific diagnoses, and the measures should capture those characteristics. Several measures show utility in this endeavor, such as the FBI with frontal dementia (Kertesz, 2000; Kertesz et al., 2003), the FrSBe with several types of dementia (Boyle et al., 2003), and the BRIEF with ADHD (Gioia & Isquith, 2001; Isquith & Gioia, 2000).

Rating scales, in general, are useful tools with multiple clinical and research applications. They are typically less expensive and less time consuming to administer, require less clinician or researcher time and involvement, and can capture important and useful data about individuals' everyday functioning. Many studies cited above have used the executive function rating scales described in this chapter to describe profiles of executive function in a broad spectrum of specific developmental and acquired disorders. In some studies, they serve as actuarial measures of self-regulation in the everyday environment against which the veridicality of performance measures can be assessed. Yet other studies have employed executive function rating scales to measure the real-world implications of biological markers, such as phenylalanine levels in individuals with PKU (Antshel & Waisbren, 2003).

In addition to the research applications described throughout this discussion, these executive function rating instruments have potential uses for clinical treatment design, monitoring, and outcome measurement. As broad spectrum screening tools, data culled from behavioral measures of executive function in advance of an appointment can help the clinician focus on potentially problematic areas requiring further assessment, while spending less time on interview and formal testing on areas that are not described as problematic. The same data may inform decisions about targets for treatment and types of interventions based on the potential for ameliorating real-world problems. Given that they capture patients' everyday functioning, the scales may reveal or suggest specific problems for which treatment goals and strategies can be targeted. For example, an individual who is described as disinhibited in the everyday world might have treatments and supports targeted specifically toward boosting inhibitory control or limiting opportunity for impulsive behavior. A child with difficulties shifting set might benefit from teaching and intervention strategies that incorporate use of routines and schedules to reduce agitation and anxiety when change is needed.

Behavioral assessment of executive function can also facilitate treatment monitoring and eventual outcome evaluation. Given the inherent difficulty in administering performance measures of executive function in a repeated fashion, behavioral measures may be more suited to such within-subjects methods. For example, a patient concerned about attentional difficulties might reveal problems with inhibitory control and working memory on a rating scale. After appropriate interview and clinical diagnosis, treatment methods might include medication and cognitive-behavior therapy. To evaluate effectiveness of treatment, the measure might be administered again after starting medication, and again after a longer period to determine whether the effects of treatment are maintained. Ratings can be provided by the individual themselves or an informant in their environment who has the opportunity to observe regularly their behavior (e.g., parent, teacher, spouse). More frequent monitoring might also be appropriate in some cases, such as for individuals who sustain a concussion in sports, where full neuropsychological evaluation may not be feasible or appropriate at the time, but rapid, timely assessment of functioning is important for determining when the individual may return to play or engage in normal activities. Limited data are available at this time, however, regarding how these executive function scales operate under such multiple administration conditions. Future applicability of statistical measures of change, such as the reliable change index or standardized regression-based change scores (Chelune, 2003; Jacobson & Truax, 1991) will be important.

Conclusion

Executive dysfunction is a common outcome in individuals with developmental or acquired neurological disorders across the life span. Appropriate assessment of executive functions is critical in order to fully define the individual's neuropsychological profile, and plan necessary interventions and/or supports. Because executive functions are a complex, environmentally sensitive set of interrelated processes, their assessment challenges our traditional testing methodologies. Specifically, performance-based tests of executive function administered in the laboratory are designed to be high in internal validity to allow examination of components of the executive control system in a somewhat fractionated manner. Tests can vary in the degree to which they are structured and controlled, such as in a laboratory or clinical setting versus a less structured real-world setting. They can also vary in terms of their face and content validity, as well as in their ability to predict real-world behavior. As such, traditional methods do not necessarily capture the integrated, multidimensional, relativistic, priority-based decision making demanded in everyday, real-world situations (Goldberg & Podell, 2000; Shallice & Burgess, 1991). Given an increasing emphasis in neuropsychology on understanding the real world functional implications of laboratory test findings, ecological validity has become an important focus in neuropsychological assessment with a number of authors articulating the critical issues (e.g., Cripe, 1996; Silver, 2000). To address this need, several behavioral measures of executive function have been developed over the past decade to capture specific behavioral manifestations of executive dysfunction in the everyday, real world, environment of the individual. Our review of these behavioral assessment tools suggests that, in addition to meeting traditional standards of reliability and validity appropriate for rating scales, these measures offer the benefit of enhanced ecological validity with their inherent focus on the actual, everyday behaviors of the individual.

While rating scales of executive function offer a time and cost efficient method of capturing individuals' executive function in the everyday environment, we do not suggest that they are sufficient alone. Instead, we advocate a multi-level approach to understanding executive function in developmental and neurological disorders across the life span. In this model, traditional test-based measures of executive function are given to tap specific components of executive function such as working memory, inhibition, and organization. One might describe this level as the component or molecular level. Additionally, assessment of everyday behavior characterizes the molar level of function in the individual, describing the ways that the specific components might play out in terms of everyday behaviors. In the behavioral assessment of executive function, this ecologically valid information provides an important bridge toward understanding how the component-level (i.e., test-based) deficits impact on the individual's everyday adaptive functioning. Given advances in neuroimaging and in genetics, the near future will likely show expansion of this multi-faceted approach to understanding executive function. Indeed, functional imaging studies of executive function abound (see Wood & Smith, this volume; Roth, Randolph, Koven, & Isquith, 2006, for a recent review) and correlations between genetic markers and executive functions (e.g., Goldberg & Weinberger, 2004; Wetter et al., 2005) and behavior in general are increasingly understood (e.g., Bartels et al., 2004; Hudziak et al., 2004; Rietveld, Hudziak, Bartels, van Beijsterveldt, & Boomsma, 2004). The future model for understanding executive function from life span developmental and psychopathological perspectives will truly range from microlevel analysis of genetics as well as functional and structural imaging of underlying neuropathophysiology, to intermediate level assessment of performance testing, to macrolevel ecological assessment via behavior rating scales.

References

Achenbach, T. (1991a). *Manual for the Child Behavior Checklist/4-18 and 1991 profile.* Burlington, VT: University of Vermont Department of Psychiatry.

Achenbach, T. (1991b). *Manuals for the Teacher's Report Form and 1991 profile.* Burlington: University of Vermont, Department of Psychiatry.

Alderman, N., Dawson, K., Rutterford, N. A., & Reynolds, P. J. (2001). A comparison of the validity of self-report measures amongst people with acquired brain injury: A preliminary study of the usefulness of EuroQol-5D. *Neuropsychological Rehabilitation, 11*(5), 529–537.

Allain, P., Roy, A., Kefi, Z., Pinon, K., Etcharry-Bouyx, F., & Le Gall, D. (2004). Executive functions in patients with severe closed-head injury: Assessment with the "behavioral assessment of the dysexecutive syndrome"/Fonctions exécutives et traumatisme crânien sévère: Évaluation à l'aide de la "behavioral assessment of the dysexecutive syndrome." *Revue de Neuropsychologie, 14*(3), 285–323.

Amieva, H., Phillips, L., & Sala, S. D. (2003). Behavioral dysexecutive symptoms in normal aging. *Brain and Cognition, 53*(2), 129–132.

Anderson, V. A., Anderson, P., Northam, E., Jacobs, R., & Mikiewicz, O. (2002). Relationships between cognitive and behavioral measures of executive function in children with brain disease. *Child Neuropsychology Special Issue: Behavior Rating Inventory of Executive Function (BRIEF), 8*(4), 231–240.

Anderson, S. W., & Tranel, D. (1989). Awareness of disease states following cerebral infarction, dementia, and head trauma. *The Clinical Neuropsychologist, 3*, 327–339.

Annoni, J. M., Devuyst, G., Carota, A., Bruggimann, L., & Bogousslavsky, J. (2005). Changes in artistic style after minor posterior stroke. *Journal of Neurology, Neurosurgery & Psychiatry, 76*(6), 797–803.

Antshel, K. M., Conchelos, J., Lanzetta, G., Fremont, W., & Kates, W. R. (2005). Behavior and corpus callosum morphology relationships in velocardiofacial syndrome (22q11.2 deletion syndrome). *Psychiatry Research: Neuroimaging, 138*(3), 235–245.

Antshel, K. M., Epstein, I. O., & Waisbren, S.E. (2004). Cognitive strengths and weaknesses in children and adolescents homozygous for the galactosemia Q188R mutation: A descriptive study. *Neuropsychology, 18*(4), 658–664.

Antshel, K. M., & Waisbren, S. E. (2003). Timing is everything: Executive functions in children exposed to elevated levels of phenylalanine. *Neuropsychology, 17*(3), 458–468.

Azouvi, P., Couillet, J., Leclercq, M., Martin, Y., Asloun, S., & Rousseaux, M. (2004). Divided attention and mental effort after severe traumatic brain injury. *Neuropsychologia, 42*(9), 1260–1268.

Azzara, L. E. (2005). A normative study of the Frontal Lobe Personality Scale (FLOPS). *Dissertation Abstracts International: Section B, 65,* 6705.

Bartels, M., van den Oord, E. J. C. G., Hudziak, J.J., Rietveld, M. J. H., van Beijsterveldt, C. E. M., & Boomsma, D. I. (2004). Genetic and environmental mechanisms underlying stability and change in problem behaviors at ages 3, 7, 10 and 12. *Developmental Psychology, 40*(5), 852–867.

Bathgate, D., Snowden, J. S., Varma, A., Blackshaw, A., & Neary, D. (2001). Behavior in frontotemporal dementia, Alzheimer's disease and vascular dementia. *Acta Neurologica Scandinavica, 103*(6), 367–378.

Beck, A. T., Steer, R. A., & Brown, G. K. (1996). *Manual for Beck Depression Inventory II (BDI-II).* San Antonio, TX: Psychology Corporation.

Beebe, D. W., & Gozal, D. (2002). Obstructive sleep apnea and the prefrontal cortex: Towards a comprehensive model linking nocturnal upper airway obstruction to daytime cognitive and behavioral deficits. *Journal of Sleep Research, 11*(1), 1–16.

Beebe, D. W., Wells, C. T., Jeffries, J., Chini, B., Kalra, M., & Amin, R. (2004). Neuropsychological effects of pediatric obstructive sleep apnea. *Journal of the International Neuropsychological Society, 10*(7), 962–975.

Beldarrain, M. G., Garcia-Monco, J. C., Astigarraga, E., Gonzalez, A., & Grafman, J. (2005). Only spontaneous counterfactual thinking is impaired in patients with prefrontal cortex lesions. *Cognitive Brain Research, 24*(3), 723–726.

Bellebaum, C., Schäfers, L., Schoch, B., Wanke, I., Stolke, D., & Forsting, M. (2004). Clipping versus coiling: Neuropsychological follow up after aneurysmal subarachnoid hemorrhage (SAH). *Journal of Clinical and Experimental Neuropsychology, 26*(8), 1081–1092.

Benke, T., Karner, E., Seppi, K., Delazer, M., Marksteiner, J., & Donnemiller, E. (2004). Subacute dementia and imaging correlates in a case of fahr's disease. *Journal of Neurology, Neurosurgery & Psychiatry, 75*(8), 1163–1165.

Bennett, P. C., Ong, B., & Ponsford, J. (2005). Measuring executive dysfunction in an acute rehabilitation setting: Using the Dysexecutive Questionnaire (DEX). *Journal of the International Neuropsychological Society, 11*(4), 376–385.

Bernstein, J. H., & Waber, D. P. (1990). Developmental neuropsychological assessment: The systemic approach. In A. A. Boulton, G. B. Baker, & M. Hiscock (Eds.), *Neuromethods: Vol. 17 Neuropsychology.* Clifton, N.J.: Humana.

Bogod, N. M., Mateer, C. A., & Macdonald, S. W. S. (2003). Self-awareness after traumatic brain injury: A comparison of measures and their relationship to executive functions. *Journal of the International Neuropsychological Society, 9*(3), 450–458.

Boyle, P. A., & Malloy, P. F. (2003). Treating apathy in Alzheimer's disease. *Dementia and Geriatric Cognitive Disorders, 17*(1–2), 91–99.

Boyle, P. A., Malloy, P. F., Salloway, S., Cahn-Weiner, D. A., Cohen, R., & Cummings, J. L. (2003). Executive dysfunction and apathy predict functional impairment in Alzheimer disease. *American Journal of Geriatric Psychiatry, 11*(2), 214–221.

Bracken, B. A., & Keith, L. K. (2004). *Clinical Assessment of Behavior professional manual.* Lutz, FL: Psychological Assessment Resources.

Broadbent, D. E., Cooper, P. F., Fitzgerald, P., & Parkes, K. R. (1982). The Cognitive Failures Questionnaire (CFQ) and its correlates. *British Journal of Clinical Psychology, 21,* 1–16.

Brookshire, B., Levin, H. S., Song, J. X., & Zhang, L. (2004). Components of executive function in typically developing and head-injured children. *Developmental Neuropsychology, 25*(1–2), 61–83.

Brunswick, E. (1955). Symposium of the probability approach in psychology: Representative design and probabilistic theory in a functional psychology. *Psychological Review, 62,* 193–217.

Burgess, P. W. (1997). Theory and methodology in executive function and research. In P. Rabbitt (Ed.), *Methodology of Frontal and Executive Function* (pp. 81–116). Hove, U.K.: Psychology Press.

Burgess, P. W., Alderman, N., Evans, J., Emslie, H., & Wilson, B. A. (1998). The ecological validity of tests of executive function. *Journal of the International Neuropsychological Society, 4,* 547–558.

Burgess, P., & Shallice, T. (1997). *The Hayling and Brixton tests (two tests of dysexecutive syndrome.* Bury St. Edmonds, England: Thames Valley Test.

Burmeister, R., Hannay, H. J., Copeland, K., Fletcher, J. M., Boudousquie, A., & Dennis, M. (2005). Attention problems and executive functions in children with spina bifida and hydrocephalus. *Child Neuropsychology, 11*(3), 265–283.

Cahn-Weiner, D. A., Grace, J., Ott, B. R., Fernandez, H. H., & Friedman, J. H. (2002). Cognitive and behavioral features discriminate between Alzheimer's and Parkinson's disease. *Neuropsychiarty, Neuropsychology, & Behavioral Neurology, 15*(2), 79–87.

Chan, R. C. K. (2001). Dysexecutive symptoms among a non-clinical sample: A study with the use of the Dysexecutive Questionnaire. *British Journal of Psychology, 92*(3), 551–565.

Chan, R. C. K., & Chen, E. Y. H. (2004). Executive dysfunctions and neurological manifestations in schizophrenia. *Hong Kong Journal of Psychiatry, 14*(3), 2–6.

Chan, R. C. K., Chen, E. Y. H., Cheung, E. F. C., & Cheung, H. K. (2004). Executive dysfunctions in schizophrenia: Relationships to clinical manifestation. *European Archives of Psychiatry and Clinical Neuroscience, 254*(4), 256–262.

Chan, R. C. K., Hoosain, R., Lee, T. M. C., Fan, Y. W., & Fong, D. (2003). Are there subtypes of attentional deficits in patients with persisting post-concussive symptoms? A cluster analytical study. *Brain Injury, 17*(2), 131–148.

Chan, R. C. K., & Manly, T. (2002). The application of "dysexecutive syndrome" measures across cultures: Performance and checklist assessment in neurologically healthy and traumatically brain-injured Hong Kong chinese volunteers. *Journal of the International Neuropsychological Society, 8*(6), 771–780.

Channon, S., Mockler, C., & Lee, P. (2005). Executive functioning and speed of processing in phenylketonuria. *Neuropsychology, 19*(5), 679–686.

Chelune, G. (2003). Assessing reliable neuropsychological change. In R. D. Franklin (Ed.), *Prediction in Forensic and Neuropychology: Sound Statistical Practices* (pp. 123–147). Mahwah, NJ: Lawrence Erlbaum Associates.

Chiaravalloti, N. D., & DeLuca, J. (2003). Assessing the behavioral consequences of multiple sclerosis: An application of the Frontal Systems Behavior Scale (FrSBe). *Cognitive & Behavioral Neurology, 16,* 54–67.

Cripe, L. I. (1996). The ecological validity of executive function testing. In R. J. Sbordone, & C. J. Long (Eds.), *Ecological Validity of Neuropsychological Testing* (pp. 171–202). Delray Beach, FL: St Lucie Press, Inc.

Cummings, J. L. (1993). Frontal-subcortical circuits and human behavior. *Archives of Neurology, 50*(8), 873–880.

Cummings, D. D., Singer, H. S., Krieger, M., Miller, T. L., & Mahone, E. M. (2002). Neuropsychiatric effects of guanfacine in children with mild tourette syndrome: A pilot study. *Clinical Neuropharmacology, 25*(6), 325–332.

Davis, M. H. (1980). A multidimensional approach to individual differences in empathy. *Catalog of Selected Documents in Psychology, 10*(MS. 2124), 85–100.

Denckla, M. B. (1989). Executive function, the overlap zone between attention deficit hyperactivity disorder and learning disabilities. *International Pediatrics, 4*, 155–160.

Detzer, M. J., Whitaker, K. R., Isquith, P. K., Christiano, A. S., & Casella, S. J. (June, 2004). Self-reported executive function in adolescents with type 1 diabetes mellitus (T1DM). *Diabetes Supplement.*

Evans, J. J., Chua, S. E., McKenna, P. J., & Wilson, B. A. (1997). Assessment of the dysexecutive syndrome in schizophrenia. *Psychological Medicine, 27*, 635–646.

Fernandez-Duque, D., & Black, S. E. (2005). Impaired recognition of negative facial emotions in patients with frontotemporal dementia. *Neuropsychologia, 43*(11), 1673–1687.

Franzen, M. D., & Wilhelm, K. L. (1996). Conceptual foundations of ecological validity in neuropsychological assessment. In R. J. Sbordone, & C. J. Long (Eds.), *Ecological Validity of Neuropsychological Testing* (pp. 91–112). Boca Raton, FL: St. Lucie Press.

García-Villamisar, D., & Della Sala, S. (2002). Dual-task performance in adults with autism. *Cognitive Neuropsychiatry, 7*(1), 63–74.

Gilotty, L., Kenworthy, L., Sirian, L., Black, D. O., & Wagner, A. E. (2002). Adaptive skills and executive function in autism spectrum disorders. *Child Neuropsychology. Special Issue: Behavior Rating Inventory of Executive Function (BRIEF), 8*(4), 241–248.

Gioia, G. A., Espy, K. A., & Isquith, P. K. (2003). *Behavior Rating Inventory of Executive Function-Preschool Version*, Odessa, FL: Psychological Assessment Resources.

Gioia, G. A., & Isquith, P. K. (2004). Ecological assessment of executive function in traumatic brain injury. *Developmental Neuropsychology, 25*, 135–158.

Gioia, G. A., & Isquith, P. K. (2001). Executive function and ADHD: Exploration through children's everyday behaviors. *Clinical Neuropsychological Assessment, 2*, 61–84.

Gioia, G. A., Isquith, P. K., Guy, S. C., & Kenworthy, L. (2000). *Behavior Rating Inventory of Executive Function.* Odessa, FL: Psychological Assessment Resources.

Gioia, G. A., Isquith, P. K., Kenworthy, L., & Barton, R. M. (2002). Profiles of everyday executive function in acquired and developmental disorders. *Child Neuropsychology, 8*, 121–137.

Gioia, G. A., Isquith, P. K., Retzlaff, P. D., & Espy, K. A. (2002). Confimatory factor analysis of the Behavior Rating Inventory of Executive Function (BRIEF) in a clinical sample. *Child Neuropsychology, 8*, 249–257.

Goldberg, E., & Podell, K. (2000). Adaptive decision making, ecological validity, and the frontal lobes. *Journal of Clinical and Experimental Neuropsychology, 22*, 56–68.

Goldberg, T. E., & Weinberger, D. R. (2004). Genes and the parsing of cognitive processes. *Trends in Cognitive Sciences, 8*, 325–335.

Grace, J., & Malloy, P. F. (2001). *Frontal Systems Behavior Scale.* Lutz, FL: Psychological Assessment Resources, Inc.

Grace, J., Stout, J. C., & Malloy, P. F. (1999). Assessing frontal behavior syndromes with the Frontal Lobe Personality Scale. *Assessment, 6*, 269–284.

Guy, S. C., Isquith, P. K., & Gioia, G. A. (2004). *Behavior Rating Inventory of Executive Function—Self Report Version.* Odessa, Fla.: Psychological Assessment Resources, Inc.

Hart, T., Whyte, J., Kim, J., & Vaccaro, M. (2005). Executive function and self-awareness of "real-world" behavior and attention deficits following traumatic brain injury. *Journal of Head Trauma Rehabilitation. Special Issue: Disorders of Self-awareness, 20*(4), 333–347.

Heffernan, T., Ling, J., & Bartholomew, J. (2004). Self-rated prospective memory and central executive deficits in excessive alcohol users. *Irish Journal of Psychological Medicine, 21*(4), 122–124.

Hudziak, J. J., van Beijsterveldt, C. E. M., Althoff, R. R., Stanger, C., Rettew, D. C., Nelson, E. C., et al. (2004). Genetic and environmental contributions to the Child Behavior Checklist obsessive-compulsive scale. *Archives of General Psychiatry, 61*, 608–616.

Isquith, P. K., & Gioia, G. A. (2000). Brief predictions of ADHD: Clinical utility of the Behavior Rating Inventory of Executive Function for detecting ADHD subtypes in children [Abstract]. *Archives of Clinical Neuropsychology, 15*, 780–781.

Isquith, P. K., Gioia, G. A., & Espy, K. (2004). Executive function in preschool children. Examination through everyday behavior. *Developmental Neuropsychology, 26*, 403–422.

Jacobs, R., & Anderson, V. (2002). Planning and problem solving skills following focal frontal brain lesions in childhood: Analysis using the tower of London. *Child Neuropsychology, 8*(2), 93–106.

Jacobson, N. S., & Truax, P. (1991). Clinical significance: A statistical approach to defining meaningful change in psychotherapy research. *Journal of Consulting and Clinical Psychology, 59*, 12–19.

Janusz, J., Ahluvalia, T., & Gioia, G. A. (2002). The relationship between executive function and adaptive behavior [Abstract]. *Journal of the International Neuropsychological Society, 8*, 304.

Jarratt, K. P., Riccio, C. A., & Siekierski, B. M. (2005). Assessment of attention deficit hyperactivity disorder (ADHD) using the BASC and BRIEF. *Applied Neuropsychology. Special Issue: Attention Deficit Hyperactivity Disorder (ADHD) and Neuropsychology, 12*(2), 83–93.

Kahokehr, A., Siegert, R. J., & Weatherall, M. (2004). The frequency of executive cognitive impairment in elderly rehabilitation inpatients. *Journal of Geriatric Psychiatry and Neurology, 17*(2), 68–72.

Kaplan, E. (1988). A process approach to neuropsychological assessment. In T. Boll, & B. K. Bryant (Eds.), *Clinical Neuropsychology and Brain Function: Research, Measurement and Practice*. Washington, D.C.: American Psychological Association.

Kenealy, L.E. (2002). Executive functioning ability in children with ADHD: Effects of subtype and comorbidity. *Dissertation Abstracts International: Section B: The Sciences and Engineering, 63*(1-B), 530.

Kertesz, A. (2000). Behavioral and psychological symptoms and frontotemporal dementia (pick's disease). *International Psychogeriatrics, 12*(Suppl1), 183–187.

Kertesz, A., Davidson, W., & Fox, H. (1997). Frontal Behavior Inventory: Diagnostic criteria for the frontal lobe dementia. *The Canadian Journal of Neurological Sciences, 24*(1), 29–36.

Kertesz, A., Davidson, W., McCabe, P., & Munoz, D. (2003). Behavioral quantitation is more sensitive than cognitive testing in frontotemporal dementia. *Alzheimer Disease and Associated Disorders, 17*, 223–229.

Kertesz, A., Nadkarni, N., Davidson, W., & Thomas, A. W. (2000). The Frontal Behavioral Inventory in the differential diagnosis of frontotemporal dementia. *Journal of the International Neuropsychological Society, 6*, 460–468.

Kiley-Brabeck, K. (2004). Social skills of children with 22q11 deletion syndrome: A social cognitive neuroscience approach. *Dissertation Abstracts International: Section B: The Sciences and Engineering, 64*(12-B), 6332.

Kleeberg, J., Bruggimann, L., Annoni, J., van Melle, G., Bogousslavsky, J., & Schluep, M. (2004). Altered decision-making in multiple sclerosis: A sign of impaired emotional reactivity? *Annals of Neurology, 56*(6), 787–795.

Kral, M. C., & Brown, R. T. (2004). Transcranial doppler ultrasonography and executive dysfunction in children with sickle cell disease. *Journal of Pediatric Psychology, 29*(3), 185–195.

Landry, S. H., Swank, P., Stuebing, K., Prasad, M., & Ewing-Cobbs, L. (2004). Social competence in young children with inflicted traumatic brain injury. *Developmental Neuropsychology, 26*(3), 707–733.

Lawrence, V., Houghton, S., Douglas, G., Durkin, K., Whiting, K., & Tannock, R. (2004). Executive function and ADHD; A comparison of children's performance during neuro-psychological testing and real-world activities. *Journal of Attention Disorders, 7*(3), 137–149.

Lezak, M. (1995). *Neuropsychological Assessment* (3rd ed.). New York: Oxford University Press.

Mahone, E. M., Cirino, P. T., Cutting, L. E., Cerrone, P. M., Hagelthorn, K. M., Hiemenz, J. R., et al. (2002). Validity of the Behavior Rating Inventory of Executive Function in children with ADHD and/or tourette syndrome. *Archives of Clinical Neuropsychology, 17*(7), 643–662.

Mahone, E. M., Koth, C. W., Cutting, L., Singer, H. S., & Denckla, M. B. (2001). Executive function in fluency and recall measures among children with Tourette syndrome or ADHD. *Journal of the International Neuropsychological Society, 7*, 102–111.

Mahone, E. M., Zabel, T. A., Levey, E., Verda, M., & Kinsman, S. (2002). Parent and self-report ratings of executive function in adolescents with myelomeningocele and hydro-cephalus. *Child Neuropsychology. Special Issue: Behavior Rating Inventory of Executive Function (BRIEF), 8*(4), 258–270.

Malloy, P., & Grace, J. (2005). A review of rating scales for measuring behavior change due to frontal systems damage. *Cognitive and Behvaioral Neurology, 18*(1), 18–27.

Manchester, D., Priestley, N., & Jackson, H. (2004). The assessment of executive functions: Coming out of the office. *Brain Injury, 18*(11), 1067–1081.

Mangeot, S., Armstrong, K., Colvin, A. N., Yeates, K. O., & Taylor, H. G. (2002). Long-term executive deficits in children with traumatic brain injuries. *Child Neuropsychology.*

Marczinski, C. A., Davidson, W., & Kertesz, A. (2004). A longitudinal study of behavior in frontotemporal dementia and primary progressive aphasia. *Cognitive and Behavioral Neurology, 17*(4), 185–190.

Mathias, J. L. (2003). Neurobehavioral functioning of persons with Parkinson's disease. *Applied Neuropsychology, 10*(2), 57–68.

Mega, M. S., & Cummings, J. L. (1994). Frontal-subcortical circuits and neuropsychiatric disorders. *Journal of Neuropsychiatry and Clinical Neurosciences, 6*, 358–370.

Norris, G., & Tate, R. L. (2000). The Behavioral Assessment of Dysexecutive Syndrome (BADS): Ecological, concurrent and construct validity. *Neuropsychological Rehabilitation, 10*(1), 33–45.

Norton, L. E., Malloy, P. F., & Salloway, S. (2001). The impact of behavioral symptoms on activities of daily living in patients with dementia. *American Journal of Geriatric Psychiatry, 9*, 41–48.

Odhuba, R. A., van den Broek, M. D., & Johns, L. C. (2005). Ecological validity of measures of executive functioning. *British Journal of Clinical Psychology, 44*, 269–279.

Patton, J. H., Stanford, M. S., & Barratt, E. S. (1995). Factor structure of the Barratt impulsiveness scale. *Journal of Clinical Psychology, 51*(6), 768–774.

Pennington, B. F., Bennetto, L., McAleer, O. K., & Roberts, R. J. (1996). Executive functions and working memory: Theoretical and measurement issues. In G. R. Lyon, & N. A. Krasnegor (Eds.), *Attention, Memory and Executive Function*. Baltimore: Paul H. Brookes Publishing Co.

Rabin, L. (2001). Test Usage Patterns and Perceived Ecological Utility of Neuropsychological Assessment Techniques: A Survey of North American Clinical Neuropsychologists. Unpublished doctoral dissertation, Oxford University.

Rabin, L. A., Roth, R. M., Isquith, P. K., Wishart, H. A., Nutter-Upham, K. E., Pare, N., Flashman, L. A., & Saykin, A. J. (2006). Self and informant reports of executive function in mild cognitive impairment and older adults with cognitive complaints. *Archives of Clinical Neuropsychology, 21*, 721–732.

Ready, R. E., Ott, B. R., Grace, J., & Cahn-Weiner, D. A. (2003). Apathy and executive dysfunction in mild cognitive impairment and alzheimer disease. *American Journal of Geriatric Psychiatry, 11*(2), 222–228.

Rietveld, M. J. H., Hudziak, J. J., Bartels, M., van Beijsterveldt, C. E. M., & Boomsma, D. I. (2004). Heritability of attention problems in children: Longitudinal results from a study of twins, age 3 to 12. *Journal of Child Psychology and Psychiatry, 45*(3), 577–588.

Reynolds, C. R., & Kamphaus, R. W. (1992). *Behavior Assessment System for Children*. Circle Pines, MN: *American Guidance Service, Inc.*

Roth, R. M., Isquith, P. K., & Gioia, G. A. (2005). BRIEF-A: Behavior Rating Inventory of Executive Function-Adult Version. Odessa, FL: Psychological Assessment Resources.

Roth, R. M., Randolph, J. J., Koven, N. S., & Isquith, P. K. (2006). Neural substrates of executive functions: Insights from functional neuroimaging. In F. Columbus (Ed.), *Focus on Neuropsychology Research*. Hauppauge, NY: Nova Science Publishers, Inc.

Sbordone, R. J. (1996). Ecological validity: Some critical issues for the neuropsychologist. In R. J. Sbordone, & C. J. Long (Eds.), *Ecological Validity of Neuropsychological Testing* (pp. 91–112). Boca Raton, FL: St. Lucie Press.

Shallice, T., & Burgess, P. W. (1991). Deficits in strategy application following frontal lobe damage in man. *Brain, 114*, 727–741.

Shear, P. K., DelBello, M. P., Rosenberg, H. L., & Strakowski, S. M. (2002). Parental reports of executive dysfunction in adolescents with bipolar disorder. *Child Neuropsychology. Special Issue: Behavior Rating Inventory of Executive Function (BRIEF), 8*(4), 285–295.

Silver, C. (2000). Ecological validity in neuropsychological assessment in childhood traumatic brain injury. *Journal of Head Trauma Rehabilitation, 15*, 973–988.

Skjerve, A., & Brenne, L. (2003). Frontotemporal dementia–characteristics, diagnostics and treatment/Frontotemporal demens–kjennetegn, diagnostikk og behandlingstiltak. *Tidsskrift for Norsk Psykologforening, 40*(5), 390–397.

Spielberger, C. D. (1983). *Manual for the State-Trait Anxiety Inventory (STAI)*. PaloAlto, CA: Consulting Psychologists Press.

Spinella, M. (2005). Self-rated executive function: Development of the Executive Function Index. *International Journal of Neuroscience, 115*, 649–667. Philadelphia: Taylor & Francis.

Spinella, M. (2005a). Self-rated executive function: Development of the Executive Function Index. *International Journal of Neuroscience, 115*, 649–667.

Spinella, M. (2005b). *The Executive Function Index*. Unpublished manual.

Spinella, M., & Lyke, J. (2004). Executive personality traits and eating behavior. *International Journal of Neuroscience, 114*(1), 95–104.

Starkstein, S. E., Garau, M. L., & Cao, A. (2004). Prevalence and clinical correlates of disinhibition in dementia. *Cognitive and Behavioral Neurology, 17*(3), 139–147.

Stout, J. C., Ready, R. E., Grace, J., Malloy, P. F., & Paulsen, J. S. (2003). Factor analysis of the Frontal Systems Behavior Scale (FrSBe). *Assessment, 10,* 79–85.

Stout, J. C., Wyman, M. F., Johnson, S. A., Peavy, G. M., & Salmon, D. P. (2003). Frontal behavioral syndromes and functional status in probable Alzheimer disease. *American Journal of Geriatric Psychiatry Special Issue: Schizophrenia in late life, 11*(6), 683–686.

Stuss, D. T., & Benson, D. F. (1986). *The frontal lobes.* New York: Raven.

Velligan, D. I., Ritch, J. L., Sui, D., DiCocco, M., & Huntzinger, C. D. (2002). Frontal Systems Behavior Scale in schizophrenia: Relationships with psychiatric symptomatology, cognition and adaptive function. *Psychiatry Research, 113*(3), 227–236.

Vogel, A., Hasselbalch, S. G., Gade, A., Ziebell, M., & Waldemar, G. (2005). Cognitive and functional neuroimaging correlates for anosognosia in mild cognitive impairment and alzheimer's disease. *International Journal of Geriatric Psychiatry, 20*(3), 238–246.

Vriezen, E. R., & Pigott, S. E. (2002). The relationship between parental report on the BRIEF and performance-based measures of executive function in children with moderate to severe traumatic brain injury. *Child Neuropsychology. Special Issue: Behavior Rating Inventory of Executive Function (BRIEF), 8*(4), 296–303.

Waber, D. P., Gerber, E. B., Turcios, V. Y., Wagner, E. R., & Forbes, P. W. (2006). Executive functions and performance on high-stakes testing in children from urban schools. *Developmental Neuropsychology, 29,* 459–477.

Walley, R. M., & Donaldson, M. D. C. (2005). An investigation of executive function abilities in adults with Prader-Willi syndrome. *Journal of Intellectual Disability Research, 49*(8), 613–625.

Welsh, M. C., Pennington, B. F., & Grossier, D. B. (1991). A normative-developmental study of executive function: A window on prefrontal function in children. *Developmental Neuropsychology, 7,* 131–149.

Wetter, S. R., Delis, D. C., Houston, W. S., Jacobson, M. W., Lansing, A., Cobell, K., et al. (2005). Deficits in inhibition and flexibility are associated with the APOE-E4 allele in nondemented older adults. *Journal of Clinical and Experimental Neuropsychology, 27,* 943–952.

Whitaker, K. R., Detzer, M. J., Isquith, P. K., Christiano, A. S., & Casella, S. J. (June, 2004). Parent report of executive function in adolescents with Type 1 Diabetes Mellitus (T1DM). *Diabetes Supplement.*

Williams, W. H., Evans, J. J., Needham, P., & Wilson, B. A. (2002). Neurological, cognitive and attributional predictors of posttraumatic stress symptoms after traumatic brain injury. *Journal of Traumatic Stress, 15*(5), 397–400.

Wilson, B. A., Alderman, N., Burgess, P. W., Emslie, H., & Evans, J. J. (1996). *Behavioral Assessment of the Dysexecutive Syndrome.* Bury St Edmonds, England: Thames Valley Test.

Zawacki, T. M., Grace, J., Paul, R., Moser, D. J., Ott, B. R., & Gordon, N., et al. (2002). Behavioral problems as predictors of functional abilities of vascular dementia patients. *Journal of Neuropsychiatry and Clinical Neurosciences, 14*(3), 296–302.

9 Pediatric neuroimaging studies: A window to neurocognitive development of the frontal lobes

Amanda G. Wood and Elizabeth Smith

Contents

Behavioral and neuroimaging studies of children with brain lesions have greatly contributed to our understanding of the dynamic process of neurocognitive development. Carefully designed behavioral research on the nature and timing of cognitive skill acquisition in the normally developing brain has corroborated these data, although the relationship between neural substrate and typical cognitive development is relatively poorly understood. The ability to obtain measures of structural and functional brain changes in children noninvasively has triggered a new era. Models of neurocognitive development can now be tested, and disorders of childhood development with cognitive or behavioral components can be more precisely characterized.

A wide range of neuropsychological studies have documented developmental trajectories in healthy children across a variety of tasks that incorporate executive abilities. The different time course of the emergence of skills and attainment of adult ability levels supports a model of executive function comprised of discrete components. Elements of executive function include attentional control, goal-directedness, and mental flexibility. It is well established that the frontal lobes, and in particular the prefrontal cortex, have a significant role in mediating these abilities. Nevertheless, there is little data on how development of different brain regions might contribute to the successful attainment of relevant skills. These data would not only advance our theoretical appreciation of brain-behavioral relationships within the unique developmental context but also provide important information on the breakdown of these relationships in childhood-onset disorders. This chapter outlines the advances made in this area using magnetic resonance imaging (MRI).

Methodological issues

MRI scanning techniques and the analysis of brain images have advanced significantly in recent years. For example, traditional approaches to summarizing data on structural MRI scans for research purposes included visual ratings of lesion location or manual tracings of cortical structures on hard copy films. In contrast, sophisticated, computationally demanding statistical techniques to provide details of not only volume or location but also morphological features such as shape or thickness are now employed. In addition to structural morphology, different MRI sequences can be used to quantify neuronal integrity (for example, using T2 relaxometry or magnetic resonance spectroscopy) and of course, the functional neuroanatomy associated with cognition (using functional MRI; fMRI).

fMRI activation studies rely on the notion that regional changes in neural activity occur in response to task performance. Increased neural activity is associated with increases to blood flow, volume, and oxygenation. This *hemodynamic* response is exploited in fMRI by assessing its relative magnitude for an active versus a resting state. This is made possible by the different magnetic properties—and the associated magnetic resonance signals—of oxyhemoglobin (diamagnetic) and deoxyhemoglobin (paramagnetic). In essence, when a task is introduced and oxygenated blood is more prevalent, there is a reduction in the ratio of deoxygenated to oxygenated hemoglobin, which causes signal to increase (Thulborn, Waterton, Matthews, & Radda, 1982). The change in MRI signal, therefore, is dependent of the level of oxygenated blood (blood-oxygen-level dependent [BOLD]).

Some preliminary comments regarding the feasibility of scanning children with MRI and particularly fMRI are warranted. Children with developmental disorders and very young children in clinical settings are typically scanned under sedation. Apart from avoiding any potential distress to the child, this approach ensures that the images are of the highest possible quality. MRI scans are notoriously sensitive to movement artifact. When it comes to fMRI it is of course imperative that the child is alert, although some have trialed approaches that passively induce cortical activations (Souweidane et al., 1999). This requirement raises several potential problems, including gaining compliance getting into a confined and noisy space, remaining still for up to 45 min, and performing the task when prompted. In our own experience, children aged six and above took part in a practice session which replicated the scanning experience including lying on a purpose-built mock scanner and being exposed to the noises of the MRI sequences they would subsequently hear during the formal scanning session. Children were also given the opportunity to draw on their own thermoplastic face masks which were later used in the true scanning condition to prevent head motion (Wood et al., 2004). Compliance was excellent, with only 2 of 48 (4%) children who commenced scanning unable to complete the session. Our clinical use of fMRI technology has included successful testing of children as young as 5 years old, as reported by other research and clinical groups internationally.

Postprocessing of research fMRI data comprises a number of steps to ensure that the identification of brain regions is accurate and reliable, and these groups of images can be interpreted. The details of these steps are beyond the scope of this chapter and the reader is referred to Toga and Mazziota (2002) for further information.

Of relevance to pediatric imaging studies is the need to transpose individual brain images into a standard co-ordinate space (most often that of Talairach & Tournoux 1988). This process essentially allows like to be compared with like and relies on warping brains to match their major features. Reservation has been expressed about the appropriateness of transforming small brains, which may comprise proportionately different tissue types to a standard template based on mature structure. Similarly it has been argued that physiological differences in children and adults could affect group analyses of fMRI data. If the hemodynamic response, which is fundamental to the detection of signal change in fMRI experiments, differs then interpretation is problematic. It appears, however, that only minimal differences in these parameters exist between children and adults and their magnitude is smaller than other sources of noise (Kang, Burgund, Lugar, Petersen, & Schlaggar, 2003). Aside from this issue, many sophisticated image analysis techniques are available for use in pediatrics populations and the field is advancing rapidly in the absence of any significant limitations on collecting structural and fMRI data in healthy young children. In the next section, we turn to data derived from structural MRI studies on regional cortical development.

Cortical development

The bulk of cortical development occurs either in utero or in the early postnatal period, with increases in total brain volume tapering off after 5 or 6 years of age (for reviews refer to Durston et al., 2001; Giedd, 2003; Paus et al., 2001). Aside from the difficulty of studying structural development of the typically developing brain in infancy, the power of MRI lies in its ability to map the time course of regional changes in different tissue types, ideally by employing longitudinal designs. Observation of the dynamics of regional gray and white matter changes during childhood and adolescence may then provide unique data from which to map the timing of skill emergence. Here we focus on the available longitudinal structural MRI data.

White matter development

There are some conflicting results amongst structural neuroimaging investigations attempting to elucidate regional patterns of white matter development. A large longitudinal study of children and adolescents revealed linear increases in white matter volume that were not region specific (Giedd et al., 1999). In contrast, in a volumetric whole brain MRI study, Reiss, Abrams, Singer, Ross, and Denckla (1996) reported prominent regional increases in frontal white matter volume during childhood. An increase in white matter was found in dorsal prefrontal cortex, but there was no increase in ventral prefrontal regions. Another study with children and adolescents demonstrated age-related increases in white matter density in corticospinal and thalamocortical tracts bilaterally, and in left fronto-temporal pathways, providing evidence for maturation of fiber pathways supporting motor and speech functions, but did not find increases in frontal regions (Paus et al., 1999).

The largest white matter tract, the corpus callosum, plays a major role in integrating the activities of the left and right hemispheres. This region also continues to increase in size through childhood, seen mostly in increases of cross-sectional area measurements (refer to Thompson et al., 2000). Giedd, Snell, Lange, Rajapakse, Casey, Kozuch et al. (1996) found that cross-sectional area increased on average 2% per year in a group aged 4–18 years. Further, regionally specific changes have been identified in the splenium and isthmus of the corpus callosum. Further refinement of the regional specificity of white matter changes may be gained from diffusion tensor imaging (DTI), a rapidly developing technique that assesses the regularity and myelination of fibers by quantifying the diffusion of water molecules in the brain. Information about the orientation of white matter fibers is made available by exploiting the tendency for water molecules to move more readily along than across fibers and can be quantified as fractional anisotropy (FA). DTI has been used successfully in children and offers insight into the underlying basis for known white matter volume changes in childhood and adolescence (Barnea-Goraly et al., 2005; Klingberg, Vaidya, Gabrieli, Moseley, & Hedehus, 1999; Olesen, Nagy, Westerberg, & Klingberg, 2003; Schneider, Il'yasov, Hennig, & Martin, 2004; Snook, Paulson, Roy, Phillips, & Beaulieu, 2005). Increased white matter FA is seen throughout infancy and the first decade of life (see Barnea-Goraly et al., 2005). Studies investigating white matter development beyond childhood have found age related increases in white matter anisotropy in frontal and prefrontal regions (Barnea-Goraly et al., 2005; Klingberg et al., 1999) as well as in a range of other structures, including the internal capsule, basal ganglia and thalamic pathways and the corpus callosum (Barnea-Goraly et al., 2005), and the corticospinal tracts and the left arcuate fasciculus (Schmithorst, Wilke, Dardzinski, & Holland, 2002). Future studies may incorporate DTI and fMRI (Toosy et al., 2004) to further characterize the contribution of white matter changes to cognitive development.

MRI studies of gray matter development

Cortical gray matter exhibits a significant net decrease in volume from childhood to adulthood. Cross-sectional studies suggest initial increase in gray matter volume and density during early childhood followed by a decrease before adulthood. The age at which the rate of decrease slows varies, with some authors indicating little change after 20 years (Pfefferbaum et al., 1994) yet others indicating 50–60 years (Sowell et al., 2003). Developments in MRI measures of cortical thickness reveal average thickness in children 5–9 years of age ranging from 1.5 to 5.5 mm over the lateral and medial surfaces. One of the few longitudinal studies in this area reveals cortical thinning over large areas of cortex in this age range, with rates of loss in the order of 0.1–0.3 mm per year (Sowell et al., 2004). A further longitudinal study characterized gray matter density (which is a combined measure of glial, neuronal, and vascular tissue, in this case at the cortical surface) in a small group that was followed up repeatedly at regular intervals (Gogtay et al., 2004). It is often stated that the frontal lobes are the last to develop, but Gogtay and colleagues highlight the regional specificity of protracted development within the frontal lobe, with the frontal pole maturing early yet the dorsolateral prefrontal region maturing in adolescence (refer to Figure 9.1). This study also demonstrated ongoing loss of gray matter density in the orbitofrontal regions of the young adults they studied (Gogtay et al., 2004). Their

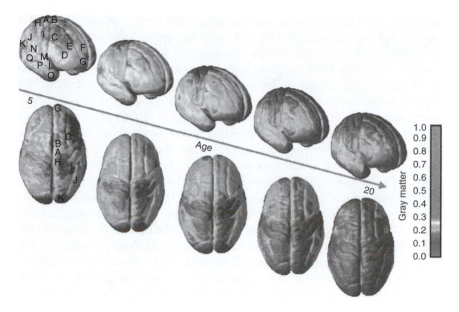

Figure 9.1 Longitudinal analysis of cortical development demonstrates ongoing loss of cerebral gray matter, particularly anteriorly. From "Dynamic mapping of human cortical development during childhood through early adulthood," by N. Gogtay, J. N. Giedd, L. Lusk, K. M. Hayashi, D. Greenstein, A. C. Vaituzis et al., 2004, *Proceedings of the National Academy of Science U S A., 101,* p. 8174.

data also suggest that the posterior temporal region continues to mature beyond the maturation of frontal association cortices.

From the point of view of the putative structural underpinnings of executive function development, these data indicate clearly that modifications of cerebral architecture continue in the prefrontal region until at least adolescence. Although this concept is not new, the contribution of neuroimaging lies in its capacity to delineate the localization of changes, the relative preservation or loss of specific tissue types, and—with large longitudinal studies—the precise timing of these changes. Future longitudinal studies may extend current knowledge by examining the precise timing of changes within the prefrontal cortex in larger cohorts. A striking feature identified by longitudinal studies is the nonlinear pattern of change reported (Giedd et al., 1999, Sowell et al., 2003), which is reminiscent of developmental "spurts" in cognitive skill acquisition. We turn next to studies that address this issue directly, using cognitive correlates of structural brain changes across childhood and adolescence.

Interaction between cerebral and cognitive development

Structural neuroimaging research to date demonstrates that cognitive development throughout childhood and adolescence is underpinned by an increase in volume, density, and coherence of cerebral white matter alongside a decline in cortical and subcortical gray matter density and thickness in the context of subtle overall brain growth. Although changes in gray and white matter during childhood and adolescence are now well described, there is a dearth of studies directly examining their cognitive correlates. Those that have measured aspects of cognition have not focused on specific cognitive processes, but rather on more global measures of ability. Earlier work showed that variance in full-scale IQ scores was explained by volume of gray matter, particularly of the prefrontal cortex (Reiss et al., 1996). More refined analysis of MRI data, this time using DTI of white matter fibers, confirms an association between frontal lobe development and IQ scores (Schmithorst et al., 2005). More rigorous assessment of specific cognitive domains is somewhat limited. Variance in prefrontal volume of healthy children is associated with performance on measures of response inhibition (Casey, Castellanos et al., 1997), and this group also showed an association between size of the anterior cingulate and speed of attentional set-shifting (Casey, Trainor et al., 1997). Changes in frontal lobe cortical thickness in children and adolescents have also been associated with verbal memory performance (Sowell, Delis, Stiles, & Jernigan, 2001) and left frontal cortical thinning in association with increases in vocabulary was demonstrated in a longitudinal study where thickness rather than density was used to measure cortical change (Sowell et al., 2004). Together, these data support the notion that acquisition of new cognitive skills is time-locked to changes in cortical development, which has implications for the timing of disease processes and their cognitive consequences. Nevertheless, increasingly sophisticated brain image analysis techniques are being reported internationally. To date, the association between structural and cognitive changes in the typically developing brain has not been fully determined. This will be an important area of future research with potentially significant implications for clinical practice.

Functional imaging

In contrast to the relative paucity of structure–function relationships reported in healthy children, there is a growing body of fMRI research on the development of cognitive processes, including executive functioning. fMRI studies to date have primarily focused on different aspects of attention and higher-order controlled processing, leaving a void in the study of more complex behavioral features of executive function. Nevertheless, data now reveal how the functional neuroanatomical networks supporting discrete skills are established at different times. A significant issue arising from existing studies is the difference in activation between children and adults. We discuss this issue below, following a review of studies on working memory and higher-order attentional control.

The development of working memory is a critical precursor to the acquisition of a range of multifaceted cognitive skills such as mental arithmetic and reading. It is also a prominent feature of disorders characterized by frontal lobe function impairment. Consistent with work performed in adults, fMRI studies in children or adolescents have employed the *n*-back paradigm. This comprises a 0-back condition in which participants respond to a presented stimulus as well as a condition in which the required response is whether the current stimulus matches that of the previous trial (1-back) or two trials previously (2-back), and so on. An early pediatric fMRI study using a 2-back (*n*-back) paradigm showed that activation during a verbal working memory task was similarly located in the prefrontal region of adults and children (Casey et al., 1995), although children had proportionately greater signal change. During a spatial *n*-back working memory task, activation in children (aged 8–10) and adults was present in the right dorsolateral prefrontal cortex, although children failed to exhibit activation in anterior cingulate cortex (Thomas et al., 1999). The absence of adult-like activation in specific regions for which cognitive processing requirements have been previously characterized offers to identify critical time-points at which developmental gains are typically made. Thomas et al. (1999) proposed that, on the basis of their fMRI data, a child's ability to "modulate competition," which is a core feature of the cingulate, emerges later at around 10 years of age.

More recent work examining spatial working memory has set out to develop tasks that ensure that children perform at similar levels to adults. The argument for this approach is that it permits the investigator to examine changes in brain activity in relation to age without concern about differences in performance between groups (Klingberg, Forssberg, & Westerberg, 2002). The alternative stance is that by creating a ceiling effect for the groups, you remove the fundamental construct of interest, namely the acquisition of specific skills throughout development. Nevertheless, Klingberg et al. (2002) combined an in-scanner paradigm that children and adults performed equally well and out of scanner testing of the extent of working memory capacity. They found greater activation in superior frontal and intraparietal regions in older children, and reported that activation in these regions was related to working memory capacity.

Other facets of executive function have been studied including the ability to inhibit an undesirable or prepotent response, which improves dramatically throughout childhood to adolescence and in adults is mediated by a network involving frontal and parietal regions. There is considerable interest in understanding the development of this network using fMRI because of its relationship to childhood-onset neuropsychiatric disorders which manifest in poor inhibitory control, such as ADHD, OCD, and Tourette's syndrome (Wright, McMullin, Martis, Fischer, & Rauch, 2005).

A useful approach to examining age-related brain–behavior skill changes is to employ one paradigm that taps into well-established skills and another whose developmental trajectory is relatively more protracted. Comparing children (9- to 12-year-olds) and adults on a selective visual attention task and one requiring inhibition of response inhibition, Booth et al. (2003) found only subtle differences on the former, whereas marked differences were observed for response inhibition. Children showed greater activation than adults across a range of prefrontal, limbic, and striatal regions. These data mirrored the behavioral results, in which children performed more poorly than adults overall.

Children (aged 8–10 years) were more susceptible to interference and less proficient on reorienting their attention than adults in an fMRI study that used modified flanker and cued reaction time tasks (Konrad et al., 2005). These behavioral features were associated with differences in the patterns of activation during task performance. Using a priori-defined regions of interest based on the behavioral literature, adults showed significant activation in expected areas, whereas children largely did not. Indeed, children displayed a more widespread pattern of activation across the whole brain. Direct comparison of activation maps showed that adults had greater activation in right prefrontal and left superior parietal cortex, whereas children showed greater activation than adults in right superior temporal and left superior frontal gyri. The different regions of activation noted in children and adults as well as the laterality differences were interpreted as support for immature fronto-striatal networks for this aspect of executive control. This study also examined the contribution of structural group differences to the observed functional activation patterns. In agreement with other groups, they observed larger gray matter volume in the temporal, frontal, and parietal lobes of children, perhaps supporting the hypothesis that reductions in neuron extent underlie apparent focalization of activation from childhood to adulthood (Konrad et al., 2005). Nevertheless, there was only limited overlap in the structure–function differences in adult and child brains.

Some studies have identified differences in the laterality of activation when children and adults were required to suppress interfering information (Bunge, Dudukovic, Thomason, Vaidya, & Gabrieli, 2002). In adults, activation occurred in the right ventrolateral prefrontal cortex, whereas in children frontal activation was left sided. The unique aspect of this study was its approach to examining children's performance, which as a group was significantly worse than adults. Bunge et al. (2002) selected a group of children whose performance was closer to that of adults, with the expectation that these children would show a similar, mature, pattern of activation. On the contrary, this group retained the left-lateralized focus of activation, albeit of greater magnitude than those with poor performances. This study is a good example of the elegant manner in which fMRI can be used to explore neurocognitive development.

The studies described here have focused on young children in whom executive skills are largely immature. Better insight to the temporal dynamics of skill emergence is gleaned from reports that include adolescents, whose performance on executive tasks often reaches adult levels. Interestingly, however, although adolescents' behavioral performance may be similar to that of adults, fMRI studies demonstrate differences in the functional neuroanatomy underlying these performances (Rubia et al., 2000). Furthermore, it is now possible, using event-related paradigms and carefully designed paradigms, to begin to tease apart which aspects of a task are associated with discrepancies in developmental functional neuroanatomy. Even when there is a correlation between age and performance, however, there is not necessarily a linear increase in activation across brain regions from childhood through to adulthood (see Luna et al., 2001). Comparison of fMRI activation in children (aged 7–11) and adolescents (aged 12–16) with adults (over 18) reveals regional differences in the age at which adult-like activation levels are achieved (Adleman et al., 2002). Activation patterns during Stroop performance typically involve the anterior cingulate, lateral prefrontal, and parietal cortices. By adolescence, parietal activation is similar to that of adults, whereas prefrontal activation continues to be significantly reduced in both children and adolescents. These data may be assumed to illustrate the development of the component cognitive processes in this type of executive task. Furthermore, other studies have identified a dissociation of prefrontal cortex function during the development of response inhibition, with some regions more activated with age and others less significantly involved (Tamm, Menon, & Reiss, 2002). Thus, an account of the functional neuroanatomy of aspects of executive development begins to emerge. It is worth noting that, without exception, these studies are cross sectional in design. Although the differences in brain regions involved in task performance identified between younger and older participants are compelling, it would be beneficial to confirm these patterns longitudinally.

One of the prevailing issues in developmental fMRI studies is an understanding of the basis for differences in adults and younger cohorts. A key issue is whether regional brain activity differences in children and adults reflect performance discrepancies or changes in the underlying neural substrate (i.e., maturation). Some authors have argued that the greater magnitude and more diffuse activation in children relative to adults supports the view that increasing cognitive capacity during childhood may coincide with a gradual loss rather than formation of new synapses and presumably a strengthening of remaining synaptic connections (Casey, Giedd, & Thomas, 2000). By and large though, adults show greater activation than younger cohorts (although this may well depend on the region of interest used, refer to Luna et al., 2001) and thus differences between children and adults in the magnitude or spatial extent of activation may of course merely reflect the known performance discrepancies in the groups. By measuring the behavioral response during scanning or gauging performance outside the scanner, one can begin to piece together the relationship between physiological changes and the activation paradigms used. Consistent with many other studies, in our own work, we identified a greater activation in adults than children (Wood et al., 2004) and this correlated with task performance measured outside the scanner. Nevertheless, the positive association between task performance and degree of activation is more broadly reflected in detailed studies of adults (Wood, Saling, Abbott, & Jackson, 2001). Thus, this is not specifically a parameter that affects pediatric neuroimaging studies but one that pertains to data on individual differences in cognitive skills. Nevertheless, it is possible to match performance on any given task and examine differences in regional brain activity, which should reflect only maturational processes. An argument against the matching strategy is that even though children and adults may be equally proficient on the task being examined children require more "effort" to perform it, therefore giving rise to differences in activation patterns. This explanation—often used post hoc to account for unexpected findings—is unsatisfactory, particularly when the dynamic nature of cognitive development is the key variable. Effort is not a cognitive process and cannot have functional neuroanatomy attributed to it. To make sense of this anecdotal construct in pediatric imaging research, we must reconceptualize it in terms of its component cognitive parts. A more constructive way to conceive this issue is to consider the additional or alternative strategies a child may use to realize a similar level of performance. By disentangling the qualitative differences in task performance of children and adults, we can move toward more sophisticated experimental designs that will better elicit true developmental differences in functional neuroanatomy. Taken together with developments in event-related imaging and the ability to suppress scanner noise during presentation of stimuli and recording of, for example, vocal responses, an approach that focuses on cognitive processing differences, rather than effort, may yield important insights into normal and abnormal cognitive development.

Steps toward resolving these issues in developmental fMRI of executive function are evident in the recent work on selective attention and response inhibition in a group of children with a small age range (9.3–11.7 years) (Booth et al., 2004). Behavioral performance was examined in relation to the intensity of activation within task-specific regions of interest (superior parietal lobule in selection attention and prefrontal cortex and basal ganglia for response inhibition). Greater activation in these network regions of interest was associated with better performance on the response inhibition task, but worse performance on selective attention. The conflicting association of activation levels with performance levels may be evidence in support of different trajectories of both these tasks (Booth et al., 2003), with selective attention being well developed in this age group relative to response inhibition. It certainly highlights the importance of identifying the relative contribution of specific cognitive components to overall activation levels in the developmental context. There is, however, still a reliance on the notion that poor performance can be associated with greater activation because of inefficient use of cognitive networks. This interpretation is akin to the role of "effort" in different activation levels and requires closer examination in the future.

Outside the realm of executive function, an elegant body of work on single-word processing captures the essence of the performance/maturation dilemma (Schlaggar et al., 2002). Participants were adults and children (aged 7–years), whose performance at a group level was statistically different but overlapping. Thus, the authors were able to systematically evaluate the reliance of activation in regions of interest on performance and age (refer to Figure 9.2). In this manner, they identified regions of activation that were performance independent, allowing them to confidently interpret their data in the context of ongoing brain development.

In this section we have described fMRI studies of aspects of executive function. Whilst these data begin to shed light on the emergence of functional neuroanatomical networks and will no doubt contribute to a better understanding of disorders in which executive dysfunction is a core feature, they also have significant implications for the interpretation of other developmental neuroimaging research in which an influence of executive functions on task performance may be occurring. For example, our own research on language lateralization in children and adults used two verbal fluency tasks, noun–verb generation and orthographic lexical retrieval (letter fluency; Wood et al., 2004). In adults there was no difference in the asymmetry of activation seen in both tasks. Conversely, in children there was more pronounced asymmetry for noun–verb generation than letter fluency. A greater role for the right hemisphere during children's performance of the latter language task was identified. Rather than interpret this as a difference in language lateralization per se, we feel that that pattern can be attributed to the letter fluency task's reliance on self-monitoring, set-shifting, and memory load, skills which are known to continue developing throughout childhood. By contrast, the verb generation task, which was similarly lateralized in children and adults, does not rely so heavily on these additional cognitive processes. These data highlight the importance of having a sound understanding of the cognitive components of fMRI tasks, without which it is possible to make erroneous judgments about brain–behavior relationships.

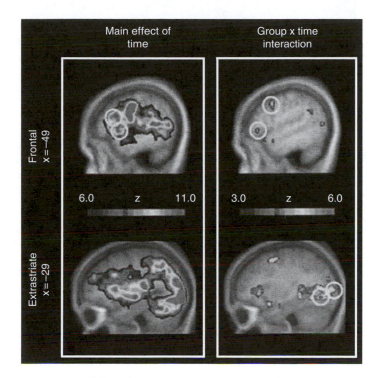

Figure 9.2 Regional relationships with age and performance in children and adults are identified and an elegant approach to identifying brain maturation is described. From "Functional neuroanatomical differences between adults and school-age children in the processing of single words," by B. L. Schlaggar, T. T. Brown, H. M. Lugar, K. M. Visscher, F. M. Miezin, and S. E. Petersen, 2002, *Science, 296*, p. 1476.

Conclusions

In their treatise on the cerebral localization of language in the context of brain injury, Penfield and Lamar Roberts (1959) remarked that a child's brain "is subject to inexorable change with the passage of time." We are now in a strong position to begin to unravel the complex story of how changes in brain structure during development enable gains of function to be made. Ultimately, of course, it is our intention that this will directly inform our models of disease processes and management of affected children. The challenges to be addressed in the pediatric neuroimaging field will be to continue to disambiguate the contribution of maturation and skill acquisition to differences in regional brain activity identified during development; it will be useful to combine fMRI with other measures of tissue integrity and some recent advances have been made using this approach (Kim & Kim 2005). Furthermore, fMRI studies may also be extended, particularly in clinical populations, by use of pharmacological interventions, which when coupled with knowledge of drug actions may in turn may provide insight to pathophysiological mechanisms of developmental disorders. Pediatric imaging studies possess enormous potential to clarify the neural differences in childhood-onset disorders involving the frontal lobes as well as learning disabilities that manifest in this age group. Both structural and fMRI may be used fruitfully to explore neuroanatomical predictors of outcome, and assess the effects of interventions.

Acknowledgments

Amanda Wood is supported by the National Health and Medical Research Council of Australia (Fellowship ID 251755).

References

Adleman, N. E., Menon, V., Blasey, C. M., White, C. D., Warsofsky, I. S., Glover, G. H., et al. (2002). A developmental fMRI study of the Stroop Color-Word Task. *Neuroimage, 16*(1), 61–75.

Barnea-Goraly, N., Menon, V., Eckert, M., Tamm, L., Bammer, R., Karchemskiy, A., et al. (2005). White matter development during childhood and adolescence: A cross-sectional diffusion tensor imaging study. *Cerebral Cortex, 15*(12), 1848–1854.

Booth, J. R., Burman, D. D., Meyer, J. R., Lei, Z., Trommer, B. L., Davenport, N. D., et al. (2003). Neural development of selective attention and response inhibition. *Neuroimage, 20*(2), 737–751.

Booth, J. R., Burman, D. D., Meyer, J. R., Trommer, B. L., Davenport, N. D., Parrish, T. B., et al. (2004). Brain–behavior correlation in children depends on the neurocognitive network. *Human Brain Mapping, 23*(2), 99–108.

Bunge, S. A., Dudukovic, N. M., Thomason, M. E., Vaidya, C. J., & Gabrieli, J. D. (2002). Immature frontal lobe contributions to cognitive control in children: Evidence from fMRI. *Neuron, 33*(2), 301–311.

Casey, B. J., Castellanos, F. X., Giedd, J. N., Marsh, W. L., Hamburger, S. D., Schubert, A. B., et al. (1997). Implication of right frontostriatal circuitry in response inhibition and attention-deficit/hyperactivity disorder. *Journal of the American Academy of Child & Adolescent Psychiatry, 36*(3), 374–383.

Casey, B. J., Cohen, J. D., Jezzard, P., Turner, R., Noll, D. C., Trainor, R. J., et al. (1995). Activation of prefrontal cortex in children during a nonspatial working memory task with functional MRI. *Neuroimage, 2*(3), 221–229.

Casey, B. J., Giedd, J. N., & Thomas, K. M. (2000). Structural and functional brain development and its relation to cognitive development. *Biological Psychology, 54*(1–3), 241–257.

Casey, B. J., Trainor, R., Giedd, J., Vauss, Y., Vaituzis, C. K., Hamburger, S., et al. (1997). The role of the anterior cingulate in automatic and controlled processes: A developmental neuroanatomical study. *Developmental Psychobiology, 30*(1), 61–69.

Durston, S., Hulshoff, H. E., Casey, B. J., Giedd, J. N., Buitelaar, J. K., & van Engeland, H. (2001). Anatomical MRI of the developing human brain: What have we learned? *Journal of the American Academy of Child and Adolescent Psychiatry, 40*, 1012–1020.

Giedd, J. N. (2003). The anatomy of mentalization: A view from developmental neuroimaging. *Bulletin of the Menninger Clinic, 67*, 132–142.

Giedd, J. N., Blumenthal, J., Jeffries, N. O., Castellanos, F. X., Liu, H., Zijdenbos, A., et al. (1999). Brain development during childhood and adolescence: A longitudinal MRI study. *Nature Neuroscience, 2*(10), 861–863.

Giedd, J. N., Snell, J. W., Lange, N., Rajapakse, J. C., Casey, B. J., Kozuch, P. L., et al. (1996). Quantitative magnetic resonance imaging of human brain development: Ages 4–18. *Cerebral Cortex*, 6(4), 551–560.

Gogtay, N., Giedd, J. N., Lusk, L., Hayashi, K. M., Greenstein, D., Vaituzis, A. C., et al. (2004). Dynamic mapping of human cortical development during childhood through early adulthood. *Proceedings of the National Academy of Science U S A.*, *101*, 8174–8179.

Kang, H. C., Burgund, E. D., Lugar, H. M., Petersen, S. E., & Schlaggar, B. L. (2003). Comparison of functional activation foci in children and adults using a common stereotactic space. *Neuroimage*, *19*(1), 16–28.

Kim, D. S., & Kim, M. (2005). Combining functional and diffusion tensor MRI. *Annals of the New York Academy of Sciences*, *1064*, 1–15.

Klingberg, T., Forssberg, H., & Westerberg, H. (2002). Increased brain activity in frontal and parietal cortex underlies the development of visuospatial working memory capacity during childhood. *Journal of Cognitive Neuroscience*, *14*(1), 1–10.

Klingberg, T., Vaidya, C. J., Gabrieli, J. D., Moseley, M. E., & Hedehus, M. (1999). Myelination and organization of the frontal white matter in children: A diffusion tensor MRI study. *Neuroreport*, *10*(13), 2817–2821.

Konrad, K., Neufang, S., Thiel, C. M., Specht, K., Hanisch, C., Fan, J., et al. (2005). Development of attentional networks: An fMRI study with children and adults. *Neuroimage*, *28*(2), 429–439.

Luna, B., Thulborn, K. R., Munoz, D. P., Merriam, E. P., Garver, K. E., Minshew, N. J., et al. (2001). Maturation of widely distributed brain function subserves cognitive development. *Neuroimage*, *13*(5), 786–793.

Olesen, P. J., Nagy, Z., Westerberg, H., & Klingberg, T. (2003). Combined analysis of DTI and fMRI data reveals a joint maturation of white and grey matter in a fronto-parietal network. *Cognitive Brain Research*, *18*(1), 48–57.

Paus, T., Collins, D. L., Evans, A. C., Leonard, G., Pike, B. & Zijdenbos, A. (2001). Maturation of white matter in the human brain: A review of magnetic resonance studies. *Brain Research Bulletin*, *54*, 255–266.

Paus, T., Zijdenbos, A., Worsley, K., Collins, D. L., Blumenthal, J., Giedd, J. N., et al. (1999). Structural maturation of neural pathways in children and adolescents: In vivo study. *Science*, *283*(5409), 1908–1911.

Penfield, W., & Lamar Roberts, L. (1959). *Speech and brain mechanisms*. New York: Atheneum.

Pfefferbaum, A., Mathalon, D. H., Sullivan, E. V., Rawles, J. M., Zipursky, R. B., & Lim, K. O. A. (1994). A quantitative magnetic resonance imaging study of changes in brain morphology from infancy to late adulthood. *Archives of Neurology*, *51*, 874–887.

Reiss, A. L., Abrams, M. T., Singer, H. S., Ross, J. L., & Denckla, M. B. (1996). Brain development, gender and IQ in children. A volumetric imaging study. *Brain*, *119*(Pt. 5), 1763–1774.

Rubia, K., Overmeyer, S., Taylor, E., Brammer, M., Williams, S. C., Simmons, A., et al. (2000). Functional frontalisation with age: Mapping neurodevelopmental trajectories with fMRI. *Neuroscience & Biobehavioral Reviews*, *24*(1), 13–19.

Schlaggar, B. L., Brown, T. T., Lugar, H. M., Visscher, K. M., Miezin, F. M., & Petersen, S. E. (2002). Functional neuroanatomical differences between adults and school-age children in the processing of single words [see comment]. *Science*, *296*(5572), 1476–1479.

Schmithorst, V. J., Wilke, M., Dardzinski, B. J., & Holland, S. K. (2002). Correlation of white matter diffusivity and anisotropy with age during childhood and adolescence: A cross-sectional diffusion-tensor MR imaging study. *Radiology*, *222*(1), 212–218.

Schmithorst, V. J., Wilke, M., Dardzinski, B. J., & Holland, S. K. (2005). Cognitive functions correlate with white matter architecture in a normal pediatric population: A diffusion tensor MRI study. *Human Brain Mapping, 26*(2), 139–147.

Schneider, J. F., Il'yasov, K. A., Hennig, J., & Martin, E. (2004). Fast quantitative diffusion-tensor imaging of cerebral white matter from the neonatal period to adolescence. *Neuroradiology, 46*(4), 258–266.

Snook, L., Paulson, L. A., Roy, D., Phillips, L., & Beaulieu, C. (2005). Diffusion tensor imaging of neurodevelopment in children and young adults. *Neuroimage, 26*(4), 1164–1173.

Souweidane, M. M., Kim, K. H., McDowall, R., Ruge, M. I., Lis, E., Krol, G., et al. (1999). Brain mapping in sedated infants and young children with passive-functional magnetic resonance imaging. *Pediatric Neurosurgery, 30*(2), 86–92.

Sowell, E. R., Delis, D., Stiles, J., & Jernigan, T. L. (2001). Improved memory functioning and frontal lobe maturation between childhood and adolescence: A structural MRI study. *Journal of the International Neuropsychological Society, 7*(3), 312–322.

Sowell, E. R., Peterson, B. S., Thompson, P. M., Welcome, S. E., Henkenius, A. L., & Toga, A. W. (2003). Mapping cortical change across the human life span. *Nature Neuroscience, 6*(3), 309–315.

Sowell, E. R., Thompson, P. M., Leonard, C. M., Welcome, S. E., Kan, E., & Toga, A. W. (2004). Longitudinal mapping of cortical thickness and brain growth in normal children. *Journal of Neuroscience, 24*(38), 8223–8231.

Talairach, J., & Tournoux, P. (1988). *Co-planar stereotaxic Atlas of the human brain: 3-Dimensional proportional system—an approach to cerebral imaging*, New York: Thieme Medical Publishers.

Tamm, L., Menon, V., & Reiss, A. L. (2002). Maturation of brain function associated with response inhibition. *Journal of the American Academy of Child & Adolescent Psychiatry, 41*(10), 1231–1238.

Thomas, K. M., King, S. W., Franzen, P. L., Welsh, T. F., Berkowitz, A. L., Noll, D. C., et al. (1999). A developmental functional MRI study of spatial working memory. *Neuroimage, 10*(3, Pt. 1), 327–338.

Thompson, P. M., Giedd, J. N., Woods, R. P., MacDonald, D., Evans, A. C., & Toga, A. W. (2000). Growth patterns in the developing brain detected by using continuum mechanical tensor maps. *Nature, 404*(6774), 190–193.

Toosy, A. T., Ciccarelli, O., Parker, G. J., Wheeler-Kingshott, C. A., Miller, D. H., & Thompson, A. J. (2004). Characterizing function–structure relationships in the human visual system with functional MRI and diffusion tensor imaging. *Neuroimage, 21*, 1452–1463.

Thulborn, K. R., Waterton, J. C., Matthews, P. M., & Radda, G. K. (1982). Oxygenation dependence of the transverse relaxation time of water protons in whole blood at high field. *Biochimica et Biophysica Acta, 714*, 265–270.

Toga, A. W., & Mazziotta, J. C. (2002). *Brain mapping: The methods* (2nd ed.). San Diego, CA: Academic Press.

Wood, A. G., Harvey, A. S., Wellard, R. M., Abbott, D. F., Anderson, V., Kean, M., et al. (2004). Language cortex activation in normal children. *Neurology, 63*(6), 1035–1044.

Wood, A. G., Saling, M. M., Abbott, D. F., & Jackson, G. D. (2001). A neurocognitive account of frontal lobe involvement in orthographic lexical retrieval: An fMRI study. *Neuroimage, 14*(1, Pt. 1), 162–169.

Wright, C. I., McMullin, K., Martis, B., Fischer, H., & Rauch, S. L. (2005). Brain correlates of negative visuospatial priming in healthy children. *Psychiatry Research, 139*(1), 41–52.

Section III

Impairments of executive function across the lifespan

10 Executive functioning and attention in children born preterm

Kelly Howard, Peter J. Anderson, and H. Gerry Taylor

Contents

Introduction

Infants born earlier than 32 weeks gestation now represent about 1–2% of all live births in developed countries (Tucker & McGuire, 2004). These very preterm infants are much more likely to survive today than they once were due to recent advances in obstetric management and neonatal intensive care (Hack & Fanaroff, 1999). Unfortunately, this reduction in mortality has not been associated with a decline in the frequency and severity of neurobehavioral impairment in this population, but instead has resulted in an increase in the absolute number of very preterm children presenting with adverse outcomes (Hack & Fanaroff, 1999). Adverse outcomes include severe neuromotor and sensory disabilities as well as cognitive deficits, learning difficulties, and behavior problems. Although outcomes vary widely, the prevalence of neurobehavioral problems at school age is estimated to be as high as 50% (Anderson et al., 2003; Taylor, Klein, & Hack, 2000). Of particular interest are the high rates of executive dysfunction, attentional problems, and attention deficit/hyperactivity disorder (ADHD) in children born very preterm. This chapter will review recent research examining attentional skills and executive functioning in children born very preterm, describes the neuropathology associated with prematurity, and proposes possible neural mechanisms underpinning the attentional and executive impairments associated with prematurity.

Prematurity

Infants born very preterm (<32 weeks' gestation) are at risk for a variety of medical complications in the neonatal period, many of which are associated with mortality or long-term disabilities (Ward & Beachy, 2003). The major conditions that impact on short- and long-term outcomes include chronic lung disease, necrotizing enterocolitis, sepsis, retinopathy of prematurity, and severe brain injury (see Table 10.1 for a description of these medical complications). The vulnerability of the very preterm infant to such conditions is related to the immaturity of multiple organ systems at birth. Thus, the smallest and most premature infants are at highest risk for developing medical problems and in many cases medical complications co-occur (Hack & Fanaroff, 1999).

Of particular importance to long-term neurobehavioral functioning is perinatal brain injury. During the late second and early third trimester of human gestation the brain is in a rapid state of development (Huppi et al., 1998). This is a period of

Table 10.1 Significant medical complications associated with preterm birth.

Complication	Description
Respiratory distress syndrome	This condition occurs when the newborn's lungs do not produce enough surfactant, a chemical normally produced by mature lungs to keep the air sacs within the lungs from collapsing.
Chronic lung disease (also known as bronchopulmonary dysplasia)	Refers to damage to parts of the newborn's lungs, usually as a result of prolonged ventilator support. The damaged lung tissue traps air or collapses, fills with fluid, and produces extra mucus.
Patent ductus arteriosus	A congenital heart abnormality that arises because the normal channel between the pulmonary artery and the aorta fails to close at birth.
Apnea	Temporary cessation of breathing that may be accompanied by a slow heart rate.
Retinopathy of prematurity	An abnormal growth of blood vessels in the eye. It can lead to bleeding and formation of scars that can damage the retina of the eye, sometimes resulting in vision loss and blindness.
Necrotizing enterocolitis	A potentially dangerous condition caused by inflammation of the lining of the gastrointestinal tract.
Sepsis	An infection of the blood.
Intraventricular hemorrhage	Bleeding in or around the ventricles.
Periventricular leukomalacia	Necrosis in brain regions around the ventricles.

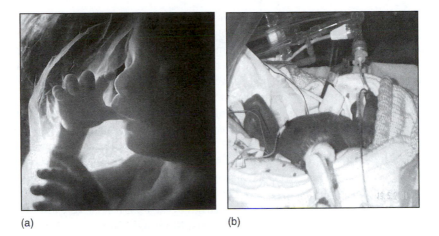

(a)   (b)

Figure 10.1   The third trimester of brain development occurring in (a) the protective intra-uterine environment and (b) the nonoptimal context of the neonatal intensive care unit.

extraordinary cerebral vulnerability, during which the formation and elaboration of dendrites and axons, proliferation and differentiation of glial cells, synaptogensis, myelination, selective cell death, and blood vessel growth takes place (Volpe, 2001). These processes are largely determined by genetic factors, although they are amendable to external influences (Monk, Webb, & Nelson, 2001). When an infant is born very preterm the immature brain develops in an environment dramatically different from the intended intrauterine one (see Figure 10.1). For example, the immature brain may be exposed to numerous medical (e.g., hypoxia, ischemia, infection, hyperbilirubinemia, inadequate nutrition, medications) and environmental (e.g., frequent noxious stimulation, the constant light and excessive sound of the neonatal intensive care unit [NICU], prolonged separation from parents) events that place it at increased risk for injury and have the potential to alter the normal maturational processes (Perlman, 2001).

The major forms of brain injury associated with preterm birth are intraventricular hemorrhage (IVH), cystic periventricular leukomalacia (PVL), and diffuse white matter abnormalities (Volpe, 2001).

An IVH is a bleed originating within the germinal matrix, a transient embryonic structure located along the lining of the lateral ventricles, and the region in which neuronal and glial cell proliferation occurs. The germinal matrix is a vascular end zone consisting of a network of fragile and immature capillaries, which are vulnerable to rupture in response to extreme fluctuations in cerebral blood flow (Roland & Hill, 2003). In the majority of cases the hemorrhage is minor and confined to the germinal matrix (Grade I) or lateral ventricles (Grade II), but in more severe cases the hemorrhage can result in ventricular dilation (Grade III) and periventricular white matter infarction (Grade IV). Hemorrhages in this region are rare in more mature infants as by 34–35 weeks' gestation the germinal matrix has completely involuted.

Cystic PVL is a nonhemorrhagic injury that is characterized by necrosis of the white matter in the periventricular region. On cranial ultrasound such lesions appear as bilateral cysts. Cystic PVL is thought to be related to hypoxic-ischemic episodes in the perinatal period and the immunological response of the mother and fetus to intrauterine infection (Dammann, Kuban, & Leviton, 2002; Volpe, 2001). Preterm infants are at an increased risk of PVL due to the immaturity of the cerebrovasculature in the periventricular region as well as the vulnerability of oligodendrocytes (i.e., the cells responsible for the production of myelin) during the third trimester. Between 23 and 32 weeks' gestation oligodendrocytes are in the active stage of proliferation and differentiation, and have been shown to be particularly susceptible during this period to hypoxic-ischemic events and inflammatory processes (Back et al., 2002). Although damage to the immature oligodendrocytes is considered the major consequence of PVL, axonal damage and injury to subplate neurons have also been noted (Dammann, Hagberg, & Leviton, 2001; Volpe, 1996).

While the incidence of Grade III/IV IVH and cystic PVL is relatively low, approximately 4% and 3%, respectively (Inder, Wells, Mogridge, Spencer, & Volpe, 2003), many researchers and clinicians now believe that diffuse noncystic white matter abnormalities are the predominant form of injury associated with preterm birth (Counsell et al., 2003; Inder, Wells et al., 2003; Maalouf et al., 1999). In the neonatal period, diffuse white abnormalities include white matter signal abnormality, enlarged lateral ventricles, reduced white matter volume, and thinning of the corpus callosum (Inder, Wells et al.). In the past, diffuse white matter abnormalities went undetected due to the insensitivity of cranial ultrasound (Maalouf, Duggan, & Counsell, 2001), which is the imaging modality most commonly employed to detect brain injury in neonates. Magnetic resonance imaging (MRI) is more sensitive to diffuse injury, and recent MRI studies conducted in the neonatal period have resulted in a better understanding of the types of brain injury associated with preterm birth. Neonatal MRI studies have demonstrated that the majority of very preterm infants display diffuse white matter abnormalities, with 20% having moderate to severe abnormalities and another 51% mild abnormalities (Inder, Wells et al.). The major pathogenetic mechanisms that underlie diffuse white matter injury are not well understood but are thought to be similar to that of cystic PVL.

Neurobehavioral outcomes

The neurobehavioral impairments associated with very preterm birth range from major disabilities to subtle neuropsychological and behavioral problems. Major disabilities occur in about 12–25% of cases and include cerebral palsy, blindness, significant hearing loss, and intellectual impairment (Hack et al., 2000; Vohr et al., 2000). An additional 40–50% of very preterm children will develop less severe neurobehavioral impairments such as specific cognitive deficits, learning disabilities, and behavioral problems (Anderson et al., 2003).

In early childhood, developmental delay is frequently reported in very preterm cohorts, particularly in the areas of language and motor development (Doyle et al., 1997; Hack et al., 2000; Vohr et al., 2000). Studies investigating school-aged outcomes have consistently found that very preterm children score lower on global measures of IQ in comparison to their term-born peers (Bhutta, Cleves, Casey,

Cradock, & Anand, 2002). Learning difficulties are also more common in very preterm children, and accordingly, rates of grade repetition and utilization of remedial educational services are significantly greater within this population (Saigal, Hoult, Streiner, Stoskopf, & Rosenbaum, 2000). Specific neuropsychological deficits include mild motor impairment or developmental coordination disorder (DCD) (Holsti, Grunau, & Whitfield, 2002), language problems (Luoma, Herrgard, Martikainen, & Ahonen, 1998), visual-motor difficulties (Goyen, Lui, & Woods, 1998), inattention (Taylor, Hack, & Klein, 1998), slow processing speed (Rose & Feldman, 1996), memory deficits (Taylor, Klein, Minich, & Hack, 2000b), and executive dysfunction (Anderson & Doyle, 2004). With regards to emotional and behavioral problems, internalizing problems such as anxiety, depression, and social withdrawal are frequently reported (Hack et al., 2004), but numerous studies have also reported an elevation in externalizing problems, in particular hyperactivity (Mick, Biederman, Prince, Fischer, & Faraone, 2002; Schothorst & van Engeland, 1996; Szatmari et al., 1990).

Some of the cognitive problems exhibited by very preterm children are short term and can be classified as developmental delay. In contrast, some cognitive concerns may increase with age, while others may not be noticeable until later in development when such skills would be expected to emerge. While there have been numerous longitudinal outcome studies, few of these have utilized a neuropsychological approach, and as a consequence, our understanding of cognitive development in this population is limited. Utilizing general cognitive measures of receptive language and IQ, some studies have reported age-related improvements across childhood (Ment et al., 2003), suggesting that this population achieves at least some catch-up. However, in contrast to these optimistic findings, several other studies have shown impairments to be stable over time (Gray, Indurkhya, & McCormick, 2004; Stevenson, Blackburn, & Pharoah, 1999). Others have reported that deficits in preterm or very low birth weight (VLBW) children relative to peers become more pronounced with age, suggesting that preterm children grow into their deficits with increasing age (Taylor, Minich, Klein, & Hack, 2004).

Marked interindividual differences are observed in this population with regards to neurobehavioral outcome. This variability is associated with multiple factors such as degree of prematurity or birth weight, neonatal complications, medical interventions, and social and environmental factors (Hack et al., 2000; Taylor, Klein, Schatschneider, & Hack, 1998). With respect to biological risk factors, studies have consistently shown that the degree of low birth weight (LBW) and gestational age at the time of delivery are strong predictors of adverse outcomes (Taylor et al., 2000). The severity of neonatal course and specific medical complications, such as severe IVH, PVL, and chronic lung disease, have also been linked to poorer outcomes (Farel, Hooper, Teplin, Henry, & Kraybill, 1998; Fletcher et al., 1997). In addition, social factors including socioeconomic status, ethnicity, parental education, family functioning, quality of home environment, social climate, access to opportunities and resources have all been shown to account for some of the variance associated with outcome (Landry, Densen, & Swank, 1997; Levy-Shiff et al., 1994; Resnick et al., 1999).

Executive function and attention studies

Problems in attention and executive function are commonly reported by parents and teachers of children and adolescents born very preterm (Anderson & Doyle, 2004; Hack et al., 2004). These children are frequently described as having difficulty thinking before acting, waiting their turn, remaining seated for long periods, and following instructions. Despite these observations, relatively few studies have administered specific cognitive tests to assess attention and executive function in very preterm children. Further, published studies vary greatly in terms of sample selection and outcome measures. For example, studies often differ in terms of (1) what birth weight and gestational age criteria were used to define groups, (2) whether samples included infants at high or low biological and social risk, (3) whether samples were drawn from a single hospital cohort or from a geographic region, and (4) when the cohort was born (e.g., before or after the introduction of certain medical interventions). With respect to outcome measures, numerous measures have been used to assess similar domains, and at times different scoring systems are utilized to score the same test. With these limitations in mind, we have reviewed previous research to determine the nature, prevalence, and severity of attentional and executive deficits in very preterm children.

Selective attention

Selective attention, the ability to focus on relevant stimuli while simultaneously ignoring irrelevant or distracting stimuli, is thought to be largely mediated by a posterior parietal system, with some involvement from the anterior cingulate gyrus and lateral prefrontal cortex (Fan, McCandliss, Fossella, Flombaum, & Posner, 2005). Visual search and letter-cancellation paradigms are commonly utilized to examine selective attention, and deficits tend to be characterized by distractibility and an inability to remain focused on the salient aspects of a task. Most, but not all (Taylor, Hack et al., 1998) studies have found that very preterm children are more likely to exhibit selective attention deficits than their term-born counterparts (Bohm, Smedler, & Forssberg, 2004; Breslau, Chilcoat, DelDotto, Andreski, & Brown, 1996; Taylor, Hack et al.; Taylor, Minich, Bangert, Filpek, & Hack, 2004; Vicari, Caravale, Carlesimo, Casadei, & Allemand, 2004), although these deficits do not always persist after controlling for IQ (Bohm et al., 2004; Taylor, Klein, Minich, & Hack, 2000a). The severity of impairment varies across studies, perhaps reflecting differences in assessment procedures and sample characteristics. Selective attention deficits in this population have been observed across childhood, from toddlerhood and early childhood (Vicari et al., 2004) to adolescence (Taylor, Minich, Bangert et al., 2004), suggesting that problems emerge at a young age and persist into adulthood. Selective attention deficits appear to be more common in infants with chronic lung disease (Taylor, Minich, Bangert et al.) and those of lower birth weights (Breslau et al., 1996). For example, Taylor et al. (2000a; 2004) found more pronounced deficits in children with birth weights less than 750 g in comparison to children with birth weights between 750 and 1499 g. Similarly, Breslau et al. (1996) found that children with birth weights less than 1500 g displayed greater impairments in selective attention than their heavier counterparts. However, while selective attention deficits appear to be more common in those children born extremely small or those who had a complicated neonatal course, impairments have also been identified in low biological risk samples (Breslau et al.; Vicari et al.).

Sustained attention

Sustained attention, or vigilance, refers to the ability to maintain concentration over an extended period of time, and is reported to be associated with a predominantly right-sided frontal-parietal network (Fan et al., 2005; Lewin et al., 1996). To assess sustained attention in very preterm children a number of studies have used continuous performance task (CPT) paradigms. In general, these studies have found that very preterm children and adolescents perform more poorly on CPT paradigms than healthy full-term children, with severity of impairment ranging from moderate to severe (Elgen, Lundervold, & Sommerfelt, 2004; Katz et al., 1996; Taylor, Hack et al., 1998; Taylor, Minich, Bangert et al., 2004). In some studies sustained attention deficits persisted even after controlling for neurosensory impairment, global intellectual deficits, and sociodemographic factors (Taylor, Hack et al.; Taylor, Minich, Bangert et al.), but other studies found these attentional deficits to be associated with IQ and parental factors (Elgen et al., 2004). Due to a lack of longitudinal research, the evolution of sustained attention deficits is not known; however, deficits have been reported at various stages of development including early childhood (Katz et al., 1996). Studies have found children with low birth weights to be at greatest risk for impairment (Taylor, Hack et al.), but this is not a universal finding (Elgen et al.). While further research is required to understand the impact of neonatal brain injury on the capacity to sustain attention, Katz et al. (1996) reported that severe lesions were related to significant deficits.

Inhibitory control

The term "inhibitory control" encompasses the ability to suppress a prepotent response, interrupt an ongoing response, and resist distraction from external stimuli (Barkley, 1997). These abilities are thought to be associated with a distributed neural network that includes the lateral prefrontal cortex, anterior cingulate, and basal ganglia (Tamm, Menon, & Reiss, 2002). Children with poor inhibitory control are often described by their parents as impulsive, careless, and intrusive. They tend to be very active children, who may interrupt or disrupt group activities and have trouble putting the breaks on their actions even after they have been asked. Go-No Go paradigms are often employed to assess inhibitory control, and commission errors, for example on CPT paradigms, are thought to reflect impulsivity. With regards to the preterm population, most of the research in this cognitive domain has been with younger children (aged between 2 and 7 years) and has found that preterm children exhibit poorer inhibitory control and a more impulsive response style than children born at term (Bohm et al., 2004; Harvey, O'Callaghan, & Mohay, 1999; Taylor, Hack et al., 1998). These impairments persist after controlling for IQ (Bohm et al.) or receptive language skills (Harvey et al., 1999), and after excluding children with neurosensory impairments (Taylor, Hack et al.). While Taylor, Klein, et al. (1998) found that decreasing birth weights (<750 g) was associated with more impulsivity, deficits in inhibitory control occur even in low-risk samples of preterm children such as children born between 28 and 36 weeks' gestation (Katz et al., 1996). Interestingly, studies involving older preterm children have reported no inhibitory control deficits (Elgen et al., 2004). These findings suggest the disinhibited behavior commonly observed in young children born very preterm may resolve with age. Alternatively, the measures used in the research to date may be insensitive to these impairments in older children born very preterm.

Working memory

Working memory, the capacity to temporarily hold and manipulate information for the purpose of guiding future responses and behaviors (Baddeley, 1998), is subserved by an integrated neural network that includes the dorsolateral prefrontal cortex, anterior cingulate, parietal and temporal cortices, hippocampus, and basal ganglia (Curtis, Zald, & Pardo, 2000; Luciana & Nelson, 1998). Children with deficits in working memory often have difficulty remembering things even for a few seconds and tend to lose track of what they are doing as they work. These problems have serious implications in the classroom as children with working memory deficits may miss important information and feel overwhelmed and frustrated. Self-ordered pointing tasks and delayed alternation paradigms require children to enlist previous memories to direct subsequent responses, and both are used to assess working memory capacity. Research clearly demonstrates depressed working memory capacity in preterm children (Bohm et al., 2004; Curtis, Lindeke, Georgieff, & Nelson, 2002; Espy et al., 2002; Frisk & Whyte, 1994; Luciana, Lindeke, Georgieff, Mills, & Nelson, 1999; Taylor, Minich, Bangert et al., 2004; Vicari et al., 2004; Woodward, Edgin, Thompson, & Inder, 2005), with the magnitude of the impairment ranging from moderate (Espy et al., 2002) to severe (Luciana et al., 1999). Working memory deficits are robust and persist after controlling for relevant sociodemographic factors (Taylor, Minich, Bangert et al.), as well as for specific cognitive skills such as verbal-semantic ability (Taylor, Minich, Bangert et al.), perceptual skills, and attentional abilities (Vicari et al.). As expected, IQ accounts for some of the variance in working memory scores in this population (Bohm et al.). Working memory deficits have been documented throughout early and middle childhood as well as during adolescence, although one study reported a "substantial" improvement between the ages 8 and 11.5 years (Curtis et al.). Working memory deficits are not restricted to preterm children with major neurosensory or intellectual impairments and have been observed in relatively low-risk samples of preterm children (Espy et al.; Vicari et al.). Decreasing birth weight and gestational age as well as neonatal complications appear to be related to later working memory impairments (Taylor, Minich, Bangert et al.; Woodward et al., 2005). More specifically, length of oxygen requirement (Taylor, Minich, Bangert et al.), cranial ultrasonic evidence of periventricular brain damage (Frisk & Whyte, 1994), and MRI-defined white matter injury (Woodward et al.) have all been associated with working memory deficits.

Mental flexibility

Mental flexibility refers to the ability to shift between different thoughts and actions according to changes in a situation, utilize feedback, generate concepts, and devise alternative problem-solving strategies (Lezak, 1993; Luria, 1973). Brain regions that have been linked to these functions include the lateral prefrontal, orbitofrontal, and parietal cortices, basal ganglia, and cerebellum (Buchsbaum, Creer, Wei-Li, & Berman, 2005). Children with problems in mental flexibility may appear rigid or inflexible and tend to have difficulties moving between activities and adjusting to new situations or changes in routine. In the classroom, these problems may manifest as difficulties with activities that require flexible problem solving. The Contingency Naming Task (CNT), intradimensional/extradimensional set shifting (ID/ED) from the Cambridge Neuropsychological Test Automated Battery (CANTAB: Luciana & Nelson, 2002) and the Trail Making Test (TMT: Army Individual Test Battery, 1994) are some examples of tasks that are used to assess mental flexibility. While several studies have reported impaired mental flexibility in very preterm children (Taylor, Hack et al., 1998; Taylor, Minich, Bangert et al., 2004; Tideman, 2000), this is not an entirely consistent finding (Curtis et al., 2002; Espy et al., 2002; Luciana et al., 1999; Rushe et al., 2001; Taylor, Minich, Bangert et al.). Differences in task demands across measures may account for these inconsistencies as certain measures, such as Spatial Reversal and ID/ED, appear to be less sensitive to impairment than other tests of set shifting (Curtis et al.; Luciana et al.; Taylor, Minich, Bangert et al.). Impaired mental flexibility has been reported in both younger (Taylor, Hack et al.) and older (Taylor, Minich, Bangert et al.) samples of very preterm children, but these deficits are at least partly related to IQ and maternal education (Taylor, Klein et al., 1998; Tideman, 2000). A longitudinal study by Taylor and colleagues (Taylor, Hack et al.; Taylor, Minich, Bangert et al.) found that children with birth weights <750 g made slower age-related gains in mental flexibility across middle childhood than children with birth weights between 750 and 1499 g or term-born controls. In addition to decreasing birth weight, IVH may be an important predictor of deficits in this executive domain. For example, Ross, Boatright, Auld, and Nass (1996) found that preterm children (between 28 and 32 weeks gestation) with low-grade IVH were less efficient in changing response set than preterm children without evidence of IVH or term-born children.

Planning ability

Planning involves the ability to look ahead, make plans, set goals, utilize problem-solving strategies, organize time and resources, and formulate the steps to complete a task (Lezak, 1993; Shallice, 1990). Several brain regions have been associated with such skills, including the dorsolateral prefrontal cortex, anterior cingulate, and caudate nucleus (Dagher, Owen, Boecker, & Brooks, 1999). Children with planning deficits may have trouble getting started with activities, may experience difficulty coping with complex situations, may struggle to plan activities in advance, tend to use inefficient strategies, and are often overwhelmed by lengthy tasks. Tasks that are used to assess planning ability include the Tower of Hanoi (TOH; Klahr 1981);

Tower of London (TOL; Shallice, 1982), and the Rey Complex Figure (RCF; Rey, 1964). Most studies have reported planning deficits in preterm children (Anderson & Doyle, 2004; Harvey et al., 1999; Luciana et al., 1999; Rickards, Kelly, Doyle, & Callanan, 2001; Taylor et al., 2000a; Taylor, Minich, Bangert et al., 2004), although the severity of impairment varies across studies. Planning deficits in the very preterm population appears robust as they are still evident after excluding children with intellectual or neurosensory deficits (Anderson & Doyle, 2004), and after controlling for adverse sociodemographic factors, IQ, and verbal functioning (Taylor, et al.; Taylor, Minich, Bangert et al.). The age at which these impairments emerge is unclear, but they are present in early to middle childhood (Harvey et al.; Luciana et al.) and adolescence (Rickards et al., 2001; Taylor, Minich, Bangert et al.). Some studies have reported more pronounced impairments in children of lower birth weights and shorter gestational ages (Anderson & Doyle, 2004; Harvey et al.; Taylor, et al.; Taylor, Minich, Bangert et al.); however, this is not a universal finding (Luciana et al.; Rickards et al.). Also, neonatal complications, such as prolonged dependency on ventilator, are associated with greater planning deficits (Harvey et al.; Luciana et al.; Taylor, Minich, Bangert et al.).

Behavioral studies of attention and executive function

On rating scales and during clinical/diagnostic interviews, parents and teachers frequently describe preterm children as inattentive and hyperactive (Anderson et al., 2003; Saigal, Pinelli, Hoult, Kim, & Boyle, 2003). While these behavioral problems have been documented across a wide age range (Anderson et al., 2003; Sommerfelt, Ellertsen, & Markestad, 1996), Stevenson et al. (1999) reported that symptoms of hyperactivity and externalizing behaviors decrease with age. It seems unlikely, however, that behavioral problems resolve entirely. In one of the few studies to follow up VLBW individuals later in life, Hack et al. (2004) found that parents continued to express concerns regarding attentional problems in their VLBW child at 20 years of age. Many studies have noted that hyperactivity and impulsivity problems are more common in preterm boys than preterm girls (Schothorst & van Engeland, 1996; Szatmari et al., 1990); however, in early adulthood preterm girls have been reported to exhibit higher rates of internalizing problems (Hack et al., 2004).

Given these findings, it is not surprising that very preterm children and adolescents are at increased risk for ADHD, a behavioral disorder characterized by symptoms of inattention, hyperactivity, and impulsivity. In fact, the rate of ADHD in the preterm population is estimated to be 2–3 times greater than that of term-born children (Bhutta et al., 2002), and it has been estimated that 14% of all cases of ADHD are attributed to prematurity (Mick et al., 2002). Szatmari, Saigal, Rosenbaum, and Campbell (1993) suggest that preterm children exhibit a relatively pure form of ADHD, as ADHD in this population is rarely diagnosed in conjunction with conduct disorder and oppositional behaviors, although it is often diagnosed with learning disabilities. In addition, very preterm children with ADHD tend to exhibit more symptoms of inattention rather than hyperactivity, especially in middle childhood and adolescence (Hack et al., 2004). Findings linking ADHD symptoms in the very preterm population to brain injury and alterations to normal brain development suggest that these symptoms have a neurological basis. Whitaker et al. (1997), for example, reported that a diagnosis of ADHD at age 6 years was four times more likely in preterm children with neonatal white matter injury, as detected by cranial ultrasound, than in preterm children without documented neonatal brain injury. Similarly, Nosarti, Allin, Frangou, Rifkin, and Murray (2005) found that increased hyperactivity in preterm adolescent boys was related to reduction in left caudate nucleus volumes.

Behavioral ratings also document executive dysfunction in very preterm children (Anderson & Doyle, 2004). Anderson et al. (2004) compared a large regional sample of extremely low birth weight (ELBW, <1000 g) children at 8 years of age with a group of term-born children on the Behavioral Rating Inventory of Executive Functioning (BRIEF; Gioia, Isquith, Guy, & Kenworthy, 2000). Analyses revealed that parents rated ELBW children as displaying more problem behaviors indicative of difficulties in working memory, planning and organization, mental flexibility, monitoring, and initiating activities. Interestingly, gestational age and birth weight correlated weakly with these behaviors, leading the researchers to speculate that social and environmental factors are likely to contribute to executive dysfunction in this population.

Summary of attentional and executive function studies

In summary, research indicates that very preterm children and adolescents are at risk of impairments across most aspects of attention and executive functioning, with the extremely premature children and those who suffer serious medical complications in the neonatal period at greatest risk (see Table 10.2 for an overview). From a clinical

Table 10.2   Summary of findings from neuropsychological studies of very preterm children and adolescents.

Cognitive domain	Summary of neuropsychological findings
Selective attention	Increased risk for deficits throughout childhood and adolescence; severity of deficits related to birth weight, although even low-risk samples perform poorer than term peers.
Sustained attention	Impairments regularly reported in younger and older samples; severity of deficits related to birth weight and possibly presence of brain injury.
Inhibitory control	Deficits reported in young samples, but rarely in older cohorts; extent of impairment related to birth weight, although low-risk children were also at risk.
Working memory	Increased risk for impairment in both younger and older samples; deficits predicted by respiratory complications and brain injury.
Mental flexibility	Findings are mixed; deficits reported to be associated with birth weight and presence of intraventricular hemorrhage (IVH).
Planning	Deficits reported across childhood and adolescence; impairments related to birth weight, gestational age, and illness related factors.

perspective, this research highlights the importance of assessing attentional and executive skills in very preterm children from an early age. Early identification of these impairments facilitates the implementation of interventions from a young age with the aim of preventing or minimizing secondary problems, such as learning difficulties and social problems.

Another common theme is the substantial variability in long-term outcome within this population. While the very preterm population performs more poorly on attentional and executive measures than their term-born peers, a significant proportion of children have no detectable impairment or subtle deficits. Further investigation may reveal subgroups of children with impairments within distinct cognitive domains, with variability in risk factors helping to explain the etiology and nature of children's cognitive impairments. For instance, our review suggests that working memory and planning deficits are strongly related to medical complications, such as respiratory problems and brain injury, whereas sustained attention, inhibitory control, and mental flexibility are more strongly related to immaturity. That is, certain medical complications may confer a specific risk on cognitive development in addition to that attributable to prematurity alone.

Neural pathways to attention and executive function deficits

Brain injury and alterations to normal brain development are likely sources of attentional and executive deficits in very preterm children (Anderson & Doyle, 2004). Neuroimaging studies in both healthy and clinical populations clearly demonstrate that attentional and executive processes are subserved by complex and interrelated neural systems (Collette et al., 2005; Fan et al., 2005), and damage to any link in these systems may result in deficits. Differentiating the neural correlates of attentional or executive deficits is a difficult task, as it may be the result of damage to the prefrontal cortex, white matter tracts, or subcortical and posterior brain regions (Anderson, 2002).

Diffuse white matter abnormalities are common in infants born before 32 weeks gestation (Inder, Wells et al., 2003). This type of diffuse injury is thought to be caused by hypoxia/ischemia and cytokine attack, both of which injure immature oligodendrocytes and can lead to axonal damage and have negative consequences for neural development (Volpe, 1997). For example, a recent series of studies has found that diffuse white matter injury affects subsequent myelination, maturation of gray matter structures (Inder et al., 1999), cerebellar growth (Shah et al., 2006), and development of subcortical structures such as the basal ganglia and thalamus (Inder, Wang, Volpe, & Warfield, 2003). Diffusion tensor imaging (DTI) has also been applied to investigate the effects of preterm birth on the integrity and connectivity of white matter tracks (Nagy et al., 2003; Partridge et al., 2004). Using this imaging technique, Huppi et al. (2001) demonstrated that neonatal white matter injury in preterm infants had "major deleterious effects on subsequent development of fiber tracts" (p. 455). Figure 10.2 provides some examples of white matter injury in the preterm infant at 40 weeks gestation. Scan (b) illustrates moderate white matter abnormalities that occur in approximately 16% very preterm infants. This scan shows white matter signal abnormality, reduction of white matter volumes, and

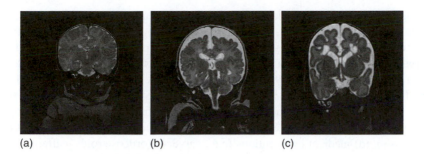

(a) (b) (c)

Figure 10.2   Qualitative magnetic resonance imaging (MRI) analysis. MRI scans (coronal T2 images) at term equivalent for (a) healthy full-term infant, (b) a very preterm infant with moderate to severe white matter injury. This scan shows signal abnormality, reduction of white matter volumes, and marked ventricular dilatation, (c) a very preterm infant with severe white matter injury. This scan shows greater loss of white matter volume and marked ventricular dilation as well as excessive cystic abnormality.

marked ventricular dilatation. Scan (c) illustrates severe white matter injury including significant loss of white matter volume, ventriculomegaly, and excessive cystic abnormality. Severe white matter injury occurs in 4% of very preterm infants.

While these diffuse white matter abnormalities may be related to the high incidence of cognitive and behavioral problems observed in preterm children (Inder, Warfield, Wang, Huppi, & Volpe, 2005), the functional significance of this pathology is not well understood. To date, there have been only a few studies that have examined the relationship between diffuse white matter abnormalities and later outcomes (Woodward, Anderson, Austin, Howard, & Inder, 2006; Woodward et al., 2005). Both these studies reported strong associations between diffuse white matter injury on MRI at term equivalent and adverse neurodevelopmental outcomes (Woodward et al., 2006) and working memory difficulties (Woodward et al.) at 2 years of age. White matter integrity is an essential component of the prefrontal neural networks associated with attentional and executive processes (Filley, 2001), and damage to periventricular white matter tracts as seen in many preterm infants may compromise these prefrontal systems, in particular the frontal-striatal pathways. In addition to a direct impact on prefrontal networks, diffuse white matter abnormalities are also likely to reduce information processing and response speed (Filley, 2001). Research from other conditions affecting the developing white matter, such as acute disseminated encephalomyelitis and childhood multiple sclerosis, has found similar evidence for disruption to frontal-subcortical circuits (Jacobs, Anderson, Neale, Shield, & Kornberg, 2004; MacAllister et al., 2005).

Volumetric studies have also demonstrated structural brain changes as a result of being born very preterm. At term equivalent (40 weeks gestation), very preterm infants have significantly less cortical and subcortical gray matter relative to term infants (Inder et al., 2005), as well as regional reductions in the parieto-occipital area (Peterson et al., 2003).

Volumetric studies with school-aged children born very preterm reveal enlarged lateral ventricles, thinning of the corpus callosum, and smaller hippocampi, basal ganglia, thalamus, amygdala, and cerebellum structures (Allin et al., 2001; Isaacs et al., 2000; Nosarti et al., 2004; Peterson et al., 2000). Overall, these findings demonstrate that prematurity, in particular extreme prematurity, alters neural development in the neonatal period and has ramifications for subsequent brain development. Factors that are likely to influence brain development in the neonatal period in this population include (a) white matter injury, (b) inadequate provision of nutritional substrates and hormones essential for brain growth and development, (c) medical complications (e.g., bronchopulmonary dysplasia, sepsis, patent ductus arterosis), (d) medical interventions (e.g., surgery, corticosteroids, caffeine, ventilation), and (e) environmental stresses (e.g., high noise levels, bright lights, prolonged separation from parents, invasive medical procedures) (Peterson et al., 2000). Few studies have explored the relationship between structural brain differences and attentional and executive impairments, although Nosarti et al. (2005) found that reduced volumes of the left caudate nucleus correlated with higher ratings of hyperactivity in adolescent boys who were born preterm (<33 weeks gestation). Similarly, Woodward et al. (2005) found significant associations between reduced cerebral tissue volumes in the dorsolateral prefrontal cortex, sensorimotor, parietoccipital, and premotor regions at term equivalent and working memory difficulties at 2 years of age. Structural brain abnormalities in preterm children and adolescents have been related to other aspects of cognitive functioning. For example, reduced hippocampal volumes have been associated with poorer performance on everyday memory and learning tasks (Isaacs et al., 2000), smaller corpus callosum volumes with weaknesses in verbal fluency (Nosarti et al., 2004), and smaller cerebellum volumes with lower IQ (Allin et al., 2001).

The pervasiveness of preterm children's deficits in attention and executive function, together with evidence that these deficits are present even in young children, implies damage to white matter tracts or subcortical and posterior brain regions, rather than direct injury to the prefrontal cortex (Luciana, 2003). Animal models of brain injury indicate that early damage to late maturing areas of the brain, such as the prefrontal cortex, may not be evident in infancy and may take several years to emerge (Goldman, 1971; Goldman, Rosvold, & Mishkin, 1970). In contrast, the functional consequences of early white matter injury or damage to early maturing areas are present from a young age and persist throughout development (Goldman & Rosvold, 1972). Furthermore, neuroimaging studies demonstrate that children display a greater reliance on subcortical systems than adults when performing attentional and executive tasks (Casey, Galvan, & Hare, 2005). In summary, while structural brain abnormalities are well documented in very preterm children, the impact of these abnormalities on attentional and executive functioning is not fully understood. Longitudinal research incorporating serial neuroimaging and neuropsychological evaluations at critical developmental stages are needed to clarify the neural basis of deficits in these skills at different ages.

Influence of social and environmental factors

Social and environmental risk factors account for variability in outcomes independent of biological risks (Taylor, Burant, Holding, Klein, & Hack, 2002). Factors such as family functioning, parenting characteristics, quality of the home environment, and socioeconomic status have the potential to moderate the effects of prematurity on cognitive and behavioral development. Few studies have systematically investigated the contribution of these factors to attentional deficits and executive dysfunction in very preterm samples. However, Robson and Peterson (1997) found that a LBW child's exposure to structured and developmentally appropriate activities in the home environment was predictive of vigilance and impulsivity. Similarly, Landry, Miller-Loncar, Smith, and Swank (2002) documented the importance of early parenting for the development of executive skills in very preterm and full-term children. These investigators found that mothers' early use and quality of verbal support to foster their children's learning (scaffolding) directly supported early language and non-verbal problem-solving skills and indirectly influenced later mental flexibility and problem-solving skills.

Other researchers have examined the effects of social risk or disadvantage on behavioral development of preterm children, although the findings are inconsistent. Levy-Shiff et al. (1994) and Taylor, Klein, et al. (1998) found that behavior problems, such as inattention and hyperactivity, were more pronounced in very preterm children at greatest social disadvantage. Conversely, studies of cognitive outcomes have reported that the effects of very preterm birth or VLBW are reduced for children from more disadvantaged backgrounds (Bendersky & Lewis, 1995; Hack et al., 1992). To explain the latter pattern of results, Hack et al. (1992) suggested that the negative consequences of birth risk on cognition may be over-whelmed by the adverse effects of the environment. These contrasting results nevertheless point to the importance of considering different moderating effects, depending on the type of outcome measured and age at assessment (Aylward, 1992; Taylor et al., 2000).

Issues for clinical practice

There are a number of issues to keep in mind when assessing a child born prematurely. First, it is important to remember that outcomes in this population are highly variable and in many cases infants born at the same gestational age or birth weight may have very different outcomes. As discussed throughout this chapter, outcomes depend on a range of medical and social factors. Thus in order to understand the context of the child's presenting problems it is important to obtain detailed information regarding the child's medical history including details about pregnancy and birth, perinatal brain injury (IVH, PVL), respiratory problems, infections, surgery, and length of hospital stay. The medical complications and interventions known to be most predictive of adverse outcomes in this group are Grade III/IV IVH, cystic PVL, bronchopulmonary dysplasia (BPD), and the administration of postnatal steroids.

Second, in addition to problems in attention and executive function, difficulties in other cognitive and behavioral domains are frequently observed, including visual-motor problems, slowed information processing, and memory and learning difficulties. At present it is not clear whether deficits in attention and executive function are more severe than deficits in other cognitive domains or whether deficits in other cognitive domains are secondary to deficits in attention and executive function.

Thus, for standard follow-up programs a broad-based assessment is warranted for children born preterm including assessment of general intellectual ability, motor skills, executive function, visual-motor skills, language, attention and behavior and educational skills. Ongoing surveillance of children born very preterm is recommended. While a number of deficits present at a young age, the nature of the impairments has been shown to change during development, and some problems may not emerge until later in life.

The effectiveness of early interventions with this population has been poorly investigated, although at some institutions early developmental programs in the NICU or shortly after discharge are standard practice. Research to date suggests that early developmental interventions tend to be associated with enhanced cognitive development in early childhood, but by middle childhood these benefits have diminished (Taylor et al., 2002). The impact these early interventions have on the development of attention and executive skills has not yet been examined.

Conclusion

While current research indicates that very preterm children and adolescents are at risk for attentional problems and executive dysfunction, further research is required to assess differential deficits. Few longitudinal studies have been conducted and the evolution of these impairments is not clear, although impairments have been consistently reported across early to middle childhood as well as adolescence. Deficits tend to be more common and severe in high-risk preterm infants, such as those with birth weights <750 g, but attentional problems and executive dysfunction have also been reported in those of relatively low medical risk and those with average intelligence. It is also important to acknowledge that outcomes in this population are variable, and a considerable proportion of children born very preterm show no attention or executive impairment. The mechanisms underlying such deficits are not well understood, but certain risk factors have been identified, such as IVH and bronchopulmonary dysplasia. The relative contribution of each of these risk factors to attentional and executive impairments needs further investigation and may vary across domains. Finally, recent neuroimaging research reveals that the majority of very preterm infants display structural abnormalities, including white matter injury and volumetric differences. These abnormalities most likely underlie the attentional and executive deficits observed in this population, although further research is required to enhance our understanding of these brain–behavior relationships.

References

Allin, M., Matsumoto, H., Santhouse, A. M., Nosarti, C., AlAsady, M. H. S., Stewart, A. L., et al. (2001). Cognitive and motor function and the size of the cerebellum in adolescents born very pre-term. *Brain, 124*, 60–66.

Anderson, P. J. (2002). Assessment and development of executive function (EF) during childhood. *Child Neuropsychology, 8*(2), 71–82.

Anderson, P. J., & Doyle, L. W. (2004). Executive functioning in school-aged children who were born very preterm or with extremely low birth weight in the 1990s. *Pediatrics*, *114*(1), 50–57.

Anderson, P. J., Doyle, L. W., Callanan, C., Carse, E., Casalaz, D., Charlton, M. P., et al. (2003). Neurobehavioral outcomes of school-age children born extremely low birth weight or very preterm in the 1990s. *Jama: Journal of the American Medical Association*, *289*(24), 3264–3272.

Aylward, G. P. (1992). The relationship between environmental risk and developmental outcome. *Journal of Developmental and Behavioral Pediatrics*, *13*(3), 222–229.

Back, S. A., Han, B. H., Luo, N. L., Chricton, C. A., Xanthoudakis, S., Tam, J., et al. (2002). Selective vulnerability of late oligodendrocyte progenitors to hypoxia-ischemia. *Journal of Neuroscience*, *22*(2), 455–463.

Baddeley, A. (1998). Recent developments in working memory. *Current Opinion in Neurobiology*, *8*, 234–238.

Barkley, R. A. (1997). Behavioral inhibition, sustained attention, and executive functions: Constructing a unifying theory of ADHD. *Psychological Bulletin*, *121*(1), 65–94.

Bendersky, M., & Lewis, M. (1995). Effects of intraventricular hemorrhage and other medical and environmental risks on multiple outcomes at age three years. *Journal of Developmental and Behavioral Pediatrics*, *16*(2), 89–95.

Bhutta, A. T., Cleves, M. A., Casey, P. H., Cradock, M. M., & Anand, K. (2002). Cognitive and behavioral outcomes of school-aged children who were born preterm: A meta-analysis. *Jama: Journal of the American Medical Association*, *288*(6), 728–737.

Bohm, B., Smedler, A. C., & Forssberg, H. (2004). Impulse control, working memory and other executive functions in preterm children when starting school. *Acta Paediatrica*, *93* (10), 1363–1371.

Breslau, N., Chilcoat, H., DelDotto, J., Andreski, P., & Brown, G. (1996). Low birth weight and neurocognitive status at six years of age. *Biological Psychiatry*, *40*(5), 389–397.

Buchsbaum, B. R., Creer, S., Wei-Li, C., & Berman, K. F. (2005). Meta-analysis of neuroimaging studies of the Wisconsin Card-Sorting Task and component processes. *Human Brain Mapping*, *25*, 35–45.

Casey, B. J., Galvan, A., & Hare, T. A. (2005). Changes in cerebral functional organization during cognitive development. *Current Opinion in Neurobiology*, *15*, 239–244.

Collette, F., Van der Linden, M., Laureys, S., Degueldre, C., Luxen, A., & Salmon, E. (2005). Exploring the unity and diversity of the neural substrates of executive functioning. *Human Brain Mapping*, *25*, 409–423.

Counsell, S. J., Allsop, J. M., Harrison, M. C., Larkman, D. J., Kennea, N. L., Kapellou, O., et al. (2003). Diffusion-weighted imaging of the brain in preterm infants with focal and diffuse white matter abnormality. *Pediatrics*, *112*(1), 1–7.

Curtis, C. E., Zald, D. H., & Pardo, J. V. (2000). Organization of working memory within the human prefrontal cortex: A PET study of self-ordered object working memory. *Neuropsychologia*, *38*(11), 1503–1510.

Curtis, W. J., Lindeke, L. L., Georgieff, M. K., & Nelson, C. A. (2002). Neurobehavioural functioning in neonatal intensive care unit graduates in late childhood and early adolescence. *Brain*, *125*, 1646–1659.

Dagher, A., Owen, A. M., Boecker, H., & Brooks, D. J. (1999). Mapping the network for planning: A correlational PET activation study with the Tower of London task. *Brain*, *122*, 1973–1987.

Dammann, O., Hagberg, H., & Leviton, A. (2001). Is periventricular leukomalacia and axonopathy as well as an oligopathy. *Pediatric Research*, *49*(4), 453–457.

Dammann, O., Kuban, K. C. K., & Leviton, A. (2002). Perinatal infection, fetal inflammatory response, white matter damage, and cognitive limitations in children born preterm. *Mental Retardation and Developmental Disabilities Research Reviews, 8*(1), 46–50.

Doyle, L. W., Bowman, E., Callanan, C., Carse, E., Charlton, M. P., Drew, J., et al. (1997). Outcome at 2 years of children 23–27 weeks' gestation born in Victoria in 1991–92. *Journal of Paediatrics and Child Health, 33*(2), 161–165.

Elgen, I., Lundervold, A. J., & Sommerfelt, K. (2004). Aspects of inattention in low birth weight children. *Pediatric Neurology, 30*(2), 92–98.

Espy, K. A., Stalets, M. M., McDiarmid, M. M., Senn, T. E., Cwik, M. F., & Hamby, A. (2002). Executive functions in preschool children born preterm: Application of cognitive neuroscience paradigms. *Child Neuropsychology, 8*(2), 83–92.

Fan, J., McCandliss, B. D., Fossella, J., Flombaum, J. I., & Posner, M. I. (2005). The activation of attentional networks. *Neuroimage, 26*(2), 471–479.

Farel, A. M., Hooper, S. R., Teplin, S. W., Henry, M. M., & Kraybill, E. N. (1998). Very-low-birthweight infants at seven years: An assessment of the health and neurodevelopmental risk conveyed by chronic lung disease. *Journal of Learning Disabilities, 31*(2), 118–126.

Filley, C. M. (2001). *The behavioural neurology of white matter.* New York: Oxford University Press.

Fletcher, J. M., Landry, S. H., Bohan, T. P., Davidson, K. C., Brookshire, B. L., Lachar, D., et al. (1997). Effects of intraventricular hemorrhage and hydrocephalus on the long-term neurobehavioral development of preterm very-low-birthweight infants. *Developmental Medicine and Child Neurology, 39*(9), 596–606.

Frisk, V., & Whyte, H. (1994). The long-term consequences of periventricular brain-damage on language and verbal memory. *Developmental Neuropsychology, 10*(3), 313–333.

Gioia, G. A., Isquith, P. K., Guy, S. C., & Kenworthy, L. (2000). *Behavior rating inventory of executive function. Professional manual.* Lutz, FL: Psychological Assessment Resources.

Goldman, P. S. (1971). Functional developmental of the prefrontal cortex in early life and the problem of neuronal plasticity. *Experimental Neurology, 32,* 366–387.

Goldman, P. S., & Rosvold, H. E. (1972). The effects of selective caudate lesions in infant and juvenile rhesus monkeys. *Brain Research, 43,* 451–485.

Goldman, P. S., Rosvold, H. E., & Mishkin, M. (1970). Selective sparing of function following prefrontal lobectomy in infant monkeys. *Experimental Neurology, 29,* 221–226.

Goyen, T. A., Lui, K., & Woods, R. (1998). Visual-motor, visual–perceptual, and fine motor outcomes in very-low-birthweight children at 5 years. *Developmental Medicine and Child Neurology, 40*(2), 76–81.

Gray, R. F., Indurkhya, A., & McCormick, M. C. (2004). Prevalence, stability, and predictors of clinically significant behavior problems in low birth weight children at 3, 5, and 8 years of age. *Pediatrics, 114*(3), 736–743.

Hack, M., Breslau, N., Aram, D., Weissman, B., Klein, N., & Borawskiclark, E. (1992). The effect of very low birth weight and social risk on neurocognitive abilities at school age. *Journal of Developmental and Behavioral Pediatrics, 13*(6), 412–420.

Hack, M., & Fanaroff, A. A. (1999). Outcomes of children of extremely low birthweight and gestational age in the 1990's. *Early Human Development, 53*(3), 193–218.

Hack, M., Wilson-Costello, D., Friedman, H., Taylor, H. G., Schluchter, M., & Fanaroff, A. A. (2000). Neurodevelopment and predictors of outcomes of children with birth weights of less than 1000 g: 1992–1995. *Archives of Pediatrics & Adolescent Medicine, 154*(7), 725–731.

Hack, M., Youngstrom, E. A., Cartar, L., Schluchter, M., Taylor, H. G., Flannery, D., et al. (2004). Behavioral outcomes and evidence of psychopathology among very low birth weight infants at age 20 years. *Pediatrics, 114*(4), 932–940.

Harvey, J. M., O'Callaghan, M. J., & Mohay, H. (1999). Executive function of children with extremely low birthweight: A case control study. *Developmental Medicine and Child Neurology, 41*(5), 292–297.

Holsti, L., Grunau, R. V. E., & Whitfield, M. F. (2002). Developmental coordination disorder in extremely low birth weight children at nine years. *Journal of Developmental and Behavioral Pediatrics, 23*(1), 9–15.

Huppi, P. S., Maier, S. E., Peled, S., Zientara, G. P., Barnes, P. D., Jolesz, F. A., et al. (1998). Microstructural development of human newborn cerebral white matter assessed in vivo by diffusion tensor magnetic resonance imaging. *Pediatric Research, 44*(4), 584–590.

Huppi, P. S., Murphy, B., Maier, S. E., Zientara, G. P., Inder, T. E., Barnes, P. D., et al. (2001). Microstructural brain development after perinatal cerebral white matter injury assessed by diffusion tensor magnetic resonance imaging. *Pediatrics, 107*(3), 455–460.

Inder, T. E., Huppi, P. S., Warfield, S., Kikinis, R., Zientara, G. P., Barnes, P. D., et al. (1999). Periventricular white matter injury in the premature infant is followed by reduced cerebral cortical gray matter volume at term. *Annals of Neurology, 46*(5), 755–760.

Inder, T. E., Wang, H., Volpe, J. J., & Warfield, S. (2003). Premature infants with PVL have altered deep nuclear structures—A volumetric MR study. *Pediatric Research, 53*(4), 538A.

Inder, T. E., Warfield, S. K., Wang, H., Huppi, P. S., & Volpe, J. J. (2005). Abnormal cerebral structure is present at term in premature infants. *Pediatrics, 115*(2), 286–294.

Inder, T. E., Wells, S. J., Mogridge, N. B., Spencer, C., & Volpe, J. J. (2003). Defining the nature of the cerebral abnormalities in the premature infant: A qualitative magnetic resonance imaging study. *Journal of Pediatrics, 143*(2), 171–179.

Isaacs, E. B., Lucas, A., Chong, W. K., Wood, S. J., Johnson, C. L., Marshall, C., et al. (2000). Hippocampal volume and everyday memory in children of very low birth weight. *Pediatric Research, 47*(6), 713–720.

Jacobs, R. K., Anderson, A. V., Neale, J. L., Shield, L. K., & Kornberg, A. J. (2004). Neuropsychological outcomes after acute disseminated encephalomyelitis: Impact of age at illness onset. *Pediatric Neurology, 31*, 191–197.

Katz, K. S., Dubowitz, L. M. S., Henderson, S., Jongmans, M., Kay, G. G., Nolte, C. A., et al. (1996). Effect of cerebral lesions on continuous performance test responses of school age children born prematurely. *Journal of Pediatric Psychology, 21*(6), 841–855.

Klahr, D. (1981). Formal assessment of problem solving and planning processes in preschool children. *Cognitive Psychology, 13*, 113–148.

Landry, S. H., Densen, S. E., & Swank, P. R. (1997). Effects of medical risk and socio-economic status on the rate of change in cognitive and social development for low birth weight children. *Journal of Clinical and Experimental Neuropsychology, 19*(2), 261–274.

Landry, S. H., Miller-Loncar, C. L., Smith, K. E., & Swank, P. R. (2002). The role of early parenting in children's development of executive processes. *Developmental Neuropsychology, 21*(1), 15–41.

Levy-Shiff, R., Einat, G., Mogilner, M. B., Lerman, M., & Krikler, R. (1994). Biological and environmental correlates of developmental outcome of prematurely born infants in early adolescence. *Journal of Pediatric Psychology, 19*(1), 63–78.

Lewin, J. S., Friedman, L., Wu, D., Miller, D. A., Thompson, L. A., Klein, S. K., et al. (1996). Cortical localization of human sustained attention: Detection with functional MR using a visual vigilance paradigm. *Journal of Computer Assisted Tomography*, *20*(5), 695–701.

Lezak, M. (1993). *Neuropsychological assessment*. New York: Oxford University Press.

Luciana, M. (2003). Cognitive development in children born preterm: Implications for theories of brain plasticity following early injury. *Development and Psychopathology*, *15*(4), 1017–1047.

Luciana, M., Lindeke, L., Georgieff, M., Mills, M., & Nelson, C. A. (1999). Neurobehavioral evidence for working memory deficits in school-aged children with histories of prematurity. *Developmental Medicine and Child Neurology*, *41*(8), 521–533.

Luciana, M., & Nelson, C. A. (1998). The functional emergence of prefrontally-guided working memory systems in four- to eight-year-old children. *Neuropsychologia*, *36* (3), 273–293.

Luciana, M., & Nelson, C. A. (2002). Assessment of neuropsychological function through use of the Cambridge Neuropsychological Testing Automated Battery: Performance in 4- to 12-year-old children. *Developmental Neuropsychology*, *22*(3), 595–624.

Luoma, L., Herrgard, E., Martikainen, A., & Ahonen, T. (1998). Speech and language development of children born at ≤32 weeks' gestation: A 5-year prospective follow-up study. *Developmental Medicine and Child Neurology*, *40*(6), 380–387.

Luria, A. R. (1973). *The working brain*. New York: Basic Books.

Maalouf, E. F., Duggan, P. J., & Counsell, S. J. (2001). Comparison of findings on cranial ultrasound and magnetic resonance imaging in preterm infants. *Pediatrics*, *107*, 719–727.

Maalouf, E. F., Duggan, P. J., Rutherford, M. A., Counsell, S. J., Fletcher, A. M., Battin, M., et al. (1999). Magnetic resonance imaging of the brain in a cohort of extremely preterm infants. *Journal of Pediatrics*, *135*(3), 351–357.

MacAllister, W. S., Belman, A. L., Milazzo, M., Weisbrot, D. M., Christodoulou, C., Scherl, W.F., et al. (2005). Cognitive functioning in children and adolescents with multiple sclerosis. *Neurology*, *64*(8), 1422–1425.

Ment, L. R., Vohr, B., Allan, W., Katz, K. H., Schneider, K. C., Westerveld, M., et al. (2003). Change in cognitive function over time in very low-birth-weight infants. *Jama: Journal of the American Medical Association*, *289*(6), 705–711.

Mick, E., Biederman, J., Prince, J., Fischer, M. J., & Faraone, S. V. (2002). Impact of low birth weight on attention-deficit hyperactivity disorder. *Journal of Developmental and Behavioral Pediatrics*, *23*(1), 16–22.

Monk, C. S., Webb, S. J., & Nelson, C. A. (2001). Prenatal neurobiological development: Molecular mechnaisms and anatomical change. *Developmental Neuropsychology*, *19* (2), 211–236.

Nagy, Z., Westerberg, H., Skare, S., Andersson, J. L., Lilja, A., Flodmark, O., et al. (2003). Preterm children have disturbances of white matter at 11 years of age as shown by diffusion tensor imaging. *Pediatric Research*, *54*(5), 672–679.

Nosarti, C., Allin, M. P., Frangou, S., Rifkin, L., & Murray, R. M. (2005). Hyperactivity in adolescents born very preterm is associated with decreased caudate volume. *Biological Psychiatry*, *57*(6), 661–666.

Nosarti, C., Rushe, T. M., Woodruff, P. W. R., Stewart, A. L., Rifkin, L., & Murray, R. M. (2004). Corpus callosum size and very preterm birth: Relationship to neuropsychological outcome. *Brain*, *127*, 2080–2089.

Partridge, S. C., Mukherjee, P., Henry, R. G., Miller, S. P., Berman, J. I., Jin, H., et al. (2004). Diffusion tensor imaging: Serial quantitation of white matter tract maturity in premature newborns. *Neuroimage*, *22*(3), 1302–1314.

Perlman, J. M. (2001). Neurobehavioral deficits in premature graduates of intensive care—Potential medical and neonatal environmental risk factors. *Pediatrics*, *108*(6), 1339–1348.

Peterson, B. S., Anderson, A. W., Ehrenkranz, R., Staib, L. H., Tageldin, M., Colson, E., et al. (2003). Regional brain volumes and their later neurodevelopmental correlates in term and preterm infants. *Pediatrics*, *111*(5), 939–948.

Peterson, B. S., Vohr, B., Staib, L. H., Cannistraci, C. J., Dolberg, A., Schneider, K. C., et al. (2000). Regional brain volume abnormalities and long-term cognitive outcome in preterm infants. *Jama: Journal of the American Medical Association*, *284*(15), 1939–1947.

Resnick, M. B., Gueorguieva, R. V., Carter, R. L., Ariet, M., Sun, Y. S., Roth, J., et al. (1999). The impact of low birth weight, perinatal conditions, and sociodemographic factors on educational outcome in kindergarten. *Pediatrics*, *104*(6).

Rey, A. (1964). *L'examen clinique en psychologie*. Paris: Presses Universitaires de France.

Rickards, A. L., Kelly, E. A., Doyle, L. W., & Callanan, C. (2001). Cognition, academic progress, behavior and self-concept at 14 years of very low birth weight children. *Journal of Developmental and Behavioral Pediatrics*, *22*(1), 11–18.

Robson, A. L., & Pederson, D. R. (1997). Predictors of individual differences in attention among low birth weight children. *Journal of Developmental and Behavioral Pediatrics*, *18*(1), 13–21.

Roland, E. H., & Hill, A. (2003). Germinal matrix-intraventricular hemorrhage in the premature newborn: Management and outcome. *Neurologic Clinics*, *21*(4), 833–851.

Rose, S. A., & Feldman, J. F. (1996). Memory and processing speed in preterm children at eleven years: A comparison with full-terms. *Child Development*, *67*(5), 2005–2021.

Ross, G., Boatright, S., Auld, P. A. M., & Nass, R. (1996). Specific cognitive abilities in 2-year-old children with subependymal and mild intraventricular hemorrhage. *Brain and Cognition*, *32*(1), 1–13.

Rushe, T. M., Rifkin, L., Stewart, A. L., Townsend, J. P., Roth, S. C., Wyatt, J. S., et al. (2001). Neuropsychological outcome at adolescence of very preterm birth and its relation to brain structure. *Developmental Medicine and Child Neurology*, *43*(4), 226–233.

Saigal, S., Hoult, L. A., Streiner, D. L., Stoskopf, B. L., & Rosenbaum, P. L. (2000). School difficulties at adolescence in a regional cohort of children who were extremely low birth weight. *Pediatrics*, *105*(2), 325–331.

Saigal, S., Pinelli, J., Hoult, L., Kim, M. M., & Boyle, M. (2003). Psychopathology and social competencies of adolescents who were extremely low birth weight. *Pediatrics*, *111*(5), 969–975.

Schothorst, P. F., & van Engeland, H. (1996). Long-term behavioral sequelae of prematurity. *Journal of the American Academy of Child and Adolescent Psychiatry*, *35*(2), 175–183.

Shah, D. K., Anderson, P. J., Carlin, J. B., Pavlovic, M., Howard, K., Thompson, D. K., et al. (2006). Reduction in cerebeller volumes in preterm infants: Relationships to white matter injury and neurodevelopment at two years of age. *Pediatric Research*, *60*(1), 97–102.

Shallice, T. (1982). Specific impairments of planning. *Philosophical Transcripts of the Royal Society of London*, *298*, 199–209.

Shallice, T. (1990). *From neuropsychology to mental structure*. New York: Cambridge University Press.

Sommerfelt, K., Ellertsen, B., & Markestad, T. (1996). Low birthweight and neuromotor development: A population based, controlled study. *Acta Paediatrica*, *85*(5), 604–610.

Stevenson, C. J., Blackburn, P., & Pharoah, P. O. D. (1999). Longitudinal study of behaviour disorders in low birthweight infants. *Archives of Disease in Childhood*, *81*(1), F5–F9.

Szatmari, P., Saigal, S., Rosenbaum, P., & Campbell, D. (1993). Psychopathology and adaptive functioning among extremely low birthweight children at eight years of age. *Development and Psychopathology, 5*(3), 345–357.

Szatmari, P., Saigal, S., Rosenbaum, P., Campbell, D., et al. (1990). Psychiatric disorders at five years among children with birthweights <1000 g: A regional perspective. *Developmental Medicine and Child Neurology, 32*(11), 954–962.

Tamm, L., Menon, V., & Reiss, A. L. (2002). Maturation of brain function associated with response inhibition. *Journal of the American Academy of Child and Adolescent Psychiatry, 41*(10), 1231–1238.

Taylor, H. G., Burant, C. J., Holding, P. A., Klein, N., & Hack, M. (2002). Sources of variability in sequelae of very low birth weight. *Child Neuropsychology, 8*(3), 163–178.

Taylor, H. G., Hack, M., & Klein, N. K. (1998). Attention deficits in children with <750 gm birth weight. *Child Neuropsychology, 4*(1), 21–34.

Taylor, H. G., Klein, N., & Hack, M. (2000). School-age consequences of birth weight less than 750 g: A review and update. *Developmental Neuropsychology, 17*(3), 289–321.

Taylor, H. G., Klein, N., Minich, N. M., & Hack, M. (2000a). Middle-school-age outcomes in children with very low birthweight. *Child Development, 71*(6), 1495–1511.

Taylor, H. G., Klein, N., Minich, N. M., & Hack, M. (2000b). Verbal memory deficits in children with less than 750 g birth weight. *Child Neuropsychology, 6*(1), 49–63.

Taylor, H. G., Klein, N., Schatschneider, C., & Hack, M. (1998). Predictors of early school age outcomes in very low birth weight children. *Journal of Developmental and Behavioral Pediatrics, 19*(4), 235–243.

Taylor, H. G., Minich, N., Bangert, B., Filpek, P. A., & Hack, M. (2004). Long-term neuropsychological outcomes of very low birth weight: Associations with early risks for periventricular brain insults. *Journal of the International Neuropsychological Society, 10*(7), 987–1004.

Taylor, H. G., Minich, N. M., Klein, N., & Hack, M. (2004). Longitudinal outcomes of very low birth weight: Neuropsychological findings. *Journal of the International Neuropsychological Society, 10*(2), 149–163.

Tideman, E. (2000). Longitudinal follow-up of children born preterm: Cognitive development at age 19. *Early Human Development, 58*(2), 81–90.

Tucker, J., & McGuire, W. (2004). ABC of preterm birth—Epidemiology of preterm birth. *British Medical Journal, 329*(7467), 675–678.

Vicari, S., Caravale, B., Carlesimo, G. A., Casadei, A. M., & Allemand, F. (2004). Spatial working memory deficits in children at ages 3–4 who were low birth weight, preterm infants. *Neuropsychology, 18*(4), 673–678.

Vohr, B. R., Wright, L. L., Dusick, A. M., Mele, L., Verter, J., Steichen, J. J., et al. (2000). Neurodevelopmental and functional outcomes of extremely low birth weight infants in the National Institute of Child Health and Human Development Neonatal Research Network, 1993–1994. *Pediatrics, 105*(6), 1216–1226.

Volpe, J. J. (1996). Subplate neurons—Missing link in brain injury of the premature infant. *Pediatrics, 97*, 112–113.

Volpe, J. J. (1997). Brain injury in the premature infant—Neuropathology, clinical aspects, pathogenesis, and prevention. *Clinics in Perinatology, 24*(3), 567–587.

Volpe, J. J. (2001). *Neurology of the newborn* (4th ed.). Philadelphia: WB Saunders.

Ward, R. M., & Beachy, J. C. (2003). Neonatal complications following preterm birth. *BJOG: An International Journal of Obstetrics and Gynaecology, 110*, 8–16.

Whitaker, A. H., Van Rossem, R., Feldman, J. F., Schonfeld, I. S., Pinto-Martin, J. A., Torre, C., et al. (1997). Psychiatric outcomes in low-birth-weight children at age 6 years: Relation to neonatal cranial ultrasound abnormalities. *Archives of General Psychiatry*, *54*(9), 847–856.

Woodward, L. J., Anderson, P. J., Austin, N. C., Howard, K., & Inder, T. E. (2006). Neonatal MRI to predict neurodevelopmental outcomes in preterm infants. *New England Journal of Medicine*, *355*(7), 685–694.

Woodward, L. J., Edgin, J. O., Thompson, D., & Inder, T. E. (2005). Object working memory deficits predicted by early brain injury and development in the preterm infant. *Brain*, *128*, 2578–2587.

11   Childhood traumatic brain injury, executive functions, and social outcomes: Toward an integrative model for research and clinical practice

Keith Owen Yeates and Vicki Anderson

Contents

Traumatic brain injury (TBI) is a leading cause of death and disability in youth under the age of 15, and therefore represents a major public health problem (Bruns & Hauser, 2003; Centers for Disease Control and Prevention, 1999). In the United States, for instance, more than 1 million children and adolescents sustain TBI annually, resulting in approximately 150,000 hospitalizations and 5,000 deaths (Kraus, 1995; Langlois, Rutland-Brown, & Thomas, 2005). Similar rates are reported in other industrialized nations (O'Connor, 2002). Injury severity is strongly related to the outcomes associated with TBI, so that moderate and severe injuries account for most of the mortality and morbidity associated with pediatric TBI, despite representing only about 15% of all cases (Kraus, 1995). As improved medical treatment has led to more frequent survival, concern has increasingly focused on the subsequent cognitive, emotional, and behavioral morbidity, especially among children with more severe injuries (Yeates, 2000), leading to significant economic and social burden for the community.

Despite the growing interest in postacute sequelae, the social outcomes of childhood TBI remain largely uncharacterized and poorly understood. Although social competence is an important predictor of numerous other outcomes, including psychological adjustment, academic performance, and health status (Cacioppo et al., 2002; Rubin, Bukowski, & Parker, 2006), we know little about social outcomes among children with TBI. Nevertheless, because of its critical developmental implications, poor social functioning is likely to play a major role in the reductions in quality of life reported following childhood TBI (Stancin et al., 2002).

Several different lines of research suggest that children with TBI are vulnerable to poor social outcomes. First, children with developmental disabilities and chronic health conditions affecting the central nervous system, such as epilepsy and cerebral palsy, are rated as less socially accepted and less socially competent than peers (Nassau & Drotar, 1997). Second, neuroimaging research has revealed an anterior–posterior gradient in the focal lesions associated with TBI. Larger and more numerous lesions are found in frontal and anterior temporal regions (Levin et al., 1989; Mendelsohn et al., 1992; Wilde et al., 2005), which are the same regions that have been implicated as the neural substrates of social information processing and the regulation of social behavior (Adolphs, 2001; Grady & Keightley, 2002). Third, the few previous studies of social outcomes in childhood TBI have shown that children with severe TBI are less skilled at social problem solving and are rated as less socially competent and lonelier than healthy children or children with injuries not involving the brain and that their poor social outcomes persist over time (Andrews, Rose, & Johnson, 1998; Bohnert, Parker, & Warschausky, 1997; Dennis, Guger, Roncadin, Barnes, & Schachar, 2001; Janusz, Kirkwood, Yeates, & Taylor, 2002; Max et al., 1998; McGuire & Rothenberg, 1986; Papero, Prigatano, Snyder, & Johnson, 1993; Yeates et al., 2004).

Nevertheless, previous research on the social outcomes of childhood TBI is limited in quantity and has not made use of state-of-the-art measures and models of social function, thereby precluding a comprehensive portrayal of social consequences following childhood TBI. Now is an excellent time to consider social outcomes in children with TBI. The emerging field of social cognitive neuroscience provides a critical perspective on the social impact of childhood TBI. Social neuroscience not only supplies research tools needed to better understand the neural substrates and social cognitive processes associated with social functioning, but also provides a foundation for a multilevel, integrative analysis of the social difficulties arising from brain insults (Brothers, 1990; Cacioppo, Berntson, Sheridan, & McClintock, 2000; Moss & Damasio, 2001; Ochsner & Lieberman, 2001; Posner, Rothbart, & Gerardi-Caulton, 2001), and in particular the role of the frontal lobes and executive functions in these processes.

The methods and models derived from social neuroscience will be particularly powerful when combined with those associated with the study of social competence in developmental psychology and developmental psychopathology (Parker et al., 2006; Rubin et al., 2006). The latter approaches reflect a developmental perspective that can enhance the field of social neuroscience. In short, we now have the tools and models to begin to understand how children's abilities to identify, think about, produce, and regulate emotions; to consider other people's perspectives, beliefs, and intentions; and to solve interpersonal problems are associated with their daily functioning in the social world. Furthermore, we can model this association in terms of developmental processes and brain pathology.

The goal of this chapter is to describe the relationship between childhood TBI and social outcomes. The chapter begins with a description of the major elements of social development as currently conceptualized by developmental psychologists, and continues with a description of how social cognitive neuroscience informs our understanding of the neural substrates of social behavior. The chapter next summarizes developmental issues that arise in the study of social outcomes in childhood TBI. This methodological and conceptual knowledge base is then applied to childhood TBI, by showing how it affects the frontal lobes, executive functions, social information processing, and social behavior, as well as their respective linkages. It concludes with the presentation of an integrative model of social outcomes of TBI and with a discussion of future research needs and possible clinical implications.

Perspectives on social development

Research in developmental psychology has provided a detailed characterization of the individual characteristics and social skills, interactions, and various aspects of social adjustment that constitute social competence. Additionally, it has shown how deficits in those areas are linked to social maladaptation. At the level of individual characteristics and social skills, *social information processing* is frequently seen as a critical determinant of social competence (Crick & Dodge, 1994; Rubin & Krasnor, 1986). Social information processing is conceived as involving a series of distinct problem-solving steps that are implemented when children respond to social situations. Such steps would commonly involve interpreting cues, clarifying goals, generating alternative responses, selecting and implementing a specific response, and evaluating the outcome. Social problem solving is often assessed by asking children to reflect on and answer questions about hypothetical social dilemmas (Dodge, Laird, Lochman, & Zelli, 2002).

Recent theorists have recognized that social information processing depends on other cognitive and affective factors, and have incorporated into their models such constructs as language pragmatics, executive function, and emotion regulation (Dodge et al., 2002; Guralnick, 1999; Lemerise & Arsenio, 2000). The latter variables are typically treated as stable individual characteristics (i.e., latent knowledge [Dodge et al., 2002]; foundation processes [Guralnick, 1999]). They are assumed to play a critical role in the implementation of interpersonal problem solving, which is seen as a more situation-specific and online social skill. The models assume that the effects of these cognitive and affective factors on social interaction and adjustment are partially mediated through their effects on social problem solving.

Research on children's *social interactions* has shown that they vary depending on both the type of social situation and the nature of children's relationships with the individuals with whom they interact (Parker et al., 2006; Rubin et al., 2006). For instance, children exhibit different behaviors when attempting to enter a peer group activity than when responding to peer provocation, and they use different strategies when attempting to gain access to objects than when attempting to gain the attention of others (Krasnor & Rubin, 1983). Similarly, children interact differently with friends than with unfamiliar peers (Dunn, Cutting, & Fisher, 2002; Newcomb & Bagwell, 1995). Notably, the range and flexibility of children's interactions across different contexts, defined both by situations and actors, is often considered a hallmark of social competence (Dodge et al., 1986; Rose-Krasnor, 1997; Rubin, Booth, Krasnor, & Mills, 1995).

Research on *social adjustment* has shown that it too varies along several important dimensions. One critical distinction is whether adjustment is evaluated based on self-perceptions versus the perceptions of others, such as peers, parents, or teachers (Parker et al., 2006; Rubin et al., 2006). This distinction may be especially important for children with TBI, who may be unaware of their own deficits and tend to evaluate their social adjustment more positively than do others. Important distinctions also exist within the broad domains of self- and other perceptions. For example, classroom peer nominations and ratings can be used to provide measures of peer acceptance, behavioral reputation, or reciprocal friendships. These outcomes are not independent of one another, but are conceptually and empirically distinct and have different implications for long-term adjustment (Asher, Parker, & Walker, 1996; Gest, Graham-Bermann, & Hartup, 2001; Nangle, Erdley, Newman, Mason, & Carpenter, 2003).

A substantial literature suggests that social information processing, social inter-action, and social adjustment are closely related to one another (Parker et al., 2006; Rubin et al., 2006). Children who display deficits in social information processing are more often aggressive or socially anxious and withdrawn. Their interactions result in being rejected by peers and being considered less desirable as friends. Anxious and withdrawn children tend to view themselves and their social skills relatively negatively, whereas aggressive children often have an exaggerated opinion of their social competence. In contrast, children whose social information-processing skills are intact tend to be more skilled in initiating and maintaining positive relationships, and rely on behaviors that are more prosocial. They are more likely to be socially accepted by peers and to have satisfactory friendships.

Contributions of social cognitive neuroscience

Until recently, the study of social behavior has not been strongly informed by neuroscience. The emerging field of social cognitive neuroscience, however, now provides a basis for integrating knowledge about brain structure and function into the study of children's social development. The field promotes integrative, multilevel studies of the links between brain, emotion and cognition, and social behavior (Brothers, 1990; Cacioppo et al., 2000; Moss & Damasio, 2001; Ochsner & Lieberman, 2001; Posner et al., 2001).

A growing literature in social cognitive neuroscience indicates that a distributed network of interdependent brain regions subserve discrete cognitive and affective processes that are integrated during the course of social behavior and development (Adolphs, 2001; Grady & Keightley, 2002). Specific brain structures that appear to play an especially critical role in social cognition include the temporal cortices, amygdala, anterior cingulate, and ventromedial, orbital and dorsolateral prefrontal cortex (Adolphs, 2001, 2002, 2003; Adolphs, Baron-Cohen, & Tranel, 2002; Allman, Hakeem, Erwin, Nimchinsky, & Hof, 2001; Anderson, Bechara, Damasio, Tranel, & Damasio, 1999; Bechara, Damasio, & Damasio, 2000; Frith & Frith, 2001; Goel, Grafman, Sadato, & Hallett, 1995; Grattan & Eslinger, 1989; Couper, Jacobs, & Anderson, 2002; Mah, Arnold, & Grafman, 2004; Siegal, & Varley, 2002). These regions have been shown to be involved in a variety of affective and cognitive processes that play important roles in social behavior: (a) emotion recognition; (b) emotion regulation; (c) the understanding of others' mental states (i.e., theory of mind); (d) social judgment and decision-making; and (e) certain cognitive-executive functions, such as inhibitory control, working memory, processing speed, and cognitive flexibility.

Notably, the brain regions known to regulate cognitive function overlap substantially with those implicated in the regulation of social-emotional functioning. For instance, the dorsolateral prefrontal cortex has been implicated in cognitive-executive functions, whereas the orbital and ventromedial prefrontal cortex plays a critical role in social-affective functions (Cummings, 1993). Thus, injury to fronto-temporal and limbic regions is likely to affect both the cognitive and emotional aspects of social behavior in children with TBI (Levin & Hanten, 2005). Of particular interest to neuropsychologists is the observation of the dual role that many of these regions play, not only in social cognition but in various aspects of memory and executive function.

Thus, social cognitive neuroscience provides a more detailed picture of the cognitive and affective constructs that also are incorporated in recent developmental models of social information processing, and also points to potential neural substrates for specific types of social interactions. More broadly, the cognitive and emotional processes that are the focus of social cognitive neuroscience provide a critical bridge between knowledge regarding the brain substrates of social behavior and models of social competence from developmental psychology. Specifically, cognitive-executive and social-affective functions reflect aspects of social information processing that are linked to a network of specific brain regions (Adolphs, 2001; Grady & Keightley, 2002). At the same time, they also represent the stable individual characteristics (i.e., latent knowledge or foundation processes) described in recent models of social competence (Dodge et al., 2002; Guralnick, 1999; Lemerise & Arsenio, 2000).

Social cognitive neuroscience has the potential to link research on children's social development to the study of childhood TBI. Childhood TBI often involves insults to the anterior brain regions implicated in social information processing. Deficits in social information processing, in turn, are known to be associated with atypical social interactions and poor social adjustment. The brain insults arising from childhood TBI, therefore, are likely to have negative consequences for children's social competence at multiple levels. By linking specific brain regions to deficits in discrete cognitive and emotional processes, social cognitive neuroscience provides a foundation for a multilevel analysis of the social problems arising from childhood TBI—an analysis that bridges brain, cognition and emotion, and action (Brothers, 1990; Cacioppo et al., 2000; Moss & Damasio, 2001).

Developmental considerations

The brain regions implicated in social behavior are subject to changes with age, just as social behavior is itself. The changes are likely related, moreover, such that brain maturation correlates with increases in children's capacities for social information processing, which in turn are related to changes in the complexity of their social behavior (Dennis, 2006; Paus, 2005; Stuss & Anderson, 2004). Understanding the distinct but linked developmental trajectories within these domains, and how they may be altered by childhood TBI, will be important for understanding social outcomes.

Brain development

The anterior regions of the brain that are linked to social behavior undergo gradual development, and the prefrontal cortex is particularly slow to mature. Morphological development of the frontal cortex is not complete until around puberty, with further changes continuing into adulthood (Klingberg, Vaidya, Gabrieli, Moseley, & Hedehus, 1999; Orzhekhovskaya, 1981; Yakovlev, 1962). Similarly, the prefrontal cortex is not fully myelinated until mid-to-late adolescence (Giedd et al., 1999; Klingberg et al., 1999; Sowell et al., 1999; Yakovlev, 1962; Yakovlev & Lecours, 1967). Synaptogenesis occurs at the same rate in most cortical regions (Rakic, Bourgeois, Eckenhoff, Zecevic, & Goldman-Rakic, 1986), although the prefrontal cortex may lag behind the rest of the brain (Chugani, Phelps, & Mazziotta, 1987; Huttenlocher, 1979). White matter may also undergo protracted development within anterior brain regions (Klingberg et al.; Sowell et al.).

Magnetic resonance imaging (MRI) studies have shown rapid growth spurts in the frontal lobes relative to the temporal lobes in the first 2 years after birth (Matsuzawa et al., 2001). After age 5, brain volumes remain relatively stable (Reiss, Abrams, Singer, Ross, & Denckla, 1996), but the ratio of gray to white matter lessens with increasing age (Pfefferbaum et al., 1994; Sowell & Jernigan, 1998) because of decreases in gray matter volumes between childhood and early adulthood (Gogtay et al., 2004; O'Donnell, Noseworthy, Levine, Brandt, & Dennis, 2005). Gray matter loss progresses evenly across the brain at an early age; by adolescence, though, the decreases are localized to the frontal and parietal lobes (Sowell et al., 1999; Sowell, Trauner, Gamst, & Jernigan, 2002). Recent longitudinal studies of cortical gray matter development have shown that higher order association cortices mature only after lower order somatosensory and visual cortices (Gogtay et al., 2004). Within the frontal lobes, maturation proceeds in a back-to-front direction, beginning in the primary motor cortex (precentral gyrus) and spreading anteriorly over the superior and inferior frontal gyri, with the prefrontal cortex developing last. Within the prefrontal cortex, the frontal pole and precentral cortex mature early and the dorsolateral cortex matures last, coinciding with its later myelination.

Development of social information processing

Social information processing also shows developmental changes, in a manner that likely relates to brain development (Anderson, Levin, & Jacobs, 2002; Diamond,

2002). The cognitive-executive functions involved in social behavior, particularly inhibitory control and working memory, undergo gradual development. For instance, during the preschool years, children become more able to delay responses, to suppress responses in a go–no go paradigm, and to respond correctly in the presence of a conflicting response option (Diamond & Taylor, 1996; Gerstadt, Hong, & Diamond, 1994; Kochanska, Murray, Jacques, Koenig, & Vandegeest, 1996; Livesey & Morgan, 1991). The development of working memory and inhibitory control occurs in tandem (Cowan, 1997; Hulme & Roodenrys, 1995), with a close relationship between working memory and inhibitory control beginning to emerge during the preschool years (Dowsett & Livesey, 2000). In some views, inhibitory control accounts for working memory growth during childhood (Bjorkland & Harishfeger, 1990).

Theory of mind is a more specific form of social information processing that also demonstrates ongoing development. Theory of mind involves the ability to think about mental states and to use them to understand and predict what other people know and how they will act (Bibby & McDonald, 2005). In adults, frontal lesions impair performance on theory of mind tasks (Stuss, Gallup, & Alexander, 2001). Theory of mind begins to become apparent early in childhood; infants display expectations about the actions of others and by 18 months, they are able to understand intentions (Kain & Perner, 2003; Meltzoff, 1995; Meltzoff, Gopnik, & Repacholi, 1999). Children first become able to understand desires and intentions (Bartsch & Wellman, 1989), and later begin to understand false beliefs (Sodian, Taylor, Harris, & Perner, 1991). The emergence of theory of mind appears to be closely related to executive functions, such as working memory and inhibitory control (Moses, 2001). Indeed, the emergence of theory of mind correlates closely with the development of executive skills, although they become less closely coupled at later ages (Carlson & Moses, 2001; Gordon & Olson, 1998; Hughes, 2002; Rowe, Bullock, Polkey, & Morris, 2001).

The ability to use and understand forms of nonliteral language, such as irony and empathy, in which a speaker's affective message does not correspond to the words spoken, also follows a protracted developmental course (Dennis et al., 2001). Early in development, children do not understand the concept of saying one thing while meaning another (Demorest, Meyer, Phelps, Gardner, & Winner, 1984). Later in development, children are able to recognize deliberate falsehoods and take into consideration both the facts of the situation and what they believe the speaker believes (Demorest et al., 1984). By middle childhood, children begin to correctly interpret white lies (Demorest et al., 1984). They also begin to understand ironic criticism and to distinguish it from deceptive intent (Demorest et al., 1984). The ability to understand ironic criticism becomes well established by early adolescence (Winner, 1988).

As they mature, children also are increasingly able to think reflectively about more complex social dilemmas, and their growing social problem-solving skills contribute to more successful social function (Crick & Dodge, 1994; Dodge et al., 2002). Young children have knowledge about prosocial problem solving that is not reflected in their spontaneous behavior (Rudolph & Heller, 1997). Children become more skilled at several different aspects of social problem solving, ranging from the retrieval or construction of possible solutions to the evaluation, selection, and enactment of behavioral responses (Mize & Ladd, 1988; Yeates, Schultz, & Selman,

1991). These changes may reflect an increasingly sophisticated ability to coordinate social perspectives (Yeates et al., 1991).

Development of social behavior

With increasing age and brain maturation, children's social information-processing abilities grow and their social behavior becomes more diverse, complex, and integrated (Rubin et al., 2006). Changes are apparent both in children's specific interactions and in their relationships (e.g., friendships). For instance, as their motor and language skills grow, toddlers begin to engage in increasingly more lengthy interactions with peers and their play becomes more organized (Eckerman & Stein, 1990). They also display the beginnings of meaningful relationships, preferring to play and engage in complex interactions with familiar as opposed to unfamiliar playmates (Howes, 1988; Howes & Phillipsen, 1998).

Pretend play is a particularly important form of social interaction during the preschool years (Goncu, Patt, & Kouba, 2002). By the third year of life, children are able to share symbolic meanings through social pretense (Howes, 1988). Goncu (1993) has reported quantitative differences in the extent to which the social interchanges of three versus four and a half-year-olds reflect shared meaning. For example, the social interactions of older preschoolers involve longer sequences or turns. With increasing age, play partners become better able to agree with each other about the roles, rules, and themes of their pretense. They are also better able to maintain their play interactions by adding new dimensions to their expressed ideas. These developments reflect preschoolers' growing capacity to take the perspective of the play partner and the increasing sophistication of their nascent theory of mind (Watson, Nixon, Wilson, & Capage, 1999).

By middle childhood, children spend significantly more time interacting with peers than they did when younger, and their peer interactions are less supervised. Pretend and rough-and-tumble play becomes less common, and is replaced by games and activities structured by adults (Pellegrini, 2002). Children become increasingly concerned with acceptance by peers during middle childhood (Kuttler, Parker, & LaGreca, 2002). Verbal and relational aggression (i.e., insults, derogation, threats, and gossip) gradually replaces direct physical aggression when conflict occurs. Children's conceptions of friendship begin to shift from being more instrumental to more empathic, perhaps contingent on their growing ability to coordinate social perspectives (Selman & Schultz, 1990). Their friendships become more stable and are more likely to be reciprocated (Berndt & Hoyle, 1985).

Many of these trends continue during adolescence. Adolescents spend almost one third of their waking hours with peers, nearly double what they spend with parents and other adults (Csikszentmihalyi & Larson, 1984). Their interactions are more likely to occur outside adult guidance and control than they were at their earlier ages, and more likely to involve members of the opposite sex (Brown & Klute, 2003). Friends become increasingly important sources of support and advice, and friendship begins to involve more intimacy and self-disclosure (Buhrmester & Furman, 1986). Adolescents develop clear conceptions of the distinctions between romantic relationships and friendships, and the two kinds of relationships have distinct implications for adolescent adjustment (Collins, 2003; Connolly, Craig, Goldberg, & Pepler, 1999).

Developmental dimensions in childhood TBI

The outcomes associated with childhood TBI are themselves dependent on developmental factors. Specifically, outcomes vary along three distinct but interrelated dimensions: the age of the child at the time of injury, the amount of time that has passed since the injury occurred, and the child's age at the time of outcome assessment (Taylor & Alden, 1997). Most studies of school-age children and adolescents have not found a strong relationship between age at injury and outcomes. However, recent studies of preschool children with TBI indicate that injuries sustained during infancy or early childhood are associated with more persistent deficits than are brain insults occurring during later childhood and adolescence (Anderson & Moore, 1995; Anderson et al., 1997; Ewing-Cobbs et al., 1997).

With regard to time since injury, longitudinal studies indicate that children generally display a gradual recovery over the first few years after TBI, with the most rapid improvement occurring soon after the insult. The initial rate of recovery is often more rapid among children with severe injuries than among those with milder injuries, but severe injuries are also associated with persistent deficits after the rate of recovery slows (Taylor et al., 2002; Yeates et al., 2002). Because very few long-term follow-up studies lasting 5 or more years have been completed, we do not know if children with TBI show any progressive deterioration in functioning relative to healthy peers after their initial recovery. However, young children appear to demonstrate a slower rate of change over time and more significant residual deficits after their recovery plateaus than do older children with injuries of equivalent severity (Anderson & Moore, 1995; Anderson et al., 1997; Ewing-Cobbs et al., 1997).

The influence of age at testing has been the focus of the least research. The effects of age at testing would be reflected in demonstrations of latent or delayed sequelae resulting from children's failure to meet new developmental demands following a TBI. For instance, because adolescence is associated with substantial maturational changes in the frontal lobes, the effects of frontal lesions might not become fully apparent until then, even if they occurred much earlier in life. The phenomena of "growing into a lesion" or time-lagged effects have been reported in case studies showing the delayed onset of social problems in children with early frontal lobe lesions (Eslinger, Gratten, Damasio, & Damasio, 1992), but group studies illustrating this phenomenon are difficult to locate. Latent effects are especially difficult to detect because they require evidence that differences in the consequences of TBI are due specifically to age at testing, as opposed to age at injury or time since injury. Disentangling these dimensions is difficult, even in the context of longitudinal research (Taylor & Alden, 1997).

An integrative, multilevel model of social outcomes in childhood TBI

Figure 11.1 represents an integrative, multilevel model of the social outcomes of childhood brain disorder grounded in concepts and methods drawn from both the

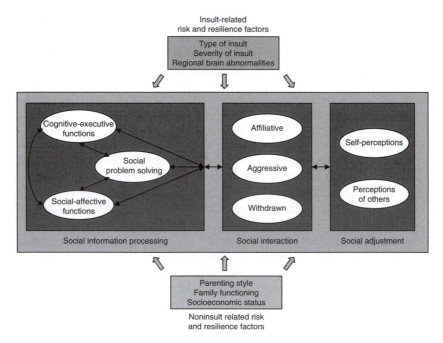

Figure 11.1   An integrative, heuristic model of social competence in children with brain disorder.

emerging field of social cognitive neuroscience and the study of social competence in developmental psychology (Yeates et al., 2007). The model specifies general relationships among social information processing, social interaction, and social adjustment, and reflects the possibility of bidirectional relations among those different levels of social competence (e.g., self-perceptions of adjustment may affect social interactions and vice versa). The model acknowledges the brain substrates for social cognition and affect regulation, and indicates that factors related directly to the neurological insult, as well as those independent of it, can influence social competence at all levels and the relations among them. The model as portrayed in Figure 11.1 is largely heuristic in nature, in that it portrays the relationships among the levels of social competence and their association with insult related and non-insult related risk and resilience factors in a general fashion that does not necessarily lead to specific predictions. However, when the existing research literature about the individual components of the model is taken into account, the model can give rise to more specific hypotheses.

For instance, this model implies that children with TBI often sustain focal lesions or other insults leading to damage to the temporal cortices, amygdala, anterior cingulate, basal forebrain, and prefrontal cortex. As a result of this selective damage, children will have difficulties understanding the emotional expressions and mental states of others, as well as regulating their own emotions. Additionally, because of deficits in executive functions, the children will have difficulty thinking about multiple social perspectives while deciding how to respond to social stimuli.

They will have difficulty thinking flexibly about how to respond, and instead may act impulsively because of their poor inhibitory control. The combination of deficits in these cognitive-executive and social-affective functions will influence children's reflective social problem solving. They will tend to (a) choose instrumental over prosocial goals; (b) misinterpret the intent of others; and (c) generate fewer and less effective responses to social dilemmas.

In their actual interactions, children with TBI will tend to behave in ways that do not promote social affiliation but rather involve aggression, social withdrawal, or other inappropriate social behaviors. As a result, they will tend to be poorly accepted by peers. They also will have fewer reciprocal friendships, and their friendships will be characterized by more avoidance or discord. Peers, teachers, and parents will describe them as less socially competent and as displaying more social problems than other children. Additionally, the children will tend to report low levels of social self-esteem and high levels of emotional distress, and negative social relationships. However, some children with TBI may be relatively unaware of their social problems and may actually overestimate their social functioning, as aggressive children have been shown to do.

The social outcomes of TBI are likely to be moderated by the developmental factors outlined earlier, particularly age at injury and time since injury. An earlier age at injury appears to be a risk factor for a number of negative social outcomes, such as persistent deficits in the social understanding of emotions (Dennis, Barnes, Wilkinson, & Humphreys, 1998). Social information processing may be particularly vulnerable at early ages because executive functions and theory of mind are more tightly linked during childhood than adulthood (Hughes, 2002). Children with early TBI may tend to show little or no improvement in their social adjustment across time, despite recovery of other cognitive abilities. Indeed, focal frontal lobe lesions in young children appear to result in more persistent social deficits than are sometimes apparent in older children and adults (Eslinger, Biddle, & Grattan, 1997).

The poor social outcomes that occur after TBI may tend to persist even when they occur later in childhood (Yeates et al., 2004). Deficits in social information processing might limit social experiences and hinder peer interactions, so that social functioning may become more divergent from that of peers with increasing time since insult. Indeed, given the transactional nature of social competence, negative social outcomes might persist even in the face of partial or complete recovery of social information processing. A cascade of negative changes in peer interactions and relationships, and consequently in broader aspects of social adjustment, including the perceptions of peers and adults, could engender a negative developmental spiral leading to chronic social problems that become very difficult to reverse even if children's social information processing improves following a TBI (Coie, 1990).

Recent research on childhood TBI

Regional brain damage in childhood TBI

Clinical neuroimaging studies have shown that childhood TBI often results in focal frontal lesions, but it is not clear if these insults result in structural changes to the broader regions implicated in social information processing. Wilde et al. (2005)

recently used in vivo MRI volumetric analysis to evaluate the extent of tissue loss following childhood TBI. The study is the first of which we are aware to examine specific subregions of the prefrontal and temporal lobes, which are the regions implicated by social neuroscience as critical for social information processing and social interaction. Volumetric MRI was used to evaluate brain volume differences in the whole brain, as well as prefrontal, temporal, and posterior regions. Participants included 16 children with moderate to severe TBI ranging from 9 to 16 years of age and 16 uninjured children of similar age and demographic characteristics. The children had been injured between 3 and 13 years of age and were between 1 and 10 years postinjury at the time of the study.

The TBI group had significantly reduced whole brain, prefrontal, and temporal regional tissue volumes, as well as increased cerebrospinal fluid (CSF). Specific regional differences were found for gray matter (GM) and white matter (WM) in the superior medial and ventromedial prefrontal regions, WM in the lateral frontal region, and GM, WM, and CSF in the temporal region. In the TBI group, whole brain volume and total brain GM were reduced, and total ventricular volume, total CSF volume, and ventricle-to-brain ratio were increased. Comparisons of volumetric data from typically developing children and subgroups of children who sustained TBI with and without regional focal lesions suggested that GM loss in frontal regions was primarily attributable to focal injury (i.e., GM loss occurred only in the TBI subgroup with focal frontal lesions). In contrast, WM loss in the frontal and temporal lobes was related to both diffuse and focal injury (i.e., WM loss occurred in TBI subgroups both with and without focal lesions).

Notably, volumetric measures of preserved frontotemporal tissue were related to functional recovery as measured by the Glasgow Outcome Scale, with greater tissue preservation predicting better recovery. Tissue preservation in the posterior cortex was not related to recovery. These results indicate that tissue loss may occur in many of the regions implicated in social information processing. However, the study did not include specific measurement of all the structures that have been implicated in research on the neural substrates of social behavior, such as the cingulate gyrus and the amygdala.

Social-affective functions in childhood TBI

A variety of studies have shown that children with TBI display impairments in social-affective functions, including pragmatic language, understanding of emotions, and appreciation of mental states. For instance, Didus, Anderson, and Catroppa (1999) investigated pragmatic language skills in 30 children with TBI ranging in severity from mild to severe, as compared to a group of 20 healthy children. Children were either between 8 and 10 years of age or between 11 and 12 years of age. The children with TBI were on average about 3 years postinjury at the time of the study. They completed two tasks, one requiring them to negotiate requests in hypothetical situations and another that assessed their ability to use hints to meet their needs. Children with TBI performed poorer than the healthy children on both tasks. Injury severity, however, was not a significant predictor of performance.

Dennis et al. (1998) examined the effect of TBI on children's appreciation of emotional states and ability to differentiate between internally experienced versus socially expressed emotion. The sample consisted of 59 children with TBI ranging from 6 to 15 years of age and 87 normally developing, age-matched controls. The children with TBI sustained their injuries between 1 and 15 years of age, and were from 6 months to 14 years postinjury at the time of the study. They completed a task that assesses the ability to understand real and deceptive emotions in brief narratives. Children with TBI were able to identify felt emotions, but had difficulty identifying expressed emotions when they were incongruent with the actual emotion. Children who sustained their TBI before age 7, or who had associated frontal lobe injury, were the most impaired.

In a separate study, Dennis and her colleagues examined the appreciation of mental states and affective communication in children with TBI (Dennis, Purvis, Barnes, Wilkinson, & Winner, 2001). The sample of 42 school-age children included 13 with severe TBI, 13 with mild TBI, and 16 age-matched, healthy controls. On average, the children with TBI were injured at 7 years of age and were 4 years postinjury. The participants were administered a task that involves the presentation of a pictured scenario and a tape-recorded speech act made by one participant to another. The speech acts take the form of literal truth, ironic criticism, or empathic praise. Children were asked a series of questions to determine their understanding of the protagonist's intentions (as reflected in literal truth statements) and emotive communication (as reflected in ironic criticism and empathic praise). Overall, children with TBI did not differ from controls in understanding literally true statements, but performed poorer than controls in understanding statements involving ironic criticism or empathic praise. Although children with severe TBI were most impaired, even children with mild TBI were less able than controls to differentiate ironic from empathic statements.

Collectively, the three studies indicate that children with TBI display deficits in social-affective functions, such as pragmatic language, affective communication, and theory of mind, that have been linked to specific neural substrates by research in social neuroscience, and also have been incorporated in recent models of social problem solving drawn from developmental psychology. However, we cannot tell from the results whether deficits in social-affective functions are directly related to social behavior or adjustment.

Social problem solving in childhood TBI

Research has also shown that social problem solving is impaired in children with TBI. Janusz et al. (2002) examined social problem solving in a sample of 6-to-12-year old children recruited prospectively from several hospitals (Janusz et al., 2002). Participants included 53 children with severe TBI, 56 with moderate TBI, and 80 with orthopedic injuries but without TBI who were part of a larger study of the outcomes of childhood TBI (Taylor et al., 2002; Yeates et al., 2002). The groups did not differ in age, gender, race, or socioeconomic status. The children and their families were assessed on three occasions, at baseline and at 6 and 12 months postinjury. Three additional assessments occurred at yearly intervals, beginning on average 4 years postinjury.

The long-term effects of childhood TBI on social problem solving were examined using data collected on average 4 years postinjury, when the participants were between 9 and 18 years of age. Data were available for 35 children with severe TBI, 40 children with moderate TBI, and 46 children with orthopedic injuries (OI). The children were administered a semistructured interview to assess the developmental level of their responses to hypothetical social dilemmas (Yeates, Schultz, & Selman, 1991; Yeates, Selman, & Schultz, 1990). Children in the severe TBI group defined social dilemmas and generated alternative strategies to solve dilemmas at the same developmental level as did children in the OI group. However, they articulated lower-level strategies as the best way to solve dilemmas and used lower-level reasoning to evaluate the effectiveness of their chosen strategies. In regression analyses controlling for group membership, race, socioeconomic status, IQ, and age, the level of children's strategies for resolving conflicts predicted parents' ratings of social competence, aggressive behavior, and academic performance. The findings suggest that children with severe TBI demonstrate long-term deficits in their social problem-solving skills that help to account for their poor social outcomes. However, the assessment of social outcomes was limited to parent report; future research is needed that examines social interaction and adjustment using methods such as peer assessments and behavioral observations.

Social information processing and social outcomes in childhood TBI

Yeates et al. (2004) subsequently conducted a more detailed examination of social outcomes of pediatric TBI and their relationships to social information processing using data from the same project. They conducted growth curve analyses of social outcomes across the first four assessments, from baseline to the 4-year follow-up. Additionally, they performed path analyses focusing on the prediction of social outcomes at the 4-year follow-up using contemporaneous measures of executive functions, language pragmatics, and social problem solving. Outcome measures included the Socialization scale from the Vineland Adaptive Behavior Scales (Sparrow, Balla, & Cicchetti, 1984) and the Social Competence and Social Problems scales from the Child Behavior Checklist (Achenbach, 1991).

Growth curve analyses revealed that childhood TBI was associated with adverse long-term social outcomes, which were exacerbated by fewer family resources and poorer family functioning. The path analyses indicated that social outcomes were accounted for, in part, by specific social-affective and cognitive-executive skills and by social problem solving, even after controlling for group membership, age, race, socioeconomic status, and IQ. The findings show that the social outcomes of childhood TBI are moderated by environmental risks, and they also illustrate how cognitive-executive and social-affective functions and social problem solving collectively are related to social adjustment. However, the assessment of cognitive-executive and social-affective functions was limited in breadth and the measurement of social outcomes relied exclusively on parent reports.

Social outcomes and frontal lobe injury in childhood TBI

Few studies have examined the link between focal brain injury and social outcomes in childhood TBI. Levin et al. (2004) recently published a study that focused on psychosocial outcomes in children with TBI, with and without focal frontal lesions (Levin et al., 2004). They compared 22 school-aged children who sustained TBI with unilateral frontal lesions to a matched sample of 22 children with TBI and nonfrontal focal lesions. They also compared 18 children who sustained a TBI with nonfrontal focal lesions to 18 children with TBI but without focal lesions. Participants were drawn from both a prospective cohort who sustained their injuries between 5 and 15 years of age and completed MRI at 3 months postinjury and from a cross-sectional cohort who were between 5 and 18 years of age at the time of the study and at least 2 years postinjury. The primary outcome measure was the Vineland Adaptive Behavior Scales (VABS; Sparrow et al., 1984). Children with frontal lesions displayed deficits on the VABS Socialization scale and Maladaptive Behavior scale when compared to children with nonfrontal lesions, despite the absence of differences on the VABS Communication scale or on cognitive tests of memory, expressive language, and processing speed. The volume of frontal lesions was a significant predictor of the VABS Socialization scale, with larger lesions associated with poorer outcomes. Nonfrontal lesions were not associated with poorer psychosocial outcomes. These findings confirm the importance of the frontal lobes in social functioning, but they are limited by the omission of measures of lesions in other brain regions implicated in social information processing and by the restricted assessment of social outcomes. For example, the authors did not distinguish between aggression and social withdrawal as potential outcomes, although those behaviors are qualitatively different outcomes and may reflect the lateralization of frontal lobe injury (Fox, Calkins, & Bell, 1994; Fox et al., 1995, 2001). Furthermore, the quality of children's relationships in the peer group at large, and more specifically with friends, was not assessed.

In another recent study, changes in social behavior were linked to lesions in the dorsal prefrontal cortex. Max et al. (2005) studied 177 children between 5 and 14 years of age who were recruited prospectively following TBI and followed to 6 months postinjury. They completed the Neuropsychiatric Rating Scale (Max et al., 1998), a semistructured psychiatric interview designed to identify symptoms of personality change due to TBI. Persistent personality change occurred in 18% of the children with TBI, with the most common changes involving affective lability, aggressive behavior, and poor social judgment (e.g., tactless comments about the listener, inappropriate sharing of personal information). Persistent personality change was more common among children with more severe injuries, and was associated with lesions to several distinct regions as seen on MRI, but only lesions in the superior frontal gyrus accounted for unique variance. This dorsal prefrontal region is connected to the ventral system discussed previously, and likely plays a key role in the effortful regulation of affective states produced by that system. The findings again point the role of the frontal lobes in social functioning, although the Neuropsychiatric Rating Scale is clearly limited as a measure of social outcomes.

Research needs, future directions, and clinical significance

Only a handful of researchers have examined social adjustment in children with TBI. The few existing studies have been characterized by a limited range of outcome measures, usually relying on parent or teacher ratings, which are subject to bias and provide only an indirect index of social functioning. Only two studies have examined self-perceptions of social competence among children with TBI (Andrews et al., 1998; Bohnert et al., 1997). These studies indicate that children report concern about losing friends and describe themselves as less socially competent and lonelier than children without TBI, but they do not report fewer or qualitatively different friendships. We are unaware of any previous studies in which classroom peer nominations or ratings were used to examine peer acceptance, behavioral reputation, or reciprocal friendships in children with TBI; yet these kinds of measures may provide more valid indices of social outcomes than lab-based cognitive measures or parent-rated questionnaires.

Broader aspects of peer interactions and social communication also have not been observed directly in previous research on childhood TBI. In addition, only a few studies have examined social information processing in children with TBI, although they have consistently documented deficits in abilities such as the understanding of mental states and the generation of effective solutions to social dilemmas (Janusz et al., 2002; Warschausky, Cohen, Parker, Levendosky, & Okun, 1997; Yeates et al., 2004). The two recent studies described earlier apparently are the only ones that have investigated the relation between social information processing in children with TBI and their social adjustment (Janusz et al.; Yeates et al., 2004).

As noted earlier, neuroimaging studies of childhood TBI have suggested that focal lesions are larger and more numerous in the brain's anterior regions, which have been broadly implicated in social behavior (Levin et al., 1989; Mendelsohn et al., 1992). However, with the exception of the recent study by Wilde et al. (2005), existing neuroimaging studies were not designed to examine the discrete brain regions specifically implicated in social cognition. Moreover, no previous studies of childhood TBI have attempted to link the results of neuroimaging analyses directly to variations in social information processing, although preliminary links between frontal lobe lesions and poor social outcomes have been demonstrated (Levin et al., 2004; Max et al., 2005).

Previous research also has largely not attended to developmental considerations. Most studies of TBI in preschool children have focused on cognitive outcomes, so that the impact of early injuries on social outcomes is largely unknown. Additionally, social outcomes after TBI have been examined longitudinally in only a few studies. Although the existing research provides evidence of persisting deficits in social adjustment despite considerable cognitive recovery (Yeates et al., 2004), the neural and social information-processing substrates of the persisting deficits are unclear.

An integrated, multilevel model, such as the one summarized in this chapter, is critical to understanding social outcomes and addressing these shortcomings (Cacioppo et al., 2000). More restricted models do not promote an examination of the links between brain, cognition and emotion, and action, as portrayed in Figure 11.1. Future research is likely to be especially informative if it entails a contemporaneous examination of each level in the model (focal brain abnormalities, social information processing, social interaction, and social adjustment) and their interrelationships in children with TBI.

The selection of constructs included in the model was made in a principled fashion, so as to avoid its being overly inclusive. For instance, the model does not encompass all possible neuropsychological outcomes, but instead focuses on specific cognitive-executive functions that have been shown empirically to relate to social cognition, particularly those implicated in studies of theory of mind (Grattan & Eslinger, 1989; Hughes, 1998). Because of its comprehensive approach to the study of social competence, however, the model may nevertheless encourage a major expansion of knowledge about the outcomes of childhood TBI. Additionally, the model is potentially germane not only to children with TBI, but also to those with neurodevelopmental disorders and to healthy children, and therefore may inform research regarding the neural and cognitive-affective substrates of social behavior more generally.

Currently, we know relatively little about outcomes at each level of the model and even less about the connections among them. Children with TBI are likely to exhibit deficits at each level, but the magnitude of deficits may vary across the different levels as a function of the specific types of injury involved. We also are unsure which levels will prove to have stronger relations and whether the relations will be different for children with TBI than for healthy children. Future research will be needed to examine whether childhood TBI alter the connections between levels of social competence.

For instance, the association between social problem solving and social interaction may be weaker among children with TBI, who may be able to articulate more appropriate responses in a reflective interview than they can actually implement during ongoing interactions. In other words, they may know more than they can do (Dennis, Wilkinson, & Humphreys, 1998). One potential explanation for a mismatch between thought and behavior is that children with TBI know what to do in a wide variety of social circumstances, but they are unable to regulate emotions adequately; as a consequence, their emotions override competent thinking, thereby resulting in incompetent social behavior. The multilevel, integrated nature of the model proposed here will allow future research to address this sort of possibility in children with TBI.

Practically speaking, the clinical application of more sensitive measures, such as those used to assess emotion understanding or the comprehension of mental states, may help clinicians target children with poor social outcomes following TBI for further intervention. In turn, the refinement of a multilevel, integrated model should prove valuable in designing interventions to promote better social outcomes following childhood TBI (Bierman, 2004; Cooley, Glang, & Voss, 1997; Glang, Todis, Cooley, Wells, & Voss, 1997; Guralnick, 1989, 1990). In this sense, a comprehensive model will afford an opportunity to improve the long-term quality of life of children and families affected by TBI.

Acknowledgments

The primary author (K.O.Y.) wishes to acknowledge the contributions of his coauthors on the following article, which served as the primary impetus for this chapter: Yeates, K. O., Bigler, E. D., Dennis, M., Gerhardt, C. A., Rubin, K. A., Stancin, T., Taylor, H. G., and Vannatta, K. (2007). Social outcomes in childhood brain disorder: A heuristic integration of social neuroscience and developmental psychology. *Psychological Bulletin, 133*, 535–556.

References

Achenbach, T. M. (1991). *Manual for the child behavior checklist/4–18 and 1991 profile.* Burlington, VT: Department of Psychiatry, University of Vermont.

Adolphs, R. (2001). The neurobiology of social cognition. *Current Opinion in Neurobiology, 11*, 231–239.

Adolphs, R. (2002). Neural systems for recognizing emotion. *Current Opinion in Neuro-biology, 12*, 169–177.

Adolphs, R. (2003). Cognitive neuroscience of human social behaviour. *Nature Neuroscience Review, 4*, 165–178.

Adolphs, R., Baron-Cohen, S., & Tranel, D. (2002). Impaired recognition of social emotions following amygdala damage. *Journal of Cognitive Neuroscience, 14*, 1264–1274.

Allman, J., Hakeem, A., Erwin, J., Nimchinsky, E., & Hof, P. (2001). The anterior cingulate cortex. The evolution of an interface between emotion and cognition. *Annals of the New York Academy of Sciences, 935*, 107–117.

Anderson, S., Bechara, A., Damasio, H., Tranel, D., & Damasio, H. (1999). Impairment of social and moral behavior related to early damage in human prefrontal cortex. *Nature Neuroscience, 2*, 1032–1037.

Anderson, V., Levin, H. S., & Jacobs, R. (2002). Executive functions after frontal lobe injury: A developmental perspective. In D. T. Stuss & R. T. Knight (Eds.), *Principles of frontal lobe function* (pp. 504–527). New York: Oxford University Press.

Anderson, V., & Moore, C. (1995). Age at injury as a predictor of outcome following pediatric head injury: A longitudinal perspective. *Child Neuropsychology, 1*, 187–202.

Anderson, V. A., Morse, S. A., Klug, G., Catroppa, C., Haritou, F., Rosenfeld, J., & Pentland, L. (1997). Predicting recovery from head injury in young children: A prospective analysis. *Journal of the International Neuropsychological Society, 3*, 568–580.

Andrews, T. K., Rose, F. D., & Johnson, D. A. (1998). Social and behavioural effects of traumatic brain injury in children. *Brain Injury, 12*, 133–138.

Asher, S. R., Parker, J. G., & Walker, D. L. (1996). Distinguishing friendship from acceptance: Implications for intervention and assessment. In W. M. Bukowski, A. F. Newcomb, & W. W. Hartup (Eds.), *The company they keep: Friendship in childhood and adolescence* (pp. 366–405). New York: Cambridge University Press.

Bartsch, K., & Wellman, H. M. (1989). Young children's attribution of action to beliefs and desires. *Child Development, 60*, 946–964.

Bechara, A., Damasio, H., & Damasio, A. R. (2000). Emotion, decision making and the orbitofrontal cortex. *Cerebral Cortex, 10*, 295–307.

Berndt, T. J., & Hoyle, S. G. (1985). Stability and change in childhood and adolescent friendships. *Developmental Psychology, 21*, 1007–1015.

Bibby, H., & McDonald, S. (2005). Theory of mind after traumatic brain injury. *Neuropsy-chologia, 43*, 99–114.

Bierman, K. L. (2004). *Peer rejection: Developmental processes and intervention.* New York: Guilford Publications.

Bjorkland, D. F., & Harishfeger, K. K. (1990). The resources construct in cognitive develop-ment: Diverse sources of evidence and a theory of inefficient inhibition. *Developmental Review, 10*, 48–71.

Bohnert, A. M., Parker, J. G., & Warschausky, S. A. (1997). Friendship and social adjustment of children following a traumatic brain injury: An exploratory investigation. *Developmental Neuropsychology*, *13*, 477–486.

Brothers, L. (1990). The social brain: A project for integrating primate behavior and neurophysiology in a new domain. *Concepts in Neuroscience*, *1*, 27–51.

Brown, B. B., & Klute, C. (2003). Friends, cliques, and crowds. In G. R. Adams & M. D. Berzonsky (Eds.), *Blackwell Handbook of Adolescence* (pp. 330–348). Malden, MA: Blackwell.

Bruns, J., & Hauser, W. (2003). The epidemiology of traumatic brain injury: A review. *Epilepsia*, *44* (Suppl. 10), 2–10.

Buhrmester, D., & Furman, W. (1986). The changing functions of friends in childhood. A neo-Sullivan perspective. In V. J. Derlega & B. A. Winstead (Eds.), *Friendship and social interaction* (pp. 41–62). New York: Springer-Verlag.

Cacioppo, J. T., Berntson, G. G., Sheridan, J. F., & McClintock, M. K. (2000). Multilevel integrative analyses of human behavior: Social neuroscience and the complementing nature of social and biological approaches. *Psychological Bulletin*, *126*, 829–843.

Cacioppo, J. T., Hawkley, L. C., Crawford, L. E., Ernst, J. M., Burleson, M. H., Kowalewski, R. B. et al. (2002). Loneliness and health: Potential mechanisms. *Psychosomatic Medicine*, *64*, 407–417.

Carlson, S. M., & Moses, L. J. (2001). Individual differences in inhibitory control and children's theory of mind. *Child Development*, *72*, 1032–1053.

Centers for Disease Control and Prevention, National Center for Injury Prevention and Control. (1999). *Traumatic brain injury in the United States: A report to congress*. Atlanta, GA: US Department of Health and Human Services, Centers for Disease Control and Prevention.

Chugani, H. T., Phelps, M. E., & Mazziotta, J. C. (1987). Positron emission tomography study of human brain functional development. *Annals of Neurology*, *22*, 487–497.

Coie, J. D. (1990). Toward a theory of peer rejection. In S. R. Asher & J. D. Coie (Eds.), *Peer rejection in childhood* (pp. 365–401). Cambridge, England: Cambridge University Press.

Collins, W. A. (2003). More than a myth: The developmental significance of romantic relationships during adolescence. *Journal of Research on Adolescence*, *13*, 1–24.

Connolly, J., Craig, W., Goldberg, A., & Pepler, D. (1999). Conceptions of cross-sex friendships and romantic relationships in early adolescence. *Journal of Youth & Adolescence*, *28*, 481–494.

Cooley, E. A., Glang, A., & Voss, J. (1997). Making connections: Helping children with ABI build friendships. In A. Glang, G. H. S. Singer, & B. Todis (Eds.), *Students with acquired brain injuries: The school's response* (pp. 255–275). Baltimore: P.H. Brookes.

Couper, E., Jacobs, R., & Anderson, V. (2002). Adaptive behaviour and moral reasoning in children with frontal lobe lesions. *Brain Impairment*, *3*, 105–113.

Cowan, N. (1997). The development of working memory. In N. Cowan & C. Hulme (Eds.), *The development of memory in childhood* (pp. 163–200). Hove, UK: Psychology Press.

Crick, N. R., & Dodge, K. A. (1994). A review and reformulation of social information-processing mechanisms in children's social adjustment. *Psychological Bulletin*, *115*, 74–101.

Csikszentmihalyi, M., & Larson, R. (1984). *Being adolescent*. New York: Basic Books.

Cummings, J. L. (1993). Frontal-subcortical circuits and human behavior. *Archives of Neurology*, *50*, 873–880.

Demorest, A., Meyer, C., Phelps, E., Gardner, H., & Winner, E. (1984). Words speak louder than actions: Understanding deliberately false remarks. *Child Development*, *55*, 1527–1534.

Dennis, M. (2006). Prefrontal cortex: Typical and atypical development. In J. Risberg & J. Grafman (Eds.) *The frontal lobes: Development, function and pathology* (pp. 128–162). New York: Cambridge University Press.

Dennis, M., Barnes, M. A., Wilkinson, M., & Humphreys, R. P. (1998). How children with head injury represent real and deceptive emotion in short narratives. *Brain and Language, 61*, 450–483.

Dennis, M., Guger, S., Roncadin, C., Barnes, M., & Schachar, R. (2001). Attentional-inhibitory control and social-behavioral regulation after childhood closed head injury: Do biological, developmental, and recovery variables predict outcome? *Journal of the International Neuropsychological Society, 7*, 683–692.

Dennis, M., Purvis, K., Barnes, M. A., Wilkinson, M., & Winner, E. (2001). Understanding of literal truth, ironic criticism, and deceptive praise after childhood head injury. *Brain and Language, 78*, 1–16.

Dennis, M., Wilkinson, M., & Humphreys, R. P. (1998). How children with head injury represent real and deceptive emotion in short narratives. *Brain and Language, 61*, 450–483.

Diamond, A. (2002). Normal development of prefrontal cortex from birth to young adulthood: Cognitive functions, anatomy, and biochemistry. In D. T. Stuss & R. T. Knight (Eds.), *Principles of frontal lobe function* (pp. 466–503). New York: Oxford University Press.

Diamond, A., & Taylor, C. (1996). Development of an aspect of executive control: Development of the abilities to remember what I said and to "Do as I say, not as I do." *Developmental Psychobiology, 29*, 315–334.

Didus, E., Anderson, V., & Catroppa, C. (1999). The development of pragmatic communication skills in head-injured children. *Pediatric Rehabilitation, 3*, 177–186.

Dodge, K. A., Laird, R., Lochman, J. E., & Zelli, A. (2002). Multidimensional latent-construct analysis of children's social information processing patterns: Correlations with aggressive behavior problems. *Psychological Assessment, 14*, 60–73.

Dodge, K. A., Pettit, G. S., McClaskey, C. L., & Brown, M. M. (1986). Social competence in children. *Monographs of the Society for Research in Child Development, 51* (Serial no. 213).

Dowsett, S. M., & Livesey, D. J. (2000). The development of inhibitory control in preschool children: Effects of "executive skills" training. *Developmental Psychobiology, 36*, 161–174.

Dunn, J., Cutting, A., & Fisher, N. (2002). Old friends, new friends: Predictors of children's perspective on their friends at school. *Child Development, 73*, 621–635.

Eckerman, C. O., & Stein, M. R. (1990). How imitation begets imitation and toddler's generation of games. *Developmental Psychology, 26*, 370–378.

Eslinger, P. J., Biddle, K. R., & Grattan, L. M. (1997). Cognitive and social development in children with prefrontal cortex lesions. In N. A. Krasnegor, G. R. Lyon, & P. S. Goldman-Rakic (Eds.), *Development of the prefrontal cortex: Evolution, neurobiology, and behavior* (pp. 295–336). Baltimore: Paul H. Brookes.

Eslinger, P. J., Grattan, L. M., Damasio, H., & Damasio, A. R. (1992). Developmental consequences of childhood frontal lobe damage. *Archives of Neurology, 49*, 764–769.

Ewing-Cobbs, L., Fletcher, J. M., Levin, H. S., Francis, D. J., Davidson, K., & Miner, M. E. (1997). Longitudinal neuropsychological outcome in infants and preschoolers with traumatic brain injury. *Journal of the International Neuropsychological Society, 3*, 581–591.

Fox, N. A., Calkins, S. D., & Bell, M. A. (1994). Neural plasticity and development in the first two years of life: Evidence from cognitive and socioemotional domains of research. *Development and Psychopathology, 6*, 677–696.

Fox, N. A., Henderson, H. A., Rubin, K., Calkins, S. D., & Schmidt, L. A. (2001). Continuity and discontinuity of behavioral inhibition and exuberance: Psychophysiological and behavioral influences across the first 4 years of life. *Child Development, 72*, 1–21.

Fox, N. A., Rubin, K. H., Calkins, S. D., Marshall, T. R., Coplan, R. J., Porges, S. W., Long, J., & Stewart, S. (1995). Frontal activation asymmetry and social competence at four years of age. *Child Development, 66*, 1770–1784.

Frith, U., & Frith, C. (2001). The biological basis of social interaction. *Current Directions in Psychological Science, 10*, 151–155.

Gerstadt, C. L., Hong, Y. J., & Diamond, A. (1994). The relationship between cognition and action: Performance of children 3.5–7 years old on a Stroop-like day–night test. *Cognition, 53*, 129–153.

Gest, S., Graham-Bermann, S., & Hartup, W. (2001). Peer experience: Common and unique features of number of friendships, social network centrality, and sociometric status. *Social Development, 10*, 23–40.

Giedd, J. N., Blumenthal, J., Jeffries, N. O., Castellanos, F. X., Lui, J., Zijdenbos, A. et al. (1999). Brain development during childhood and adolescence: A longitudinal MRI study. *Nature Neuroscience, 2*, 861–863.

Glang, A., Todis, B., Cooley, E., Wells, J., & Voss, J. (1997). Building social networks for children and adolescents with traumatic brain injury: A school-based intervention. *Journal of Head Trauma Rehabilitation, 12*, 32–47.

Goel, V., Grafman, J., Sadato, N., & Hallett, M. (1995). Modeling other minds. *NeuroReport, 6*, 1741–1746.

Gogtay, N., Giedd, J. N., Lusk, L., Hayashi, K. M., Greenstein, D., Vaituzis, A. C. et al. (2004). Dynamic mapping of human cortical development during childhood through early adulthood. *Proceedings of the National Academy of Sciences, 101*, 8174–8179.

Goncu, A. (1993). Development of intersubjectivity in the dyadic play of preschoolers. *Early Childhood Research Quarterly, 8*, 99–116.

Goncu, A., Patt, M. B., & Kouba, E. (2002). Understanding young children's pretend play in context. In P. K. Smith & C. H. Hart (Eds.), *Blackwell handbook of childhood social development* (pp. 418–437). Malden, MA: Blackwell.

Gordon, A. C., & Olson, D. R. (1998). The relation between acquisition of a theory of mind and the capacity to hold in mind. *Journal of Experimental Child Psychology, 68*, 70–83.

Grady, C. L., & Keightley, M. L. (2002). Studies of altered social cognition in neuropsychiatric disorders using functional neuroimaging. *Canadian Journal of Psychiatry, 47*, 327–336.

Grattan, L., & Eslinger, P. (1989). Higher cognition and social behavior: Changes in cognitive flexibility and empathy after cerebral lesions. *Neuropsychology, 3*, 175–185.

Guralnick, M. J. (1989). Social competence as a future direction for early intervention programs. *Journal of Mental Deficiency Research, 33*, 275–281.

Guralnick, M. J. (1990). Social competence and early intervention. *Journal of Early Intervention, 14*, 3–14.

Guralnick, M. J. (1999). Family and child influences on the peer-related social competence of young children with developmental delays. *Mental Retardation and Developmental Disabilities Research Reviews, 5*, 21–29.

Howes, C. (1988). Peer interaction of young children. *Monographs of the Society for Research in Child Development, 53* (Serial No. 217).

Howes, C., & Phillipsen, L. (1998). Continuity in children's relationships with peers. *Social Development, 7*, 340–349.

Hughes, C. (1998). Executive function in preschoolers: Links with theory of mind and verbal ability. *British Journal of Developmental Psychology*, *16*, 233–253.

Hughes, C. (2002). Executive functions and development: Emerging themes. *Infant and Child Development*, *11*, 201–209.

Hulme, C., & Roodenrys, S. (1995). Practitioner review: Verbal working memory development and its disorders. *Journal of Child Psychology and Psychiatry*, *36*, 373–398.

Huttenlocher, P. R. (1979). Synaptic density in human frontal cortex—developmental changes and effects of aging. *Brain Research*, *163*, 195–205.

Janusz, J. A., Kirkwood, M. W., Yeates, K. O., & Taylor, H. G. (2002). Social problem-solving skills in children with traumatic brain injury: Long-term outcomes and prediction of social competence. *Child Neuropsychology*, *8*, 179–194.

Kain, W., & Perner, J. (2003). Do children with ADHD not need their frontal lobes for theory of mind? A review of brain imaging and neuropsychological studies. In M. Brune, H. Ribbert, & W. Schiefenhovel (Eds.), *The social brain: Evolution and pathology* (pp. 197–230). Chichester, UK: Wiley.

Klingberg, T., Vaidya, C. J., Gabrieli, J. D. E., Moseley, M. E., & Hedehus, M. (1999). Myelination and organization of the frontal white matter in children: A diffusion tensor MRI study. *Neuroreport*, *10*, 2817–2821.

Kochanska, G., Murray, K., Jacques, T. Y., Koenig, A. L., & Vandegeest, K. A. (1996). Inhibitory control in young children and its role in emerging internalization. *Child Development*, *67*, 490–507.

Krasnor, L., & Rubin, K. H. (1983). Preschool social problem solving: Attempts and outcomes in naturalistic interaction. *Child Development*, *54*, 1545–1558.

Kraus, J. F. (1995). Epidemiological features of brain injury in children: Occurrence, children at risk, causes and manner of injury, severity, and outcomes. In S.H. Broman & M. E. Michel (Eds.), *Traumatic head injury in children* (pp. 22–39). New York: Oxford University Press.

Kuttler, A. F., Parker, J. G., & La Greca, A. M. (2002). Developmental and gender differences in preadolescents' judgments of the veracity of gossip. *Merrill-Palmer Quarterly*, *48*, 105–132.

Langlois, J. A., Rutland-Brown, W., & Thomas, K. E. (2005). The incidence of traumatic brain injury among children in the United States: Differences by race. *Journal of Head Trauma Rehabilitation*, *20*, 229–238.

Lemerise, E. A., & Arsenio, W. F. (2000). An integrated model of emotion processes and cognition in social information processing. *Child Development*, *71*, 107–118.

Levin, H., Amparo, E., Eisenberg, H., Miner, M., High, W. Jr., Ewing-Cobbs, L. et al. (1989). MRI after closed head injury in children. *Neurosurgery*, *24*, 223–227.

Levin, H. S., & Hanten, G. (2005). Executive functions after traumatic brain injury in children. *Pediatric Neurology*, *33*, 79–93.

Levin, H. S., Zhang, L., Dennis, M., Ewing-Cobbs, L., Schachar, R., Max, J. et al. (2004). Psychosocial outcome of TBI in children with unilateral frontal lesions. *Journal of the International Neuropsychological Society*, *10*, 305–316.

Livesey, D. J., & Morgan, G. A. (1991). The development of response inhibition in 4- and 5-year-old children. *Australian Journal of Psychology*, *43*, 133–137.

Mah, L., Arnold, M. C., & Grafman, J. (2004). Impairment of social perception associated with lesions of the prefrontal cortex. *American Journal of Psychiatry*, *161*, 1247–1255.

Matsuzawa, J., Matsui, M., Konishi, T., Noguchi, K., Gur, R. C., Bilker, W. et al. (2001). Age-related volumetric changes of brain gray and white matter in healthy infants and children. *Cerebral Cortex*, *11*, 335–342.

Max, J. E., Koele, S. L., Lindgren, S. D., Robin, D. A., Smith, W. L. Jr., Sato, Y. et al. (1998). Adaptive functioning following traumatic brain injury and orthopedic injury: A controlled study. *Archives of Physical Medicine and Rehabilitation, 79,* 893–899.

Max, J. E., Levin, H. S., Landis, J., Schachar, R. J., Saunders, A. E., Ewing-Cobbs, L., Chapman, S. B., & Dennis, M. (2005). Predictors of personality change due to traumatic brain injury in children and adolescents in the first six months after injury. *Journal of the American Academy of Child & Adolescent Psychiatry, 44,* 432–435.

McGuire, T. L., & Rothenberg, M. B. (1986). Behavioral and psychosocial sequelae of pediatric head injury. *Journal of Head Trauma Rehabilitation, 1,* 1–6.

Meltzoff, A. N. (1995). Understanding of the intentions of others: Reenactment of intended acts by 18-month-old children. *Developmental Psychology, 31,* 838–850.

Meltzoff, A. N., Gopnik, A., & Repacholi, B. M. (1999). Toddlers understanding of intentions, desires and emotions: Explorations of the dark ages. In P. D. Zelazo, J. W. Astington, & D. R. Olson (Eds.), *Developing theories of intention: Social understanding and self-control* (pp. 17–41). Mahwah, NJ: Erlbaum.

Mendelsohn, D., Levin, H. S., Bruce, D., Lilly, M., Harward, H., Culhane, K. A. et al. (1992). Late MRI after head injury in children: Relationship to clinical features and outcome. *Childs Nervous System, 8,* 445–452.

Mize, J., & Ladd, G. W. (1988). Predicting preschoolers' peer behavior and status from their interpersonal strategies: A comparison of verbal and enactive responses to hypothetical social dilemmas. *Developmental Psychology, 24,* 782–788.

Moses, L. J. (2001). Executive accounts of theory of mind development. *Child Development, 72,* 688–690.

Moss, H., & Damasio, A. (2001). Emotion and the human brain. *Annals of the New York Academy of Sciences, 935,* 101–106.

Nangle, D. W., Erdley, C. A., Newman, J. E., Mason, C. A., & Carpenter, E. (2003). Popularity, friendship quantity, and friendship quality: Interactive influences on children's loneliness and depression. *Journal of Clinical Child and Adolescent Psychology, 32,* 546–555.

Nassau, J. H., & Drotar, D. (1997). Social competence among children with central nervous system-related chronic health conditions: A review. *Journal of Pediatric Psychology, 22,* 771–793.

Newcomb, A., & Bagwell, C. (1995). Children's friendship relations: A meta-analytic review. *Psychological Bulletin, 117,* 306–347.

Ochsner, K. N., & Lieberman, M. D. (2001). The emergence of social cognitive neuroscience. *American Psychologist, 56,* 717–734.

O'Conner, P. (2002). Hospitalisation due to traumatic brain injury (TBI), Australia 1997–1998. *Injury Research and Statistics Series* (No. 11). Adelaide:AIHW (AIHW cat no. INJCAT 43).

O'Donnell, S., Noseworthy, M., Levine, B., Brandt, M., & Dennis, M. (2005). Cortical thickness of the frontopolar area in typically developing children and adolescents. *Neuroimage, 24,* 948–954.

Orzhekhovskaya, N. S. (1981). Fronto-striatal relationships in primate ontogeny. *Neuroscience and Behavioural Physiology, 11,* 379–385.

Papero, P. H., Prigatano, G. P., Snyder, H. M., & Johnson, D. L. (1993). Children's adaptive behavioural competence after head injury. *Neuropsychological Rehabilitation, 3,* 321–340.

Parker, J., Rubin, K. H., Erath, S., Wojslawowicz, J. C., & Buskirk, A. A. (2006). Peer relationships and developmental psychopathology. In D. Cicchetti & D. Cohen (Eds.), *Developmental psychopathology: Risk, disorder, and adaptation* (2nd ed.), Vol. 2. (pp. 419–493). New York: Wiley.

Paus, T. (2005). Mapping brain maturation and cognitive development during adolescence. *Trends in Cognitive Sciences*, *9*, 60–68.

Pellegrini, A. D. (2002). Rough-and-tumble play from childhood through adolescence: Development and possible functions. In P. K. Smith & C. H. Hart (Eds.), *Blackwell handbook of childhood social development* (pp. 438–453). London: Blackwell.

Pfefferbaum, A., Mathalon, D. H., Sullivan, E. V., Rawles, J. M., Zipursky, R. B., & Lim, K. O. (1994). A quantitative magnetic resonance imaging study of changes in brain morphology from infancy to late adulthood. *Archives of Neurology*, *51*, 874–887.

Posner, M., Rothbart, M., & Gerardi-Caulton, G. (2001). Exploring the biology of socialization. *Annals of the New York Academy of Sciences*, *935*, 208–216.

Rakic, P., Bourgeois, J. P., Eckenhoff, M. F., Zecevic, N., & Goldman-Rakic, P. S. (1986). Concurrent overproduction of synapses in diverse regions of the primate cerebral cortex. *Science*, *232*, 232–235.

Reiss, A. L., Abrams, M. T., Singer, H. S., Ross, J. L., & Denckla, M. B. (1996). Brain development, gender and IQ in children. *Brain*, *119*, 1763–1774.

Rose-Krasnor, L. (1997). The nature of social competence: A theoretical review. *Social Development*, *6*, 111–135.

Rowe, A. D., Bullock, P. R., Polkey, C. E., & Morris, R. G. (2001). "Theory of mind" impairments and their relationship to executive functioning following frontal lobe excisions. *Brain*, *124*, 600–616.

Rubin, K. H., Booth, C., Krasnor, L. R., & Mills, R. S. L. (1995). Social relationships and social skills: A conceptual and empirical analysis. In S. Shulman (Ed.), *Close relationships and socioemotional development* (pp. 63–95). Norwood, NJ: Ablex.

Rubin, K. H., Bukowski, W., & Parker, J. (2006). Peer interactions, relationships, and groups. In N. Eisenberg (Ed.), *Handbook of child psychology* (6th ed.): *Social, emotional, and personality development* (pp. 571–645). New York: Wiley.

Rubin, K. H., & Krasnor, L. R. (1986). Social-cognitive and social behavioral perspectives on problem solving. In M. Perlmutter (Ed.), *Cognitive perspectives on children's social and behavioral development. The Minnesota symposia on child psychology* (Vol. 18, pp. 1–68). Hillsdale, NJ.: Erlbaum.

Rudolph, K., & Heller, T. (1997). Interpersonal problem solving, externalizing behavior, and social competence in preschoolers: A knowledge-performance discrepancy? *Journal of Applied Developmental Psychology*, *18*, 107–117.

Selman, R. L., & Schultz, L. H. (1990). *Making a friend in youth: Developmental theory and pair therapy*. University of Chicago Press.

Siegal, M., & Varley, R. (2002). Neural systems involved in "theory of mind." *Nature Reviews/Neuroscience*, *3*, 463–471.

Sodian, B., Taylor, C., Harris, P. L., & Perner, J. (1991). Early deception and the child's theory of mind: False trails and genuine markers. *Child Development*, *62*, 468–483.

Sowell, E. R., & Jernigan, T. L. (1998). Further MRI evidence of late brain maturation: Limbic volume increases and changing asymmetries during childhood and adolescence. *Developmental Neuropsychology*, *14*, 599–617.

Sowell, E. R., Thompson, P. M., Holmes, C. J., Batth, R., Jernigan, T. L., & Toga, A. W. (1999). Localizing age-related changes in brain structure between childhood and adolescence using statistical parametric mapping. *NeuroImage*, *9*, 587–597.

Sowell, E. R., Trauner, D. A., Gamst, A., Jernigan, T. L. (2002). Development of cortical and subcortical brain structures in childhood and adolescence: A structural MRI study. *Developmental Medicine and Child Neurology*, *44*, 4–16.

Sparrow, S. S., Balla, D. A., & Cicchetti, D. V. (1984). *Vineland Adaptive Behavior Scales: Interview Edition*. Circle Pines, MN: American Guidance Service.

Stancin, T., Drotar, D., Taylor, H. G., Yeates, K. O., Wade, S. L., & Minich, N. M. (2002). Health-related quality of life of children and adolescents following traumatic brain injury. *Pediatrics [On-line]*, *109*, e34. (http://www.pediatrics.org/cgi/content/full/109/2/e34)

Stuss, D. T., & Anderson, V. (2004). The frontal lobes and theory of mind: Developmental concepts from adult focal lesion research. *Brain and Cognition*, *55*, 69–83.

Stuss, D. T., Gallup, G. G., & Alexander, M. P. (2001). The frontal lobes are necessary for 'theory of mind.' *Brain*, *124*, 279–286.

Taylor, H. G., & Alden, J. (1997). Age-related differences in outcome following childhood brain injury: An introduction and overview. *Journal of the International Neuropsychological Society*, *3*, 555–567.

Taylor, H. G., Yeates, K. O., Wade, S. L., Drotar, D., Stancin, T., & Minich, N. (2002). A prospective study of short- and long-term outcomes after traumatic brain injury in children: Behavior and achievement. *Neuropsychology*, *16*, 15–27.

Warschausky, S., Cohen, E. H., Parker, J. G., Levendosky, A. A., & Okun, A. (1997). Social problem-solving skills of children with traumatic brain injury. *Pediatric Rehabilitation*, *1*, 77–81.

Watson, A. C., Nixon, C. L., Wilson, A., & Capage, L. (1999). Social interaction skills and theory of mind in young children. *Developmental Psychology*, *35*, 386–391.

Wilde, E. A., Hunter, J. V., Newsome, M. R., Scheibel, R. S., Bigler, E. D., Johnson, J. L. et al. (2005). Frontal and temporal morphometric findings on MRI in children after moderate to severe traumatic brain injury. *Journal of Neurotrauma*, *22*, 333–344.

Winner, E. (1988). *The point of words: Children's understanding of metaphor and irony*. Cambridge, MA: Harvard University Press.

Yakovlev, P. I. (1962). Morphological criteria of growth and maturation of the nervous system in man. *Research Publications Association for Research in Nervous and Mental Disease*, *39*, 3–46.

Yakovlev, P. I., & Lecours, A. R. (1967). The myelogenetic cycles of regional maturation of the brain. In A. Minkowski (Ed.), *Regional development of the brain in early life* (pp. 3–70). Oxford: Blackwell.

Yeates, K. O. (2000). Closed-head injury. In K. O. Yeates, M. D. Ris, & H. G. Taylor (Eds.), *Pediatric neuropsychology: Research, theory, and practice* (pp. 92–116). New York: Guilford.

Yeates, K. O., Schultz, L. H., & Selman, K. O. (1991). The development of interpersonal negotiation strategies in thought and action: A social-cognitive link to behavioral adjustment and social status. *Merrill-Palmer Quarterly*, *37*, 369–406.

Yeates, K. O., Selman, R. L., & Schultz, L. H. (1990). Bridging the gaps in child-clinical assessment: Toward the application of social-cognitive developmental theory. *Clinical Psychology Review*, *10*, 567–588.

Yeates, K. O., Swift, E., Taylor, H. G., Wade, S. L., Drotar, D., Stancin, T. et al. (2004). Short- and long-term social outcomes following pediatric traumatic brain injury. *Journal of the International Neuropsychological Society*, *10*, 412–426.

Yeates, K. O., Taylor, H. G., Wade, S. L., Drotar, D., Stancin, T., & Minich, N. (2002). A prospective study of short- and long-term neuropsychological outcomes after pediatric traumatic brain injury. *Neuropsychology*, *16*, 514–523.

Yeates, K. O., Bigler, E. D., Dennis, M., Gerhardt, C. A., Rubin, K. A., Stancin, T. et al. (2007). Social outcomes in childhood brain disorder: A heuristic integration of social neuroscience and developmental psychology. *Psychological Bulletin*, *133*, 535–556.

12 Executive functions after frontal lobe insult in childhood

Vicki Anderson, Rani Jacobs, and A. Simon Harvey

Contents

Until recently the development of the frontal lobes and the functions they subsume in children have received relatively little attention. Early researchers argued that these brain regions were silent in infancy and early childhood, only becoming functional once they were fully developed in later childhood and adolescence (Golden, 1981). Today, this traditional view is being questioned, with research demonstrating that, even while in a process of maturation, the frontal regions of the brain are fully active and engaged, although activation patterns may differ to those observed in the adult brain (Wood et al., 2004). Further, evidence is mounting that the integrity and efficiency of these developing frontal regions is essential for normal development, due to their extensive connections with other cerebral regions and their central role in mediating executive functions (EF). It is now argued that damage or disruption to prefrontal regions while they are rapidly developing during infancy and early childhood may cause irreversible changes in brain organization and connectivity as well as associated impairments in cognitive and social function, which impact on the child's capacity to interact with his/her environment in an adaptive manner, and reduce the capacity for independence in adulthood (Anderson, Anderson, Northam, Jacobs, & Mikiewicz, 2002; Eslinger, Flaherty-Craig, & Benton, 2004; Jacobs, Anderson, & Harvey, 2001; Jacobs, Harvey, & Anderson, 2007; Johnson, 2001; Kolb, Pellis, & Robinson, 2004).

Converging evidence from the neurosciences and psychology illustrates the importance of prefrontal regions documenting that, from an evolutionary perspective, these regions are disproportionately represented in humans (27% of brain size) compared to cats (3.5%) and chimpanzees (17%) (Fuster, 2002). Frontal structures and connections mature rapidly through childhood and early adolescence, and this development is paralleled by specific increases in intellectual skills (Shaw et al., 2006) and executive abilities, such as attentional control, planning and mental flexibility (Anderson, Anderson, Northam, Jacobs, Catroppa, 2001; Fuster, 2002; Gogtay et al., 2004). An understanding of these normal developmental processes provides a backdrop for interpreting the possible impairments of children who have sustained frontal injuries. This chapter aims to: (a) briefly examine the structural development of the frontal lobes and the corresponding maturation of EF; (b) establish the cognitive and behavioral consequences of damage to frontal regions during childhood; (c) compare these consequences to other developmental insults; and (d) to explore the impact of time of insult to outcomes.

Frontal lobe development

The frontal lobes are organized in a largely hierarchical manner. The prefrontal cortices (PFC) and their association areas receive input from posterior and subcortical cerebral regions (Barbas, 1992; Fuster, 1993, 2002). While the PFC has been purported to be critical for efficient EF, it has also been acknowledged that these regions are functionally heterogeneous, with different skills subsumed by different subregions. Specifically, Fuster (2002) proposes that anterior cingulate and medial regions are critical for drive and motivation, lateral cortices for working memory and set shifting, and orbito-frontal (and medial) regions for impulse control and interference. In contrast, he describes attentional skills as requiring the efficient involvement of all areas.

Based on recent findings from brain imaging research it is evident that the frontal lobes are the last area of the brain to develop (Giedd et al., 1999; Jernigan & Tallal, 1990). Prefrontal grey matter tends to increase postnatally and then plateaus between the ages of 4 and 12, and declines again in association with the development of functional systems (Edelman, 1987; Giedd et al., 1999). In contrast, white matter volume increases through childhood and adolescence, reaching maturity sometime in early adulthood (Klinberg, Vaidya, Gabrieli, Moseley, & Hedehus, 1999; Sowell, Delis, Stiles, & Jernigan, 2001), and is mainly associated with the ongoing process of myelination (Fuster, 2002).

An overview of developmental processes within the brain indicates that frontal lobe maturation tends to lag behind other brain regions (Fuster, 2002; Scheibel, 1990; Yakovlev & Lecours, 1967), thus limiting the efficiency of cortical connectivity. Postnatally, a number of critical growth periods have been documented within frontal regions, using methodologies such as EEG, functional and structural imaging, and metabolic analyses. The first of these has been found to occur between birth and 2 years, another from 7 to 9 years, with a final spurt in late adolescence (16–19 years) (Casey, Giedd, & Thomas, 2000; Diamond, 2002; Fuster, 1993; Hudspeth & Pribram, 1990; Huttenlocher & Dabholkar, 1997; Jernigan & Tallal, 1990; Klinberg et al., 1999;

Sowell et al., 2003; Thatcher, 1991, 1992, 1997). Progressive myelination of frontal structures, prefrontal ribonucleic acid development, and changes in patterns of metabolic activity have been documented (Chiron et al., 1997; Chugani, Phelps, & Mazziota, 1987; Fuster, 1993, 2002; Giedd et al., 1996; Hale, Bronik, & Fry, 1997; Hudspeth & Pribram, 1990; Huttenlocher & Dabholkar, 1997; Jernigan & Tallal, 1990; Kennedy, Sakurada, Shinohara, & Miyaoka, 1982; Klinberg et al., 1999; Staudt et al., 1993; Uemura & Hartmann, 1978; Yakovlev & Lecours, 1967). Not all central nervous system (CNS) development conforms to this hierarchical model. Synaptogenesis appears to be simultaneous in multiple areas and layers of the cortex (Rakic, Bourgeois, Eckenhoff, Zecevic, & Goldman-Rakic, 1986), with neurotransmitter receptors throughout the brain reported to mature at the same time (Lidow & Goldman-Rakic, 1991). Such findings suggest concurrent development, where posterior and anterior structures develop along approximately the same timetable. Other neuronal elements display a different style of maturation, exhibiting periods of regression, characterized by an initial overproduction, followed by an elimination of redundant elements (Blatter et al., 1995; Pfefferbaum et al., 1994).

The frontal lobes are intimately connected with all other brain regions, and specific prefrontal regions—medial, lateral, and orbital—are connected to each other and to a wide range of extra-frontal structures (Fuster, 2002) (see Figures 12.1 and 12.2). Thus, while prefrontal regions may "orchestrate" behavior, they are also dependent on other cerebral areas for input, with efficient functioning reliant upon the quality of

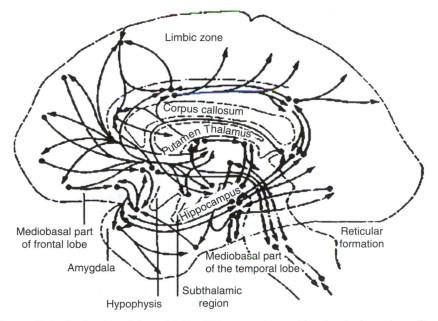

Figure 12.1 Intricacies of frontal lobe (FL) connections with other brain regions. From *The Working Brain*, by A. R. Luria, 1973, New York: Oxford.

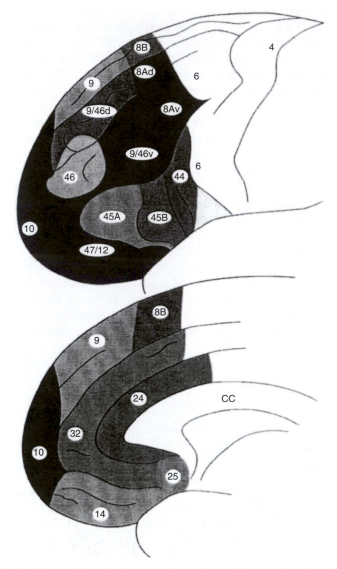

Figure 12.2   Petrides and Pandya's cytoarchitectonic revisions to the frontal lobes (FL). From "Dorsolateral prefrontal cortex: Comparative cytoarchitectonic analysis in human and macaque brain and cortico-cortical connection patterns," by M. Petrides and D. N. Pandya, 1999, *European Journal of Neuroscience*, *11*, pp. 1011–1036.

information transmitted from other cerebral regions. This pattern of connectivity has significant implications during childhood, when brain development is rapid and connections are in the process of being established. Even in the context of normal development, the frontal lobes will need to "wait" for these connections to come "online" before being optimally functional. Where a cerebral injury or insult occurs to the developing brain, the genetically orchestrated process of cerebral connectivity is disrupted. As a result, cerebral networks may be abnormal, or never mature, leading to a limitation in the neural transmission to or within the frontal regions, with the potential for a severe impact on both lower-order and higher-order functions, and a likely picture of global impairment. The frontal lobes, with their very protracted developmental trajectory, are particularly vulnerable to these influences.

Previous arguments purporting the plasticity of the young brain argue that reorganization of function can occur after such disruptions, due to a lack of early structural and functional specialization, resulting in minimal, if any, functional consequences. However, more recent models argue for "early vulnerability," where early brain injury disrupts ongoing neural and behavioral maturation significantly and may lead to abnormal and often maladaptive consequences. Thus, even if the young brain has the capacity to reorganize, this may not necessarily lead to functional advantage. Pascual-Leone and colleagues (Pascual-Leone, Armdi, Fregni, & Merobet, 2005) as has been demonstrated for children sustaining very early trauma (e.g., stroke, head injury), who tend to present with more global impairments, and certainly not the more specific "frontal lobe syndrome" that is described following frontal injury in adults (Anderson, Levin, & Jacobs, 2002; Anderson, Northam, Wrennall, & Hendy, 2001; Eslinger, Biddle, & Grattan, 1997). Further, reorganization may be more common following focal lesions to regions believed to subsume critical functions such as language and motor skills (Aram & Eisele, 1994).

Development of executive functions

Executive function is an umbrella term which refers to a complex set of psychological constructs encompassing a number of separate, but integrated processes that are responsible for goal-directed behavior (Lezak, 1995). It is generally agreed that these skills are primarily subsumed by the PFC (Benton, 1968; D'Esposito et al., 1995; Harlow, 1868; Luria, 1973; Milner, 1963; Stuss & Benson, 1986; Walsh, 1978), although some adult studies have also demonstrated that the integrity of posterior and subcortical regions is also important for efficient overall function (Dhager, Owen, Boecker, & Brooks, 1999; Dias, Robbins, & Roberts, 1996; Eslinger, Warner, Grattan, & Easton, 1991; Mesulam, 1981, 1990; Moll et al., 2002; Passingham, Toni, & Rushworth, 2000; Stuss, Alexander et al., 1994; Stuss, Toth et al., 1999). These findings suggest a distributed but integrated network for effective executive function (Alivisatos & Petrides, 1997; Klinberg, O'Sullivan, & Roland, 1997; Knight, 1996, 1997; Passingham et al., 2000; Stuss, Alexander et al., 2002; Stuss, Toth et al., 1999). Neuroanatomical data also support the notion of a distributed cerebral system for EF, identifying strong links between frontal, and posterior/subcortical (extra-frontal) brain regions (Barr & Kiernan, 1993; Öngür & Price, 2000; Stuss & Benson, 1986).

The rarity of focal frontal pathology and resultant limited sample sizes have hampered progress in understanding the role of the frontal lobes and their association with EF in childhood. An alternative method of examining this association is to take advantage of parallels identified between normal developmental processes within the PFC and increases in efficiency of EF. A number of studies have focussed on documenting the developmental trajectories of executive processes throughout childhood and adolescence (Anderson, Anderson, & Garth, 2001; Anderson, P.,

Anderson, V., & Lajoie, 1995; Delis, Kaplan, & Kramer, 2001; Espy, 1997; Jacobs et al., 2001; Korkman, Kirk, & Kemp, 1998). Based on these data, Anderson (2002; this volume) has derived a model of EF specifically relevant for childhood and adolescence. He proposes four separate but integrated subdomains for EF, each with its own developmental trajectory.

The first domain is labeled *Attentional Control* and includes self-regulation, self-monitoring, and the capacity to selectively attend to important information while ignoring extraneous details, and to focus attention for extended periods. Skills in this domain emerge earliest, developing rapidly from age 4, and are relatively mature by 6–7 years of age (Anderson, 2002; Diamond & Taylor, 1996; Espy, 1997; Smidt, Jacobs, & Anderson, 2004). The domain of *Goal Setting* refers to strategic processes including the ability to develop new concepts, devise and implement strategies prior to commencing a problem, and execute these in an organized, efficient manner. A third domain, *Cognitive Flexibility*, entails the capacity to shift between response sets, learn from mistakes and devise alternate strategies, and concurrently process multiple sources of information. Skills within the latter two domains (goal setting and cognitive flexibility) appear to come online late in the preschool period, and then undergo rapid development in middle childhood, with marginal improvements seen on some tasks in 14–15 year olds (Anderson, 2002; Anderson, Anderson, & Lajoie, 1996; Anderson, P. et al., 2001; Kelly, 2000; Kirk, 1985; Krikorian & Bartok, 1998; Levin et al., 1991; Smidt et al., 2004; Waber & Holmes, 1985; Welsh, Pennington, & Grossier, 1991). The final domain of *Information Processing* is more general and involves fluency of responses as well as efficiency and speed of output. These aspects of performance are generally reflected in the timed component of EF measures or in the volume of output generated under a particular time constraint, and appear to undergo rapid development between 6 and 12 years of age (Kelly, 2000; Levin et al., 1991; Welsh et al., 1991). Further gains in processing skills have been documented into mid-adolescence and these skills appear to stabilize at around 15 years of age, with marginal improvements beyond this time (Kail, 1986).

Relationship between frontal lobes and executive function: A developmental perspective

Before moving to discuss the relationship between frontal brain pathology and EF after early brain damage, a number of definitional and psychometric issues need to be considered. The various controversies surrounding these issues have been discussed in detail in previous chapters and so will be briefly summarized here.

Traditionally, in the neuropsychology literature there has been conceptual debate regarding discrimination of the concepts of frontal lobe function and EF. Even today, researchers tend to confuse the terms, leading to the assumption that the two are interchangeable. For the purposes of this chapter, and particularly within a developmental context, it is important to tease out this distinction, as we argue that frontal lobe function and EF are not synonymous in the context of early brain insult, or even normal development. Specifically, we will consider frontal lobe function to be a biological term referring to activity occurring within the frontal lobes, which may or may not be related to EF. Conversely, we view the term EF as a psychological construct, referring to a set of behaviors important for goal-directed activities (Stuss, 1992). The frontal lobes, and PFC specifically, may play a role in these executive skills, but the term itself does not incorporate a reference to underlying brain regions. In adult studies, researchers have been able to fractionate out different processes on EF tasks, identifying distinct impairments depending on the specific site of prefrontal pathology (Mesulam, 1981, 1990; Stuss et al., 1998). We would argue that, in the developmental context, the integrity of the brain appears to be important for EF, but that *frontal lobe type* symptomatology may occur with disruption to areas of the brain other than prefrontal cortex (Anderson, Jacobs, & Harvey, 2005; Jacobs & Anderson, 2002). Thus, frontal lobe lesions may produce unique patterns of performance on EF measures reflecting the specific contributions to cognition provided by these brain regions, and their level of maturity and connectivity at time of insult.

Two separate lines of inquiry lend support to the dependence of the PFC on input from extra-frontal brain regions for effective development. First, and as noted above, many aspects of cortical development in humans proceed in a hierarchical manner, with development of posterior/subcortical brain regions typically preceding development of the corresponding prefrontal region to which they form connections (Hudspeth & Pribram, 1990). This implies that adequate maturation of prefrontal cortex is likely to be dependent on development of extra-frontal brain regions. Animal studies provide direct evidence for this notion, showing that medial temporal damage early in life can permanently alter the structure and function of the prefrontal cortex (Beauregard, Malkova, & Bachevalier, 1995; Bertolino et al., 1997; Kolb & Gibb, 2002; Raedler, Knable, & Weinberger, 1998), and cause deficits in EF similar to those seen following prefrontal damage (Goldman-Rakic, 1987). Conversely, early frontal lobe damage has been reported to alter the structure of corresponding extra-frontal regions if damage occurs prior to these areas reaching maturity, causing permanent changes in brain morphology and function (Kolb & Gibb, 2002).

The importance of the entire brain for EF in childhood has been further highlighted in a recent imaging study. Using a Go/No Go paradigm, Tamm, Menon, and Reiss (2002) demonstrated a different pattern of activation in younger, compared with older, participants and argued that the differing activation is possibly due to the adoption of less efficient strategies in children for completing the same EF task and suggest that there may be increasing specialization of prefrontal regions with age. Bunge, Dudukovik, Thomason, Vaidya, and Gabrieli (2002) documented a similar pattern of age-related differences when comparing children and adults on tasks of interference suppression and inhibition. Thus, the integrity of the entire brain appears to be more critical for carrying out executive tasks in childhood than in adulthood, when the CNS is mature.

In keeping with the notion that there is less specificity in the brain regions subsuming EF in childhood, Alexander and Stuss (2000) have suggested that tasks that are routine for some people may be novel for others and therefore become a measure of EF. This may be particularly pertinent to childhood populations where life experience is limited, and children are therefore more likely to encounter situations that are novel and may be perceived by them as complex. These tasks then would necessarily recruit prefrontal cortex in children more frequently than perhaps would be seen in an adult population.

Assessing the frontal lobes versus executive function

Multi-determined test measures are often described as tapping EF, or even frontal lobe function, ignoring the clear involvement of lower-order skills and other brain regions in the mediation of test performances. For example, the Complex Figure of Rey (1964) is often considered to be a measure of EF. However, task analysis reveals that efficient performance requires motor and perceptual abilities, in addition to goal setting skills. Thus, traditional accuracy scores on the task will reflect multiple cognitive skills and their neurological underpinnings. Use of more specific perform-ance variables, reflective of specific aspects of EF (e.g., organizational or process scores) needs to be considered to truly evaluate EF. To illustrate the relative discriminability of multidimensional scores versus those more directly assessing EF, we developed a process score for the Rey Complex Figure (RCF; Anderson, P. et al., 2001), and then employed it, along with traditional accuracy and recall measures, in children with focal frontal lesions ($n = 15$), focal temporal lesions ($n = 30$), generalized brain damage ($n = 16$), and healthy controls ($n = 37$). Children with generalized damage achieved poor results on all three measures, reflecting global cognitive impairment. However, there were no differences across other groups for accuracy, questioning the utility of this measure in identifying impairments specific to frontal lobe pathology. In contrast, frontal lesions were associated with reduced process scores, with productions being fragmented and poorly planned (Matthews, Anderson, & Anderson, 2001).

Levin et al. (1994) also supported the importance of considering aspects of test performance relevant to frontal lobe function. They reported that there were no correlations between global scores on the Tower of London (TOL; Shallice, 1982) and frontal lobe volumes in children with traumatic brain injury (TBI). Poorer performances on the more sensitive measures of planning and inhibition (e.g., number of extra attempts required) were associated with less frontal lobe volume.

Stuss and colleagues (1999) also highlight this notion of "micro-analysis" of test performance in an adult sample. They showed that although attentional problems were evident following either focal frontal or posterior damage, the nature of this impaired performance varied according to the site of pathology. Right and bilateral PFC damage was associated with impaired selective attention, or difficulty with-holding attention to distracting information, but only when tasks became more difficult. Right PFC and right posterior damage were associated with deficits inhibi-ting responses to spatial locations across all levels of complexity. Left and bilateral PFC damage also produced deficits in this ability but only at the highest level of task complexity, suggesting that greater frontal lobe resources are required, as tasks become more complex. Finally, damage to the left PFC produced deficits inhibiting motor responses to novel and previously reinforced locations, with left posterior damage also producing these deficits at the highest level of task complexity.

In children, the contribution of extra-frontal and frontal brain regions to specific executive processes may be less clearly delineated than in adults, due to the immaturity of cerebral structures particularly the PFC, at the time of insult (Chugani et al., 1987; Hudspeth & Pribram, 1990; Huttenlocher & Dabholkar, 1997; Klinberg et al., 1999; Thatcher, 1997). Given the strong connections between prefrontal and extra-frontal brain regions and the later maturation of the PFC compared with other brain regions, it is likely that prefrontal development is intimately dependent on efficient input from extra-frontal brain regions. Consequently, extra-frontal damage occurring during development may not only result in primary impairments as a direct result of the site of damage, but may also impede prefrontal development and therefore function.

Functional brain imaging research has contributed to our knowledge in this area, demonstrating combined activation of frontal and other brain regions on a number of EF tasks including the Stroop (Leung, Skudlarski, Gatenby, Peterson, & Gore, 2000) and the Revised Strategy Application Test (Levine et al., 1998) as well as working memory (Alivisatos & Petrides, 1997; Klinberg et al., 1997), associative learning (Passingham et al., 2000), selective attention (Corbetta, Miezin, Dobmeyer, Shulman, & Petersen, 1991) and problem solving (Dhager et al., 1999; Dias et al., 1996) paradigms.

In summary then, data from child and adult lesion studies, together with functional imaging research in adults, suggest that both frontal and extra-frontal brain regions are required for efficient EF, and that it is likely that these regions play different roles in this complex system.

Early frontal lobe damage: Developmental consequences

Until recently, there has been limited examination of the impact of early frontal lobe injury, and related executive deficits, on long-term development. Further, few studies have distinguished between cognitive and affective consequences. Mateer (1990) conducted one of the earliest studies in this area, reporting on a small group of children with early brain insult. She identified evidence of cognitive dysfunction, including perseveration, reduced attention, rigidity, lability, and social difficulties, alongside intact or mildly depressed intellectual ability, consistent with adult patterns of impairment. Following on from this work, several case studies of adults sustaining frontal lobe damage in childhood have emerged in the literature, revealing the expected pattern of poor problem solving, reduced planning and inappropriate social skills (Anderson, 1988; Anderson, Damasio, Tranel, & Damasio, 2000; Eslinger et al., 1997; Eslinger, Biddle, Pennington, & Page, 1999; Eslinger, Grattan, Damasio, & Damasio, 1992; Marlowe, 1992). Eslinger and colleagues (1992, 2004) report a pattern of delayed onset of impairments, with increasing difficulties identified as executive skills fail to come online and mature at critical stages throughout development.

Several group studies have recently reported on the effects of specific frontal pathology in children with TBI (Anderson & Catroppa, 2005; Anderson & Moore,

1995; Garth, Anderson, & Wrennall, 1997; Levin et al., 1994, 1997, 2000; Pentland, Todd, & Anderson, 1998; Todd, Anderson, & Lawrence, 1996). Each of these authors has documented the expected cognitive deficits in aspects of EF in children and adolescents with brain injury. There is also a description of poorer outcomes following younger age at insult and a "relative deterioration" or lack of normal development in children with frontal pathology over time since insult. Such ongoing difficulties may reflect the inadequacy of the young damaged brain to acquire skills in the normal manner, and has major implications for the needs of these children through their lifetime.

Behavioral and social impairments in association with frontal lobe pathology have received recent attention. Diminished affective response, apathy and reduced motivation, poor social judgment, inadequate self-control, disturbed self-awareness, and poor interpersonal skills and reduced moral judgment have all been described (Anderson et al., 2002; Couper, Jacobs, & Anderson, 2002; Damasio, 1994; Eslinger et al., 1999; Stuss, Gallup, & Alexander, 2001). Such deficits have been reported to be more severe following early frontal lobe damage (Anderson, S. W. et al., 2000), perhaps suggesting that these deficits may be a characteristic feature of early frontal lobe damage. Of note, such impairments have also been described in many developmental and acquired pediatric conditions including ADHD (Barkley, 1996), head injury (Pentland et al., 1998), and epilepsy (Anderson et al., 2001).

Case illustration

This hypothesized lack of normal development, or "emergence of deficits," may be best illustrated on an individual case basis. The following case description plots the progress of a young child, who suffered a severe head injury, and later demonstrated a lack of expected development, and gradual fall-off in performance relative to age-peers.

Mark's development had been normal to advanced, with no significant medical history, when he sustained a severe head injury as a result of falling beneath a tractor at age 3 years. Mark was initially unconscious and transferred to hospital via air ambulance. On admission to hospital, radiological investigation confirmed bilateral frontal lobe contusions and hemorrhage (see Figure 12.3), requiring surgical intervention including dural repair and debriding in the region of injury. Mark remained unconscious for 4 weeks, and received intensive rehabilitation over the months postinjury.

On discharge, 2 months postinjury, Mark's residual difficulties included restricted expressive and receptive language, severely limited attention, impaired mobility, significant gross and fine motor problems, and poor impulse control. At 12 months postinjury, Mark continued to experience difficulties with mobility and coordination. His speech was slow and labored, restricting his capacity for normal communication. Attentional and behavioral problems had emerged as major concerns and his parents reported significant difficulties managing his behavior.

Mark was first comprehensively assessed at 6 months postinjury, and then on a number of subsequent occasions until the age of 16 years. On each occasion, qualitative features of presentation included high levels of distractibility and impulsivity.

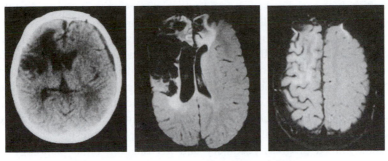

Acute   10 years postinjury

Figure 12.3   Acute CT scan and repeat MRI scans 10 years postinjury for Mark, who was aged 3 years when he sustained a severe traumatic brain injury (TBI), including bilateral frontal pathology.

Figure 12.4 plots his performances at each assessment across intellectual, memory, and visuo-motor domains, with scores presented as age equivalents to enable direct comparison across tests. As these results illustrate, Mark exhibited age expected progress in the first 12 months, probably reflecting some recovery of function in addition to some limited developmental progress. After this time his development (as measured by psychometric testing) slowed, with minimal improvement over the following years. By 12 years postinjury, Mark's best results on neuropsychological test measures were at the level expected for an 8-year old child.

This lack of developmental progress recorded on testing is consistent with Mark's school history. He commenced mainstream school at age 6 years, requiring full-time support and a modified educational curriculum. By mid-primary school, Mark's considerable cognitive, social, and behavioral impairments became difficult to manage within the classroom, and he was transferred to a special school for children with intellectual impairment. Despite this change, Mark experienced continued

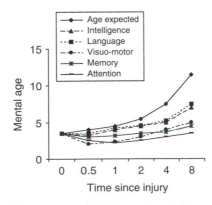

Figure 12.4   Mark's cognitive recovery/development postinjury.

difficulties, both social and academic. By 'late' adolescence, it was evident that Mark would be unable to live independently, or to attain unsupported employment. At age 16, he remained dependent for daily living skills including basic hygiene and dressing. Consistent with these problems, Mark was unable to engage in complex activities, for example cooking, travel on public transport, or shopping without supervision. He was socially isolated, with no close friendships and minimal peer contact, however, it was his behavioral difficulties—impulsivity, poor self-monitoring, and poor anger control—which were most debilitating, and led to his family reducing their social activities and seeking frequent respite care.

Mark's limited progress postinjury and his ongoing brain pathology illustrate the potential impact of disruption to frontal regions during early development. In contrast to the specific deficits often reported in adults, it appears that children may experience more global impairment, with a pattern of emerging deficits with time since injury, as the child fails to acquire expected skills and knowledge. While case studies such as Mark's provide some insight into the effects of early frontal lobe injury, systematic, group-based research is required to fully understand the impact of such insults.

Traumatic brain injury and executive dysfunction

Researchers investigating children following TBI argue that, because the frontal regions are frequently damaged as a result of TBI, this group can provide insights for understanding the long-term implications of frontal lobe pathology and associated impairments of EF. There are now a large number of studies which report executive problems following childhood TBI using traditional psychometric measures, although such standard measures have been argued to lack sensitivity to day-to-day executive abilities (Anderson, 1998; Gioia, Isquith, Guy, & Kenworthy, 2000), and thus may underestimate their severity. Our own research supports these findings, suggesting that, while gross measures such as intelligence scores and memory quotients are often intact, clinically significant deficits are evident in planning ability (Todd et al., 1996), high-level attentional skills and information processing speed (Fenwick & Anderson, 1999; Anderson & Pentland, 1998), adaptive function (Anderson et al., 1997), social and behavioral competence (Anderson et al., 2000; Yeates & Anderson, this volume), and high-level language (Didus, Anderson, & Catroppa, 2000).

In response to discrepancies between test findings and day-to-day performance, researchers have begun to employ experimental tasks specifically designed to tap executive skills. Dennis and colleagues have employed this approach, conducting several studies examining aspects of high-level language function and communication following childhood TBI. Results indicate that children with severe head injury, and probable frontal lobe damage, exhibit deficits in integrating knowledge and knowing when it is appropriate to make inferences as opposed to accept literal translations (Barnes & Dennis, 2001). These researchers identified impaired sensitivity to social cues and messages, with specific problems dealing with subtleties of language, in particular the language of mental states and intention, including irony and deception (Dennis & Barnes, 2001; Dennis, Purvis, Barnes, Wilkinson, & Winner, 2001).

Levin and colleagues have attempted to extend these findings, by linking performances on tests of EF with indices from structural brain imaging. Studies from their group and others document deficits in a range of executive skills following TBI in childhood, associated with structural and functional changes within prefrontal regions, including reduced inhibition and mental flexibility (Levin et al., 1993), poor planning, reduced memory capacity and strategic learning, as well as high-level aspects of linguistic function (Anderson, Levin, & Jacobs, 2002).

Despite these remarkably consistent findings, this line of research is unable to isolate the specific effects of frontal lobe pathology from additional pathology commonly present in TBI. In particular, diffuse white matter pathology and disruption, which may influence information processing speed, attention and memory function, clearly have the potential to impact on performance on measures tapping executive abilities.

Focal frontal pathology

Another, more precise approach to understanding the role of the frontal lobes and PFC in early development is to investigate the effects of localized damage to these regions during childhood. In adults, focal frontal lesions involving PFC have been shown to cause behavioral and executive dysfunction. It is unclear whether, in young children, the same pattern will emerge. Over the past few years we have investigated this possibility by examining the neuropsychological abilities of children with PFC pathology (Anderson et al., 2002, 2005; Couper et al., 2002; Jacobs et al., 2001, 2007; Matthews et al., 2001). This research program has employed a number of clinical measures purported to assess specific components of EF, in keeping with the definition provided earlier in this chapter: attentional control, goal setting, and cognitive flexibility. One of the novel aspects of the study was the implementation of the scoring method described by Garth et al. (1997) that included traditional summary scores, but also acknowledged that such scores represent the contribution of a range of lower-level cognitive abilities, in addition to executive skills (described in Anderson, Anderson, & Jacobs, this volume). It was predicted that, while summary scores would detect general levels of cognitive impairment, more "process-orientated" scores would enable discrimination within frontal groups.

In contrast to the previous studies, this research excluded children who had sustained closed head injury, in an attempt to focus on the impact of pathology confined to the frontal lobes, and including PFC. The sample included 38 children, aged 7–16 years, with focal brain lesions, involving the PFC, as documented on MRI scan. Children with additional pathology were excluded from participation. Etiology of frontal pathology was diverse and included stroke, penetrating head injury, tumor, and dysplasia. A healthy control group ($n = 40$) was also recruited to the study to match the demographic characteristics of the frontal group (gender, age, SES) as closely as possible.

While trends for poorer performance were evident for children with pathology within the PFC, group differences identified across mastery and rate measures were surprisingly small. For mastery scores, children with PFC lesions exhibited poorer attentional control and reduced high-level language skills. Mastery level scores on tasks tapping goal setting and planning abilities were unimpaired relative to controls. Contrary to expectations, children with PFC pathology generally recorded shorter completion times than controls across all EF tasks. Such quick performances are not necessarily advantageous, however, as overall efficiency may be compromised. Certainly, in this study faster response speeds were not related to better overall performances. One interpretation of these findings is that the quicker responses of the frontal group are abnormal, possibly reflecting impulsive responses, or lack of attention to detail. This suggestion is supported by higher error rates recorded by the group, suggesting where speed-accuracy trade-offs are acting, children with frontal lesions are more likely to choose speed, which may indicate impulsivity.

In the domain of strategy, results were more consistent with adult findings. As illustrated in Table 12.1, children with focal PFC lesions demonstrated frequent perseverative errors, were less efficient on tasks tapping reasoning skills, with a lower capacity for strategic behavior and evidence of cognitive inflexibility. There was also a trend for poorer attentional control, higher error levels, and reduced self-monitoring (see Anderson et al., 2005 for further detail).

Table 12.1   Results for executive function components across groups.

Measure/Variable	Frontal n = 38 Adj M (SE)	Control n = 40 Adj M (SE)	Effect Size
Attentional control			
TOL: no. rule breaks*	1.8 (0.3)	0.5 (0.3)	.88
COWAT: % rule breaks**	21.4 (3.4)	5.4 (3.0)	.96
CNT1% SC**	6.1 (0.6)	4.6 (0.6)	.69
CNT2% SC*	2.4 (0.5)	1.2 (0.5)	.36
CNT3% SC*	11.3 (1.4)	6.7 (1.4)	.58
CNT4% SC**	16.2 (2.0)	10.4 (1.9)	.49
COWAT: % repetitions	2.1 (0.5)	0.8 (0.5)	.89
Score DT: no both correct**	4.4 (0.4)	6.8 (0.4)	.85
Goal setting			
COWAT: no. words	16.9 (1.2)	26.1 (1.1)	1.0
CGT-C sorts correct	2.9 (0.3)	4.2 (0.3)	.63
CGT-C explicit cues	0.7 (0.1)	0.2 (0.1)	.67
CNT3: efficiency	0.8 (0.08)	1.2 (0.07)	.28
CNT4: efficiency	1.8 (1.2)	4.0 (0.2)	.46
Goal setting			
TOL: no. failed attempts	9.4 (0.6)	7.2 (0.5)	.57
RCF: copy accuracy	25.0 (1.0)	28.5 (1.0)	.43

* Impaired on one measure only.
** Impaired on more than one measure (or where only one measure, ** impaired).
TOL: Tower of London; COWAT: Controlled Oral Word Association Test; CNT: SC: Contingency Naming Test Self-Corrections; Score DT: Score Dual Task; CGT-C: Concept Generation Test–Categories; RCF: Rey Complex Figure.

As is often argued within the adult literature, simple comparisons of clinical and control groups may mask subtle deficits demonstrated by subsets within the clinical sample. In an attempt to address this issue, we further divided children according to laterality of pathology. We expected that children with lesions within left PFC would perform more poorly on tasks requiring primarily verbal skills, while those with right PFC pathology would achieve poorest results for non-verbal tasks and attentional control. Findings, however, suggested that left PFC lesions were generally associated with better performance, regardless of task modality. In contrast, presence of right PFC pathology added to the risk of impairments in a range of executive domains including attentional control, goal setting, and cognitive flexibility, regardless of the primary modality of the task. These results cannot be explained in terms of severity, timing, or size of lesion, as no group differences were identified for these factors.

On the basis of this pattern of findings it may be postulated that, in early childhood, EFs are primarily subsumed by the right PFC, or that damage to right PFC impacts in a global manner on the development of executive skills. As the brain matures, executive skills may become progressively lateralized, leading to the verbal/non-verbal distinction described in the adult domain. Thus, when right PFC damage occurs in childhood, the efficient maturation and transfer of these skills may be disrupted. However, where early left PFC damage occurs, development can continue unaffected in the right hemisphere. Transfer of function may then not occur at all, with all functions maintained within healthy right hemisphere, or transfer may occur after some recovery to the damaged left frontal regions. Some evidence to support this hypothesis derives from a number of studies which have examined both structural and functional aspects of brain development. Findings suggest greater maturation and activation within the right frontal regions in children between 1 and 3 years of age (Basser, 1962; Chi et al., 1991; Chiron et al., 1997; Goldberg, Podell, & Lovell, 1994; Simonds & Scheibel, 1989). Further, such an interpretation is consistent with the notion of non-verbal learning disability (Rourke, 1987), a developmental syndrome, which describes the right hemisphere as particularly vulnerable to early insult. Future research is needed to further examine these potential developmental asymmetries.

Frontal versus extra-frontal damage in early childhood

On the basis of developmental literature and animal studies that suggest that the integrity of the brain appears to be important for prefrontal development, it is likely that extra-frontal damage prior to the maturation of prefrontal structures may disrupt the development of these regions, leading to aberrant connections and abnormal function in these regions. As a consequence we predict that, contrary to the focal deficits seen following focal pathology in adults, executive dysfunction will be a common feature of all childhood cerebral insult, irrespective of the location of injury. Using the sample described above and two additional groups, with either extra-frontal ($n = 20$) or generalized ($n = 21$) brain pathology, we investigated whether there was less differentiation between performance of the frontal and extra-frontal pathology groups on EF measures than has been described in the adult literature.

Table 12.2   Summary of executive function results for clinical groups according to each subdomain.

Executive subdomains	Frontal	Extra-frontal	Generalized
Attentional control			
Self-monitoring	*	**	**
Self-regulation	**	—	**
Goal setting			
Concept formation	**	**	**
Planning/Organization	**	**	**
Cognitive flexibility			
Mental flexibility	**	**	**
Verbal working memory	—	**	—
Shifting attention/Switching	*	**	*
Divided attention-verbal	**	**	**
Divided attention-verbal/non-verbal	*	—	**

No significant group differences; * impaired on one measure only; ** impaired on more than one measure (or where only one measure, ** impaired).

Overall, results were as predicted, that is, children with cerebral pathology, irrespective of the site of damage, demonstrated deficits on measures of EF, with all clinical groups performing more poorly than controls, regardless of lesion location. There were a few exceptions, with some statistically significant differences detected between clinical groups, suggesting greater specificity of certain brain regions in some aspects of EF during childhood. These results are summarized in Table 12.2. Notably, the generalized group had greatest problems with self-monitoring on early trials (trials 1 and 2) of the Contingency Naming Test, which taps into both attentional control and conceptual flexibility elements of EF. The extra-frontal group also performed more poorly than the frontal and control groups on trial 2 of this task. As the task became more difficult, however, differences between the clinical groups were less obvious with all groups performing significantly more poorly than the control group on trials with increased demands on working memory and cognitive flexibility.

Subtle differences among the clinical groups were also detected, suggesting that while many brain regions may be required to perform certain executive tasks, some regions may be relied upon more heavily than others. The frontal group consistently demonstrated greatest problems on measures of self-regulation and divided attention. As expected, given involvement of both frontal and extra-frontal regions, the generalized group exhibited impairments across most EF domains. While it may be that the lack of differentiation between the frontal and extra-frontal pathology groups is due to insensitivity of measures, these findings may also be due to the immaturity of skills at the time of testing (Anderson, 2002; Kelly, 2000). Of note, our analysis of the potential generalized impact of seizure activity and EEG abnormalities, which are common across all these clinical groups, suggest that such factors did not explain the pattern of EF impairments described.

Additional support for the validity of these findings is derived from brain imaging studies, using healthy children and from animal research. For example, Tamm et al. (2002) report less intense activation of a greater number of brain regions in children compared with adults using an activation paradigm tapping response inhibition. This may be particularly pertinent to tasks that depend on later developing executive processes such as working memory, planning, and cognitive flexibility. However, whether increasing differentiation in executive processes can be seen with age as these skills reach maturity, or whether such early damage interrupts this developmental process, leading to permanent deficits in these later developing executive processes, remains unclear.

Animal work also suggests that extra-frontal damage early in life may disrupt ongoing development of the PFC, leading to changes in prefrontal morphology and function (Beauregard et al., 1995; Bertolino et al., 1997; Goldman-Rakic, 1987). Thus, extrapolating to humans, children with extra-frontal damage may exhibit similar executive impairments to those seen in children with frontal lobe insults, in addition to impairments in lower-level skills typically subsumed by the damaged region such as memory and visuo-spatial ability.

Irrespective of the mechanism involved, we believe that our findings, together with animal lesion research and imaging studies in normally developing children, suggest that in early childhood, the integrity of the entire brain is essential for adequate EF. In other words, cerebral damage in childhood, irrespective of the site of pathology, may render the child vulnerable to a range of executive deficits, which in turn may impact on learning and social interaction. Further, later developing skills may be more vulnerable to all forms of childhood cerebral insult, with frontal, extra-frontal, and generalized groups all exhibiting impaired performance on measures of cognitive flexibility and goal setting. In contrast, only frontal pathology was associated with significant deficits (relative to controls) on tasks tapping self-regulation, an aspect of EF that develops relatively early in childhood (Diamond & Taylor, 1996; Espy, 1997).

The lack of statistically significant findings between the clinical groups also lends support to the notion of an integrated system for executive processes. This may be particularly important for childhood cerebral injury, as it would be anticipated that most aspects of EF would be immature at the time of insult, particularly following damage in early childhood. Such damage, irrespective of the site of injury, may have detrimental consequences for the development of later emerging executive skills (as predicted by Dennis' 1989 model), such as those within the domains of goal setting and cognitive flexibility.

In summary, where prefrontal pathology occurs in childhood, there is evidence for a systemic framework where efficient prefrontal function (and thus, executive function) is dependent on effective development of connected brain regions. This reliance on more widely distributed brain regions in early childhood for completing complex tasks highlights the vulnerability of EF development to cerebral insult in a number of brain regions in childhood, not just those restricted to prefrontal regions. Longitudinal follow-up of this sample into mid-adolescence, using both standard neuropsychological assessment techniques and functional imaging paradigms, may shed further light on the nature of EF impairments following early focal damage to frontal or extra-frontal brain regions. Studies using very large samples of children with focal brain lesions will also enhance our understanding of the complex relationship between age at injury and executive function in childhood.

Age at onset

The degree to which the immature brain is able to recover from a brain lesion has been reported to depend, in part, on the timing and nature of the injury. For focal frontal lesions, both language and motor skills show relatively better outcome following early damage (Basser 1962; Kennard, 1936, 1940, 1942; Vargha-Khadem, O'Gorman, & Watters, 1985). However, the consequence of focal frontal lesions on the development of more complex skills such as EF remains unclear.

Using the sample described above, we were interested to examine the impact of focal frontal lesions sustained at varying stages during development on EFs (Jacobs et al., n.d.). To do this, we divided our total sample into five groups (prenatal lesions, acquired injuries between 0 and 3 years, 4 and 6 years, and 7 and 9 years or 10 years and older) based on timing of lesion. These groups were derived from animal models of focal frontal injuries (Kolb & Gibb, 1993, 2002), models of EF development (Anderson, V., 1998, 2002; Diamond & Goldman-Rakic 1985; Diamond & Taylor, 1996; Kelly, 2000; Levin et al., 1991) and cerebral maturation (Hudspeth & Pribram, 1990; Huttenlocher & Dabholkar, 1997; Thatcher, 1997) and thought to reflect potential stages for critical development of different executive processes.

Results showed that the prenatal lesion group obtained the lowest FSIQ, with all other groups performing within the low average to average range. This pattern is somewhat similar to that described for children with generalized cerebral pathology, with a younger age at injury associated with poorer intellectual capacity (Anderson et al., 1997; Anderson & Moore, 1995; Ewing-Cobbs et al., 1997; Taylor & Alden, 1997; Yeates et al., 2002). Results are also consistent with case reports, documenting reduced intellectual capacity for children with frontal lobe injuries sustained early in life (Ackerly & Benton, 1948; Eslinger & Biddle, 2000; Eslinger et al., 1999; Marlowe, 1992), with such early lesions interfering with a child's capacity to acquire new knowledge and skills effectively.

Findings suggest a non-linear relationship between age at injury and EF performance as described for animal models (Kolb & Gibb, 1993, 2002; Kolb, Gibb, & Gorny, 2000), but with differences dependent on the task used. Consistent with Dennis' (1989) developmental model and data from Bates and colleagues (Bates, Vicari, & Trauner, 1999), the group with prenatal lesions performed most poorly across the majority of measures, indicating that they may be most vulnerable to global executive impairments due to the disruption such damage causes to early developing executive processes and consequently all subsequent development, and possibly also reflecting the lack of opportunity for reorganization of synapses.

Children with lesions sustained between 7 and 9 years performed most closely to controls for EF measures. Consistent with this positive outcome, a number of cerebral processes occur during this time, e.g., synaptogenesis (Thatcher, 1997; peak in prefrontal brain activity Hudspeth & Pribram, 1990), which have been associated with cerebral reorganization in animal models (see chapter 4, for review), facilitating better capacity for compensation or recovery during this time.

The pattern of deficits for children with lesions acquired during infancy/early childhood (0–3 years) appeared to be related to primary impairments in self-regulation. This group responded impulsively on many multi-step tasks of planning and organization, obtaining significantly poorer "strategy/process" scores on these measures, which resulted in lower "mastery" scores. In contrast, injuries between 4 and 6 years tended to result in language-based executive deficits and is in keeping with previous reports of the vulnerability of language functions to insult during this period (Dennis, 1989).

The group with lesions beyond 9 years of age appeared to experience focal deficits, much like those documented following focal frontal lesions in adulthood, where neuronal pathways are already established at the time of insult and deficits are closely linked to lesion location within the prefrontal cortex.

Interestingly, behavioral outcome did not follow the same pattern as cognitive executive processes. All lesion groups obtained elevated ratings on some scales of the Behavior Rating Inventory of Executive Function (BRIEF; Gioia et al., 2000). Of particular interest, while the group with injuries between 7 and 9 years did not display significant deficits on cognitive measures of EF, they obtained scores in the clinically significant range for Initiation, Working Memory and Shift scales from the BRIEF, suggesting problems with complex behavioral functions, which may not be apparent in structured assessment settings.

In summary, these results lend support to the notion of a non-linear relationship between age at injury and EF, with the period between 7 and 9 years being a potential "window of opportunity" for relatively better outcome following focal frontal lobe injuries. This period is associated with the emergence and rapid development of more complex executive skills including planning and organization, concept formation, working memory and cognitive flexibility (Anderson, 2001, 2002; Kelly, 2000; Welsh et al., 1991). In parallel with this development, a number of developmental changes occur within the frontal lobes including a period of synaptogenesis around 7 years (Thatcher, 1997) and a peak in prefrontal brain activity between 7 and 8 years (Hudspeth & Pribram, 1990). It is important to note that this group did not escape EF deficits entirely, but did experience behavioral problems as well as subtle difficulties on many EF tasks, with slightly impaired performances observed relative to the control group. Whether these impairments will become more apparent over time as skills are expected to emerge cannot be determined until the sample reaches maturity. Results highlight the importance of delineating executive processes and taking into account the differing developmental trajectories of these when determining the nature and severity of executive impairments following frontal lobe lesions at varying stages of development.

Socio-moral reasoning

In addition to their role in cognitive processes, the frontal lobes play a critical role in mediating social behavior. Case studies of adults sustaining focal frontal damage in infancy or childhood suggest that deficits in socio-moral behavior are the most disabling of all impairments (Ackerly & Benton, 1948; Anderson, Bechara, Damasio, Tranel, & Damasio, 1999), with personality development and aspects of social behavior argued to be the most compromised aspects of EF following early frontal damage (Tranel & Eslinger, 2000), as the child is unable to acquire complex social knowledge (Anderson et al., 1999). While there does not appear to be a specific profile of cognitive executive deficits following early frontal lesions, problems in the social sphere are consistently reported, highlighting the severity of these problems in children and suggesting that they may be a characteristic feature of childhood frontal pathology. In fact, deficits in social functioning can be so severe following early frontal lesions that Anderson and colleagues (1999) argue that it is a syndrome resembling psychopathy. Tranel (2002) describes five characteristic features of this syndrome including: (a) a dampening of emotions including apathy; (b) poor modulation of emotional experience such as low frustration tolerance or irritability; (c) reduced decision making, particularly in relation to social function (e.g., inflexibility, poor judgment, social inappropriateness); (d) difficulties perceiving the future consequences of one's decisions; and (e) marked lack of insights into one's difficulties. Cohort studies of children with TBI report similar findings, consistently documenting social and behavioral deficits in children following frontal lobe damage (Anderson et al., 1997; Papero, Prigatano, Snyder, & Johnson, 1993; Prigatano, O'Brien, & Klonoff, 1993), and argue that these represent the greatest challenge for professionals working with these children in a rehabilitation setting.

Given the severity of social deficits in children with damage that incorporates the frontal lobes, we recently conducted a pilot study to examine the specific role of the frontal lobes and PFC in moral behavior (Couper, Jacobs, & Anderson, 2003). In this study only children with focal PFC damage were recruited. We compared the performance of 11 children with lesions in PFC in childhood and 10 age-matched controls on a measure of socio-moral reasoning (Socio-moral Reflection Questionnaire; Gibbs, Basinger, & Fuller, 1992). Children were required to (a) have general intellectual abilities in the low average range or higher (that is, full-scale IQ $> = 80$); (b) speak English at home; and (c) be aged between 8 and 16 years at initial assessment. The Socio-moral Reflection Measure, Short Form (SRM-SF) is based on Kolhberg's (1984) stages of moral maturity but uses moral dilemmas that are more likely to be encountered by children. The SRM-SF provides a measure of moral maturity and values in the following domains: contract and truth, affiliation, life, property and law and, finally, justice.

Results of this study showed significant delays in social maturation of children with PFC lesions. Children in the study were reassessed 3 years after their initial assessment and results showed significant lag in moral development in the PFC group (see Figure 12.5). These results are comparable with case reports and reflect an increasing gap between actual and expected capacity to acquire social knowledge over time. Individual case analysis revealed that the mild improvement of the PFC group over time was accounted for by three cases only. All other cases were reasoning at the same level as they were 3 years prior. These findings are particularly concerning given the importance of social and moral values in our society, with deficits linked to higher rates of incarceration in brain injured populations. Given the critical importance of these skills in everyday life, further investigations with larger samples of children are required, with a long-term aim of targeting intervention programs at these skills to support children in

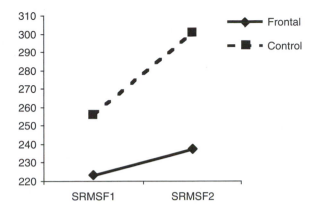

Figure 12.5   Socio-moral reasoning of children with frontal lobe (FL) lesions and controls over time.

developing socially appropriate responses to everyday situations, and to become a valuable, contributing member of society.

Conclusions

Multiple lines of evidence now provide a picture of ongoing development of EF throughout childhood. Physiological research describes substantial brain development continuing at least into adolescence, with anterior cerebral regions maturing relatively late, and showing a series of growth spurts. Neuropsychological studies have also identified growth spurts represented by distinct improvements in performance on tests purported to measure EF. There is growing consensus that these physiological and cognitive spurts may occur in parallel, with transitions in cognitive development reflecting ongoing cerebral development.

To accurately describe the development of executive skills in both healthy and clinical populations, there is a need to identify developmentally appropriate measures tapping these skills in assessment protocols. Of those currently employed, most have been designed for adult populations. Many lack standardized administration and scoring procedures. Few have adequate developmental norms, precluding accurate interpretation of developmentally appropriate levels of performance. There is an over-reliance on less sensitive "summary scores," with little emphasis on more microanalytic techniques which may have the capacity to isolate specific executive skills from lower-order cognitive abilities. Consequently, clinicians are often required to base their analysis of executive function on qualitative observation and contextual data.

The immaturity of executive skills through childhood suggests that they may be vulnerable to the impact of early cerebral insult, where emerging and developing abilities have been noted to be particularly at risk. The presence of executive impairments early in life may have significant implications for ongoing cognitive, social, and emotional development. The lack of ability to maintain attention, plan, reason, abstract, think flexibly, and regulate behavior may impinge on a child's capacity to learn and benefit from the environment, and to interact with others effectively. Clinical observations of brain injured children support this notion. Further, in contrast to the often focal consequences observed in adults, in the context of intact scores on intellectual measures, children who sustain frontal lobe pathology are likely to present with more globally depressed cognitive profiles, as evidenced by impaired intellectual quotients, with the likelihood of emerging deficits over time. The possible explanations for these generalized impairments may relate to the impact of such injuries on the child's capacity to acquire new skills.

Alternatively, there may be a biological basis, reflecting the timing of injury, the capacity for functional reorganization and recruitment within the developing brain, and the relative vulnerability of the right frontal cortex early in development.

Current research limitations restrict our ability to come to any firm conclusions regarding the role of prefrontal regions for the development of efficient executive abilities in children. Conclusions from previous research are limited by methodological flaws, including problems in the accurate detection and characterization of frontal pathology, confounding effects of extra-frontal injury, and lack of consensus regarding the essential features of EF, as well as their most appropriate indicators in children, and expected developmental trajectories. Hypothesis driven studies using tasks designed to measure specific cognitive processes could contribute to advancements in assessment and cognitive intervention. Additionally, advances in the neurosciences, specifically the pharmacologic modulation of executive functioning and effects on prefrontal cortex, and increased capacity to directly measure brain function via functional imaging techniques, provide a great opportunity to develop more accurate diagnostic procedures and treatment strategies for children with frontal dysfunction.

References

Ackerly, S., & Benton, A. (1948). Report of a case of bilateral frontal lobe defect. *Association for Research on Nervous and Mental Disorders, 27*, 479–504.

Alexander, M., & Stuss, D. (2000). Disorders of frontal lobe functioning. *Seminars in Neurology, 20*(4), 427–437.

Alivisatos, B., & Petrides, M. (1997). Functional activation of the human brain during mental rotation. *Neuropsychologia, 35*(2), 111–118.

Anderson, P. (2002). Assessment and development of executive function (EF) during childhood. *Child Neuropsychology, 8*(2), 71–82.

Anderson, P., Anderson, V., & Garth, J. (2001). A process-oriented approach to scoring the Complex Figure of Rey. *The Clinical Neuropsychologist, 15*, 81–94.

Anderson, P., Anderson, V., & Lajoie, G. (1995). The Tower of London Test: Validation and standardization for pediatric populations. *The Clinical Neuropsychologist, 10*, 54–65.

Anderson, S. W., Bechara, A., Damasio, H., Tranel, D., & Damasio, A. R. (1999). Impairment of social and moral behavior related to early damage in human prefrontal cortex. *Nature Neuroscience, 2*, 1032–1037.

Anderson, S. W., Damasio, H., Tranel, D., & Damasio, A. R. (2000). Long-term sequelae of prefrontal cortex damage acquired in early childhood. *Developmental Neuropsychology, 18*, 281–296.

Anderson, V. (1988). Recovery of function in children: The myth of cerebral plasticity. In M. Matheson & H. Newman (Eds.), *Brain impairment* (pp. 223–247). Proceedings from the Thirteenth Annual Brain Impairment Conference, Sydney.

Anderson, V. (1998). Assessing executive functions in children: Biological, psychological, and developmental considerations. *Neuropsychological Rehabilitation*, *8*, 319–349.

Anderson, V., Anderson, P., Northam, E., Jacobs, R., & Catroppa, C. (2001a). Development of executive functions through late childhood and adolescence in an Australian sample. *Developmental Neuropsychology*, *20*, 385–406.

Anderson, V., Anderson, P., Northam, E., Jacobs, R., & Mikiewicz, O. (2002). Relationships between cognitive and behavioral measures of executive function in children with brain disease. *Child Neuropsychology*, *8*, 231–240.

Anderson, V., Bond, L., Catroppa, C., Grimwood, K., Nolan, T., & Keir, E. (1997). Childhood bacterial meningitis: Impact of age at illness and medical complications on long-term outcome. *Journal of the International Neuropsychological Society*, *3*, 147–158.

Anderson, V., & Catroppa, C. (2005). Recovery of executive skills following pediatric traumatic brain injury (TBI): A two year follow-up. *Brain Injury*, *19*(6), 459–470.

Anderson, V., Jacobs, R., & Harvey, A. H. (2005). Prefrontal lesions and attentional skills in childhood. *Journal of the International Neuropsychological Society*, *11*, 817–831.

Anderson, V., Levin, H., & Jacobs, R. (2002). Developmental and acquired lesions of the frontal lobes in children: Neuropsychological implications. In D. Stuss & R. Knight (Eds.), *Principles of frontal lobe function* pp. 504–527. New York: OUP.

Anderson, V., & Moore, C. (1995). Age at injury as a predictor of outcome following pediatric head injury. *Child Neuropsychology*, *1*, 187–202.

Anderson, V., Northam, E., Wrennall, J., & Hendy, J. (2001b). *Developmental neuropsychology: A clinical approach*. London: Erlbaum.

Anderson, V., & Pentland, L. (1998). Attention deficit following paediatric head injury. *Neuropsychological Rehabilitation*, *8*, 283–300.

Aram, D., & Eisele, J. (1994). Intellectual stability in children with unilateral brain lesions. *Neuropsychologia*, *32*, 85–95.

Barbas, H. (1992). Architecture and cortical connections of the prefrontal cortex in the rhesus monkey. In P. Chauvel & A. Delgado-Esceuta (Eds.), *Advances in neurology* (pp. 91–115). New York: Raven Press.

Barkley, R. A. (1996). Linkages between attention and executive functions. In G. R. Lyon & N. A. Krasnegor (Eds.), *Attention, memory and executive function* (pp. 307–326). Baltimore: Paul H. Brookes.

Barnes, M. A., & Dennis, M. (2001). Knowledge-based inferencing after childhood head injury. *Brain and Language*, *76*, 253–265.

Barr, M., & Kiernan, J. (1993). *The human nervous system: An anatomical viewpoint* (6th ed., pp. 173–179). Philadelphia: Harper & Row.

Basser, L. (1962). Hemiplegia of early onset and the faculty of speech with special reference to the effects of hemispherectomy. *Brain: A Journal of Neurology*, *85*, 428–460.

Bates, E., Vicari, S., & Trauner, D. (1999). Neural mediation of language development: Perspectives from lesions studies of infants and children. In H. Tager-Flusberg (Ed.), *Neurodevelopmental disorders* (pp. 533–581). Cambridge, MA: MIT.

Beauregard, M., Malkova, L., & Bachevalier, J. (1995). Stereotypies and loss of social affiliation after early hippocampectomy in primates. *Neuroreport*, *6*, 2521–2526.

Benton, A. (1968). Differential behavioral effects in frontal lobe disease. *Neuropsychologia*, *6*, 53–60.

Bertolino, A., Sauders, R. C., Mattay, V. S., Bachevalier, J., Frank, J. A., & Weinberger, D. R. (1997). Altered development of prefrontal neurons in rhesus monkeys with neonatal mesial temporo-limib lesions: A proton magnetic resonance imaging study. *Cerebral Cortex, 7*, 740–748.

Blatter, D., Bigler, E., Gale, S., Johnson, S., Anderson, C., Burnett, B. et al. (1995). Quantitative volumetric analysis of brain MR: Normative data base spanning five decades of life. *American Journal of Neuroradiology, 16*, 241–251.

Bunge, S., Dudukovik, N., Thomason, M., Vaidya, C., & Gabrieli, J. (2002). Immature frontal lobe contributions to cognitive control in children: Evidence from fMRI. *Neuron, 33*, 301–311.

Casey, B. J., Giedd, J. N., & Thomas, K. M. (2000). Structural and functional brain development and its relation to cognitive development. *Biological Psychology, 54*, 241–257.

Chi, J., Dooling, E., & Gilles, F. (1991). Lest-right asymmetries of the temporal speech areas of the human Fetus. *Archives of Neurology, 34*, 346–248.

Chiron, C., Jambaque, I., Nabbout, R., Lounes, R., Syrota, A., & Dulac, O. (1997). The right brain hemisphere is dominant in human infants. *Brain: A Journal of Neurology, 120*, 1057–1065.

Chugani, H. T., Phelps, M. E., & Mazziotta, J. C. (1987). Positron emission tomography study of human brain functional development. *Annals of Neurology, 22*, 287–297.

Corbetta, M., Miezin, F. M., Dobmeyer, S., Shulman, G. L., & Petersen, S. E. (1991). Selective and divided attention during visual discriminations of shape, color, and speed: Functional anatomy by positron emission tomography. *The Journal of Neuroscience, 11*(8), 2383–2402.

Couper, E., Jacobs, R., & Anderson, V. (2002). Adaptive behaviour and moral reasoning in children with frontal lobe lesions. *Brain Impairment, 3*, 105–113.

Damasio, A. (1994). Descartes error and the future of human life. *Scientific American, 271*, 144.

Delis, D., Kaplan, E., & Kramer, J. (2001). *Delis–Kaplan Executive Function System (D-KEFS): Examiner's manual.* San Antonio, TX: Psychological Corporation.

Dennis, M. (1989). Language and the young damaged brain. In T. Boll & B. K. Bryant (Eds.), *Clinical neuropsychology and brain function: Research, measurement and practice* (pp. 89–123). Washington: American Psychological Association.

Dennis, M., & Barnes, M. A. (2001). Comparison of literal, inferential and intentional text comprehension in children with mild or severe closed head injury. *Journal of Head Trauma Rehabilitation, 16*, 456–468.

Dennis, M., Purvis, K., Barnes, M. A., Wilkinson, M., & Winner, E. (2001). Understanding of literal truth, ironic criticism, and deceptive praise following childhood head injury. *Brain and Language, 78*, 1–16.

D'Esposito, M., Detre, J. A., Alsop, D. C., Shin, R. K., Atlas, S., & Grossman, M. (1995). The neural basis of the central executive system of working memory. *Nature, 378*, 279–281.

Dhager, A., Owen, A. M., Boecker, H., & Brooks, D. J. (1999). Mapping the network for planning: A correlational PET activation study with the Tower of London task. *Brain: A Journal of Neurology, 122*(10), 1973–1987.

Diamond, A. (2002). Normal development of prefrontal cortex from birth to young adulthood: Cognitive functions, anatomy, and biochemistry. In D. Stuss & R. Knight (Eds.), *Principles of frontal lobe function* (pp. 466–503). New York: Oxford University Press.

Diamond, A., & Goldman-Rakic, P. S. (1985). Evidence for involvement of prefrontal cortex in cognitive changes during the first year of life: Comparison of human infants and rhesus monkeys on a detour task with transparent barrier. *Neurosciences Abstracts (Pt. II), 11*, 832.

Diamond, A., & Taylor, C. (1996). Development of an aspect of executive control: Development of the abilities to remember what I said and to "do as I say, not as I do." *Developmental Psychobiology, 29*(4), 315–334.

Dias, R., Robbins, T. W., & Roberts, A. C. (1996). Dissociation in prefrontal cortex of affective and attentional shifts. *Nature, 380*, 69–72.

Didus, E., Anderson, V., & Catroppa, C. (2000). The development of pragmatic communication skills in head-injured children. *Pediatric Rehabilitation, 3*, 177–186.

Edelman, G. (1987). *Neural Darwinism.* New York: Basic Books.

Eslinger, P., & Biddle, K. (2000). Adolescent neuropsychological development after early right prefrontal cortex damage. *Developmental Neuropsychology, 18*, 297–329.

Eslinger, P., Biddle, K., & Grattan, L. (1997). Cognitive and social development in children with prefrontal cortex lesions. In N. Krasnegor, G. Lyon, & P. S. Goldman-Rakic (Eds.), *Development of the prefrontal cortex: Evolution, neurology, and behavior* (pp. 295–336). Baltimore: Brookes.

Eslinger, P., Biddle, K., Pennington, B., & Page, R. (1999). Cognitive and behavioral development up to 4 years after early right frontal lobe lesion. *Developmental Neuropsychology, 15*, 157–191.

Eslinger, P., Flaherty-Craig, C., & Benton, A. (2004). Developmental outcomes after early prefrontal cortex damage. *Brain and Cognition, 55*, 84–103.

Eslinger, P., Grattan, L., Damasio, H., & Damasio, A. (1992). Developmental consequences of childhood frontal lobe damage. *Archives of Neurology, 49*, 764–769.

Eslinger, P. J., Warner, G. C., Grattan, L. M., & Easton, J. D. (1991). "Frontal lobe" utilization behavior associated with paramedian thalamic infarction. *Neurology, 41*, 450–452.

Espy, K. (1997). The Shape School: Assessing executive function in preschool children. *Developmental Neuropsychology, 13*(4), 495–499.

Ewing-Cobbs, L., Fletcher, J., Levin, H., Francis, D., Davidson, K., & Miner, M. (1997). Longitudinal neuropsychological outcome in infants and preschoolers with traumatic brain injury. *Journal of the International Neuropsychological Society, 3*, 581–591.

Fenwick, T., & Anderson, V. (1999). Impairments of attention following childhood traumatic brain injury. *Child Neuropsychology, 5*, 213–223.

Fuster, J. (1993). Frontal lobes. *Current Opinion in Neurobiology, 3*, 160–165.

Fuster, J. (2002). Frontal lobe and cognitive development. *Journal of Neurocytology, 31*, 373–385.

Garth, J., Anderson, V., & Wrennall, J. (1997). Executive functions following moderate-to-severe frontal lobe injuries: Impact of injury and age at injury. *Pediatric Rehabilitation, 1*, 99–108.

Gibbs, J. C., Basinger, K. S., & Fuller, D. (1992). *Moral maturity: Measuring the development of sociomoral reflection.* Hillsdale, NJ: Lawrence Erlbaum.

Giedd, J., Blumenthal, J., Jeffries, N., Castellanos, F., Liu, H., Zijdenbos, A., et al. (1999). Brain development during childhood and adolescence: A longitudinal MRI study. *Nature Neuroscience, 2*, 861–863.

Giedd, J., Snell, J., Lange, N., Rajapaske, J., Casey, B., Kozuch, P., et al. (1996). Quantitative magnetic resonance imaging of human brain development: Ages 4–18. *Cerebral Cortex, 6*, 551–560.

Gioia, G., Isquith, P., Guy, S., & Kenworthy, L. (2000). *The behavior rating inventory of executive function.* Odessa, FL: PAR Inc.

Gogtay, N., Giedd, J., Lusk, L., Hayashi, K., Greenstein, D., Vaituzis, C. et al. (2004). Dynamic mapping of human cortical development during childhood and early adulthood. *Proceedings of the National Academy of Science, 101*, 8174–8179.

Goldberg, E., Podell, K., & Lovell, M. (1994). Lateralization of frontal lobe functions and cognitive novelty. *Journal of Neuropsychiatry, 6*, 371–378.

Golden, C. J. (1981). The Luria-Nebraska Children's Battery: Theory and formulation. In G. W. Hynd & J. E. Obrzut (Eds.), *Neuropsychological assessment of the school-aged child* (pp. 277–302). New York: Grune & Stratton.

Goldman-Rakic, P. S. (1987). Development of cortical circuitry and cognitive function. *Child Development, 58*, 601–622.

Hale, S., Bronik, M., & Fry, A. (1997). Verbal and spatial working memory in school-aged children: Developmental differences in susceptibility to interference. *Developmental Psychology, 33*, 364–371.

Harlow, J. M. (1868). Recovery from the passage of an iron bar through the head. *Publications of the Massachusetts Medical Society (Boston), 2*, 327–346.

Hudspeth, W., & Pribram, K. (1990). Stages of brain and cognitive maturation. *Journal of Educational Psychology, 82*, 881–884.

Huttenlocher, P., & Dabholkar, A. (1997). Developmental anatomy of prefronatl cortex. In N. Krasnegor, G. Reid Lyon, & P. Goldman-Rakic (Eds.), *Development of the prefrontal cortex: Evolution, neurobiology, and behavior* (pp. 69–84). Baltimore: Brookes.

Jacobs, R., & Anderson, V. (2002). Planning and problem solving skills following focal frontal brain lesions in childhood: Analysis using the Tower of London. *Child Neuropsychology, 8*, 93–106.

Jacobs, R., Anderson, V., & Harvey, A. S. (2001). Concept Generation Test: A measure of conceptual reasoning skills in children. Examination of developmental trends. *Clinical Neuropsychological Assessment, 2*, 101–117.

Jacobs, R., Harvey, A. S., & Anderson, V. (2007). Executive functions following focal frontal lobe lesions: Impact of timing of lesion on outcome. *Cortex, 43*, 792–805.

Jernigan, T. L., & Tallal, P. (1990). Late childhood changes in brain morphology observable with MRI. *Developmental Medicine and Child Neurology, 32*, 379–385.

Johnson, M. (2001). Functional brain development in infants: Elements of an interactive specialization framework. *Child Development, 71*, 75–81.

Kail, R. (1986). Sources of age differences in speed of processing. *Child Development, 57*, 969–987.

Kelly, T. (2000). The development of executive function in school-aged children. *Clinical Neuropsychological Assessment, 1*, 38–55.

Kennard, M. A. (1936). Age and other factors in motor recovery from precentral lesions in monkeys. *American Journal of Physiology, 115*, 138–146.

Kennard, M. A. (1940). Reorganization of motor function in cerebral cortex of monkeys deprived of motor and pre-motor areas in infancy. *Journal of Neurophysiology, 1*, 477–496.

Kennard, M. A. (1942). Cortical reorganization of motor function. *Archives of Neurology and Psychiatry, 48*, 227–240.

Kennedy, C., Sakurada, O., Shinohara, M., & Miyaoka, M. (1982). Local cerebral glucose utilization in the newborn macaque monkey. *Annals of Neurology, 12*, 333–340.

Kirk, U. (1985). Hemispheric contributions to the development of graphic skill. In C. Best (Ed.), *Hemispheric function and collaboration in the child* (pp. 193–228). Orlando, FL: Academic Press.

Klinberg, T., O'Sullivan, B. T., & Roland, P. E. (1997). Bilateral activation of fronto-parietal networks by incrementing demand in a working memory task. *Cerebral Cortex, 7*, 465–471.

Klinberg, T., Vaidya, C., Gabrieli, J., Moseley, M., & Hedehus, M. (1999). Myelination and organization of the frontal white matter in children: A diffusion tensor study. *Neuroreport, 10*, 2817–2821.

Knight, R. T. (1996). Contribution of human hippocampal region to novelty detection. *Nature, 383,* 256–259.

Knight, R. T. (1997). Distributed cortical network for visual attention. *Journal of Cognitive Neuroscience, 9,* 75–91.

Kohlberg, L. (1984). *The psychology of moral development.* San Francisco, CA: Harper & Row.

Kolb, B., & Gibb, R. (1993). Possible anatomical basis of recovery of function after neonatal frontal lesions in rats. *Behavioral Neuroscience, 107,* 799–811.

Kolb, B., & Gibb, R. (2002). Frontal plasticity and behavior. In D. Stuss & R. Knight (Eds.), *Principles of frontal lobe function* (pp. 541–556). New York: Oxford University Press.

Kolb, B., Gibb, R., & Gorny, G. (2000). Cortical plasticity and the development of behavior after early frontal cortical injury. *Developmental Neuropsychology, 18,* 423–444.

Kolb, B., Pellis, S., & Robinson, T. (2004). Plasticity and functions of the orbital frontal cortex. *Brain and Cognition, 55,* 104–115.

Korkman, M., Kirk, U., & Kemp, S. (1998). *Manual for the NEPSY.* San Antonio, TX: Psychological Corporation.

Krikorian, R., & Bartok, J. (1998). Developmental data for the Porteus Maze Test. *The Clinical Neuropsychologist, 12*(5), 305–310.

Leung, H. C., Skudlarski, P., Gatenby, J., Peterson, B., & Gore, J. (2000). An event-related functional MRI study of the Stroop Word Interference Task. *Cerebral Cortex, 10,* 552–560.

Levin, H. S., Culhane, K. A., Hartmann, J., Evankovich, K., Mattson, A. J., Harward, H., et al. (1991). Developmental changes in performance on tests of purported frontal lobe functioning. *Developmental Neuropsychology, 7,* 377–395.

Levin, H. S., Culane, K. A., Mendelsohn, D., Lily, M. A., Bruce, D., Fltecher, J., et al. (1993). Cognition in relation to magnetic resonance imaging in head-injured children and adolescents. *Archives of Neurology, 50,* 897–905.

Levin, H. S., Mendelsohn, D., Lily, M. A., Fletcher, J. M., Culhane, K. A., Chapman, S. B., et al. (1994). Tower of London performance in relation to magnetic resonance imaging following closed head injury in children. *Neuropsychology, 8,* 171–179.

Levin, H., Song, J., Scheibel, R., Fletcher, J., Harward, H., Lilly, M., et al. (1997). Concept formation and problem solving following closed head injury in children. *Journal of the International Neuropsychological Society, 3,* 598–607.

Levin, H. S., Benavidez, D. A., Verger-Maestre, K., Perachio, N., Song, J. X., Mendelsohn, D., et al. (2000). Reduction of corpus callosum growth after severe traumatic brain injury in children. *Neurology, 54,* 647–653.

Levine, B., Black, A., Cabeza, R., Sinden, M., McIntosh, A., Toth, J., et al. (1998). Episodic memory and self in the case of isolated retrograde amnesia. *Brain: A Journal of Neurology, 121,* 1951–1973.

Lezak, M. (1995). *Neuropsychological assessment.* New York: Oxford.

Lidow, M., & Goldman-Rakic, P. S. (1991). Synchronised overproduction of neurotransmitter receptors in diverse regions of the primate cerebral cortex. *Proceedings of the National Academy of Science, 88,* 10218–10221.

Luria, A. R. (1973). *The working brain.* New York: Basic Books.

Marlowe, W. B. (1992). The impact of a right prefrontal lesion on the developing brain. *Brain and Cognition, 20,* 205–213.

Mateer, C. A. (1990). Cognitive and behavioral sequalae of face and forehead injury in childhood. *Journal of Clinical and Experimental Neuropsychology, 12,* 95.

Matthews, L., Anderson, V., & Anderson, P. (2001). Assessing the validity of the Rey Complex Figure as a diagnostic tool: Accuracy, recall and organisational strategy scores in children with brain insult. *Clinical Neuropsychological Assessment, 2,* 85–100.

Mesulam, M. M. (1981). A cortical network for directed attention on unilateral neglect. *Annals of Neurology, 10*, 309–325.

Mesulam, M. M. (1990). Large-scale neurocognitive networks and distributed processing for attention, language and memory. *Annals of Neurology, 28*(5), 597–613.

Milner, B. (1963). Effects of different brain lesions on card sorting. *Archives of Neurology, 9*, 90–100.

Moll, J., de Oliveira-Souza, R., Eslinger, P., Bramati, I., Mourão-Miranda, J., Andreiuolo, P. A., et al. (2002). The neural correlates of moral sensitivity: A functional magnetic resonance imaging investigation of basic and moral emotions. *The Journal of Neuroscience, 22*(7), 2730–2736.

Öngür, D., & Price, J. L. (2000). The organization of networks within the orbital and medial prefrontal cortex of rats, monkeys and humans. *Cerebral Cortex, 10*, 206–219.

Papero, P., Prigatano, G., Snyder, H., & Johnson, D. (1993). Children's adaptive behavioral competence after head injury. *Neuropsychological Rehabilitation, 3*, 321–340.

Pascual-Leone, A., Armdi, A., Fregni, F., & Merobet, L. (2005). The plastic human brain cortex. *Annual Reviews in Neuroscience, 28*, 377–401.

Passingham, R. E., Toni, I., & Rushworth, M. F. S. (2000). Specialisation within the prefrontal cortex: The ventral prefrontal cortex and associative learning. *Experimental Brain Research, 133*, 103–113.

Pentland, L., Todd, J. A., & Anderson, V. (1998). The impact of head injury severity on planning ability in adolescence: A functional analysis. *Neuropsychological Rehabilitation, 8*, 301–317.

Petrides, M., & Pandya, D. N. (1999). Dorsolateral prefrontal cortex: Comparative cytoarchitectonic analysis in human and macaque brain and cortico-cortical connection patterns. *European Journal of Neuroscience, 11*, 1011–1036.

Pfefferbaum, A., Mathalon, D., Sullivan, E., Rawles, J., Zipursky, R., & Lim, K. (1994). A quantitative magnetic resonance imaging study of changes in brain morphology from infancy to late adulthood. *Archives of Neurology, 34*, 227–234.

Prigatano, G., O'Brien, K. M., & Klonoff, P. (1993). Neuropsychological rehabilitation of young adults who suffer brain injury in childhood: Clinical observations. *Neuropsychological Rehabilitation, 3*, 411–414.

Rakic, P., Bourgeois, J. P., Eckenhoff, M., Zecevic, N., & Goldman-Rakic, P. (1986). Concurrent overproduction of synapses in diverse regions of the primate cerebral cortex. *Science, 232*, 232–235.

Raedler, T. J., Knable, W. B., & Wienberger, D. R. (1998). Schizophrenia as a developmental disorder of the cerebral cortex. *Current Opinion in Neurobiology, 8*, 157–161.

Rey, A. (1964). *L'examen clinique en psychologie*. Paris: Presses Universitaires de France.

Rourke, B. P. (1987). Syndrome of nonverbal learning disabilities: The final common pathway of white-matter disease/dysfunction. *The Clinical Neuropsychologist, 1*, 209–234.

Scheibel, A. (1990). Dendritic correlates of higher cognitive function. In A. Scheibel & A. Wechsler (Eds.), *Neurobiology of higher cortical function* (pp. 239–270). New York: Guilford Press.

Shallice, T. (1982). Specific impairments of planning. *Philosophical Transcripts of the Royal Society of London, 298*, 199–209.

Shaw, P., Greenstein, D., Lerch, L., Lenroot, N., Gogtay, N., Evans, A., et al. (2006). Intellectual ability and cortical development in children and adolescents. *Nature, 440*, 676–679.

Simonds, R., & Scheibel, A. (1989). The post-natal development of the motor speech area: A preliminary analysis. *Brain and Language, 37*, 42–58.

Smidt, D., Jacobs, R., & Anderson, V. (2004). The Object Classification Task for Children (OCTC): A measure of concept generation and mental flexibility in early childhood. *Developmental Neuropsychology*, *26*, 385–402.

Sowell, E., Delis, D., Stiles, J., & Jernigan, T. (2001). Improved memory functioning and frontal lobe maturation between childhood and adolescence: A structural MRI study. *Journal of the International Neuropsychological Society*, *7*, 312–322.

Sowell, E., Thompson, P., Welcome, S., Henkenius, A., Toga, A., & Petersen, B. (2003). Cortical abnormalities in children and adolescents with attention deficit/hyperactivity disorder. *Lancet*, *362*, 1699–1707.

Staudt, M., Schropp, C., Staudt, F., Obletter, N., Bise, K., & Breit, A. (1993). Myelination of the brain in MRI: A staging system. *Pediatric Radiology*, *23*, 169–176.

Stuss, D. (1992). Biological and psychological development of executive functions. *Brain and Cognition*, *20*, 8–23.

Stuss, D., Alexander, M., Floden, D., Binns, M., Levine, B., McIntosh, A. R., et al. (2002). Fractionation and localization of distinct frontal lobe processes: Evidence from focal lesions in humans. In D. Stuss & R. Knight (Eds.), *Principles of frontal lobe function* (pp. 392–407). New York: Oxford University Press.

Stuss, D., Alexander, M., Hamer, L., Palumbo, C., Dempster, R., Binns, M., et al. (1998). The effects of focal anterior and posterior brain lesions in verbal fluency. *Journal of the International Neuropsychological Society*, *4*, 265–278.

Stuss, D., Alexander, M., Palumbo, C., Buckle, L., Sater, L., & Pogue, J. (1994). Organizational strategies of patients with unilateral or bilateral frontal lobe injury in word list learning tasks. *Neuropsychology*, *8*, 355–373.

Stuss, D. T., & Benson, D. F. (1986). *The frontal lobes*. New York: Raven Press.

Stuss, D., Gallup, G., & Alexander, M. (2001). The frontal lobes are necessary for 'theory of mind.' *Brain: A Journal of Neurology*, *124*, 279–286.

Stuss, D. T., Toth, J., Franchi, D., Alexander, M., Tipper, S., & Craik, F. (1999). Dissociation of attentional processes in patients with focal frontal and posterior lesions. *Neuropsychologia*, *37*, 1005–1027.

Tamm, L., Menon, V., & Reiss, A. L. (2002). Maturation of brain function associated with response inhibition. *Journal of the American Academy of Child and Adolescent Psychiatry*, *41*, 1231–1238.

Taylor, H. G., & Alden, J. (1997). Age-related differences in outcomes following childhood brain insults: An introduction and overview. *Journal of the International Neuropsychological Society*, *3*, 555–567.

Thatcher, R. W. (1991). Maturation of the human frontal lobes. Physiological evidence for staging. *Developmental Neuropsychology*, *7*, 397–419.

Thatcher, R. W. (1992). Cyclical cortical reorganization during early childhood. *Brain and Cognition*, *20*, 24–50.

Thatcher, R. W. (1997). Human frontal lobe development: A theory of cyclical cortical reorganization. In N. Krasnegor, G. Reid Lyon, & P. Goldman-Rakic (Eds.), *Development of the prefrontal cortex: Evolution, neurobiology, and behavior* (pp. 85–116). Baltimore: Brookes.

Todd, J. A., Anderson, V. A., & Lawrence, J. (1996). Planning skills in head injured adolescents and their peers. *Neuropsychological Rehabilitation*, *6*, 81–89.

Tranel, D. (2002). Emotion, decision making and the ventromedial prefrontal cortex. In D. Stuss & R. Knight (Eds.), *Principles of frontal lobe function* (pp. 338–353). New York: Oxford University Press.

Tranel, D., & Eslinger, P. J. (2000). Effects of early onset brain injury on the development of cognition and behavior: Introduction to the special issue. *Developmental Neuropsychology, 18*, 273–280.

Uemura, E., & Hartmann, H. A. (1978). RNA content and volume of nerve cell bodies in human brain: I. Prefrontal cortex in aging normal and demented patients. *Journal of Neuropathology and Experimental Neurology, 37*, 487–496.

Vargha-Khadem, F., O'Gorman, A., & Watters, G. (1985). Aphasia and handedness in relation to hemispheric side, age at injury and severity of cerebral lesion during childhood. *Brain: A Journal of Neurology, 108*, 677–696.

Waber, D. P., & Holmes, J. M. (1985). Assessing children's copy productions of the Rey-Osterreith Complex Figure. *Journal of Clinical and Experimental Neuropsychology, 7*, 264–280.

Walsh, K. W. (1978). *Neuropsychology: A clinical approach*. New York: Churchill Livingston.

Welsh, M. C., Pennington, B. F., & Groisser, D. B. (1991). A normative-developmental study of executive function: A window on prefrontal function in children. *Developmental Neuropsychology, 7*, 131–149.

Wood, A., Harvey, A. S., Wellard, M., Abbott, D., Anderson, V., Kean, M., et al. (2004). Language cortex activation in normal children. *Neurology, 63*, 1035–104.

Yakovlev, P. I., & Lecours, A. R. (1967). The myelogenetic cycles of regional maturation of the brain. In A. Minkiniwski (Ed.), *Regional development of the brain in early life*. (pp. 3–70). Oxford, England: Blackwell.

Yeates, K. O., Taylor, H. G., Wade, S. L., Drotar, D., Stancin, T., & Minich, N. (2002). A prospective study of short- and long-term neuropsychological outcomes after pediatric traumatic brain injury. *Neuropsychology, 16*, 514–523.

13   Prefrontal cortex and the maturation of executive functions, cognitive expertise, and social adaptation

Paul J. Eslinger and Kathleen R. Biddle

Contents

Introduction

Neuropsychological maturation is a complex process of developmental brain reorganization that involves numerous brain systems interacting through genetic, neurobiological, and experiential forces. Among these systems, the prefrontal cortex plays a leading role in fostering life span maturation, particularly coordinating the physiology of multiple neural networks, enabling self-regulation, and mediating the many executive and social–emotional processes that underlie goal-directed behavior and adaptive social actions (Blair, Zelazo, & Greenberg, 2005; Eslinger, 1996; Eslinger & Grattan, 1991; Segalowitz & Rose-Krasnor, 1992; Stuss, 1992; Tranel & Eslinger, 2000). The rate and trajectory of prefrontal cortical change during development has a reverberating effect on maturation of the many brain systems that underlie adaptive behavior (Eslinger, Grattan, & Damasio, 1992; Goldman & Galkin, 1978; Kolb, Gibb, & Gorny, 2000). Such prefrontal neurophysiology facilitates the adaptive plasticity and organization of functional cortical and subcortical systems. In this way, the potential resources of multiple neuropsychological processes can be coordinated and harnessed for the difficult tasks of childhood and adolescent maturation. In this chapter, we address clinical, cognitive, and neuroscience aspects of developmental prefrontal cortex lesions and typical prefrontal cortical maturation. Several approaches, which altogether help us to understand the impact of prefrontal pathophysiology on development, will be discussed. To date, case studies of the natural history of prefrontal lesions in children have provided invaluable insights into these complex issues. More recently fine-grained cognitive analyses coupled with contemporary functional brain imaging methods allow us to take a broader perspective on the role of the prefrontal cortex in development. Moreover, maturation of the prefrontal cortex and related networks constitutes one of the most important challenges of childhood, adolescence, and early adulthood and a major neurobiological foundation for independent and adaptive adult functioning.

Developmental outcomes after early prefrontal cortex damage

Isolated prefrontal cortex damage in childhood has been considered a rare clinical condition. Until the 1990s there was only one detailed developmental case study of early prefrontal cortex damage reported in the medical literature (see Finger, 1991, for case descriptions of early frontal damage and aphasia in the 19th century). Ackerly and Benton (1948) first described case JP at a December 1947 scientific meeting of the Association for Research in Nervous and Mental Disease. Both subsequently provided thoughtful follow-up analysis and reflection on JP's problematic develop- ment and abnormal maturation into early adulthood (Ackerly, 1964; Benton, 1991). Their major conclusion was that JP demonstrated a primary social defect not explained by general cognitive, environmental-rearing, socioeconomic, psychiatric, or biomedical deficits other than his congenital bilateral prefrontal cortex lesions. In the neurodevelopmental literature, the significance of JP's case is comparable in magnitude to that of Phineas Gage in the adult frontal lobe literature (Harlowe, 1868) and HM in the adult amnesia literature (Scoville & Milner, 1957), that is, JP remains perhaps the most exemplary and instructive clinical case revealing the crucial import- ance of the prefrontal cortex in psychological development and maturation.

Some of JP's neurobehavioral deficits were evident from 2–3 years of age, though not fully appreciated until later retrospective analysis. Among the earliest behavioral problems was recurrent wandering from home, often some distance away. JP appeared unconcerned about his wanderings and did not come to appreciate the anxiety it caused others. These behaviors did not respond to reprimands and punish- ment, and forecast what were to become lifelong impairments in social self-regulation, learning from experience (particularly negative consequences), social sensitivity, and perspective-taking. The early behavioral deficits are noteworthy observations because the prefrontal cortex was not thought to play a very significant role in early childhood behavior and certainly not as a mediator of childhood executive functions and self- regulation. However, its role in acquiring self-regulation, early executive capacities, and contingency-based learning within these early years has become more clearly recognized (Blair, Zelazo, et al., 2005).

The etiology of JP's prefrontal cortex damage was ascribed to a congenital condition causing significant atrophy. We reconstructed the estimated lesions based on the surgical report that was part of his comprehensive medical evaluation. The lesion reconstruction is shown in Figure 13.1 and is notable for damage involving virtually all right prefrontal cortex, the frontal poles bilaterally, and lesser atrophy of the remaining left prefrontal cortex. Thus, the lesion can be considered bilateral but asymmetric. In adults, greater pathophysiology of right prefrontal regions has been associated with many social–cognitive and emotional impairments affecting theory of mind, solving social dilemmas, and decision-making abilities (Eslinger et al., in press; Tranel, Bechara, & Denburg, 2002). Hence, the extensive

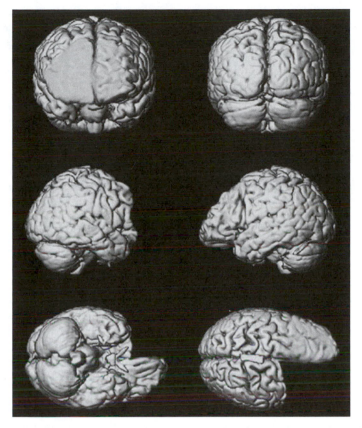

Figure 13.1   Reconstruction of the bilateral paranatal prefrontal cortex lesions of JP from available surgical report presented by Ackerly and Benton (1948). The lesions encompassed the frontal poles and orbital–medial prefrontal cortex bilaterally.

early right prefrontal damage in JP may be an important factor in his developmental impairments and poor outcome.

JP's social–emotional impairments and real-life adaptive deficits became increasingly evident in adolescence and continued in varying severity throughout his known adult life. Although he possessed an expressed sense of right and wrong, this often did not guide his actions and he progressively ran afoul of social norms and committed minor legal transgressions. The psychological testing of JP in adolescence, when he was brought to a child guidance clinic, revealed an average range of general intelligence in a young man who could be exceedingly polite. Despite limitations of available instruments of the day, cognitive testing provided sufficient differentiation to suggest executive processing impairments. Ackerly and Benton's rich psychological observations and behavioral descriptions provide many others clues to the social–emotional and social–cognitive impairments. For example, it is evident that JP's theory of mind and empathic capabilities were extremely limited and associated with a boastful, self-centered view of the social world. While he initiated actions in typical manner, his goal-oriented behaviors, working memory, cognitive flexibility, self-awareness, inhibitory control, and ability to delay gratification were quite deficient and changed little throughout development. Although he could eventually work within certain semi-skilled positions, his independent goal direction, consistency, and productivity posed continuing problems. Socially, he remained devoid of friends and intimate relationships (as best as could be determined), yet he did not appear distressed by limited and distant social engagement.

Because of the limitations of single case studies, it is important to compare and contrast the findings to other available cases and to group studies. Such comparisons help address concerns about sampling biases, reliability of identified structure–function relationships, generalizability of results, and role of factors such as lesion size, location, type, and age of onset. Pervasive developmental impairments similar to JP have been reported in case studies by Price, Daffner, Stowe, and Mesulam (1990), Eslinger et al. (1992), Marlowe (1992), Eslinger, Biddle, and Grattan (1997), Eslinger, Biddle, Pennington, and Page (1999), and Anderson, Damasio, Tranel, and Damasio (2000) (see Eslinger, Flaherty-Craig, & Benton, 2004; for comparative analysis of these and other cases). The most common lesion sites were unilateral or bilateral frontal polar cortex and ventromedial prefrontal cortex. Bilateral and right prefrontal lesions were more frequent in these reports, similar to the sites of orbital prefrontal damage in adults most closely associated with poor adjustment and adaptive outcomes (Tranel et al., 2002). Interestingly, the single case with left polar and mesial prefrontal cortex structural lesion at 7 years of age showed bilateral low blood flows in prefrontal regions when studied with single-photon emission computed tomography (SPECT) as a young adult. Thus, developmental conse-quence of some early prefrontal lesions may include contralateral pathophysiological effects, as reported in animal model studies by Goldman and Galkin (1978). The structure–function relationships identified in JP are also supported by group studies. Mateer and Williams (1991) emphasized the large dissociation between preserved general cognitive functions and impaired attentional, self-regulatory, and social maturation in children with early traumatic frontal damage. The deficits not only persisted but could also lead to progressive adaptive deficits. Jacobs and Anderson (2002) studied a sample of 31 children with focal frontal pathology and reported that early right prefrontal damage was associated with impaired spatial problem solving and more frequent self-regulatory errors. Significant atten-tional deficits after early prefrontal damage were also identified by Anderson, Jacobs, and Harvey (2005) in a sample of 36 children with prefrontal cortical lesions and related principally to right and bilateral lesions. The bilateral lesion sample were found to be at a disadvantage in resource-dependent tasks such as divided attention, while the right prefrontal lesion sample showed shifting, monitor-ing, and inhibitory control deficits. Levin et al. (2004) reported that unilateral frontal traumatic lesions in a sample of 22 school age children were associated with poorer Daily Living and Socialization Scores on the Vineland Adaptive Behavior Scale as well as more maladaptive behaviors. Volume of frontal lesion was significantly related to the Socialization domain but side of lesion did not appear to have differential effects.

The magnitude of neurobehavioral deficits after early prefrontal cortex lesions can be very significant and dramatically affect the lives of affected individuals.

These clinical and psychometric observations pose an interesting problem for the so-called Kennard effect, named after the researcher Margaret Kennard after her seminal studies in the 1930s and 1940s (see Finger, 1991; for a contemporary analysis). Kennard demonstrated that recovery of motor functions in nonhuman primates after early cerebral damage was comparatively better than adult-onset damage, with return of functional capabilities, suggesting that the brain has a larger reserve or potential for recovery and compensation if neural damage occurred early. Why didn't the above-mentioned cases that were followed developmentally show functional recovery or compensation? In fact, most showed the opposite pattern, that is, progressive worsening of adaptive capacities and behavior. If one relies solely on an age reserve hypothesis, the childhood prefrontal findings cannot be squared with the Kennard proposal. Fortunately, Kolb et al. (2000) have investigated these issues ingenious animal model studies and have identified several reasons for these discrepancies. Frontal cortical damage during the first few post-natal days of the rat, after neurogenesis is complete and intense cortical migration is occurring, was associated with the poorest developmental outcomes than earlier and later lesions. Anatomical pathology included both small brains and abnormal connectivity. Besides age of onset, recovery after early frontal cortical damage in the rat was influenced by lesion size, sex, age at assessment, and nature of behavioral testing. After comparison of cortical development stages in rats and humans, Kolb et al. suggested that human frontal lesions occurring in late gestation and the first few postnatal months may be happening during the most vulnerable period for adaptive outcomes, while damage around 1–2 years of age may carry comparatively greater potential for adaptive recovery. In addition, we propose that the specific location of the early prefrontal damage is likely to be another significant determinant of adaptive outcome. That is, damage encompassing the frontal poles and ventromedial prefrontal cortices will lead to poorer adaptive outcomes, particularly because of their indispensable roles in maturation of executive function, self-regulatory processes, and the delicate interplay of emotional and cognitive systems. There are still many other outstanding issues regarding size, etiology, and momentum of lesions, unilateral versus bilateral lesion effects, the respective roles of right versus left prefrontal systems, and the potential modulating effects of behavior therapy, trophic factors, neuromodulators, and prescription medicines such as stimulants on developmental outcomes.

Adaptive outcome after early prefrontal cortex damage

Although several reports clearly document clinically problematic outcomes after early prefrontal cortex damage, as described above, there are cases whose developmental histories have been much more adaptive and positive. We have observed and examined two of these cases for more than 10 years and both are now young adults who are working and living independently (Eslinger et al., 2004). Both suffered right dorsolateral prefrontal damage, one at 3 years of age and the other at 7 years, yet their developmental challenges have been very different. JC initially presented with left hemispatial neglect, constructional apraxia, distractibility, impulsive responding, impaired visual memory for designs, difficulties completing multistep tasks, emotional lability and left hemiparesis 6 months after successful resection of a deep intraventricular arteriovenous malformation (AVM) with intraparenchymal hematoma, when he was 7 years of age (Eslinger et al., 1999). These deficits were very similar to those associated with adult-onset right dorsolateral prefrontal lesion, and suggest that neural mediation of several important cognitive–behavioral processes (spatial, attentional, executive, and self-regulation) was well-differentiated within right prefrontal cortical systems by this age. These observations are consistent with those of Reuda, Posner, and Rothbart (2005) who demonstrated improving performance on resolution of visual conflict tasks, use of attentional controls, and decreased response latencies by children between the ages of 4 and 7 years and no significant differences or improvements in performance of 7-year-olds as compared to adults. JC's first neurobehavioral examination 6 months after surgery also revealed atypical smelling of everyday nonfood items (clothing, carpet, and objects), short attention span, reduced initiation, inability to play by himself, and preference for younger playmates—all premorbidly uncharacteristic for him. His brain magnetic resonance imaging (MRI) scan revealed a large right dorsolateral prefrontal lesion that extended deep to near the head of the caudate, dorsal premotor cortex, and the anterior insula (see Figure 13.2).

Despite profound postacute deficits, JC has recovered remarkably over the past 15 years. He has not developed social or adaptive impairments and has remained in stable and supportive relationships with his family, girlfriend, friends, and coworkers. Despite early left hemispatial neglect, his perceptual–motor recovery was so good that he eventually participated in competitive sports for many years through

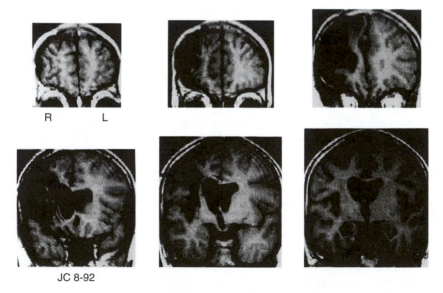

R   L

JC 8-92

Figure 13.2 Chronic phase brain MRI scan showing extensive localized right dorsolateral prefrontal cortex damage from AVM ablation at 7 years of age in patient JC. Notably, there was sparing of orbital and polar prefrontal regions bilaterally.

school, and overcame a spatial working memory deficiency that manifested initially as losing track of offensive and defensive ends of a sports field.

Prior to his AVM, JC had been described by his elementary school teachers as a bright creative youngster with great academic potential. Following his injury, JC's academic progress remained steady but was not as proficient due to residual attentional difficulties. A trial of low dose stimulant medication led not only to improved classroom performance but also attenuated his spontaneity and outgoing personality, and he chose not to continue with it. His educational performance was also impacted by subtle language impairments that negatively affected his communicative competence. His high school teachers indicated that although he was talkative, JC's written expression was not commensurate with his oral abilities. Experimental analysis of his personal discourse style and language skills indicated subtle yet persistent deficits in several pragmatic areas of language development. In comparison to his typically developing adolescent peers, JC's discourse was vague and unelaborated. He did not appear to understand the listener's needs when he engaged in personal narratives. He also demonstrated difficulties with metaphoric language. Despite being eligible to receive academic support services in high school, JC usually declined participation, preferring not to be seen as having learning differences. Although he had some pragmatic difficulties in language areas, his social judgment in this area was quite typical for an adolescent.

One of the major psychosocial tasks of adolescence is the formation of a coherent identity (Erikson, 1968). For JC, the period of exploration and eventual commitment to an identity may have been prolonged as a result of his subtle differences in attention and comprehending social nuances that typically developing teens understand easily. The peer group is a potent source of feedback in adolescence contributing to one's self-esteem, self-concept, and identity. JC experienced some late adolescent emotional upheaval that appeared related to continuing difficulties in understanding other people (likely to entail subtle theory of mind and social–emotional perceptual difficulties), but he has learned to manage these adjustment challenges and maintain his progress.

Despite these developmental trials, JC has shown a consistent resilience of character that has carried him through many social, emotional, and cognitive tasks. For example, following high school, he completed graphic design school and has since maintained full-time employment in newspaper advertising and freelance design, managing his own finances and life decisions. He reports a stable and mutually supportive relationship with his girlfriend. Importantly, he has remained persistent in his goal-directed behavior, well-connected to his family and friends, and continually seeks new compensatory strategies. In analyzing his brain injury characteristics, we are persuaded that the sparing of orbital and polar prefrontal regions, the unilateral location of prefrontal injury, and the onset of damage at 7 years of age are all likely to be important neurobiological factors associated with his adaptive developmental outcome. There are also personal, family, and social support factors that we believe critically supported JC's continuing recovery, adaptive compensations, acceptance of certain limitations, and optimism that he could accomplish what he set out to do. Powell and Voeller (2004) describe the management of any child with a prefrontal executive dysfunction as a team endeavor in

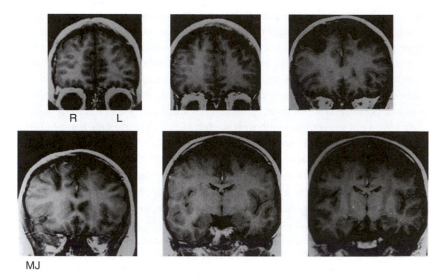

Figure 13.3   Chronic phase brain MRI scan showing isolated right dorsolateral prefrontal lesion with onset at 3 years of age in patient MJ.

which families and schools contribute resources and support for each child's deficits and structure the environment for success. They suggest that parents "Learn to be a good accessory frontal lobe" (p. 795). JC's family was actively involved in his recovery and in supporting his continued growth and development in family, social, and academic areas. They were steadfast in their confidence in his ability to over-come or compensate for any persisting deficits resulting from his neural injury.

In contrast to JC, MJ suffered localized right dorsolateral prefrontal damage at 3 years of age, from an abscess that required surgical evacuation. Brain MRI findings are shown in Figure 13.3. In the early recovery phases, MJ showed a mixture of attentional and interpersonal difficulties that required evaluation and close follow-up care both at home and in school. Cognitive testing in adolescence revealed detectable but not severe deficiencies in visuospatial aspects of executive functions such as spatial planning, working memory, and organizational strategies even a decade after his illness. Despite these limitations MJ continued to progress academically. Because of his interpersonal difficulties, he fared better in a large public high school setting than a small private school. As he matured, he preferred a smaller college setting where he completed studies and performed very well. His family setting and parental support were exceptional. These supports were steadfast despite MJ's tendency to be emotionally indifferent and detached from them. Parents reported that they noticed a clear difference in his temperament and behavior soon after his illness. He forged rare friendships, was frequently in conflict with siblings over usually minor matters (often acting rude, indifferent, or with inappropriate joking), and was awkward in emotional and pragmatic communication. Despite interpersonal problems, MJ has always been kind to family pets, regulated his behavior within legal bounds, and has not developed any delinquent or conduct problems. As he matured in later adolescence, he thrived academically and within certain social settings.

He completed college and has worked successfully within a business office setting that requires primarily telephone and computer communication skills. He has a similarly aged girlfriend who finds him "funny" and is now considering graduate education options. Despite his developmental challenges with spatial executive functions and interpersonal processes of emotional communication, empathy, and perspective-taking, MJ has found several niches in which he can thrive and certainly continues to show adaptive and maturational progress. His right dorsolateral prefrontal injury at 3 years of age likely altered the maturational rate and trajectory of several cognitive, emotional, and behavioral processes associated with the right prefrontal region, rather than causing a single isolated deficit. This accords well with the observations of Max et al. (2006) who reported that traumatic lesions of the superior frontal gyrus was most associated with significant personality change in the first 12 months after injury in a large sample of school age children. Early damage to this prefrontal region has also been related to developmental alterations in anatomy and physiology of other prefrontal and related cortical regions (Goldman & Galkin, 1978; Kolb et al., 2000). Despite these neurodevelopmental concerns, MJ has thrived and continues to show adaptive behavior. As with JC's case mentioned above, the unilateral extent of the lesion and sparing of the frontal polar and ventromedial prefrontal cortical regions may be important anatomical contributors to continuing adaptive development.

Summary

Longitudinal examination of single cases with specific prefrontal cortex lesions at early ages provides an opportunity to document and experimentally explore the natural history of recovery and the potential maturational plasticity of this important brain region within a neurodevelopmental framework. There are several neurobiological and environmental variables that contribute to differences in developmental outcome, among them lesion characteristics of location, size, momentum, and age of onset as well as age of testing and nature of testing, respectively. Given the small sample of cases reported thus far, the relative importance of several of these variables is not yet clear. A potentially critical factor, in our view, is the location of lesion. Damage to ventromedial prefrontal cortex and frontal polar cortex has been associated with chronic cognitive, emotional, and self-regulatory impairments that escalate in adolescence and continue as adaptive deficits in adulthood. Bilateral, right- and left-sided lesions in these areas can lead to negative developmental outcomes, a pattern we have also observed in adults (Eslinger & Geder, 2000). In contrast, early dorsolateral prefrontal lesions, at least of a unilateral nature (no developmental bilateral lesions have been reported), may be associated with more delimited deficits that preserve many executive, emotional, and self-regulatory processes.

The increasing adaptive deficits in adolescence, we have proposed, arise from a more intense interaction among postlesion deficits, arrested neural and neuropsychological development, and increasing environmental and cognitive demands that are placed on teenagers. Academic and social pressures mount as adults and peers expect that individuals have reached a stage of formal operational reasoning and self-regulation that permits them to engage in hypothetical and deductive reasoning, considering and weighing alternatives and conditional probabilities in order to eventually make sound decisions. In a study of typically developing adolescents Anderson, Anderson, Northam, Jacobs, and Catroppa (2001) noted that attentional control, cognitive flexibility, and goal-setting behaviors, each identified as components of executive function, had different developmental trajectories. For example, adolescents appeared to undergo a surge in growth of goal-setting skills at age 12, while 15-year-olds prevailed as being faster and possessing better attentional capacities. Such results support the contention that adolescents are typically more efficient and capable in problem solving and planning than young children.

Given the highly integrative nature of prefrontal cortical systems, particularly throughout development, we hypothesize that such damage cause an altered inter-play of cognitive, emotional, and self-regulatory processes that is expressed as a diversity of impairments and developmental challenges that unfold over at least two decades. The resulting alteration of neurodevelopmental trajectories for cognition, emotion, and self-regulation, in turn, changes the formation of knowledge struc-tures, decision-making strategies, personal habits, identity formation, and interper-sonal processing that guide perception, moral behavior, flexible problem solving, learning from experience, and social interaction. Extant data from case studies suggest that early prefrontal cortex damage does not lead to a single deficit or outcome, but rather diverse deficits and outcomes that are likely influenced by anatomy and physiology of the damage as well as family and social influences. These observations provide several ideas for the experimental measurement and analysis to be undertaken in larger clinical samples. Functional brain imaging studies of healthy children and adolescents, which are described below, may further elucidate prefrontal neurodevelopmental deficits as well as how the prefrontal cortex influences typical development.

Social moral emotions, prefrontal cortex, and development

Moral behavior and moral emotions are important processes for social adaptation and maturation at personal, interpersonal as well as community and societal levels. Acquiring social sensitivity and associated cognitive and emotional self-regulation are crucial developmental challenges that involve prefrontal cortex and related networks of subcortical and cortical regions. For many decades, the so-called moral psychology was focused on processes of cognition and knowledge as the key mediators of moral behavior and decision making (Kohlberg & Kramer, 1969; Piaget, 1932). As applied to the often murky issues of morality and other interpersonal actions, moral reasoning was conceptualized as a uniquely rational human capability that provided a clear basis for deciding issues of fairness, equity, justice, and even fundamental bases for government, legal systems, and social order. There are several problems with this conceptual approach, and the foremost is that moral reasoning is not necessarily predictive of moral behavior. Both sociopaths and select patients with acquired prefrontal damage can demonstrate normal moral reasoning on standardized tests (such as moral dilemmas) but act quite differently in real-life, being impaired in social judgment and sensitivity (Eslinger & Damasio, 1985; Moll et al., 2002). To help address this huge gap, a moral emotion correction has been proposed by Haidt (2003) who elaborates on several families of social–moral emotions that have significant influences on social–moral behaviors. These include, for example, social emotions of disgust and contempt that are other-condemning and contribute to social dissolution and distancing; compassion, awe and gratitude that are important prosocial emotions; and self-conscious emotions of guilt, embarrassment and shame that contribute importantly to self-regulation. This has led us to investigate if there are different neural systems for social–moral processing based on cognitive appraisal versus emotional mediation. If so, this would support the contention that moral actions may be influenced by more than just reasoning capabilities, and that cognitive and emotional processing streams for the social–moral domain may be different from each other and potentially dissociable.

In a series of functional brain imaging studies in healthy young adults, we discovered that cognitive judgments about right and wrong actions activated principally frontal polar and anterior temporal regions. In contrast, when healthy adults viewed scenes of moral violations as passive witnesses, without any requirement to make decisions about the materials, they not only reported the experience of moral emotions, but also showed activations that shifted to medial orbitofrontal, inferior frontal polar, medial frontal, and superior temporal sulcus regions, principally in the right hemisphere (see Moll, de Olivera-Souza, & Eslinger, 2003; for review). Therefore, moral reasoning and moral emotions appeared to emanate from different neural systems. In a further study, response to moral emotional stimuli highly associated with basic disgust and social contempt, similar significant activations were evident in the orbitofrontal cortices (Moll et al., 2005; see Figure 13.4). When viewed within a neurodevelopmental framework, these results suggest that an important neural substrate for acquiring social sensitivity and empathy may involve frontal polar and orbitofrontal cortices, among other areas. Studies of adult patients with orbitofrontal damage suggest that their social–moral emotions, particularly

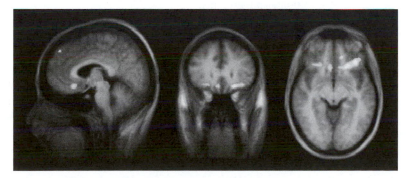

Figure 13.4 Summary fMRI figure showing brain activations in healthy adults during social–moral emotion processing of basic disgust and social contempt, with specific involvement of orbital prefrontal regions. The social–moral emotion of contempt may depend, in part, on a common neural substrate with primal representation of disgust. From "The Moral Affiliations of Disgust: A Functional MRI Study," by J. Moll, R. de Oliveira-Souza, F. T. Moll, F. A. Ignacio, I. E. Bramati, E. M. Caparelli-Daquer, et al. (2005). *Cognitive and Behavioral Neurology, 18*, 68–78.

self-conscious emotions, are impaired (Beer, Heerey, Keltner, Scabini & Knight, 2003). Preliminary data from a sample of community sociopaths also show that their appreciation of guilt, embarrassment, and pity in social scenarios was significantly lower than controls, despite the fact their moral reasoning was not significantly different (J. Moll, personal communication). These are social–moral emotions from the self-conscious and other-suffering clusters that are intimately related to social sensitivity, empathy, and self-regulation in relationship to behavioral norms. Hence, sociopathy, whether developmental or acquired, may involve pathophysiology of some common neural substrates that are crucial for mediation of social–moral emotions rather than moral reasoning. One of these potential neural regions, the orbitofrontal cortex, has extensive connections with medial prefrontal regions, the amygdala, temporal pole, insula, and other paralimbic structures and appears to be crucial for mediation of diverse autonomic, visceral, and somatic effector systems that shape emotional reactivity and subsequent contingency-based learning (Eslinger, 1999). Thus, we hypothesize that early disruption of orbitofrontal and frontal polar regions may well alter the basic kinds of social–emotional processing that can occur and can be linked to perceptions, language, actions, and reinforcement-based outcomes that inform social knowledge structures inter-relating the self with significant others, various social groupings, and the sets of social norms and legal statutes that govern human behavior. Deficits in social–moral emotions may not be reflected by tests of moral reasoning or cognitively based moral judgment. Incorporating assessment of social–moral emotions may help address the chasm sometimes found in prefrontal lesion samples between intact cognitive assessment of moral processing and impaired moral judgment and behavior in the real world.

At this time, we are planning to directly investigate these processing systems in typically developing children and adolescents with various functional MRI (fMRI) paradigms. Such data may help complement the available adult studies and experimental studies of various clinical neurodevelopmental samples that experience significant social–emotional impairments.

Prefrontal cortex and the development of cognitive expertise

While clinical case and group studies provide sometimes striking examples of impairments related to cerebral damage, interpreting these findings with regard to typical neurodevelopmental processes can be challenging. To help bridge this gap, we have begun exploring functional neuromaturational changes involving the prefrontal cortex in typically developing children and adolescents with cognitive tasks sensitive to prefrontal maturation. In relational reasoning tasks (such as the Raven's Progressive Matrices), stimulus sets are structured so that individuals have to derive and manipulate relations among stimulus features for purposes of reasoning, planning, and problem solving. Relational dimensions can include color, size, shape, sequence, etc. Computation of solutions is based not on a priori memorized or semantic knowledge per se, but rather on the active perceptual and representational analysis of novel stimulus arrays. Such tasks are often described as requiring fluid reasoning, and clinical studies support important roles for frontal-parietal and frontal-striatal networks in fluid cognitive ability. Recent historical analyses of elementary mathematical education have confirmed a large contemporary shift from counting and memorization to emphasis on problem-solving skills, relational reasoning, and manipulation of information (Blair, Gamson, Thorne, & Baker, 2005). Among other factors, such early educational training may be influencing cognitive development and the increasing rate of fluid intelligence capabilities known as the Flynn effect.

We undertook fMRI BOLD analysis of brain activation patterns that typically developing children and adolescents 8–19 years of age generated while completing relational reasoning and calculation tasks in a 3 T magnet. The relational reasoning stimuli were similar to those developed for the Raven's Progressive Matrices, and required problem solving when there are two or more relations among a set of geometric designs. The calculation tasks entailed straightforward addition and subtraction problems and more complex coin calculation problems that are common in math education today. The resulting data, processed with SPM2 software and mapped onto anatomical images of the brain, revealed common areas of activation principally in the right dorsolateral prefrontal cortex, the superior parietal cortices including the region of the intraparietal sulcus, and the occipital lobe. To explore specific neurodevelopmental changes, we computed age regressions in order to identify cerebral regions that changed with age, becoming either more active with age (positive regressions) or less active with age (negative regressions). A summary of 3-dimensional representation of these age regression results is presented in Figure 13.5 for the relational reasoning data set. Red areas represent significant positive regressions and green areas represent significant negative regressions with age. Data analysis indicated that areas of increasing activation with age during relational reasoning were localized to superior parietal cortices, whereas prefrontal and anterior cingulate areas became significantly less active with age. We interpret these findings as support for the conclusion that younger children activate more prefrontal and anterior cingulate regions because of the greater attentional and executive resources needed for relational reasoning in comparison to adolescents who are more proficient and efficient at such tasks. Similar neurodevelopmental shifts in activation were evident for the number and coin calculation tasks. Thus, prefrontal cortex and associated anterior cingulate regions appear to play a key role in the acquisition of fluid types of executive intelligence as well as computational proficiency and efficiency. We suspect that similar types of neuroplasticity may underlie the acquisition of everyday expertise across a variety of cognitive domains, and that the pivotal role of prefrontal cortical systems may naturally diminish as posterior cortical regions consolidate more information processing efficiency and automaticity. This pattern of neurophysiological change may be related to the pruning and sculpting of neural networks throughout development. For example, in tasks of visual conflict resolution (Rueda, Posner, Rothbart, & Davis-Stober, 2004), the evoked response potential (ERP) distributions of adults was localized to midline frontal regions, in contrast to the ERP's of 4-year-old children that were distributed more widely to midline and lateral prefrontal regions. Their results suggest an increasing efficiency in functional brain networks, which supports improved performance and time on tasks requiring conflict resolution. The results support the supposition that insults to the developing prefrontal cortex at an early age, when there is rapid development

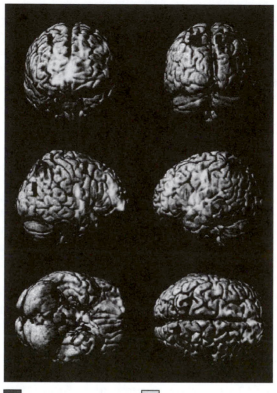

■ Positive age regression   □ Negative age regression

Figure 13.5   Summary 3-D rendering fMRI BOLD activations that show significant positive correlations and negative correlations with age during a relational reasoning task requiring fluid intelligence. Results were generated from a sample of healthy children and adolescents 8–19 years of age. The positive age regression areas became more active with age (suggesting consolidated cognitive skills) whereas the negative age regression regions became less active with age (suggesting less need for executive resources) while solving relational reasoning problems.

of top-down mediated skills, could potentially alter neurocognitive capacities by interfering with the appropriate connectivity to necessary neural substrates that are critical to skill acquisition.

In a secondary fMRI analysis, we also compared significant activation clusters for the three cognitive tasks across the typical developmental sample. Results are summarized in Figure 13.6 represented by colocalization of three different colors on a sagittal cut of the brain (blue: coin calculation task; yellow: number calculation task; cyan: relational reasoning task). These clusters represent average activation effects and show a high degree of overlap. We interpret these results as showing that the three kinds of cognitive processing generated common activations in the prefrontal and parietal regions associated with working memory, computational skill, and spatial fluid intelligence. The data illustrate important interactions of prefrontal

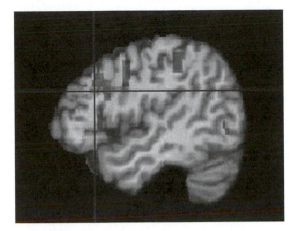

Figure 13.6 Summary figure showing fMRI brain activations in a typical developmental sample 8–19 years of age. Specific areas of activity were prominent in the prefrontal cortex and superior parietal cortex during related cognitive tasks. There were very similar regions of activation in the dorsolateral prefrontal cortex (commonly associated with working memory demands, attentional control, and problem-solving strategies) and the superior parietal region (commonly associated with number processing, spatial working memory, and spatial problem solving) that occurred for all three tasks, suggesting an important degree of related processing between prefrontal and parietal cortices during typical neuromaturation of higher cognitive capacities.

cortex with posterior cortical processing regions that are dedicated to more domain-specific functions. It is our view that prefrontal cortex provides vital domain neutral executive resources for problem solving and decision making such as attentional control, working memory, organizational, and manipulative abilities that are crucial during development. When prefrontal cortical regions are disrupted by injury or other pathology, we suspect that networks such as these have a severely altered rate and trajectory of maturation.

Conclusion

Studies of prefrontal cortex and its role in development and neuromaturation support a pivotal role for this cortical region in the integration of cognition, social emotions, and behavior throughout childhood and adolescence, and the acquisition of executive functions and self-regulation that are vital for everyday expertise and adaptation. Early damage to the prefrontal cortex disrupts not only local prefrontal physiology but also the inter-related plasticity and maturation of many neural networks that are linked to prefrontal cortex. Unlike other cortical regions, the effects of such injury early in life may have burgeoning and reverberating effects for decades, causing significant problems for patients and families, particularly when damage invades the frontal polar and ventromedial prefrontal regions. However, some individuals with limited prefrontal lesions outside these areas fare well and can develop adaptive compensatory behaviors that allow them to function independently as adults. The study of these differences in outcome, together with emerging methodologies in functional brain imaging and other modalities, have the potential to advance the treatment of prefrontal syndromes and promote the health of typical children.

Acknowledgment

This work was supported in part by Pennsylvania State University Tobacco Settlement Funds and the Children, Youth and Family Consortium. Special thanks to Jianli Wang, MD, PhD for expertise in reconstructing the cerebral lesions of case JP. This chapter is dedicated to the memory of Professor Arthur L. Benton—mentor, neighbor, and friend.

References

Ackerly, S. S. (1964). A case of paranatal bilateral frontal lobe defect observed for thirty years. In J. M. Warren & K. Akert (Eds.), *The frontal granular cortex and behavior* (pp. 192–218). New York: McGraw-Hill.

Ackerly, S. S., & Benton, A. L. (1948). Report of a case of bilateral frontal lobe defect. *Proceedings of the Association for Research in Nervous and Mental Disease, 27,* 479–504.

Anderson, S. W., Damasio, H., Tranel, D., & Damasio, A. R. (2000). Long-term sequelae of prefrontal cortex damage acquired in early childhood. *Developmental Neuropsychology, 18,* 281–296.

Anderson, V., Anderson, P., Northam, E., Jacobs, R., & Catroppa, C. (2001). Development of executive functions through late childhood and adolescence in an Australian sample. *Developmental Neuropsychology, 20*(1), 385–406.

Anderson, V., Jacobs, R., & Harvey, A. S. (2005). Prefrontal lesions and attentional skills in childhood. *Journal of the International Neuropsychological Society, 11,* 817–831.

Beer, J. S., Heerey, E. A., Keltner, D., Scabini, D., & Knight, R. T. (2003). The regulatory function of self-conscious emotion: Insights from patients with orbitofrontal damage. *Journal of Personality and Social Psychology, 85,* 594–604.

Benton, A. L. (1991). Prefrontal injury and behavior in children. *Developmental Neuropsychology, 7,* 275–281.

Blair, C., Gamson, D., Thorne, S., & Baker, D. (2005). Rising mean IQ: Changing cognitive demand of mathematics education for young children, population exposure to formal schooling, and the neurobiology of the prefrontal cortex. *Intelligence, 33,* 93–106.

Blair, C., Zelazo, P. D., & Greenberg, M. T. (2005). The measurement of executive function in early childhood. *Developmental Neuropsychology, 28,* 561–572.

Erikson, E. H. (1968). *Identity: Youth and crisis.* New York: Norton.

Eslinger, P. J. (1996). Conceptualizing, describing, and measuring components of executive functions. In G. R. Lyon & N. A. Krasnegor (Eds.), *Attention, memory and executive function* (pp. 367–395). Baltimore: Paul H. Brookes.

Eslinger, P. J. (1999). Orbital frontal cortex: Historical and contemporary views about its behavioral and physiological significance. *Neurocase, 5,* 225–230.

Eslinger, P. J., Biddle, K. R., & Grattan, L. M. (1997). Cognitive and social development in children with prefrontal cortex lesions. In N. A. Krasnegor, G. R. Lyon, & P. S. Goldman-Rakic (Eds.), *Development of the prefrontal cortex: Evolution, neurobiology, and behavior* (pp. 295–335). Baltimore: Paul H. Brookes.

Eslinger, P. J., Biddle, K. R., Pennington, B., & Page, R. B. (1999). Cognitive and behavioral development up to 4 years after early right frontal lobe lesion. *Developmental Neuropsychology, 15*, 157–191.

Eslinger, P. J., & Damasio, A. R. (1985). Severe disturbance of higher cognition after bilateral frontal lobe ablation: Patient EVR. *Neurology, 35*, 1731–1741.

Eslinger, P. J., Flaherty-Craig, C. V., & Benton, A. L. (2004). Developmental outcomes after early prefrontal cortex damage. *Brain and Cognition, 55*, 84–103.

Eslinger, P. J., & Geder, L. (2000). Behavioral and emotional changes after focal frontal lobe damage. In J. Bogousslavsky & J. L. Cummings (Eds.), *Focal brain lesions and emotion* (pp. 217–260). Cambridge, UK: Cambridge University Press.

Eslinger, P. J., & Grattan, L. M. (1991). Perspectives on the developmental consequences of early frontal lobe damage: Introduction. *Developmental Neuropsychology, 7*, 257–260.

Eslinger, P. J., Grattan, L. M., & Damasio, A. R. (1992). Developmental consequences of childhood frontal lobe damage. *Archives of Neurology, 49*, 764–769.

Eslinger, P. J., Moore, P., Antani, S., et al. (in press). Resolving social dilemmas in fronto-temporal dementia. *Journal of Neurology, Neurosurgery and Psychiatry.*

Finger, S. (1991). Brain damage, development, and behavior: Early findings. *Developmental Neuropsychology, 7*, 261–274.

Goldman, P. S., & Galkin, T. W. (1978). Prenatal removal of frontal association cortex in fetal rhesus monkey: Anatomical and functional consequences in postnatal life. *Brain Research, 12*, 451–485.

Haidt, J. (2003). The moral emotions. In R. J. Davidson, K. R. Scherer, & H. H. Goldsmith (Eds.), *Handbook of affective sciences.* Oxford, UK: Oxford University Press.

Harlowe, J. M. (1868). Recovery from severe injury to the head. *Publication of the Massachusetts Medical Society, 2*, 327–346.

Jacobs, R., & Anderson, V. (2002). Planning and problem solving skills following focal frontal lesions in childhood: Analysis using the tower of London. *Child Neuropsychology, 8*, 93–106.

Kohlberg, L., & Kramer, R. (1969). Continuities and discontinuities in childhood and adult moral development. *Human Development, 12*, 93–120.

Kolb, B., Gibb, R., & Gorny, G. (2000). Cortical plasticity and the development of behavior after early frontal cortical injury. *Developmental Neuropsychology, 18*, 423–444.

Levin, H. S., Zhang, L., Dennis, M., Ewing-Cobbs, L., Schachar, R., Max, J., et al. (2004). Psychosocial outcome of TBI in children with unilateral frontal lesions. *Journal of the International Neuropsychological Society, 10*(3), 305–316.

Marlowe, W. (1992). The impact of right prefrontal lesion on the developing brain. *Brain and Cognition, 20*, 205–213.

Mateer, C. A., & Williams, D. (1991). Effects of frontal lobe injury in childhood. *Developmental Neuropsychology, 7*, 359–376.

Max, J. E., Levin, H. S., Schachar, R. J., Landis, J., Saunders, A. E., Ewing-Cobbs, L., et al. (2006). Predictors of personality change due to traumatic brain injury in children and adolescents six to twenty-four months after injury. *Journal of Neuropsychiatry and Clinical Neurosciences, 18*(1), 21–32.

Moll, J., de Olivera-Souza, R., & Eslinger, P. J. (2003). Morals and the human brain: A working model. *NeuroReport, 14*, 299–305.

Moll, J., de Oliveira-Souza, R., Eslinger, P. J., Bramati, I. E., Mourao-Miranda, J., Andreiuolo, P. A., et al. (2002). The neural correlates of moral sensitivity: A functional magnetic resonance imaging investigation of basic and moral emotions. *Journal of Neuroscience, 22*, 2730–2736.

Moll, J., de Oliveira-Souza, R., Moll, F. T., Ignacio, F. A., Bramati, I. E., Caparelli-Daquer, E. M., et al. (2005). The moral affiliations of disgust: A functional MRI study. *Cognitive and Behavioral Neurology, 18,* 68–78.

Piaget, J. (1968). *Six psychological studies* (A. Tenzer, Trans.). New York: Vintage Books.

Powell, K. B., & Voeller, K. S. (2004). Prefrontal executive syndromes in children. *Journal of Child Neurology, 19*(10), 785–797.

Price, B. H., Daffner, K. R., Stowe, R. M., & Mesulam, M. M. (1990). The comportmental learning disabilities of early frontal lobe damage. *Brain, 113,* 1383–1393.

Rueda, M. R., Posner, M. I., Rothbart, M. K., & Davis-Stober, C. P. (2004). Development of the time course for processing conflict: An ERP study with four year olds and adults. *BMC Neuroscience, 5,* 39.

Scoville, W. B., & Milner, B. (1957). Loss of recent memory after bilateral hippocampal lesions. *Journal of Neurology, Neurosurgery and Psychiatry, 20,* 11–212.

Segalowitz, S. J., & Rose-Krasnor, L. (1992). The construct of brain maturation in theories of child development. *Brain and Cognition, 20,* 1–7.

Stuss, D. T. (1992). Biological and psychological development of executive functions. *Brain and Cognition, 20,* 8–23.

Tranel, D., Bechara, A., & Denburg, N. (2002). Asymmetric functional roles of right and left ventromedial prefrontal cortices in social conduct, decision-making, and emotional processing. *Cortex, 38*(4), 589–612.

Tranel, D., & Eslinger, P. J. (2000). Effects of early onset brain injury on the development of cognition and behavior: Introduction to the special issue. *Developmental Neuropsychology, 18,* 273–280.

14   Attention deficits and the frontal lobes

Vicki Anderson

Contents

From a functional perspective, attentional skills are of particular significance during childhood, being critical for the development of cognitive and neuropsychological systems, which in turn influence adaptive, social, and academic functioning (Cooley & Morris, 1990; Dennis, Wilkinson, Koski, & Humphreys, 1995; Douglas, 1983). If attentional skills are impaired, then children may be less able to learn and acquire skills from their environment, to function independently in day-to-day life, and to make use of teaching and instruction. Accurate mapping of a child's attentional profiles may enable the implementation of appropriate and accurately targeted intervention.

Recent research has identified anterior brain regions as critical for effective attention. The frontal lobes, particularly the prefrontal cortices, are intimately involved in normal development of attention, because of their rich connections with many cerebral regions and their unique role in efficient executive function. As has been observed in previous chapters, these structures develop rapidly through childhood and early adolescence, paralleled by increases in "higher-order" executive abilities, including those related to attention, such as attentional control, shifting, and divided attention (Gogtay et al., 2004). Research is emerging to suggest that damage to prefrontal regions during childhood may interrupt normal maturational processes, leading to irreversible changes in brain structure and organization, and associated impairments in the development of these higher-order attentional skills (Anderson, Jacobs, & Harvey, 2005; Anderson, Levin, & Jacobs, 2002).

Adult research examining the consequences of frontal lobe injury has consistently identified impairments in attention including distractibility, and impulsivity, as well as reduced sustained and shifting attention (Knight & Stuss, 2002; Ponsford & Kinsella, 1992; Stuss et al., 1999, 1994; Wilkins, Shallice, & McCarthy, 1987). Developmental researchers have made similar observations with respect to the cerebral underpinnings of conditions known to impact attentional abilities, such as attention deficit hyperactivity disorder (ADHD), learning disabilities, Aspergers syndrome, and autism (August & Garfinkel, 1990; Casey, Gordon, Mannheim, & Rumsey, 1993; Castellanos & Tannock, 2002; Durston et al., 2003; Klin, Sparrow, Volkman, Cicchetti, & Rourke, 1995; Schulz, Newcorn, Fan, Tang, & Halparin, 2005a; Schulz et al., 2005b; Wainwright-Sharp & Bryson, 1993). More recently morphological and activation studies have also supported this link, documenting anomalies in structure and function of anterior brain regions where attentional deficits are present (Anderson, Catroppa, Morse, Haritou, & Rosenfeld, 2005; Castellanos & Tannock, 2002; Sowell et al., 2003). This chapter will review some of this literature, in the context of recent theoretical and developmental models of attention.

Neuropsychological theories of attention

The application of neuropsychological models of attention and information processing skills has provided some insight regarding links between frontal pathology, lesion laterality and neurobehavioral function. One of the earliest neuropsychological models of attention was that postulated by Alexander Luria (1973), and was based on localizationist thinking characteristic of that era. Luria proposed that two attention systems could be identified within the brain: a posterior and an anterior system. The first he described as a reflexive, or environmentally triggered, system that responded primarily to novel, biologically meaningful stimuli. Luria (1973) observed that this system was characterized by rapid habituation, with higher-order cognition largely unnecessary to its efficient functioning. The second unit, responsible for "volitional attention," he identified as a system involving a person's interpretation of environmental stimuli. He suggested that this system was mediated by more sophisticated cognitive processes. Luria went further to postulate that these two systems work in parallel in the mature brain, allowing the individual to monitor the environment for events that might require a response, while pursuing various goals guided by intentional behaviors. Luria's model did not address possible developmental aspects of these two systems, except to suggest that the more primitive attention system emerges first, soon after birth, with the second, more sophisticated system developing along with increasing experience and maturation.

Posner (1988; Posner, & Petersen, 1990) also supports a dual system model of attention, and has been an influential figure in the development of a robust theoretical neuropsychological model of attention. Consistent with Luria's (1973) earlier model, Posner suggested two components to attentional processing, derived from findings from his extensive empirical research. First, he described a system predominantly located in the posterior cerebral cortex, in particular the parietal lobes, and parts of the thalamus and midbrain. This system is primarily directed towards selective attention, and directs shifts in spatial attention. Posner has argued that there is evidence that this system is functional very early in life, as young as 4 months of age, in keeping with PET studies showing mature metabolism within the parietal lobes around this stage of development (Chugani, Phelps, & Mazziotta, 1987). He also postulated a second, anterior system, which is a higher-order system, with substantial neural links to the posterior system. This system is more associated with enhancing the intensity of the attention directed towards particular cognitive tasks. Citing both PET studies and behavioral data, Posner and colleagues have speculated that the anterior cingulate gyrus and areas of the prefrontal cortex are important in the mediation of this more executive aspect of attention, with development of these elements more protracted, due to the immaturity of cerebral areas under-pinning them.

Attempts to describe attention have been hindered by inconsistencies in termino-logy. In the 1800s William James argued that "focalisation, concentration, and consciousness" were the key elements (1890, pp. 403–404). A more contemporary description states that attention refers to "...all those aspects of human cognition that the subject can control...and to all aspects of cognition having to do with limited resources or capacity..." (Shiffrin, 1988, p. 739). Recently, in an attempt to develop a more fine-grained understanding of attentional processes, attempts have been made to compartmentalize attention into a number of separate, interacting components, forming a functional system (Dove, Pollman, Schubert, Wiggins, & van Cramon, 2000; Mirsky, Anthony, Duncan, Ahearn, & Kellam, 1991; Rubia et al., 1999; Shimamura, 1995; Stuss, Shallice, Alexander, & Picton, 1995), each subsumed by particular cerebral regions and forming an integrated cerebral system. Any disruption to this system has been argued to be likely to result in deficits in one or more aspects of attention (Mirsky et al., 1991; Mirsky, 1996; Stuss et al., 1995). Specific details of these models remain controversial. However, in keeping with current brain–behavior models, which frequently argue that aspects of cognition are underpinned by distributed neural networks, it is generally agreed that attention is subsumed by an integrated neuroanatomical system. Based on mainly behavioral data, this system has been argued to incorporate the brain stem, aspects of the subcortex and posterior cortical regions, and prefrontal cortex, with a critical role for the right hemisphere (Mirsky et al., 1991; Posner & Petersen, 1990; Stuss et al., 1995, 1999; Woods & Knight, 1986). Recent brain imaging work, using samples with impaired attention (e.g., ADHD, focal frontal lesions), has provided supporting evidence for such a distributed neural basis for attention (Castellanos et al., 2001; Sowell et al., 2003; Stuss et al., 2002, 1999; Stuss, 2006).

Definitions and operationalization of the attentional system remain problematic, but a number of separate, interdependent components are consistently identified. *Sustained attention* refers to the ability to maintain attention for prolonged periods to stimuli which occur at a low and often unpredictable rate. Where this component is inefficient, the specific characteristic of performance is a quicker than expected deterioration in the ability to maintain attention, or a fluctuating response pattern including omissions and episodes of lack of response (Anderson, Anderson, & Anderson, 2006). Using data from his own research to support his hypothesis, as well as that from a variety of animal studies, Mirsky (1996) postulates that this element of attention is mediated to a large extent by the reticular formation, other brain stem structures, and the medial thalamus (Bakay Pragay, Mirsky, Fullerton, Oshima, & Arnold, 1975; Bakay Pragay, Mirsky, & Nakamura, 1987; Ray, Mirsky, & Bakay Pragay, 1982). In his most recent publication Mirsky (1996) includes a fifth attentional component, stability of attentional effort, which he suggests is mediated by brain stem and midline thalamic structures. Others (Heilman, Voeller, & Nadeau, 1991; Mesulam, 1985; Stuss et al., 1995) argue that this concept is better incorporated into sustained attention, with anterior cerebral structures implicated (Anderson et al., 2005; Stuss et al., 1995, 1999; Van Zomeren & Brouwer, 1994).

Selective attention is defined as the capacity to attend to, and focus on, relevant stimuli, while filtering out extraneous information or to identify salient stimuli and perform motor responses in the presence of background distraction. Mirsky and colleagues (1991) suggest that focussed attention is associated with the superior temporal, inferior parietal and striatal regions. There is also evidence that this aspect of attention may be represented throughout the attentional system. For example, Stuss et al. (1995, 1999) argue that the cingulate and other anterior cerebral structures play a role in this aspect of attention, while others implicate parietal regions as well (Posner & Petersen, 1990).

In keeping with its role as "manager" or "central executive" of the brain, the prefrontal cortex is argued to be critical to all aspects of the system, but primarily higher-order components of the attentional system, including shifting and divided attention (Dove et al., 2000; Mesulam, 1981; Mirsky et al., 1991; Shimamura, 1995; Stuss et al., 1995, 1999). The ability to *shift attentional focus* relates to mental flexibility or the capacity to shift attention from one aspect of a stimulus to another in a flexible, efficient manner, and as such, is thought to be subsumed by the prefrontal cortex, including the anterior cingulate gyrus (Mirsky et al.; Stuss, 2006).

Of particular relevance in the developmental context are *divided attention* and *inhibition/impulsivity*. Divided attention refers to the capacity to simultaneously attend to multiple tasks/stimuli, and is generally argued to be a function of the frontal regions of the brain (Stuss et al., 1995). A number of studies have now been reported which support the involvement of these regions in effective divided attention (Anderson et al., 2005; Stuss et al., 1999, 2000). The ability to inhibit prepotent responses, or to suppress impulsive responses, has also been linked with frontal lobe function (Barkley, 1997, 2000). Deficits in these processes are commonly described as a characteristic of both developmental and acquired disorders involving the frontal lobes (Anderson et al., 2005; Anderson, Fenwick, Robertson, & Manly, 1998; Barkley, 1990; Drechsler, Brandeis, Foldenyi, Imhof, & Steinhausen, 2005; Wu, Anderson, & Castiello, 2002).

Some theorists have also argued that attentional functions may be lateralized, suggesting a specific role for the right hemisphere (Heilman et al., 1991; Mesulam, 1985; Robertson, 1999). Right hemisphere dysfunction has been associated with deficits in arousal, sustained attention, selective attention, response speed, response inhibition, self-monitoring, and motor activation (Heilman et al., 1991; Mesulam, 1981; Posner, 1988; Robertson, 1999; Stuss et al., 1995, 1999; Woods & Knight, 1986). In contrast, for patients with left frontal pathology, deficits are reported to be primarily language-based, with some suggestion that skills in initiation and divided attention may also be impaired (Godefroy, Lhullier, & Rousseaux, 1996; Godefroy & Rousseaux, 1996; Mecklinger, von Cramon, Springer, & Matthes-von-Cramon, 1999; Smith & Jonides, 1999). Lesions to either hemisphere may result in deficits in attentional shift and cognitive flexibility (Grattan, Bloomer, Archambault, & Eslinger, 1994; Owen, Roberts, Polkey, Sahakian, & Robbins, 1991).

Within the developmental literature, recent imaging studies have identified a specific role for the right frontal cortex for children with ADHD (Semrud-Clikeman et al., 2000; Sowell et al., 2003), suggesting that lateralization of attentional skills may be present early in childhood. These findings have been supported in a recent study from our laboratory, which identified a unique role for right prefrontal regions in attention in children with prefrontal pathology, regardless of whether the cerebral insult was either acquired or developmental (Anderson et al., 2005).

In summary, while contemporary brain–behavior models of attention argue that these skills are mediated by a distributed neural network, there is clear evidence for the importance of frontal regions within this system. Research implicates these regions in executive aspects of attention, such as shifting and divided attention. In addition, and consistent with Anderson's (2002) model of executive function, aspects of attention that may be defined as associated with "control" (e.g., stability of attentional effort, impulsivity/inhibition) are also noted to have links with the frontal lobes. However, to date few of these models have provided any insight into the development of attentional skills, nor do they consider whether their theories have relevance for children and adolescents, or for older adults. Thus, there is a challenge for those working within a developmental context to establish the relevance of such models, using the range of approaches at our disposal, such as examination of brain-behavior links in healthy samples via innovative structural and functional imaging techniques, as well as by employing more traditional methods for studying the consequences of brain damage for attention.

Development of attention

To fully understand the potential impact of prefrontal pathology on attentional skills in children, it is critical to have some understanding of normal maturational processes in this domain. Without such developmental markers, it is difficult to discriminate normal from deviant levels of ability. If a child is unable to attend efficiently to the environment, learning of new skills and knowledge may be limited, resulting in cumulative deficits, as is evidenced in the gradual deterioration in IQ scores in a number of CNS conditions where children exhibit attention deficits (Anderson & Moore, 1995; Anderson, Smibert, Godber, & Ekert, 1994; Ewing-Cobbs et al., 1997; Gronwall, Wrightson, & McGinn, 1997). Thus, a thorough understanding of the nature of attention and its development across childhood, and appropriate methods of assessment, are vital.

Developmental research demonstrates that the young child has a limited attentional capacity, possibly reflecting the immaturity of underlying neural substrates, for example, unmyelinated axons and developing frontal lobes (McKay, Halperin, Schwartz, & Sharma, 1994; Ruff & Rothbart, 1996). Kinsbourne (1996) argues that the development of attention is characterized by a systematic increase in the child's ability to override innate response tendencies, and replace them with more appropriate ones, in situations where it is advantageous to do so. He suggests that these increases in attentional capacity depend on the ability to transmit information both within the cortex and via subcortical–cortical connections. It is argued (Hudspeth & Pribram, 1990; Klingberg, Vaidya, Gabrieli, Moseley, & Hedehus, 1999; Thatcher,

1991) that the development of these tracts occurs in a set order, and within a set time frame, with anterior–posterior connections not fully developed until late child-hood. Consistent with such a perspective are observations from the developmental psychology literature that attentional skills improve with age (Cooley & Morris, 1990; Lane & Pearson, 1982; Lane, 1978; Manly et al., 2001; McKay et al., 1994; Shepp, Barrett, & Kolbet, 1987), with different developmental trajectories identified for the separate elements of attention.

Infancy and preschool periods

Attentional control, incorporating the ability to inhibit prepotent responses, or to suppress impulsive responses, has been reported to be the first aspect of attention to develop. While infants younger than 9 months of age have been shown to have difficulty inhibiting previously learned responses, by 12 months most infants can inhibit certain behaviors and shift response set, with continued improvements indi-cated until 3 years (Diamond, 1985; Diamond, 2002; Diamond & Doar, 1989; Gerardi-Caulton, 2000; Kochanska, Murray, & Harlan, 2000). By 3 years, children also demonstrate the capacity to inhibit "instinctive" behaviors (Diamond & Taylor, 1996; Espy, 1997), and improvements in speed and accuracy are evident on tasks of impulse control until around age six (Diamond & Taylor, 1996; Espy, Kaufmann, McDiarmid, & Glisky, 1999; Smidt, Jacobs, & Anderson, 2004).

Ruff and Rothbart (1996) track attentional development through infancy and childhood, describing a variety of experimental approaches to measurement. They argue that the development of attention is closely linked with progress in other cognitive domains, as well as to social development. They support an interactional process, whereby underlying neural substrates dictate potential development, with environmental input determining the extent to which development approximates this potential. In their view, specific components of attention are separable even very early in development, with more automatic, reflex aspects on line initially in early infancy, and volitional attention emerging in later childhood. Their model is consistent with current thinking in the neurosciences, and with neuropsychological theories put forward by Luria (1973), and more recently by Posner and Petersen (1990).

School-aged children

Not surprisingly, attention is difficult to measure accurately in infants and young children, and the bulk of the literature on attentional developmental has focused on the school-aged population. For example, McKay and coworkers (1994) have plotted the development of sustained and selective attention skills and response speed in a normative sample of children aged between 6 and 13 years, and compared their performances to that of an adult sample. They report relatively early maturation of selective attention, with adult level performances achieved in their youngest children on tasks tapping these skills. For sustained attention, abilities appeared relatively stable through childhood, with a developmental spurt around age eleven. Tests of response speed showed more gradual progress, with increments in performance observed up until 11 years of age.

Using a rigorous longitudinal design, Rebok et al. (1997) reported on the development of attention skills in 435 children assessed at ages 8, 10, and 13 years. A computer-based Continuous Performance Test (CPT) paradigm (Rosvold, Mirsky, Sarason, Bransome, & Beck, 1956) was employed in this study, with outcome measures of reaction time (RT), accuracy (correct responses and correct omissions), and omission errors. Rebok and colleagues detected significant age effects on all measures. Reaction times improved between 8 and 10 and again from 10 to 13 years. Accuracy dramatically improved from 8 to 10 years then showed gradual improvement from 10 to 13 years. Errors declined by about half from 8 to 10 years with more gradual declines from 10 to 13 years. Contrary to McKay et al. (1994), Rebok et al. (1997) concluded that sustained attention develops rapidly from 8 to 10 then plateaus from 10 to 13 years, with only gradual improvements during that period. More recent cross-sectional research has supported Rebok et al.'s (1997) findings, suggesting that, regardless of the outcome measure employed, there is continued improvement in attention skills from 8 to 16, but with the magnitude of gains reducing from around 10 to 11 years (Klenberg, Korkman, & Lahti-Nuuttila, 2001; Manly et al., 2001).

These important studies have contributed to our knowledge and understanding of the development of attention in school-aged children. However, they have also focused on lower level attentional skills, including sustained and selective attention, and have not reported on aspects of performance that might specifically reflect anterior brain function. To address these outstanding issues, Betts et al. (Betts, McKay, Maruff, & Anderson, 2006) have considered the developmental trajectories associated with sustained attention, and incorporated the effect of task load on children's performance. They examined three age groups, with a computerized attention battery (CogState, 2001), illustrated in Figure 14.1, and found that,

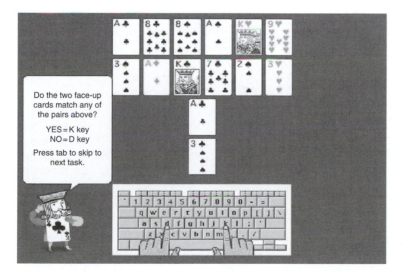

Figure 14.1   Matching task (the keyboard and instructions disappear after the practice trials).

as expected, sustained attention developed throughout the school-aged period, with improvements recorded for all measures (speed, errors, accuracy, and variability).

Overall, rapid growth occurred from 5–6 to 8–9 years, and then a developmental plateau was evident from 8–9 to 11–12 years with only minor improvement, consistent with previous research showing sustained attention to develop throughout childhood, with rapid improvements to age 10, then gradual improvements thereafter (Klenberg et al., 2001; Manly et al., 2001; Rebok et al., 1997), as illustrated in Figure 14.2. Specifically, 5–6 year-olds committed significantly more errors than the 8–9 year-olds who committed significantly more errors than the 11–12 year-olds. Measures of variability (standard deviation and mean absolute deviation from the median (MAD) demonstrated that 5–6 year-olds showed more variability in their responses than 8–9 year-olds, who in turn, were less consistent than 11–12 year-olds. Further, 8–9 year-olds recorded response speeds as short as the 11–12 year-old group, but with less accuracy. This pattern of less accurate performance may reflect emerging, but not yet established sustained attention skills in the 8–9 year-old children (Anderson, Anderson, & Lajoie, 1996; Kirk, 1985). Task complexity also influenced children's performances, with poorer results evident on the high load tasks than the low load tasks, regardless of age (Figure 14.3).

Additional research from our group, obtained while developing normative data for the Test of Everyday Attention for Children (TEA-Ch; Manly, Robertson, Anderson, & Nimmo-Smith, 1999), has also documented developmental trends in attention skills. From 6 to 15 years children showed definite advances in their performances on a range of attentional components and across modalities. The TEA-Ch is a modified version of the Test of Everyday Attention (Robertson, Ward, Ridgeway, & Nimmo-Smith, 1994), designed to be appealing to children. The aim of the test is to employ ecologically relevant and reliable measures of attention, derived from cognitive theory, to assess current multicomponent views of attention. The TEA-Ch includes a number of subtests, and has been designed to measure various aspects of attention including sustained, focussed, divided and

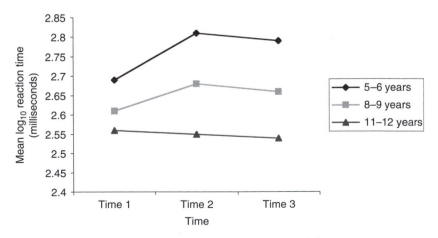

Figure 14.2   The mean $\log_{10}$ reaction time (RT) across age and time.

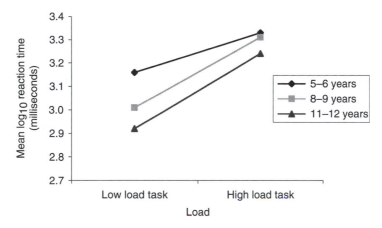

Figure 14.3 The mean log$_{10}$ reaction time (RT) across age and task load.

shifting attention skills, across both auditory/verbal and visual/spatial modalities. To examine sustained attention skills the "Score" paradigm has been utilized. On these tasks children are asked to listen and count a series of tones, which are auditorily presented to them at irregular intervals. The baseline task, Score includes 10 items where only the tones are presented. A second task, Score Dual Task, includes a divided attention component where the child needs to count the tones as well as identify an animal name embedded in a simulated news broadcast presented simultaneously with tones. Figure 14.4 shows the performances of different age groups on these measures. Results show a gradual increment in sustained attention skills through childhood, with older children achieving consistently higher scores. In addition, while interference reduces overall level of performance, the age effects are similar. For the divided attention task (Score Dual), children 9 years and older

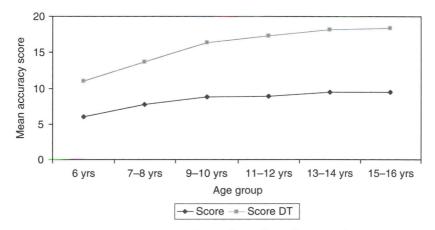

Figure 14.4 Developmental trajectories for the "Score" and "Score DT" subtests (TEA-Ch).

are less disadvantaged by task complexity, suggesting a possible developmental spurt in these divided attention skills around age nine. This possibly reflects the frontal underpinnings of these aspects of attention, and the relative immaturity of these cerebral regions in early to middle childhood.

A second paradigm employed in the TEA-Ch examines visual attention, including sustained and divided attention. On the initial Sky Search task, children are required to circle target stimuli, in this case spaceships, on a coloured sheet. The measures recorded include number of targets detected (visual selective attention) and time to completion (response speed), and a time-per-target measure. A variation of this task, Sky Search Dual Task (divided attention), requires the child to continue this basic task while counting a series of tones presented to them via audio-tape. Figure 14.5 illustrates age-related trends on these measures, showing gradual improvement in visual selective attention skills (time-per-target) from 6 to 16 years (Figure 14.5a). Similar to findings in the auditory modality, where the attentional demands are greater (Sky Search Dual Task), younger children (less than 9 years) perform significantly more poorly, taking longer to complete tasks (Figure 14.5b). This discrepancy is less evident in the older age groups, with a plateau in performance from 9–16 years.

In summary, developmental research has identified different developmental trajectories for specific attentional components. For example, a number of studies

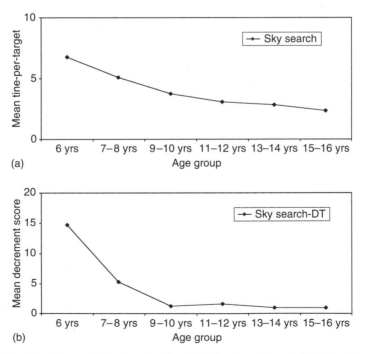

Figure 14.5   Developmental trajectories for (a) "Sky Search" and (b) "Sky Search-DT" subtests (TEA-Ch).

document relatively early development of basic selective attention skills, indicating rapid maturation in infancy and early childhood, with adult level performances demonstrated by children as young as age 6 (McKay et al., 1994; Manly et al., 2001; Rebok et al., 1997; Ruff & Rothbart, 1996). Shifting and divided attention skills have been found to progress slowly in early childhood, with more dramatic development into adolescence (Anderson, Anderson, Northam, Jacobs, & Catroppa, 2001; Chelune & Baer, 1986; Manly et al., 1999, 2001). Processing speed, which underpins performance on many attentional tasks, shows a gradual progression, with regular increments documented from 6 years to mid-adolescence (Anderson et al., 2001; Kail, 1986, 1988). These late developing skills may be particularly susceptible to the effects of disruption from cerebral insult due to their protracted developmental course (Dennis, 1989).

Disruptions to the attentional system

Abnormalities in attentional development are seen in a range of developmental and acquired disorders, for example, autism (Casey et al., 1993; Wainwright-Sharp & Bryson, 1993), attention deficit/hyperactivity disorder (August & Garfinkel, 1990), Asperger's syndrome (Klin et al., 1995), traumatic brain injury (TBI; Anderson & Pentland, 1998; Anderson et al., 1998; Catroppa, Anderson, & Stargatt, 1999; Ewing-Cobbs et al., 1998; Kaufmann, Fletcher, Levin, Miner, & Ewing-Cobbs, 1993), insulin dependent diabetes myelitis (Northam et al., 1998), cranial irradiation (Anderson, Godber, Smibert, Weiskop, & Ekert, 2004; Brouwers, Riccardi, Fedio, & Poplack, 1985), and Tourettes Syndrome (Lang, Athanasopoulous, & Anderson, 1998; Yeates & Bornstein, 1994).

The nature of attention deficits appears to vary across these groups, perhaps due to different underlying cerebral pathology, or to timing of onset of the condition. The influence of such factors is well illustrated in the case of TBI (Ponsford & Kinsella, 1992). Within the adult literature, many researchers now argue that attentional skills are intact following TBI, but speed of processing is reduced. When injury is sustained during childhood, the pattern of deficits appears to be more global. While children do exhibit slowed processing speed, they also display deficits in other aspects of attention, including sustained attention and shifting attention in particular (Anderson & Pentland, 1998; Catroppa et al., 1999; Ewing-Cobbs et al., 1998; Kaufmann et al., 1993). Further, deficits vary according to injury severity, with minimal evidence of attentional deficits following mild TBI, but significant impairment in moderate and severe TBI (Catroppa & Anderson, 2005; Catroppa et al., 1999; Willmott, Anderson, & Anderson, 2000).

Traumatic brain injury and impaired attention

Traumatic brain injury is characterized by diffuse axonal injury and more focal lesions in vulnerable brain regions including frontal and temporal cortex. In the absence of group studies examining the impact of focal frontal pathology, TBI has provided a model for the evaluation of the behavioral correlates of frontal lobe injury in childhood. To date, a limited number of studies have reported on attentional outcomes following childhood TBI, with somewhat inconsistent results. In one such study, Mateer and Williams (1991) examined a small group of children who had sustained early cerebral insult. Their findings documented intact or mildly depressed intellectual ability, despite presence of frontal pathology, consistent with adult findings (Walsh, 1978, 1985). In contrast, these children demonstrated behavioral symptoms of perseveration, reduced attention, rigidity, and social difficulties. Several other studies (Anderson & Moore, 1995; Garth, Anderson, & Wrennall, 1997; Levin et al., 1997; Pentland, Todd, & Anderson, 1998; Todd, Anderson, & Lawrence, 1996), also employing samples of children with TBI, have reported similar findings. In one of the earliest studies to employ standardized measures of attention, researchers (Timmermans & Christensen, 1991) investigated TBI children, aged 5 to 16 years, and found evidence for impairments in sustained attention, with selective attention skills intact. More recently, others (e.g., Dennis et al., 1995) have reported that children and adolescents with a history of TBI demonstrate impairments of both vigilance and selective attention. Anderson and Pentland (1998) examined a group of children and adolescents who had suffered moderate-to-severe TBI in early childhood, prior to the maturation of cerebral regions underpinning attentional processes. They described a pattern of global attention deficits, even in the long-term postinjury. They argued that such generalized attentional and information processing deficits represent permanent impairments for children with moderate-to-severe TBI, with greatest problems in the areas of speed of processing and shifting attention.

In recent years, variations of the Continuous Performance Paradigm (CPT; Rosvold et al., 1956) have become widely used as measures of attention, especially of sustained attention. The CPT is a computer-based procedure where the subject is required to attend to a computer screen for an extended period of time (e.g., 20 min), while identifying "target" stimuli embedded in a series regular stimulus presentations by pressing a response button which records accuracy and RT. The sensitivity of the CPT paradigm to sustained attention is believed to result from such signals being presented rapidly over a lengthy period of time, requiring subjects to maintain attention continuously throughout the task. Further, as the CPT provides no opportunity to correct an error once a response is given, then even brief periods of inattention can be detected (Halperin, 1991).

A number of cross-sectional studies have employed CPT paradigms to investigate attention following TBI in pediatric populations. Kaufmann et al. (1993) examined attention in a group of mild, moderate, and severe TBI children, aged 7–16 years, at 6 months post-TBI. Poorer performance was documented, that is more errors and slower responses, for children who had suffered a severe TBI, suggesting poor sustained attention for these children. The investigations of this group (Kaufmann et al.) were extended by Anderson and Pentland (1998), using a CPT paradigm with 22 adolescents who had sustained moderate or severe TBI and 22 healthy age-matched controls. In this study, the CPT task was divided into 4 time blocks (each of 5 minutes) to determine any fall off in performance with time on task. While children with TBI made more errors than healthy controls on all time blocks, their performance across sequential time blocks did not deteriorate at a greater rate than that of the controls, suggesting no clear evidence for any an impairment of sustained attention. However, these findings, as well as those of others (Catroppa et al., 1999; Fenwick & Anderson, 1999), did demonstrate a slowed rate of processing for the TBI group, suggesting that this may be a crucial factor underlying performance following TBI in childhood.

Very few authors have attempted a fine-grained analysis of component processes involved in performances on such attentional tasks (e.g., stimulus complexity, processing speed) that may be contributing to poor performance on the CPT task. An earlier study attempting to understand attentional sequelae post-TBI in children was conducted using an experimental approach to investigate four different stages of information processing: feature extraction and identification, response selection, and motor adjustment. While these authors did not control for important predictors such as injury severity, age at injury and time since injury, they were able to demonstrate a relationship between history of TBI and specific deficits in response selection and rate of motor execution, with feature extraction and identification intact (Murray, Shum, & McFarland, 1992). Unfortunately, while research has advanced with respect to tighter definition of TBI and acknowledgment of the importance to outcome of factors such as injury age and recovery profiles, there have been few attempts to replicate such careful delineation of specific attentional and related abilities in this population.

A longitudinal study of attention post-TBI has been conducted by Catroppa and colleagues (Catroppa & Anderson, 1999, 2003, 2005; Catroppa et al., 1999). Children were assessed during the acute stage postinjury, using a CPT paradigm similar to that of Anderson and Pentland (1998). Results revealed that, in the early stages of recovery, the severe TBI group demonstrated a difficulty in sustained attention when compared to mild and moderate TBI children. By 24 months post-injury, no significant differences were evident among the TBI groups on a measure of simple RT; however, there was a difference between the mild and severe TBI groups on the most complex task, which required speed, accuracy, and decision-making, suggesting that these factors underlie impaired performances previously identified on the CPT in children with severe TBI.

A small number of studies have examined higher-order attentional skills, as more appropriate assessment tools for these domains have emerged. Anderson et al. (1998) used the TEA-Ch (Manly et al., 1999) to fractionate attentional skills in children with TBI. They assessed 18 children with moderate-severe TBI and compared them to healthy age-, gender-, and SES-matched controls, aged 8–14 years. They argued, consistent with other researchers, that attentional skills appear to be differentially impaired after significant TBI. Specifically, components of attention found to be deficient were those that have been argued to be subserved by frontal brain regions, and included sustained attention, divided attention, and response inhibition.

These findings provide some support for involvement of frontal systems in the mediation of attention. However, the additional presence of diffuse axonal injury complicates interpretation as such, pathology has also been noted to impact on attentional function.

Focal frontal pathology in children

Evidence supporting the presence of attentional difficulties in the context of early focal prefrontal pathology derives primarily from a small number of human case studies. These cases are characterized by disinhibition, reduced attention and executive deficits in association with prefrontal pathology (Ackerly & Benton, 1948; Anderson, 1988; Anderson, Damasio, Tranel, & Damasio, 2000; Eslinger & Biddle, 2000; Eslinger, Biddle, & Grattan, 1997; Eslinger, Biddle, Pennington, & Page, 1999; Eslinger, Grattan, Damasio, & Damasio, 1992; Marlowe, 1992). In keeping with the developmental model of emerging deficits (Dennis, 1989), Eslinger and colleagues (1992) report a pattern of delayed onset of impairments, with difficulties only identified over time as new skills fail to "come on-line" and mature at critical stages throughout development. In particular, these authors identify poor development of attention and self-regulation as core deficits following prefrontal lesions sustained in childhood.

To date, group-based studies of this population are rare. Even in the adult literature, seminal studies have included participants with extra-frontal injuries in addition to the more focal prefrontal pathology of interest (Stuss et al., 1999, 2000; Stuss, Gallup, & Alexander, 2001). In our laboratory we have recently conducted a study which has examined the impact of focal frontal lesions, involving prefrontal cortex, on a range of attention measures, and employing the theoretical models described earlier in the chapter (Anderson et al., 2005). The measures employed in the study, and the attentional components underpinning performances are listed in Table 14.1. The sample for the study included 36 children with MRI evidence of focal frontal pathology, with no evidence of extra-frontal involvement and 40 age- and gender-matched healthy controls. Results from this study are provided in Table 14.2.

Results illustrated that children with prefrontal pathology performed more poorly than controls on higher-order measures of attention, including shifting and divided attention, and parents reported higher levels of disinhibition and impaired self-monitoring. In contrast, measures of selective attention and processing speed were

Table 14.1 Attention measures used in focal frontal lesion study.

	Verbal measures	*Spatial measures*
Selective attention	Digit Span (scaled score, total correct-forward span)	TMT A (time, errors)
	CNT:1&2 (efficiency)	Sky Search (attention score)
Shifting attention	CNT:3 &4 (time, efficiency) CC (no. correct)	TMT B (errors, (Time B−Time A)/Time A)
Divided attention	Score DT (games, animals, scaled score)	SS-DT (time-per-target, proportion of games correct)
Processing speed	CNT1 & 2 (time) CC (s/switch)	SS Motor (time)

CNT: Contingency Naming Test; CC: Creature Counting; Score DT: Score Dual Task; SS-DT: Sky Search Dual Task; SS Motor: Sky Search Motor; TMT: Trail Making Test.

Table 14.2 Mean adjusted scores, F-, p-values, and partial eta-squared values for attention measures across prefrontal and control groups.

		Prefrontal Adj M (SE)	Control Adj M (SE)	F-value	p-value	Partial Eta^2
Selective attention	Digit Span	7.8 (0.5)	10.1 (0.4)	11.9	.001	.16
	Digits forwards	3.8 (0.3)	4.9 (0.2)	13.8	.001	.23
	CNT trial 1: efficiency	4.5 (0.2)	5.0 (0.2)	3.0	.09	.04
	CNT trial 2: efficiency	3.8 (0.2)	4.1 (0.2)	1.2	.30	.02
	TMT:A: time (s)	26.9 (1.9)	24.1 (1.6)	1.3	.30	.02
	TMT:A: errors	0.08 (.05)	0.05 (.04)	0.3	.60	.01
	Sky Search: attention score	5.4 (0.4)	4.5 (0.4)	2.2	.14	.03
Shifting attention	CNT trial 3: efficiency	1.5 (0.1)	1.9 (1.0)	8.3	.01	.12
	CNT trial 4: efficiency	0.9 (0.1)	1.2 (.07)	8.2	.01	.13
	CC: no correct	4.6 (0.3)	5.6 (0.3)	4.8	.03	.08
	TMT:(B − A)/A	1.2 (0.2)	1.2 (0.1)	0.04	.84	.00
	TMT:B: errors+	0.95 (0.2)	0.33 (0.2)	4.1	.05	.06
Divided attention	Score DT: animals correct	8.8 (0.2)	9.5 (0.2)	4.3	.04	.06
	Score DT: games correct	4.8 (0.4)	7.2 (0.4)	18.9	<.001	.23
	Score DT total	13.6 (0.5)	16.6 (0.4)	21.5	>.001	.26
	SS-DT: time/target (s)	6.5 (0.5)	6.4 (0.4)	0.03	1.0	.00
	SS-DT DT: % correct	0.7 (0.04)	0.8 (0.03)	6.3	.01	.09
Processing speed	CNT trial 1: time (s)	25.4 (1.5)	21.0 (1.3)	4.5	.04	.07
	CNT trial 2: time (s)	28.3 (1.8)	27.8 (1.8)	0.04	.84	.00
	CC: s/switch	4.6 (0.2)	4.1 (0.2)	3.1	.09	.05
	SS Motor: time (s)	24.4 (1.2)	21.1 (1.1)	4.2	.05	.06
Behaviour rating inventory of executive function (BRIEF)	Inhibit: T score	62.4 (1.9)	51.8 (2.3)	12.6	.001	.22
	Shift: T score	59.0 (2.4)	51.2 (2.8)	4.5	.04	.09
	Monitor: T score	60.8 (1.9)	49.7 (2.2)	14.4	<.001	.24

CNT: Contingency Naming Test; CC: Creature Counting; Score DT: Score Dual Task; SS-DT: Sky Search Dual Task; SS Motor: Sky Search Motor; TMT: Trail Making Test.

less deviant. Impairments in attention were most evident for children with right-sided pathology. Such results imply that the right prefrontal cortex plays a critical role in the early development of basic attentional skills.

This study then investigated the impact of frontal pathology in comparison to extra-frontal and generalized pathology, in keeping with arguments that cognitive and attention skills may be less differentiated in the developing brain, and thus executive aspects of attention may be less localized following damage to the immature brain, than is seen in similar injuries occurring in adulthood. The sample was divided according to lesion location as follows: frontal pathology ($n = 38$), extra-frontal pathology ($n = 20$), generalized pathology ($n = 21$) and healthy controls ($n = 40$). Using the theoretical framework described by Anderson (2002), these groups were compared on a range of domains including: attentional control, shifting, and divided attention. Contrary to adult studies, there was very little differentiation in attentional processes between frontal and extra-frontal pathology groups. Analysis of the attention profile demonstrated by the frontal lobe group suggests that these children did experience more difficulties than other pathology groups on measures of attentional control, including both inhibitory control and self-regulation. They had trouble adhering to task rules, for tasks involving both verbal and nonverbal components, with performances characterized by rule breaks, poor self-monitoring, and repeated errors. However, in the areas of shifting and divided attention, children with frontal lobe lesions often performed most similarly to controls, with greater deficits observed in association with both extra-frontal and generalized pathology, suggesting that the integrity of the entire brain is necessary for adequate attentional functions in childhood. In other words, cerebral damage in childhood, irrespective of the site of pathology, may render the child vulnerable to a range of attention deficits, which in turn may impact on learning and social interaction.

Attention deficit/hyperactivity disorder, attention, and the frontal lobes

Attention deficit hyperactivity disorder is among one of the most common and well-studied childhood psychiatric disorders. The disorder is characterized by impaired attention, hyperactivity and impulsivity, and has been related to secondary deficits in academic achievement, social functioning and executive dysfunction. While the underlying causes of ADHD have been debated in the past, recent advances in neuroimaging, as well as positive responses to medication, have provided strong support for a neural basis for the disorder (Halperin & Schulz, 2006). There has now been a considerable amount of energy directed towards identifying specific neural substrates for ADHD, however, results are not always consistent. Structural imaging research has identified reductions in brain volume, cerebellar involvement, small corpus callosal regions and subcortical asymmetries as potential candidates to explain ADHD (Baumgardner, Singer, & Denckla, 1996; Castellanos & Tannock, 2002; Filipek et al., 1997; Semrud-Clikeman et al., 2000). However, the most consistent findings document frontal lobe involvement, and disruption to frontal–striatal circuitry and dorso-lateral regions in particular (Filipek et al., 1997; Semrud-Clikeman et al., 2000; Solanto, 2002; Sowell et al., 2003). Functional imaging research supports these findings (Barry, Clarke, & Johnstone, 2003;

Langleben et al., 2001; Spalletta et al., 2001). Providing further support for these findings, recent studies have reported correlations between structural and functional abnormalities in these regions and executive deficits and behavioral problems in ADHD populations (Durston et al., 2003; Rubia, Smith, Brammer, Toone, & Taylor, 2005; Schulz et al., 2004, 2005a, 2005b).

Impairments in attention are considered the key feature of ADHD, with response inhibition the primary deficit (Lajoie, Anderson, Tucker, Robertson, & Manly, 2005; Manly et al., 2001). Theoretical models have suggested that inhibitory dysfunction in ADHD is consistent with the executive dysfunction theory of ADHD developed by Barkley (1994, 1997). According to the model, behavioral inhibition is the primary deficit in ADHD, specifically for the subtypes with hyperactivity (i.e., the predominantly hyperactive-impulsive type and combined type). The model hypothesises that ineffective execution of behavioral inhibition leads to secondary impairments in four domains: (a) working memory; (b) self-regulation of affect-motivation-arousal; (c) internalization of speech; and (d) reconstitution. In turn, these functions interfere with effective self-regulation and adaptive functioning. Barkley also cites excessive and impulsive responding in interpersonal communication, as evidence for these children's inability to delay responding. According to this theory, children with ADHD of these types are capable of performing appropriately if they allow themselves the time to do so. However, they usually fail to inhibit their responses before they have had enough time to assess the task and arrive at the correct response. Thus, the theory accounts for impulsive errors, but does not explain so easily why children with ADHD of these types are often found to be slow and variable in RT tasks.

Others have reported that sustained attention is the component of attention most reliably impaired in ADHD. In support of this view, children exhibiting the disorder are commonly described as having "short attention spans" and being unable to follow through on instructions and tasks. Some researchers have noted, on the basis of overall performance, that children with ADHD are unable to mobilize the effort required to meet the demands of sustained attention tasks (Douglas & Peters, 1979; Douglas, 1983; Loge, Staton, & Beatty, 1990; Sykes, Douglas, & Morgenstern, 1973). Others have found a greater decrement in the performance of ADHD samples over time (Hooks, Milich, & Lorch, 1994; Seidel & Joshcko, 1990). However, there is also a body of evidence which has been unable to document any evidence of sustained attention deficits in ADHD samples (Michael, Klorman, Salzman, Borgstedt, & Dainer, 1981; Prior, Freethy, & Geffen, 1985; van der Meere & Sergeant, 1988).

To gain further understanding of attentional impairments in children with ADHD, we recently conducted a study in our lab (Anderson et al., 2006), where we used a modified version of the CPT paradigm (see Figure 14.6) and compared attentional profiles of children with ADHD ($n = 27$) to those of children with acquired conditions impacting on the CNS: (a) moderate traumatic brain injury (TBI: $n = 41$); (b) acute lymphoblastic leukemia (ALL: $n = 31$); and (c) insulin dependent diabetes mellitus (IDDM: $n = 39$). A healthy control group ($n = 46$) was also examined. Groups were compared on measures of sustained attention, selective attention, and response inhibition. In addition, measures of performance variability and deterioration, and processing speed were examined. Results showed that children with ADHD exhibited global and severe attentional impairments in contrast to all other groups.

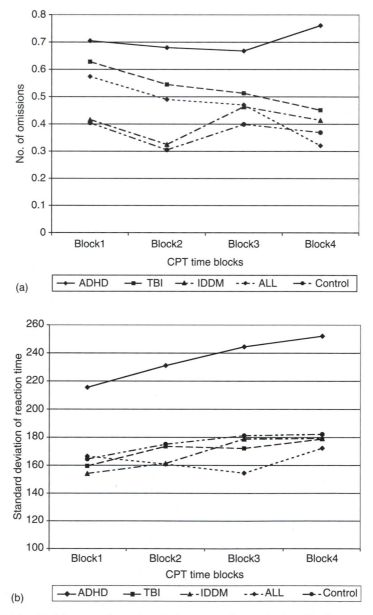

Figure 14.6 (a) Mean number of omission errors for each time block across groups. (b) Standard deviation of reaction times for each time block across groups.

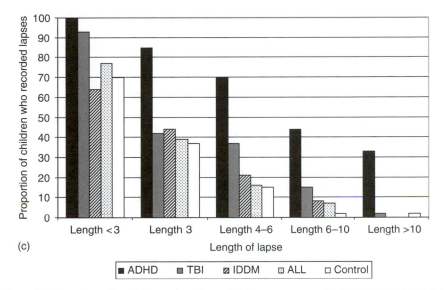

Figure 14.6 (continued)   (c) Length of lapse (LAP) across groups for total CPT task. LAP is defined as two or more consecutive responses from any of the following categories: incorrect response (omission, commission), delayed or "no" response (>1500 ms), or impulsive response (<200 ms). ADHD = attention deficit hyperactivity disorder; TBI = traumatic brain injury; IDDM = insulin dependent diabetes mellitus; ALL = acute lymphoblastic leukemia.

More recently Manly et al. (2001) have reported on the attentional profiles of 24 boys recently diagnosed with ADHD, but not yet on medication. Using the TEA-Ch, they identified deficits in executive aspects of attention for this group, including reduced sustained attention and attentional control, consistent with a number of previous reports (Douglas, 1972; Swanson et al., 1998). In contrast, and again in keeping with previous findings, selective attention skills were largely intact (Douglas & Peters, 1979; Hooks et al., 1994; van der Meere & Sergeant, 1988).

Very similar findings have recently been reported in a study from our laboratory. Using a range of clinical and experimental measures, Wu et al. (2002) and Micallef, Anderson, Anderson, Robertson, and Manly (2001) have compared attentional skills in a sample of children with pure ADHD to children with ADHD and learning disability (LD) and those with pure LD. These authors replicated the findings of Manly et al. (2001), documenting deficits in attentional control and sustained attention for their ADHD sample. In contrast, children with comorbid LD exhibited impaired selective attention and attentional capacity, suggesting that, when examining the specific impact of ADHD, it may be important to exclude children with comorbidities, which may contaminate findings.

Conclusions

Attentional skills are critical to normal development. Research shows that these skills develop through infancy and childhood, only reaching maturity during late adolescence. There continues to be a debate regarding terminology and conceptualization of this complex construct; however, there is general agreement that the attention system is multicomponent, with both lower- and higher-order components important for efficient function. Divided attention and shifting attention may be seen as the "executive" elements of the system, with several converging lines of evidence suggesting an important role for the frontal lobes, and prefrontal cortex in particular, in subsuming these particular skills.

References

Ackerly, S., & Benton, A. (1948). Report of a case of bilateral frontal lobe defect. *Association for Research on Nervous and Mental Disorders*, *27*, 479–504.

Anderson, P. (2002). Assessment and development of executive function (EF) during childhood. *Child Neuropsychology*, *8*(2), 71–82.

Anderson, P., Anderson, V., & Lajoie, G. (1996). Standardization of the tower of London test. *The Clinical Neuropsychologist*, *10*, 54–65.

Anderson, S., Damasio, H., Tranel, D., & Damasio, A. (2000). Long-term sequelae of prefrontal cortex damage acquired in early childhood. *Developmental Neuropsychology*, *18*, 281–296.

Anderson, V. (1988). Recovery of function in children: The myth of cerebral plasticity. In M. Matheson & H. Newman (Eds.), *Brain impairment. Proceedings from the thirteenth annual brain impairment conference* (pp. 223–247). Sydney: ASSBI.

Anderson, V. (1998). Assessing executive functions in children: Biological, psychological, and developmental considerations. *Neuropsychological Rehabilitation*, *8*, 319–349.

Anderson, V., Anderson, P., & Anderson, D. (2006). Comparing attention skills in children with acquired and developmental disorders. *Journal of the International Neuropsychological Society*, *12*, 519–531.

Anderson, V., Anderson, P., Northam, E., Jacobs, R., & Catroppa, C. (2001). Development of executive functions through late childhood and adolescence in an Australian sample. *Developmental Neuropsychology*, *20*, 385–406.

Anderson, V., Catroppa, C., Morse, S., Haritou, F., & Rosenfeld, J. (2005). Attention skills two years after traumatic brain injury in early childhood. *Brain Injury*, *19*, 699–710.

Anderson, V., Fenwick, T., Robertson, I., & Manly, T. (1998). Attentional skills following traumatic brain injury in children: A componential analysis. *Brain Injury*, *12*, 937–949.

Anderson, V., Godber, T., Smibert, E., Weiskop, S., & Ekert, H. (2004). Impairments of attention following treatment with cranial radiation and chemotherapy with children. *Journal of Clinical and Experimental Neuropsychology*, *26*, 684–697.

Anderson, V., Jacobs, R., & Harvey, A. H. (2005). Prefrontal lesions and attentional skills in childhood. *Journal of the International Neuropsychological Society*, *11*, 817–831.

Anderson, V., Levin, H., & Jacobs, R. (2002). Developmental and acquired lesions of the frontal lobes in children: Neuropsychological implications. In D. Stuss & R. Knight (Eds.), *Principles of frontal lobe function* (pp. 504–527). New York: Oxford University Press.

Anderson, V., & Moore, C. (1995). Age at injury as a predictor of outcome following pediatric head injury. *Child Neuropsychology*, *1*, 187–202.

Anderson, V., & Pentland, L. (1998). Attention deficit following paediatric head injury. *Neuropsychological Rehabilitation*, *8*, 283–300.

Anderson, V., Smibert, E., Godber, T., & Ekert, H. (1994). Intellectual, educational and behavioural sequelae following cranial irradiation and chemotherapy. *Archives of Disease in Childhood*, *70*, 476–483.

August, G. J., & Garfinkel, B. D. (1990). Comorbidity of ADHD and reading disability among clinic referred children. *Journal of Abnormal Child Psychology*, *18*, 29–45.

Bakay Pragay, E., Mirsky, A. F., & Nakamura, R. K. (1987). Attention-related unit activity in the frontal association cortex during a go/no go discrimination task. *Experimental Neurology*, *96*, 481–500.

Bakay Pragay, E., Mirsky, A. F., Fullerton, B. C., Oshima, H. I., & Arnold, S. W. (1975). Effect of electrical stimulation of the brain on visually controlled (attentive) behaviour in the *Macaca mulatta*. *Experimental Neurology*, *49*, 203–220.

Barkley, R. (1990). *ADHD: A Handbook of Diagnosis and Treatment*. New York: Guilford Press.

Barkley, R. A. (1994). Impaired delayed responding: A unified theory of attention deficit disorder. In D. K. Routh (Ed.), *Disruptive behaviour disorders: Essays in honour of Herbert Quay* (pp. 11–57). New York: Plenum.

Barkley, R. A. (1997). Behavioural inhibition, sustained attention, and executive functions: Constructing a unified theory of ADHD. *Psychological Bulletin*, *121*, 65–94.

Barkley, R. A. (2000). Genetics of childhood disorders: XVII, ADHD, Part 1, The executive functions and ADHD. *Journal of the American Academy of Child and Adolescent Psychiatry*, *39*, 1064–1068.

Barry, R. J., Clarke, A., & Johnstone, S. (2003). A review of electrophysiology in attention deficit/hyperactivity disorder: I, qualitative and quantitative electroencephalography. *Clinical Neurophysiology*, *114*, 171–183.

Baumgardner, T., Singer, H., & Denckla, M. (1996). Corpus callosum morphology in children with Tourette syndrome and attention deficit hyperactivity disorder. *Neurology*, *47*, 477–482.

Betts, J., McKay, J., Maruff, P., & Anderson, V. (2006). The development of sustained attention in children: The effect of age and task load. *Child Neuropsychology*, *12*, 205–222.

Brouwers, P., Riccardi, R., Fedio, R., & Poplack, D. (1985). Long-term neuropsychological sequelae of childhood leukemia: Correlation with CT brain scan abnormalities. *Journal of Pediatrics*, *106*, 723–728.

Casey, B., Gordon, C., Mannheim, G., & Rumsey, J. (1993). Dysfunctional attention in autistic savants. *Journal of Clinical and Experimental Neuropsychology*, *15*, 933–946.

Castellanos, F. X., & Tannock, R. (2002). Neuroscience of attention-deficit/hyperactivity disorder: The search for endophenotypes. *Nature Reviews Neuroscience*, *3*, 617–628.

Castellanos, F. X., Giedd, J. N., Berquin, P. C., Walter, J. M., Sharp, W., Tran, T. et al. (2001). Quantitative brain magnetic resonance imaging in girls with attention-deficit/hyperactivity disorder. *Archives of General Psychiatry*, *58*, 289–295.

Catroppa, C., & Anderson, V. (1999). Attention in the acute phase following pediatric head injury. *Child Neuropsychology*, *5*, 251–265.

Catroppa, C., & Anderson, V. (2003). Children's attentional skills two years post-TBI. *Developmental Neuropsychology*, *23*, 359–373.

Catroppa, C., & Anderson, V. (2005). A prospective study of the recovery of attention from acute to 2 years post pediatric traumatic brain injury. *Journal of the International Neuropsychological Society*, *11*, 84–98.

Catroppa, C., Anderson, V., & Stargatt, R. (1999). A prospective analysis of the recovery of attention following pediatric head injury. *Journal of the International Neuropsychological Society*, *5*, 48–57.

Chelune, G. J., & Baer, R. A. (1986). Developmental norms for the Wisconsin Card Sorting Test. *Journal of Clinical and Experimental Neuropsychology*, *8*, 219–228.

Chugani, H. T., Phelps, M. E., & Mazziotta, J. C. (1987). Positron emission tomography study of human brain functional development. *Annals of Neurology*, *22*, 487–497.

Cooley, E. L., & Morris, R. D. (1990). Attention in children: A neuropsychologically based model for assessment. *Developmental Neuropsychology, 6*, 239–274.

CogState Ltd. (2001). *A scientifically validated measure of cognitive performance*. Melbourne, Australia: CogState Ltd.

Dennis, M. (1989). Language and the young damaged brain. In T. Boll & B. K. Bryant (Eds.), *Clinical neuropsychology and brain function: Research, measurement and practice* (pp. 85–124). Washington: American Psychological Association.

Dennis, M., Wilkinson, M., Koski, L., & Humphreys, R. P. (1995). Attention deficits in the long term after childhood head injury. In: S.H. Broman & M.E. Michel (Eds.), *Traumatic head injury in children*. New York: Oxford University Press.

Diamond, A. (1985). Development of the ability to use recall to guide action, as indicated by the infant's performance on A-not-B. *Child Development, 56*, 868–883.

Diamond, A. (2002). Normal development of prefrontal cortex from birth to young adulthood: Cognitive functions, anatomy, and biochemistry. In D. T. Stuss & R. T. Knight (Eds.), *Principles of frontal lobe function* (pp. 466–503). New York: Oxford University Press.

Diamond, A., & Doar, B. (1989). The performance of human infants on a measure of frontal cortex function, the delayed response task. *Developmental Psychobiology, 22*, 271–294.

Diamond, A., & Taylor, C. (1996). Development of an aspect of executive control: Devcelopment of the abilities to remember what I said and to "do as I say not as I do." *Developmental Psychobiology, 29*, 315–334.

Douglas, V. I. (1972). Stop, look and listen: The problem of sustained attention and impulse control in hyperactive and normal children. *Canadian Journal of Behavioural Science, 4*, 259–281.

Douglas, V. I. (1983). Attentional and cognitive problems. In M. Rutter (Ed.), *Developmental neuropsychiatry* (pp. 280–329). New York: Guilford Press.

Douglas, V. I., & Peters, K. G. (1979). Towards a clearer definition of the attention deficit of hyperactive children. In G. A. Hale & M. Lewis (Eds.), *Attention and development of cognitive skills* (pp. 173–248). New York: Plenum.

Dove, A., Pollman, S., Schubert, T., Wiggins, C., & van Cramon, D. (2000). Prefrontal cortex activation in task switching: an event-related fMRI study. *Cognitive Brain Research, 9*, 103–109.

Drechsler, R., Brandeis, D., Foldenyi, M., Imhof, K., & Steinhausen, H. (2005). The course of neurophysiological functions in children with attention deficit hyperactivity disorder from late childhood to early adolescence. *Journal of Child Psychology and Psychiatry, 46*, 824–836.

Durston, S., Tottenham, N., Thomas, K., Davidson, M., Eigsti, I., & Yang, Y. (2003). Differential patterns of striatal activation in young children with and without ADHD. *Biological Psychiatry, 53*, 871–878.

Eslinger, P., & Biddle, K. (2000). Adolescent neuropsychological development after early right prefrontal cortex damage. *Developmental Neuropsychology, 18*, 297–330.

Eslinger, P., Biddle, K., & Grattan, L. (1997). Cognitive and social development in children with prefrontal cortex lesions. In N. Krasnegor, G. Lyon, & P. Goldman-Rakic (Eds.), *Development of the prefrontal cortex: Evolution, neurology, and behavior* (pp. 295–336). Baltimore: Brookes.

Eslinger, P., Biddle, K., Pennington, B., & Page, R. (1999). Cognitive and behavioral development up to 4 years after early right frontal lobe lesion. *Developmental Neuropsychology, 15*, 157–191.

Eslinger, P., Grattan, L., Damasio, H., & Damasio, A. (1992). Developmental consequences of childhood frontal lobe damage. *Archives of Neurology, 49*, 764–769.

Espy, K. A. (1997). The Shape school: Assessing executive function in preschool children. *Developmental Neuropsychology*, *13*(4), 495–499.

Espy, K. A., Kaufmann, P. M., McDiarmid, M. D., & Glisky, M. L. (1999). Executive functioning in preschool children: Performance on A-not-B and other delayed response format tasks. *Brain and Cognition*, *41*, 178–199.

Ewing-Cobbs, L., Fletcher, J., Levin, H., Francis, D., Davidson, K., & Miner, M. (1997). Longitudinal neuropsychological outcome in infants and preschoolers with traumatic brain injury. *Journal of the International Neuropsychological Society*, *3*, 581–591.

Ewing-Cobbs, L., Prasad, M., Fletcher, J. M., Levin, H. S., Miner, E., & Eisenberg, H. (1998). Attention after pediatric traumatic brain injury: A multidimensional assessment. *Child Neuropsychology*, *4*, 35–48.

Fenwick, T., & Anderson, V. (1999). Impairments of attention following childhood traumatic brain injury. *Child Neuropsychology*, *5*, 213–223.

Filipek, P. A., Semrud-Clikeman, M., Steingard, R. J., Renshaw, P. F., Kennedy, D. N., & Biederman, J. (1997). Volumetric MRI analysis comparing subjects having attention-deficit/hyperactivity disorder with normal controls. *Neurology*, *48*, 589–601.

Garth, J., Anderson, V., & Wrennall, J. (1997). Executive functions following moderate to severe frontal lobe injury: Impact of injury and age at injury. *Pediatric Rehabilitation*, *1*, 99–108.

Gerardi-Caulton, G. (2000). Sensitivity to spatial conflict and the development of self-regulation in children 24–36 months of age. *Developmental Science*, *3*, 294–298.

Godefroy, O., Lhullier, C., & Rousseaux, M. (1996). Non-spatial disorders in patients with frontal or posterior brain damage. *Brain*, *119*, 191–202.

Godefroy, O., & Rousseaux, M. (1996). Divided and focussed attention in patients with lesion of the prefrontal cortex. *Brain and Cognition*, *30*, 155–174.

Gogtay, N., Giedd, J., Lusk, L., Hayashi, K., Greenstein, D., Vaituzis, C. et al. (2004). Dynamic mapping of human cortical development during childhood and early adulthood. *Proceedings of the National Academy of Science*, *101*, 8174–8179.

Grattan, L. M., Bloomer, R. H., Archambault, F. X., & Eslinger, P. J. (1994). Cognitive flexibility and empathy after frontal lobe lesion. *Neuropsychiatry, Neuropsychology, and Behavioral Neurology*, *7*, 251–259.

Gronwall, D., Wrightson, P., & McGinn, V. (1997). Effect of mild head injury during the preschool years. *Journal of the International Neuropsychological Society*, *3*, 592–597.

Halperin, J. M. (1991). The clinical assessment of attention. *International Journal of Neuroscience*, *58*, 171–182.

Halperin, J. M., & Schulz, K. (2006). Revisiting the role of the prefrontal cortex in the pathophysiology of attention deficit/hyperactivity disorder. *Psychological Bulletin*, *132*, 560–581.

Heilman, K., Voeller, K., & Nadeau, S. (1991). A possible pathophysiologic substrate of attention deficit hyperactivity disorder. *Journal of Child Neurology*, *6*(suppl.), 76–81.

Hooks, K., Milich, R., & Lorch, E. (1994). Sustained and selective attention in boys with attention deficit hyperactivity disorder. *Journal of Clinical Child Psychology*, *23*, 69–77.

Hudspeth, W., & Pribram, K. (1990). Stages of brain and cognitive maturation. *Journal of Educational Psychology*, *82*, 881–884.

James, W. (1890). *The principles of psychology*. New York: Henry Holt.

Kail, R. (1986). Sources of age differences in speed of processing. *Child Development*, *57*, 969–987.

Kail, R. (1988). Developmental processes for speed of cognitive processes. *Journal of Experimental Child Psychology*, *45*, 339–364.

Kaufmann, P., Fletcher, J., Levin, H., Miner, M., & Ewing-Cobbs, L. (1993). Attention disturbance after pediatric closed head injury. *Journal of Child Neurology*, *8*, 348–353.

Kinsbourne, M. (1996). Models of consciousness: Serial and parallel in the brain. In M. Gazzaniga (Ed.), *The cognitive neurosciences*. Cambridge, MA: MIT Press.

Kirk, U. (1985). Hemispheric contributions to the development of graphic skills. In C. Best (Ed.), *Hemispheric function and collaboration in the child* (pp. 193–228). New York: Academic Press.

Klenberg, L., Korkman, M., & Lahti-Nuuttila, P. (2001). Differential development of attention and executive functions in 3- to 12-year-old Finnish children. *Developmental Neuropsychology, 20*(1), 407–428.

Klin, A., Sparrow, S., Volkman, F., Cicchetti, D., & Rourke, B. (1995) Asperger syndrome. In B. Rourke (Ed.), *Syndrome of non-verbal learning disabilities* (pp. 93–119). New York: Guilford.

Klingberg, T., Vaidya, C. J., Gabrieli, J. D., Moseley, M. E., & Hedehus, M. (1999). Myelination and organization of the frontal white matter in children: A diffusion tensor MRI study. *Neuroreport, 10*, 2817–2821.

Knight, R., & Stuss, D. (2002). Prefrontal cortex: The present and the future. In D. Stuss & R. Knight (Eds.), *Principles of frontal lobe function* (pp. 573–59). New York: Oxford University Press.

Kochanska, G., Murray, K., & Harlan, E. (2000). Effortful control in early childhood: Continuity and change, antecedents, and implications for social development. *Developmental Psychology, 36*, 220–232.

Lajoie, G., Anderson, V., Tucker, A., Robertson, I., & Manly, T. (2005). Effects of methylphenidate on attention skills in children with attention deficit/hyperactivity disorder. *Brain Impairment, 6*, 21–32.

Lane, D. M. (1978). Developmental changes in attention deployment skills. *Journal of Experimental Child Psychology, 28*, 16–29.

Lane, D. M., & Pearson, D. A. (1982). The development of selective attention. *Merrill-Palmer Quarterly, 28*, 317–337.

Lang, W., Athanasopoulous, O., & Anderson, V. (1998). Do attentional profiles differ across developmental disorders. *Journal of the International Neuropsychological Society, 4*, 221.

Langleben, D., Austin, G., Krikorian, G., Ridlehuber, H., Goris, M., & Strauss, H. (2001). Interhemispheric asymmetry of regional cerebral blood flow in prepubescent boys with attention deficit hyperactivity disorder. *Nuclear Medicine Cummunications, 22*, 1333–1340.

Levin, H., Song, J., Scheibel, R., Fletcher, J., Harward, H., Lilly, M. et al. (1997). Concept formation and problem solving following closed head injury in children. *Journal of the International Neuropsychological Society, 3*, 598–607.

Loge, D. V., Staton, R. D., & Beatty, W. W. (1990). Performance of children with ADHD on tests sensitive to frontal lobe dysfunction. *Journal of the American Academy of Child and Adolescent Psychiatry, 29*, 540–545.

Luria, A. R. (1973). *The working brain*. New York: Basic Books.

McKay, K., Halperin, J., Schwartz, S., & Sharma, V. (1994). Developmental analysis of three aspects of information processing: Sustained attention, selective attention, and response organization. *Developmental Neuropsychology, 10*, 121–132.

Manly, T., Anderson, V., Nimmo-Smith, I., Turner, A., Watson, P., & Robertson, I. (2001). The differential assessment of children's attention: The Test of Everyday Attention for Children (TEA-Ch): Normative sample and ADHD performance. *Journal of Child Psychology and Psychiatry, 42*, 1065–1087.

Manly, T., Robertson, I. H., Anderson, C., & Nimmo-Smith, I. (1999). *TEA-CH: The test of everyday attention for children*. Bury St Edmunds, UK: Thames Valley Test Company.

Marlowe, W. (1992). The impact of a right pre-frontal lesion on the developing brain. *Brain and Cognition, 20,* 205–213.

Mateer, C. A., & Williams, D. (1991) Effects of frontal lobe injury in childhood. *Developmental Neuropsychology, 7,* 69–86.

Mecklinger, A., von Cramon, D., Springer, A., & Matthes-von Cramon, G. (1999). Executive control functions in task switching: Evidence from brain injured patients. *Journal of Clinical and Experimental Neuropsychology, 21,* 606–619.

Mesulam, M. (1981). A cortical network for directed attention on unilateral neglect. *Annals of Neurology, 10,* 309–325.

Mesulam, M. (1985). Attention, confusional states and neglect. In M. M. Mesulam (Ed.), *Principles of behavioural neurology* (pp. 125–168). Philadelphia: F.A. Davis Company.

Micallef, S., Anderson, J., Anderson, V., Robertson, I., & Manly, T. (2001). Sustained and selective attention in children with attention deficit/hyperactivity disorder and specific learning disabilities. *Clinical Neuropsychological Assessment, 2,* 1–23.

Michael, R. M., Klorman, R., Salzman, L. F., Borgstedt, A. D., & Dainer, K. B. (1981). Normalizing effects of methylphenidate on hyperactive children's vigilance performance and evoked potentials. *Psychophysiology, 18,* 665–677.

Mirsky, A. F. (1996). Disorders of attention: A neuropsychological perspective. In G. Lyon & N. Krasnegor (Eds.), *Attention, memory and executive function* (pp. 71–95). Baltimore: Paul H. Brookes Publishing.

Mirsky, A. F., Anthony, B. J., Duncan, C. C., Ahearn, M. B., & Kellam, D. G. (1991). Analysis of the elements of attention: A neuropsychological approach. *Neuropsychology Review, 2,* 109–145.

Murray, R., Shum, D., & McFarland, K. (1992) Attentional deficits in head-injured children: An information processing analysis. *Brain and Cognition, 18,* 99–115.

Northam, E., Anderson, P., Werther, G., Warne, G., Adler, R., & Andrewes, D. (1998). Neuropsychological complications of insulin dependent diabetes in children two years after disease onset. *Diabetes Care, 21,* 379–384.

Owen, A. M., Roberts, A. C., Polkey, C. E., Sahakian, B. J., & Robbins, T. W. (1991). Extra-dimensional versus intra-dimensional set shifting performance following frontal lobe excisions, temporal lobe excisions or amygdalo-hippocampectomy in man. *Neuropsychologia, 29,* 993–1006.

Pentland, L., Todd, J., & Anderson, V. (1998). The impact of head injury on planning ability in adolescence: A functional analysis. *Neuropsychological Rehabilitation, 8,* 301–317.

Ponsford, J., & Kinsella, G. (1992). Attentional deficits following closed head injury. *Journal of Clinical and Experimental Neuropsychology, 14,* 822–838.

Posner, M. (1988). Structures and functions of selective attention. In T. Boll & B. K. Bryant (Eds.), *Clinical neuropsychology and brain function: Research, measurement and Practice* (pp. 173–202). Washington: American Psychological Association.

Posner, M. I., & Petersen, S. E. (1990). The attention system of the human brain. *Annual Review of Neuroscience, 13,* 25–42.

Prior, M., Freethy, L., & Geffen, G. (1985). Auditory attentional abilities in hyperactive children. *Journal of Child Psychology and Psychiatry, 26,* 289–304.

Ray, C. L., Mirsky, A. F., & Bakay Pragay, E. (1982). Functional analysis of attention-related unit activity in the reticular formation of the monkey. *Experimental Neurology, 77,* 544–562.

Rebok, G., Smith, C., Pascualvaca, D., Mirsky, A., Anthony, B., & Kellam, S. (1997). Developmental changes in attentional performance in urban children from eight to thirteen years. *Child Neuropsychology, 3,* 47–60.

Robertson, I. (1999). The rehabilitation of attention. In D. Stuss, G. Winocur, & I. Robertson (Eds.), *Cognitive neurorehabilitation* (pp. 302–313). Cambridge, UK: Cambridge University Press.

Robertson, I., Ward, A., Ridgeway, V., & Nimmo-Smith, I. (1994). *Test of everyday attention.* Bury St Edmunds, UK: Thames Valley Test Company.

Rosvold, H. E., Mirsky, A. F., Sarason, I., Bransome, E. D., & Beck, L. H. (1956). A continuous performance test of brain damage. *Journal of Consulting Psychology, 20,* 343–350.

Rubia, K., Overmeyer, S., Taylor, R., Brammer, M., Williams, S., & Simmons, A. (1999). Hypofrontality in attention deficit hyperactivity disorder during higher-order motor control: A study with functional MRI. *American Journal of Psychiatry, 156,* 891–896.

Rubia, K., Smith, A., Brammer, M., Toone, B., & Taylor, E. (2005). Abnormal brain activation during inhibition and error detection in medication-naïve adolescents with ADHD. *American Journal of Psychiatry, 162,* 1067–1075.

Ruff, H., & Rothbart, M. (1996). *Attention in early development: Themes and variations.* New York: Oxford University Press.

Schulz, K., Fan, J., Tang, C., Newcorn, G., Buchsbaum, M., Cheung, A. et al. (2004). Response inhibition in adolescents diagnosed with attention deficit/hyperactivity disorder during childhood: An event-related fMRI study. *American Journal of Psychiatry, 161,* 1150–1165.

Schulz, K., Newcorn, G., Fan, J., Tang, C., & Halparin, J. (2005a). Brain activation gradients in ventrolateral prefrontal cortex related to persistence of ADHD in adolescent boys. *Journal of the American Academy of Child & Adolescent Psychiatry, 44,* 47–54.

Schulz, K., Tang, C., Fan, J., Marks, D., Cheung, A., Newcorn, J. et al. (2005b). Differential prefrontal cortex activation during inhibitory control in adolescents with and without childhood ADHD. *Neuropsychology, 19,* 390–402.

Seidel, W. T., & Joshcko, M. (1990). Evidence of difficulties in sustained attention in children with ADHD. *Journal of Abnormal Child Psychology, 18,* 217–229.

Semrud-Clikeman, M., Steingard, R., Filipek, P., Biederman, J., Bekken, K., & Renshaw, P. (2000). Using MRI to examine brain–behavior relationships in males with attention deficit hyperactivity disorder. *Journal of the American Academy of Child and Adolescent Psychiatry, 39,* 477–484.

Shepp, B. E., Barrett, S. E., & Kolbet, L. I. (1987). The development of selective attention: Holistic perception versus resource allocation. *Journal of Experimental Child Psychology, 43,* 159–180.

Shiffrin, R. M. (1988). Attention. In R. C. Atkinson, R. J. Herrnstein, G. Lindzey, & R. D. Luce (Eds.), *Stevens' handbook of experimental psychology, 2nd Edition* (pp. 739–811). New York: Wiley.

Shimamura, A. (1995). Memory and frontal lobe function. In M. Gazzaniga (Ed.), *The cognitive neurosciences* (pp. 803–813). Cambridge: MIT Press.

Smidt, D., Jacobs, R., & Anderson, V. (2004). The object classification task for children (OCTC): A measure of concept generation and mental flexibility in early childhood. *Developmental Neuropsychology, 26,* 385–402.

Smith, E., & Jonides, J. (1999). Storage and executive processes in the frontal lobes. *Science, 282,* 1657–1661.

Solanto, M. (2002). Dopamine dysfunction in ADHD: Integrating clinical and neuroscience research. *Brain Behavior Research, 130,* 65–71.

Sowell, E., Thompson, P., Welcome, S., Henkenius, A., Toga, A., & Peteresen, B. (2003). Cortical abnormalities in children and adolescents with attention deficit/hyperactivity disorder. *Lancet, 362,* 1699–1707.

Spalletta, G., Pasini, A., Pau, F., Guido, G., Menghini, L., & Caltagirone, C. (2001). Prefrontal blood flow dysregulation in drug naïve ADHD children without structural abnormalities. *Journal of Neural Transmission, 108*, 1203–1216.

Stuss, D. (2006). Frontal lobes and attention: Processes and networks, fractionation and integration. *Journal of the International Neuropsychological Society, 12*, 261–271.

Stuss, D., Alexander, M., Floden, D., Binns, M., Levine, B., McIntosh, A. R. et al. (2002). Fractionation and localization of distinct frontal lobe processes: Evidence from focal lesions in humans. In D. Stuss & R. Knight (Eds.), *Principles of frontal lobe function* (pp. 392–407). New York: Oxford University Press.

Stuss, D., Alexander, M., Palumbo, C., Buckle, L., Sater, L., & Pogue, J. (1994). Organizational strategies of patients with unilateral or bilateral frontal lobe injury in word list learning tasks. *Neuropsychology, 8*, 355–373.

Stuss, D., Gallup, G., & Alexander, M. (2001). The frontal lobes are necessary for 'theory of mind.' *Brain, 124*, 279–286.

Stuss, D. T., Levine, B., Alexander, M., Hong, J., Palumbo, C., Hamer, L. et al. (2000). Wisconsin Card Sorting Test performance in patients with focal frontal and posterior brain damage: Effects of lesion location and test structure on separable cognitive processes. *Neuropsychologia, 38*, 388–402.

Stuss, D. T., Shallice, T., Alexander, M., & Picton, T. (1995). A multidisciplinary approach to anterior attentional functions. *Annals of the New York Academy of Science, 769*, 191–211.

Stuss, D. T., Toth, J. P., Franchi, D., Alexander, M., Tipper, S., & Craik, F. (1999). Dissociation of attentional processes in patients with focal frontal and posterior lesions. *Neuropsychologia, 37*, 1005–1027.

Swanson, J., Posner, M., Cantwell, D., Wigal, S., Crinella, F., Filipek, P. et al. (1998). Attention-deficit/hyperactivity disorder: Symptom domains, cognitive processes, and neural networks. In R. Parasuraman (Ed.), *The attentive brain* (pp. 445–460). Cambridge, MA: MIT Press.

Sykes, D., Douglas, V. I., & Morgenstern, G. (1973). Sustained attention in hyperactive children. *Journal of Child Psychology and Psychiatry, 14*, 213–220.

Thatcher, R. W. (1991). Maturation of the human frontal lobes. Physiological evidence for staging. *Developmental Neuropsychology, 7*, 397–419.

Timmermans, S. R., & Christensen, B. (1991). The measurement of attention deficits in TBI children and adolescents. *Cognitive Rehabilitation, 9*(4), 26–31.

Todd, J., Anderson, V., & Lawrence, J. (1996). Planning skills in head injured adolescents and their peers. *Neuropsychological Rehabilitation, 6*, 81–99.

van der Meere, J. J., & Sergeant, J. A. (1988). Controlled processing and vigilance in hyperactivity: Time will tell. *Journal of Abnormal Child Psychology, 16*, 641–655.

van Zomeren, A. H., & Brouwer, W. (1994). *Clinical neuropsychology of attention.* New York: Oxford University Press.

Walsh, K. W. (1978). *Neuropsychology: A clinical approach.* New York: Churchill Livingstone.

Walsh, K. W. (1985). *Understanding brain damage: A primer of neuropsychological evaluation.* New York: Churchill Livingston.

Wainwright-Sharp, J., & Bryson, S. (1993). Visual orienting deficits in high functioning people with autism. *Journal of Autism and Developmental Disorders, 23*, 1–13.

Wilkins, A., Shallice, T., & McCarthy, R. (1987). Frontal lesions and sustained attention. *Neuropsychologia, 25*, 359–365.

Willmott, C., Anderson, V., & Anderson, P. (2000). Attention following pediatric head injury: A developmental perspective. *Developmental Neuropsychology, 17*, 361–379.

Woods, D. L., & Knight, R. T. (1986). Electrophysiological evidence of increased distractibility after dorsolateral prefrontal lesions. *Neurology, 36*, 212–216.

Wu, K., Anderson, V., & Castiello, U. (2002). Neuropsychological evaluation of deficits in executive functioning for ADHD children with or without LD. *Developmental Neuropsychology, 22,* 501–531.

Yeates, K., & Bornstein, R. (1994). Attention deficit disorder and neuropsychological functioning in children with Tourette's syndrome. *Neuropsychology, 8,* 65–74.

15　Frontotemporal dementia: Correlations between pathology and function

Julie Snowden

Contents

Introduction

A striking feature of degenerative diseases of the brain, which affect people in middle and old age, is that they can be remarkably circumscribed both in terms of the distribution of brain atrophy and the resulting changes in mental function. As a consequence of this selectivity, degenerative disorders can represent a natural model for assisting understanding of brain function.

Frontotemporal dementia (FTD) is the prototypical and most common "focal" dementia syndrome. It is characterized by profound character change and alteration in a person's social conduct and is associated with a range of executive impairments. In keeping with the clinical picture, the degenerative process preferentially involves the frontal lobes and anterior parts of the temporal lobes, more posterior parts of the brain remaining relatively unaffected even in advanced disease. The precise distribution of pathology within the anterior hemispheres differs across individual patients and reflects phenotypic variations within FTD. This chapter describes the characteristics of this intriguing and challenging disorder and examines the relationship of behavioral and cognitive features to the underlying structural changes in the brain.

Demographic features

FTD is an early onset dementia, affecting people most commonly in middle age. Symptoms typically begin between the ages of 45 and 65, although there are exceptions. The youngest recorded onset in a pathologically confirmed case is 21 years (Snowden, Neary, & Mann, 2004). Occasionally, initial symptoms may present in the elderly. The onset and progression of illness is insidious, with death occurring between 2 and 20 years following onset of symptoms. The high variability in duration of disease is influenced by patients' physical well-being. Many patients with FTD remain physically well, with few neurological signs. However, Parkinsonian features of akinesia and rigidity may develop particularly in the later stages. Moreover, a minority of patients with established FTD develops the physical signs of motor neuron disease/amyotrophic lateral sclerosis (MND/ALS) (Neary et al., 1990). Patients who remain physically well typically have a prolonged course, whereas those who develop neurological abnormalities, which compromise their level of physical activity, have an attenuated course. A short course is particularly evident in the minority of FTD patients with MND/ALS (Hodges, Davies, Xuereb, Kril, & Halliday, 2003; Neary et al.). FTD is strongly a familial disorder. A positive family history of a similar dementing illness in a first-degree relative is recorded in about 40% of cases. There are no obvious environmental determinants and patients come from a wide variety of cultural, socioeconomic, and geographic backgrounds. Men and women are affected with comparable frequency (Rosso et al., 2003). In people presenting with a dementing illness before the age of 65, the frequency of occurrence of FTD compared to Alzheimer's disease is about 1:3.

Clinical presentation

Personality change and breakdown in social conduct dominate the clinical presentation and are core features of current diagnostic criteria (Gustafson, 1987; Neary, Snowden, Northen, & Goulding, 1988, Neary et al., 1998; Snowden, Neary, & Mann, 1996). From being responsible citizens, people with FTD become uncaring and lacking in concern, leading to neglect of domestic and occupational responsibilities and breakdown in interpersonal relationships. Because of the insidious evolution the precise onset of disease is difficult to determine. Nevertheless, particular events may impress themselves sufficiently on the patient's family that they lead to a realization that something is seriously wrong, and precipitate medical referral. For example, Patient A, formerly a conscientious and respected employee, was dismissed from his job as an electrician because he acted the fool, while working at great height, thereby endangering the lives of himself and his colleagues. He put on a monkey's mask in order to amuse his colleagues and placed a bucket on his head. Patient B incurred huge debts by making unnecessary and extravagant purchases. He purchased a caravan even though the family had no car capable of pulling it and had no inclination to take a caravanning holiday. Patient C's husband was perturbed to find, on returning home one day, his wife sitting in the car in the driveway. She had returned from a shopping expedition several hours earlier, but had remained in the car and made no attempt to unload the shopping. She could not account for her inaction. Patient D told lewd jokes and laughed uproariously at the funeral of his mother to whom he had previously been devoted and respectful. His family was shocked at the complete absence of signs of grief. Patient E's wife was taken aback when, on her return from work one day, patient E showed no concern that their beloved dog had died and was lying on the garden path. In all cases, the patients showed a total lack of insight into the inappropriateness of their behavior and denied that anything was wrong.

Changes in emotion

Changes in affect are a central, defining feature of FTD and, as noted above, may be a prominent presenting symptom. Affect is typically bland, shallow, and indifferent. Some patients have a fatuous appearance, and may make puerile jokes or puns, whereas other patients show generalized flattening or blunting of emotions. There is a loss of emotional warmth and rapport with others. In keeping with this, relatives report a loss of feelings of empathy, sympathy, and compassion; patients are described as selfish and self-centered. Patients no longer exhibit social emotions of shame or embarrassment, reflected in a loss of personal modesty.

Emotional changes cover the range of primary (e.g., sadness, fear) and social (e.g., empathy, compassion) emotions. It is the lack of appropriate affective response to situations that sets FTD patients apart from patients with other forms of dementia (Bathgate, Snowden, Varma, Blackshaw, & Neary, 2001). In Alzheimer's disease, for example, amnesic patients may have reduced cognitive insight into their condition for the understandable reason that they forget that they have forgotten. Yet, these same patients, when confronted with tasks that are beyond their capabilities, display appropriate signs of anxiety, distress, or concern. By contrast, FTD patients readily respond "don't know" to questions while displaying no signs of frustration or concern regarding their poor performance.

Changes in conduct

Alterations occur both in patients' personal and social conduct. Patients neglect personal hygiene and if left to their own devices may no longer wash or change their clothes. They cease to show interest in their personal appearance and may put on esthetically and seasonally inappropriate combinations of clothing (e.g., a floral summer frock, combined with heavy winter boots and gloves). They may be incontinent without concern. Neglect extends not only to personal care but also domestic and occupational responsibilities. A formerly house-proud individual may no longer bother to carry out household tasks, such as cleaning and tidying the home. Some patients are overactive and restless, rushing from one task to another. Yet, their activity lacks goal-direction and persistence and tasks remain incomplete. Other patients show a notable lack of initiative and spend all day watching television or doing nothing. Sometimes apathy can be the presenting symptom, as in the case of patient C. More usually, there is a gradual increase in apathy over the course of the disease.

There is a decline in manners, social graces, and decorum. Formerly courteous and attentive individuals may simply ignore friends and relatives who visit their homes. Alternatively, they may be disinhibited, making personal, sexually explicit or potentially insulting comments about people within earshot. Disinhibited patients may approach and talk to strangers in the street. They may laugh or sing in inappropriate social settings. They may make social faux-pas or breaches of etiquette, such as drinking from the wine bottle in a sophisticated restaurant.

Rituals and stereotypes

Behavior in FTD often has a stereotypic quality (Bathgate et al., 2001; Mendez, Perryman, Miller, Swartz, & Cummings, 1997; Nyatsanza et al., 2003; Snowden et al., 1996). Stereotypies range from simple motor mannerisms, such as repetitive hand rubbing, foot tapping, humming, or grunting to highly complex daily routines. Patients may repeatedly hum the same tune, sing the same song, clap the same rhythm, or dance the same steps. They may repeatedly say the same word or phrase or relate the same anecdote or repertoire of remarks. Overactive patients may pace the room repetitively, or wander the streets, following an identical route. Rituals may have a compulsive quality. Patients may clock-watch, carrying out a particular activity at precisely the same time each day. They may constantly align objects, or may count the number of steps as they walk. Occasionally rituals are of a superstitious nature, such as avoidance of walking on the gaps between paving stones or on a creaking floorboard in the home. Occasionally rituals have a bizarre quality. One patient would touch each of the four walls upon entering a room, before spitting on the floor. Sometimes a repetitive behavior is elicited by a particular situation. One patient invariably sang "Rule Britannia" as she went through the door from the living room into her kitchen.

Repetitive and stereotyped behaviors are significantly more common in FTD than in the common forms of dementia of Alzheimer's disease and vascular dementia (Bathgate et al., 2001), and as such their presence is a strong discriminator in differential diagnosis.

Hoarding and environmental dependency

Some patients collect up and hoard objects. For example, they may cram their pockets with debris found on the street. They may refuse to discard old newspapers, which increasingly pile up in the home. One patient, who lived alone, was found in a state of neglect, surrounded by dozens of empty fruit juice cartons, which he had aligned around the room.

Hoarding can be seen as one form of stimulus-bound or environmentally driven behavior. An extreme form of environmental dependency is utilization behavior. This behavior, associated with frontal lobe pathology and described initially by Lhermitte (1983), refers to the tendency to use objects within reach, even when the context is inappropriate. For example, a patient may carry on the action of drinking from a cup long after the cup is empty. A patient, on visiting the home of neighbors, may proceed to comb his or her hair using the neighbors' comb, or cut up the newspaper using the neighbors' scissors, if those objects happen to lie within the patient's grasp. A patient may put on multiple layers of the same type of clothing (e.g., four shirts) if those articles of clothing happen to be in view.

Utilization behavior is not seen in all FTD patients and is typically a relatively late development in the disease course. Nevertheless, it has diagnostic value, because of its high degree of specificity for FTD, and for this reason it is included in current diagnostic criteria for FTD (Neary et al., 1998).

Eating and oral behaviors

Changes in eating and other oral behavior frequently occur (Ikeda, Brown, Holland, Fukuhara, & Hodges, 2002; Miller, Darby, Swartz, Yener, & Mena, 1995; Neary et al., 1998; Snowden et al., 1996). Some changes appear to be linked to patients' stimulus-bound behavior. Thus, patients may eat excessively and indiscriminately, cramming food and stealing food from the plates of others. Relatives may report that the patient would carry on eating so long as food is present and they have to actively remove food from view to prevent the patient becoming obese. Similarly, patients may drink to excess. In cases where the preferred beverage is alcoholic this may raise the erroneous suspicion of alcohol abuse as a cause rather than symptom of the patient's disorder. Patients who smoke may increase their daily cigarette consumption. Yet, this commonly results from patients' tendency to light up and stub out cigarettes repeatedly, despite each cigarette being unfinished.

Some alterations in eating habits cannot simply be attributed to environmentally driven behavior. FTD patients commonly develop a preference for sweet food, and they may actively seek these out. Some patients develop food fads that are part of a ritual or routine. For example, one patient insisted on eating the same flavor of ice cream at precisely the same time each day, while he watched a particular television program. Another patient ate one brand of mints, while waiting in the car for his wife when she shopped in the supermarket. He refused all other brands. Another patient ate two of an identical brand of chocolate bar each day.

Hyperorality may extend to the tendency to eat nonedible objects. This symptom of Klüver–Bucy syndrome is normally associated with late-stage disease.

Structural and functional brain imaging

Structural imaging reveals cerebral atrophy, with prominence in the frontal and anterior temporal lobes. The atrophy is bilateral (Figure 15.1), although sometimes asymmetrical in distribution affecting either the left or right hemisphere to a greater

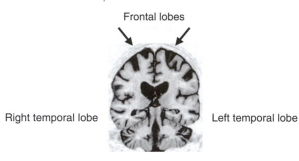

Figure 15.1   Magnetic resonance (MR) scan (coronal view) of a frontotemporal dementia (FTD) patient showing atrophy in the anterior cerebral hemispheres. The arrows draw attention to the frontal lobe atrophy, which is present in both hemispheres.

extent. The atrophy is commonly most pronounced in the frontal lobes (Figure 15.1), although the temporal poles are invariably affected to some degree.

Functional imaging, using positron emission tomography (PET), functional magnetic resonance imaging (fMRI), and single-photon emission computed tomography (SPECT), shows abnormalities in the frontal and anterior temporal lobes with normal appearances in the posterior cerebral hemispheres (Figure 15.2). As with structural imaging, the changes are bilateral but may be asymmetric. Functional imaging is even more sensitive to changes in the anterior hemispheres than structural brain imaging. Studies using fMRI have shown loss of frontal activation in early FTD patients in whom structural MRI is normal (Rombouts et al., 2003). Some authors have argued that the ventromedial frontal cortex is likely to be the earliest

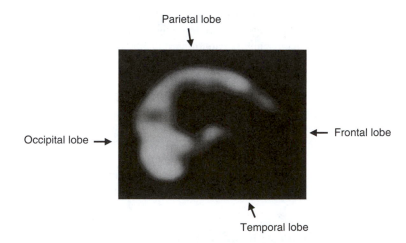

Figure 15.2   Single-photon emission computed tomography (SPECT) scan (sagittal view) of a frontotemporal dementia (FTD) patient showing reduced uptake of tracer in the fronto-temporal regions. (Normal perfusion is light (parietal and occipital regions). The dark areas (frontal and temporal) indicate underperfusion, reflecting loss of function.)

site of pathology in FTD on the basis that PET studies have shown this to be an affected area common to all patients (Salmon et al., 2003).

Pathology

Macroscopic changes

Atrophy in FTD is most marked in the frontal neocortex, anterior temporal neocortex, amygdala, and basal ganglia (Brun, 1987, 1993; Kril, Macdonald, Patel, Png, & Halliday, 2005; Mann & South, 1993; Mann, South, Snowden, & Neary, 1993). The histological changes in neocortex involve mainly layers II and III, the origin of cortico-cortical associational neurones, and spare layer V, the major source of cortico-subcortical neurones. The precise distribution of pathology may differ, with some patients showing atrophy relatively confined to the orbital parts of the frontal lobe and extending posteriorly into the temporal lobe, whereas others show widespread frontal lobe atrophy extending into dorsolateral regions. The atrophy is invariably bilateral but asymmetries may be present in some patients. FTD patients who develop MND/ALS, who have an attenuated course of illness because of their physical symptoms, show relatively circumscribed frontotemporal atrophy compared to patients with more prolonged course (Snowden et al., 1996). Typically, the orbital parts of the frontal lobes are most affected and dorsolateral cortex relatively preserved. These findings are in keeping with imaging findings (Salmon et al., 2003) that suggest that these regions to be the earliest site of pathology.

Microscopic changes

On immunohistochemical analysis, up to half the cases display pathological changes linked to the tau protein and are referred to as "tauopathies." Some of these cases show swollen neurones (Pick cells) and inclusion bodies (Pick bodies), fulfilling former pathological definitions of Pick's disease. In other cases, without tau pathology, most show ubiquitinated inclusions, referred to as ubiquitin-type or MND-type histology. The remaining cases show no specific histological features aside from cortical microvacuolation giving rise to a spongy appearance. The distribution of pathology within the frontal and temporal lobes is the same regardless of underlying histological characteristics.

Causes of FTD

Patients' symptoms reflect the progressive impairment of function and loss of cells in frontal and temporal neocortex. There is clear evidence that this degenerative process has a genetic substrate. In familial cases showing tau-based histology, mutations have been identified in the *tau* gene on chromosome 17 (Hutton et al., 1998). More recently, in familial non-tau cases, mutations have been discovered in the growth factor, progranulin gene, also on chromosome 17 (Baker et al., 2006). Some cases of FTD/ALS have shown linkage to chromosome 9 (Hosler et al., 2000). At present the cause of sporadic FTD remains unspecified, although it is suspected that here too there will be genetic determinants, i.e., intrinsic programming faults that lead certain individuals to be vulnerable to the degenerative process. No external, environmental influences (e.g., toxins) have been identified.

Executive impairments in FTD

Executive function is a broad term that refers to a range of capacities that permit a person to regulate and modulate behavior appropriately. It includes the capacity for foresight: to be able to see what needs to be done and to set goals or plan. It includes the ability to organize plans of actions, to attend to what is relevant and ignore what is not relevant and to sustain attention over time. It includes the ability to abstract information, to monitor one's own performance/actions in relation to an intended goal and to have the mental flexibility to shift actions/behavior if circumstances change. A range of cognitive tests are available that are designed to tap these executive skills. The prevailing pattern of cognitive change in FTD is one of executive failure. Many patients fail a wide variety of standard tests of executive function, and the quality of their errors has a distinctly frontal flavor. Thus, on the modified version of the Wisconsin Card Sorting Test (Nelson, 1976) which requires the patient to sort cards according to a common rule (shape, color, or number), and then to shift to an alternative method of sorting after six consecutive correct responses, it is not uncommon for patients to achieve one category only and for 100% of errors to be perseverative. That is, the patient identifies one possible method of sorting (e.g., color), but cannot thereafter see alternative possibilities and persists in sorting according to the original rule, despite constant feedback that their responses are incorrect. The same pattern of behavior is seen in the less demanding Weigl's block test (De Renzi, Faglioni, Savoiardo, & Vignolo, 1966), which requires the patient to group solid, colored shapes according a common feature (color, shape, or motif). The patient typically groups blocks successfully according to one dimension (e.g., color) but fails to see alternative methods of grouping (e.g., shape) even when the examiner cues the patient by providing a partial sort. Indeed, patients have a tendency to dismantle the examiner's grouping, saying that it is wrong, and to regroup the blocks according to the original sorting method (Thompson, Stopford, Snowden, & Neary, 2005). Such a pattern of performance provides a compelling demonstration of lack of mental flexibility and an inability to switch mental set. Also on fluency tests patients may show not only an economy of response, indicating a lack of novel ideas, but also a failure to shift from one response or response type to another. For example, in a category fluency task, patients may generate names of domestic animals, but then come to a rapid halt, failing to move on to other sources of animal names, such as farm animals and wild animals. In a Design Fluency Test (Jones-Gotman & Milner, 1977), in which the patient is requested to generate novel, abstract designs limited to four lines, their responses are commonly limited to a few ideas, which are perseverated multiple times (Figure 15.3).

Design Fluency Tests provide scope for yielding a variety of performance patterns and in FTD there is frequently more than one error type. Figure 15.3 shows that the patient not only produce perseverations but also rule violations. The test instructions state that designs (a) should be abstract and therefore not depict concrete objects

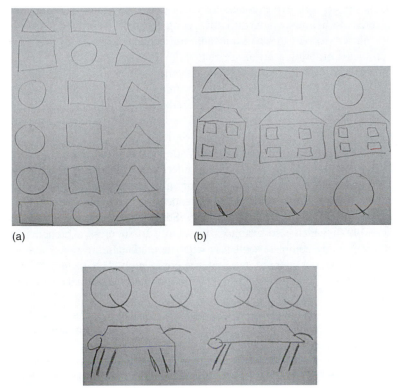

(a)   (b)

(c)

Figure 15.3   Design fluency performance in a frontotemporal dementia (FTD) patient. (a) The initial items produced during the course of the test show violation of the 4-line rule and response perseveration. (b) and (c) The later items show, in addition, an increased concrete tendency. The patient draws concrete objects rather than abstract, nonrepresentational designs as instructed.

and (b) should be confined to four lines. The figure reveals rule violations in both respects: the patient draws shapes that do not have four lines and gradually resorts to the depiction of concrete objects. It should be stressed that such errors are not a consequence of difficulty remembering the instructions. Patients may repeat instructions correctly while proceeding to violate them. Moreover, such errors arise even when the patient is constantly reminded of the instructions throughout the course of the task. Such performance provides a striking illustration of *loss of goal-direction*. The patient's behavior is no longer guided or constrained by the goals or demands of the task at hand.

FTD patients commonly fail tasks that require *organization* or *sequencing*. On clinical bedside testing a typical finding is that although patients are able to point to named objects in the room, they have considerable difficulty doing so in sequence (e.g., desk, light, door, window), and make order errors. In the motor domain, they have problems in copying sequences of hand postures (e.g., palm down, fist, palm up), even though they can copy individual postures accurately. In the verbal domain they have difficulty reordering a set of printed words (e.g., care sick for nurses people) to make a meaningful sentence. In the visual domain, they have problems ordering a set of six pictures to conform to a logical narrative, even though they can describe accurately the contents of individual pictures.

FTD patients show impairments in voluntary aspects of attention, exhibiting problems in sustained attention, selective attention, suppression of attention and attentional switching, and they may fail a variety of standard attentional tests (Robertson, Ward, Ridgeway, & Nimmo-Smith, 1994). On a standard Stroop test (Golden, 1978; Stroop, 1935), patients may show a complete inability to suppress the natural/dominant response. Thus, in the interference condition in which they are required to name the ink color (e.g., red) or an incongruous color word (e.g., blue), they are totally unable to inhibit the natural tendency to read out the word (blue) instead of naming the ink color. On the Haylings Sentence Completion Test (Burgess & Shallice, 1997), which also examines the ability to suppress a prepotent response, patients commonly complete sentences with the predictable response and are totally unable to generate an unconnected sentence completion. This pattern of response on both Stroop and Haylings tests exemplify the stimulus-bound character of patients' behavior.

As noted above, a common error type on Design Fluency Tests is the production of concrete responses. Patients draw identifiable objects rather than abstract designs as instructed. *Concreteness of thought* may also be evident in verbal fluency performance. Patients produce category exemplars exclusively that relate to their own personal experience. Thus, when asked to generate animals a patient might respond "dog, two cats. We used to have a budgerigar." When provided with the prompt "Tell me any animals, from anywhere in the world" the patient might respond "No more. We've only got a dog and two cats. Max, Tabatha and Lucy."

Impact of executive deficits on other cognitive domains

Executive failures in FTD predictably have a secondary impact on performance on tests that do not explicitly test executive function. Lack of adherence to the task goal, poor sustained and selective attention, failure of checking, concreteness of thought, failure of mental set shifting, inability to inhibit previous responses, lack of strategic search, organizational, and sequencing difficulties may all contribute to reduced efficiency on tests of language, perception, spatial abilities, and memory. For example, on a simple spatial test that requires the patient to count an array of dots, FTD patients may fail because of rapid, impulsive responding without checking. They give a rapid response based on an immediate estimate, without attempting to count the dots systematically. However, they do not have a fundamental inability to appreciate the spatial array and can locate and count individual dots accurately when requested to do so, in keeping with the preservation of parietal lobe function. Similarly, drawings may be poorly organized, without regard to accuracy of detail, and may show perseveration of strokes. Yet, overall spatial configuration is well preserved. On language tasks, responses may be characterized by economy of output, concreteness of thought, stereotyped word usage, echolalia, and perseveration.

Patients may recite without difficulty well-rehearsed verbal series, yet fail to generate novel utterances in conversational speech, reflecting an absence of mental plans or goals. They may ostensibly be able to understand word meanings and yet their understanding of the intention underlying utterances (pragmatics) may be impaired. For example, in bedside tests of comprehension the generic question "Do you cut meat with a spoon?" might yield the self-referential response "I don't eat meat. I'm a vegetarian"; the question "Do you use a saw to cut wood?" might yield "My husband does that. I never use his tools." Thus, the patient provides a concrete, person-centered response to what is intended as a simple exploration of understanding of word meaning.

The secondary impact of executive failure on cognitive performance is most clearly seen in the domain of memory. Relatives may report that patients' memory is selective and that they "remember what they want to remember." Consistent with this report, formal testing may reveal variability and inconsistencies in performance, suggesting that factors related to the encoding and subsequent retrieval of material, such as attention, may be influential. Indeed, memory performance depends crucially on how memory is probed. It is particularly poor in open-ended recall tasks, such as the recall of a short story, which makes demands on active retrieval, organization, and generation of information. Commonly, patients provide economical and un-elaborated or "do not know" responses. When memory is probed using direct questions or multiple-choice alternatives, which reduce the executive demands, the performance shows a dramatic (and disproportionate) improvement. Performance is maintained over a delay (e.g., 30 min), with no evidence of rapid information loss.

Impact of executive deficits on behavior

Much of the behavioral change in FTD can be seen as a manifestation of patients' executive impairments (Table 15.1). Patients' failure to initiate activities and tendency to sit idle or conversely, their purposeless, undirected activity can both be seen as a consequence of *failure of goal-direction and planning*. They no longer see what needs to be done and do not generate "plans of action." They may react to the environment, but are no longer proactive. Reckless and impulsive behavior may be seen as a reflection of patients' *impaired judgment and foresight*. They are unable to see the future consequences of their actions. Behavior is driven by stimuli in the immediate vicinity rather than by forward planning and forethought, hence the environmental dependency. Immediate stimuli override more abstract goals. Patients' chaotic, disorganized lifestyle reflects an *inability to organize and sequence* components of activities. A lack of persistence on tasks reflects a failure to *sustain attention* and distractibility from extraneous environmental stimuli. Behavioral rigidity and adherence to routine reflects a *loss of mental flexibility* and ability to see things from alternative points of views.

Social cognition in FTD

A salient clinical feature of FTD is breakdown in interpersonal relationships. Patients are regarded as totally changed, and from being thoughtful, compassionate

Table 15.1   Executive deficits in frontotemporal dementia and their
behavioral consequences.

Executive deficit	Behavioral consequences
Planning/foresight	Apathy, inertia
	Purposeless, undirected activity
	Neglect of self-care
	Neglect of domestic and occupational responsibilities
	Behavior governed by immediate wants rather than long-term goals
	Behavior driven by environmental stimuli (stimulus bound)
	Unable to foresee consequences of actions
Organization/sequencing	Disorganized behavior; breakdown in sequence of actions (action program)
Attention	Fails to sustain attention on task
	Distracted by irrelevant environmental stimuli
	Difficult to engage and maintain attention
Abstraction	Literal thinking; responses to questions are self-referential (concrete)
	Fails to grasp intention underlying utterances
Self-monitoring	Fails to detect own mistakes
	Loss of insight
Mental flexibility/set shifting	Rigid, poorly adaptable; preservative
	Unable to see other points of view; loss of sympathy and empathy

individuals become self-centered and apparently oblivious of the needs of others. For example, one patient's wife reported that when she left hospital following major abdominal surgery her husband made no attempt to assist her in carrying her luggage and seemed oblivious of her difficulties and obvious discomfort. Impaired mental flexibility and inability to switch mental set may be seen as factors that contribute to the very severe breakdown in social, interpersonal relationships in FTD. That is, patients are no longer able to see things from an alternative perspective so cannot put themselves in another person's shoes. Aside from these general executive impairments, there is accumulating evidence that other specific impairments may contribute to the impairment of interpersonal functioning in FTD. "Theory of mind" refers to the ability to infer what a person feels or thinks when that person's mental state differs from one's own (Baron-Cohen, Leslie, & Frith, 1985; Leslie, 1987). The prototypical theory of mind task involves a scenario of the following type: Person A puts an object in location X (e.g., a cupboard) and then leaves the room. Person B moves the object from location X to location Y (e.g., a drawer). Person A returns. The question is where person A thinks the object is located. Control subjects infer that person A will think the object is still in location X even though they know that it is in location Y. That is, they appreciate that person A may have a different belief than his or her own. FTD patients, by contrast, commonly respond that person A thinks the object is in location Y, reflecting their own knowledge/belief. Impairments in FTD have been demonstrated on a variety of tests of theory of mind (Gregory et al.,

Figure 15.4   Example of test material used in a study of social cognition/theory of mind.

2002; Lough, Gregory, & Hodges, 2001; Snowden et al., 2003), which require the patient to draw inferences about another person's mental state. Of course, specific deficits in social cognition are not always easy to disentangle from more general impairments in executive function. Tests of theory of mind, by their very nature, are typically mentally demanding, involving holding in mind and mentally manipulating multiple elements of information. This is particularly true of tasks involving second-order false belief (What does person A think, person B thinks?). Such tasks might feasibly be failed for general executive reasons rather than specific deficits in theory of mind. Nevertheless, some patients perform poorly even on very simple theory of mind tasks that make few mental executive demands. For example, when patients are asked to indicate which of four items another person, depicted by a line drawing of a face (Figure 15.4) "likes best," some FTD patients respond according to their own personal preference rather than on the basis of eye gaze of the face, as used by normal controls. Thus the patient might choose strawberry as the preferred item, whereas controls select apple. This pattern of performance cannot be ascribed simply to lack of comprehension or failure of compliance. These same patients who respond on the basis of personal preference when asked to indicate which item the face likes best may have no difficulty indicating correctly which item the face is looking at. The former task requires the patient to infer an independent mental state to another person on the basis of eye gaze, whereas the latter task requires the patient only to comment on physical properties of that person (i.e., to state the direction of eye gaze). Such performance provides compelling evidence that the patient has an egocentric worldview and is no longer able to attribute independent mental states to others.

Another source of evidence for specific impairments in social cognition is the finding that impaired performance on theory of mind tasks may occur in some patients in the absence of detectable abnormalities on traditional frontal lobe executive tests (Lough et al., 2001). That is, tests of social cognition and other aspects of executive function are potentially dissociable.

Emotion processing

A functional domain allied to social cognition is the processing of emotions. As noted above, alteration in the expression of emotion is a ubiquitous symptom, and FTD patients are commonly emotionally blunted or fatuous. In keeping with the impairment in emotional expression they also show impairments in the recognition of emotion. This is not limited to a single input modality. Patients have been shown to be impaired in their recognition of both facial emotions (Keane, Calder, Hodges, & Young, 2002; Lavenu, Pasquier, Lebert, Petit, & van der Linden, 1999) and vocal expressions of emotion (Keane et al., 2002). Such deficits are likely to contribute to patients' loss of capacity for sympathy and empathy.

Phenotypic variations and their relation to pathology

It has been indicated above that FTD patients exhibit a wide variety of executive deficits. Although this is true of many patients, it is not invariably the case. Some FTD patients perform surprisingly well on traditional frontal executive tests, despite severe character and behavioral change in their daily lives (Gregory, Serra-Mestres, & Hodges, 1999; Neary et al., 1988; Snowden et al., 1996). The difference between those who perform poorly and those who perform relatively well reflects distinct phenotypic variation within FTD. Stage of disease contributes to but does not account entirely for such patient variation.

Disinhibited versus apathetic FTD

Some patients' behavior is characterized by fatuousness, impulsivity, distractibility, social disinhibition, and purposeless overactivity, giving a picture reminiscent of hypomania (Snowden et al., 1996). Other patients exhibit a picture of emotional blunting, apathy, inertia, loss of volition, and economy of effort, which may be mistaken for depression. Overactive, disinhibited patients typically become increasingly apathetic over the course of the disease. Nevertheless, even at the time of initial presentation some patients show the pseudo-hypomanic picture and others are pseudo depressed. An example of the latter is patient C, described above, whose apathy and inertia was exemplified by her failure to get out of the car for several hours following a shopping expedition.

The disinhibited, "pseudo-hypomanic" phenotype is associated with a more circumscribed distribution of frontal lobe atrophy than the apathetic pseudo-depressed type. In disinhibited patients, the orbital parts of the frontal lobes as well as the temporal poles are predominantly affected. Dorsolateral frontal cortices are well preserved. By contrast, in apathetic pseudo-depressed patients atrophy is widespread throughout the frontal lobes, including dorsolateral frontal cortices. Apathetic patients, with extensive frontal involvement, typically exhibit severe and widespread impairment on traditional executive tests. It is these patients whose performance is most likely to be characterized by response economy, concreteness of thought, striking verbal and motor perseveration, and in whom executive impairments are likely to have a pervasive secondary effect on performance in other cognitive domains.

By contrast, patients with relatively restricted orbitofrontal lobe atrophy may perform well on a range of traditional executive tests (Gregory et al., 1999; Neary et al., 1988; Snowden et al., 1996). Sometimes close examination may reveal subtle, circumscribed deficits. Rahman, Sahakian, Hodges, Rogers, and Robbins (1999), for example, demonstrated impairment on a decision-making task but not on a range of other executive tests. Their patients showed an overall increase in risk-taking behavior and failure to make personally advantageous decisions. The pattern of behavior, which was similar to that shown in other patients with acquired lesions of the orbitofrontal cortex (Bechara, Damasio, Damasio, & Anderson, 1994), could not be ascribed merely to impulsivity or a failure of inhibitory control as the patients exhibited prolonged deliberation times. Rather, it was interpreted as representing a failure to anticipate expected outcomes, consistent with a failure of forward planning.

The apparent preservation of performance on many traditional executive tasks in patients with restricted orbitofrontal cortical atrophy contrasts with the severe breakdown in their social interpersonal conduct. Patient A, described above, is a case in point. He was inappropriately jocular, fatuous, and lacking in sympathy and empathy. His behavior was puerile, disinhibited, and socially inappropriate. He showed a total lack of concern at the loss of his job and lacked insight that there was anything wrong. Yet, he performed normally on a range of standard executive tests. The latter make substantial demands on problem-solving skills, but few demands on social skills. The dissociation reinforces the view of Damasio, Tranel, and Damasio (1990) that the orbitofrontal lobes have a crucial role in social functioning. In keeping with this view Lough et al. (2001) found, in an FTD patient with relatively selective orbitofrontal pathology, impaired social cognition in the absence of detectable abnormalities on traditional frontal lobe executive tests.

Left and right hemisphere contributions to behavior

FTD is a bilateral disease. However, it can be asymmetric with one hemisphere being affected disproportionately, and occasionally the asymmetry is substantial. When the atrophic process is relatively confined to one frontal lobe executive and behavioral changes are much less striking than in patients in whom both frontal lobes are significantly affected. This observation is an important one in that it explains why patients with acquired frontal lobe lesions due to nondegenerative pathologies, such as vascular insults, space-occupying lesions, or neurosurgical resections of the frontal lobes, so rarely exhibit the gross behavioral change and magnitude of executive impairment that is so prototypical of FTD. In nondegenerative pathologies the damage is typically unilateral, or at least predominantly involving one hemisphere, whereas in FTD it is not. It would seem that both frontal lobes contribute to executive function and that it is when both hemispheres are compromised that the behavioral and cognitive consequences are so pronounced.

The finding that both hemispheres contribute to behavioral and executive impairments in FTD does not necessarily mean that they contribute equally. A recent pathological study of 17 FTD patients (Kril et al., 2005) reported symmetrical atrophy in most brain regions, but in the frontal lobes significantly greater atrophy in the right than left hemisphere. The difference was numerically quite small (58% versus 54% atrophy) and the study cohort small, so that it is difficult to know to what extent the patients are representative of the FTD population. Nevertheless, the authors interpreted their findings as evidence for the particular importance of the right frontal lobe in governing social behavior. A similar argument has been proposed by other authors (Liu et al., 2004), who reported greater behavioral impairment and social breakdown in FTD patients who had more severe atrophy on the right side than on the left. Another study using voxel-based morphometry (Williams, Nestor, & Hodges, 2005) showed that behavioral changes in FTD correlated with loss of gray matter in the paracingulate frontal region, particularly on the right side.

Systematic evaluation of different components of executive function related to hemispheric emphasis of pathology has yet to be undertaken. However, clinical observation suggests that FTD patients with more right-sided pathology tend to be more inattentive and difficult to engage than those with more left-sided pathology, suggesting that attentional factors may contribute to phenotypic differences, and perhaps to the greater observed social breakdown in patients with more right-sided disease.

Frontal and temporal lobe contributions to function

Although FTD is frequently construed as a frontal lobe dementia, it needs to be emphasized that the anterior parts of the temporal lobes, especially the temporal poles, are invariably involved. Given the strong anatomical links between orbitofrontal cortex and anterior temporal lobes by the uncinate fasciculus it would not be surprising to find the two regions to be functionally linked. Care needs to be taken therefore in ascribing all behavioral and executive changes in FTD automatically and exclusively to frontal lobe pathology. Nevertheless, within the FTD population, there are behavioral differences that permit some conclusions to be drawn about the relative contributions of frontal and temporal lobes. Repetitive and stereotyped behaviors are a common feature of all FTD patients. However, in apathetic patients with widespread frontal lobe atrophy stereotypies are more likely to take the form of simple motor mannerisms, such as repetitive foot tapping, humming, or hand rubbing (Snowden et al., 2001). By contrast, in disinhibited patients with relatively circumscribed orbitofrontal atrophy they may comprise relatively complex behavioral routines. Interestingly, when stereotyped rituals represent a dominant presenting feature of the disease (as in the case of the patient who would touch each wall in turn on entering a room and then spit on the floor) the atrophy is found to be most marked in temporal lobes and striatum, with relatively lesser involvement of the frontal lobes (Snowden et al., 1996).

Independent findings from patients with semantic dementia reinforce and complement this observation. Semantic dementia is another focal syndrome, arising from circumscribed degeneration of the anterior hemispheres. It is characterized by a progressive loss of understanding of the meaning of words and other conceptual knowledge about the world (Hodges, Patterson, Oxbury, & Funnell, 1992; Snowden, Goulding, & Neary, 1989; Snowden et al., 1996), and is associated with striking, selective atrophy of the temporal lobes. In pure cases, the frontal lobes are relatively unaffected, thereby providing a valuable comparison for disentangling frontal and temporal lobe contributions to cognition and behavior. Semantic dementia patients commonly perform well on standard executive tasks, provided that the task does not depend on word comprehension or object identity, confirming the assumption that executive deficits do indeed arise as a result of frontal lobe pathology. However, semantic dementia patients superficially share some of the behavioral changes of FTD (Snowden et al., 2001). In particular they exhibit repetitive, stereotyped behaviors. They are typically markedly time-bound, having to carry out activities at precisely the same time each day, and adhering to a strict daily routine. They are preoccupied by a limited range of activities, which they carry out repetitively in precisely the same way each time. This compulsive quality is seen to some extent in disinhibited FTD patients with relatively confined frontal lobe atrophy, but rarely in FTD patients with widespread frontal lobe atrophy, in whom unconcern and general loss of interest in activities is more prevalent. The findings in semantic dementia highlight the importance of the temporal rather than frontal lobes in influencing compulsive behavior.

Conclusions

FTD is a devastating degenerative disorder of the frontal and anterior temporal lobes that affects people in the middle years of their life and gives rise to profound character change, breakdown in social, interpersonal functioning and impairment on neuropsychological tests of executive function. From a clinical perspective, the disorder represents a considerable challenge for management. From a theoretical point of view, FTD represents an important natural model for facilitating understanding of the functions of the frontal lobes, yielding data that complements that obtained from the study of child development and its disorders. It emphasizes, in particular, the fact that the impact of impaired executive functioning goes far beyond failure on a set of cognitive tests. It has profound impact on the way a person behaves and functions in daily life. Indeed, conduct in daily life may be severely compromised even when performance on formal executive tests is normal. This finding highlights the importance of thorough history-taking and qualitative observations in identifying executive breakdown, and underscores the fact that executive failure is a behavioral construct that cannot be fully captured by structured cognitive tasks alone. FTD epitomizes its multifaceted and complex nature.

References

Baker, M., Mackenzie, I. R., Pickering-Brown, S. M., Gass, J., Rademakers, R., Lindholm, C., et al. (2006). Mutations in progranulin cause tau-negative frontotemporal dementia linked to chromosome 17. *Nature, 442,* 916–919.

Baron-Cohen, S., Leslie, A. M., & Frith, U. (1985). Does the autistic child have a theory of mind? *Cognition, 21,* 37–46.

Bathgate, D., Snowden, J. S., Varma, A., Blackshaw, A., & Neary, D. (2001). Behaviour in frontotemporal dementia, Alzheimer's disease and vascular dementia. *Acta Neurologica Scandinavica, 103*, 367–378.

Bechara, A., Damasio, A. R., Damasio, H., & Anderson, S. W. (1994). Insensitivity to future consequences following damage to human prefrontal cortex. *Cognition, 50*, 7–15.

Brun, A. (1987). Frontal lobe degeneration of non-Alzheimer type. I. Neuropathology. *Archives of Gerontology and Geriatrics, 6*, 193–208.

Brun, A. (1993). Frontal lobe degeneration of non-Alzheimer type revisited. *Dementia, 4*, 126–131.

Burgess, P. W., & Shallice, T. (1997). *The Hayling and Brixton Tests*. Bury St Edmunds, Suffolk, U.K: Thames Valley Test Company.

Damasio, A. R., Tranel, D., & Damasio, H. (1990). Individuals with sociopathic behavior caused by frontal damage fail to respond automatically to social stimuli. *Behavioral Brain Research, 41*, 81–94.

De Renzi, E., Faglioni, P., Savoiardo, M., & Vignolo, L. A. (1966). The influence of aphasia and of the hemispheric side of the lesion on abstract thinking. *Cortex, 2*, 399–420.

Golden, C. J. (1978) *Stroop Color and Word Test*. Chicago: Stoelting.

Gregory, C. A., Serra-Mestres, J., & Hodges, J. R. (1999). Early diagnosis of the frontal variant of frontotemporal dementia: How sensitive are standard neuroimaging and neuropsychologic tests? *Neuropsychiatry Neuropsychology and Behavioral Neurology, 12*, 128–135.

Gregory, C., Lough, S., Stone, V., Erzinclioglu, S., Martin, L., Baron-Cohen, S., et al. (2002). Theory of mind in patients with frontal variant frontotemporal dementia and Alzheimer's disease: Theoretical and practical implications. *Brain, 125*, 752–764.

Gustafson, L. (1987). Frontal lobe degeneration of non-Alzheimer type. II. Clinical picture and differential diagnosis. *Archives of Gerontology Geriatrica, 6*, 209–223.

Hodges, J. R., Patterson, K., Oxbury, S., & Funnell, E. (1992). Semantic dementia. Progressive fluent aphasia with temporal lobe atrophy. *Brain, 115*, 1783–1806.

Hodges, J. R., Davies, R., Xuereb, J., Kril, J., & Halliday, G. (2003). Survival in frontotemporal dementia. *Neurology, 61*, 349–354.

Hosler, B., Siddique, T., Sapp, P. C., Sailor, W., Huang, M. C., Hossain, A., et al. (2000). Linkage of familial amyotrophic lateral sclerosis with frontotemporal dementia to chromosome 9q21–22. *Journal of the American Medical Association, 284*, 1664–1669.

Hutton, M., Lendon, C. L., Rizzu, P., Baker, M., Froelich, S., Houlden, H., et al. (1998) Association of missense and 5 splice site mutations in *tau* with the inherited dementia FTDP-17. *Nature, 393*, 702–705.

Ikeda, M., Brown, J., Holland, A. J., Fukuhara, R., & Hodges, J. R. (2002). Changes in appetite, food preference and eating habits in frontotemporal dementia and Alzheimer's disease. *Journal of Neurology Neurosurgery and Psychiatry, 73*, 371–376.

Jones-Gotman, M., & Milner, B. (1977). Design fluency: The invention of nonsense drawings after focal cortical lesions. *Neuropsychologia, 15*, 653–674.

Keane, J., Calder, A. J., Hodges, J. R., & Young, A. W. (2002). Face and emotion processing in frontal variant frontotemporal dementia. *Neuropsychologia, 40*, 655–665.

Kril, J. J., Macdonald, V., Patel, S., Png, F., & Halliday, G. M. (2005). Distribution of brain atrophy in behavioral variant frontotemporal dementia. *Journal of the Neurological Sciences, 232*, 83–90.

Lavenu, I., Pasquier, F., Lebert, F., Petit, H., & van der Linden, M. (1999). Perception of emotion in frontotemporal dementia and Alzheimer's disease. *Alzheimer's Disease and Associated Disorders, 13*, 96–101.

Leslie, A. M. (1987). Pretense and representation: The origins of 'theory of mind.' *Psychological Review*, *94*, 412–426.

Lhermitte, F. (1983). Utilization behaviour and its relation to lesions of the frontal lobes. *Brain*, *106*, 237–255.

Liu, W., Miller, B. L., Kramer, J. H., Rankin, K., Wyss-Coray, C., Gearhart, R., et al. (2004). Behavioral disorders in the frontal and temporal variants of frontotemporal dementia. *Neurology*, *62*, 742–748.

Lough, S., Gregory, C., & Hodges, J. R. (2001). Dissociation of social cognition and executive function in frontal variant frontotemporal dementia. *Neurocase*, *7*, 123–130.

Mann, D. M. A., & South, P. W. (1993). The topographic distribution of brain atrophy in frontal lobe dementia. *Acta Neuropathologica*, *85*, 334–340.

Mann, D. M. A., South, P. W., Snowden, J. S., & Neary, D. (1993). Dementia of frontal lobe type; neuropathology and immunohistochemistry. *Journal of Neurology, Neurosurgery and Psychiatry*, *56*, 605–614.

Mendez, M. F., Perryman, K. M., Miller, B. L., Swartz, J. R., & Cummings, J. L. (1997). Compulsive behaviours as presenting symptoms of frontotemporal dementia. *Journal of Geriatrics, Psychiatry and Neurology*, *10*, 154–157.

Miller, B. L., Darby, A. L., Swartz, J. R., Yener, G. G., & Mena, I. (1995). Dietary changes, compulsions and sexual behaviour in frontotemporal degeneration. *Dementia*, *6*, 195–199.

Neary, D., Snowden, J. S., Northen, B., & Goulding, P. J. (1988). Dementia of frontal lobe type. *Journal of Neurology, Neurosurgery and Psychiatry*, *51*, 353–361.

Neary, D., Snowden, J. S., Mann, D. M. A., Northen, B., Goulding, P. J., & Mcdermott, N. (1990). Frontal lobe dementia and motor neuron disease. *Journal of Neurology, Neurosurgery and Psychiatry*, *53*, 23–32.

Neary, D., Snowden, J. S., Gustafson, L., Passant, U., Stuss, D., Black, S., et al. (1998). Frontotemporal lobar degeneration. A consensus on clinical diagnostic criteria. *Neurology*, *51*, 1546–1554.

Nelson, H.E. (1976). A modified card sorting test sensitive to frontal lobe defects. *Cortex*, *12*, 313–324.

Nyatsanza, S., Shetty, T., Gregory, C., Lough, S., Dawson, K., & Hodges, J. R. (2003). A study of stereotypic behaviours in Alzheimer's disease and frontal and temporal variant frontotemporal dementia. *Journal of Neurology, Neurosurgery and Psychiatry*, *74*, 1398–1402.

Rahman, S., Sahakian, B. J., Hodges, J. R., Rogers, R. D., & Robbins, T. W. (1999). Specific cognitive deficits in mild frontal variant frontotemporal dementia. *Brain*, *122*, 1469–1493.

Robertson, I. H., Ward, T., Ridgeway, V., & Nimmo-Smith, I. (1994). *The test of everyday attention*. Bury St Edmunds, Suffolk, U.K: Thames Valley Test Company.

Rombouts, S. A., Van Swieten, J. C., Pijnenburg, Y. A., Goekoop, R., Barkhof, F., & Scheltens, P. (2003). Loss of frontal fMRI activation in early frontotemporal dementia compared to early AD. *Neurology*, *60*, 1904–1908.

Rosso, S. M., Donker Kaat, L., Baks, T., Joosse, M., de Koning, I., Pijnenburg, Y., et al. (2003). Frontotemporal dementia in the Netherlands: Patient characteristics and prevalence estimates from a population-based study. *Brain*, *126*, 2016–2022.

Salmon, E., Garraux, G., Delbeuck, X., Collette, F., Kalbe, E., Zuendorf, G., et al. (2003). Predominant ventromedial frontopolar metabolic impairment in frontotemporal dementia. *Neuroimage*, *20*, 435–440.

Snowden, J. S., Goulding, P. J., & Neary, D. (1989). Semantic dementia: A form of circumscribed atrophy. *Behavioural Neurology*, *2*, 167–182.

Snowden, J. S., Neary, D., & Mann, D. M. A. (1996). *Frontotemporal lobar degeneration: Frontotemporal dementia, progressive aphasia, semantic dementia.* London: Churchill Livingstone.

Snowden, J. S., Bathgate, D., Varma, A., Blackshaw, A., Gibbons, Z. C., & Neary, D. (2001). Distinct behavioural profiles in frontotemporal dementia and semantic dementia. *Journal of Neurology, Neurosurgery and Psychiatry, 70*, 323–332.

Snowden, J. S., Gibbons, Z. C., Blackshaw, A., Doubleday, E., Thompson, J., Craufurd, D. et al. (2003). Social cognition in frontotemporal dementia and Huntington's disease. *Neuropsychologia, 41*, 688–701.

Snowden, J. S., Neary, D., & Mann, D. M. A. (2004). Autopsy proven, sporadic frontotemporal dementia, due to microvacuolar histology, with onset at 21 years of age. *Journal of Neurology, Neurosurgery and Psychiatry, 75*, 1337–1339.

Stroop, J. R. (1935). Studies of interference in serial verbal reactions. *Journal of Experimental Psychology, 18*, 643–662.

Thompson, J. C., Stopford, C. L., Snowden, J. S., & Neary, D. (2005). Qualitative neuropsychological performance characteristics in frontotemporal dementia and Alzheimer's disease. *Journal of Neurology, Neurosurgery, and Psychiatry, 76*, 920–927.

Williams, G. B., Nestor, P. J., & Hodges, J. R. (2005). Neural correlates of semantic and behavioural deficits in frontotemporal dementia. *Neuroimage, 24*, 1042–1051.

16 From α-synucleinopathy to executive dysfunction: Early-stage parkinson's disease

Michael M. Saling and Jennifer Bradshaw

Contents

Executive functions come into play when two or more sources of information, streams of thought, or behavioral tendencies need to be processed in the interests of establishing, maintaining, and appropriately terminating planful, goal-directed action. It is underpinned by protocognitive or fundamental processes such as attentional focus and selectivity, inhibition and suppression of irrelevant, misdirected, or superfluous behaviors, and ultimately the sequential organization of output. Demands on executive function are greatest when remembered or habitual solutions to external challenges are inadequate, necessitating the elaboration of novel solutions. At this level, executive processing is a controlled process, involving the ability to represent the elements of the problem in a temporary and accessible "online" store, to manipulate them strategically, and to shift flexibly from approaches that are unlikely to be effective or appropriate to those which have a greater chance of success. Controlled processing occurs within a capacity-limited, and frequently refreshed group of subsystems collectively referred to as working memory.

The neurocognitive architecture of executive function is inescapably hierarchical. Much of the current edifice of our understanding of executive process was built on a study of cases with primary injury to frontal cortex with little or no involvement of basal forebrain, diencephalic, or brain stem mechanisms of behavior. In parallel with this dominant trend, however, there was a growing view that the motor functions of the basal ganglia are complex enough to merit descriptors, such as programming, sequencing, and motor planning (Delwaide & Gonce, 1993; Marsden, 1982). Anatomical studies began to overturn the classical notion that output from the basal ganglia terminates in a single nucleus of the thalamus, which in turn projects to premotor cortex. It is now clear that the basal ganglia are in a position to gain access to much wider regions of the frontal cortex on the medial and lateral aspects of the cerebrum. Recent years have seen an explosion of interest in the behavioral implications of the frontostriatal circuitry. Parkinson's disease (PD), together with its clinical and pathological congeners, has been one of the major drivers of this quest, and much of what is now known about the frontostriatal basis of executive dysfunction has come from research on this condition.

In an ironic counterpoint to James Parkinson's original assertion (Goldman & Goetz, 2005) that the "intellect is uninjured," PD has been the subject of a voluminous body of neuropsychological research (Henry & Crawford, 2004; Levin, Tomer, & Rey, 1992; Rashkin, Borod, & Tweedy, 1990). Psychometric studies, predominantly from the 1970s onwards showed that patients with PD performed poorly on a wide range of tasks when compared with healthy controls (Pirozzolo, Swihart, Rey, Mahurin, & Jankovic, 1993), suggesting multiple cognitive impairments, even at a relatively early stage of the disease. With a growing recognition of the possibility that this very general performance failure might be an artifact of the cardinal motor features of the disease, attempts were made to define the nature of the putative cognitive disorder more precisely. The most commonly reported impairment fell within the visuospatial domain. Nevertheless, convincing evidence of a fundamental spatial disturbance was not forthcoming. Before long the visuospatial impairment of PD came to be seen as a by-product of executive disturbances such as attentional set shifting or disturbances in the sequential execution of movement in the absence of external guidance (Brown & Marsden, 1990; Freeman et al., 2000). Increasing attention was drawn to the fact that executive-like disturbances were not restricted to tasks with visuospatial content, bolstering the notion that higher cognitive impairment in PD was indeed of an executive type (Brown & Marsden, 1990; Taylor, Saint-Cyr, & Lang, 1986), with greater similarities to frontal than to posterior cortical disorders.

This picture has emerged against a background of disagreement (Saint-Cyr, Taylor, & Nicholson, 1995). PD is a heterogeneous and progressive condition. Variations in the pattern of motor signs and stage of disease have, in all likelihood, played a major role in the complexity of the neuropsychological findings over the past 40 years. Cognitive impairments become more extensive as the disease progresses, and around 20% of patients develop a dementia. By contrast, the early phases of the disease are characterized by circumscribed losses of cognitive function, often restricted to particular forms of executive dysfunction. This is paralleled by restriction of the anatomical pathology to the nigrostriatal system, and involvement of nondopaminergic systems is not as extensive as it is in later stages of the disease. As two authorities have remarked, "Parkinson's disease has become the prototypic disorder of a single neurochemical deficiency affecting a primary anatomical system" (Goetz & Kompoliti, 2005, p. 561). Its earlier stages, therefore, constitute an informative model of the striatal contribution to the expression of executive function, and in this chapter we focus on current developments in this line of research.

Clinical features of parkinson's disease

The clinical features of PD can be grouped into cardinal and secondary manifest-ations. The cardinal manifestations are tremor, rigidity, akinesia, and postural instability.

Tremor

This is the most obvious manifestation in PD, and is commonly the earliest clinical indication of the disease. In its earliest stages, the tremor is usually unilateral and confined to the arm. It is maximal when the limb is at rest, and abates when the limb is voluntarily moved. The oscillations are coarse and slow (around 3–5 cycles per second). With progress of the disease, the tremor spreads proximally and ipsilaterally before it involves the contralateral limbs.

Rigidity

Patients with PD often complain of a feeling of "weakness" in the limbs. This subjective change is underpinned by stiffness or rigidity of the limbs. Rigidity manifests as resistance to passive movement. The resistance can be smooth and constant (leadpiping), or step like (cogwheeling), giving the impression of a lever moving over a ratchet system. Rigidity, like tremor, often has a unilateral onset.

Akinesia

PD is characterized by a diminution of voluntary movement, which manifests in a variety of ways. Initiation of movement becomes increasingly delayed, the excursion of individual movements is reduced (hypokinesia), and movement becomes slower (bradykinesia). In general, sequential and alternating movements are impaired, and repetitive movement shows rapid fatigue. Specific manifestations of akinesia include decreased eyeblink and mask-like face (hypomimia), a loss of volume in voice (hypophonia), dysarthria, excessively small writing (micrographia), and loss of arm swing.

Postural instability

This is a late-occurring feature, and its appearance heralds a particularly disabling stage of the disease. Posture becomes stooped, and in combination with a loss of postural reflexes, the patient is at risk of falling either forward or backward. A characteristic shuffling or festinating gait, with small quick steps, can be regarded as a complex by-product of postural instability and hypokinesia.

The secondary features of PD, which are beyond the scope of this chapter, are considered to include behavioral, affective, ocular, autonomic, and sleep-related dysfunction (Pfeiffer & Bodis-Wollner, 2005).

Classical cognitive features: Primary or secondary?

PD has been the subject of decades of intense cognitive research. Deficits in visuospatial function, memory, and language comprehension have been described at relatively early stages of the disease, but the extent to which the cardinal motor features or impairments in protocognitive function confound the interpretation of cognitive task performances is still debated. Within the domain of visuospatial function, for example, complex figure copying in PD is abnormal at an early stage, but can be accounted for in terms of executive (Freeman et al., 2000) and motor programming (Marsden, 1982) dysfunctions. Deficits in the perception of line orientation or facial discrimination have also been documented. These are uncorrelated with severity of motor features, and tend place a low demand on controlled processing resources (Foti & Cummings, 1997). Electrophysiological evidence suggests that posterior cortico-subcortical circuits are involved in visuocognitive impairments in PD (Bodis-Wollner & Antal, 2005). Some degree of spatial disorientation might also be part of the clinical picture (Bowen, Hoehn, & Yahr, 1972; Hovestadt, De Jong, & Meerwaldt, 1987). The case for primary impairments in memory and language is less convincing. Memory difficulties in PD manifest predominantly at a retrieval level, particularly in the application of recall strategies. On the other hand, learning within cued paradigms, such as verbal paired associates, is unaffected (Taylor, Saint-Cyr, & Lang, 1990). From a clinical perspective, amnesia is not a feature of PD (Foti & Cummings, 1997; Paulson & Stern, 1997). Similarly, patients with uncomplicated PD are not dysphasic (Foti & Cummings, 1997; Paulson & Stern, 1997). On formal examination impairments in the comprehension of embedded, grammatically complex sentences are noted (Grossman, Lee, Morris, Stern, & Hurtig, 2002), as well as reduced performance on word generation (Bokura, Yamaguchi, & Kobayashi, 2005; Bouquet, Bonnaud, & Gil, 2003; Lange et al., 2003) paradigms. This language pattern is readily explained in terms of reduced executive resources (Gilbert, Belleville, Bherer, & Chouinard, 2005; Grossman et al., 2002).

Pathology of parkinson's disease: α-synuclein and lewy inclusions

While parkinsonism can be a feature of a number of other syndromes, such as Lewy body dementia, progressive supranuclear palsy, multiple system atrophy, Wilson's disease, or corticobasal degeneration, PD is distinguished by the fact that the cardinal features initially occur in isolation of any other neurological impairments. Less than 10 years ago, in what has been described as a "stunning" discovery, it was shown that the α-synuclein protein is a unifying factor of a spectrum of degenerative conditions which include PD, Lewy body dementia, and multiple system atrophy (Giasson, Lee, & Trojanowski, 2004). At a pathological level they are all characterized by abnormal filamentous aggregations of α-synuclein protein, which eventually contribute to neuronal demise. This protein occurs naturally in presynaptic terminals.

The functions of α-synuclein are not well understood at this stage, but its expression is upregulated when neuronal remodeling occurs (Kahle, Neumann, Ozmen, & Haass, 2000), suggesting that it plays a role in synaptic plasticity. It is strongly associated with the regulation of presynaptic dopaminergic vesicles. Pathological aggregation of α-synuclein appears to be encouraged by oxidative stress, and the specificity of its association with dopaminergic systems appears to be brought about by dopamine's proclivity for accumulating oxidants as a by-product of its metabolism. α-Synuclein forms the main fibrillary component of Lewy bodies. Mesencephalic Lewy bodies represent the pathologic sine qua non for the diagnosis of PD (Hughes, Daniel, & Lees, 2001). Almost all cases have a few Lewy bodies in cingulate cortex, but not in frontal, temporal, or parietal association cortex (Harding & Halliday, 2001). Lewy neurites are also rich in α-synuclein. With progression of the disease, neuritic inclusions become more profuse than Lewy bodies, with a distribution in medial temporal structures and cingulate cortex. Braak and others have drawn attention to the "hierarchical susceptibility" of cortical structures in the progress of PD, with initial involvement of anterior temporal mesocortex, followed by anterior cingulate, insular, and subgenual mesocortex. Important for our consideration of executive dysfunction is the finding that pathological involvement of the prefrontal cortex occurs only during the late stages of PD (Braak, Rub, Steur, Del Tradici, & de Vos, 2005, p. 1407).

The focus of this chapter is early-stage idiopathic PD, prior to the onset of PD dementia. In their work on the staging of PD, by tracing the anatomical distribution of α-synuclein-immunopositive Lewy neurites and Lewy bodies, Braak and others (Braak et al., 2002, 2003, 2005) have shown that the disease begins in medullary nuclei (preclinical stages 1–2), and then proceeds to involve the substantia nigra and other mesencephalic nuclei (stages 3–4), at which time the cardinal motor features of the disease begin to appear. In the end (stages 5–6), cerebral cortex becomes involved (Braak et al., 2002). In neuropathological and clinical terms, early-stage PD is synonomous with Braak stages 3 and 4.

Anatomical and functional aspects of early-stage PD

The clinical phase of PD begins with degeneration of mesencephalic dopaminergic neurons, predominantly in the pars compacta of the substantia nigra. The meso-striatal pathways from the substantia nigra terminate in the two structures of the dorsal striatum, namely the putamen and the caudate nucleus (De Ybenes & Gomez, 1993). The net result is a dopaminergic denervation lesion in the putamen and the adjacent mediodorsal portion of the head of the caudate nucleus. Dopamine reduction is most obvious in the striatum, with little reduction in prefrontal cortex, anterior cingulate cortex or the hippocampus; this relative pattern can be maintained quite late into the course of the disease (Scatton, Rouquier, Javoy-Agid, & Agid, 1982). Functional neuroimaging with [(18)F]-dopa suggests that dopamine might be upregulated in frontal cortex in the earlier stages of the disease (Rakshi et al., 1999). As further evidence of neuronal integrity in early-stage PD, cortical metabolic activity in nondemented patients with PD does not differ from that of controls (Otsuka et al., 1991; Otsuka et al., 1996; Peppard et al., 1992; Sasaki et al., 1992).

Putaminal dopamine depletion is the primary cause of the motor features of PD. The putamen receives inputs from premotor and sensorimotor cortices, and in turn influences activity in these cortices via specific projection channels through the globus pallidus interna and the thalamus (Middleton & Strick, 1997). This motor circuit represents the basic ground plan of frontostriatal circuitry in general (Alexander, Crutcher, & DeLong, 1990). While caudate depletion is not as severe as that in the putamen, it is substantial. Caudate depletion is important from a cognitive point of view because it is part of the circuitry involving prefrontal cortex. The caudate receives regionally segregated inputs from the dorsolateral prefrontal cortex (which projects to the dorsolateral aspect of the head of the caudate nucleus), and from the lateral orbitofrontal cortex (which projects to the ventromedial aspect of the caudate) (Alexander, DeLong, & Strick, 1986). Consistent with the general structure of frontostriatal circuitry, the caudate nucleus is in a position to influence prefrontal cortex via segregated channels through the globus pallidus interna and thalamus. These are thought to be separate from the transpallidal projections of the motor system (Middleton & Strick, 1997), although the extent to which the segregation is absolute is unresolved (Percheron & Filion, 1991). Dopamine depletion in the caudate nucleus is not uniform, with relative sparing of the ventral aspects (Kish, Shannak, & Hornykiewicz, 1988). Ventrolateral prefrontal circuitry, therefore, is likely to function normally for longer into the course of the disease than the dorsolateral prefrontal circuit, with implications for the patterning of executive function in early PD (Owen, 2004).

Executive dysfunction in early PD

Recent research has continued to support previous findings that patients with early PD have impairments on a variety of tasks that are considered to tap executive function, leaving little doubt that early-stage PD is characterized by well-differentiated and selective executive dysfunction (Brown & Marsden, 1990; Owen, 2004; Robbins, Owen, & Sahakian, 1998; Saint-Cyr et al., 1995; Zgaljardic, Borod, Foldi, & Mattis, 2003). These impairments occur within the visuospatial (Bradley, Welch, & Dick, 1989; Hodgson, Tiesman, Owen, & Kennard, 2002; Kemps, Szmalec, Vandierendonck, & Crevits, 2005; Weintraub et al., 2005) and verbal–symbolic (Bouquet et al., 2003; Brown, Soliveri, & Jahanshahi, 1998; Dirnberger, Frith, & Jahanshahi, 2005; Gilbert et al., 2005; Lewis, Cools et al., 2003; Tamura, Kikuchi, Otsuki, Kitagawa, & Tashiro, 2003) domains. Impairments in planning (Dagher, Owen, Boecker, & Brooks, 2001; Lewis, Cools et al., 2003; Taylor et al., 1986; Weintraub et al., 2005), set shifting (Hayes, Davidson, Keele, & Rafal, 1998; Lewis, Slabosz, Robbins, Barker, & Owen, 2005; Richards, Cote, & Stern, 1993; Rogers et al., 1998), and manipulation of information in working memory (Bradley et al., 1989; Bublak, Muller, Gron, Reuter, & von Cramon, 2002; Fournet, Moreaud, Roulin, Naegele, & Pellat, 1996; Gilbert et al.; Jahanshahi et al., 2002; Lewis, Cools et al., 2003; Lewis, Dove, Robbins, Barker, & Owen, 2004; Lewis et al., 2005; Tamura et al., 2003) have been demonstrated.

Executive function shares the properties of the construct of controlled processing, and the two concepts are essentially synonymous (Casey, 2005). Controlled processes require attention, involve the activation of sequences of elements which can be manipulated rapidly and flexibly in the face of novel problems. Key aspects of controlled processing are a top-down inhibition of irrelevant or competing actions, the significant demand it places on attentional resources, and its dependence on capacity-limited systems (Casey, 2005; Posner & Snyder, 1975). It follows that reductions in short-term and working memory systems exert a compromising effect on executive function. Working memory impairments are prominent in early PD. In the verbal domain, these are quite selective, manifesting as a specific disturbance in the rule-based *manipulation* of verbal information in working memory, but not in the maintenance of the same information in memory, or its retrieval (Bublak et al., 2002; Gilbert et al., 2005; Lewis et al., 2003, 2005). Manipulation of material in working memory in early PD is oversensitive to increasing information load, leading to a rapid exhaustion of working memory capacity and executive function in general (Bublak et al.).

The dissociation between manipulation and maintenance of information in working memory corresponds with the distinction between the function of the dorsolateral prefrontal and ventrolateral prefrontal cortices (Owen, 2004). The latter, which lies approximately in the mid-region of the inferior frontal gyrus, mediates lower level processes, such as storage and retrieval of sequentially arranged elements in short-term memory. The dorsolateral prefrontal cortex, lying in the mid-region of the middle frontal gyrus, mediates active manipulation of elements in short-term storage, and other aspects of high-level executive function (Petrides, 1994). The dorsolateral prefrontal-caudate circuit is impaired earlier in PD than the ventrolateral prefrontal-caudate circuit, and appears to be the basis for the now well-documented manipulation–maintenance dissociation. This also explains the widening of the cognitive impairment to include more fundamental function that occurs with disease progression.

Functional neuroanatomy of executive dysfunction in early PD

Despite the strong and well-established association between executive function and the frontal lobes (Petrides, 1994; Ramnani & Owen, 2004), the pattern of executive impairment seen in early PD differs in some respects from that seen in patients with structural damage to the frontal cortex (Owen et al., 1992; Robbins et al., 1998; Saint-Cyr et al., 1995). Patients with PD do not show the extent of impairment often seen in frontal lobe damage (Robbins et al.). While differences have not been fully delineated in more specific terms, one distinction is that patients with early PD do not exhibit the fixity or perseveration seen in frontal lobe damage. Instead of persisting with a newly irrelevant set or strategy, they have trouble with the formation of newly relevant sets (Saint-Cyr et al.).

Although there is no evidence of frontal lobe damage or persisting dopaminergic depletion in early-stage PD, there is also no recent evidence to suggest that the frontal lobes are completely uninvolved in the executive impairments of early-stage PD. Some form of frontostriatal interaction would seem to be a minimal requirement. Given the anatomy of dopaminergic pathways, there are two potential models (Figure 16.1). The first hypothesis would postulate that the underlying impairment

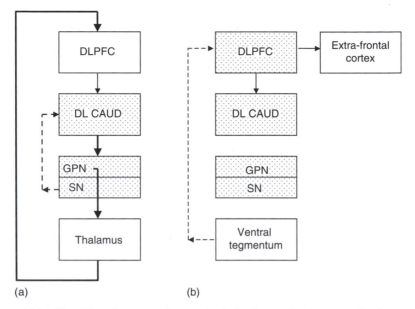

Figure 16.1   Simplified diagram of frontostriatal circuitry underlying executive impairment in PD. Panel (a) shows disrupted connectivity postulated by the nigrostriatal hypothesis of executive dysfunction in PD. The broken line represents the nigrostriatal dopaminergic pathway, and the stippled areas indicate the structures directly affected by dopamine depletion. The heavy solid lines show the bottom-up effect of a dopamine-depleted dorsolateral caudate nucleus on an intact dorsolateral prefrontal cortex. The mesocortical hypothesis (panel b) attributes the executive dysfunction in PD to a direct dopaminergic effect on frontal cortex mediated by the mesocortical pathway (broken line). A dysfunctional or damaged dorsolateral prefrontal cortex, in turn, exerts a top-down effect on other parts of the brain. (DLPFC = dorsolateral prefrontal cortex; DL CAUD = dorsolateral head of caudate nucleus; GPN = globus pallidus; SN = substantia nigra.)

is in the mesostriatal pathway, primarily affecting putamen-caudate function, and that striatal outflow to normal frontal cortex causes the executive dysfunction. This hypothesis is still current, and is supported by the finding that while striatal blood flow during the performance of planning and spatial working memory tasks is reduced, there is no parallel hypoperfusion in frontal cortex (Dagher et al., 2001; Dirnberger et al., 2005; Owen, Doyon, Petrides, & Evans, 1996). The second hypothesis implicates the mesocortical dopaminergic pathway, with a direct task-related effect of frontal activity, and a top-down degradation of prefrontal input into an already dysfunctional striatum. These models are not mutually exclusive, and findings supporting each are not necessarily contradictory (Owen, 2004).

Activation studies

The Tower of London (TOL) has been an important paradigm in studies of planning in early PD. The underlying neural network for this task has been characterized in healthy individuals (Dagher, Owen, Boecker, & Brooks, 1999). Two analytic approaches were employed: a comparison between rest and task conditions to identify all structures involved in TOL performance, and a correlational analysis to identify those structures in which cerebral blood flow correlated with task complexity, and therefore demand on executive resources. Structures that did not correlate with task complexity were those involved in visual processing (occipital and posterior parietal cortex), and those involved in sequencing and execution of arm movement (right cerebellum, left primary motor cortex, and supplementary motor cortex). On the other hand, premotor cortex, rostral anterior cingulate cortex, and dorsolateral prefrontal cortex bilaterally, as well as the right dorsal caudate nucleus, did correlate with the complexity measure. This finding suggests the existence of a network in which there is a co-operative interaction between lateral and medial frontal cortices, and basal ganglia in planned, strategically based response selection.

Regional cerebral blood flow using a touch screen version of the TOL paradigm in an early and mildly affected PD group was compared with that in healthy controls (Dagher et al., 2001). Patients and controls were well matched in terms of TOL performance. The controls showed task-related activation in essentially the same network as that described by Dagher et al. (1999). The patients also showed activation in prefrontal cortex (mid-dorsolateral prefrontal cortex, lateral premotor cortex, and frontopolar region). Unlike the controls, however, the patients did not show task-related activation in the right caudate nucleus, or in the right anterior cingulate cortex. These findings were interpreted as evidence for the notion that planning impairments in early PD are primarily mediated by a mesostriatal dysfunction. A further and interesting difference emerged in patterns of hippocampal activity: while the control group showed task-related decrements in hippocampal activation, the patients showed task-related increments in hippocampal activation. This finding provides a glimpse into the complexity of secondary neurocognitive effects of striatal impairment. The patient sample was not impaired on the TOL at a group level. It is possible that their planning function was based on a compensatory mechanism, mediated by recruitment of the hippocampal system in the presence of a failing striatal system. In cognitive terms, patients might have supported their planning function by declarative processing, that is, solving the immediate problem on the basis of remembered solutions, in the place of procedural and capacity-limited processing that normally underpins TOL performance (Dagher et al., 1999).

Perhaps a more focussed way of addressing the neural basis of executive dysfunction in early PD is to compare patients with and without executive disorders, but who are nevertheless matched in other respects. There is a degree of cognitive heterogeneity in early PD in the sense that patients who are equivalent in terms of demographic factors and degree of motor impairment might differ in terms of their performance on tests of executive function (Lewis, Cools et al., 2003). Patients who perform poorly on the TOL also exhibit a specific impairment in the manipulation of information in verbal working memory, against the background of a normal ability to maintain information in working memory. When these groups were compared by means of fMRI, using a verbal working memory paradigm, the executive-impaired group showed significant underactivity in caudate nucleus and in dorso- and ventrolateral frontal cortex (Lewis, Dove, Robbins, Barker, & Owen, 2003).

This study is unusual in that it compares two groups of early-stage PD patients, well equated in terms of noncognitive disease characteristics; that is, both groups have putatively equivalent involvement of mesostriatal pathways. One group, however, performed well on tests of executive function, whereas the other was impaired. This, in itself, suggests that mesostriatal involvement is not a sufficient condition for the emergence of an executive dysfunction. The demonstration of task-related prefrontal underactivity implies a mesocortical contribution in addition.

Is dopamine involved?

On anatomical grounds, the imaging studies described above suggest a potential role for mesostriatal and mesocortical dopaminergic pathways, but do not specifically implicate dopamine in the executive dysfunction of early PD. Evidence for improvements in cognition with dopamine therapy is inconsistent (Carbon & Marie, 2003; Zgaljardic, Foldi, & Borod, 2004), although dopamine withdrawal can induce executive deficits (Lange et al., 1992). Dopamine effects on executive function might be specific to some aspects, such as manipulation in working memory or planning (Lewis et al., 2005; Owen et al., 1995), leaving other aspects, such as attentional set shifting, unaffected (Lewis et al.). In other studies improvements in planning and working memory with L-dopa were not found (Cools, Stefanova, Barker, Robbins, & Owen, 2002; Mattay et al., 2002).

Inconsistent drug effects on executive dysfunction, and indeed PD cognitive dysfunction in general, might be the result of differential dopamine concentrations in striatal and frontal cortex, the latter being consistently higher than striatal levels, and above the threshold for impairment in terminal stage PD (Kish et al., 1988). As a result, doses effective in alleviating motor symptoms at a striatal level might represent an overdose in frontal cortex, with the effect of *disturbing* executive function is some cases (Gotham, Brown, & Marsden, 1988).

Patients taken off L-dopa therapy can show increased task-related rCBF in frontal cortex, which can be normalized by L-dopa administration. These changes in frontal rCBF correlate with executive performance, and suggest that dopaminergic pathways are capable of modulating frontal function in PD in response to task-related demands (Cools et al., 2002). Increasing the executive demand in random number generation, by manipulating rates of production, in healthy controls is associated with increased blood flow in the right globus pallidus interna, and decreased blood flow in the right frontal cortex. Patients with PD showed a decrement in pallidal rCBF together with an increment in frontal cortex (Dirnberger et al., 2005). This pattern suggests that PD causes a loss of striatal modulation of frontal cortex in the face of increasing executive demand.

Metabolic and transmitter ligand correlational studies

This approach maps cognitive function by determining how variations in task performance correlate with regional variation in resting brain glucose uptake. A further PET study by Lozza, Baron, Eidelberg et al. (2004) defined a network involving ventromedial frontal cortex bilaterally, left hippocampus, left pallidum, and mediodorsal thalamus. Glucose uptake in these regions was related to strategic, planning, and working memory aspects of executive dysfunction. The relationship between frontal and striatal glucose uptake and executive function was positive, but negative in the thalamus, again raising the possibility of modulatory effects within the network.

PET research using 11C-S-Nomifensine (11C-S-NMF), which is a marker of striatal dopaminergic denervation, showed that binding in the caudate nucleus correlated selectively with a measure of set shifting (Marie et al., 1999), adding support to the involvement of mesostriatal dopaminergic neurotransmitter systems in executive dysfunction (Marie & Defer, 2003).

Clinical and functional implications

The motor manifestations in early PD are the most obvious features of the disease, and cognitive changes are often overlooked. The emergence of difficulties in absorbing complex instructions, errors of capture, poor multitasking, of general daily forgetfulness, should alert the clinician to the possibility of an early executive dysfunction. On clinical examination, executive impairments in early PD do not occur in isolation. Rather, they are seen against a background of slowed information processing and secondary effects on other cognitive domains. Thus, executive dysfunctions are seen together with reduced reaction time, impaired visuospatial function, poor retrieval on measures of free recall, and generative verbal fluency. Cued recall and confrontation naming are usually normal. This profile is not necessarily associated with significant difficulties in the usual activities of daily living, and therefore does not fulfill the criteria for the diagnosis of a dementia (Foti & Cummings, 1997). Some studies, however, suggest that early cognitive dysfunction in PD is prodromal to PDD in the moderate to advanced stages of the disease (Kavanagh & Marder, 2005; Levy et al., 2002; Woods & Troster, 2003).

Conclusions

While we have not attempted an exhaustive review of the relevant literature in this chapter, there is now strong evidence for a selective executive dysfunction as an intrinsic feature of PD without dementia. Previous resistance to this notion is partly attributable to the view that the basal ganglia do not mediate cognitive function, as well as the absence of evidence of frontal lobe involvement in PD. The emergence of the concept of an integrated frontostriatal network as a functional entity was a fundamental point of departure in accounting for disorders of executive function in a variety of neurological and neuropsychiatric conditions (Cummings, 1993). Referring to the seminal work of Alexander and others on frontostriatal circuitry (Alexander et al., 1990; Alexander et al., 1986), Saint-Cyr et al. (1995) summed up the essential dilemma and its solution as follows: "Studies of the encoding of movement control at cortical and subcortical levels indicate that there is a great deal of parallel processing and self-organization, forcing the final abandonment of the serial model of top-down processing from cortex to striatum. Because cognitive operations and decision making are probably restricted to the cortical level of processing, the ultimate will to act cannot be made at the striatal level. However, the striatum is in the important position of integrating cortical and subcortical information through which the cortical threshold for initiation may be altered" (p. 9–10).

In the context of PD primary pathology in prefrontal cortex in the earlier stages is unlikely, but at most, minimal. This is the sticking point in neurocognitive models of executive dysfunction which postulate an exclusively top-down mechanism. Alexander's concept of the frontostriatal networks embodies the notion of parallel striatal outflow, via the globus pallidus to frontal cortices, allowing for regional demand-related modulation of prefrontal activity, and this mechanism is well supported by recent cognitive activation studies in early-stage PD. Concomitantly, there is no suggestion from recent studies that the prefrontal cortex is primarily functionally impaired, consistent with a purely mesostriatal basis for PD executive dysfunction. The findings of Lewis, Dove et al. (2003), however, suggest that the executive dysfunction in PD depends on the additional involvement of mesocortical pathways, perhaps on a purely demand-related basis.

Although largely speculative at this stage, the α-synucleinopathies might also be unified in terms of their neurocognitive phenotype, and one obvious candidate is a commonality in executive impairment caused by dysfunction in mesostriatal-mesocortical pathways. Although there are some neurobiological differences between PD with dementia (PDD) and dementia with Lewy bodies (DLB) (Aarsland, Ballard, & Halliday, 2004), there are also similarities which suggest that PDD and DLB are pathologically continuous (Braak et al., 2005; Jellinger, 2004; McKeith & Mosimann, 2004). DLB patients do not appear to have dopaminergic depletion in ventrolateral nigral neurons as seen in PD, but they do show significant dopamine depletion in all regions of the striatum (Walker et al., 2004). Executive dysfunction is a prominent component of the clinical picture in DLB (Collerton, Burn, McKeith, & O'Brien, 2003). There is also considerable overlap in the distribution of dopamine depletion between PD and multiple system atrophy (MSA), but additional mesencephalic reduction occurs MSA (Scherfler et al., 2005). Executive disorders have been documented in MSA (Robbins et al., 1994), but these are more severe than in non-demented patients with PD (Dujardin, Defebvre, Krystkowiak, Degreef, & Destee, 2003; Meco, Gasparini, & Doricchi, 1996). Further characterization of executive dysfunction in DLB and MSA might help to draw out potential links between the molecular biology of the synucleinopathies and the neurocognitive architecture of executive dysfunction.

References

Aarsland, D., Ballard, C. G., & Halliday, G. (2004). Are Parkinson's disease with dementia and dementia with Lewy bodies the same entity? *Journal of Geriatric Psychiatry Neurology, 17*(3), 137–145.

Alexander, G. E., Crutcher, M. D., & DeLong, M. R. (1990). Basal ganglia thalamocortical circuits: Parallel substrates for motor, oculomotor, 'prefrontal' and 'limbic' functions. *Progress in Brain Research, 85*, 119–146.

Alexander, G. E., DeLong, M. R., & Strick, P. L. (1986). Parallel organization of functionally segregated circuits linking basal ganglia and cortex. *Annual Review of Neuroscience, 9*, 357–381.

Bodis-Wollner, I., & Antal, A. (2005). Primary visual and visuocognitive deficits. In R. F. Pfeiffer & I. Bodis-Wollner (Eds.), *Parkinson's disease and non-motor function* (pp. 233–244). Totowa, NJ: Humana Press.

Bokura, H., Yamaguchi, S., & Kobayashi, S. (2005). Event-related potentials for response inhibition in Parkinson's disease. *Neuropsychologia, 43*(6), 967–975.

Bouquet, C. A., Bonnaud, V., & Gil, R. (2003). Investigation of supervisory attentional system functions in patients with Parkinson's disease using the Hayling task. *Journal of Clinical and Experimental Neuropsychology, 25*(6), 751–760.

Bowen, F. P., Hoehn, M. M., & Yahr, M. D. (1972). Parkinsonism: Alterations in spatial orientation as determined by a route-walking test. *Neuropsychologia, 10,* 355–361.

Braak, H., Del Tredici, K., Bratzke, H., Hamm-Clement, J., Sandmann-Keil, D., & Rub, U. (2002). Staging of the intracerebral inclusion body pathology associated with idiopathic Parkinson's disease (preclinical and clinical stages). *Journal of Neurology, 249* (Suppl. 3), III/1–5.

Braak, H., Del Tredici, K., Rub, U., de Vos, R. A., Jansen Steur, E. N., & Braak, E. (2003). Staging of brain pathology related to sporadic Parkinson's disease. *Neurobiology of Aging, 24*(2), 197–211.

Braak, H., Rub, U., Steur, E., Del Tredici, K., & de Vos, R. A. I. (2005). Cognitive status correlates with neuropathological stage in Parkinson disease. *Neurology, 64,* 1404–1410.

Bradley, V. A., Welch, J. L., & Dick, D. J. (1989). Visuospatial working memory in Parkinson's disease. *Journal of Neurology, Neurosurgery, and Psychiatry, 52,* 1228–1235.

Brown, R. G., & Marsden, C. D. (1990). Cognitive function is Parkinson's disease: From description to theory. *Trends in the Neurosciences, 13,* 21–29.

Brown, R. G., Soliveri, P., & Jahanshahi, M. (1998). Executive processes in Parkinson's disease—random number generation and response suppression. *Neuropsychologia, 36* (12), 1355–1362.

Bublak, P., Muller, U., Gron, G., Reuter, M., & von Cramon, D. Y. (2002). Manipulation of working memory information is impaired in Parkinson's disease and related to working memory capacity. *Neuropsychology, 16*(4), 577–590.

Carbon, M., & Marie, R. M. (2003). Functional imaging of cognition in Parkinson's disease. *Current Opinion in Neurology, 16*(4), 475–480.

Casey, B. J. (2005). Frontostriatal and frontocerebellar circuitry underlying cognitive control. In S. W. Keele (Ed.), *Developing individuality in the human brain: A tribute to Michael I. Posner* (pp. 141–166). Washington, DC: American Psychological Association.

Collerton, D., Burn, D., McKeith, I., & O'Brien, J. (2003). Systematic review and meta-analysis show that dementia with Lewy bodies is a visual–perceptual and attentional–executive dementia. *Dementia and Geriatric Cognitive Disorders, 16*(4), 229–237.

Cools, R., Stefanova, E., Barker, R. A., Robbins, T. W., & Owen, A. M. (2002). Dopaminergic modulation of high-level cognition in Parkinson's disease: The role of the prefrontal cortex revealed by PET. *Brain, 125,* 584–594.

Cummings, J. L. (1993). Frontal-subcortical circuits and human behavior. *Archives of Neurology, 50,* 873–880.

Dagher, A., Owen, A. M., Boecker, H., & Brooks, D. J. (1999). Mapping the network for planning: A correlational PET activation study with the Tower of London. *Brain, 122,* 1973–1987.

Dagher, A., Owen, A. M., Boecker, H., & Brooks, D. J. (2001). The role of the striatum and hippocampus in planning: A PET activation study in Parkinson's disease. *Brain, 124,* 1020–1032.

De Ybenes, J. G., & Gomez, M. A. M. (1993). Dopamine systems in the mammalian brain. In E. Tolosa (Ed.), *Parkinson's disease and movement disorders* (pp. 13–34). Baltimore: Williams and Wilkins.

Delwaide, P. J., & Gonce, M. (1993). Pathophysiology of Parkinson's signs. In J. Jankovic & E. Tolosa (Eds.), *Parkinson's disease and movement disorders* (pp. 77–92). Baltimore: Williams and Wilkins.

Dirnberger, G., Frith, C. D., & Jahanshahi, M. (2005). Executive dysfunction in Parkinson's disease is associated with altered pallidal-frontal processing. *Neuroimage, 25*(2), 588–599.

Dujardin, K., Defebvre, L., Krystkowiak, P., Degreef, J. F., & Destee, A. (2003). Executive function differences in multiple system atrophy and Parkinson's disease. *Parkinsonism & Related Disorders, 9*(4), 205–211.

Foti, D., & Cummings, J. L. (1997). Neurobehavioral aspects of movement disorders. In R. L. Watts & W. C. Koller (Eds.), *Movement disorders: Neurologic principles and practice* (pp. 15–30). New York: McGraw-Hill.

Fournet, N., Moreaud, O., Roulin, J. L., Naegele, B., & Pellat, J. (1996). Working memory in medicated patients with Parkinson's disease: The central executive seems to work. *Journal of Neurology, Neurosurgery, and Psychiatry, 60*(3), 313–317.

Freeman, R. Q., Giovannetti, T., Lamar, M., Cloud, B. S., Stern, R. A., Kaplan, E., et al. (2000). Visuoconstructional problems in dementia: Contribution of executive systems functions. *Neuropsychology, 14*(3), 415–426.

Giasson, B. I., Lee, V. M. -Y., & Trojanowski, J. Q. (2004). Parkinson's disease, dementia with Lewy bodies, multiple system atrophy and the spectrum of diseases with α-synuclein inclusions. In J. Q. Trojanowski (Ed.), *The neuropathology of dementia* (2nd ed., pp. 353–375). Cambridge University Press.

Gilbert, B., Belleville, S., Bherer, L., & Chouinard, S. (2005). Study of verbal working memory in patients with Parkinson's disease. *Neuropsychology, 19*(1), 106–114.

Goetz, C. G., & Kompoliti, K. (2005). Parkinson's disease. In A. C. Ludolph (Ed.), *Neurodegenerative diseases: Neurobiology, pathogenesis, and therapeutics* (pp. 561–574). Cambridge University Press.

Goldman, J. G., & Goetz, C. G. (2005). James Parkinson. In R. F. Pfeiffer (Ed.), *Parkinson's disease* (pp. 1–10). Boca Raton, FL: CRC Press.

Gotham, A. M., Brown, R. G., & Marsden, C. D. (1988). Frontal cognitive function in patients with Parkinson's disease on and off levodopa. *Brain, 111*, 299–321.

Grossman, M., Lee, C., Morris, J., Stern, M. B., & Hurtig, H. I. (2002). Assessing resource demands during sentence processing in Parkinson's disease. *Brain and Language, 80*(3), 603–616.

Harding, A. J., & Halliday, G. M. (2001). Cortical Lewy body pathology in the diagnosis of dementia. *Acta Neuropathologica (Berlin), 102*(4), 355–363.

Hayes, A. E., Davidson, M. C., Keele, S. W., & Rafal, R. D. (1998). Toward a functional analysis of the basal ganglia. *Journal of Cognitive Neuroscience, 10*(2), 178–198.

Henry, J. D., & Crawford, J. R. (2004). Verbal fluency deficits in Parkinson's disease: A meta-analysis. *Journal of the International Neuropsychological Society, 10*, 608–622.

Hodgson, T. L., Tiesman, B., Owen, A. M., & Kennard, C. (2002). Abnormal gaze strategies during problem solving in Parkinson's disease. *Neuropsychologia, 40*, 411–422.

Hovestadt, A., De Jong, G. J., & Meerwaldt, J. D. (1987). Spatial disorientation as an early symptom of Parkinson's disease. *Neurology, 37*, 485–487.

Hughes, A. J., Daniel, S. E., & Lees, A. J. (2001). Improved accuracy of clinical diagnosis of Lewy body Parkinson's disease. *Neurology, 57*(8), 1497–1499.

Jahanshahi, M., Rowe, J., Saleem, T., Brown, R. G., Limousin-Dowsey, P., Rothwell, J. C., et al. (2002). Striatal contribution to cognition: Working memory and executive function in Parkinson's disease before and after unilateral posteroventral pallidotomy. *Journal of Cognitive Neuroscience, 14*(2), 298–310.

Jellinger, K. A. (2004). Lewy body-related alpha-synucleinopathy in the aged human brain. *Journal Neural Transmission, 111*(10–11), 1219–1235.

Kahle, P. J., Neumann, M., Ozmen, L., & Haass, C. (2000). Physiology and pathophysiology of alpha-synuclein. Cell culture and transgenic animal models based on a Parkinson's disease-associated protein. *Annals of the New York Academy of Sciences, 920*, 33–41.

Kavanagh, P., & Marder, K. (2005). Dementia. In R. F. Pfeiffer & I. Bodis-Wollner (Eds.), *Parkinson's disease and nonmotor dysfunction* (pp. 35–47). Totowa, NJ: Humana Press.

Kemps, E., Szmalec, A., Vandierendonck, A., & Crevits, L. (2005). Visuo-spatial processing in Parkinson's disease: Evidence for diminished visuo-spatial sketch pad and central executive resources. *Parkinsonism & Related Disorders, 11*(3), 181–186.

Kish, S. J., Shannak, K., & Hornykiewicz, O. (1988). Uneven patterns of dopamine loss in the striatum of patients with idiopathic Parkinson's disease: Pathophysiologic and clinical implications. *New England Journal of Medicine, 318*, 876–880.

Lange, K. W., Robbins, T. W., Marsden, C. D., James, M., Owen, A. M., & Paul, G. M. (1992). L-dopa withdrawal in Parkinson's disease selectively impairs cognitive performance in tests sensitive to frontal dysfunction. *Psychopharmacology, 107*, 394–404.

Lange, K. W., Tucha, O., Alders, G. L., Preier, M., Csoti, I., Merz, B., et al. (2003). Differentiation of parkinsonian syndromes according to differences in executive functions. *Journal of Neural Transmission, 110*(9), 983–995.

Levin, B. E., Tomer, R., & Rey, G. J. (1992). Cognitive impairments in Parkinson's disease. *Neurology Clinics, 10*, 471–485.

Levy, G., Jacobs, D. M., Tang, M. X., Cote, L. J., Louis, E. D., Alfaro, B., et al. (2002). Memory and executive function impairment predict dementia in Parkinson's disease. *Movement Disorders, 17*(6), 1221–1226.

Lewis, S. J., Cools, R., Robbins, T. W., Dove, A., Barker, R. A., & Owen, A. M. (2003). Using executive heterogeneity to explore the nature of working memory deficits in Parkinson's disease. *Neuropsychologia, 41*(6), 645–654.

Lewis, S. J., Dove, A., Robbins, T. W., Barker, R. A., & Owen, A. M. (2003). Cognitive impairments in early Parkinson's disease are accompanied by reductions in activity in frontostriatal neural circuitry. *Journal of Neuroscience, 23*(15), 6351–6356.

Lewis, S. J., Dove, A., Robbins, T. W., Barker, R. A., & Owen, A. M. (2004). Striatal contributions to working memory: A functional magnetic resonance imaging study in humans. *The European Journal of Neuroscience, 19*(3), 755–760.

Lewis, S. J., Slabosz, A., Robbins, T. W., Barker, R. A., & Owen, A. M. (2005). Dopaminergic basis for deficits in working memory but not attentional set-shifting in Parkinson's disease. *Neuropsychologia, 43*(6), 823–832.

Lozza, C., Baron, J. C., Eidelberg, D., Mentis, M. J., Carbon, M., & Marie, R. M. (2004). Executive processes in Parkinson's disease: FDG-PET and network analysis. *Human Brain Mapping, 22*, 236–245.

Marie, R. M., Barre, L., Dupuy, B., Viader, F., Defer, G., & Baron, J. C. (1999). Relationships between striatal dopamine denervation and frontal executive tests in Parkinson's disease. *Neuroscience Letters, 260*(2), 77–80.

Marie, R. M., & Defer, G. L. (2003). Working memory and dopamine: Clinical and experimental clues. *Current Opinion in Neurology, 16*(Suppl. 2), S29–S35.

Marsden, C. D. (1982). The mysterious motor function of the basal ganglia: The Robert Wartenberg lecture. *Neurology, 32*, 514–539.

Mattay, V. S., Tessitore, A., Callicott, J. H., Bertolino, A., Goldberg, T. E., Chase, T. N., et al. (2002). Dopaminergic modulation of cortical function in patients with Parkinson's disease. *Annals of Neurology, 51*(2), 156–164.

McKeith, I. G., & Mosimann, U. P. (2004). Dementia with Lewy bodies and Parkinson's disease. *Parkinsonism & Related Disorders, 10*(Suppl. 1), S15–S18.

Meco, G., Gasparini, M., & Doricchi, F. (1996). Attentional functions in multiple system atrophy and Parkinson's disease. *Journal of Neurology Neurosurgery and Psychiatry, 60*(4), 393–398.

Middleton, F. A., & Strick, P. L. (1997). New concepts about the organization of basal ganglia output. In J. A. Obeso, M. R. DeLong, C. Ohye, & C. D. Marsden (Eds.), *The basal ganglia and new surgical approaches for Parkinson's disease: Advances in neurology* (Vol. 74, pp. 57–68). Philadelphia: Lippincot-Raven.

Otsuka, M., Ichiya, Y., Hosokawa, S., Kuwabara, Y., Tahara, T., Fukumura, T., et al. (1991). Striatal blood flow, glucose metabolism and 18F-dopa uptake: Difference in Parkinson's disease and atypical parkinsonism. *Journal of Neurology Neurosurgery and Psychiatry, 54*(10), 898–904.

Otsuka, M., Ichiya, Y., Kuwabara, Y., Hosokawa, S., Sasaki, M., Yoshida, T., et al. (1996). Glucose metabolism in the cortical and subcortical brain structures in multiple system atrophy and Parkinson's disease: A positron emission tomographic study. *Journal of Neurological Science, 144*(1–2), 77–83.

Owen, A. M. (2004). Cognitive dysfunction in Parkinson's disease: The role of frontostriatal circuitry. *Neuroscientist, 10*(6), 525–537.

Owen, A. M., Doyon, J., Petrides, M., & Evans, A. C. (1996). Planning and spatial working memory: A positron emission tomography study in humans. *European Journal of Neuroscience, 8*, 353–364.

Owen, A. M., James, M., Leigh, P. N., Summers, B. A., Marsden, C. D., Quinn, N. P., et al. (1992). Fronto-striatal cognitive deficits at different stages of Parkinson's disease. *Brain, 115*, 1727–1751.

Owen, A. M., Sahakian, B. J., Hodges, J. R., Summers, B. A., Polkey, C. E., & Robbins, T. W. (1995). Dopamine-dependent frontostriatal planning deficits in early Parkinson's disease. *Neuropsychology, 9*, 126–140.

Paulson, H. L., & Stern, M. B. (1997). Clinical manifestations of Parkinson's Disease. In R. L. Watts & W. C. Koller (Eds.), *Movement disorders: Neurologic principles and practice* (pp. 183–199). New York: McGraw-Hill.

Peppard, R. F., Martin, W. R., Carr, G. D., Grochowski, E., Schulzer, M., Guttman, M., et al. (1992). Cerebral glucose metabolism in Parkinson's disease with and without dementia. *Archives of Neurology, 49*(12), 1262–1268.

Percheron, G., & Filion, M. (1991). Parallel processing in the basal ganglia: Up to a point. *Trends in the Neurosciences, 14*, 55–56.

Petrides, M. (1994). Frontal lobes and behavior. *Current Opinion in Neurobiology, 4*, 207–211.

Pfeiffer, R. F., & Bodis-Wollner, I. (Eds.) (2005). *Parkinson's disease and nonmotor dysfunction*. Totowa, NJ: Humana Press.

Pirozzolo, F. J., Swihart, A. A., Rey, G. J., Mahurin, R., & Jankovic, J. (1993). Cognitive impairments associate with Parkinson's disease and other movement disorders. In J. Jankovic & E. Tolosa (Eds.), *Parkinson's disease and movement disorders* (pp. 493–510). Baltimore: Williams and Wilkins.

Posner, M. I., & Snyder, R. R. (1975). Attention and cognitive control. In R. Solso (Ed.), *Information processing and cognition* (pp. 55–85). Hillsdale, NJ: Lawrence Erlbaum.

Rakshi, J. S., Uema, T., Ito, K., Bailey, D. L., Morrish, P. K., Ashburner, J., et al. (1999). Frontal, midbrain and striatal dopaminergic function in early and advanced Parkinson's disease A 3D [(18)F]dopa-PET study. *Brain, 122*(Pt. 9), 1637–1650.

Ramnani, N., & Owen, A. M. (2004). Anterior prefrontal cortex: Insights into function from anatomy and neuroimaging. *Nature Neuroscience, 5*, 185–194.

Rashkin, S. A., Borod, J. C., & Tweedy, J. (1990). Neuropsychological aspects of Parkinson's disease. *Neuropsychological Review, 1*, 185–219.

Richards, M., Cote, L. J., & Stern, Y. (1993). Executive function in Parkinson's disease: Set-shifting or set-maintenance? *Journal of Clincal and Experimental Neuropsychology, 15*(2), 266–279.

Robbins, T. W., James, M., Owen, A. M., Lange, K. W., Lees, A. J., Leigh, P. N., et al. (1994). Cognitive deficits in progressive supranuclear palsy, Parkinson's disease, and multiple system atrophy in tests sensitive to frontal lobe dysfunction. *Journal of Neurology Neurosurgery and Psychiatry, 57*(1), 79–88.

Robbins, T. W., Owen, A. M., & Sahakian, B. J. (1998). The neuropsychology of basal ganglia disorders: An integrative cognitive and comparative approach. In M. A. Ron & A. S. David (Eds.), *Disorders of brain and mind* (pp. 57–83). Cambridge University Press.

Rogers, R. D., Sahakian, B. J., Hodges, J. R., Polkey, C. E., Kennard, C., & Robbins, T. W. (1998). Dissociating executive mechanisms of task control following frontal lobe damage and Parkinson's disease. *Brain, 121*(Pt. 5), 815–842.

Saint-Cyr, J. A., Taylor, A. E., & Nicholson, K. (1995). Behavior and the basal ganglia. In W. J. Weiner & A. E. Lang (Eds.), *Advances in neurology: Behavioral neurology of movement disorders* (Vol. 65, pp. 1–28). New York: Raven Press.

Sasaki, M., Ichiya, Y., Hosokawa, S., Otsuka, M., Kuwabara, Y., Fukumura, T., et al. (1992). Regional cerebral glucose metabolism in patients with Parkinson's disease with or without dementia. *Annals of Nuclear Medicine, 6*(4), 241–246.

Scatton, B., Rouquier, L., Javoy-Agid, F., & Agid, Y. (1982). Dopamine deficiency in the cerebral cortex in Parkinson's disease. *Neurology, 32*, 1039–1040.

Scherfler, C., Seppi, K., Donnemiller, E., Goebel, G., Brenneis, C., Virgolini, I., et al. (2005). Voxel-wise analysis of [123I]beta-CIT SPECT differentiates the Parkinson variant of multiple system atrophy from idiopathic Parkinson's disease. *Brain, 128*(Pt. 7), 1605–1612.

Tamura, I., Kikuchi, S., Otsuki, M., Kitagawa, M., & Tashiro, K. (2003). Deficits of working memory during mental calculation in patients with Parkinson's disease. *Journal of the Neurolological Sciences, 209*(1–2), 19–23.

Taylor, A. E., Saint-Cyr, J. A., & Lang, A. E. (1986). Frontal lobe dysfunction in Parkinson's disease: The cortical focus of neostriatal outflow. *Brain, 109*, 845–883.

Taylor, A. E., Saint-Cyr, J. A., & Lang, A. E. (1990). Memory and learning in early Parkinson's disease. *Brain and Cognition, 2*, 211–232.

Walker, Z., Costa, D. C., Walker, R. W., Lee, L., Livingston, G., Jaros, E., et al. (2004). Striatal dopamine transporter in dementia with Lewy bodies and Parkinson disease: A comparison. *Neurology, 62*(9), 1568–1572.

Weintraub, D., Moberg, P. J., Culbertson, W. C., Duda, J. E., Katz, I. R., & Stern, M. B. (2005). Dimensions of executive function in Parkinson's disease. *Dementia and Geriatric Cognitive Disorders, 20*(2–3), 140–144.

Woods, S. P., & Troster, A. I. (2003). Prodromal frontal/executive dysfunction predicts incident dementia in Parkinson's disease. *Journal of International Neuropsychological Society, 9*(1), 17–24.

Zgaljardic, D. J., Borod, J. C., Foldi, N. S., & Mattis, P. (2003). A review of the cognitive and behavioral sequelae of Parkinson's disease: Relationship to frontostriatal circuitry. *Cognitive and Behavioral Neurology*, *16*(4), 193–210.

Zgaljardic, D. J., Foldi, N. S., & Borod, J. C. (2004). Cognitive and behavioral dysfunction in Parkinson's disease: Neurochemical and clinicopathological contributions. *Journal of Neural Transmission*, *111*(10–11), 1287–1301.

Section IV

Rehabilitation of impairments in executive function

17 Models for the rehabilitation of executive impairments

Barbara A. Wilson and Jonathan Evans

Contents

Introduction

"A patient with frontal lobe disease will retain the ability to move around, use language, recognise objects, and even memorize information. Yet like a leaderless army, cognition disintegrates and ultimately collapses with the loss of the frontal lobes." (Goldberg, 2001, p. 23)

In his excellent book, *The Executive Brain*, Goldberg tells us that the brain's chief executive is the frontal lobes. This is so often the area damaged after traumatic brain injury (TBI), and so often the cause of bewilderment to relatives of the survivors of TBI, not to mention the frustration of rehabilitation staff trying to remediate executive deficits. We have known for many years that frontal lobe damage can lead to devastating social consequences, one of the earliest case descriptions being that of the famous Phineas Gage (Harlow, 1868). Although Gage survived after an iron rod had been blown through his frontal lobes in a dynamiting accident, he became a changed character who suffered dire consequences, many of which are described in scholarly detail by Macmillan (2000). Treatment for damage to the frontal lobes has continued to develop since those early attempts to come to terms with such a disabling condition, and much of this treatment has benefited by a growth in understanding among scientists and researchers, some of whom have built their own models to explain a number of its complexities. Neuropsychologists have drawn help from these models of executive functioning and brain–behavior relationships and it is the aim of this chapter to focus on those models that seem to be most relevant to neuropsychological rehabilitation.

A model is a representation that can help us understand and predict related phenomena. Models range from simple analogies such as that of the faulty switch to explain distractibility, through to complex computer models to explain how damaged systems learn new information. In rehabilitation, models are useful for facilitating thinking about assessment and treatment, for explaining deficits to therapists, relatives and patients, and for enabling us to conceptualize outcomes. There are several models that can guide our choice of rehabilitation strategy and among these perhaps the three most relevant for understanding deficits of executive functioning are (a) the Working Memory Model (WM; Baddeley, 1986; Baddeley & Hitch, 1974); (b) the Supervisory Attentional System Model (SAS; Norman & Shallice, 1986; Shallice & Burgess, 1996); and (c) Duncan's Model of Goal Neglect (Duncan, 1986; Duncan, Burgess, & Emslie, 1995). These will be described below and evaluated in terms of their contribution to rehabilitation.

Before doing this, however, it is perhaps timely here to remind ourselves that in rehabilitation we address a wide range of issues and not simply a discrete problem that can be adequately explained by one particular model. Even for patients whose primary presenting disorder can be described as a Dysexecutive Syndrome, there will be other issues such as anxiety, stress, social and work related matters that must be addressed if rehabilitation is to improve functioning in everyday life. Consequently, we need to draw on a wide range of models including those that involve learning, behavior and emotion. Drawing upon a synthesis of several models is probably the best way to accomplish optimum effectiveness in rehabilitation and, in an attempt to achieve this goal, Wilson (2002) combined several current models to build an overarching framework of models to inform the complex everyday problems faced by survivors of brain injury, many of whom will experience executive impairments. A brief account of this broad and inclusive structure will therefore be offered in conclusion to this chapter.

Working memory model

This model (Baddeley, 1986; Baddeley & Hitch, 1974) categorizes memory according to the length of time information is stored. *Sensory memory* holds information for less than a quarter of a second. *Working memory* holds information for a few seconds and this can be extended by rehearsal and *Long-term memory* which is potentially limitless and can hold information for decades. It is the working memory section of the model that is particularly relevant to executive functioning. Baddeley (1997) says working memory "can be defined as a system for temporary maintenance and manipulation of information" (p. 64). The core component is the *Central Executive* (CE) which can be considered to be the general controller or allocator of attentional resources. It is involved in decision making, judgment, reasoning, planning, divided attention and dual tasking. If, for example, we are going to do two things at once such as driving a car and talking to a passenger, the CE allows us to allocate sufficient attentional resources to the control of the car and road conditions and sufficient resources to talk to our passenger. If something unexpected or complex happens such as having to join a busy road, we will probably stop talking to our passenger and concentrate our resources on the busy traffic conditions.

The CE is aided by two slave systems namely the *phonological loop* and the *visuospatial scratch pad* or *sketchpad*. The phonological route may have evolved for the purpose of language acquisition (Baddeley, 2002) as people with deficits in this system have difficulty learning to read, find it hard to acquire a foreign language and cannot manipulate words such as omitting the initial sounds of words (e.g., when hearing "land" say "and"). The visuospatial sketchpad allows for the temporary storage and manipulation of visual and spatial information. Patients with deficits in this component of the model will be unable to do such tasks as mentally count the number of windows in their house. One patient described how she was unable to imagine holding her new grandchild; nor could she work out what items of clothing would go together (Wilson, Baddeley, & Young, 1999). Della Sala and Logie (2002) provide convincing evidence to show that the visual and spatial aspects of the sketchpad are dissociable, with some patients having deficits in visual but not spatial tasks and vice versa.

In order to demonstrate that the CE co-ordinates these two slave systems, Baddeley, Logie, Bressi, Della Sala, and Spinnler (1986) carried out an ingenious study with patients diagnosed as having Alzheimer's Disease (AD) and age matched healthy controls. All participants were required to track a target moving round a computer. The level of difficulty was manipulated so that all participants were at the same level (for example, all were close to 70% of time on target). In addition, all were given a forward digit span task and each individual's span was established. Thus all participants were matched on the individual tasks, one of which involved the visuospatial sketchpad and one the phonological loop. Then participants were asked to carry out the two tasks simultaneously. Performance of the control subjects went down a little but the performance of the AD patients was very impaired even though all were matched on the single tasks. Baddeley et al. (1986) interpreted this as an impairment of the CE. Hartman, Pickering, and Wilson (1992) replicated this study with survivors of TBI and controls who had sustained orthopaedic injuries. Essentially they found the same phenomenon, i.e., that TBI patients had a CE deficit.

In what ways can this model help our work in rehabilitation? It can be used to plan assessment, influence treatment, explain deficits, and understand outcomes. When a patient with a TBI is admitted for rehabilitation, we will probably assess executive functioning and this assessment will be informed by our understanding of the CE component of the model. We may look at the patient's ability to do two tasks simultaneously and follow the procedure used by Baddeley et al. (1986) with the AD patients. For a patient who has problems with forward digit span we may decide to introduce tasks involving the phonological loop in more detail. If the patient complains of not being able to see how things go together it is possible that the visuospatial sketchpad is impaired and we may want to look at this. Many survivors of brain injury will have episodic memory difficulties and we would almost certainly screen for these by giving tests of visual and verbal recall and recognition. In addition to these assessment issues we might use the model to help us plan treatment: for example, we might want to identify the person's strengths so these can be used to help compensate for the weaknesses. Alderman (1996) used the CE component of the model to conceptualize the deficits of a severely impaired brain-injured patient and selected an operant conditioning approach to deal with her particular problem.

Patients, therapists, and family members may be surprised that scores are so good on some tests (perhaps on immediate and semantic memory tasks) yet so disastrous on others (perhaps delayed recall and recognition). Here we can use the model to explain that different memory systems hold information for differing lengths of time. Finally, we may find the model useful to conceptualize response to rehabilitation. The reason why some people compensate well, for example, may be because they have a good CE and no problems with planning and organization. In contrast, the reason why some people can only function in a structured environment is because they have a dysexecutive syndrome with its associated difficulties in problem solving, planning, organization, initiation, self-monitoring, error correction, and behavior regulation.

The limitations of this model for rehabilitation are, first, that it does not specify in sufficient detail how to deal with the resultant deficits, and second, that it does not address the concomitant difficulties such as anxiety, depression or behavioral difficulties. To be fair, however, the model was not designed to do this. Its strengths lie in the help it gives in understanding why certain problems occur in people with brain injury; in making predictions about the kind of behavior to expect (for example people with the amnesic syndrome have a normal phonological loop and do well on forward digit span tasks); and in providing us with new assessment procedures such as the Doors and People Test of Visual and Verbal Recall and Recognition (Baddeley, Emslie, & Nimmo-Smith, 1994), The Visual Patterns Test (Della Sala, Gray, Baddeley, & Wilson, 1997) and the Behavioural Assessment of the Dysexecutive Syndrome (BADS; Wilson, Alderman, Burgess, Emslie, & Evans, 1996).

Supervisory attentional system model

Although there is great variability in the extent and degree of impairment in patients with frontal lobe deficits, certain features are highly characteristic. Rylander (1939) described them as "disturbed attention, increased distractibility...a difficulty grasping the whole of a complicated state of affairs...well able to work along routine lines (but) cannot learn to master new types of task" (p. 22). Shallice (1982) believed this pattern of deficit could be due to an impairment of attentional control. Norman and Shallice (1986) explained this in terms of a model of attention in which a supervisory attentional system exerts an executive function to deal with novel or nonroutine tasks. It is involved in

"...producing a response to novelty that is planned rather than one that is routine or impulsive. The situations in which it [a Supervisory Attentional System] is required are those where the routine triggering by the environment of the organism's battery of specialised thought or action schemata is insufficient to produce an appropriate response. Instead, some form of problem-solving behaviour, trying out hypotheses and learning from failed attempts, is required." (Shallice, 1988, p. 345)

The SAS is required in five situations: (a) for planning and trouble shooting; (b) for error correction or trouble shooting; (c) when responses are not well learned or when they contain novel sequences; (d) when the situation is dangerous or technically difficult; and (e) when there is a need to overcome a strong habitual response or overcome temptation (Norman & Shallice, 1986). Another system, the contention scheduling system deals with routine or automatic tasks. Baddeley (1986) suggests that the SAS is analogous to the CE component of the WM model.

A considerable amount of work has investigated the fractionation of The Dysexecutive Syndrome. Shallice and Burgess (1996) argue that the SAS can be fractionated into a set of basic subcomponents or sub processes and provide evidence both from imaging studies and from double dissociations in patients with neurological deficits. Burgess and Alderman (2004) suggest that the SAS plays a part in at least eight different processes, which may be impaired in isolation. These are: working memory, monitoring, rejection of schema, spontaneous schema generation, adoption of processing mode, goal setting, delayed intention marker realization, and episodic memory retrieval.

Evans (2001, 2003) believes that the SAS model is essentially a detailed problem-solving framework that is closely related to Luria's (1966) conception of problem solving. Shallice and Burgess (1996) say that in order to respond to novelty we need to (a) create a new schema as we cannot rely on the old schema that govern routine behavior; (b) use a special purpose working memory to hold on to and implement this new schema; and (c) incorporate a system that monitors and evaluates and accepts and rejects actions depending on how successful they are at solving the novel problem. Luria (1966) also argues for three stages in the problem-solving process: namely, strategy selection, application of operations and evaluation of outcomes. Not only can patients have a deficit in any one of these stages but also each stage requires the contribution of a number of underlying cognitive processes for successful functioning (Evans, 2001). The treatment approaches of Evans (2001, 2003, 2005) have been influenced by the SAS model. He argues that when we treat executive deficits we are in essence treating a problem-solving deficit. Like Shallice and Burgess (1996) and Luria (1966), Evans also identifies three broad processes involved in problem solving, similar to those described earlier: first, it is necessary to notice that a problem exists and monitor and evaluate the solutions one implements (online monitoring); second, a plan of action must be developed (planning); and third, a solution must be initiated (translation of intention into action). Evans has employed the Shallice and Burgess (1996) model to help plan the rehabilitation needs of patients. This model, shown in Figure 17.1, enables us to pinpoint the particular deficits of individual patients. Evans (2001, 2003) also describes strategies to improve online monitoring, planning and translating plans into actions.

Clinically, we can see people who show deficits in each of these stages. There are patients who have no awareness that there is anything the matter and fail to recognize that a problem exists. Here is a comment from an employer of a man with executive deficits following TBI:

> "My employee used to be very quick at his job. Since he has returned to work after his injury, he seems to have great difficulty learning from his mistakes. I had to tell him several times about a mistake he kept making at work, but he simply couldn't see it as a problem."

Some people can recognize they have a problem but do not know what to do about it, so stage one is working but not stage two. This is a comment from one patient with planning difficulties:

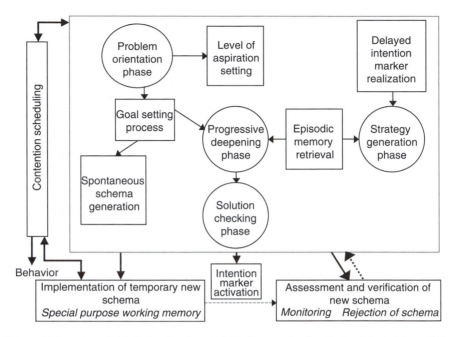

Figure 17.1   A model to help plan the rehabilitation needs of patients. Adapted from "The domain of the supervisory process and temporal organization of behaviour," by T. Shallice and P. Burgess, 1996, *Philosophical Transactions of the Royal Society B: Biological Sciences, 351*, pp. 1405–1412.

"I used to be a chef in a very busy kitchen. I organised all the food we needed to order, what we could put on the menu and what each member of kitchen staff had to do. After my accident I just couldn't get my head around it all. I couldn't organise the kitchen so I lost my job."

Some people know there is a problem and can think what they should do but they cannot put the plan into action. So here the difficulty is in stage three. An example of such a patient is RP, reported by Evans, Emslie, and Wilson (1998). Following hemorrhages in both frontal lobes, RP was unable to carry out the plans necessary to manage household tasks such as cooking a meal, washing her clothes, watering the plants or taking medication. She knew what she was supposed to do, she had a plan but when she went to start one of these tasks, such as going to the kitchen to do the washing, she became distracted and started counting the cars going past the window or she engaged in some other unnecessary activity. She was unable to carry out many of the household tasks with the help of a pager. The alarm on the pager and the written message provided seemed to keep her attention on the task in hand. Wilson, Emslie, Quirk, and Evans (2001) and Wilson, Evans, Emslie, and Malinek (1997) describe further research on the benefits of this pager.

Before introducing treatment we need to administer an assessment. The SAS model has certainly been influential in the assessment of executive deficits. Shallice and Burgess (1991) classic paper described the Six Elements and Multiple Errands Test developed for three patients with normal intellectual functioning and normal performance on traditional frontal lobe tests. Despite this normal performance on tests they were unable to cope in everyday life because of severe executive deficits. Shallice and Burgess summed up the weaknesses of traditional frontal lobe tests very well when they stated: "...the patient typically has a single explicit problem to tackle at any one time, the trials tend to be short, task initiation is strongly prompted by the examiner and what constitutes successful trial completion is clearly characterised." (pp. 727, 728). This is in contrast to a problem arising in day-to-day living where there may be more than one solution and when a task may extend over a period of time. The Six Elements Test captures these everyday intricacies as participants are asked to carry out 6 subtasks over a period of time and follow certain rules. Similarly the Multiple Errands Test requires a participant to carry out tasks in a shopping center also following specified rules. These ecological tests tap real-life functioning in a way tests like The Wisconsin Card Sorting Test, The Trail Making Test and Verbal Fluency do not (although of course these tests are relevant in other situations). The Six Elements Test has been modified and incorporated into the BADS (Wilson et al., 1996), while the Multiple Errands Test has been modified for use in hospital settings (Alderman, Burgess, Knight, & Henman, 2003). Evans (2001) suggests that assessment can be conducted at the level of basic cognitive skills required to problem solve, such as memory, language and attention; or through the presentation of problems to be solved in the form of standardized tests or everyday functional tasks such as making a coat hanger by following the instructions provided (a task in The Chessington Occupational Therapy Neurological Assessment Battery [COTNAB; Tyerman, Tyerman, Howard, & Hadfield, 1986]). Impairments may be seen in each stage of the problem-solving process or in the co-ordination of these stages. It is often necessary to carry out a systematic analysis of an individual's performance to determine where the failure occurs. Burgess, Simons, Dumontheil, and Gilbert (2005) provide a good example of how to determine which process is impaired when people carry out multiple tasks. Problem-solving deficits can also be assessed through systematic observation of an everyday task such as shopping or preparing a meal.

Once the particular deficits have been identified one can plan treatment. How does the SAS model help here? Let us remind ourselves of the five situations when we need the SAS to take over from the more automatic Contention Scheduling System: (a) for planning and trouble shooting; (b) for error correction or trouble shooting; (c) when responses are not well learned or when they contain novel sequences; (d) when the situation is dangerous or technically difficult; and (e) when there is a need to overcome a strong habitual response or overcome temptation (Norman & Shallice, 1986). We can target intervention programmes to deal with any one or all of these situations. One approach is to employ problem-solving therapy. This has been used with psychiatric patients well before the SAS model was published. D'Zurilla and Goldfried (1971) adopted a "problem-solving" approach to psychological (psychiatric) problems emphasizing the following stages:

1. Problem orientation
2. Problem definition and formulation
3. Generating potential alternative solutions
4. Decision making concerning the best approach
5. Solution implementation and
6. Solution verification

This approach is similar to the Problem Solving Training programme developed for brain-injured patients with executive deficits (von Cramon, Cramon, & Mai, 1991; von Cramon & Matthes-von Cramon, 1992, 1994). In their 1991 paper the authors describe the training as:

> "...providing patients with techniques enabling them to reduce the complexity of a multi-stage problem by breaking it down into more manageable portions. A slowed down, controlled and stepwise processing of a given problem should replace the unsystematic and often rash approach these patients spontaneously prefer." (1991, p. 46)

The purpose of problem-solving therapy (PST) is to enable patients to (a) identify and analyze problems; (b) separate relevant from irrelevant information; (c) recognize the relationship between different relevant pieces of information and if necessary combine them; (d) produce ideas or solutions; (e) use different mental representations such as flow charts; and (f) monitor the implementation of solutions and evaluate outcome. PST is based on group work over a period of about 6 weeks with an average of 25 sessions. Individuals who they feel will benefit from this approach are listed as follows: (a) those who show difficulty in responding appropriately to feedback; (b) those who do not consider alternative solutions when the chosen course of action is unsuccessful (c) those who do not notice obvious mistakes or cannot correct them even if they are recognized; (d) those who carry out tasks in a sloppy or incorrect way; (e) those who do not recognize what has to be done or have to be told specifically what to do; (f) those who cannot make decisions on their own; and (g) those who fail to anticipate the consequence of their actions.

Patients accepted for PST should be able to concentrate for more than 20 min; show willingness to make an effort; have at least a vague understanding that their thinking ability has been impaired; have some (maybe limited) ability to think in abstract terms (e.g., to be able to recognize common features between exercises worked through with a therapist and exercises done individually); have some learning capacity; and should not have severe perceptual or language deficits.

There is some, albeit limited, evidence for the success of this type of therapy. von Cramon et al. (1991) compared a PST group ($N = 20$) with a control "memory therapy" (MT) group ($N = 17$) and found that those in the PST group were significantly better than the control group on ratings of problem-solving ability and some test performances (e.g., The Tower of Hanoi). However, some patients in the PST group were worse after PST (and MT). von Cramon et al. (1991) suggest this may be due to an increased awareness of the complexity of problems leading to confusion, in contrast to their pretreatment propensity towards premature and ill-considered actions.

A more recent study of problem-solving training was that of Rath, Simon, Langenbahn, Sherr, and Diller (2003), who treated 60 outpatients, all at least 1 year postinjury and compared a group receiving "conventional neuropsychological rehabilitation" with a problem-solving group. All participants were assessed on (a) a number of cognitive tests (including the Stroop, The Controlled Oral Word Association Test and the Wisconsin Card Sorting Test); (b) measures of psychosocial functioning (including The Sickness Impact Profile, the Community Integration Questionnaire and The Rosenburg Self-Esteem Scale); (c) a self-appraisal question-naire (of problem solving, clear thinking, and emotional regulation); and (d) observer ratings of role-played scenarios. Those in the problem-solving group (and not conventional group) improved on the WCST, the self-appraisal problem-solving questionnaire, self-appraisal of clear thinking and self-appraisal of emotional regu-lation together with observer ratings of role-played scenarios. These gains were maintained at a 6-month follow-up. Other than the self-appraisal reports, we are not told of any functional gains in everyday life and, apart from the WCST, no other standardized tests showed improvement.

PST is appropriate for treating difficulties in any one of the three stages outlined by Evans (2001), i.e., online monitoring, planning and translation of intention into action and it can also deal with some of the eight different processes dealt with by the SAS outlined by Burgess and Alderman (2004).

Some of the treatment approaches for individual cognitive deficits such as impaired working memory, delayed episodic memory and dual tasking or divided attention deficits also play a part in rehabilitation because, as Evans (2001) reports, these are required for adequate performance of executive activities. While the evidence for the treatment of attentional deficits is mixed (Manly & Mattingley, 2004), there is certainly evidence that some kinds of attentional impairments can be treated effectively (Robertson, Hogg, & McMillan, 1998; Robertson, Tegnér, Tham, Lo, & Nimmo-Smith, 1995). Again, although the SAS model has encouraged ideas for treatment, it remains limited in rehabilitation because executive deficits have to be regarded in the context of the wider picture, taking on board the individual's additional problems and needs.

Goal neglect theory

People with goal neglect disregard the requirements of a task even though the task has been understood and remembered. It appears as if the main purpose of the task has slipped the subject's mind. Goal neglect has similarities to the SAS model as problems occur only in situations involving novelty, inadequate or weak error feedback, or when there are many concurrent demands (multi tasking) (Duncan, Emslie, Williams, Johnson, & Freer, 1996). The essential message of this model is that disorganization of behavior after frontal lobe damage reflects a defect in goal-based search and a failure to constrain the choice of action by its intended results. People without brain damage also show goal neglect under some circumstances, particularly people with a low measure of general intelligence (Spearman, 1927). Patients are able to report what they intend to do, or have been told to do, and yet this intention does not adequately control their subsequent actions. Goal neglect is confined entirely to novel behavior as once the neglect has been pointed out most people no longer show the neglect. Thus, it is extremely sensitive to verbal and other prompts that draw attention to the neglected task requirement. This has similarities to Luria's explanations for the impairments seen in frontal lobe patients (Luria, 1963, 1966, 1973). He suggests that the frontal lobes contain a system for the programme, regulation and verification of voluntary action with an emphasis on action that is normally controlled by inner speech. "In these patients the verbal command remained in their memory, but it no longer controlled the initiated action and lost its regulating influence" (Luria, 1973, p. 200). Complex behaviors are frequently replaced by simpler and more basic stereotypes, "they lose not only control over their actions, but also the ability to check their results, although frequently they remember the task assigned" (Luria, 1973, p. 210).

Goal neglect is hard to measure in test situations, occurring as it does in more open-ended unstructured, real-life situations when overlearned behaviors will not suffice. In order to achieve goals and not let them slip through our minds we need to exert higher level control over basic cognitive and motor processes. An important aspect of goal-directed behavior is the selection of new actions when previously selected actions fail to achieve the goal. Based on Duncan's model, Robertson (1996) produced a manual of goal management training (GMT) to overcome the problems of goal neglect. It is essentially a list of what needs to be done but, unlike other lists, this is one that tries to prevent actions that hinder goal achievement and promote actions likely to enhance goal achievement. Duncan (1986) believes that goal neglect occurs in patients who are unable to construct such lists or use those they do construct in an ineffective manner. Paper and pencil exercises are used to train people to use the five-step list. For example, if your task is to arrange a birthday party for a relative, you would need to (a) stop and think what you had to do; (b) define the main task and plan the party; (c) list the steps required to carry out the plan, e.g., check that the date is convenient for your relative, book a room at the local hotel, send invitations, order food, drink and a band etc.; (d) learn these steps (if necessary) and put them into action; and (e) monitor the situation to ensure the plans had been achieved. The list of steps can be seen in Figure 17.2.

Levine et al. (2000) wanted to determine the effectiveness of Robertson's (1996) Goal Management Training. In their first study, 30 patients with TBI were randomly allocated to GMT or motor skills training. The GMT was carried out in one session, which lasted between four and six hours. Those in the GMT group improved on paper and pencil tasks including proof-reading and grouping items according to

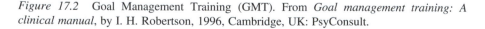

- STOP!   🛑   "What am I doing? Check the mental blackboard"
- DEFINE   The main task
- LIST   The steps
- LEARN   The steps
- DO IT!
- CHECK   "Am I doing what I planned?"

Figure 17.2   Goal Management Training (GMT). From *Goal management training: A clinical manual*, by I. H. Robertson, 1996, Cambridge, UK: PsyConsult.

certain criteria. The authors claim these were similar to tasks that are problematic in everyday life for patients with executive deficits. In the second study the GMT was given to KF, a 35-year-old university graduate who had survived herpes simplex encephalitis. She had a range of cognitive deficits including attention, executive and memory problems. One of her major real-life difficulties was with the preparation of meals. Meal planning involves the management of multiple sub goals, foresight, working memory and prospective memory and thus is a good practical example of a task likely to benefit from GMT. KF reported four particular problems with meal preparation: (a) failure to assemble the necessary ingredients; (b) focussing on irrelevant details when reading a menu; (c) repeatedly checking instructions; and (d) sequencing difficulties, i.e., carrying out steps in the wrong order or omitting steps. The total number of problematic steps in each category was taken as the measure of performance. Three sessions were spent collecting baseline data on the same paper and pencil tasks used in study 1. KF then completed a self-report diary before two sessions of GMT were given. This was followed by 10 sessions in which KF had to implement GMT to meal preparation using recipes that were graded in difficulty. The stages from the GMT were implemented using errorless learning techniques (Wilson et al., 1994). KF showed significant improvement both on the paper and pencil tasks and on meal preparation.

GMT has also been modified for more general use in rehabilitation. Evans (2001) combined aspects of Von Cramon's PST with GMT to plan and run a group for patients with executive deficits. This is the Attention and Goal Management Group which is part of a holistic rehabilitation programme (Wilson, Evans et al., 2000). The group runs twice a week for six to eight weeks. The first few sessions address issues of attention and then a problem-solving framework is introduced. The framework is similar to the one described by Levine et al. (2000) and comprises a checklist together with a template that enables clients to work through the checklist. The checklist and template can be seen in Figures 17.3 and 17.4. After practice with this framework clients are encouraged to internalize it in the hope that it will become automatic. A self-monitoring sheet is also used to enable patients to keep track of problems with attention, concentration, planning and problem solving (also influenced by GMT). A self-monitoring sheet is also used (see Figure 17.5).

Miotto and Evans (2005) have evaluated this group format and found it to be effective in leading to improvements on both neuropsychological tests and everyday ratings of executive functioning.

Of course this group therapy is in many ways similar to the problem-solving treatments that were influenced by the SAS model described above. We should not really be surprised by this similarity as all the models described so far are trying to explain executive deficits and thus they are bound to lead to similar treatment approaches. The same can be said of self-instructional techniques described by Robertson, Nico, and Hood (1995) and others. On the one hand we could argue that these techniques are influenced by the theory of goal neglect as they are prompting people to achieve their goals. On the other hand one could argue that they are more akin to the SAS model as they allow people to deal with novel, nonroutine situations.

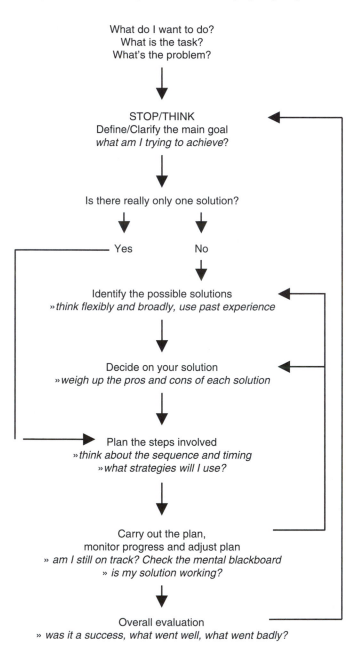

Figure 17.3 Goal Management (Problem Solving) Framework. From *Neurobehavioural disability and social handicap following traumatic brain injury* (p. 209), by J. J. Evans, 2001, Hove: Psychology Press.

1. Main goal _____

2. If there is really only one obvious solution go to section 5 and plan the steps.
   If there is more than one possible solution, go to section 3.

3. *Alternative solutions*   *Pros*   *Cons*

4. Decision: _____

5. Plan

Steps	Strategies	Done? Y or N
1.		
2.		
3.		
4.		

Remember to monitor and evaluate!

Figure 17.4   Planning and Problem-Solving Template.

Self instruction has been used as a treatment for unilateral neglect (Robertson et al., 1998; Robertson, Nico et al., 1995) where it functions as an alerting system to improve sustained attention. It has also been used to improve problem solving. Cicerone and Wood (1987) reported a study using self-instructional training to improve problem solving in a 20-year-old man who had sustained a severe head injury. Although the man was functioning independently, he was impulsive, interrupted conversations, and appeared not to think before he did something. The Tower of London (Shallice, 1982) was used as a training task. Treatment involved three stages. In stage one the man was asked to describe aloud each move before he made it and while he was making it. In stage two he was asked to whisper the move to himself before and while making the move. In stage three he was required to describe the move sub vocally (or in other words think through the move). This training was successful at improving the man's performance on the trained task (The Tower of London) and on two other untrained tasks. With some generalization training, there were improvements in his general social behavior, as rated by family.

Another example of self-instructional training is reported by von Cramon and Matthes-von Cramon (1994). This paper describes how a 33-year-old physician was enabled to return to work through self-instructional training. The man sustained a TBI at the age of 24 years. He was in coma for 2 days and in Post Traumatic Amnesia for 10 weeks. An MRI scan showed discrete bilateral frontal lobe damage. Although he managed to pass his medical examinations postinjury, this was only after several failures. He found employment but all jobs were short term in neurosurgery, pathology and the pharmaceutical industry. He was described as having a

Please use this sheet to keep a record of problems that arise during the course of the programme.
Your specific areas to focus on are attention, concentration, planning, and problem solving.

Date and time	What was the situation and what was the problem?	What was the cause of the problem? e.g., difficulty remembering, concentrating, planning or problem solving, managing my mood, or behavior	Did I use a strategy to help myself? If so, which strategy did I use? If not, could I have used a strategy to help myself? If so, which strategy could I have used?
18.01.01	I was on a train having a conversation with a friend and I was just about to say something when my friend spoke. I was distracted by what she said and forgot what I was going to say.	Memory; "Working memory"	As I was being distracted by what my friend said I could have made a mental note, i.e., tried to keep in mind what I was wanting to say.
18.01.01	I asked my colleague if they wanted a drink and what sort. On arrival in the kitchen I found that I could not recall what they had said.	Working memory; Attention	I could clarify what they had said by repeating back "so you want a black coffee with one sugar?" I could also try and ensure that I'm actually listening to the answer and not just pre-empting their response.
20.01.01	A friend called while I was watching the football results on the TV and found it difficult to listen to the conversation with my friend.	Attention—being distracted by the TV	I could have turned the TV off or asked if I could ring my friend back in a short while after the results had finished.

Figure 17.5   Oliver Zangwill Centre self-monitoring sheet.

"lack of overview," and being dependent upon meticulous instructions. He did not benefit from feedback, spent too much time on routine activities, and was unable to adapt to novel or changing situations. Neuropsychological assessment showed normal performance on tests of perception, language, calculation and memory. He also scored well on traditional executive tasks (Weigl Sorting Task, Cognitive Estimates, Tower of London and the WCST).

A protected work trial in the hospital pathology laboratory was the setting for the man's treatment. He was provided with prototypical reports on autopsies to guide him in his report writing. Staff noted that he tended to jump to conclusions about the diagnoses he was supposed to make so he was taught a set of rules and guidelines for the systematic process of diagnosis. Initially these rules and guidelines were provided externally and before the man internalized or learned them. The guidelines were

1. Identify main clinical data
2. Describe pathological features by microscopic examination
3. Look up observations in a textbook
4. Generate hypotheses about diagnosis
5. Evaluate pros and cons of each hypothesis
6. Decide which diagnosis most likely
7. Judge the certainty of the diagnosis (1–10)
8. If more than 5, write report
9. If less than 5, discuss case with superiors

If discussing case, elaborate arguments concerning potential diagnosis and identify questions.

As a result of this training the man's correct diagnoses increased and his reports slowly improved. However, the improvement did not generalize to a novel planning task. In addition there was some indication of better, albeit still limited, insight into his difficulties. Thus, self-instruction techniques would appear to have some modest benefits for people with executive deficits.

Self alerting strategies to improve sustained attention (Robertson, Tegnér et al., 1995) have been used to help those with executive deficits. Manly, Hawkins, Evans, Woldt, and Robertson (2001) trained 10 patients with TBI on the "hotel task" which is similar in principle to the Six Elements task (Shallice & Burgess, 1996) Periodic noncontingent alerting versus no alert conditions were given in counterbalanced order. While working on the task patients were told *"If you hear a bleep just try think about what you are doing."* Tones were presented at random intervals. Half the patients completed the "cued" version first and half completed the noncued version first. Performance improved with the noncontingent cueing. At The Oliver Zangwill Centre we have sent alerting messages through a paging system to maintain attention. Messages include, *"Am I pacing myself?"* and *"Stop think!"* One could argue that this is a form of managing goal neglect as it helps people focus on the task in hand. Alternatively, one could argue that it improves online monitoring and is therefore more in step with the SAS model. Once again, it is not surprising that different models of executive functioning lead to similar treatment strategies.

A broader view of rehabilitation

As has been argued earlier, executive deficits are so broad ranging that no one single treatment approach is sufficient to deal with all the manifestations of these deficits and added to this is the fact that such deficits are often accompanied by other cognitive, emotional, social, and behavioral problems. Consequently, no one single model is going to be sufficient on its own in the rehabilitation of people with brain injury. In the practice of rehabilitation we do not, as a rule, target a hypothetical construct such as a deficit of the CE or a failure to deal with nonroutine tasks but instead tend to deal with the consequences or the manifestations of such deficits and failures. We might for example try to help someone learn to problem solve or teach the use of a pager to remind someone to carry out household tasks. We need to remember that any specific intervention needs to be set in the wider context of the individual's needs and take into account family circumstances, social relationships, personal preferences and vocational aspirations. Interventions need to be practical, applicable and of use to the individual. Thus, however good the various models of executive functioning are, they will rarely be sufficient on their own to deal with the variety and complexity of the problems faced by people requiring rehabilitation.

Two basic assumptions in brain injury rehabilitation are, first, that neuropsychological rehabilitation is concerned with the amelioration of cognitive, social and emotional deficits caused by an insult to the brain, and second, the main aims of such rehabilitation are to enable people with disabilities to (a) achieve their optimum level of well being; (b) reduce the impact of their problems on everyday life; and (c) help them return to their own, most appropriate environments. From this it follows that no one model, theory or framework can deal with all the difficulties facing people with brain impairments. These often include multiple cognitive impairments as well as accompanying social, emotional and behavioral problems. This being the reality, what additional models do we need? Some of the influential theories and models in rehabilitation over the years are described in Wilson (2002, 2004) and include theories and models of behavior, learning, emotion, assessment, recovery, and plasticity. In an attempt to incorporate many of these models into a broad structure, Wilson (2002) published a tentative comprehensive model of cognitive or neuropsychological rehabilitation (see Figure 17.6).

Starting with the patient and his or her family, we will probably need to know about the premorbid personality and lifestyle of the brain-injured person (and perhaps other family members) as this is likely to impact on the needs and desires of these people and thus on the rehabilitation offered. We may need to examine the nature, extent, and severity of the brain damage through such sources as hospital notes and/or the referral forms, neurological investigations and imaging studies. We are very likely to administer a neuropsychological assessment, which in turn will be influenced by different approaches such as psychometric, ecologically valid and theoretically driven assessment procedures. We may well supplement the neuropsychological measures with behavioral or functional assessments procedures because, while information from standardized tests helps us understand cognitive strengths and weaknesses, their test scores do not help us understand real-life problems and how to tackle their manifestations in everyday life. Thus,

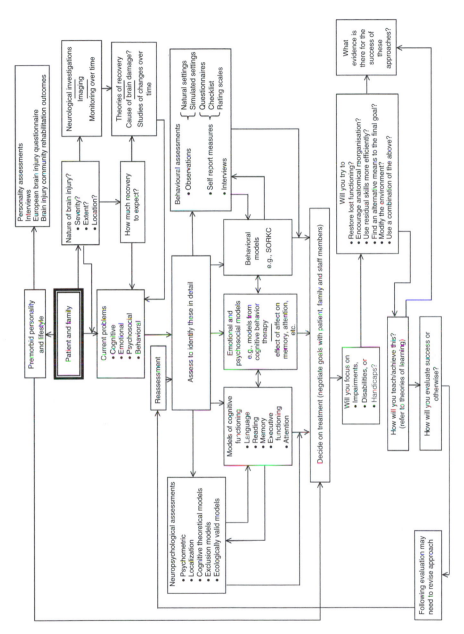

Figure 17.6   A provisional model of cognitive rehabilitation.

the neuropsychological test results need to be complemented by information from functional or behavioral assessments in order to build up a complete picture of someone's difficulties. If we need to follow people over time and repeat assessments we should also recognize that repeating neuropsychological tests may not provide reliable information as improvement in scores may simply reflect a practice effect whereas no change in scores may mask deterioration, again because of a practice effect (Wilson, Watson, Baddeley, Emslie, & Evans, 2000). This is particularly true of executive tests, which are very sensitive to practice effects and are often "one shot tests."

We may be interested in whether or not further recovery is to be expected, especially if the person with brain injury is seen in the early days, weeks, or months after an insult. Theories of recovery are relevant here. The cause of brain damage is also important. People with TBI, for example, may show recovery for a longer time than, say, someone with encephalitis (Wilson, 1998).

Cognitive, emotional, psychosocial, and behavioral problems should be evaluated more thoroughly through reference to a more detailed model. Models of language, reading, memory, attention, and perception (in addition to models of executive functioning already discussed), can provide details about cognitive strengths and deficits. Models from cognitive behavior therapy, such as the one by Beck (1996) contribute to understanding emotional and psychosocial problems, while a behavioral model such as the SORKC of Kanfer and Saslow (1969) allows better conceptualization of disruptive or inappropriate behaviors. SORKC stands for stimulus, organism, response, contingency, and consequence. According to Ciminero, Calhoun, and Adams (1977) *stimulus* refers to the antecedent events or discriminative stimuli that trigger problem behaviors (these can be physical, social, or internal events). *Organism* refers to a person's biological condition and to individual differences resulting from previous experiences. *Response* refers to the behaviors of concern and these can be motor, cognitive or physiological behaviors. *Contingency* refers to the schedules of reinforcement in operation. *Consequence* refers to events that follow behavior and these can be physical, social or self-generated. While this is not an exhaustive list of the type of problems faced by survivors of brain injury, other problems such as motor or sensory deficits are more likely to be treated by physiotherapists or other staff. Neuropsychologists, of course, can work together successfully with others and may need to incorporate models of motor and sensory functioning and recovery in their work.

Once the problems are identified, one can decide on the rehabilitation strategies. This is likely to involve the negotiation of suitable goals. Given that one of the main goals of rehabilitation is to enable people to return to their own most appropriate environment, the person with brain injury, family members, and rehabilitation staff should all be involved in the negotiating process. The main goals may aim to improve impairments, disabilities, or handicaps. Although there may be times or stages in the recovery process where it is appropriate to focus on impairments, the majority of goals for those engaged in cognitive rehabilitation will address disabilities and handicaps. There is obviously more than one way to try to achieve any goal. Sometimes we try to restore lost functioning (Evans, 2005). Occasionally we may try to encourage anatomical reorganization (Robertson & Murre, 1999).

We frequently help people use their residual skills more efficiently (as described earlier in many of the treatments for executive deficits). Many rehabilitation practices help people find alternative means to a final goal (functional adaptation) and this, too, is the focus of some of the treatments for executive deficits mentioned above. We can also use environmental modifications to bypass problems (Burgess & Alderman, 2004). It is likely that most rehabilitation programmes will use a combination of some of the above methods. Whichever approach is selected, one should be aware of theories of learning. In Baddeley's words, "A theory of rehabilitation without a theory of learning is a train without an engine" (Baddeley, 1993, p. 235).

Evidence for the success of these approaches also needs to be taken into account. The final question is: "How best to evaluate success or otherwise?" Consider Whyte's (1997) view that outcome should be congruent with the level of intervention. If intervening at the disability level then outcome measures should be measures of disability and so forth. As most rehabilitation is concerned with the reduction of disabilities and handicaps, outcome measures should reflect changes in disability and handicap: for example, how well does someone who forgets to do things, now remember to do things? There are studies which directly assess such changes. For example, the paging system referred to earlier (Wilson et al., 2001; Wilson et al., 1997) that helped people with executive or memory deficits or both, measured success in achieving everyday targets before, during, and after the provision of a pager. This study demonstrated convincingly that pagers can reduce the everyday problems of people with memory and planning problems following brain injury. Finally, we should always be aware that in designing rehabilitation studies, it is desirable and possible to combine theory, scientific methodology and clinical relevance.

Conclusions

This chapter has described the main problems faced by people with executive deficits following an injury or insult to the brain. Three major models are considered within the context of the light they shed on our understanding of the nature of executive functioning. The first of these is The WM Model (Baddeley, 1986; Baddeley & Hitch, 1974). The second is The SAS model (Norman & Shallice, 1986; Shallice & Burgess, 1991) and the third is that of Goal Neglect (Duncan, 1986; Duncan et al., 1995). These models are described and their contribution to rehabilitation considered. All have helped us to understand the nature of executive functioning and why certain problem behaviors occur. Two in particular, the WM model and the SAS model, have led to new assessment procedures to identify executive deficits, and all have promoted new ways of treatment, with, perhaps, the SAS model leading to the greatest number of ideas in this domain. However successful these models are in providing increased understanding, all are limited in their application to rehabilitation of the individual client in his or her own daily life if seen only in specific terms of executive deficits in separation from all other rehabilitation issues. Their strength is most apparent when set alongside other cognitive, behavioral, social and emotional difficulties faced by people with brain injury. A more embracing, provisional fourth model of Cognitive Rehabilitation is therefore considered (Wilson, 2002). This model or "framework" synthesizes some of the major models influencing neuropsychological rehabilitation, and serves to remind us that good clinical practice will be enhanced if we draw our ideas and inspirations from the broadest possible and indeed growing range of ideas, studies, models and theories.

References

Alderman, N. (1996). Central executive deficit and response to operant conditioning methods. *Neuropsychological Rehabilitation, 6*, 161–186.

Alderman, N., Burgess, P. W., Knight, C., & Henman, C. (2003). Ecological validity of a simplified version of the multiple errands shopping test. *Journal of the International Neuropsychological Society, 9*, 31–44.

Baddeley, A. D. (1986). *Working memory*. Oxford: Clarendon Press.

Baddeley, A. D. (1993). A theory of rehabilitation without a model of learning is a vehicle without an engine: A comment on Caramazza and Hillis. *Neuropsychological Rehabilitation, 3*, 235–244.

Baddeley, A. D. (1997). *Human memory: Theory and practice* (Revised ed.). Hove: Psychology Press.

Baddeley, A. D. (2002). The psychology of memory. In A. D. Baddeley, B. A. Wilson, & M. Kopelman (Eds.), *Handbook of memory disorders* (2nd ed., pp. 3–15). Hove: Psychology press.

Baddeley, A. D., Emslie, H., & Nimmo-Smith, I. (1994). *Doors and people: A test of visual and verbal recall and recognition*. Bury St Edmunds: Thames Valley Test Company.

Baddeley, A. D., & Hitch, G. (1974). Working memory. In G. H. Bower (Ed.), *The psychology of learning and motivation* (Vol. 8, pp. 47–89). New York: Academic Press.

Baddeley, A. D., Logie, R., Bressi, S., Della Sala, S., & Spinnler, H. (1986). Dementia and working memory. *Quarterly Journal of Experimental Psychology, 38*, 603–618.

Beck, A. T. (1996). Beyond belief: A theory of modes, personality, and psychopathology. In P. M. Salkovskis (Ed.), *Frontiers of cognitive therapy* (pp. 1–25). New York: The Guilford Press.

Burgess, P. W., & Alderman, N. (2004). Executive dysfunction. In L. H. Goldstein & J. E. McNeil (Eds.), *Clinical Neuropsychology: A practical guide to assessment and management for clinicians* (pp. 185–209). Chichester: John Wiley & Sons Ltd.

Burgess, P. W., Simons, J. S., Dumontheil, I., & Gilbert, S. J. (2005). The gateway hypothesis of rostral PFC function. In J. Duncan, L. Phillips, & P. McLeod (Eds.), *Speed, control and ageing: In honour of Patrick Rabbitt* (pp. 215–246). Oxford: Oxford University Press.

Cicerone, K. D., & Wood, J. C. (1987). Planning disorder after closed head injury: A case study. *Archives of Physical Medicine and Rehabilitation, 68*, 111–115.

Ciminero, A. R., Calhoun, K. S., & Adams, H. E. (Eds.) (1977). *Handbook of behavioural assessment*. New York: Wiley.

Della Sala, S., Gray, C., Baddeley, A. D., & Wilson, L. (1997). *Visual Patterns Test*. Bury St Edmunds: Thames Valley Test Company.

Della Sala, S., & Logie, R. H. (2002). Neuropsychological impairments of visual and spatial working memory. In A. D. Baddeley, M. D. Kopelman, & B. A. Wilson (Eds.), *Handbook of memory disorders* (2nd ed., pp. 271–292). Chichester: John Wiley.

Duncan, J. (1986). Disorganisation of behaviour after frontal lobe damage. *Cognitive Neuropsychology, 3*, 271–290.

Duncan, J., Burgess, P., & Emslie, H. (1995). Fluid intelligence after frontal lobe lesions. *Neuropsychologia, 33*, 261–268.

Duncan, J., Emslie, H., Williams, P., Johnson, R., & Freer, C. (1996). Intelligence and the frontal lobe: The organization of goal-directed behavior. *Cognitive Psychology, 30*, 257–303.

D'Zurilla, T. J., & Goldfried, M. R. (1971). Problem solving and behavior modification. *Journal of Abnormal Psychology, 78*, 107–126.

Evans, J. J. (2001). Rehabilitation of the dysexecutive syndrome. In T. M. McMillan (Ed.), *Neurobehavioural disability and social handicap following traumatic brain injury* (pp. 209–227). Hove: Psychology Press.

Evans, J. J. (2003). Rehabilitation of executive deficits. In B. A. Wilson (Ed.), *Neuropsychological rehabilitation: Theory and practice* (pp. 53–70). Lisse, The Netherlands: Swets & Zeitlinger.

Evans, J. J. (2005). Can executive impairments be effectively treated? In P. Halligan & D. Wade (Eds.), *The effectiveness of rehabilitation for cognitive deficits*. Oxford: Oxford University Press.

Evans, J. J., Emslie, H., & Wilson, B. A. (1998). External cueing systems in the rehabilitation of executive impairments of action. *Journal of the International Neuropsychological Society, 4*, 399–408.

Goldberg, E. (2001). *The executive brain: Frontal lobes and the civilized mind*. New York: Oxford University Press.

Harlow, J. M. (1868). Recovery from the passage of an iron bar through the head. *Publications of the Massachusetts Medical Society, 2*, 327–346.

Hartman, A., Pickering, R. M., & Wilson, B. A. (1992). Is there a central executive deficit after severe head injury? *Clinical Rehabilitation, 6*, 133–140.

Kanfer, F. H., & Saslow, G. (1969). Behavioral diagnosis. In C. Franks (Ed.), *Behavior therapy: Appraisal and status* (pp. 417–444). New York: McGraw Hill.

Levine, B., Robertson, I. H., Clare, L., Carter, G., Hong, J., Wilson, B. A., et al. (2000). Rehabilitation of executive functioning: An experimental–clinical validation of Goal Management Training. *Journal of the International Neuropsychological Society, 6*, 299–312.

Luria, A. (1966). *Higher cortical functions in man*. New York: Basic Books.

Luria, A. R. (1963). *Restoration of function after brain injury*. New York: Pergamon Press.

Luria, A. R. (1973). *The working brain*. New York: Basic Books.

Macmillan, M. (2000). *An odd kind of fame: Stories of Phineas Gage*. Cambridge, MA: The MIT Press.

Manly, T., Hawkins, K., Evans, J. J., Woldt, K., & Robertson, I. H. (2001). Rehabilitation of executive function: Facilitation of effective goal management on complex tasks using periodic auditory alerts. *Neuropsychologia, 40*, 271–281.

Manly, T., & Mattingley, J. B. (2004). Visuospatial and attentional disorders. In L. H. Goldstein & J. E. McNeil (Eds.), *Clinical Neuropsychology: A practical guide to assessment and management for clinicians* (pp. 229–252). Chichester: John Wiley & Sons Ltd.

Miotto, E., & Evans, J. J. (2005). *Rehabilitation of executive functioning: A controlled cross-over study of an attention and problem solving group intervention*. Paper presented at the Neuropsychological Rehabilitation Conference, Galway, July 2005.

Norman, D. A., & Shallice, T. (1986). Attention to action: Willed and automatic control of behaviour. In R. J. Davidson, G. E. Schwartz, & D. E. Shapiro (Eds.), *Consciousness and self-regulation* (Vol. 4, pp. 1–18). New York: Plenum Press.

Rath, J. F., Simon, D., Langenbahn, D. M., Sherr, R. L., & Diller, L. (2003). Group treatment of problem-solving deficits in outpatients with traumatic brain injury: A randomised outcome study. *Neuropsychological Rehabilitation, 13*, 461–488.

Robertson, I. H. (1996). *Goal management training: A clinical manual.* Cambridge, UK: PsyConsult.

Robertson, I. H., Hogg, K., & McMillan, T. M. (1998). Rehabilitation of unilateral neglect: Improving function by contralesional limb activation. *Neuropsychological Rehabilitation, 8*, 19–29.

Robertson, I. H., & Murre, J. M. J. (1999). Rehabilitation of brain damage: Brain plasticity and principles of guided recovery. *Psychological Bulletin, 125*, 544–575.

Robertson, I. H., Nico, D., & Hood, B. M. (1995). The intention to act improves unilateral neglect: Two demonstrations. *NeuroReport, 17*, 246–248.

Robertson, I. H., Tegnér, R., Tham, K., Lo, A., & Nimmo-Smith, I. (1995). Sustained attention training for unilateral neglect: Theoretical and rehabilitation implications. *Journal of Clinical and Experimental Neuropsychology, 17*, 416–430.

Rylander, G. (1939). Personality changes after operation on the frontal lobes. *Acta Psychiatrica et Neurologica, 20* (Suppl.), 1–327.

Shallice, T. (1982). Specific impairments of planning. *Philosophical Transactions of the Royal Society of London B, 298*, 199–209.

Shallice, T. (1988). *From neuropsychology to mental structure.* Cambridge: Cambridge University Press.

Shallice, T., & Burgess, P. (1991). Deficit in strategy application following frontal lobe damage in man. *Brain, 114*, 727–741.

Shallice, T., & Burgess, P. (1996). The domain of the supervisory process and temporal organization of behaviour. *Philosophical Transactions of the Royal Society B: Biological Sciences, 351*, 1405–1412.

Spearman, C. (1927). *The abilities of man.* New York: Macmillan.

Tyerman, R., Tyerman, A., Howard, P., & Hadfield, C. (1986). *Chessington Occupational Therapy Neurological Assessment Battery (COTNAB).* Nottingham: Nottingham Rehab.

von Cramon, D. Y., Cramon, G. M. -V., & Mai, N. (1991). Problem solving deficits in brain injured patients: A therapeutic approach. *Neuropsychological Rehabilitation, 1*, 45–64.

von Cramon, D. Y., & Matthes-von Cramon, G. (1992). Reflections on the treatment of brain injured patients suffering from problem-solving disorders. *Neuropsychological Rehabilitation, 2*, 207–230.

von Cramon, D. Y., & Matthes-von Cramon, G. (1994). Back to work with a chronic dysexecutive syndrome: A case report. *Neuropsychological Rehabilitation, 4*, 399–417.

Whyte, J. (1997). Distinctive methodologic challenges. In M. J. Fuhrer (Ed.), *Assessing medical rehabilitation practices: The promise of outcomes research.* Baltimore, MD: Paul H Brookes Publishing Co.

Wilson, B. A. (1998). Recovery of cognitive functions following non-progressive brain injury. *Current Opinion in Neurobiology, 8*, 281–287.

Wilson, B. A. (2002). Towards a comprehensive model of cognitive rehabilitation. *Neuropsychological Rehabilitation, 12*, 97–110.

Wilson, B. A. (2004). Theoretical approaches to cognitive rehabilitation. In L. H. Goldstein & J. McNeil (Eds.), *Clinical neuropsychology: A guide to assessment and management for clinicians* (pp. 345–366). Chichester: John Wiley.

Wilson, B. A., Alderman, N., Burgess, P., Emslie, H., & Evans, J. (1996). *Behavioural Assessment of the Dysexecutive Syndrome.* Bury St Edmunds: Thames Valley Test Company.

Wilson, B. A., Baddeley, A. D., Evans, J. J., & Shiel, A. (1994). Errorless learning in the rehabilitation of memory impaired people. *Neuropsychological Rehabilitation*, *4*, 307–326.

Wilson, B. A., Baddeley, A. D., & Young, A. W. (1999). LE, A person who lost her 'mind's eye.' *Neurocase*, *5*, 119–127.

Wilson, B. A., Emslie, H. C., Quirk, K., & Evans, J. J. (2001). Reducing everyday memory and planning problems by means of a paging system: A randomised control crossover study. *Journal of Neurology, Neurosurgery and Psychiatry*, *70*, 477–482.

Wilson, B. A., Evans, J., Brentnall, S., Bremner, S., Keohane, C., & Williams, H. (2000). The Oliver Zangwill Centre for Neuropsychological Rehabilitation: A partnership between health care and rehabilitation research. In A. -L. Christensen & B. P. Uzzell (Eds.), *International handbook of neuropsychological rehabilitation* (pp. 231–246). New York: Kluwer Academic/Plenum Publishers.

Wilson, B. A., Evans, J. J., Emslie, H., & Malinek, V. (1997). Evaluation of NeuroPage: A new memory aid. *Journal of Neurology, Neurosurgery and Psychiatry*, *63*, 113–115.

Wilson, B. A., Watson, P. C., Baddeley, A. D., Emslie, H., & Evans, J. J. (2000). Improvement or simply practice? The effects of twenty repeated assessments on people with and without brain injury. *Journal of the International Neuropsychological Society*, *6*, 469–479.

18 Helping children without making them helpless: Facilitating development of executive self-regulation in children and adolescents

Mark Ylvisaker and Timothy Feeney

Contents

The goals of this chapter are to clarify the concept of executive function/self-regulatory (EF/SR) capacity and skills, to describe factors that influence development of EF/SR in children, and to present intervention themes under the following headings: intervention within a community context, general management guidelines, SR scripts, intervention for organizational impairment, teaching compensatory cognitive and academic strategies, and behavioral interventions. Pharmacologic options are often relevant for children with EF/SR impairment, but are not within the scope of this chapter.

We intend the themes of this chapter to be relevant to children from preschool age through adolescence. Furthermore, despite frequent references to children with frank brain injuries, the themes are applicable to a variety of etiologies associated with EF/SR impairment, including autism (Hill, 2004; Laurent & Rubin, 2004; Russell, 1998), attention-deficit/hyperactivity disorder (ADHD) (Barkley, 1997), fetal alcohol syndrome (Kaemingk & Paquette, 1999), and others. Children from socially disadvantaged environments are also at risk for EF/SR weakness, despite no clinical diagnosis (Waber et al., 2006). Most of the intervention approaches that we describe have a theoretical and research base, which we summarize. However, it is important to note that our orientation to serving children and adolescents with EF/SR impairment derives largely from a combined 45 years of work in two pediatric rehabilitation facilities and consultation in over 500 schools. This experience has led us to emphasize the role of everyday contexts in providing interventions and supports for children with EF/SR impairment and the critical role of everyday people within those contexts. These emphases can also be justified with reference to the large experimental literature on transfer of training as well as the growing literature on effectiveness of interventions for the populations under consideration. Interventions as we use the term include what is commonly referred to as rehabilitation as well as educational, cognitive, communication, and behavioral interventions and supports for a wide variety of clinical populations.

Self-regulation in a developmental context

An important goal for parents and the educational system is to have children learn how to regulate their emotions, cognition, and social behavior so that they act in a way that is consistent with family, school, and society standards and the needs of others, and that is also strategic in relation to their learning, academic, and social success. The same EF/SR skills underlie emotional/social/behavioral self-regulation (e.g., controlling affective states, inhibiting impulses, deferring gratification, communicating respectfully, benefiting from feedback [Vohs & Ciarocco, 2004]) and cognitive/academic self-regulation (e.g., strategic reading, effective studying, taking responsibility for academic success [Meichenbaum & Biemiller, 1998]) and thus should be viewed within one consistent intervention framework (Ylvisaker, Jacobs, & Feeney, 2003).

Other chapters in this book present considerations related to the definition of EFs as a neuropsychological construct (see also Anderson, Levin, & Jacobs, 2002). Consistent with our previous work on the subject, we have chosen a functional definition of the construct, based on an analysis of prerequisites for successful performance of difficult tasks. These include some degree of awareness of ones strengths and weaknesses (thereby enabling a judgment of task difficulty) and an ability to set reasonable goals, organize plans to achieve the goals, initiate goal-directed behavior, inhibit impulses that interfere with goal achievement, monitor behavior and evaluate it in relation to the goals, benefit from feedback, flexibly select and modify strategies in response to performance feedback, and flexibly perceive situations from a variety of possible perspectives. Each of these components falls on a continuum of performance and develops gradually in childhood, in dynamic interaction with each other and with related domains of cognitive and social development (Flavell, Miller, & Miller, 2002). Because the term *self-regulation* is better understood by those unfamiliar with neuropsychological discussions of the topic and because that term brings to the table a large literature in related fields of psychology, we have chosen to combine the terms to form the general construct, EF/SR.

The growing literature on self-regulation has close theoretical ties with psychological theory construction regarding the self and clinical ties with fields like substance abuse, eating disorders, health problems, crime, motivation, procrastination, and the like (Baumeister & Vohs, 2004). Self-regulation and *self-determination* have also come to be used as the central terms within theory construction and research related to intrinsic motivation (Ryan & Deci, 2000, 2002). Within this theory, innate human needs include competence, autonomy, and relatedness, each of which is woven into the intervention sections of this chapter. The literature on EFs has close theoretical ties with neuro-psychological investigations and clinical ties with rehabilitation for individuals with frank neurologic impairment (Burgess & Robertson, 2002; Cicerone, 2005; Shallice & Burgess, 1991; Ylvisaker, Szekeres, & Feeney, 1998). In educational psychology and special education, the term *metacognition* has historically been used to refer to "execu-tive self-regulatory" control over cognitive processes in the context of learning and academic performance (Flavell ct al., 2002); and "self-determined or self-regulated learning" is increasingly used to describe these approaches, which have been validated by recent studies (Graham & Harris, 2003; Martin et al., 2003; Meichenbaum & Biemiller, 1998). Finally, the term self-determination is commonly used to cover much the same ground in discussions of intellectual impairment (developmental disabilities) (Wehmeyer, Agran, & Hughes, 1998). We have attempted to mine all these fields in formulating a theoretically informed, but practice-based approach to serving children and adolescents with EF/SR impairment.

The importance of EF/SR in adult outcomes for children with and without disability has been documented in many studies. For example, Mischel and Ayduk (2004) summarized research showing an association between performances on deferred gratification tasks at age four (e.g., one cookie now or two cookies later) and later Scholastic Aptitude Test results, as well as better social-cognitive, personal, and interpersonal indices in adolescence. Similarly, McCabe, Cunnington, and Brooks-Dunn (2004) reviewed several studies demonstrating that preschool self-regulation predicts later social competence and resiliency. Waber and colleagues (2006) found that low scores on academic testing of children from disadvantaged environments corresponded closely with their scores on ecologically valid measures of EF/SR, despite normal performance on many important neuropsychological tests. Wehmeyer and Schwartz (1997) found that important markers of successful adult outcome (e.g., working for pay) were better predicted by adolescent scores on the Self-Determination Scale (Wehmeyer, 1995) than by IQ measures in students with learning disabilities and those with mild mental retardation.

In the case of children who incur traumatic brain injury (TBI) early in life, sense of personal identity (measured at age 18) was found to be a strong predictor of adult employment outcome, whereas IQ measures and academic success were not (Nybo & Koskiniemi, 1999). Similarly, Cattelani, Lombardi, Brianti, and Mazucchi (1998) followed children injured in middle childhood (age 8–14) and found that behavioral and psychosocial disorders persisted and had a negative impact on general quality of life far in excess of that resulting from intellectual problems. Neuropsychological studies of children with early frontal lobe injury have been uniformly pessimistic about adult social outcome, but with no descriptions of the nature and quality of inter-ventions provided over the course of childhood (Eslinger, Biddle, & Grattan, 1997;

Tranel, 2002). One outcome of our work over the years has been to inject a tone of optimism into the pediatric brain injury literature (Feeney & Ylvisaker, 1995, 2003, 2006, in press; Ylvisaker & Feeney, 1998).

Factors that influence development of self-regulation

Self-regulation, including "the many processes by which the human psyche exercises control over its functions, states, and inner processes" (Vohs & Baumeister, 2004, p. 1), develops gradually and in a nonlinear way in children, beginning in infancy and continuing through adolescence and into the young adult years. Furthermore, there is a variability in development across children and across tasks and settings. For example some 4-year-olds are capable of delaying gratification whereas others are not, and a child may delay gratification within some tasks and settings and not others.

Catroppa and Anderson (2006) reviewed the evidence for different developmental trajectories for various dimensions of EF/SR. Anderson et al. (2002) argued for a stage-wise understanding of EF/SR, despite the near unanimous rejection of Piagetian stages in developmental cognitive psychology (Flavell et al., 2002). Although these neuropsychological studies, based on selected test performance, contribute to an understanding of child development, conclusions must be guarded because success on EF/SR tasks is as dependent on the selection of tasks as on the child's development. For example, Kelly (2000) highlighted the period between ages 9 and 13 years as critical for development of planning and strategic behavior. However, with developmentally appropriate tasks, one could equally highlight the period from age one to five. Similarly, Anderson et al. described three bursts of frontal lobe and EF/SR development: birth to two, seven to nine, and late adolescence. However the most cursory real-world comparison of 3- and 6-year-olds leads inevitably to the conclusion that there is profound development of EF/SR during those years. More importantly, intervention decisions should not be held hostage to any theory of developmental stages. With appropriate task modifications, all the interventions and supports described in this chapter are relevant for children of all ages beyond infancy.

Of special importance for educators and providers of pediatric rehabilitation are studies of factors that positively influence EF/SR development (Table 18.1; Bronson, 2000). Many of these factors are environmental and thus controllable, including environmental predictability, opportunities and rewards for effective self-regulation, intelligent mediation of natural problem-solving opportunities, reward systems that highlight intrinsic as opposed to extrinsic reinforcement, scripts of interaction designed to be internalized by the child as SR self-talk, and facilitation of a positive sense of self. The effects of parent–child interaction on the development of EF/SR in young children have been documented in a series of studies by Landry et al. (2001, 2002, 2003). The findings of Waber and colleagues (2006) suggest that general social disadvantage during childhood can result in ineffective development of meta-cognitive and self-regulatory functions. The fact that EF/SR development has a variety of environmental contributors underlies the nonpharmacologic interventions described later in this chapter.

Many children arrive at school with relative (and in some cases extreme) SR immaturity or they become poorly regulated as a result of acquired neurologic impairment, such as TBI. They may regulate their behavior poorly (e.g., impulsively

Table 18.1   Factors that influence the development of self-regulation in children.

- Neurologic maturation, especially development of the frontal lobes
- Stability, organization, and predictability in the home environment
- Reasonable emotional attachment to important adults in the child's life
- Adequate opportunities for children to exercise control over events in their life
- A parenting style that steers between the extremes of permissiveness (at one end) and an overly authoritarian and controlling style (at the other end). Many people call this middle ground an "authoritative/responsive" style of parenting
- An environment at home and at school that models, values, and rewards self-regulation, autonomy, and personal responsibility
- Identification with more mature individuals who actively use self-regulatory (SR) strategies
- Reasonably effective development of language, for communication as well as for problem-solving and SR self-talk
- Positive adult–child interactions that include the regulatory words, procedures, and themes that will eventually be internalized by children to become their SR system. Adult interaction with children, if well conceived and frequently repeated, ultimately becomes appropriated by the children as an internal self-regulation system (see below)
- Development of a coherent and positive sense of personal identity that includes SR strategies

grabbing or lashing out at other children); they may regulate their emotions poorly (e.g., crying when impulses cannot be satisfied); they may regulate their academic behavior poorly (e.g., failing to notice and repair errors or comprehension gaps). In these respects they may be much like younger children even though their physical and perhaps intellectual development is at a higher level. The following categories of children often have relatively weak self-regulation:

- Children with neurologic impairment or immaturity in the brain systems that support self-regulation (notably prefrontal cortex). This includes the following diagnoses: ADHD, autism spectrum disorders, anxiety disorders, TBI, frontal lobe tumors, fetal alcohol syndrome, Tourette's syndrome, some types of mental retardation, and others.
- Children from chaotic, unpredictable, disorganized home environments.
- Children with weak emotional attachments to the important adults in their lives (e.g., multiple foster placements).
- Children who have been given few opportunities for legitimate control over events in their lives, and who have learned to control events through manipulation and defiance. This may include diagnoses like oppositional defiant disorder, conduct disorder, and intermittent explosive disorder.
- Children who are simply immature developmentally.

Intervention themes

The following sections sketch intervention themes that are elaborated in cited publications, from which additional procedural details can be obtained. Most of the interventions are based on interactions known to facilitate EF/SR development in typically developing children, but are more explicit and intense with clinical populations. Using a typical developmental template for developing intervention and support strategies is consistent with a general Vygotskian approach, which we embrace. This chapter closes with an emphasis on systematically reducing supports for children with disability so that they can develop maximal autonomy consistent with their disability.

Community involvement as a foundation for the meaningful pursuit of goals

Helping children with EF/SR impairment become more strategic learners and better regulated socially should not be viewed as a discrete intervention to be delivered in a therapeutic context by an EF specialist for a limited period. This negative judgment is supported by an extensive experimental literature on transfer of training (Detterman & Sternberg, 1993) and by unpromising reviews of both compensatory strategy interventions delivered outside of the academic curriculum (Baker, Gersten, & Scanlon, 2002; Resnick, 1987) and cognitive behavior modification (CBM) delivered as a clinical intervention outside of the context of everyday social interaction (Abikoff, 1991; Barkley, 2004). Rather EF/SR interventions and supports should be understood as components of a general community culture in which development of self-regulation or autonomy is a primary value. Such a culture can be constructed in family homes and schools alike.

Cultures can be defined in part by their shared values and often unspoken rules. The values and rules embraced within a community's culture dictate roles, routines, action strategies, rewards, and communication systems that guide day-to-day interactions with others and development of sense of self. Communities are the places in which individuals practice action strategies and self-regulatory scripts, receive feedback about their behavior, and alter patterns of interaction so that they become consistent with community values. Communities also provide the background of meaning and importance that sustains motivation to succeed.

In a community that values development of self-regulation, the mentors (e.g., parents, instructional staff, therapists) do not simply impart knowledge and skill while ensuring acceptable patterns of behavior. In addition they see themselves as models and facilitators of the child's development of autonomy, requiring attention to all aspects of EF/SR intervention and support described below. Within this framework, the roles of adults—parents and rehabilitation/education staff alike— include being an expert/model of effective self-regulation, facilitator (helping to articulate the community culture and the goals for the child as a member of the community), coach (providing planned supports, scripts, and on-the-spot coaching), and cheerleader (facilitating internalization of intrinsic motivation so that the child pursues goals motivated by a desire to succeed at culturally valued tasks).

Within such communities, individual children are not viewed as collections of discrete behaviors and academic, physical, cognitive, and social competencies. Rather they are viewed as unique individuals who (a) pursue meaningful goals; (b) as they participate in culturally valued activities; (c) within cultural contexts; (d) with support and expert mediation as needed from more proficient individuals within that context; and (e) using and mastering cultural tools, such as language, mathematics, category schemes, organizational supports, and domain-specific strategies as they participate successfully in valued activities. Instructional and rehabilitation objectives are therefore ideally formulated as, "John will successfully complete ___ activity related to personally meaningful goal ___, with ___ supports and mediation, and using ___ tools and strategies to ensure success." Framing objectives in this manner orients staff to the desired long-term outcome for the child, namely success as a self-regulated and strategic adult. It also mandates ongoing attention to the procedural elements described below. This framework is in sharp contrast to the standard formulation of instructional and therapeutic objectives in rehabilitation and special education settings.

Just as adults within a community that values EF/SR have varied roles, so do the children. To be sure, children are learners who need to be engaged in relevant instructional activities. In addition, they should have contributory roles (e.g., special jobs, meaningful projects, peer support roles) that encourage higher levels of self-regulation and that associate EF/SR with positive personal identities. Supports for higher levels of autonomy include those discussed in subsequent sections of this chapter.

Procedures for maintaining the culture of autonomy within learning communities include regular attention to needed supports, adjustments in supports as children improve, and routine community meetings in which roles are reviewed and adjustments made. These reviews should be framed within a perspective that views each interaction with others as an opportunity to create and solidify an identity, based on the feedback in that context and on the individual's ability to profit from that feedback. Communities become the context in which young people create identity and establish routine behaviors that are consistent with that identity, increasing the probability that they will engage in behaviors needed to develop the desired identity. Ylvisaker and Feeney (2000) described specific procedures that can be used to help individuals and those who support them construct an identity that is at the same time compelling and inclusive of the hard strategic effort needed to be successful with a disability.

Case illustration

When EF/SR intervention began, Jim was a 17-year-old with classic autism and a measured intelligence quotient of less than 60. He attended school in his community high school, with some integrated classes. Most of his day was spent in a special education resource room. His most salient disability was prompt dependence; he required near total one-to-one prompting to complete any task that was not a very well-established routine for him. When not prompted, he would become confused and do nothing. Initiation outside of well-rehearsed routines was never observed. In addition, his speech tended to be echolalic and rarely spontaneous.

His intervention focused on self-prompting and was coordinated among all his teachers, assistants, and later work supervisors. With the help of staff, Jim created brief (4–7 min) videos of himself in real school settings engaged in school day transitions, academic activities, and interactions with staff. The videos also included his own voice-over narration of the activities. For example, the narration might include, "I walk to computer class; I take my seat; I listen to my teacher; I follow her instructions; I ask for help if unsure." The purpose of the videos and their repeated viewings prior to the activity was to help Jim internalize the self-prompts needed to engage independently in successful school behavior. The same procedure was used when Jim began paid part-time employment in community settings. Later these self-talk prompts were imported into a handheld Palm Pilot. As he internalized the self-prompts, the use of the Palm Pilot was faded.

Because routines change and novelty is a fact of life that was difficult for Jim, his Palm Pilot also included a fallback strategy, that he named the "Oh crap plan." This plan was essentially a routine to deal with changes in routine. When confused about what to do, Jim would hit the "Oh crap" icon on his Palm Pilot, which then produced a prompt for Jim to seek relevant help.

Two years after initiation of these self-prompt strategies, Jim had progressed from total external prompt dependence to substantial independence. He made no use of paraprofessional support at school and successfully self-initiated within reasonably familiar routines. Staff continued to develop new videos and self-prompting instructions for new activities. In addition, Jim held two part-time jobs in the community: mail delivery in the town hall and a clerk job for a not-for-profit agency. In both cases, supervisors used the same procedures to help Jim internalize his routines and self-prompts. Jim's successful intervention illustrates the power of community involvement, context sensitivity, meaningful participation, and EF/SR scripts in helping a previously dependent adolescent become an independent and successful student and employee.

General management guidelines to facilitate development of self-regulation

Maturation of self-regulation is very gradual from infancy to adulthood (Bronson, 2000). In supporting students who are immature in this domain, it is useful to consider how mature adults support typically developing young children in the design of both physical and interpersonal environments. The 10 principles outlined in Table 18.2 are critical elements of this support. Supports are necessary for children with immature self-regulation, but may create over-dependence and helplessness if not properly modulated and reduced over time. Later we discuss the dangers inherent in overreliance on a "prosthetic executive system" approach to supporting children with EF/SR impairment.

Self-regulatory scripts and development of autonomy

Our goal in this section is to describe routines or scripts of interaction organized in such a way that the child gradually internalizes the script as automatic SR self-talk. Thus the theme is facilitation of *automatic self-regulation* or *EF/SR habits* via internalized SR self-talk. The section ends with two case illustrations and a discussion of empirical evidence.

The general notion that thinking, including SR self-talk, is internalized speech has a varied and venerable lineage, including classical philosophy (e.g., Plato in the *Phaedrus*), classical behavioral psychology (Skinner, 1953), and classical developmental cognitive psychology (Vygotsky, 1962). Often the operation of these SR, EFs is assumed to be conscious and deliberate. Indeed, many theorists draw a sharp contrast between self-regulated behavior, on the one hand, and automatic or habitual behavior on the other. Fitzsimons and Bargh (2004) disputed this dichotomy by summarizing

Table 18.2 Ten general principles of executive function/self-regulatory support.

1. "Childproof" the environment to a degree consistent with the child's EF/SR development:
   - Childproof the *physical environment* (e.g., reduce dangers, temptations, and distractions)
   - Childproof the *activity environment* (e.g., provide supports so that all activities can be successfully completed)
   - Childproof the *social environment* (e.g., ensure that children are with other children with whom they are reasonably compatible)
   - Childproof the *expectation environment* (e.g., adjust expectations to fit the child's abilities, stressors, moods, illness, tough times, and the like)
   - Childproof the *stressor environment* (e.g., provide adequate preparation and supports for stressful times, such as transitions, changes in routine, and the like)
2. Create everyday routines of activity and interaction that are well understood by the children and effectively supported, so that the children experience success in their lives.
3. Expect impulsive and poorly regulated behavior from time to time, especially if the child is tired or stressed, there are changes in routine, the environment is overly stimulating, or demands are high. Remain calm. Adult anxiety and agitation increase the child's anxiety and agitation.
4. Do not expect immature children to routinely regulate their emotions and behavior effectively—control impulses and defer gratification—in relation to a distant goal (e.g., control impulses now to get a reward or avoid a punishment at the end of the day) or an abstract rule (e.g., think about others' needs, not just your own).
5. Use behavior management procedures that are proactive, positive, and supportive. That is, set the child up for success rather than reacting to the child's failures. Negativity and punishment predictably breed a downward cycle of more negativity and punishment with poorly regulated children. (See behavioral interventions below.)
6. Use an interactive and teaching style that is positive and supportive (versus threatening and testing).
7. Use everyday conversational routines of interaction that are designed to become internalized by the children as their own SR system. (See self-regulation scripts below.)
8. Ensure that instructions and expectations are clear. Use concrete (e.g., graphic) organizational supports as needed. (See intervention for organizational impairment below.)
9. Use rewards, including praise, and other motivational procedures that highlight intrinsic motivation. Intrinsically motivated behaviors increase willingness to try hard tasks and to sustain effort. Extrinsically motivated behaviors (done for a payoff) reduce intrinsic motivation and sustained effort (Ryan & Deci, 2002).
10. Help the child develop a sense of self that includes competence and a desire for self-regulation. The more a child sees an activity as related to sense of self, the more intrinsic the motivation and the more sustained the effort (Deci, Koestner, & Ryan, 1999).

evidence showing that self-regulation (i.e., "...the capacity of individuals to guide themselves...toward important goal states." p. 151) can be active, dynamic, complex, *and automatic*. Automatic EF/SR behavior in adults is illustrated by the habit or automatically triggered routine of fastening the seat belt when entering an automobile. The clinical need to automatize EF/SR scripts is based on studies (reviewed by Schmeichel & Baumeister, 2004) showing that SR resources are depleted with effortful self-regulation. Individuals with frontal lobe or diffuse neuronal pathology often have limited processing resources without placing additional demands on those resources with deliberate self-regulation (Schmitter-Edgecombe, 1996).

Consistent with the Vygotskian theme of thinking as self-talk internalized from interaction with more competent members of the culture, Landry and colleagues have recently documented a significant association between parents' interactive style and growth in preschool children's executive SR functions, specifically problem-solving skills (Landry et al., 2001, 2002, 2003). Effective parental scaffolding (including hints, prompts, and other verbal supports) at age three predicted high scores on EF measures at age six. In educational psychology, teacher "scaffolding" for problem solving (hints that facilitate success without taking over the problem-solving activity) have been shown to facilitate self-determined learners (Graham & Harris, 2003; Reeve, Bolt, & Cai, 1999; Reeve, 2002). Because many adults take over the executive, SR aspects of functioning for children with disability, they should be alerted to the importance of engaging their children in scripted EF/SR routines, providing whatever support may be necessary, but stopping short of threatening learned helplessness in the child. Larsen and Prizmic (2004) reviewed the available developmental evidence regarding *affect-regulation* strategies, including self-talk strategies that might be encouraged within these everyday routines of interaction.

Ylvisaker and Feeney (2002) proposed a rehabilitation framework within which the executive, SR aspects of behavior become a component of everyday adult–child interaction. Table 18.3 includes examples of specific EF/SR scripts as well as the most general Goal-Obstacle-Plan-Do-Review script, listed first because it is a

Table 18.3   Examples of executive function/self-regulatory scripts of interaction designed to be used at appropriate times in real-world contexts with the goal of having the child internalize EF/SR self-talk. The words can be customized for individual children and delivery should be conversational, nonpunitive, and motivating.

General EF/SR Script: Goal-Obstacle-Plan-Do-Review
1. This is the goal (What do you want to accomplish, make happen; what will it look like when you're done?)
2. This might be hard because...
3. So we need a plan; how about...?
4. Do it
5. Review it: How did it work out? What worked for you? What didn't work? What adjustments need to be made?

Hard/Easy Script
1. This seems to be kind of hard (or easy) for you
2. I think it's hard (easy) because...
3. Because it's hard, you should probably...
4. There's always something that works

Ready/Not Ready Script
1. I think you are ready (or not ready) now
2. You look ready (or not ready) because...
3. Because you're ready, you can... (or this is what you need to do to be ready)
4. There's always something that works

Table 18.3 (continued)   Examples of executive function/self-regulatory scripts of
interaction designed to be used at appropriate times in real-world contexts with the goal of
having the child internalize EF/SR self-talk. The words can be customized for individual
children and delivery should be conversational, nonpunitive, and motivating.

Problem-Solving Script
1. This seems to be a problem
2. It's a problem because...
3. Let's see if this works...
4. There's always something that works

Big Deal/Little Deal Script
1. I think this is a big deal (or not a big deal)
2. It's a big (or little) deal because...
3. Because it's a big (little) deal, you...
4. There's always something that works

Scary/Not Scary Script
1. This is kind of scary/dangerous (or not scary/dangerous)
2. It's scary (or not) because....
3. Because it's scary, you...
4. There's always something that works

What About You Script
1. It's important to know what John thinks/John feels
2. It's important because...
3. Here's a way to find out...
4. There's always something that works

Experimental Script
1. You and I have different ideas about how to get this done
2. We disagree because...
3. Let's try it both ways and see what works best
4. There's always something that works

Responsibility Script
1. This is my deal (or not my deal)
2. It's my deal because...
3. Because it's my deal, I will...
4. There's always something that works

Play to Change Plays Script
1. Identify the issue: Change or deviation from routine
2. State the reason
3. Generate a strategy (e.g., ask for help)
4. General reassurance

See text for modified *self-coaching* scripts for developmentally more mature adolescents.

Note: Video illustrations of most of these SR scripts can be viewed on the following web site:
www.bianys.org/learnet/tutorials/sr_ef_routines.html.

simple operational definition of executive, SR functioning that should pervade the
facilitation process from preschool through adolescence.

Scripts similar to those listed in Table 18.3 can be devised for strategy exploration
routines, social self-control, and the like. The goal is to associate the scripts with

the everyday occurrences for which that SR thought process would be helpful. With repetition and gradual reduction of supports, these scripts can then be internalized by the child as relatively automatic SR thought processes, triggered by relevant environmental events. For some children, the scripts can be framed as questions (e.g., Is this a big deal or a little deal?); for others, questions should be avoided, particularly children whose anxiety is aroused by questions or who would have difficulty answering the question accurately. In both cases, the scripts should be delivered in a supportive, conversational manner, using language that the child understands and to which the child reacts positively. Ideally these scripts are used frequently (while avoiding boredom and nagging) and at times within everyday action contexts when the child ideally should have the use of the script as SR self-talk. To avoid negative associations with the scripts, the positive versions (e.g., easy, little deal, not a problem, not scary) should predominate early in the facilitation process.

For many adolescents, particularly those with experience in sports (strongly valued in many adolescent cultures), we have framed this SR self-talk as self-coaching (Ylvisaker, 2006). Individualized SR (self-coaching) "plays" can be negotiated with the student and then video-taped during role-playing activities in which the "self-coach's" words are used by the student and perhaps negotiated cuing words can be used by staff. The video should also include a meaningful rationale for the play, possibly including relevant information about brains and also about social situations. That is, the goal is not only to improve self-regulation of behavior and emotions but also to increase understanding of the personal and social worlds—all within the compelling context of personally meaningful sports metaphors. The video can then be repeatedly viewed, much as an athlete views game films, to improve performance by internalizing the self-coaching script.

Commonly used adolescent and young adult "self-coaching plays" include the following:

- **"Am I ready?"** For example, do I have what I need for school today? (Sports: Does an athlete have the necessary equipment?)
- **"Am I sure?"** For example, am I sure that John is angry at me; did I interpret his behavior correctly? (Sports: Has the quarterback called the right play for this defense or should he change the play at the line of scrimmage?)
- **"What exactly am I trying to accomplish?"** For example, do I have a major test to study for or a large paper to write? (Sports: Who's the opponent this week?)
- **"What's the game plan? What do I need to do to win?"** For example, what do I need to do to prepare for this test? (Sports: What's the game plan?)
- **"How'd I do?"** For example, did I get a low grade because I didn't study enough? What will I do the next time? (Sports: Review the game films.)
- **"Call time out! Spike the ball! Get organized!"** For example, I feel over-whelmed, but maybe if I just stop and organize my tasks I'll get back on track. (Sports: Call time out.)
- **"Let's think about that"** For example, I feel like smacking him, but maybe I'd better get the facts. (Sports: Should the coach throw the replay flag or not?)
- **"Is it a big deal or a little deal?"** For example, I'm upset that I can't go out this weekend, but it's really not the biggest deal in the world.

For sports-minded adolescents, sports metaphors can be used liberally to create positive associations with effortful self-regulation. For those who are not sports minded, a variety of other positive metaphors are available: "self-direction" (drama, film); "self-guiding" (hiking); "self-choreographing" (dance); "self-supervising" (business); "self-conducting" (music).

Case illustration: Adolescent

As a result of years of context-sensitive coaching (largely provided by her parents), by age 16, Sally had mastered SR self-talk. She had learned to think out loud both as a self-calming procedure and as a problem-solving procedure when faced with difficult academic or other problems. She said that it was important for her to actually talk out loud; silent self-talk simply did not work for her. Her high school mathematics teacher objected to this "distraction," in part because Sally's out-loud thinking helped other students during exams. The teacher was counseled to accept Sally's strategy during regular classes, and offer her a separate space for exams. Sally's chemistry teacher, in contrast, recognized that other students could benefit from Sally's audible thought processes; therefore, she encouraged Sally to continue the processes, invited other students to "tune in" and to begin thinking out loud themselves. In this way, a wise teacher turned an apparent "disability" into an individual and classroom strength.

Case illustration: Child with severe impairment

When self-regulation intervention began, John was 12-years-old receiving services in a self-contained special education classroom. He was classified as a student with a TBI. His cognitive and EF/SR functioning was judged to be at an 18–30 month level of development. He also had moderate sensory (mainly visual) and motor impairments. John's severe disabilities were a result of physical abuse suffered as an infant. Salient problems for staff included anxiety, often resulting in extreme self-stimulatory behavior or physical aggression when he experienced confusion or other forms of discomfort, and extremely poor safety judgment.

The two SR scripts targeted by staff were the "big deal/little deal" script, to reduce anxiety, and the "scary/not scary" script, to improve safety judgment. At that time, John's physical therapy program was focused on safe walking on uneven surfaces or in distracting circumstances. His physical therapist and other staff were urged to use the scary/not scary script routinely during this training. The script, uttered calmly and slowly, would go something like this: "John, we are coming to stairs; this can be scary because you could fall; but if you hold onto the railing and my hand, you will be safe; there is always something that works." John was presented with this script hundreds of times over the school year.

The following year, John had advanced to a middle school with entirely new staff. During a visit to the school, the program consultant observed the following interaction. John was about to get up from a table following an academic period. His assistant teacher said that it was time to walk to the bathroom, which was at the end of a busy corridor. As John rose, he said in a barely audible manner, "Gotta be safe."

When asked, the assistant said that he always said those words when heading out of the room or walking on the playground. She was not aware of the origin of the script, but it was clear that John had internalized the SR scary/not scary script targeted by the previous year's staff and that the script had a positive effect on his self-regulation.

Evidence for self-regulatory/self-talk interventions

In addition to the evidence from normal child development cited earlier, self-talk interventions have been studied with a variety of disability populations. The most thoroughly studied self-talk/self-regulation intervention is CBM (Meichenbaum, 1977). Barkley (2004) reviewed the reviews and meta-analyses of CBM applied to adolescents with ADHD (understood as an EF disorder) and concluded that, despite documentation of statistically significant improvements, literature has failed to demonstrate clinically meaningful outcomes. However, missing from Barkley's review was a meta-analysis in which the investigators restricted their review to studies in which the intervention was delivered in the setting in which the problems were occurring. Robinson, Smith, Miller, and Brownell (1999) wisely restricted the scope of their meta-analysis to studies implemented in everyday school settings for students with aggressive behavior associated with ADHD. Twelve studies (with 36 effect size measures) yielded a large mean effect size of 0.64, or a 24 percentile rank increase for the CBM subjects compared to controls.

It is reasonable to interpret this positive meta-analysis, particularly in contrast to earlier pessimistic reviews, as underscoring the importance of a culture in which the interventions are embedded within the routines of everyday life, particularly for children and adolescents with EF/SR impairment. Consistent with this interpretation, Berk (2001) pointed out that *clinic-based* CBM is not consistent with its purported Vygotskian roots. Rather, modeling and coaching for SR self-talk should be provided within the individual's authentic tasks and settings. The approach described in this chapter is fully consistent with Berk's authoritative advice.

Reid, Trout, and Schartz (2005) completed a meta-analysis of peer-reviewed studies that examined the effectiveness of more specific self-regulation interventions for children with ADHD. The four interventions examined were self-monitoring training, self-monitoring plus reinforcement, self-reinforcement, and self-management (combining self-monitoring, self-rating, and self-evaluating). Each of these interventions can be readily incorporated within the scripts listed in Table 18.3. The 16 studies, which included 51 participants, were mainly single-subject experiments with elementary school students, implemented in their educational setting. Large effect sizes (greater than 0.8) were found for most of the interventions in relation to most of the outcome variables: on-task behavior, socially appropriate behavior, and academic accuracy and productivity. Furthermore, the self-regulation interventions showed a strong additive effect in those cases in which the children were simultaneously treated pharmacologically. Averaging across all interventions and outcomes, the effect sizes were greater than 1.0.

The Reid and colleagues meta-analysis of EF interventions for children with ADHD contrasts sharply with the results of a randomized controlled clinical trial reported by Abikoff and colleagues (Abikoff et al., 2004; Hechtman et al., 2004).

These investigators found that none of the behavioral or psychosocial interventions for students with ADHD added to the effect size produced by medication alone. These contradictory findings can perhaps be explained by some combination of the following two differences: (a) the behavioral and social interventions in the Abikoff study were decontextualized and therefore poorly conceived in relation to what is known about the underlying impairment. For example, the social skills intervention was delivered once a week in a clinic setting and not directly tied to the contexts of the students' social lives. In a review of meta-analyses of social skills intervention studies, Gresham, Sugai, and Horner (2001) found that traditional decontextualized social skills training of this sort has a minimal effect on real-world social success for high incidence disabilities (learning disabilities; emotional-behavioral disturbance). One would expect even less impact on those students known to have special difficulty with transfer of training and therefore in need of "point of participation" interventions and supports. (b) The positive meta-analysis of Reid and colleagues mainly considered single-subject experiments. Single-subject studies tend to use highly individualized and context-sensitive interventions (in contrast to group intervention protocols like those used in the Abikoff et al. study), to select subjects likely to benefit from the intervention, and to terminate the study in the event of likely failure of the intervention.

Graham and Harris (2003) reported the results of a meta-analysis of 18 studies of the effectiveness of Self-Regulated Strategy Development, a strategy intervention approach that includes facilitation of self-regulatory scripts (self-assessment, goal setting, self-instructing, self-monitoring, self-reinforcing). Large to very large effect sizes were found for students with no disability, high risk students, and students with learning disabilities from grade 2 through high school. This approach is consistent with the themes of this chapter in that scripts of self-regulation are embedded in everyday instructional routines for the teaching of reading, writing, mathematics, and content courses.

At least two studies have evaluated the effectiveness of teaching–learning routines in which the student is trained to use something like the Goal-Obstacle-Plan-Do-Review EF/SR routine described in Table 18.3. Martin et al. (2003) found that a Plan-Work-Evaluate-Adjust routine, delivered in the context of everyday academic lessons, improved the self-regulated learning of intellectually normal 9- and 10-year-olds in a residential school for students with severe emotional and behavioral problems.

Wehmeyer, Palmer, Agran, Mithaug, and Martin (2000) evaluated the effectiveness of the self-determined learning model as applied to 40 adolescents with mild mental retardation, learning disabilities, or emotional/behavioral disturbance. Teaching–learning routines included 12 self-addressed questions that the students used to guide their learning behavior. Again the Goal-Obstacle-Plan-Do-Review EF/SR routine described in Table 18.3 was represented in these questions: *Goal*: "What do I want to learn?"; *Obstacle*: "What could keep me from taking action?"; *Plan*: "What can I do to make this happen?"; *Do*: "When will I take action?"; *Review*: "Do I now know what I want to know?". Teacher facilitation of these self-talk questions resulted in goal attainment beyond teacher expectations and improvements on standardized measures of self-determination. There were no significant differences among the three disability groups, suggesting equal effectiveness across disabilities.

SR script intervention is a not-too-distant cousin of social stories as used with children and adolescents on the autism spectrum. In both cases, the goal is improved understanding as well as increased self-regulation of emotions and behavior by framing the improvements positively within personally compelling stories (social stories) or plays (self-coaching). Samsoti, Powell-Smith, and Kincaid (2004) reviewed the available evidence for social stories in autism. The 10 published reports (all single-subject studies or case studies) all had positive outcomes, but serious methodological flaws were common. Therefore, the authors concluded that the evidence base is not yet strong enough to honor the intervention with the title "evidence based"; however, the evidence is accumulating and the procedure remains a clinical recommendation.

Consistent with the reviews of compensatory strategy intervention, described below, it is likely that EF/SR scripts need to be employed for extended periods (months or years) and in the context of personally relevant activities to produce meaningful outcomes. Braga, Campos da Paz, and Ylvisaker (2005) presented data from a randomized controlled clinical trial showing that cognitive and physical aspects of children's functioning are more effectively facilitated after brain injury by training parents to provide appropriate functional stimulation within the routines of everyday life versus treating the child using a traditional clinic-based model of professional intervention. It is likely that the EF/SR dimensions of functioning are best approached in a similar indirect, context-sensitive, and long-term manner.

Intervention and supports for developing organizational skills

Organizational difficulties as a component of EF/SR impairment often result in difficulty organizing thoughts and behavior for effective learning and performance of activities of daily living, complex play activities, efficient word retrieval and expressive discourse tasks (speaking and writing), extended text comprehension, and other complex social, educational, or vocational tasks that require organization. Grafman's neuropsychological theory of specific event complexes and managerial knowledge units (MKUs) (Grafman, 1995; Grafman, Sirigu, Spector, & Hendler, 1993) maintains that the foundation for focused attention, organized thinking and talking, efficient remembering, effective planning, and success with any organizationally demanding task lies in the effective use of organized knowledge structures (schemas), of greater or lesser generality with respect to domains of content. Effective application of these knowledge schemas relies on maturation, growth of domain-specific knowledge, and intactness of frontal lobe structures, explaining much of the disorganized behavior, inefficient attending, and ineffective problem solving of individuals with EF/SR impairment associated with prefrontal brain pathology (e.g., TBI, ADHD).

Ylvisaker, Szekeres, and Haarbauer-Krupa (1998) discussed organizational impairment within a neuropsychological framework and presented a variety of intervention and support approaches. Advance organizational supports for complex tasks, including graphic organizers of a variety of types, have become an evidence-based standard of practice in many settings in which disorganized children are supported (Bulgren &

Schumaker, 2006; Kim et al., 2004). Graphic organizers are also commonplace supports for non-disabled adults, including maps, blueprints, and sequences of pictures to guide individuals through the assembly of products that are sold unassembled.

Swanson and Hoskyn (2001) completed a meta-analysis of 93 group experiments involving students with learning disabilities and found that effective advance organization for learning tasks was one of the two best predictors of positive student learning outcomes (the other being amount of practice). Kim and colleagues (2004) identified large effect sizes in their meta-analysis of studies using graphic and other types of advance organizer with students with learning disabilities. Although students with EF/SR impairment have not been specifically studied, it is reasonable to expect that their characteristic organizational impairments would make them especially strong candidates for organizational supports in their academic and possibly also daily living tasks. As with EF/SR scripts, the goal of graphic advance organization (e.g., sequences of photographs, flow diagrams, checklists, and the like) is to help the child internalize the organizational structure of the task so that the organizational supports can then be gradually reduced, resulting in increased task competence and independence for the child.

For example, students in the early grades benefit from a clear flow diagram that includes the components of a narrative as they attempt to comprehend and produce stories more effectively. (See Figure 18.1) As the components of story structure are internalized, the diagram is gradually faded. Bulgren and Schumaker (2006) and Ylvisaker, Szekeres, and Haarbauer-Krupa (1998) presented a variety of graphic advance organizers and procedures for their implementation. A critical feature of organizers is that they accurately capture the organization of that which is to be organized. Many graphic organizers available in special education materials are visually attractive, but fail to meet this obvious standard (e.g., representing a narrative as circular rather than linear).

Viewing organization as based on domain-specific knowledge structures (such as MKUs) is inconsistent with the common practice among many rehabilitation and special education professionals of drilling children with decontextualized cognitive/organizational exercises in sequencing, categorizing, associating, and the like. Many studies of cognitive training have shown that organizational improvement is not a matter of "sharpening the organizational tools of the mind" (like categorizing and sequencing) with cognitive exercises of this sort. (See Mann, 1979, for a thorough summary of the history of cognitive process training.) Ylvisaker (2003) presented the theoretical base for the alternative "context-and-content-sensitive" approach to cognitive intervention, along with a summary of supportive research.

Teaching compensatory cognitive and academic strategies

Strategic academic behavior is a critical component of EF/SR for school-age children and adolescents. For example, students with poor reading comprehension need to acquire habits of strategic behavior before reading (e.g., reviewing the text for orientation to its content; presetting with questions that need to be answered), during reading (e.g., periodically trying to summarize; dealing with comprehension breakdowns), and after reading (e.g., summarizing, reacting to the content). Ylvisaker,

Figure 18.1   Simple graphic organizer for narrative structure (story grammar) representing the components: Setting (characters, place, time), initiating event, characters' reactions, plan, carrying out of the action, resolution. From *Traumatic brain injury rehabilitation: Children and adolescents* by M. Ylvisaker, S. F. Szekeres, and J. Haarbauer-Krupa, 1998, Boston: Butterworth-Heinemann. Reproduced with permission.

Szekeres, and Feeney (1998) comprehensively discussed considerations related to teaching compensatory cognitive and academic strategies to students with EF/SR impairment after TBI. Our goal in this section is merely to call attention to important aspects of strategy intervention and to bring this large literature to bear on the more general topic of EF/SR intervention.

Critical features of successful strategy intervention have been elaborated by Pressley and his colleagues in a variety of publications (Pressley, 1995; Pressley et al., 1995). These include the following:

- *Context sensitivity*: Cognitive/educational strategy interventions need to be delivered within the context of everyday teaching–learning routines and relevant curricular content.
- *Direct and intensive instruction*: Strategic academic skills require direct instruction along with a large number and variety of authentic application trials.

- *Long term*: The shaping of effective cognitive and academic strategic habits and skills requires years of high-quality instruction and successful practice.
- *Intensive*: Strategy intervention needs to be part of the daily regimen.
- *Personally meaningful, with a focus on correct attribution*: Students need to know that they are responsible for their academic success and that their strategic efforts will be meaningfully rewarded.

The well documented success of the Self-Regulated Strategy Development approach (Graham & Harris, 2003) supports the addition of a sixth feature to this list, namely the embedding of self-regulation scripts within the strategy instruction.

Early strategy intervention in special education was often short term and delivered outside of the context of the student's curricular content. Resnick's (1987) narrative review documented the disappointing results of these early efforts. Recent curriculum-embedded approaches to strategy intervention have been more successful. In their narrative review of research on cognitive strategy approaches to improving reading comprehension for students with varied disabilities, Baker et al. (2002) described the progression from decontextualized to context- and content-sensitive strategy intervention. Reviews of the large research literature on reading comprehension instruction for students without identified disability have similarly highlighted this theme of context- and content-embedded intervention (Sweet & Snow, 2002). The same themes were demonstrated in a meta-analysis of 180 group studies (1537 effect sizes) of strategy intervention in special education generally (Swanson, 1999). Swanson concluded that there was ample evidence for a combined model that integrates direct intensive instruction with curriculum-embedded strategy intervention in teaching students with learning problems (independent of etiology).

We highlight these themes in strategy intervention across disability populations because practitioners of neuropsychological rehabilitation often fall prey to the temptation to deliver strategy intervention in a way that is separated from the child's academic curriculum and social culture, and of insufficient duration to have a meaningful and enduring impact on self-regulated learning and social behavior. Validated curriculum-based strategy intervention procedures have been described by several investigators in educational psychology (Block & Pressley, 2002; Brown, Pressley, Van Meter, & Schuder, 1996; Guthrie, Wigfield, & VonSecker, 2000; Meichenbaum & Biemiller, 1998; Palinscar & Brown, 1989; Pressley, 2002) and special education (Bulgren & Schumaker, 2006; Deshler & Schumaker, 1988; Gersten, Fuchs, Williams, & Baker, 2001; Graham & Harris, 2003; Wehmeyer et al., 2000).

Furthermore, Borkowski has repeatedly found that an intervention focus on correct attribution for success and failure and attention to the student's sense of personal identity as a potentially successful strategic student (i.e., self-efficacy beliefs) are both critical additions to strategy intervention for struggling students (Borkowski & Burke, 1996; Borkowski, Carr, Rellinger, & Pressley 1990; Borkowski, Chan, & Muthukrishna, 2000; Borkowski, Weyhing, & Carr, 1988). Ylvisaker and Feeney (2002) argued that assistance in constructing an organized and motivating sense of self is particularly important in the case of young people with acquired brain injury, and they described intervention procedures designed to assist with this process (Ylvisaker & Feeney, 2000). Positive identity construction is motivated in part by studies that connect self-efficacy beliefs (i.e., I am capable of achieving this outcome) with willpower (Mischel & Ayduk, 2004). Ylvisaker and Feeney's practice of linking personal heroes with effortful strategic behavior in the identity construction process is indirectly supported by studies of typically developing children, demonstrating that reminders of individuals who represent strength before tasks requiring self-regulation improve performance on those tasks (Vohs & Ciarocco, 2004).

Executive function/self-regulatory and positive behavior supports

Feeney and Ylvisaker have described several successful single-subject experiments and case studies in which children and adolescents with challenging behavior associated with EF/SR impairment after brain injury were taught to regulate their behavior sufficiently to meet standards in community schools (Feeney & Ylvisaker, 1995, 2003, 2006, in press; Ylvisaker & Feeney, 1998). Although the need for intervention in these cases was based on behavioral concerns, the impairments and interventions/ supports clustered within that domain in which cognitive, EF/SR, communication, social, academic, and behavioral concerns overlap and dynamically interact. Because the intervention/support plans had several components, it was impossible to identify the specific contributions of individual components to the positive outcomes. However, EF/SR components were central in each case. The approach that we have used for many years is organized around the following components. (See Ylvisaker et al. [2003] for a discussion of the theoretical and empirical supports for this approach. See Ylvisaker et al. [2007] for a systematic review of the evidence for behavioral interventions for children and adults with behavior disorders after TBI.)

- *Cognitive/EF/SR Focus*: *Daily Routine*: *Negotiation and choice*: Daily routines in school (and often at home as well) are analyzed collaboratively and decisions about the minimum amount of work to be accomplished and support plans for achieving the goals (within limits set by general classroom routines) are made collaboratively with the student. Specific time demands (e.g., You must finish these 10 problems in 5 minutes) are often eliminated from the routine, because they frequently evoke oppositional behavior.
- *EF/SR Focus*: *Goal-Obstacle-Plan-Do-Review Routine*: The students are given a graphic map that represents the general sequence of activities from an EF/SR perspective: negotiation of the goal (i.e., What are you trying to accomplish?); identification of difficulty level and obstacles (i.e., Is this going to be hard or easy? What might stand in the way?); creation of a plan: (i.e., How do you plan to get this done? What do you need? What are the steps? How long will this take?); review following task completion (i.e., What were you trying to accomplish? How'd it work out? What worked for you? What didn't work? What was easy? difficult? What adjustments need to be made). These interactions with staff are brief and collaborative (versus a performance-oriented quiz).
- *Cognitive/EF focus*: *Graphic advance organizers*: Because of significant organizational impairment, students are generally provided with photograph or other graphic cues. In some cases, one photograph or drawing is sufficient to orient the student to the task; in others, a sequence of photos/drawings is used

to guide the student through organizationally demanding tasks. Staff work with the students to choose the content of the photographs/drawings, which could include the student engaged in the activity with or without staff, critical materials, important places, and the like. The photos or drawings are placed in small binders that could be hidden in a pouch or pocket.

- *Behavioral focus*: *Positive momentum*: Staff ensure that the plan includes relatively easy tasks with a guaranteed high level of success and reinforcement before difficult or stressful work is introduced, and if possible, a student-preferred activity precedes every mandated activity. Thus "positive momentum" is created prior to potentially stressful tasks.
- *Cognitive/behavioral focus*: *Reduction of errors*: In addition to eliminating time demands and negotiating amount of work to be completed, instructional staff are trained to provide sufficient modeling and assistance so that the students experience few errors (which tend to evoke negative behavior and interfere with learning). Thus instruction is consistent with the principles of "errorless learning," which has been shown to be important for individuals with significant memory impairment (Evans et al., 2000).
- *Behavioral/communication focus*: *Escape communication*: Because the functional behavior assessment often indicates that many occurrences of challenging behavior serve to communicate a need to escape a task or place, the students are taught positive communication alternatives (e.g., I'm done or I need a break). Staffs are trained to encourage these alternatives at natural transition times and when the students begin to appear anxious or upset, and to reward the students' use of positive escape communication.
- *Communication focus*: *Adult communication style*: Instructional assistants are trained to (a) increase their frequency of supportive and reinforcing interactions with the students, (b) anticipate students' difficulties and offer assistance or model escape utterances, and (c) avoid nagging (as perceived by the students).

The emphasis on cognitive, EF/SR, and behavioral antecedent supports is based in part on the repeated finding that individuals with ventral prefrontal damage (common in TBI and other EF/SR diagnoses) learn at best inefficiently from the consequences of their behavior (Bechera, Damasio, Damasio, & Anderson, 1994; Bechera, Tranel, Damasio, & Damasio, 1996; Damasio, 1994; Rolls, 1998, 2000; Schlund, 2002a, b). This finding is especially important in light of the fact that most school-based behavior management programs are organized almost exclusively around the consequences of behavior. Similarly, classroom instruction tends to be organized around demands for performance followed by feedback. Thus students with EF/SR impairment may routinely receive interventions that are incompatible with their primary neuropsychological impairment.

Wade, Michaud, and Maines-Brown (2006) reported the results of a randomized controlled clinical trial comparing usual care (UC: $N = 16$, procedures not described) in pediatric rehabilitation units with a fairly intensive family-centered, problem-solving intervention (FPS: $N = 16$) that included many of the EF/SR components used by Feeney and Ylvisaker in their intervention studies. The FPS group received seven standardized sessions and up to four additional individualized sessions as needed, with the general goal of equipping families with a simple but effective routine for collaboratively solving behavioral and cognitive problems that are common after TBI. The sessions, which involved parents, the child with TBI, and possibly siblings, were spread over 6 months and offered the family coaching in identifying and solving everyday behavioral problems (e.g., how do you respond to teasing?) and cognitive/academic problems (e.g., how do you focus attention while doing homework?). FPS sessions covered many domains of content, but focused heavily on behavioral issues, using a general antecedent-focused, self-regulatory, positive behavior supports framework.

Results suggest that the program was well received by parents and children alike; both parents and children noted increased knowledge and skills, and improved relationships compared to the UC group; and parents in the FPS group reported greater improvements in child behavior. Standardized assessment demonstrated significant reduction in internalizing behavioral symptoms in the FPS versus UC group, with large effect sizes. This study offers preliminary RCT support for a context-sensitive, EF/SR-oriented, positive, proactive, and family-centered approach to serving children with cognitive and behavior problems after moderate or severe TBI.

In addition to the randomized controlled study of Wade et al. (2006), Ylvisaker et al. (2007) identified 16 reports of studies (11 single-subject experiments, 5 case studies) in which positive behavior support procedures were used, possibly in conjunction with traditional contingency management. The 30 participants were all children or adolescents at the time of the intervention. In most cases, explicit training in self-monitoring and self-direction was a component of the intervention. All of the studies reported a positive outcome, indicating that this approach can be said to be evidence based, according to criteria established for the evaluation of single-subject designs in evidence-based practice (Horner et al., 2005).

Case illustration

The following case illustration effectively illustrates the connections among behavior management, EF/SR scripts, and organizational intervention. Ben was 11-years-old at the time of the intervention. He was diagnosed with high functioning autism and was placed in a typical classroom in his community school. Most aspects of cognitive functioning were within normal limits, despite great difficulty processing subtleties in language. Ben also had significant difficulty with social communication. It was hard for him to read social cues, resulting in frequent misinterpretation of peers' communication. For example, he often thought that peers were making fun of him when they were not. He occasionally responded with physical aggression (e.g., pushing), which resulted in two suspensions from school.

Ben adhered rigidly to the rules that he understood, and often admonished peers for violating the rules. Rigidity also manifested itself in inflexibility in topic shifts in conversation. His organizational impairment was evidenced by a messy desk, an inability to find things, and frequent forgetting of homework. His impulse control problems included refusing teacher instructions when they did not fit with what he was doing.

Most components of Ben's intervention were also applied to the other students in his classroom, with or without disability, although the delivery for Ben was more targeted and intensive. All of the students learned to organize their work around the Goal-Obstacle-Plan-Do-Review routine discussed earlier. In addition, every academic task began with identification of difficulty level (hard or easy), prediction of level of success with the task, and determination of possible need for help. Each task ended with a review, including both teacher and student answers to the questions, "Did I do as well as I thought I would do?" and "Did I get the help that I needed?" Teacher and student evaluations were then compared and identified difficulties were transformed into suggestions for the next activity. In addition, Ben began each school day by writing his plan for the day and answering the question, "What kind of student am I going to be today?" To self-cue all of these SR activities, Ben chose the words, "I need to think" and staff would cue him by asking, "Are you thinking?" or "What are you thinking?"

By the end of the academic year, Ben progressed from struggling academically, behaviorally, and socially to a zero incidence rate of behavior problems and homework completion from less than 25% to more than 75%. Late in the year he was named student of the month and was invited to a peer's birthday party for the first time in his life. He also helped other students, not by admonishing them for rule violation (his earlier practice), but by suggesting that it helps to think about what you are doing.

Support-oriented interventions and avoidance of helplessness

As consultants in schools, we often receive negative responses from staff to recommendations for support-oriented teaching and behavior management, and for apprenticeship teaching versus the more traditional performance-oriented teaching common in schools. Frequently this objection is expressed with words like, "What you propose is not the real world! If John receives this level of support, he'll never learn to deal with the demands and frustrations of the real world. We'll make him helpless if we continue this level of support."

The first response to this legitimate concern is to point out that the intervention process does not stop with intensive supports in place. Rather the goal is to enable the individual to be successful and then reduce supports systematically as it becomes possible to do so. An elaborated response to the concern adds that learned helplessness at its core is a settled disposition to believe that one is unable to have a positive impact on the important events of ones life (Peterson, Maier, & Seligman, 1993). This belief may result in passivity, depression, or anger and oppositional behavior. Transforming learned helplessness into learned optimism requires creating an environment in which the child experiences success in pursuing personally meaningful goals. Within this framework of generally successful behavior, children can gradually gain greater control over their supports, which can be gradually withdrawn as the child's skills improve. Gradual withdrawal of supports as the child's competence increases requires ongoing assessments and flexibility on the part of educators and parents. Avoidance of helplessness presupposes a commitment to such assessments and flexible adjustments.

Living optimally is more than the absence of pathology (Gillham, 2000). Helping children and their families to create positive interactions and achieve meaningful outcomes requires more than identifying the disabilities associated with neurological impairment; it requires helping them identify their strengths and barriers to success and then creating positive approaches to achieve their desired outcomes. Pathology-oriented interventions that focus predominantly on identifying deficits for purposes of their amelioration are less likely to have a sustained effect. A positive, strength-oriented approach does not entail ignoring problems and impairments, but rather helping individuals identify the difficulties they are confronting within a larger context of meaningful goal pursuit and potential to succeed, and creating supports that focus on achieving outcomes (and making adaptations) that are meaningful in that context (Aspinwall & Brunhart, 2000).

The themes of learned helplessness and learned optimism are connected to the popular clinical recommendation that adults must play the role of "prosthetic executive system" for children with EF/SR impairment. Despite its kernel of wisdom, this recommendation suffers from two fatal flaws. First, it implicitly assumes that children categorically are or are not capable of self-regulation. In contrast, the developmental reality is that there are thousands of degrees of SR capacity from the total dependence of a newborn to the high levels of self-regulation of a mature, successful young adult. Similarly, EF/SR impairments range from mild to profound. In addition to the construct falling on a continuum, there is variability in SR performance at any given level of development relative to internal states (e.g., level of fatigue, hunger, fright), and setting and activity (e.g., level of novelty, complexity).

Second, children with EF/SR impairment can improve their SR functioning, at least within specific action contexts. Thus the level of EF/SR support must regularly be adjusted to fit the child's needs, with adults playing the "prosthetic executive system" role flexibly and decreasingly over time. These adjustments are made within the context of ensuring sufficient success for ongoing motivation and persistence (i.e., intrinsic motivation), but not so much help that the helper takes over. To ensure that this proceeds systematically, criteria must be established in advance for reducing or increasing levels of support. When the support offered by others encourages autonomy, there is a well-documented increase in participation in activities and also in the self-regulation of behavior (Grolnick & Ryan, 1987, 1989; Martin et al., 2003; Wehmeyer et al., 2000; Williams & Deci, 1996).

Conclusion

Our goals in this chapter have been to propose a broad cultural framework within which development of executive self-regulation can be fostered and to summarize procedural recommendations designed to achieve that goal. Long-term social, academic, and vocational outcomes for children with and without disability are determined in large part by their ability to regulate their emotions, cognitive functions, and social behavior. Children with EF/SR impairments are candidates for intensified supports and interventions provided by all adults in the child's everyday environments. These supports and interventions take the form of scripted interaction designed to facilitate internalization of SR self-talk, organizational supports, cognitive and academic strategies, and positive supports for behavioral self-regulation. To avoid helplessness and foster optimism, the supports must be effectively modulated over time so that individuals experience success while at the same time learning that success is a product of their strategic effort.

References

Abikoff, H. (1991). Cognitive training in ADHD children: Less to it than meets the eye. *Journal of Learning Disabilities, 24,* 205–209.

Abikoff, H., Hechtman, L., Klien, R. G., Gallagher, R., Fleiss, K., Etcovitch, J., et al. (2004). Social functioning in children with ADHD treated with long-term methylphenidate and multimodal psychosocial treatment. *Journal of the American Academy of Childhood and Adolescent Psychiatry, 43*(7), 820–829.

Anderson, V., Levin, H. S., & Jacobs, R. (2002). Executive functions after frontal lobe injury: A developmental perspective. In D. T. Stuss & R. T. Knight (Eds.), *Principles of frontal lobe function* (pp. 504–527). New York: Oxford University Press.

Aspinwall, L. G., & Brunhart, S. M. (2000). What I do know won't hurt me: Optimism, attention to negative information, coping and health. In J. E. Gillham (Ed.), *The science and of optimism and hope* (pp. 163–200). Radnor, PA: Templeton Foundation Press.

Baker, S., Gersten, R., & Scanlon, D. (2002). Procedural facilitators and cognitive strategies: Tools for unraveling the mysteries of comprehension and the writing process, and for providing meaningful access to the general curriculum. *Learning Disabilities Research & Practice, 17*(1), 65–77.

Barkley, R. A. (1997). *ADHD and the nature of self-control.* New York: Guilford Press.

Barkley, R. A. (2004). Adolescents with attention-deficit/hyperactivity disorder: An overview of empirically based treatments. *Journal of Psychiatric Practice, 10*(1), 39–56.

Baumeister, R. F., & Vohs, K. D. (2004). *Handbook of self-regulation: Research, theory, and applications.* New York: Guilford Press.

Bechera, A., Damasio, A., Damasio, H., & Anderson, S. (1994). Insensitivity to future consequences following damage to human prefrontal cortex. *Cognition, 50,* 7–15.

Bechera, A., Tranel, D., Damasio, H., & Damasio, A. (1996). Failure to respond autonomically to anticipated future outcomes following damage to prefrontal cortex. *Cerebral Cortex, 6,* 215–225.

Berk, L. A. (2001). *Awakening children's minds: How parents and teachers can make a difference.* New York: Oxford.

Block, C. C., & Pressley, M. (2002). *Comprehension instruction: Research-based best practices.* New York: Guilford Press.

Borkowski, J. G., & Burke, J. E. (1996). Theories, models, and measurements of executive functioning: An information processing perspective. In G. R. Lyon & N. A. Krasnegor (Eds.), *Attention, memory, and executive function* (pp. 235–261). Baltimore: Paul Brookes Publishing.

Borkowski, J. G., Carr, M., Rellinger, E., & Pressley, M. (1990). Self-regulated cognition: Interdependence of metacognition, attributions, and self-esteem. In B. F. Jones & L. Idol (Eds.), *Dimensions of thinking and cognitive development* (pp. 53–92). Hillsdale, NJ: Erlbaum.

Borkowski, J. G., Chan, K. S., & Muthukrishna, N. (2000). A process-oriented model of metacognition: Links between motivation and executive functioning. In G. Shraw (Ed.), *Issues in measurement of metacognition.* Lincoln, NB: University of Nebraska Press.

Borkowski, J. G., Weyhing, R. S., & Carr, M. (1988). Effects of attributional training on strategy-based reading comprehension in learning disabled students. *Journal of Educational Psychology, 80,* 46–53.

Braga, L. W., Campos da Paz, A., & Ylvisaker, M. (2005). Direct clinician-delivered versus indirect family-supported rehabilitation of children with traumatic brain injury: A randomized controlled trial. *Brain Injury, 19*(10), 819–831.

Bronson, M. B. (2000). *Self-regulation in early childhood*. New York: Guilford Press.

Brown, R., Pressley, M., Van Meter, P., & Schuder, T. (1996). A quasi-experimental validation of transactional strategies instruction with low-achieving second grade readers. *Journal of Educational Psychology, 88*, 18–37.

Bulgren, J. A., & Schumaker, J. B. (2006). Teaching practices that optimize curriculum access. In D. D. Deshler & J. B. Schumaker (Eds.), *Teaching adolescents with disabilities: Accessing the general curriculum* (pp. 79–120). Thousand Oaks, CA: Corwin Press.

Burgess, P. W., & Robertson, I. H. (2002). Principles of the rehabilitation of frontal lobe function. In D. T. Stuss & R. T. Knight (Eds.), *Principles of frontal lobe function* (pp. 557–572). New York: Oxford University Press.

Cattelani, R., Lombardi, F., Brianti, R., & Mazucchi, A. (1998). Traumatic brain injury in childhood: Intellectual, behavioral and social outcome into adulthood. *Brain Injury, 12* (4), 283–296.

Catroppa, C., & Anderson, V. (2006). Planning, problem-solving and organizational abilities in children following traumatic brain injury: Intervention techniques. *Pediatric Rehabilitation, 9*(2), 89–97.

Cicerone, K. (2005). Rehabilitation of executive function deficits. In W. M. High, A. M. Sander, M. A. Struchen, & K. A. Hart (Eds.), *Rehabilitation interventions following traumatic brain injury: State of the science* (pp. 71–87). New York: Oxford University Press.

Damasio, A. R. (1994). *Descartes' error: Emotion, reason, and the human brain*. New York: Avon Books.

Deci, E. L., Koestner, R., & Ryan, R. M. (1999). A meta-analytic review of experiments examining the effects of extrinsic rewards on intrinsic motivation. *Psychological Bulletin, 125*, 627–668.

Deshler, D. D., & Schumaker, J. B. (1988). An instructional model for teaching students how to learn. In J. L. Graden, J. E. Zins, & M. J. Curtis (Eds.), *Alternative educational delivery systems: Enhancing instructional options for all students* (pp. 391–411). Washington, DC: National Association of School Psychologists.

Detterman, D. K., & Sternberg, R. J. (Eds.) (1993). *Transfer on trial: Intelligence, cognition, and instruction*. Norwood, NJ: Ablex.

Eslinger, P. J., Biddle, K. R., & Grattan, L. M. (1997). Cognitive and social development in children with prefrontal cortex lesions. In N. A. Krasnegor, G. R. Lyon, & P. S. Goldman-Rakic (Eds.), *Development of the prefrontal cortex: Evolution, neurobiology, and behavior* (pp. 295–235). Baltimore: Paul Brookes Publishing.

Evans, J. J., Wilson, B. A., Schuri, U., Andrade, J., Baddeley, A., Bruna, O., et al. (2000). A comparison of "errorless" and "trial-and-error" learning methods for teaching individuals with acquired memory deficits. *Neuropsychological Rehabilitation, 10*(1), 67–101.

Feeney, T., & Ylvisaker, M. (1995). Choice and routine: Antecedent behavioral interventions for adolescents with severe traumatic brain injury. *Journal of Head Trauma Rehabilitation, 10*(3), 67–82.

Feeney, T., & Ylvisaker, M. (2003). Context-sensitive behavioral supports for young children with TBI: Short-term effects and long-term outcome. *Journal of Head Trauma Rehabilitation, 18*(1), 33–51.

Feeney, T., & Ylvisaker, M. (2006). Context-sensitive cognitive-behavioral supports for young children with TBI: A replication study. *Brain Injury, 20*(6), 629–645.

Feeney, T., & Ylvisaker, M. (in press) Context-sensitive cognitive-behavioral supports for young children with TBI: A second replication study. *Journal of Positive Behavior Supports*.

Flavell, J. H., Miller, P. H., & Miller, S. A. (2002). *Cognitive development* (4th ed.). Upper Saddle River, NJ: Prentice Hall.

Fitzsimons, G. M., & Bargh, J. A. (2004). Automatic self-regulation. In R. F. Baumeister & K. D. Vohs (Eds.), *Handbook of self-regulation: Research, theory and applications* (pp. 151–170). New York: Guilford Press.

Gillham, J. E. (2000). Introduction. In J. E. Gillham (Ed.), *The science of optimism and hope* (pp. 3–10). Radnor, PA: Templeton Foundation Press.

Gersten, R., Fuchs, L. S., Williams, J. P., & Baker, S. (2001). Teaching reading comprehension strategies to students with learning disabilities: A review of research. *Review of Educational Research, 71*(2), 279–320.

Grafman, J. (1995). Similarities and distinctions among current models of prefrontal cortical functions. In J. Grafman, K. J. Holyoak, & F. Boller (Eds.), *Structure and function of the human prefrontal cortex* (pp. 337–368). New York: The New York Academy of Sciences.

Grafman, J., Sirigu, A., Spector, L., & Hendler, J. (1993). Damage to the prefrontal cortex leads to decomposition of structured event complexes. *Journal of Head Trauma Rehabilitation, 8*, 73–87.

Graham, S., & Harris, K. R. (2003). Students with learning disabilities and the process of writing: A meta-analysis of SRSD studies. In H. L. Swanson, K. R. Harris, & S. Graham (Eds.), *Handbook of learning disabilities* (pp. 323–344). New York: Guilford.

Gresham, F. M., Sugai, G., & Horner, R. H. (2001). Interpreting outcomes of social skills training for students with high-incidence disabilities. *Exceptional Children, 67*(3), 331–344.

Grolnick, W. S., & Ryan, R. M. (1987). Autonomy in children's learning: An experimental and individual difference investigation. *Journal of Personality and Social Psychology, 52*, 890–898.

Grolnick, W. S., & Ryan, R. M. (1989). Parent styles associated with children's self-regulation and competence in school. *Journal of Educational Psychology, 81*, 143–154.

Guthrie, J. T., Wigfield, A., & VonSecker, C. (2000). Effects of integrated instruction on motivation and strategy use in reading. *Journal of Educational Psychology, 92*, 331–341.

Hechtman, L., Abikoff, H., Klien, R. G., Weiss, G., Respitz, C., Kouri, J., et al. (2004). Academic achievement and emotional status of children with ADHD treated with long-term methylphenidate and multimodal psychosocial treatment. *Journal of the American Academy of Childhood and Adolescent Psychiatry, 43*(7), 812–819.

Hill, E. L. (2004). Executive dysfunction in autism. *Trends in Cognitive Sciences, 8*(1), 26–32.

Horner, R. D., Carr, E. G., Halle, J., McGee, G., Odom, S., & Wolery, M. (2005). The use of single-subject research to identify evidence-based practice in special education. *Exceptional Children, 71*, 165–180.

Kaemingk, K., & Paquette, A. (1999). Effects of alcohol exposure on neuropsychological functioning. *Developmental Neuropsychology, 15*(1), 111–140.

Kelly, T. P. (2000). The development of executive function in school age children. *Clinical Neuropsychological Assessment, 1*, 38–55.

Kim, A., Vaughn, S., Wanzek, J., & Wei, S. (2004). Graphic organizers and their effect on the reading comprehension of students with LD: A synthesis of research: *Journal of Learning Disabilities, 37*(2), 105–118.

Landry, S. H., Miller-Loncar, C. L., Smith, K. E., & Swank, P. R. (2002). The role of early parenting in children's development of executive processes. *Developmental Neuropsychology, 21*(1), 15–41.

Landry, S. H., Smith, K. E., & Swank, P. R. (2003). The importance of parenting during early childhood for school-age development. *Developmental Neuropsychology, 24*(2/3), 559–591.

Landry, S. H., Smith, K. E., Swank, P. R., Assel, M. A., & Vellet, S. (2001). Does early responsive parenting have a special importance for children's development or is consistency across early childhood necessary? *Developmental Psychology, 37*, 387–403.

Larsen, R. J., & Prizmic, Z. (2004). Affect regulation. In R. F. Baumeister & K. D. Vohs (Eds.), *Handbook of self-regulation: Research, theory and applications* (pp. 40–61). New York: Guilford Press.

Laurent, A. C., & Rubin, E. (2004). Challenges in emotional regulation in Asperger Syndrome and high-functioning autism. *Topics in Language Disorders, 24*(4), 286–297.

Mann, L. (1979). *On the trail of process: A historical perspective on cognitive processes and their training.* New York: Grune and Stratton.

Martin, J. E., Mithaug, D. E., Cox, P., Peterson, L. Y., Van Dyke, J. L., & Cash, M. E. (2003). Increasing self-determination: Teaching students to plan, work, evaluate, and adjust. *Exceptional Children, 69*(4), 431–447.

McCabe, L. A., Cunnington, M., & Brooks-Dunn, J. (2004). The development of self-regulation in young children: Individual characteristics and environmental contexts. In R. F. Baumeister & K. D. Vohs (Eds.), *Handbook of self-regulation: Research, theory and applications* (pp. 340–356). New York: Guilford Press.

Meichenbaum, D. (1977). *Cognitive behavior modification: An integrative approach.* New York: Plenum Press.

Meichenbaum, D., & Biemiller, A. (1998). *Nurturing independent learners: Helping students take charge of their learning.* Cambridge, MA: Brookline Books.

Mischel, W., & Ayduk, O. (2004). Willpower in a cognitive-affective processing system: The dynamics of delay of gratification. In R. F. Baumeister & K. D. Vohs (Eds.), *Handbook of self-regulation: Research, theory and applications* (pp. 99–129). New York: Guilford Press.

Nybo, T., & Koskiniemi, M. (1999) Cognitive indicators of vocational outcome after severe traumatic brain injury in childhood. *Brain Injury, 13*(10), 759–766.

Palinscar, A. S., & Brown, A. L. (1989). Classroom dialogues to promote self-regulated comprehension. In J. Brophy (Ed.), *Teaching for understanding and self-regulated learning* (Vol. 1). Greenwich, CT: JAI Press.

Peterson, C., Maier, S. F., & Seligman, M. E. P. (1993). *Learned helplessness: A theory for the age of control.* New York: Oxford University Press.

Pressley, M. (1995). *Cognitive strategy instruction that really improves children's academic performance.* Cambridge, MA: Brookline Books.

Pressley, M. (2002) *Reading instruction that works: The case for balanced teaching* (2nd ed.). New York: Guilford Press.

Pressley, M. and Associates (1995). *Cognitive strategy instruction that really improves children's academic performance* (Rev. ed.). Cambridge, MA: Brookline Books.

Reeve, J. (2002). Self-determination theory applied to educational settings. In E. L. Deci & R. M. Ryan (Eds.), *Handbook of self-determination research* (pp. 183–203). University of Rochester Press.

Reeve, J., Bolt, E., & Cai, Y. (1999). Autonomy-supportive teachers: How they teach and motivate students. *Journal of Educational Psychology, 91*, 537–548.

Reid, R., Trout, A. L., & Schartz, M. (2005). Self-regulation interventions for children with attention deficit/hyperactivity disorder. *Exceptional Children, 71*(4), 361–377.

Resnick, L. B. (1987). *Education and learning to think.* Washington, DC: National Academy Press.

Robinson, T. R., Smith, S. W., Miller, M. D., & Brownell, M. T. (1999). Cognitive behavior modification of hyperactivity-impulsivity and aggression: A meta-analysis of school-based studies. *Journal of Educational Psychology, 91*, 195–203.

Rolls, E. T. (1998). The orbotofrontal cortex. In A. C. Roberts, T. W. Robbins, & L. Weiskrantz (Eds.), *The prefrontal cortex: Executive and cognitive functions* (pp. 67–86). Oxford University Press.

Rolls, E. T. (2000). The orbitofrontal cortex and reward. *Cerebral Cortex, 10*(3), 284–294.

Russell, J. (Ed.). (1998). *Autism as an executive disorder*. New York: Oxford University Press.

Ryan, R. M., & Deci, E. L. (2000). Self-determination theory and the facilitation of intrinsic motivation, social development, and well-being. *American Psychologist, 55*, 68–78.

Ryan, R. M., & Deci, E. L. (2002). Overview of self-determination theory: An organismic dialectical perspective. In E. L. Deci & R. M. Ryan (Eds.), *Handbook of self-determination research* (pp. 3–33). University of Rochester Press.

Samsoti, F. J., Powell-Smith, K. A., & Kincaid, D. (2004). A research synthesis of social story interventions for children with autism spectrum disorders. *Focus on Autism and Other Developmental Disabilities, 19*(4), 194–204.

Schlund, M. W. (2002a). Effects of acquired brain injury on adaptive choice and the role of reduced sensitivity to contingencies. *Brain Injury, 16*, 527–535.

Schlund, M. W. (2002b). The effects of brain injury on choice and sensitivity to remote consequences: Deficits in discriminating response-consequences relations. *Brain Injury, 16*, 347–357.

Schmeichel, B. J., & Baumeister, R. F. (2004). Self-regulatory strength. In R. F. Baumeister & K. D. Vohs (Eds.), *Handbook of self-regulation*: *Research, theory and applications* (pp. 84–98). New York: Guilford Press.

Schmitter-Edgecombe, M. (1996). Effects of traumatic brain injury on cognitive performance: An attentional resource hypothesis in search of data. *Journal of Head Trauma Rehabilitation, 11*(2), 17–30.

Shallice, T., & Burgess, P. W. (1991). Deficits in strategy application following frontal lobe damage in man. *Brain, 114*, 727–741.

Skinner, B. F. (1953). *Science and human behavior*. New York: Free Press.

Swanson, H. L. (1999). Instructional components that predict treatment outcomes for students with learning disabilities: Support for a combined strategy and direct instruction model. *Learning Disabilities Research and Practice, 14*(3), 129–140.

Swanson, H. L., & Hoskyn, M. (2001). Instructing adolescents with learning disabilities: A component and composite analysis. *Learning Disabilities Research and Practice, 16* (2), 109–119.

Sweet, A. P., & Snow, C. (2002). Reconceptualizing reading comprehension. In C. C. Block, L. B. Gambrell, & M. Pressley (Eds.), *Improving comprehension instruction*: *Rethinking research, theory, and classroom practice* (pp. 17–53). San Francisco: John Wiley & Sons (Jossey-Bass).

Tranel, D. (2002). Emotion, decision making, and the ventromedial prefrontal cortex. In D. T. Stuss & R. T. Knight (Eds.), *Principles of frontal lobe function* (pp. 338–353). New York: Oxford University Press.

Vohs, K. D., & Baumeister, R. F. (2004). Understanding self-regulation: An introduction. In R. F. Baumeister & K. D. Vohs (Eds.), *Handbook of self-regulation*: *Research, theory and applications* (pp. 1–9). New York: Guilford Press.

Vohs, K. D., & Ciarocco, N. J. (2004). Interpersonal functioning requires self-regulation. In R. F. Baumeister & K. D. Vohs (Eds.), *Handbook of self-regulation*: *Research, theory and applications* (pp. 392–407). New York: Guilford Press.

Vygotsky, L. S. (1962). *Thought and language* (A. Kozulin, Trans.). Cambridge, MA: M.I.T. Press. (Original work published 1934)

Waber, D. P., Gerber, E. B., Turcios, V. Y., Wagner, E. R., & Forbes, P. W. (2006). Executive functions and performance on high-stakes testing in children from urban schools. *Developmental Neuropsychology, 29*(3), 459–477.

Wade, S. L., Michaud, L., & Maines-Brown, T. (2006). Putting the pieces together: Preliminary efficacy of a family problem-solving intervention for children with traumatic brain injury. *Journal of Head Trauma Rehabilitation, 21*(1), 57–67.

Wehmeyer, M. L. (1995). *The Arc's Self-Determination Scale: Procedural guidelines.* Arlington, TX: The Arc of the United States.

Wehmeyer, M. L., Agran, M., & Hughes, C. (1998). *Teaching self-determination to students with disabilities: Basic skills for successful transition.* Baltimore: Paul H. Brookes.

Wehmeyer, M. L., Palmer, S. B., Agran, M., Mithaug, D. E., & Martin, J. E. (2000). Promoting causal agency: The self-determined learning model of instruction. *Exceptional Children, 66*(4), 439–453.

Wehmeyer, M. L., & Schwartz, M. (1997). Self-determination and positive adult outcomes: A follow-up study of youth with mental retardation or learning disabilities. *Exceptional Children, 63*(2), 245–255.

Williams, G. C., & Deci, E. L. (1996). Internalization of biopsychosocial values by medical students: A test of self-determination theory. *Journal of Personality and Social Psychology, 70,* 767–779.

Ylvisaker, M. (2003). Context-sensitive cognitive rehabilitation: Theory and practice. *Brain Impairment, 4*(1), 1–16.

Ylvisaker, M. (2006). Self-coaching: A context-sensitive approach to social communication after traumatic brain injury. *Brain Impairment, 7,* 246–258.

Ylvisaker, M., & Feeney, T. (1998). *Collaborative brain injury intervention: Positive everyday routines.* San Diego, CA: Singular.

Ylvisaker, M., & Feeney, T. (2000). Construction of identity after traumatic brain injury. *Brain Impairment, 1,* 12–28.

Ylvisaker, M., & Feeney, T. (2002). Executive functions, self-regulation, and learned optimism in pediatric rehabilitation: A review and implications for intervention. *Pediatric Rehabilitation, 5*(2), 51–70.

Ylvisaker, M., Jacobs, H., & Feeney, T. (2003). Positive supports for people who experience disability following brain injury: A review. *Journal of Head Trauma Rehabilitation, 18*(1), 7–32.

Ylvisaker, M., Szekeres, S. F., & Haarbauer-Krupa, J. (1998). Cognitive rehabilitation: Organization, memory and language. In M. Ylvisaker (Ed.), *Traumatic brain injury rehabilitation: Children and adolescents* (Rev. ed., pp. 181–220). Boston: Butterworth-Heinemann.

Ylvisaker, M., Szekeres, S. F., & Feeney, T. (1998). Cognitive rehabilitation: Executive functions. In M. Ylvisaker (Ed.), *Traumatic brain injury rehabilitation: Children and adolescents* (Rev. ed., pp. 221–269). Boston: Butterworth-Heinemann.

Ylvisaker, M., Turkstra, L., Coehlo, C., Yorkston, K., Kennedy, M., Sohlberg, M., & Avery, J. (2007). Behavioral interventions for individuals with behavior disorders after TBI: A systematic review of the evidence. *Brain Injury, 21*(8), 769–805.

19 Intervention approaches for executive dysfunction following brain injury in childhood

Cathy Catroppa and Vicki Anderson

Contents

Introduction

Following traumatic brain injury (TBI), thousands of young lives are lost or permanent disability is sustained (Adelson et al., 2003; Goldstein & Levin, 1987; Jennett, 1996; Kraus, 1987, 1995; Mazurek, 1994). Although the pattern of sequelae for injury sustained in adulthood is now outlined with some certainty (Levine, 1988; Pruneti, Cantini, & Baracchini-Muratorio, 1988), knowledge pertaining to adults is not reliably generalizable to the pediatric population (Anderson & Moore, 1995; Jennett & Teasdale, 1981; Levine, 1988; Levin, Benton, & Grossman, 1982). In fact, there is increasing evidence that the young child's brain may be particularly vulnerable to early trauma and a number of explanations have been proposed to account for this vulnerability. Physiologically, the child's brain is incompletely developed. In comparison to adults, the child's skull is more flexible, neck control is poor, and the head is proportionally larger, leading to less focal damage, but greater diffuse injury and interruption to cerebral development (Hudpeth & Primram, 1990). With regard to cognitive and developmental factors, children possess fewer well-consolidated skills than adults as they are just beginning to accumulate skills and knowledge, therefore, have fewer established skills. Future acquisition of these skills may be compromised, depending on the nature and severity of the cerebral damage (Dennis, 1989).

The most common type of TBI in children and adolescents is closed head injury, which accounts for almost 90% of all head injuries. In closed head injury, the brain oscillates within the skull and neuronal pathways may stretch or sever within the brain or brainstem (Davis & Vogel, 1995). Pathological consequences include diffuse injury to the white matter of the brain, as well as the stretching and shearing of nerve fibers, axons, and tracts throughout the brain (diffuse axonal injury) in areas, including the frontal lobes, temporal lobes, corpus callosum, fornix, cerebellum, and ascending and descending brainstem pathways (Adams, Graham, Murray, & Scott, 1982; Levine, 1988; Mattson & Levin, 1990; Stuss & Gow, 1992). When this widespread damage occurs in a brain that is still developing, the predictability of outcome is more difficult (Pruneti et al., 1988), with such diffuse damage impacting on processes such as neuronal myelination and frontal lobe maturation (Hudpeth & Primram, 1990; Thatcher, 1991). While neuronal proliferation and synaptogenesis in the frontal cortex reaches a peak between 1 and 2 years of age, the frontal lobes and their functions continue to emerge throughout adolescence and young adulthood. These aspects of brain development have been linked to the establishment of higher order skills such as information processing, planning, social cognition, self-regulation, and executive skills (Adolfs, 2003; Cicerone & Tupper, 1990; Milner & Petrides, 1984; Stuss & Gow, 1992; Walsh, 1978). Disruption to the maturation of these functions may cause permanent impairment of established skills and reduce the child's potential to acquire new skills (Beaulieu, 2002; Dennis, 1989), often resulting in dysfunctional behaviors and poor relationships.

Over the past decade, advances have been made in rehabilitation practices to obtain the best outcome for the individual following brain injury. Mazaux and Richer (1998) distinguished three phases of rehabilitation. The first takes place during coma and during arousal states, with the primary aim of providing sensory stimulation. The second phase facilitates recovery of impairments and compensates for difficulties in areas including cognition and behavior. The third phase includes outpatient therapy, with the aim of acquiring independence in physical, social, and domestic areas, to re-enter the community successfully. While the rehabilitation given and the therapy outcome varies depending on the participant's age and nature of impairment (Chen, Heinemann, Bode, Granger, & Mallinson, 2004; Dumas, Haley, Ludlow, & Rabin,

2002), the importance of the family–professional collaboration and the use of a multidisciplinary rehabilitation service are key factors in enhancing successful functional outcomes (Barnes, 1999; Hostler, 1999; Semlyen, Summers, & Barnes, 1998; Swaine, Pless, Friedman, & Montes, 2000).

The aim of this chapter is to define executive function (EF), to outline the nature of EF impairments following acquired brain injury (ABI) using a developmental perspective, to discuss postinjury recovery processes, the commencement of rehabilitation and models of intervention. The few available evaluative intervention studies will be outlined, with focus directed to the important role of caregivers, particularly in the educational context.

Executive function

Executive functions (EFs) have been defined as a set of interrelated skills often including one or more of the following: (a) attentional control, (b) planning/goal setting and problem solving, (c) cognitive flexibility of thought and action, (d) concept formation/abstraction, (e) information processing, and (f) social cognition (Anderson, 2002; Anderson, Anderson, Northam, Jacobs, & Catroppa, 2001; Busch, McBride, Curtiss, & Vanderploeg, 2005; Ewing-Cobbs, Prasad, Landry, Kramer, & Deleon, 2004; Lezak, 1993; Stuss & Benson, 1986; Weyandt & Willis, 1994). The model proposed by Anderson (2002) has described these skills in some detail, stressing their importance in the attainment of a future goal (refer to Anderson [2002], chapter 1).

These frontally mediated executive skills begin to emerge in the first year of life and continue to develop into late adolescence and early adulthood (Casey, Giedd, & Thomas, 2000; Klinberg, Vaidya, Gabrieli, Moseley, & Hedehus, 1999; Levin et al., 1991; Stuss, 1992; Welsh & Pennington, 1988), suggesting that in younger children, the full extent of EF difficulties may not be evident for many years postinjury. As mentioned earlier, EFs are argued to be mediated by the prefrontal cortex, which is particularly vulnerable following TBI. The initial compression of the brain, in addition to acceleration–deceleration movements, forces the brain forward, backward, and side-to-side within the skull, potentially resulting in widespread damage throughout the brain (Fennell & Mickle, 1992; Hynd & Willis, 1988; Miller, 1991). The frontal lobes, due to their location and adjacent bony structures, are uniquely at risk as a consequence of such injuries (Capruso & Levin, 1992; Walsh, 1978). As the frontal lobes have reciprocal connections with cortical, subcortical, and limbic brain regions, it follows that the resultant disruption to EF may occur as a result of direct damage to prefrontal regions, or in association with disruption of connections between these areas and other brain regions (Stuss & Gow, 1992; Stuss, Mateer, & Sohlberg, 1994). Therefore, executive dysfunction may not only occur in the context of localized frontal damage, but also where diffuse axonal injury is present (Jacobs, 2003; Stuss & Gow, 1992).

Lack of executive control over cognitive, social, and behavioral functions has been found to cause major day-to-day problems for severely head-injured individuals (Goldenberg, Oder, Spatt, & Podreka, 1992), with EF deficits a hallmark of childhood TBI. The highest forms of mental activity, such as creativity, abstract reasoning, organizational capacity, judgment, conceptual abilities, and social cognition may be affected, with personality changes also reported (Anderson & Catroppa, 2005; Mattson & Levin, 1990; Milner & Petrides, 1984; Papero, Prigatano, Snyder, & Johnson, 1993; Shallice & Evans, 1978; Stuss & Anderson, 2004). Despite the diversity of deficits that may occur in the context of frontal lobe pathology (Goldstein & Levin, 1992; Stablum, Mogentale, & Umilta, 1996), few studies have investigated behavioral and cognitive recovery patterns and outcomes following TBI and frontal lobe damage, particularly in a pediatric population.

Research findings

A number of researchers (Pentland, Todd, & Anderson, 1998; Todd, Anderson, & Lawrence, 1996) examined strategic aspects of EF, in a group of adolescents who had sustained TBI during childhood. These authors designed a multidimensional party-planning task, which required participants to hold several task dimensions in mind simultaneously. Results showed that those with moderate and severe TBI were significantly impaired in their capacity to simultaneously take into account the multiple steps required to accurately complete the task. Levin and colleagues (1997) compared a group of 151 children with TBI to 89 controls, with a subsection of the children seen longitudinally at 3 and 36 months postinjury. Findings demonstrated that injury severity affected performance on all measures of EF. Garth, Anderson, and Wrennall (1997) studied a group of children with moderate to severe TBI and described executive deficits in areas including planning and problem solving, slowed speed of response, and reduced capacity for abstract thought. Harris (1996) examined nine children with TBI (mean age of 11.4 years) and compared them to control subjects on an overt rehearsal free recall task. The severe TBI group presented with impaired verbal recall, an inefficient use of a passive rehearsal strategy and used mainly simple rehearsal strategies. As a whole, children with TBI were less able to modify their rehearsal strategies, were limited in the use of metamemory, and had limited awareness of their memory skills. Dennis, Barnes, Donnelly, Wilkinson, and Humphreys (1996) also examined metacognitive skills, including knowledge appraisal and knowledge management in a group of children with an ABI and a group of normally developing children. Children with an ABI performed poorly in appraisal, management, and metacognitive areas. Hanten et al. (Hanten, Bartha, & Levin, 2000; Hanten, Dennis, Zhang, Barnes, & Roberson, 2004) reported similar results where findings suggested differences in metacognitive capabilities (e.g., clustering, categorization, prospective judgments of recall, monitoring spoken language, estimation of memory span, and overconfidence in performance) between uninjured children and those who had suffered TBI.

Focussing on high-level attentional aspects of EF following early TBI (Catroppa, Anderson, & Stargatt, 1999; Fenwick & Anderson, 1999), difficulties are most evident when tasks involve adaptive shifting from one stream of information to another, or when mental flexibility is required (e.g., holding rules in mind and alternating between the rules while completing a given task). A research program conducted in our lab (Catroppa & Anderson, 2006) identified EF as an area where both children and families report residual difficulties at 2 years postinjury, evident

Table 19.1   Executive function deficits.

	Mild traumatic brain injury (TBI)	Moderate TBI	Severe TBI
Attentional control	*	**	**
Cognitive/mental flexibility	—	—	**
Abstract reasoning	—	*	**
Planning/organization	*	**	**

—   No problems—within 1 standard deviation of the mean.
*   Mild problems—1–2 standard deviations below the mean.
**   Severe problems—greater than 2 standard deviations below the mean.

most clearly at times of developmental transition (see Table 19.1). Of note, such problems are often difficult to identify within the more structured environment of the clinic, but tend to emerge in the more complex context of day-to-day life, at home, school, and within the peer group, where individuals are expected to work independently, and adapt and function appropriately in diverse social situations.

Developmental considerations

Within the pediatric context, interpreting this field of research is problematic due to inconsistencies with definition and operationalization of the construct, but more-so because of the rapidly developing status of EF skills (Welsh & Pennington, 1988). Kelly (2000) reported different developmental trajectories for the interrelated skill areas. With regard to planning and using strategies, some development was reported between the ages of 9 and 13 years, with areas such as motor organization and verbal concept formation showing steep development between the ages of 7 and 11 years. In the areas of fluency and speed of response, a steady but shallow development was reported between the ages of 7 and 13 years. Anderson et al. (2001) also reported differing developmental trajectories for each skill area. With regard to attentional control and processing speed, there was a gradual trend for an increase in these skills through adolescence, with a growth spurt around 7–9 years of age, and another at approximately 15 years of age. No significant increments across late childhood or early adolescence were evident for cognitive flexibility and monitoring, with significant advances evident in early-to-middle childhood. Goal setting showed greatest development prior to adolescence, with gradual progression to 11–12 years and then a developmental spurt at approximately age 12. Anderson (2002) also found that executive domains mature at different rates, with attentional processes undergoing much development during infancy and middle childhood, with information processing, goal setting, and cognitive flexibility all relatively mature by 12 years of age, with many executive processes not fully established until mid-adolescence or early adulthood (See Table 19.2 for a summary of the development of EF skills). More recently, Smidt, Jacobs, and Anderson (2004) used a microanalytic approach to map and contrast developmental trajectories across a range of executive processes (attention control, cognitive flexibility, information processing, and goal setting), in children between 3 and 7 years, and again this study revealed different

Table 19.2   Development of executive function skills.

	Kelly (2000)	Anderson et al. (2001)	Anderson (2002)
1. Attentional control		7–9 years, 15 years	Infancy and middle childhood
2. Planning/goal setting	9–13 years	11–12 years	Relatively mature age 12 years
—Motor organization	7–11 years		
—Verbal concept formation	7–11 years		
3. Cognitive flexibility/ monitoring		Early-middle childhood	Relatively mature age 12 years
4. Information processing			Relatively mature age 12 years
—Processing speed		7–9 years, 15 years	
—Fluency/speed of response	7–13 years		

developmental trajectories for these executive domains (See Figure 19.1). From research findings, it may be inferred that those skills that are in a rapid state of development at the time of injury will be most vulnerable (Ewing-Cobbs et al., 2004). The full extent of executive dysfunction may only be evident in late childhood and

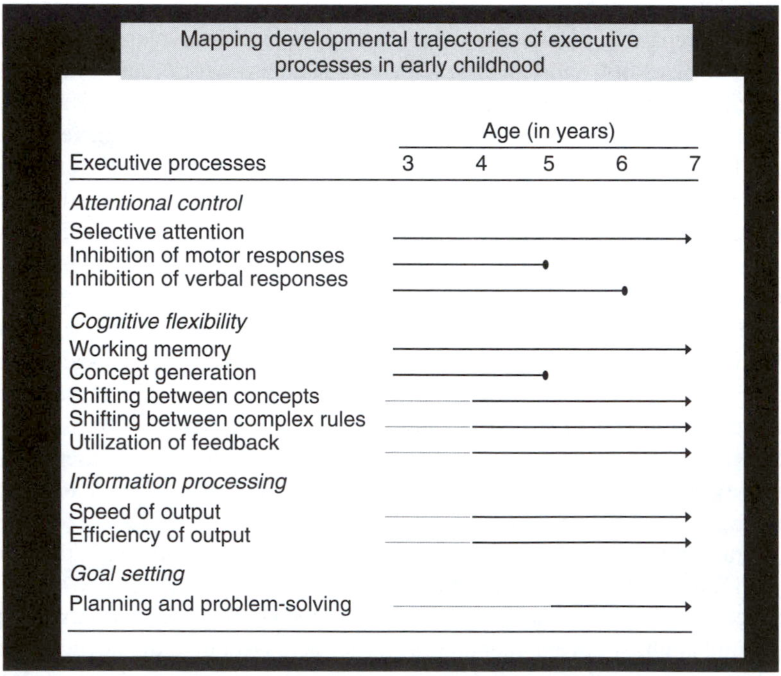

Figure 19.1   Developmental trajectories of executive processes in early childhood.

adolescence, when children are required to act more independently, and utilize planning and reasoning abilities (Anderson et al., 2001; Cronin, 2001; Dennis, 1989; Taylor & Alden, 1997).

Recovery following ABI in childhood

Brain damage results in a number of changes to the central nervous system (CNS), primarily in the acute phase postinjury, and often involving the death and shrinkage of axons and associated neural structures, and the consequent actions of glial cells in repairing the damage as much as possible. In the pediatric population, where the brain is in a process of development, there is some evidence for ongoing degeneration and cumulative pathology over time (Anderson et al., 2001; Anderson & Pentland, 1998; Paakko, Vainionpaa, Lanning, Laitinen, & Pyhtinen, 1992; Stein & Spettell, 1995; Stein, Spettell, Young, & Ross, 1995). Despite these degenerative processes, some recovery of function is evident, both biologically and functionally. Some current models of brain development assume that functional specialization of brain regions is via molecular mechanisms and genetic processes (Johnson, 1990), whereas other models also believe that brain development and specialization occurs over time, both pre- and postnatally (Johnson, 1997, 2000, 2003). Most of these recovery processes can be classified as either "restitution" or "substitution." Restitution of function suggests that spontaneous physiological recovery occurs, that is, as damaged brain tissue heals, neural pathways are reactivated and so functions are restored. Several mechanisms described within the context of restitution include regeneration, sprouting, and denervation supersensitivity (Cannon & Rosenbleuth, 1949; Kolb & Gibb, 1999; Kolb & Wishaw, 1996; Laurence & Stein, 1978; Rothi & Horner, 1983). Substitution theories refer to restoration via transfer of functions from damaged brain tissue to healthy sites, that is, system reorganization or compensation. The two mechanisms commonly described are anatomical reorganization and behavioral compensation (Kolb & Wishaw, 1996; Lashley, 1929; Luria, 1963; Munk, 1881; Rothi & Horner, 1983). While processes of restitution and substitution overlap in the acute phase of recovery, by 6 months postinjury, the process of substitution is believed to be the dominant mechanism (Kolb & Gibb, 1999; Laurence & Stein, 1978; Rothi & Horner, 1983).

Anderson and Catroppa (2005) investigated the recovery of EF in the 2 years postinjury following TBI in childhood. Four components of EF were examined and these were (a) attentional control; (b) planning, goal setting, and problem solving; (c) cognitive flexibility; and (d) abstract reasoning. This study revealed that, while children with severe TBI performed poorest during the acute stage, they exhibited greatest recovery over a 2-year-period (see Figures 19.2–19.5). Despite this recovery, which occurred without any formal intervention, functional deficits remained most severe for this group, with the possibility of further impact on ongoing development. This manuscript stresses the need for intervention to be implemented for at-risk children to prevent, or lessen, the impact of EF difficulties, and so prevent secondary problems (e.g., educationally and socially) occurring. Therefore, a description of intervention models and specific strategies that may be implemented to assist in strengthening EF skills will follow.

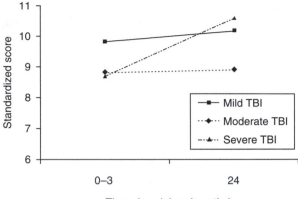

Figure 19.2   Attentional control 2 years posttraumatic brain injury (TBI).

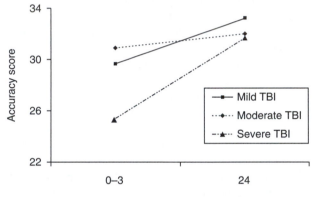

Figure 19.3   Planning, goal setting, and problem-solving 2 years posttraumatic brain injury (TBI).

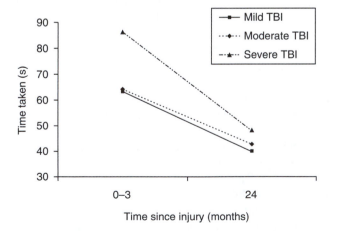

Figure 19.4   Cognitive flexibility 2 years posttraumatic brain injury (TBI).

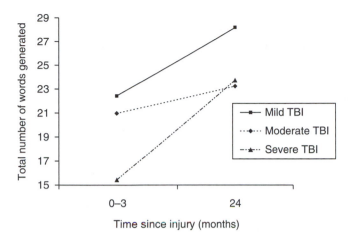

Figure 19.5 Abstract reasoning 2 years posttraumatic brain injury (TBI).

Commencement of rehabilitation/intervention

Once the injured child is stable and has emerged from coma and posttraumatic amnesia (PTA), occupational therapy, physiotherapy, speech therapy, clinical psychology, and neuropsychological services may be instituted to guide further intervention efforts. These services aim to identify areas of impaired neurobehavioral function, to treat them directly, and to begin to plan environmental and educational modifications necessary for a smoother transition to home, school, and the community. As described by Wilson (2000), the two main goals of rehabilitation or intervention are to (a) reduce the everyday consequences of impaired cognitive functioning (disabilities) and (b) reduce the level of handicap (the extent these impairments impede successful re-entry into society). Researchers have found generally, to achieve preferred outcomes, the amount and timing of rehabilitation, increasing hours of therapy given per week, and the opportunity for readmission (e.g., to identify any new problems that have arisen in the day-to-day environment) are all important factors (Cope & Hall, 1982; Shiel et al., 2001; Tuel, Presty, Meythaler, Heinemann, & Katz, 1992).

Models of intervention

Approaches to pediatric rehabilitation may be broadly classified according to the aim of the intervention. The restitution approach aims at improving the individual's capacities by restoration of function via re-establishment of impaired functions (Cicerone & Tupper, 1990; Sohlberg & Mateer, 1989). The substitution approach focuses on functional adaptation, where intact abilities are utilized to "reroute" skills that have been disrupted. Included in this latter approach are externally focused strategies that are directed toward altering the environment to meet the child's new needs, with no intention of changing the child's actual abilities (Mateer,

1999a, 1999b), and in some cases in providing education (e.g., to caregivers and teachers) to enhance understanding and consequently change behavior. The majority of intervention techniques are based on this latter approach. Of note, most interventions are focussed on cognitive or "cold" EF, with less emphasis on rehabilitation of behavioral/social or "hot" EF. Worthy of mention, while out of the scope of this chapter, researchers have also reviewed the benefits of pharmacological stimulants (Napolitano, Elovic, & Qureshi, 2005) in the management and treatment of deficits following TBI.

Direct approach

Direct interventions are designed to treat the cognitive impairments that have resulted from injury. Once impaired cognitive abilities are identified, the child is trained, using specific exercises focusing on those cognitive abilities or processes, in an attempt to improve these skills, as well as to impact more generally on all cognitive functions. Lost functions must be retrained and impaired functions must be maximally stimulated to be present and maintained (Rothi & Horner, 1983). Adult results suggest that such approaches may be more effective in certain cognitive domains, such as attention (Diller & Gordon, 1981; Gray, Robertson, Pentland, & Anderson, 1992; Mateer, Kerns, & Eso, 1996; Robertson, 1990). However, there is little evidence that this direct approach has a high level of effectiveness, or that it generalizes to other cognitive domains or daily functions (Miller, 1992; Park & Ingles, 2001; Ponsford, Sloan, & Snow, 1995; Wilson, 1996, 1997; Wood, 1988).

Behavioral compensation

This is perhaps the most popular approach to rehabilitation, where behavioral disorders are thought to result from a combination of disorganization, disinhibition, impulsivity, poor insight and mental flexibility, and family factors. This approach attempts to train individuals with TBI to perform various activities and tasks using alternative strategies, enabling the person to compensate for their cognitive deficits. Such intervention procedures are designed to improve or restore cognitive capacity or lessen the functional impact of the impairment (Rothi & Horner, 1983; Stuss et al., 1994), suggesting that compensatory approaches, rather than cognitive retraining, will lead to improved performance (Park & Ingles, 2001).

Behavior modification strategies

Behavioral strategies aim at overcoming cognitive deficits via the use of behavioral interventions. These may include the use of positive and negative reinforcement, the implementation of token economies, the writing of behavioral contracts, the use of peer facilitators, and transfer of training procedures (Kazdin, 1984). It is often less difficult to evaluate these programs because behaviors to be trained are measured directly at the same time that treatment is given (Ponsford et al., 1995), with baseline assessments often conducted before a decision to intervene is made.

Environmental modifications and supports

There are a number of studies within the adult literature that have suggested that application of these techniques is related to significant improvement in skills (Berg, Koning-Haanstra, & Deelman, 1991; Evans, Emslie, & Wilson, 1998; Mateer, 1999; Schmitter-Edgecombe, Fahy, Whelan, & Long, 1995; Wilson & Moffat, 1992). Applications may include the simplification of tasks, allowing more time to complete tasks, the reduction of noise, the removal of other potential distractions (Mateer, 1999), and the use of external aids or cues, such as lists, diaries, alarms, or paging systems. Until recently, external cueing has not been found to be a particularly successful approach for younger children; however, a recent study by Wilson and colleagues (Wilson, Emslie, Quirk, & Evans, 2001) showed that children as young as 8 years of age were able to benefit from a computerized reminder intervention program (Neuropage), showing increased ability to recall important events and information when accessing this system. To a great extent, the emphasis of pediatric rehabilitation is on modifying the child's environment (i.e., home, classroom, playground, etc.) to ensure that the context is conducive to best level of function.

Educational/instructional support

Although psycho-educational approaches are often used with adults, educating children with respect to the consequences of head injury, and its possible impact on their lives, has led to inconsistent results. Beardmore, Tate, and Liddle (1999) demonstrated that while children did not show any benefit from a single information session (perhaps due to memory difficulties following TBI), parents appeared to show improved understanding of their child's difficulty, indicating that parents may act as "tutors" for EF deficits. Of a more complex nature, children may also be taught the use of self-talk, self-instructional methods, and self-monitoring strategies to regulate behavior and achieve preferred outcomes (Mateer, 1999; Ponsford et al., 1995). For a summary of Intervention Phases/Models refer to Table 19.3.

Table 19.3 Phases/models of intervention.

Phase	Intervention	Administrator
1. During coma	Sensory stimulation	Medical staff
2. Postcoma/posttraumatic amnesia (PTA)	Intervention for difficulties in cognition and behavior	Occupational therapist Speech pathologist Neuropsychologist
3. Outpatient therapy	Intervention to assist re-entry into physical, educational, and social areas	Occupational therapist Physiotherapist
	Direct approach	Clinical psychologist
	Behavioral compensation	Neuropsychologist
	Behavior modification	Educational psychologist
	Environmental modification	Special educators
	Environmental supports	School staff
	Educational supports	Family
	Instructional strategies	Significant other(s)

Our laboratory is also involved in the implementation of an intervention program (Signposts program modified for use with an ABI population) aimed at improving parents' skills to manage their child's challenging behavior post-TBI), and more detail will be given in later sections of this chapter.

Applications of strategies for executive dysfunction

A number of researchers have stated that it is best to use a combination of intervention approaches, usually beginning with the use of external cues and behavioral strategies, and moving to strategies that establish and maintain internal self-regulatory control, with additional training using real-life situations for generalization to occur (Mateer, 1999; Ponsford et al., 1995; Sohlberg, Mateer, & Stuss, 1993). There are few studies investigating EF following childhood trauma, and even fewer rigorously evaluating the effectiveness of interventions for such dysfunction. Of these studies, when evaluating outcomes acutely and long-term following pediatric TBI, results generally support EF difficulties (Anderson and Catroppa, 2005, Levin et al., 1997; Pentland et al., 1998; Todd et al., 1996), consequently strategies to remediate EF deficits are required. Many of these strategies, employed in rehabilitation programs (Ponsford et al.; Sterling, 1994; Ylvisaker, 1985), have not undergone rigorous evaluation, therefore, long-term benefit and generalization is not fully understood. Additionally, many of the strategies have been implemented with adults and require modification to be appropriate for children.

   The remainder of this chapter focuses on studies reporting intervention techniques for EF difficulties following TBI in childhood. Pediatric research conducted to date has focused on different aspects of EF, and has adopted both broad and general intervention techniques, with little focus on rigorous evaluation studies. There is a place for both general and more specific techniques when intervening in a pediatric population, where EF difficulties become especially apparent in more demanding and complex environments. To bring some organization to the information to follow, a potentially artificial division will be made between intervention techniques for cognitive difficulties and intervention techniques for social/behavioral difficulties.

Cognitive interventions

Attentional control

When looking at attentional difficulties, defined earlier within the attentional control category (Anderson, 2002), a number of general intervention strategies have been put forth by Dawson and Guare (2004) and Ylvisaker and Feeney (2002), although only a few evaluation studies have been conducted. Dawson and Guare (2004; pp. 47, 52) discuss environmental modifications for sustained attention and response inhibition difficulties and suggestions include the following general interventions that can be implemented into a classroom setting. For a comprehensive review, refer to Dawson and Guare (2004).

Sustained attention

- Make students aware of stop and start times to increase persistence with tasks.
- Use of subtasks, allowing rest periods after each subtask is completed.
- Ensure students are alert when they are required to sustain their attention.
- It is important that students are aware of their attentional limitations, so that they can monitor their need for a break.
- Help students devise a work-plan.
- Make students aware of what keeps them motivated to sustain attention.
- Provide guidance, positive reinforcement.
- Slowly transfer the responsibility to the student.

Response inhibition

- Talk to the student about impulsive behavior.
- Discuss the possibility of a replacement behavior.
- Use strategies to encourage the use of the replacement behavior.
- Increase supervision.
- Ignore impulsive behavior and reinforce the replacement behavior.
- Slowly fade reinforcement and cueing.

Ylvisaker and Feeney (2002) provide a framework for pediatric rehabilitation, using strategies from the learned helplessness and optimism literature to provide a comprehensive approach to intervention, for children and adolescents with brain injury. These authors also provide an intervention checklist for individuals with EF impairment in areas including self-monitoring (e.g., is the individual maximally involved in charting his own performance?) and self-inhibition (e.g., if inhibition cues are needed, are they subtle and provided by peers as much as possible?). For a comprehensive review of the checklist, refer to Ylvisaker and Feeney (2002) and Ylvisaker, Szekeres, and Feeney (1998).

Only a handful of studies have evaluated the effectiveness of intervention programs directed at attentional skills in children. Of these studies conducted, the samples have been small, a control group is often not assessed, and studies predominantly consist of teenagers or individual case studies. Due to this limited research base, a study by Gray et al. (1992) is of particular interest. This group investigated skills classified as working memory, frontal functions, and other attentional skills in adults with TBI and non-TBI. Subjects received computerized attentional training or recreational computing. Only minor differences were found between groups at the end of training, but by 6-month follow-up, the experimental group performed better on two tests of attention/working memory. However, this study did not evaluate these gains in terms of everyday functioning. Robertson (1990) argues that results from attentional training as well as other cognitive skills, via use of computers, has yielded inconsistent results and procedures have not shown to generalize to real-life settings, suggesting that computers only be used as a research tool until further research indicates its benefit.

In a study by Burke et al. (Burke, Wesolowski, & Guth, 1988), a group of five adolescents, all injured in motor vehicle accidents and in coma for almost 3 weeks with primarily frontal injuries, were given cognitive training to address a number of difficulties including poor attention and concentration, reduced memory and problem-solving skills, and poor social judgment. Training to improve attention and concentration specifically involved self-control strategies and antecedent control. To improve self-regulation, small groups were taught via self-instructional training, modeling and role-playing, reinforcement, and group feedback. Staff members also assisted in organizing the injured person's environment when training was complete. Data revealed that four of five adolescents returned home to live with parents, and the same numbers were able to return to public schools, therefore suggesting that the intervention was successful.

Brett and Laatsch (1998) trained teachers to administer rehabilitation tasks in a number of attentional domains (e.g., attention and concentration) via the use of a computer and flash cards. Pre- and posttreatment results showed minimal improvement, supporting Robertson (1990) with regard to the inconsistent findings of interventions via computer tasks. Thompson (1995) and Thompson and Kerns (2000) conducted case studies as well as investigating a group of high school students using attention process training (APT). Inconsistent results were obtained, with some subjects showing improvements. Crowley and Miles (1991) reported an adolescent intervention case study, where a 16-year-old boy was provided with rehabilitation 18 months following severe TBI. A behaviorally based intervention was implemented, and analysis of behavior identified problems with self-monitoring and applying oneself consistently to tasks. Forty sessions of one hour duration over a period of 8 weeks, were used to improve self-monitoring via the use of saturated cues and by charting progress. The outcome measure was performance on an algebra review test and completion of homework. Results suggested some improvement in algebra and completion of homework. In a similar study (Selznick & Savage, 2000), self-monitoring procedures were introduced to three adolescent boys with brain injury. The outcome measures were on task behavior, accuracy, and productivity. The intervention, a behavioral compensation approach (e.g., the use of cues), assisted self-monitoring, which in turn led to positive gains on the outcome measures, with some generalization also evident when the intervention was withdrawn.

In general, these few studies examining intervention techniques in the attentional control area following childhood brain injury suggest some improvement following intervention, with more success when attention training was provided by a therapist, with or without cognitive intervention strategies, rather than on the reliance of a computerized intervention. More emphasis is required on developmental issues (e.g., are certain strategies more appropriate and effective for different age groups?) and to determine generalization of gains from the testing environment to the "real world" (Penkman, 2004).

Planning/goal setting

A number of intervention techniques, mainly broad strategies and a few evaluative studies, have been proposed in the general area of planning, organization, and problem solving (Sterling, 1994; Ylvisaker, 1985). In the childhood–adolescent domain, these approaches may be supplemented by methods employed within an educational context as "there are common interventions that apply across executive skills" (Dawson & Guare, 2004; p. 40), and these may include six steps:

1. Problem behavior should be described.
2. Goal is set that is linked to the problem behavior.
3. Set of steps is established to reach the goal.
4. Child is supervised.
5. Process is evaluated and any necessary changes are made.
6. Supervision is faded.

For planning, organization, and task initiation difficulties, Dawson and Guare (2004) propose environmental modification as the preferred intervention technique. When considering planning difficulties these authors suggest the provision of a plan or schedule, breaking long-term projects into subtasks, assigning a deadline to each subtask, and asking questions to prompt children to think about how to make a plan (e.g., What do you have to do first?). When considering organizational difficulties, strategies included the use of organizational schemas, such as a system for organizing schoolwork, for example, where the child was asked to use different colored folders to identify completed assignments from work not yet done. They found that to achieve success, children required a cue to use the schema, followed by positive reinforcement when the schema was utilized. Once the skill was overlearned, with repeated exposure to many different schemas, the cuing and reinforcement could then be faded.

In the area of initiation, another facet of planning and goal setting Dawson and Guare (2004; p. 54) also proposed interventions such as the following:

1. Use of verbal and visual cues.
2. Assist child to get started.
3. Note start and stop times.
4. Write a plan for the task.
5. Monitor the child and provide reinforcement.
6. Fade supervision over time.

Other researchers and clinicians have also reported intervention strategies that are useful in treating (a) organizational and planning, and (b) problem-solving deficits following pediatric ABI (Ponsford et al., 1995; Sterling, 1994; Ylvisaker, 1985), and these are presented in Table 19.4.

Ylvisaker and Feeney (2002), as mentioned earlier, applied strategies from learned helplessness and optimism research to develop interventions for children with brain injury. These authors also present a checklist for interventions in areas including planning, organizing and problem solving (e.g., Does the individual participate maximally in planning intervention activities? Is the organization of the session obvious to the individual? Is the individual's life organized around well-understood routines? Is the individual maximally engaged in selecting strategies?), and initiation

Table 19.4   Interventions.

Organizing and Planning
 1. Use of a "who, what, when, and where" approach to planning a task.
 2. Use of organizational aides, for example, lists.
 3. Design of step-by-step plans before commencing a complex piece of work.
 4. Use of flow diagrams, graphs, or other pictorial cues.
 5. Break tasks into smaller components and work on one component at a time.
 6. Use of external cues to monitor progress, for example, tick off a checklist.
 7. Summarize complex information focusing on key points.
 8. Bold and highlight key information.
 9. The efficient use of a diary (via training) to organize school/social events.
10. Allow time to plan/organize a task before commencing work on the given task.

Problem Solving
 1. Identify the problem. (What is the problem?)
 2. Identify the goal. (What will you gain by solving this problem?)
 3. What is the relevant information?
 4. What are the possible solutions?
 5. Evaluate the solutions.
 6. Make a decision. (What seems to be the best solution?)
 7. Formulate a plan. (How do you plan to take action?)
 8. Monitor and evaluate the results.

Source: From *Traumatic Brain Injury: Rehabilitation for Everyday Adaptive Living*, by J. Ponsford,
        S. Sloan, and P. Snow, 1995. Hove, UK: Lawrence Erlbaum Associates; Students with acquired
        brain injuries in primary and secondary schools. Project Report, by L. Sterling, 1994, Canberra,
        Australia: Australian Government Publishing Service (AGPS); *Head Injury Rehabilitation:
        Children and Adolescents*, by M. Ylvisaker (Ed.), 1985, San Diego, CA: College-Hill Press.

(e.g., Do activities engaged make demands on the individual's ability to initiate?).
For a comprehensive review of the checklist refer to Ylvisaker and Feeney (2002)
and Ylvisaker et al. (1998).

As indicated, a wide range of intervention strategies and approaches, individually
and in combination, have been implemented following pediatric TBI, for difficulties
in planning, goal setting, and problem solving. However, specific studies evaluating
the efficacy of intervention techniques with child-based samples are minimal. Levine
et al. (2000), using an adult sample, have provided encouraging results, which may
be extrapolated to child samples. Intervention for executive difficulties in an adult
sample of 30 mild-severe ABI patients, 3–4 years postinsult, assessed the effects of
a specific training procedure, goal management training (GMT) to assist in the
area of goal neglect. Goal neglect refers to difficulties in maintaining intentions in
goal-directed behavior. Goal-directed behavior has a planning and problem-solving
component, where an important aspect is the selection of new activities when
previous actions have failed to achieve a goal. These authors suggest a five-step
flowchart with feedback loops where necessary: (a) STOP—What am I doing?; (b)
DEFINE—The main task; (c) LIST—The steps; (d) LEARN—The steps and do it;
and (e) CHECK—Am I doing what I planned to do? Results showed that GMT
improved performance on pencil-and-paper activities and on a real-life task (e.g.,
meal preparation). It was concluded that further research was indicated to evaluate

the generalization of this procedure to a broader range of real-life situations. Perhaps such a procedure, if found to be generalizable, could be modified and used with a pediatric population.

Another recent study included a sample of 143 subjects that ranged in age from childhood to the elderly (8–83 years), and was predominantly restricted to ABI patients (Wilson et al., 2001). Targeted deficits included memory, attention, planning, and organizational problems. The intervention comprised a radio-paging system where reminders were transmitted to each individual on their pager. Findings indicated that the pager system significantly reduced everyday problems of memory and planning for participants with brain injury. However, due to the wide age range and to the inclusion of non-ABI participants, it was difficult to evaluate the efficacy of the pager system for those who sustained an ABI during childhood.

Case studies have also been reported, where three children who suffered a severe ABI one year previously, and aged between 6 and 10 years, were given direct instruction programs as a form of intervention (Glang, Singer, Cooley, & Tish, 1992). Behavioral principles were implemented, including task analysis, modeling, and shaping, with participants being pretaught problem-solving strategies, with practice being provided. Improvements were reported in areas such as self-monitoring and mathematics.

Suzman, Morris, Morris, and Milan (1997) investigated five children, between the ages of 6 and 11 years, who sustained severe head injuries 6–9 months previously, and presented with problem-solving difficulties. The intervention was quite complex and consisted of metacognitive training, self-instructional training, self-regulation training, attribution training, and reinforcement. A computerized problem-solving task (*Think Quick*, 1987) was used to evaluate the intervention program, as well as pre- and postintervention social validity and psychometric measures, collected via parental and teacher report. Results revealed substantial improvement on trained tasks and improvements on some of the postintervention standardized tests of problem solving.

As in the attentional control domain, although there are numerous broad strategies recommended to assist skills in the planning, organization, and problem-solving areas, there have been minimal evaluation studies. Again, studies are needed to rigorously evaluate the effectiveness of an intervention with children following TBI, before such strategies can be implemented with confidence.

Cognitive flexibility

Intervention techniques in the cognitive flexibility domain, which may include divided attention, working memory, feedback utilization, and conceptual transfer (Anderson, 2002), have also been limited. General interventions have been implemented, with few controlled trials, and minimal evaluative studies conducted. Vakil, Blachstein, Rochberg, and Vardi (2004) reported that children who sustained a brain insult had difficulty transferring information into long-term storage, reflecting an inefficient learning strategy, implicating memory deficits (e.g., working memory) on tasks of an executive nature.

Again drawing from adult research, intervention techniques that have been used for "memory" difficulties include memory book training (Sohlberg & Mateer, 1989), notebook training (Schmitter-Edgecombe et al., 1995), memory strategy training versus drill or repetitive practice on memory tasks, use of compensatory devices, and environmental modifications (Wilson, 1997; Wilson & Watson, 1996) and errorless learning (Wilson, Baddeley, & Evans, 1994), suggesting that memory strategy training (e.g., including working memory) has the potential to assist individuals in their day-to-day functioning. Wright and Limond (2004) describe implicit (e.g., skills and habits such as walking) and explicit (e.g., recollection of a piece of knowledge) memory, with the latter including working memory. These authors suggest the use of passive rehabilitation strategies for younger children, with emphasis on improving retrieval of learned information, with the use of much environmental support as offered by parents and teachers. Older children were thought to benefit more-so from strategic intervention, or assistance in improving the organization of material in memory.

As can be seen there is minimal research investigating intervention techniques for skills in areas including divided attention and working memory with children. These skills can be difficult to define and measure accurately, therefore increasingly difficult to intervene and evaluate particularly in a developmental context. Perhaps child-based rehabilitation in this area could draw on intervention techniques used with children where such cognitive impairments also exist (e.g., learning disabilities, attention deficit hyperactivity disorder).

In summary, it is clear that evaluative studies are scarce within the pediatric domain, and where conducted they often rely on case material or very small samples. It is often difficult to measure the success of an intervention program due to the many methodological differences between studies, and due to the various intervention models used alone or in combination, making it difficult to replicate findings. Furthermore, speed of processing and performance on EF tasks are linked; therefore, interventions aimed at improving EF performance may also increase speed or efficiency with which tasks are completed, and in a circular fashion, increased speed of processing will make completion of EF tasks more efficient, combining the contribution of these skills. Of note, there is much to learn from broader educational literature, where intervention approaches used may also be applicable to TBI. For a summary of intervention models used in previous TBI literature (cognitive and social/behavioral), refer to Table 19.5.

Social/behavioral interventions

Social and behavioral difficulties are often present in the context of TBI and associated EF impairments (Dykeman, 2003; Ruff & Niemann, 1990), and these often make successful integration into everyday life challenging, therefore worthy of some discussion. To target a disruptive or inappropriate behavior and to identify contributing factors, a child must be observed in his or her natural environment, most often the school and home. With regard to intervention strategies, behavior modification techniques (e.g., use of reinforcement, shaping of behavior, modeling, prompting and cuing, use of contracts, self-monitoring, cognitive strategies,

Table 19.5 Summary of interventions in pediatric literature following executive dysfunction.

Executive dysfunction	Intervention model
Cognitive Difficulties	
Attentional control	Environmental modifications
	Behavior modification techniques
	Direct approach
	Self-instructional methods
	Educational support
Planning/goal setting/problem solving	Environmental modifications
	Behavior modification Techniques
	Direct approach
	Self-instructional methods
	Problem-solving strategies
Cognitive flexibility	Environmental modifications/supports
Social/behavioral dysfunction	Environmental modifications
	Behavior modification techniques
	Self-instructional methods
	Supports—significant other(s)

anxiety-managing strategies, relaxation techniques, didactic class activities, use of peer models) may assist in reducing disruptive behavior and increasing prosocial behavior (Dykeman, 2003). There is minimal research investigating these techniques in a pediatric population and the examples below reveal the complexity involved in conducting these evaluative studies.

Feeney and Ylvisaker (2003) investigated the effects of a cognitive behavioral intervention program on two young children with behavioral concerns following TBI sustained at 5 years of age. Both children presented with frontal lobe impairment and severe challenging behavior. They were reported as having deficits in the areas of organization and planning in the classroom, and these difficulties contributed to their behavioral problems. Feeney and Ylvisaker (2003) made the point that behavioral disruption is often a consequence of complex interactions between the child and injury, abilities and impairments and supports available, suggesting that intervention should involve the child as well as the caregivers at home and at school. Behaviors were operationally defined and outcome measures were frequency and intensity of aggression and amount of work completed. An ABAB design was implemented where "A" was the baseline condition and "B" was the intervention. The intervention included (a) daily routine, (b) positive momentum, (c) reduction of errors, (d) escape communication, (e) adult communication style, (f) graphic advance organizers, and (g) goal-plan-do-review routine, with staff trained in a number of these areas. Results indicated that the challenging behavior had significantly decreased in intensity and was almost eliminated. Long-term follow-up indicated a positive long-term outcome, suggesting that a support-oriented intervention that includes both behavioral and cognitive components was successful. Maintenance of gains was facilitated by training the following year's staff and by training parents.

Mottram and Berger-Gross (2004) evaluated a behavioral intervention program at a rehabilitation hospital for three boys between the ages of 8 and 14 years with brain injury. Two control groups were also implemented: children with appropriate behavior and children with disruptive behavior. A multiple baseline design across individuals was employed, where the experimental group's disruptive behavior was seen to decrease by 69% during the intervention phase, with maintenance at follow-up. This study suggested that a behavioral package that includes program rules, a token economy with response cost and mystery motivators, was well received by children and staff, and resulted in long-term improvements. Again this study highlights the importance of training staff and caregivers in intervention techniques so that these can be implemented in various settings to assist in generalization of gains.

Role of educating caregivers

Recent literature stresses the important role of caregivers, such as families and teachers, in the recovery process following brain injury (Feeney & Ylvisaker, 2003; Mottram & Berger-Gross, 2004; Ylvisaker et al., 2001). Therefore, it follows that an essential part of the intervention program should be to educate caregivers with regard to the mechanisms of the injury, possible short- and long-term consequences of the injury, recovery process, and the role of intervention in both prevention and dealing with residual impairments. The injured children may also be included if old enough, to assist them in understanding what has happened, and more importantly, to help them understand and cope with changes that they may be aware of, both cognitively or socially, from pre- to postinjury. Only minimal research has been conducted to evaluate the efficacy of such programs following a brain injury in childhood.

One such research study (Ponsford et al., 2001) evaluated a group of children who had sustained a mild TBI, and compared them to children with minor injuries not involving the head. Measures of preinjury behavior, psychological adjustment, postconcussion symptoms, attention, speed of processing, and memory were administered. One group of children who had sustained a mild TBI were seen 1 week postinjury and their family was also given an information booklet outlining symptoms associated with mild TBI and suggested coping strategies. Another group was seen at 3 months postinjury and their family was not given a booklet. Results indicated that the latter group generally reported more symptoms and was more stressed 3 months postinjury. It was concluded that the provision of an information booklet lowers the incidence of ongoing problems by reducing anxiety.

Furthermore, limited research has been conducted evaluating parental training programs that have a focus on the social/emotional aspects of EF. The most well-established treatment of children with difficult behavior at home is training parents to implement behavior change strategies at home (Gavidia-Payne & Hudson, 2002; Sanders, 1999). The Signposts for Building Better Behavior program were developed to provide parent support to families of children with intellectual and developmental disabilities, and has resulted in significant improvements in child behavior and parental functioning (Hudson et al., 2003). Given these findings, it was expected that parents of children with TBI will also benefit from the parenting skills taught

Table 19.6   Findings from the Signposts pilot program.

Evaluation	Suggestions/recommendations
1. Content evaluation: Aims of the program (assist parents to mange difficult behavior) found to be appropriate.	—More information/skills to assist parents to teach social skills to their children.
2. Input evaluation: Generally agreed by all that parenting skills taught and information presented were appropriate and useful for parents.	—Teach parents skills in developing consistent daily routines; —Provide skills to enable parents to talk to children about appropriate and inappropriate behaviors; —More information regarding the link between cognitive limitations and difficult behavior; —More information about and child–parent adjustment difficulties postinjury.
3. Process evaluation: Parents reported high satisfaction with the parenting strategies taught and the training methods used.	
4. Product evaluation: This involved the evaluation of the application of the Signpost program.	**Results** —All children demonstrated a significant decrease in the frequency of non-compliant behavior. —Improvements in all areas of function were seen for some child from pre- to postintervention. —All parents reported a decrease in the overall frequency of parenting hassles. —Improvement was noted in parenting satisfaction following the intervention.

in the program to manage difficult behaviors, and prevent such behavior occurring in the future. A pilot study (Giallo & Matthews, in progress) has been completed to identify any amendments to the original Signposts program content that may be necessary for a group of children with ABI. A sample of four families and nine consultants were recruited to participate and a summary of results and recommendation made by participants is given above (See Table 19.6). Researchers in our laboratory are now involved in developing supplementary modules specific for a TBI population.

Works in progress

Development of intervention techniques in our laboratory

Recently, a pilot intervention program was commenced (Catroppa & Anderson, in progress), aimed at teaching strategies to improve executive functioning (e.g., planning, organizing, problem solving, maintaining positive self-esteem, etc.) with an adolescent/young adult group, at a time 8–10 years postinjury. Evaluation to date indicates some improvements in target areas. This program is continuing with the recruitment of a larger sample of adolescents/young adults postinjury.

The intervention program (The Amsterdam memory and attention training for children [Amat-c]) has been trialed successfully in Sweden and found to improve executive skills (Van't Hooft et al., 2005) and maintain these improvements over time in a pediatric group postbrain injury. This intervention is currently being translated into English, and once the translation is complete, a pilot will be conducted to ascertain its relevance and impact on an Australian TBI population.

How to bring intervention techniques into an educational setting/context

As seen by the literature presented in this chapter, while there are research papers outlining possible intervention techniques, most of these are not evaluative studies, making it difficult to accurately interpret the efficacy of the suggested intervention. Of these where evaluation of an intervention technique was conducted, it was often a case study report.

Whilst there are few evaluative studies, the theme of the existing literature suggests that optimal intervention should be focused in the educational setting or family, so that it is context based, and thus most likely to promote generalization. Furthermore, that the focus of rehabilitation is to maximize, not restore function, and this should be a goal agreed upon and understood by all involved. The following are key indicators that help devise, implement, and evaluate an intervention program in an educational setting:

1. Educate caregivers, both staff and families, as it is essential that caregivers are aware of the mechanisms of brain injury, have knowledge about recovery processes and the possibility of residual impairments. Caregivers will then be better able to identify a problem as it arises, the first step in a successful intervention program.
2. Provide general and specific training to caregivers on ways to intervene when problems do arise. Training and education with regard to behavior modification techniques may be most beneficial. Training should also be varied depending on specific needs of the caregivers.
3. Provide caregivers with support and professional contacts that they can access when further expertise is required to manage a particular problem.
4. Encourage school staff and families to work together, and to provide similar boundaries and behavioral approaches.
5. There may be some common areas of difficulty between students that have sustained a brain injury and other students in the classroom, for example, in the areas of attention, planning, problem solving, social relationships, and behavior. If so, the class as a whole may be educated and be presented with strategies to assist in these areas; therefore, benefits will be possible for a larger number of students.
6. If dealing with an older student group, education regarding brain injury, possible areas of difficulty and simple intervention techniques may be

provided to classrooms as a whole. This will help those who have had an injury to better understand any changes they are aware of in their abilities, and may also assist peers to be more understanding and accepting of difficulties they may be aware of with particular students. This classroom approach also suits those students who prefer to remain anonymous, regarding their ABI, while receiving ABI-related education.

7. For specific cases where a challenging cognitive or behavioral difficulty is evident, further implementation of a more complex intervention program aimed at decreasing the areas of difficulty and enhancing appropriate skills, via the use of compensatory strategies/behaviors will be most beneficial. Staff and families will require the support of "experts" in the area to assist with devising such a program and evaluating its efficacy.

8. The realization that there is no "cookbook" approach to intervention in the pediatric area following brain injury. While there will be commonalities in residual deficits for those who have sustained a brain injury, each individual will present with their own unique preinjury status, age at injury, family environment, severity and localization of injury, profile of strengths and weaknesses, and their potential to benefit from the intervention implemented. Intervention techniques will need to be devised, perhaps some adapted from adult models, then trialed and evaluated with children who present with challenging difficulties, with changes made to the intervention plan to suit individual needs.

9. It is of importance that a team-based approach is applied, which involves the school, parents, child/adolescent, and the health professionals.

Conclusion

Research investigating efficacy of intervention techniques following TBI is minimal, and that available is often been based on adult samples. Evaluation is also difficult due to inconsistencies across studies, such as variable preinjury characteristics, degree of severity, sites of brain damage, timing of intervention, outcome measures used (Davis, Fardanesh, Rubner, Wanlass, & MacDonald, 1997; Hawley, Taylor, Hellawell, & Pentland, 1999; Schwartz, 2006), age of the sample, length, and type of intervention, methods of data collection, use of a control group, and support provided to caregivers (Sinnakaruppan & Williams, 2001). Furthermore, as components of EF are interrelated, improvement in one skill area following intervention may influence improvements in other areas, making evaluation of outcomes less clear. However, when taking into account the small number of evaluation studies in the pediatric/adolescent area, research findings suggest some degree of improvement in executive skills following implementation of interventions. Although the current evidence supporting the benefit of intervention is not compelling, it does suggest a positive trend, providing direction for future research (Hall & Cope, 1995; High, Boake, & Lebmkubl, 1995; Mills, Nesbeda, Katz, & Alexander, 1992). Of more certainty is that executive difficulties are often evident following childhood TBI, especially for those who sustained moderate to severe injuries; therefore, it is essential that intervention programs are developed (with a team-based approach in mind), rigorously evaluated, and then implemented in the early stages following TBI, leading to prevention or decrease in disability as the child matures into adolescence and adulthood.

In summary, while it is challenging to develop and evaluate intervention programs for children with TBI, and to then generalize skills gained into the real world, interventions should be continued while gains are being made, with funds available for this to take place, especially because cost-savings and benefits will continue for years to come (Aranow, 1987; Davis et al., 1997; Eames, Cotterill, Kneale, Storrar, & Yeomans, 1995), as these individuals will be better able to function in society. As summed by Ylvisaker et al. (2005), recent findings suggest a long-term cognitive-rehabilitation program where specialists serve as consultants to teachers, parents, and significant others, where the "goal is to organise the routines of life at school and home to facilitate the child's successful participation in school and other culturally valued activities" (p. 4). Such a program will allow children to be monitored over time, so that new intervention strategies may be devised to suit the changing demands in a child's environment. Future research should focus on piloting intervention programs, and then using methods such as randomized controlled trials to rigorously evaluate the programs, to then be able to incorporate such programs into clinical practice.

References

Adams, J. H., Graham, D. I., Murray, L. S., & Scott, G. (1982). Diffuse axonal injury due to non-missile head injury in humans: An analysis of 45 cases. *Annals of Neurology, 12*(2), 557–563.

Adelson, P. D., Bratton, S. L., Carney, N. A., Chesnut, R. M., du Coudray, H. E. M., Goldstein, B., et al. (2003). Chapter 1: Introduction. *Pediatrics Critical Care Medicine, 4*(3), S2–S4.

Adolfs, R. (2003). Cognitive neuroscience of human social behavior. *Nature Reviews. Neuroscience, 4*, 165–178.

Anderson, P. (2002). Assessment and development of executive function (EF) during childhood. *Child Neuropsychology, 8*(2), 71–82.

Anderson, V., Anderson, P., Northam, E., Jacobs, R., & Catroppa, C. (2001). Development of executive functions through late childhood and adolescence: An Australian sample. *Developmental Neuropsychology, 20*, 385–406.

Anderson, V., & Catroppa, C. (2005). Recovery of executive skills following paediatric traumatic brain injury (TBI): A two year follow-up. *Brain Injury, 19*(6), 459–470.

Anderson, V., & Moore. (1995). Age at injury as a predictor following pediatric head injury: A longitudinal perspective. *Child Neuropsychology, 1*(3), 187–202.

Anderson, V., & Pentland, L. (1998). Attention Deficit following paediatric head injury. *Neuropsychoogical Rehabilitation, 8*, 283–300.

Aranow, H. U. (1987). Rehabilitation effectiveness with severe brain injury: Translating research into policy. *Journal of Head Trauma and Rehabilitation, 2*(3), 24–36.

Barnes, M. P. (1999). Rehabilitation after traumatic brain injury. *British Medical Bulletin, 55*(4), 927–943.

Beardmore, S., Tate, R., & Liddle, B. (1999). Does information and feedback improve children's knowledge and awareness of deficits after traumatic brain injury? *Neuropsychological Rehabilitation, 9*, 45–62.

Beaulieu, C. L. (2002). Rehabilitation and outcome following pediatric traumatic brain injury. *Surgical Clinics of North America, 82*, 393–408.

Berg, I., Koning-Haanstra, M., & Deelman, B. (1991). Long-term effects of memory rehabilitation: A controlled study. *Neuropsychological Rehabilitation, 1*, 97–111.

Brett, A. W., & Laatsch, L. (1998). Cognitive rehabilitation therapy of brain-injured students in a public high school setting. *Pediatric Rehabilitation, 2*, 27–31.

Burke, W. H., Wesolowski, M. D., & Guth, M. L. (1988). Comprehensive head injury rehabilitation: An outcome evaluation. *Brain Injury, 2*(4), 313–322.

Busch, R. M., McBride, A., Curtiss, G., & Vanderploeg, R. D. (2005). The components of executive functioning in traumatic brain injury. *Journal of Clinical and Experimental Neuropsychology, 27*, 1022–1032.

Cannon, W., & Rosenbleuth, A. (1949). *The supersensitivity of denervated structures.* New York: Macmillan.

Capruso, D. X., & Levin, H. S. (1992). Cognitive impairment following closed head injury. *The Neurology of Trauma, 10*(4), 879–893.

Casey, B., Giedd, J., & Thomas, K. (2000). Structural and functional brain development and its relation to cognitive development. *Biological Psychiatry, 54*, 241–257.

Catroppa, C., & Anderson, V. (2006). Planning, problem solving and organizational abilities in children following TBI: Intervention techniques. *Pediatric Rehabilitation, 9*, 89–97.

Catroppa, C., & Anderson, V. (in progress). The implementation and evaluation of a pilot rehabilitation program following paediatric traumatic brain injury.

Catroppa, C., Anderson, V., & Stargatt, R. (1999). A prospective analysis of the recovery of attention following pediatric head injury. *Journal of the International Neuropsychological Society, 5*, 48–57.

Chen, C. C., Heinemann, A. W., Bode, R. K., Granger, C. V., & Mallinson, T. (2004). Impact of pediatric rehabilitation services on children's functional outcomes. *The American Journal of Occupational Therapy, 58*(1), 44–53.

Cicerone, K., & Tupper, D. (1990). Neuropsychological rehabilitation: Treatment on errors in everyday function. In D. Tupper & K. Cicerone (Eds.), *The neuropsychology of everyday life: Issues in development and rehabilitation* (pp. 271–291). Boston: Kluwer Academic.

Cope, D. N., & Hall, K. (1982). Head injury rehabilitation: Benefit of early intervention. *Archives of Physical Medicine and Rehabilitation, 63*, 433–437.

Cronin, A. F. (2001). Traumatic brain injury in children: Issues in community function. *The American Journal of Occupational Therapy, 55*(4), 377–384.

Crowley, J. A., & Miles, M. A. (1991). Cognitive remediation in paediatric head-injury: A case study. *Journal of Pediatric Psychology, 16*, 611–627.

Davis, C. H., Fardanesh, L., Rubner, D., Wanlass, R. L., & McDonald, C. M. (1997). Profiles of functional recovery in fifty traumatically brain-injured patients after acute rehabilitation. *American Journal of Physical Medicine and Rehabilitation, 76*(3), 213–218.

Davis, M. J., & Vogel, L. (1995). Neurological assessment of the child with head trauma. *Journal of Dentistry for Children*, (March–April), 93–96.

Dawson, P., & Guare, R. (2004). *Executive skills in children and adolescents. A practical guide to assessment and intervention.* New York: The Guilford Press.

Dennis, M. (1989). Language and the young damaged brain. In T. Boll & B. Bryant (Eds.), *Clinical neuropsychology and brain function: Research, measurement and practice.* Washington, DC: American Psychological Association.

Dennis, M., Barnes, M. A., Donnelly, R. E., Wilkinson, M., & Humphreys, R. P. (1996). Appraising and managing knowledge: Metacognitive skills after childhood head injury. *Developmental Neuropsychology, 12*(1), 77–103.

Diller, L., & Gordon, W. (1981). Rehabilitation and clinical neuropsychology. In S. Filskov & T. Boll (Eds.), *Handbook of clinical neuropsychology* (pp. 702–733). New York: Wiley.

Dumas, H. M., Haley, S. M., Ludlow, L. H., & Rabin, J. P. (2002). Funtional reovery in pediatric traumatic brain injury during inpatient rehabilitation. *American Journal of Physical Medicine and Rehabilitation, 81*(9), 661–669.

Dykeman, B. F. (2003). School-based interventions for treating social adjustment difficulties in children with traumatic brain injury. *Journal of Instructional Psychology, 30*(3), 225–230.

Eames, P., Cotterill, G., Kneale, T. A., Storrar, A. L., & Yeomans, P. (1995). Outcome of intensive rehabilitation after severe brain injury: A long-term follow-up study. *Brain Injury, 10*(9), 631–650.

Evans, J. J., Emslie, H., & Wilson, W. (1998). External cueing systems in the rehabilitation of executive impairments of action. *Journal of the International Neuropsychological Society, 4*, 399–408.

Ewing-Cobbs, L., Prasad, M. R., Landry, S. H., Kramer, L., & DeLeon, R. (2004). Executive functions following traumatic brain injury in young children: A preliminary analysis. *Developmental Neuropsychology, 26*(1), 487–512.

Feeney, T. J., & Ylvisaker, M. (2003). Context-sensitive behavioural supports for young children with TBI. Short-term effects and long-term outcome. *Journal of Head Trauma and Rehabilitation, 18*(1), 33–51.

Fennell, E. B., & Mickle, J. P. (1992). Behavioural effects of head trauma in children and adolescents. In M.G. Tramontana and S. R. Hooper (Eds.), *Advances in Child Neuropsychology—Volume 1.* New York: Springer-Verlag.

Fenwick, T., & Anderson, V. (1999). Impairments of attention following childhood traumatic brain injury. *Child Neuropsychology, 5*(4), 213–223.

Garth, J., Anderson, V. A., & Wrennall, J. (1997). Executive functions following moderate to severe frontal lobe injury: Impact of injury and age at injury. *Pediatric Rehabilitation, 1*, 99–108.

Gavidia-Payne, S. T., & Hudson, A. (2002). Behavioural supports for parents of children with an intellectual disability and problem behaviours: An overview of the literature. *Journal of Intellectual and Developmental Disability, 27*, 31–55.

Giallo, R., & Matthews, J. (in progress). Treatment acceptability the Signposts program for parents of children with an acquired brain injury.

Glang, A., Singer, G., Cooley, E., & Tish, N. (1992). Tailoring direct instruction techniques for use with elementary students with TBI. *Journal of Head Trauma Rehabilitation, 7*(4), 93–108.

Goldenberg, G., Oder, W., Spatt, J., & Podreka, I. (1992). Cerebral correlates of disturbed executive function and memory in survivors of severe closed head injury: A SPECT study. *Journal of Neurology, Neurosurgery and Psychiatry, 55*, 362–368.

Goldstein, F. C., & Levin, H. S. (1987). Epidemiology of pediatric closed head injury: Incidence, clinical characteristics and risk factors. *Journal of Learning Disabilities, 20*(9), 518–525.

Goldstein, F. C., & Levin, H. S. (1992). Cognitive function after closed head injury: Sequelae and outcome. In L. J. Thal, W. H. Moos, and E. R. Gamzu (Eds.), *Cognitive disorders: Pathophysiology and treatment.* New York: Marcel Dekker.

Gray, J., Robertson, I., Pentland, B., & Anderson, S. (1992). Micro-computer based attentional training after brain damage: A randomised group controlled trial. *Neuropsychological Rehabilitation, 2*, 97–115.

Hall, K. M., & Cope, D. N. (1995). The benefit of rehabilitation in traumatic brain injury: A literature review. *Journal of Head Trauma Rehabilitation, 10*(1), 1–13.

Hanten, G., Bartha, M., & Levin, H. S. (2000). Metacognition following pediatric traumatic brain injury: A preliminary study. *Developmental Neuropsychology, 18*(3), 383–398.

Hanten, G., Dennis, M., Zhang, L., Barnes, M., & Roberson, G. (2004). Childhood head injury and metacognitive processes in language and memory. *Developmental Neuropsychology*, *25*(1/2), 85–106.

Harris, J. R. (1996). Verbal rehearsal and memory in children with closed head injury: A quantitative and qualitative analysis. *Journal of Communication Disorders*, *29*, 79–93.

Hawley, C. A., Taylor, R., Hellawell, D. J., & Pentland, B. (1999). *Journal of Neurology, Neurosurgery and Psychiatry*, *67*(6), 749–754.

High, W. M., Boake, C., & Lebmkubl, L. D. (1995). Critical analysis of studies evaluating the effectiveness of rehabilitation after traumatic brain injury. *Journal of Head Trauma Rehabilitation*, *10*(1), 14–26.

Hostler, S. L. (1999). Pediatric family-centered rehabilitation. *Journal of Head Trauma Rehabilitation*, *14*(4), 384–393.

Hudpeth, W., & Primram, K. (1990). Stages of brain and cognitive maturation. *Journal of Educational Psychology*, *82*, 881–884.

Hudson, A., Matthews, J., Gavidia-Payne, S., Cameron, C., Mildon, R., & Radler, G. (2003). Evaluation of an intervention system for parents of children with intellectual disability and challenging behaviour. *Journal of Intellectual Disability Research*, *47*, 238–249.

Hynd, G. W., & Willis, W. G. (Eds.), (1988). Intercranial injuries. *Paediatric Neuropsychology*. New York: Grune and Stratton.

Jacobs, R. (2003). *Executive skills following focal frontal lobe lesions in childhood*. Unpublished doctoral thesis. University of Melbourne, Australia.

Jennett, B. (1996). Epidemiology of head injury. *Journal of Neurology, Neurosurgery, and Psychiatry*, *60*, 362–369.

Jennett, B., & Teasdale, G. (1981). *Management of head injuries*. Philadelphia: FA Davis Company.

Johnson, M. H. (1990). Cortical maturation and the development of visual attention in early infancy. *Journal of Cognitive Neuroscience*, *2*, 81–95.

Johnson, M. H. (1997). *Developmental cognitive neuroscience: An introduction*. Oxford: Blackwell.

Johnson, M. H. (2000). Functional brain development in infants: Elements of an interactive specialisation framework. *Child Development*, *71*, 75–81.

Johnson, M. H. (2003). Development of human brain functions. *Biological Psychiatry*, *54*, 1312–1316.

Kazdin, A. E. (1984). *Behavior modification in applied settings* (3rd ed.). Chicago: The Dorsey Press.

Kelly, T. P. (2000). The development of executive function in school-aged children. *Clinical Neuropsychological Assessment*, *1*, 38–55.

Klinberg, T., Vaidya, C., Gabrieli, J., Moseley, M., & Hedehus, M. (1999). Myelination and organization of the frontal white matter in children: A diffusion tensor study. *Neuro Report*, *10*, 2817–2821.

Kolb, B., & Gibb, R. (1999). Neuroplasticity and recovery of function after brain injury. In D. Stuss, G. Winocur, & I. Robertson (Eds.), *Cognitive neurorehabilitation* (pp. 9–25). New York: Cambridge University Press.

Kolb, B., & Wishaw, Q. (1996). *Fundamentals of human neuropsychology*. (4th ed.). New York: W. H. Freeman.

Kraus, J. F. (1987). Epidemiology of head injury. In P. R. Cooper (Ed.), *Head injury* (2nd ed., pp. 1–19). Baltimore: Williams and Wilkins.

Kraus, J. F. (1995). Epidemiological features of brain injury in children: Occurrence, children at risk, causes and manner of injury, severity, and outcomes. In S. Broman &

M. E. Michel (Eds.), *Traumatic head injury in children* (pp. 22–39). New York: Oxford University Press.

Lashley, K. (1929). *Brain mechanisms and intelligence*. University of Chicago Press.

Laurence, S., & Stein, D. (1978). Recovery after brain damage and the concept of localisation of function. In S. Finger (Ed.), *Recovery from brain damage* (pp. 369–407). New York: Plenum Press.

Levin, H. S., Benton, A. L., & Grossman, R. G. (1982). *Neurobehavioural consequences of closed head injury*. New York: Oxford University Press.

Levin, H. S., Culhane, K. A., Hartmann, J., Evankovich, K., Mattson, A. J., Harward, H., et al. (1991). Developmental changes in performance on tests of purported frontal lobe functioning. *Developmental Neuropsychology, 7*, 377–395.

Levin, H. S., Song, J., Scheibel, R. S., Fletcher, J. M., Harward, H., Lilly, M. M., et al. (1997). Concept formation and problem-solving following closed head injury in children. *Journal of the International Neuropsychological Society, 3*, 598–607.

Levine, M. J. (1988). Issues in neurobehavioural assessment of mild head injury. *Cognitive Rehabilitation, 6*, 14–19.

Levine, B., Robertson, I. H., Clare, L., Carter, G., Hong, J., Wilson, B., et al. (2000). Rehabilitation of executive functioning: An experimental-clinical validation of goal management training. *Journal of the International Neuropsychological Society, 6*, 299–312.

Lezak, M. (1993). *Neuropsychological assessment*. New York: Oxford.

Luria, A. R. (1963). *Restoration of function after brain injury*. New York: Macmillan.

Mateer, C. (1999a). Executive function disorders: Rehabilitation challenges and strategies. *Seminars in Clinical Neuropsychiatry, 4*, 50–59.

Mateer, C. (1999b). The rehabilitation of executive disorders. In D. T. Stuss, G. Winocur, & I. H. Robertson (Eds.), *Cognitive neurorehabilitation*. United Kingdom: Cambridge University Press.

Mateer, C., Kerns, K., & Eso, K. (1996). Management of attention and memory disorders following traumatic brain injury. *Journal of Learning Disabilities, 29*, 6118–6632.

Mattson, A. J., & Levin, H. S. (1990). Frontal lobe dysfunction following closed head injury. *The Journal of Nervous and Mental Disease, 178*(5), 282–291.

Mazaux, J. M., & Richer, E. (1998). Rehabilitation after traumatic brain injury in adults. *Disability and Rehabilitation, 20*(12), 435–447.

Mazurek, A. J. (1994). Epidemiology of paediatric injury. *Journal of Accident and Emergency Medicine, 11*, 9–16.

Miller, J. D. (1991). Pathophysiology and measurement of head injury. *Neuropsychology, 5*(4), 235–261.

Miller, J. D. (1992). Pathophysiology and management of head injury. *Neuropsychology, 5*, 235–261.

Mills, V. M., Nesbeda, T., Katz, D. I., & Alexander, M. P. (1992). Outcomes for traumatically brain-injured patients following post-acute rehabilitation programmes. *Brain Injury, 6*(3), 219–228.

Milner, B., & Petrides, M. (1984). Behavioural effects of frontal lesions in man. *Trends in Neuroscience, 7*, 403–407.

Mottram, L., & Berger-Gross, P. (2004). An intervention to reduce disruptive behaviours in children with brain injury. *Pediatric Rehabilitation, 7*(2), 133–143.

Munk, H. (1881). Ueber die funktion der grosshirnrinde. *Gesammelte aus den Jahren* (pp. 1877–1880). Berlin, Germany: Hirschwald.

Napolitano, E., Elovic, E. P., & Qureshi, A. I. (2005). Pharmacological stimulant treatment of neurocognitive and functional deficits after traumatic and non-traumatic brain injury. *Medical Science Monitor, 11*(6), 212–220.

Paakko, E., Vainionpaa, L., Lanning, M., Laitinen, J., & Pyhtinen, J. (1992). White matter changes in children treated for acute lymphoblastic leukemia. *Cancer, 70*, 2728–2733.

Papero, P. H., Prigatano, G. P., Snyder, H. M., & Johnson, D. L. (1993). Children's adaptive behavioural competence after head injury. *Neuropsychological Rehabilitation, 3*(4), 321–340.

Park, N., & Ingles, J. (2001). Effectiveness of attention rehabilitation after acquired brain injury: A meta-analysis. *Neuropsychology, 15*, 199–210.

Penkman, L. (2004). Remediation of attention deficits in children: A focus on childhood cancer, traumatic brain injury and attention deficit disorder. *Pediatric Rehabilitation, 7*(2), 111–123.

Pentland, L., Todd, J. A., & Anderson, V. (1998). The impact of head injury severity on planning ability in adolescence: A functional analysis. *Neuropsychological Rehabilitation, 8*, 301–317.

Ponsford, J., Sloan, S., & Snow, P. (1995). *Traumatic brain injury: Rehabilitation for everyday adaptive living*. Hove, UK: Lawrence Erlbaum Associates.

Ponsford, J., Willmott, C., Rothwell, A., Cameron, P., Ayton, G., Nelms, R., et al. (2001). Impact of early intervention on outcome after mild traumatic brain injury in children. *Pediatrics, 108*(6), 1297–1303.

Pruneti, C. A., Cantini, R., & Baracchini-Muratorio, G. (1988). Prognostic value of type of coma after serious head injury in childhood. *Research Communications in Psychology, Psychiatry and Behaviour, 13*(3), 193–217.

Robertson, I. (1990). Does computerised cognitive rehabilitation work? A review. *Aphasiology, 4*, 381–405.

Rothi, L., & Horner, J. (1983). Restitution and substitution: Two theories of recovery with application to neurobehavioral treatment. *Journal of Clinical Neuropsychology, 3*, 73–81.

Ruff, R. M., & Niemann, H. (1990). Cognitive rehabilitation versus day treatment in head-injured adults: Is there an impact on emotional and psychosocial adjustment? *Brain Injury, 4*(4), 339–347.

Sanders, M. (1999). Triple P Positive Parenting Program: Towards an empirically validated multilevel parenting and family support strategy for the prevention of behavior and emotional problems in children. *Clinical Child and Family Psychology Review, 2*, 71–90.

Schmitter-Edgecombe, M., Fahy, J., Whelan, J., & Long, C. (1995). Memory remediation after severe head injury: Notebook training versus supportive therapy. *Journal of Consulting and Clinical Psychology, 63*, 484–489.

Schwartz, M. F. (2006). The cognitive neuropsychology of everyday action and planning. *Cognitive Neuropsychology, 23*(1), 202–221.

Selznick, L., & Savage, R. C. (2000). Using self-monitoring procedures to increase on-task behavior with three adolescent boys with brain injury. *Behavioral Interventions, 15*, 243–260.

Semlyen, J. K., Summers, S. J., & Barnes, M. P. (1998). Traumatic brain injury: Efficacy of multidisciplinary rehabilitation. *Archives of Physical Medicine and Rehabilitation, 79*, 678–683.

Shallice, T., & Evans, M. (1978). The involvement of the frontal lobes in cognitive estimation. *Cortex, 14*, 294–303.

Shiel, A., Burn, J. P. S., Henry, D., Clark, J., Wilson, B. A., Burnett, M. E., et al. (2001). The effects of increased rehabilitation therapy after brain injury: Results of a prospective controlled trial. *Clinical Rehabilitation, 15*, 501–514.

Sinnakaruppan, I., & Williams, D. M. (2001). Head injury and family carers: A critical appraisal of case management programmes in the community. *International Journal of Rehabilitation Research, 24*, 35–42.

Smidt, D., Jacobs, R., & Anderson, V. (2004). The Object Classification Task for Children (OCTC): A measure of concept generation and mental flexibility in early childhood. *Developmental Neuropsychology, 26*, 385–402.

Sohlberg, M., & Mateer, C. (1989). Training use of compensatory memory books: A three-stage behavioral approach. *Journal of Clinical and Experimental Neuropsychology, 11*, 871–891.

Sohlberg, M., Mateer, C., & Stuss, D. T. (1993). Contemporary approaches to the management of executive control dysfunction. *Journal of Head Trauma Rehabilitation, 8*(1), 45–58.

Stablum, F., Mogentale, C., & Umilta, C. (1996). Executive functioning following mild closed head injury. *Cortex, 32*, 261–278.

Stein, S. C., & Spettell, C. M. (1995). Delayed and progressive brain injury in children and adolescents with head trauma. *Pediatric Neurosurgery, 23*, 299–304.

Stein, S. C., Spettell, C. M., Young, G., & Ross, S. (1995). Delayed and progressive brain injury in closed-head trauma: Radiological demonstration. *Neurosurgery, 32*, 25–31.

Sterling, L. (1994). Students with acquired brain injuries in primary and secondary schools. Project Report. Canberra, Australia: Australian Government Publishing Service (AGPS).

Stuss, D. T. (1992). Biological and psychological development of executive functions. *Brain and Cognition, 20*, 8–23.

Stuss, D., & Anderson, V. (2004). The frontal lobes and theory of mind: Developmental concepts from adult focal lesion research. *Brain and Cognition, 55*, 69–83.

Stuss, D. T., & Benson, D. F. (1986). *The frontal lobes.* New York: Raven Press.

Stuss, D. T., & Gow, C. A. (1992). Frontal dysfunction after traumatic brain injury. *Neuropsychiatry, Neuropsychology and Behavioural Neurology, 5*(4), 272–282.

Stuss, D. T., Mateer, C. A., & Sohlberg, M. M. (1994). Innovative approaches to frontal lobe deficits. In M. A. J. Finlayson, & S. H. Garner (Eds.), *Brain injury rehabilitation, clinical considerations.* Baltimore: Williams & Wilkins.

Suzman, K. B., Morris, R. D., Morris, M. K., & Milan, M. A. (1997). Cognitive behavioural remediation of problem solving deficits in children with acquired brain injury. *Journal of Behavior Therapy and Experimental Psychiatry, 28*(3), 203–212.

Swaine, B. R., Pless, I. B., Friedman, D. S., & Montes, J. L. (2000). Effectiveness of a head injury program for children. *American Journal of Physical Medicine and Rehabilitation, 79*(5), 412–420.

Taylor, G. H., & Alden, J. (1997). Age-related differences in outcomes following childhood brain insults: An introduction and overview. *Journal of the International Neuropsychological Society, 3*, 555–567.

Thatcher, R. W. (1991). Maturation of the human frontal lobes. Physiological evidence for staging. *Developmental Neuropsychology, 7*, 397–419.

Think Quick, (1987). Fremont, CA: The Learning Company.

Thompson, J. (1995). Rehabilitation of high schooled individuals with traumatic brain injury through utilization of an attention training program. *Journal of the International Neuropsychological Society, 1*, 149.

Thompson, J., & Kerns, K. (2000). Mild traumatic brain injury in children. In S. A. Raskin & C. A. Mateer (Eds.), *Neuropsychological management of mild traumatic brain injury* (pp.233–251). New York: Oxford University Press.

Todd, J., Anderson, V., & Lawrence, J. (1996). Planning skills in head injured children. *Neuropsychological Rehabilitation, 6*, 81–99.

Tuel, S. M., Presty, S. K., Meythaler, J. M., Heinemann, A. W., & Katz, R. T. (1992). Functional improvement in severe head injury after readmission for rehabilitation. *Brain Injury, 6*(4), 363–372.

Vakil, E., Blachstein, H., Rochberg, J., & Vardi, M. (2004). Characterisation of memory impairment following closed head injury in children using the Rey Auditory Verbal learning Test (AVLT). *Child Neuropsychology, 10*(2), 57–66.

Van't Hooft, I., Andersson, K., Bergman, B., Sejersen, T., Von Wendt, I., & Bartfai, A. (2005). Beneficial effect from a cognitive training programme on children with acquired brain injuries demonstrated in a controlled study. *Brain Injury, 19*(7), 511–518.

Walsh, K. W. (1978). *Neuropsychology: A Clinical Approach.* New York: Churchill Livingston/Longman.

Welsh, M. C., & Pennington, B. F. (1988). Assessing frontal lobe functioning in children: Views from developmental psychology. *Development Neuropsychology, 4*(3), 199–230.

Weyandt, L. L., & Willis, W. G. (1994). Executive functions in school aged children: Potential efficacy of tasks in discriminating clinical groups. *Developmental Neuropsychology, 10*(1), 27–38.

Wilson, B. A. (1996). Rehabilitation and management of memory problems. *Acta Neurologica Belgica, 96*, 51–54.

Wilson, B. A. (1997). Cognitive rehabilitation: How it is and how it might be. *Journal of the International Neuropsychological Society, 3*, 487–496.

Wilson, B. A. (2000). Compensating for cognitive deficits following brain injury. *Neuropsychology Review, 10*(4), 233–243.

Wilson, B. A., Baddeley, A., & Evans, J. (1994). Errorless learning in the rehabilitation of memory impaired people. *Neuropsychological Rehabilitation, 4*(3), 307–326.

Wilson, B. A., Emslie, H., Quirk, K., & Evans, J. (2001). Reducing everyday memory and planning problems by means of a pager system: A randomised control crossover study. *Journal of Neurology, Neurosurgery and Psychiatry, 70*, 477–482.

Wilson, B., & Moffat, M. (1992). *Clinical management of memory problems.* London: Chapman & Hall.

Wilson, B. A., & Watson, P. C. (1996). A practical framework for understanding compensatory behaviour in people with organic memory impairment. *Memory, 4*(5), 465–486.

Wood, R. (1988). Attention disorders in brain rehabilitation. *Journal of Learning Disabilities, 21*, 327–332.

Wright, I., & Limond, J. (2004). A developmental framework for memory rehabilitation in children. *Pediatric Rehabilitation, 7*(2), 85–96.

Ylvisaker, M. (Ed.). (1985). *Head injury rehabilitation: Children and adolescents.* San Diego, CA: College-Hill Press.

Ylvisaker, M., Adelson, P. D., Willandino Braga, L. W., Burnett, S. M., Glang, A., Feeney, T., et al. (2005). Rehabilitation and ongoing support after pediatric TBI twenty years of progress. *The Journal of Head Trauma Rehabilitation, 20*(1), 95–109.

Ylvisaker, M., & Feeney, T. (2002). Executive functions, self-regulation, and learned optimism in paediatric rehabilitation: A review and implications for intervention. *Pediatric Rehabilitation, 5*(2), 51–70.

Ylvisaker, M., Szekeres, S. F., & Feeney, T. (1998). Cognitive rehabilitation: Executive functions. In M. Ylvisaker (Ed.), *Traumatic brain injury rehabilitation: Children and adolescents* (Rev. ed., pp. 221–269). Boston: Butterworth-Heinemann.

Ylvisaker, M., Todis, B., Glang, A., Urbanczyk, B., Franklin, C., DePompei, R., et al. (2001). Educating students with TBI: Themes and recommendations. *Journal of Head Trauma and Rehabilitation, 16*(1), 76–93.

20 Social information processing difficulties in adults and implications for treatment

Skye McDonald

Contents

Personality and psychosocial changes are considered hallmarks of frontal lobe damage. Insensitivity, impulsivity, disinhibited, egocentric and socially inappropriate behavior, and poor frustration tolerance are common. Conversely, there may be a generalized lack of responsivity and self-initiation. These disturbances to social functioning are commonly attributed to damage the orbitomedial aspects of the frontal lobes. Traditionally, they have been conceptualized as reflecting a loss of behavioral regulation resulting in responses that are inappropriate for the context in which they occur. More recently it has been recognized that deficits in social information processing will also impact upon the ability to respond normally in social situations. In this chapter, we will examine different facets of social information processing and disorders that reflect disruption to these processes.

Emotion perception disorders

An important source of information in social contexts is the emotional state of others. Being able to determine whether a coconversant is bored, angry, engaged, delighted, etc., is critical to successful social interaction. We use these cues in order to tailor initial social behavior appropriately and as feedback for regulating subsequent responses. There is clear evidence that emotion perception can be significantly impaired following frontal lobe lesions. Not only have emotion recognition impairments been found in people with focal neurological lesions (Angrilli, Palomba, Cantagallo, Maietti, & Stegagno, 1999; Blair & Cipolotti, 2000; Hornak et al., 2003; Hornak, Rolls, & Wade, 1996; Tranel, Bechara, & Denburg, 2002), but also in groups with more diffuse and multifocal brain lesions that implicate the prefrontal lobes, including traumatic brain injuries (TBI) (Breen, Caine, & Coltheart, 2002; Green, Turner, & Thompson, 2004; Jackson & Moffat, 1987; McDonald & Flanagan, 2004; McDonald, Flanagan, Rollins, & Kinch, 2003; Milders, Fuchs, & Crawford, 2003; Prigatano & Pribram, 1982; Spell & Frank, 2000), frontotemporal dementia (Keane, Calder, Hodges, & Young, 2002; Lavenu, Pasquier, Lebert, Petit, & Van der Linden, 1999), multiple sclerosis (Beatty, Orbelo, Sorocco, & Ross, 2003; Weinstein, Patterson, & Rao, 1996), and Parkinsons disease (Dujardin et al., 2004; Kan, Kawamura, Hasegawa, Mochizuki, & Nakamura, 2002; Weinstein et al., 1996).

While it has been well established that the right hemisphere plays a dominant role in many emotion processing tasks (Borod, 1993; Borod, Koff, Lorch, & Nicholas, 1986; Cicone, Wapner, & Gardener, 1980), more recent studies have suggested that the orbitomedial prefrontal lobes, particularly in association with the amygdalae, insula, anterior cingulate gyri, and basal ganglia, are fundamentally involved in the processing of emotionally significant stimuli including faces (e.g., Adolphs, 2002a; Adolphs, Damasio, Tranel, & Damasio, 1996; Phillips, Drevets, Rauch, & Lane, 2003). There continues to be strong support for asymmetry between hemispheres (Adolphs, 2002b; Angrilli et al., 1999; Tranel et al., 2002).

Types of emotion

Not all emotions are equally vulnerable to the effects of brain lesions. In particular, while positive emotions such as happiness and surprise are often processed normally, deficits in the processing of negative emotions such as disgust, fear, and sadness are common. This has led to speculation that the brain encompasses a number of relatively independent systems evolutionarily developed to process particular emotions (Adolphs, Russell, & Tranel, 1999; Adolphs & Tranel, 2004; Broks et al., 1998; Buchanan, Tranel, & Adolphs, 2004; Sprengelmeyer et al., 1996). For example, damage to the amygdala has been associated with deficits in fear (Adolphs, 2002a), anger (Adolphs et al., 1999), and sadness (Adolphs & Tranel, 2004), while the insula and basal ganglia are thought to play a particular role in the processing of disgust (Adolphs, 2002a). In normal adults, the orbitomedial prefrontal areas have increased activity when viewing angry faces (Blair, Morris, Frith, Perrett, & Dolan, 1999) and conversely, processing of angry faces is slowed when these areas are disrupted using transcranial magnetic stimulation (Harmer, Thilo, Rothwell, &

Goodwin, 2001). This, along with evidence for decreased experience of fear following orbitomedial lesions (Hornak et al., 1996), has led to theorizing that the medial prefrontal regions may have a specific role in the regulation of "high arousal" negative emotions (Adolphs, 2002b).

In general, examination of emotion processing disorders has been restricted to the so-called basic emotions, i.e., happiness, surprise, sadness, fear, anger, and disgust. However, problems have also emerged when patients with amygdala damage have been asked to discriminate between social emotions such as admiration and guilt (Adolphs, Baron-Cohen, & Tranel, 2002). Such social judgments have not been examined in detail in people with focal frontal lesions that exclude the amydalae. However, problems with judging complex emotions such as embarrassment and envy as well as basic emotions have been reported in adults with TBI (McDonald & Flanagan, 2004).

Medium of emotion

Interestingly, recent empirical work has suggested that emotion processing may encompass a number of systems dependent upon the nature of the task and the medium.

While it has been well established that deficits in emotion recognition can occur in both the visual (face) and auditory (voice) channels, there is some evidence to suggest that difficulties are not uniform across these media. Hornak et al. (1996) reported emotion perception deficits in adults with frontal lobe and extra-frontal lesions. While the majority of patients with ventromedial frontal damage had difficulties in both auditory and visual media, one patient was differentially impaired in recognizing emotion in voice but not face. Others with damage outside the medial prefrontal regions had the reverse pattern suggesting that the two media may rely upon separable, if overlapping systems (Adolphs, Damasio, & Tranel, 2002).

Additionally, recent evidence has emerged to suggest that dynamic, moving facial expressions may rely upon separate systems to those that mediate the processing of static images. This is intriguing because the majority of research conducted on facial expressions has used static images, typically taken from the Ekman and Freisen series (Ekman & Freisen, 1976). Such research is based upon a tacit assumption that static images reflect a valid representation of facial expressions. And yet, facial expressions as they occur in everyday contexts present a significantly different perceptual task. First, emotions evolve rapidly from one kind to another. Surprise, for example, is by its very nature a transient condition. Other emotions intensify and then fade away, or transmogrify into something else. In order to judge such transient facial expressions the viewer needs to have efficient information processing.

There are also cues available in moving faces in the expression of an emotional state that are not available from static images. When viewers are restricted to seeing white dots on (blacked out) faces actively moving they are better than chance at recognizing emotions (Bassili, 1978). A few studies have examined emotion recognition using moving facial expressions and have reported relatively normal performance when processing dynamic images compared to static following fronto-temporal lesions (Adolphs, Tranel, & Damasio, 2003) and TBI (McDonald &

Saunders, 2006), and relatively poor performance on dynamic expressions when the parietal cortices are compromised (Humphrey, Donnelly, & Riddoch, 1993). This has lead to speculation that dynamic facial movement may be processed by the parietal and dorsolateral frontal cortices while static images may be processed by temporal-medial frontal systems already described (Adolphs et al., 2003). While both systems probably contribute to competent expression processing, this disso-ciation has interesting implications for the remediation of people with emotion processing deficits, suggesting that if one mode of expression (still or dynamic) is particularly difficult to process, then the other may provide an easier set of cues to base discriminations upon.

Role of emotional responsivity in emotion recognition

There is also growing evidence that the subjective experience of emotions and the ability to recognize emotions in others are intertwined. Certainly this is well recognized in the normal emotion literature. Research in the 1970s (see McHugo & Smith, 1996, for review) established that there is reciprocity between viewing another's emotional expression, and one's own arousal (skin conductance) and facial movement, which faintly mimics that expression. Such responses suggest that empathic reactions are part and parcel of the processing of emotional expressions in others, reactions that can occur even without conscious awareness. The possi-bility that these somatic reactions actually assist emotion recognition has also been aired. As early as 1890, William James suggested that our bodily responses to external stimuli are important cues for recognizing our emotional state (Watson, 1978). This link between emotional responsivity and emotion recognition is impli-cated in clinical research. In studies of adults with focal orbitomedial frontal lesions, it has been found that changed emotional experience, as subjectively reported, was associated with reduced accuracy in the judging of emotional expressions (Breen et al., 2002; Hornak et al., 1996, 2003). A similar pattern was found in a group of people with severe TBI, i.e., those who reported a decrease in their subjective experience of various emotions were also those who were the least accurate in matching facial expressions (Croker & McDonald, 2005). At a methodological level, subjective reporting of emotional change may be criticized as inaccurate, being contaminated with psychological responses to disability, impaired insight, etc. But many of the kinds of emotional changes reported, e.g., "I have no feelings ... I can't tell if I have emotions—I can't tell if I'm saddened ... I don't get really sad" (Hornak et al., 1996 case 10, p. 261) appear to be genuine reflections of a loss of emotionality. Furthermore, some research has examined more direct measures of emotional responsivity in people with brain lesions and corroborated these sub-jective reports. According to this, people with either focal orbitomedial frontal lobe lesions or TBI appear to have decreased skin conductance (Blair & Cipolotti, 2000; Hopkins, Dywan, & Segalowitz, 2002) and reduced facial movement (Angrilli et al., 1999; McDonald, 2005) in response to emotional expressions. Apart from an isolated single case study (Blair & Cipolotti, 2000), to date, there has been little direct evidence for a relationship between impaired responsivity to emotional stimuli on these more objective measures and impaired emotion recognition. Nevertheless the potential link is an intriguing one. It parallels the recent work by Bechara, Damasio, and colleagues examining the role of prefrontal cortex in decision making. Their research suggests that somatic responses may guide decision making by providing somatic cues in anticipation of complex response contingencies even prior to conscious awareness (Bechara, Damasio, Damasio, & Anderson, 1994; Bechara, Damasio, & Damasio, 2000; Bechara, Damasio, Tranel, & Damasio, 1997; Damasio, 1996). Similarly, somatic responses to emotional expressions in others may provide important cues for the recognition and interpretation of those expressions.

Multiple routes to emotional processing

The close link between emotion recognition and affective responses fits with current theorizing that there may be an early automatic route to emotional processing (Phillips et al., 2003), that is mainly subcortical and provides a rapid but coarse evaluation of emotionally significant stimuli (LeDoux, 1995). For example, in the auditory system, there is the classic auditory pathway, and a second pathway that projects directly to the amygdalae, which is several synapses shorter than similar input to the neocortex (LeDoux, Sakaguchi, & Reis, 1984). It is thought that the rapid, initial processing of emotional information occurs via the superior colliculus, thalamus, and early visual cortices (Adolphs, 2002b) feeding into a ventral system that entails the amygdalae, insula, ventral striatum, and ventral regions of the anterior cingulate and prefrontal cortex (Phillips et al.). The automatic nature of this processing is suggested by functional MRI (fMRI) (Whalen et al., 1998) and PET research (Morris, Oehman, & Dolan, 1998) that shows that amygdala activation occurs in response to emotional faces without conscious awareness as well as when attention is diverted away from the emotional expression (Critchley et al., 2000). Similarly, skin conductance changes can occur in response to fearful and other emotional stimuli without overt recognition (Esteves, Dimberg, & Ohman, 1994; Ohman & Soares, 1994), indicating that affective responses are part of this early, preattentive processing of emotional stimuli. Such responses are possibly mediated via amygdala efferents to the hypothalamus and other connections (Ohman, Flykt, & Lundqvist, 2000). The ventral prefrontal cortices are also implicated in these affective reactions (Gorno-Tempini et al., 2001; Keightly et al., 2003) possibly as a means of regulation of the response (Phillips et al.).

A second "dorsal" route to emotional processing is thought to entail the hippocampus, dorsal aspects of the anterior cingulate gyrus and dorsolateral prefrontal cortex (Phillips et al., 2003). This system, with connections to other cortical regions is involved in the effortful processing of emotional stimuli, including the engagement of other cognitive processes, such as language or the accessing of contextual information (via the hippocampi) dependent upon the nature of the task. The two systems are intimately associated with many points of reciprocity and feedback. In particular, the dorsal system seems capable of modulating and regulating the ventral system in line with task demands. In evidence of this, emotion processing tasks requiring explicit processing or verbal mediation such as labeling are associated with increased activation of dorsolateral prefrontal cortex (Hariri, Bookheimer, &

Mazziotta, 2000; Keightly et al., 2003) and concomitant reduction of activation in both amygdalae (Hariri et al., 2000). Furthermore, in focal frontal patients, a lack of responsivity (arousal) to emotionally charged material has been found only when passively viewing the material, not when required to describe it (Damasio et al., 1990). These findings suggest that the dorsal (effortful) system can stimulate the ventral to overcome initial lack of responsivity.

Disorders in theory of mind

A second important facet of social information processing relates to the ability to infer what another person believes or thinks. This type of ability is known as having "Theory of Mind (ToM)." ToM inferences are vital in order to make sense of the behavior of others in a social context. This is clear in even the most apparently straightforward conversational exchange. For example, the words "Thankyou—you have been a great help!" may have several interpretations—they may be sincerely meant as an end to an interaction, they may be uttered as an oblique request for further assistance, or they may be uttered as a sarcastic retort to someone who has clearly been a hindrance. Interpreting such information accurately requires understanding what the speaker believes and feels and what the speaker intends the listener to believe as a result of the interaction. Correspondingly, it has been argued that there are three facets to ToM (Stone, Baron-Cohen, Calder, Keane, & Young, 2003), ability to attribute epistemic mental states (understanding what another knows or believes), affective mental states, and intentionality.

There is good evidence that ToM ability develops in distinct stages: with infants as young as 18 months being aware that they can share attention with another (Baron-Cohen, 1989), children at age 3–4 being aware that others may hold different beliefs to their own (first-order ToM) (Wimmer & Perner, 1983), and children at the age of 6–7 being able to reason that others may also be able to envisage what is on another's mind (second-order ToM) (Perner & Wimmer, 1985). There is also evidence that such abilities are universal across cultures (Avis & Harris, 1991) and, to a great extent, genetically determined (Hughes & Cutting, 1999).

Poor ToM has been thought to underscore the poor communicative competence that is typical of autism. Thus, despite the presence of fluent and articulate speech, many individuals with high functioning autism or Aspergers syndrome and normal IQ have pedantic, over-literal speech (Happe & Frith, 1996), fail to interact normally in conversation, often talk at length on obscure or inappropriate topics (Ozonoff & Miller, 1996), have inappropriate nonverbal communication and poor adherence to social rules (Bowler, 1992). They also fail to appreciate how utterances are used to convey information in a socially appropriate manner (Surian, Baron-Cohen, & Van der Lely, 1996) and misinterpret language used indirectly such as metaphor and irony (Happe, 1993). Problems with language production are surmised to reflect failure to appreciate the listener's perspective leading to a failure to tailor language and behavior toward him or her accordingly. Poor comprehension of indirect meaning is similarly attributed to a failure to understand how social partners might modify their language and behavior to meet particular social goals.

Theory of mind associated with frontal lobe systems

A range of evidence has suggested that ToM abilities are mediated by frontal systems, in particular the ventral frontal-limbic system (Stuss, Gallup, & Alexander, 2001). Firstly, similar deficits in social reasoning and social communication as seen in autism have also been reported in populations with focal or diffuse frontal injuries. Thus, patients with specific frontal lobe lesions have been described as having a social dysdecorum including lack of insight, blunted social awareness, tactlessness, and poor reasoning (Alexander, Benson, & Stuss, 1989), while adults with TBI have been described as egocentric, self-focused, lacking interest in other people, displaying inappropriate humor, making frequent interruptions, having a blunt manner, overly familiar, and disinhibited remarks or advances and inappropriate levels of self-disclosure (Crosson, 1987; Flanagan, McDonald, & Togher, 1995; Levin, Grossman, Rose, & Teasdale, 1979; McDonald, Flanagan, Martin, & Saunders, 2004; McDonald & Pearce, 1998; McDonald & van Sommers, 1992).

More particular reasoning deficits that implicate ToM have also been found. For example, adults with TBI have difficulty in filling out a questionnaire as though they were somebody else (Spiers, Pouk, & Santoro, 1994), find it difficult to identify the source of interpersonal conflict (Kendall, Shum, Halson, Bunning, & Teh, 1997) or otherwise interpret nonverbal interpersonal interactions (Cicerone & Tanenbaum, 1997) and fail to understand the intended meaning behind deliberately ambiguous or counterfactual (sarcastic) remarks (McDonald & Flanagan, 2004). Supporting these general observations, deficits on explicit ToM tasks have been reported in adults with focal frontal lesions (Channon & Crawford, 2000; Happe, Malhi, & Checkley, 2001; Stone, Baron-Cohen, & Knight, 1998; Stuss et al., 2001), specific amygdala damage (Fine, Lumsden, & Blair, 2001; Stone et al., 2003), and in those with diffuse or focal lesions implicating the frontal lobes including frontotemporal dementia (Gregory et al., 2002; Lough, Gregory, & Hodges, 2001) and TBI, both adult and child (Bibby & McDonald, 2004; Dennis, Purvis, Barnes, Wilkinson, & Winner, 2001; Turkstra, Dixon, & Baker, 2004; Santoro & Spiers, 1994; Stone et al., 1998). While some lesion studies have suggested that the right frontal regions may have a particular role in mediating ToM reasoning (Stuss et al.; Tranel et al., 2002), this is by no means a universal finding (Channon & Crawford, 2000; Fletcher et al., 1995; Goel, Grafman, Sadato, & Hallett, 1995). Neuroimaging and blood flow studies with normal individuals have provided evidence for involvement of the right and left medial and orbitofrontal regions as well as the posterior cingulate gyrus and temporal lobes in ToM reasoning dependent upon the nature of the task (Adolphs, 2001; Baron-Cohen et al., 1994; Fletcher et al.; Gallagher et al., 2000; Goel et al., 1995).

Modularity of theory of mind

An interesting aspect of ToM is that it has been considered to be a modular component of cognitive functioning that is dissociable from more general inferential and reasoning abilities. Claims of modularity are based specifically upon the findings that ToM ability and general intelligence appear to be dissociable, i.e., young people with autism may have normal intelligence despite impaired ToM (Happe, 1994) whereas in Down's syndrome and Williams syndrome, the reverse may occur (Karmiloff-Smith et al., 1995), although Zelazo, Burack, Benedetto, and Frye (1996) argue a dissenting view. More specifically, individuals with poor ToM are not necessarily impaired in other metarepresentational tasks. Autistic children can, for example, understand that a photograph represents things as they were, not as they are (Charman & Baron-Cohen, 1995; Leekam & Perner, 1991).

In general, tasks that have been used to measure ToM in neurological populations have varied in complexity from forced choice judgments of mental state terms based on photos of the eye region alone (Baron-Cohen, Jolliffe, Mortimore, & Robertson, 1997; Gregory et al., 2002; Milders et al., 2003; Stone et al., 2003) to answering simple (Bara, Tirassa, & Zettin, 1997; Bibby & McDonald, 2004) and doubly recursive questions (Santoro & Spiers, 1994; Stone et al., 1998) about the thoughts of protagonists in scripted vignettes both written (Stone et al.) and videotaped (McDonald & Flanagan, 2004; Santoro & Spiers). This diversity of assessment methods highlights the fact that ToM judgments probably call into play a variety of cognitive skills. It also provides an obstacle to claims that ToM deficits reflect disruption to a modular functional system within the brain devoted to such kinds of judgments, since ToM judgments could also be affected by broader difficulties that reflect the impact of other disorders arising from frontal lobe dysfunction. In particular, complex story comprehension tasks such as classical false belief tasks* typically used to assess ToM make heavy demands upon both working memory (in order to process complex doubly recursive questions such as "Does John believe that Sally believes...") (Stone et al.) and also general inferential reasoning skills. The consistent gradation seen across ToM task performance in developmental, autistic, and brain-injured populations whereby simple first-order ToM questions are answered more accurately than second-order ToM questions in false belief tasks which are, in turn, more accurately answered than mental inference questions related to the recognition of deception, faux pas (an unintended insult), double bluff, etc. in complex stories (Baron-Cohen, O'Riordan, Stone, Jones, & Plaisted, 1999; Happe, 1994; Stone et al.) may reflect a gradation in the sophistication of mentalizing inference required but may equally reflect increasing reliance upon working memory, language ability, and inferential reasoning (Bibby & McDonald, 2004). Stone et al. (2003), for example, have emphasized the online processing demands of complex story tasks whereby adults with focal amygdala lesions were able to make isolated ToM judgments but had difficulty marrying these to correctly interpret situations in which a faux pas has occurred.

Indeed, a number of studies have shown that young children's performances on false belief tasks are influenced by working memory capacity (Davis & Pratt, 1995; Gordon & Olson, 1998; Hughes, 1998; Keenan, 1998), although the evidence suggests that it is not the sole contributing factor (Tager-Flusberg, Sullivan, & Boshart, 1997). Similarly, working memory deficits have been found to contribute to poor ToM performance in adults with acquired brain damage (Bibby &

---

* Typically, in such tasks two protagonists hide an object which is then relocated by one of the protagonists while the other is out of the room. Questions are then asked as to where the naive protagonist is likely to look for the object (Wimmer & Perner, 1983).

McDonald, 2004; Stone et al., 1998) although it does not totally explain poor ToM performance (Bibby & McDonald, 2004).

The extent to which general inferencing deficits contribute to ToM deficits has not been resolved. Studies that report ToM deficits in people with frontal lobe injuries do not always control for nonmental inferential abilities (Channon & Crawford, 2000; Stuss et al., 2001) while those that have controlled this have reported ToM to be both independent of nonmental inference abilities (Gregory et al., 2002; Happe et al., 2001; Rowe, Bullock, Polkey, & Morris, 2001) and associated with them (Bibby & McDonald, 2004; Martin & McDonald, in press; Snowden et al., 2003). The most parsimonious explanation is that ToM deficits may arise as a consequence of more general cognitive impairments as well as specific (modular) deficits in mentalizing ability (Snowden et al.).

Although ToM judgments can be classified into three types: judgments about beliefs, intentions, and affective states there is, to date, little evidence that they represent dissociable abilities (Stone et al., 2003) and indeed, more complex ToM tasks such as the faux pas test require judgments in all three domains for their successful interpretation.

Information used to make ToM judgments

In everyday social encounters judgments concerning the mental state of others arise from two broad domains: one the demeanor and behavior of the protagonists and the other the general context in which the interaction takes place, including conceptual knowledge about the protagonists and their likely beliefs. ToM tasks have varied to the extent that they assess ability to use these two sources of information. The traditional approach to assessing ToM using false belief and other complex story tasks assesses the ability to use verbal (or pictorial) conceptual information regarding the beliefs of protagonists. On the other hand, a growing body of research has examined the ability to infer mental state on the basis of nonverbal stimuli. Interestingly, it transpires that humans readily attribute intentionality to moving figures in the environment, even attributing intentionality to abstract geometric figures made to move in a goal-directed fashion (Castelli, Frith, Happe, & Frith, 2002). Inferences about emotions and mental states can also be derived from partial facial cues such as the eye region alone (Baron-Cohen, Wheelwright, & Jolliffe, 1997) and focal light points placed on a moving figure (Heberlein, Adolphs, Tranel, & Damasio, 2004). These kinds of tasks are interesting, not only because they assess the ability to derive mental inferences from perceptual rather than conceptual information, but also because, as most rely upon single-word fixed-choice responses, they suffer less from the problem of complexity and inherent cognitive demands of fully verbally mediated tasks.

Using such tasks the role of the frontolimbic system (i.e., amygdala, superior temporal gyrus, and medial prefrontal areas) in ToM has been further implicated. These regions are active when making judgments regarding whether another is making eye contact or not (Calder et al., 2002; Kawashima et al., 1999). Conversely, deficits in judging eye-gaze direction have been reported following bilateral amygdala lesions (Young et al., 1995). Eye-gaze direction is an important cue for ToM as it enables the viewer to understand what another may have knowledge about, be attending to, etc. (Stone et al., 2003).

In addition, judgments about subtle mental states (e.g., thoughtful, bored) including social emotions that infer cognitions (e.g., guilt and flirtatiousness) derived from information in the eye region of the face are poorly performed by people with both acquired frontal lobe pathology (Gregory et al., 2002; Lough & Hodges, 2002) and autism (Baron-Cohen, Wheelright, Hill, Raste, & Plumb, 2001; Baron-Cohen, Wheelwright, Stone, & Rutherford, 1999). Such judgments are also poorly performed by adults with amygdala damage, although in this case it appears that their problems are restricted to the recognition of emotion-related mental inferences. The ability to interpret nonemotional mental states (e.g., quizzical and thoughtful) is less affected (Adolphs, Baron-Cohen et al., 2002).

Finally, the beliefs of speakers (engaged in neutral topics) and their intentions toward their interlocutors (i.e., what they want their interlocuters to think or feel) as revealed by their facial expressions, body movements, and tone of voice are poorly interpreted by adults with TBI. It should be noted, however, that this particular task relied upon verbal questions rather than rating scales or forced choice labels used in other perceptual tasks and therefore has relatively heavy verbal demands (McDonald & Flanagan, 2004).

Judgments regarding social characteristics of individuals

Competent social processing often also calls into play the ability to make judgments about more enduring characteristics of others in terms of their attractiveness, personality traits, and social position. Once again, these judgments appear to be mediated by a ventromedial frontal lobe system that includes the amygdalae. Amygdala activation has been found when assessing trustworthiness based on facial characteristics (Winston, Strange, O'Doherty, & Dolan, 2002) and conversely such judgments are impaired with amygdala damage (Adolphs, Tranel, & Damasio, 1998). Interestingly, such judgments are not affected when the stimuli are verbal descriptors rather than photographs, suggesting that the amygdala's role may be specifically related to the processing of perceptual characteristics. Personality judgments of extroversion, warmth, neuroticism, reliability, and adventurousness, which are based upon the movements of light points on a walking figure, are impaired in people with brain damage, with the relevant cortical region localized to the left frontal opercular cortices (Heberlein et al., 2004).

In a related vein, the prefrontal regions, amygdalae, and associated structures have been implicated in the social evaluation of faces according to gender, race, dominance, and general attractiveness. Adults with medial frontal damage have been reported to be less regulated by implicit gender stereotypes on a reaction time task than are people with dorsolateral frontal lesions and nonbrain-injured controls (Milne & Grafman, 2001). Degree of activation of the amygdala when viewing unfamiliar faces of another race has been associated with the strength of implicit racial stereotypes held by the participant (Phelps et al., 2000), although amygdala damage alone does not lead to a loss of access to these stereotypes (Phelps, Cannistraci, & Cunningham, 2003). While adults with ventromedial frontal lesions make generally similar ratings of dominance (based on gender, age, friendly facial expression, and clothing) to adults with brain damage outside this region or without brain damage at all, they appeared generally less sensitive to these cues, especially those of gender and age than the other groups (Karafin, Tranel, & Adolphs, 2004). Finally, preference judgments related to the visual attractiveness of faces have been reported to activate the ventral striatum (Kampe, Frith, Dolan, & Frith, 2001) and the orbitofrontal cortex (O'Doherty et al., 2003).

One explanation for the role that frontal systems play in judgments of social stereotypes has been forwarded by Grafman (1994) who argued that social schema, or social knowledge networks, are stored in the ventromedial areas of the prefrontal lobes and is used to make initial social judgments. It has been suggested that these schemata are activated rapidly and automatically, possibly influenced by somatic responses via the amygdalae (Milne & Grafman, 2001). Frontal damage that leads to the loss or degradation of these schema results in a loss of implicit social judgments while explicit processing of social information remains unaffected. Although further evidence suggests that it is specifically negative rather than positive implicit associations that are disrupted following frontal and amygdala damage (Park et al., 2001). This does not account for all the evidence regarding social judgments seen. It is not only social judgments with potentially negative expectations (such as unknown faces from a different racial group, or dominant individuals) that are altered in people with prefrontal lesions, but also evaluations based on stereotypes of gender and age, and more general attributions of personality and attractiveness that do not clearly invoke negative associations.

Morality judgments

Another important aspect of social processing is the capacity to judge social behavior according to a set of acceptable standards or mores and, yet again, these kinds of judgments appear to be mediated by the medial frontal-amygdala system. Thus, the medial prefrontal and temporal regions are activated during the detection of moral transgressions (Berthoz, Armony, Blair, & Dolan, 2002) and moral dilemmas (Greene, Sommerville, Nystrom, Darley, & Cohen, 2001) and, conversely, individuals with orbitofrontal and amygdala damage have difficulty in identifying moral transgressions (Stone, Cosmides, Toobey, Kroll, & Knight, 2002) or judging their seriousness (Blair & Cipolotti, 2000).

It is possible that poor moral reasoning reflects general reasoning deficits including but not restricted to social reasoning. A second possibility, based upon the "somatic marker theory" put forth by Bechara, Damasio, and colleagues (Bechara, 2004) is that reasoning about social consequences triggers somatic responses via an amygdala-frontal system that provides warning signals regarding poor (socially unacceptable) outcomes, just as somatic responses are triggered when contemplating risky outcomes in nonsocial tasks. Yet another possibility is that moral reasoning is reliant upon the ability to represent mental states in others (Berthoz et al., 2002).

While none of these explanations can be discounted Blair and Cipolotti argue for another explanation, based upon their work with J.S., an individual with orbitofrontal damage and associated aggression and callous disregard for others (Blair &

Cipolotti, 2000). J.S. had impaired emotion recognition, especially for negative emotions and reduced responsivity to both facial expressions and threatening objects. J.S. demonstrated awareness of social rules and could identify transgressions of these, suggesting intact access to social knowledge. However, his ability to discern more serious transgressions (e.g., moral transgressions in which there was a victim) from conventional transgressions (e.g., embarrassing incidents) was aberrant. Neither deficits in general inferencing nor specific mental inferencing could explain his poor moral reasoning. Nor could his deficits be attributed to a general loss of somatic marker activation because he was able to perform a (nonsocial) gambling task satisfactorily, a task involving the identification of risky choices and one that typically, people with somatic marker deficits fail to solve. Blair and Cipolotti (2000) argued that moral reasoning, in J.S. at least, reflected impairment to a specific system mediated by the (right) orbitofrontal system and the (left) amygdala that enables incoming social information to be evaluated in terms of its negative consequences, specifically angry reactions in others, by reference to existing schemas of social knowledge, developed and informed by prior experiences. According to these authors, frontal lesions may result in these schemas no longer being activated or, if activated, no longer able to modify ongoing behavior, including cognitive judgments. This explanation for moral reasoning deficits is not dissimilar to the somatic marker hypothesis although it focuses specifically upon social information and the effects of anger expectations. Importantly it places emotional processing centrally in moral reasoning, a view that is supported by fMRI research that has indicated that emotionally engaging moral dilemmas are more likely to activate the medial frontal regions than more impersonal moral or nonmoral dilemmas (Greene et al., 2001).

Disorders in understanding social meanings in language

Although damage to the prefrontal lobes rarely results in any aphasic condition, it is well recognized that the communicative competence of people with frontal lobe injuries, i.e., their ability to use language to communicate, is often compromised. Patients with focal frontal lesions may respond to initial, concrete associations producing confabulatory, contradictory, and disorganized discourse without apparent concern (Alexander & Freedman, 1984; Stuss, Alexander, Leiberman, & Levine, 1978) and their discourse may be disturbed by the constant intrusion of irrelevant associations (Luria, 1976). Alternatively, the patient may become mute or in lesser degrees may suffer listlessness, apathy, and greatly reduced verbal output (Alexander et al., 1989). Such patients may be incapable of producing a sustained narrative (Damasio & Van Hoesen, 1983) or the organized evolution of their narratives may be disrupted by perseveration and the incorporation of inert stereotypes (Luria, 1976). Similar patterns of impairment, i.e., an impoverishment of output or else confabulatory and tangential conversation have been described in those with more diffuse impairment implicating frontal systems including adults with frontal dementia and TBI (Barber, Snowden, & Craufurd, 1995; Gustafson, 1993; Levin et al., 1979; Milton, Prutting, & Binder, 1984; Neary, 1990; Prigatano, Roueche, & Fordyce, 1986; Thomsen, 1984).

These difficulties are particularly apparent when patients are faced with specific social communication tasks, as has been revealed in a number of studies conducted in adults and children with TBI. Thus, problems have been revealed in the production of contextually appropriate speech acts (Dennis & Barnes, 1990, 2000), paraphasing of main ideas and structuring of narratives (Chapman et al., 1991, 2004), producing diplomatic or persuasive requests (McDonald & Pearce, 1998; McDonald & van Sommers, 1992; Turkstra, McDonald, & Kaufman, 1996), providing clear and organized instruction (McDonald, 1993, 1995; Turkstra et al., 1996), and negotiation of everyday service enquiries (Togher, McDonald, Code, & Grant, 2004).

Problems with social language use are not, however, restricted to the regulation and production of socially appropriate output. There is also strong evidence that people with frontal systems damage have problems understanding the subtle social meanings inherent in all verbal communication. Every act of communication carries with it several layers of meaning. There are the conventional meanings that pertain to the semantic and syntactic rules of language use, i.e., the literal meaning associated with each word used and the specification of the topic, subject, object, etc., as revealed by word order. But beyond this there are many social meanings apparent simply from the choice of words. For example, the question "Could you tell me the way to Jordon Hall?" is seen as more polite than the equivalent "Where is Jordon Hall?" (Clark & Schunk, 1980) partly because the former is more tentative than the latter and therefore signals a hesitancy to impose upon the listener. Such devices are universally used across cultures to negotiate social encounters (Brown & Levinson, 1978) and provide a variety of implicit signals to the listener including information as to how the speaker views him or her in terms of social standing and level of intimacy. If the speaker is hesitant he or she may choose to communicate indirectly, whereby the intended meaning of the utterance is only partially revealed by the words chosen (*"it would be good to have some more air in here"*) or else only implied (*"it is very hot in here"*). In some instances of indirect language, such as sarcasm, the speaker says one thing, but means something that is often opposite in meaning to that literally asserted, e.g., "That was a great idea!" spoken to suggest the reverse. Speakers rely upon such indirect meanings frequently in normal conversation in the service of politeness or other social considerations. While language comprehension per se is usually intact in people with prefrontal lobe lesions, it is these indirect meanings in social discourse, i.e., the pragmatic dimension of language that has proven particularly difficult to process.

As with social language production, the majority of work examining pragmatic inferences following brain injury has focused upon those with TBI or else mixed neurological groups including people with TBI (e.g., Channon & Crawford, 2000). According to these studies, adults, adolescents, and children with TBI consistently demonstrate difficulties understanding nonliteral meanings such as sarcasm (Channon & Crawford, 2000; Channon & Watts, 2003; McDonald, 1992; McDonald & Pearce, 1996; McDonald et al., 2003; McDonald & Flanagan, 2004; Turkstra, McDonald, & DePompei, 2001; Turkstra, McDonald, & DePompei, 2001), humor (Docking, Jordan, & Murdoch, 1999; Docking, Murdoch, & Jordan, 2000), ironic criticism (Dennis et al., 2001), and ambiguous advertising slogans (Pearce, McDonald, &

Coltheart, 1998). In every case responses indicate a tendency to erroneously interpret the salient literal meaning as the meaning intended.

Explanations for loss of pragmatic understanding

Explanations for difficulty in the processing of indirect meaning tend to fall into two broad camps. On the one hand, there has been a great deal of interest in the role that specific social processes, such as emotion recognition and ToM abilities play in unraveling the social meanings of discourse, on the other hand, the role of more general inferential processing problems has also been examined. Both perspectives merit brief discussion.

Firstly, because some instances of pragmatic inference, notably, sarcastic inference, are associated with a particular attitude (scorn and derision), it has been argued that recognizing the attitudinal or emotional stance of the speaker is pivotal to the successful conveyance of the intended meaning (Sperber & Wilson, 1986). However, while emotion recognition is often impaired in people with frontal lobe injuries, there is no clear relationship between emotion recognition ability and the ability to understand sarcasm (McDonald & Flanagan, 2004; McDonald & Pearce, 1996).

Secondly, based upon work within autistic groups, it has been argued that ToM deficits underpin loss of pragmatic understanding. Certainly this relationship is well established in autism (Happe, 1993; Surian et al., 1996). Furthermore, within the autistic population, gradations of ToM competence have been directly linked to gradations in comprehension of indirect meanings. Thus, children with autism who could not understand first-order ToM (i.e., what another person might believe) could not understand metaphors since these rely upon understanding that someone is making an implicit comparisons between the actual state of affairs and some similar set of circumstances. Children who had first-order ToM could do this. Children who could not understand second-order ToM (i.e., what one person thinks that another person thinks) could not understand irony. In order to make sense of irony one must understand that both protagonists share a world view that the ironic statement contradicts (Happe, 1993).

A relationship between ToM abilities and the ability to understand pragmatic inferences has also emerged in people with severe TBI, that is, adults with TBI, who fail to understand sarcastic comments, are also likely to fail to understand the intentions of the speakers (McDonald & Flanagan, 2004). The question remains, however, as to whether this relationship is, indeed, causal or mediated by some other domain independent ability such as general inferential reasoning.

ToM abilities are, in fact, unlikely to account for all pragmatic processing deficits seen because there are many instances of pragmatic inference that are not reliant upon understanding the speaker's beliefs and intentions. Ambiguous advertisements, for example, whereby advertising slogans conjure up more than one meaning, rely more upon double meanings and word associations than understanding the thoughts of the advertiser and yet, people with frontal lobe injuries find the pragmatic inferred meanings in such advertisements opaque (Pearce et al., 1998). In addition, both children and adults with TBI have difficulty not only with text comprehension that requires inferring intention (i.e., ironical utterances), but also with text that requires more general inferences to be generated (e.g., inferring causal relationships) (Dennis et al., 2001; Martin & McDonald, 2005). Similarly, work using fMRI has suggested that the (medial) frontal lobes are activated not only when adults listen to sentence pairs that rely upon ToM reasoning, but also when they listen to sentence pairs that are not socially orientated, e.g., "The lights have been on since last night," "The car doesn't start" (Ferstl & Yves von Cramon, 2002).

A systematic relationship between poor pragmatic inference ability and performance on nonsocial inferential reasoning tasks has been found in people with TBI (Martin & McDonald, 2005; McDonald & Pearce, 1996) and a relationship between standard executive measures (tests of concept formation and inhibition) and pragmatic performance has also been reported (Channon & Crawford, 2000; Channon & Watts, 2003; McDonald & Pearce, 1996). Furthermore, when compared directly, general inferential reasoning was found to be strongly associated with performance on a sarcasm task in people with TBI whereas ToM ability was not (Martin & McDonald, 2005).

In general, the interpretation of conversational inference such as sarcasm by normal adults appears to be facilitated by understanding the intentions of the speaker and their attitude (emotional stance). However, these abilities are not sufficient, or even necessary for successful pragmatic processing. In contrast, the ability to make inferences in general, i.e., the ability to think at a conceptual level, appears to be fundamental to the ability to understand the many implied social meanings underlying conversation. Interestingly, this is not the case in people with Aspergers, where ToM ability has been clearly associated with ability to interpret sarcasm (Martin & McDonald, 2004). This suggests a different mechanism underlying poor pragmatic comprehension in developmental disorders such as autism compared to acquired frontal pathology.

Implications for treatment

In this review, a number of disorders of social information processing following brain impairment have been detailed including difficulties with emotion recognition, mentalizing ability, judgments about individual differences, judgments about morality, and understanding implied conversational meanings. Each of these difficulties represents obstacles that the individual with frontal damage must face when attempting to negotiate his or her social world effectively. Consequently, treatment that can ameliorate these conditions is of tantamount importance. Despite this, research into the remediation of social information processing following brain injury has been virtually nonexistent. In order to provide new directions for rehabilitation it is worth considering some general principles from the cognitive remediation literature as well as particular insights gained from the emerging body of research into social cognition disorders, and, where possible, insights gained from the treatment of other clinical populations.

Emotion processing disorders

Typically, remediation approaches have emphasized either restorative principles, whereby the impaired function is directly remediated, or compensatory approaches, whereby the patient is provided with strategies to bypass his or her difficulties. The growing sophistication of our understanding concerning the manner in which emotion processing deficits may manifest following brain injury provides new directions for rehabilitation in both restoration and compensation.

Restorative approaches to rehabilitation, in general, have regained momentum in recent years. This is based upon growing evidence concerning the capacity of the brain to reorganize and regenerate following injury. For example, work with both primates and brain-injured humans has shown that paresis can be gradually improved with targeted practice and is reflected in reorganization of the motor cortex (Nudo & Milliken, 1996; Taub, Crago, & Uswatte, 1998). Similar functional improvements with associated cortical change have been reported in neuropsychological domains including aphasia and hemineglect (Cornelissen et al., 2003; Pizzamiglio et al., 1998; Pulvermuller et al., 2001). This work suggests that skills can be re-established following brain injury, provided the remediation targets are highly specific. In particular, the evidence favors an approach aimed at focusing attention on relevant stimuli or behavior and repeated practice of target processes (see Robertson & Murre, 1999 for review). The implications for these findings are that emotion perception too may be amenable to treatment, provided that the exact nature of the deficit is elucidated and appropriately targeted in treatment. Thus a proper evaluation of the brain-injured individual's ability to process emotions under a variety of conditions (e.g., different categories of emotion, moving versus still images, audio versus visual channels) needs to occur prior to remediation. Once identified, the emotion processing impairment can be the target of repeated and increasing complex practice-based exercises (Holland & Sonderman, 1974). A rational approach to remediating emotion, based on these principles, would involve the participant practicing recognition of stylized, emotional expressions, focusing upon those aspects of the facial features that provide clear clues as to the expression conveyed. As this technique is mastered the participant would be provided with fewer and fewer instructions and more complex facial expressions.

Compensatory techniques, too, retain an important, often complementary, role in rehabilitation, helping the patient bypass their deficits using intact cognitive abilities in a strategic manner. Such approaches are particularly efficacious because they enable the patient to focus upon his or her strengths, which is more encouraging and ultimately therapeutic than repeatedly confronting impairment (Murray & Holland, 1995). Such techniques are also informed by a more precise understanding of the nature of emotion processing difficulties. For example, deficits in processing visual emotional stimuli may be bypassed by training to focus upon the auditory medium. Failure to have an autonomic response when passively viewing emotional material may be ameliorated by requiring the patient to actively focus upon and describe the image thereby, hypothetically, engaging the dorsolateral cognitive system that may in turn stimulate the ventral-frontal system to trigger an affective reaction.

A growing sophistication of our understanding of emotion processing problems will inevitably lead to better remediation techniques. In the meantime, the small amount of work that has been conducted to date to evaluate treatment for emotion perception has highlighted the potential value of this kind of approach. Treatment of emotion perception in those with brain injury is very sparse although the pre-liminary results of two randomized trial for adults with TBI emphasizing direct remediation of emotion recognition was positive (Bornhofen & McDonald, in press a,b). On the other hand, there has been increasing interest in the remediation of emotion perception deficits in other clinical populations including normal, autistic, and intellectually disabled children and adults with schizophrenia. Using a variety of treatment approaches the results have been generally positive (Bauminger, 2002; Frommann, Streit, & Wolwer, 2003; Hadwin, Baron-Cohen, Howlin, & Hill, 1996; McAlpine, Singh, Kendall, & Hampton, 1992; McKenzie, Matheson, McKaskie, Hamilton, & Murray, 2000; Penn & Combs, 2000; Stewart & Singe, 1996; van der Gaag, Kern, van den Bosch, & Liberman, 2002), although not always (see Milne & Spence, 1988) highlighting a renewed optimism in this area of remediation.

Mentalizing disorders

Deficits in mentalizing may be rehabilitated using similar principles to that already outlined. Direct remediation, for example, may involve the training of patients to practice attending to cues that enable them to consider another's perspective while compensatory techniques may include teaching patients to ask targeted questions to assist gauge the intentions of their interlocutor. Evidence regarding the efficacy of treatment for mentalizing disorders after any kind of clinical condition is limited. Several studies have aimed to teach children with autism to think about social situations from the perspective of others, using a variety of techniques including games, role plays, and training in the use of thought bubbles to represent the beliefs of others (Delmolino, 2000; Hadwin et al., 1996; Ozonoff & Miller, 1995; Wellman et al., 2002). In each case the treatment improved performance on traditional ToM measures although there was poor generalization and little improvement in social competence. Other work has reported improvements in mentalizing ability in adults with schizophrenia when provided with strategies to verbally characterize others' mental states (Roncone et al., 2004; Sarfati, Passerieux, & Hardy-Bayle, 2000).

Other aspects of social information processing

Cognitive rehabilitation of other aspects of social perception such as judging trust-worthiness, morality, and deciphering pragmatic inference have not, to date, been the subject of systematic study. Partly, this reflects the fact that problems in these areas have only recently become the subject of detailed examination. To some extent, these aspects of social perception rely upon the ability to integrate and interpret a variety of social cues, i.e., they rely upon "social intelligence" as defined in the social skills literature (McFall, 1982). On the presumption that the ability to infer these social meaning relies upon conceptual reasoning and, thus, executive function (Body, Perkins, & McDonald, 1999; McDonald & Pearce, 1996; Pearce et al., 1998; Ylvisaker, 2000) techniques that target concept formation may have direct relevance. Cognitive retraining approaches that target concept formation usually do so in the context of attempting to improve problem-solving skills by making the various stages explicit, e.g., problem identification, problem definition, generation of alternate strategies, decision making, implementation, and self-monitoring (Cramon, Matthes-von Cramon, & Mai, 1991). Problem identification and problem definition explicitly require conceptual skills. Typically, these aspects of problem solving have been addressed by training the participant to discriminate between relevant and irrelevant information, produce goal-directed ideas, practice maintaining and changing conceptual sets, and processing multiple sources of information (Cramon & Matthes-von Cramon, 1992; Delahunty & Morice, 1994; Delahunty, Morice, & Frost, 1993). Using such techniques, modest improvements have been noted in flexibility and set maintenance as measured by the Wisconsin Card Sorting Test (Delahunty et al., 1993). Such techniques may translate well to social problem solving. For example, patients may be aided by explicitly working through the implications of different moral transgressions, by explicitly verbalizing which features of a person signal approachability, etc. and by explicitly considering several sources of information to generate a nonliteral interpretation of sarcastic or otherwise ambiguous comments.

Need for appropriate social assessment measures

An important issue in the remediation of social perception is the availability of ecologically valid materials for assessment and for remediation exercises. The neuropsychological test literature has tended to lag in this area, although the treatment of emotion perception deficits in autism and other developmental conditions is rapidly developing and, as a consequence, useful resources for emotion perception exercises are becoming available on the internet, e.g., http://www.dotolearn.com/games/facialexpressions. Materials for assessing higher aspects of social perception are relatively scarce although a few useful materials are available. In particular, The Awareness of Social Inference Test (TASIT) is a commercially available test (McDonald, Flanagan, & Rollins, 2002) that uses videoed vignettes of social interactions to assess the ability to infer the emotional state of the speaker, their intentions, and the meaning of indirect conversational remarks. This test has a respectable normative sample (McDonald et al., 2003), is sensitive to social perception deficits after TBI (McDonald & Flanagan, 2004; McDonald et al.), and has established ecological validity (McDonald et al., 2004). The Social Problem-Solving Video Vignettes (Kendall et al., 1997) and the Assessment of Interpersonal Problem Solving Skills (AIPSS) (Donahoe et al., 1990) are also based upon videoed vignettes and provide stimuli that require participants to identify and describe the nature of interpersonal problems and social goals as well as examining their ability to generate and implement solutions. While these instruments are designed for assessment purposes they provide useful templates for the production of treatment resources. Videoed social information can represent useful bridging stimuli for treatment, enabling socially realistic information to be presented in a manner that is standardized and controlled.

Conclusion

Ever since the vivid description of Phineas Gage and his changed persona following his frontal lobe injury, there has been a growing interest in the frontal lobes and their disorders. While the socioemotional consequences of these have continued to be described in fascinating detail, the underpinning neuropsychological mechanisms have not been particularly well articulated. The focus of empirical research into the frontal lobes has been firmly based upon (nonsocial) cognitive processes and their disorders. But the times are changing and the proposition that social cognition, i.e., social information processing, represents a field of study in its own right has gained impetus. Certain components of social cognition, such as emotion recognition, appear to represent uniquely social, modular processes, dissociable from other cognitive systems. The extent to which other abilities, such as mentalizing and pragmatic inferential reasoning, also represent discrete social processes is yet to be determined although it does seem to be the case that these more complex judgments call into play other intellective abilities. The implications of our growing understanding of the mechanisms underpinning social processing is that we are far better able to target specific deficits in remediation. Social processing represents the challenge of the future in terms of designing targeted, ecologically valid and generalizable assessment and treatment approaches. Hopefully this review has gone some way to provide some insights into directions this might take.

References

Adolphs, R. (2001). The neurobiology of social cognition. *Current Opinion in Neurobiology, 11*, 231–239.

Adolphs, R. (2002a). Neural systems for recognizing emotion. *Current Opinion in Neurobiology, 12*(2), 169–177.

Adolphs, R. (2002b). Recognizing emotion from facial expressions: Psychological and neurological mechanisms. *Behavioral and Cognitive Neuroscience Reviews, 1*(1), 21–62.

Adolphs, R., Baron-Cohen, S., & Tranel, D. (2002). Impaired recognition of social emotions following amygdala damage. *Journal of Cognitive Neuroscience, 14*(8), 1264–1274.

Adolphs, R., Damasio, H., & Tranel, D. (2002). Neural systems for recognition of emotional prosody: A 3-D lesion study. *Emotion, 2*(1), 23–51.

Adolphs, R., Damasio, H., Tranel, D., & Damasio, A. R. (1996). Cortical systems for the recognition of emotion in facial expressions. *Journal of Neuroscience, 16*(23), 7678–7687.

Adolphs, R., Russell, J. A., & Tranel, D. (1999). A role for the human amygdala in recognizing emotional arousal from unpleasant stimuli. *Psychological Science, 10*(2), 167–171.

Adolphs, R., & Tranel, D. (2004). Impaired judgments of sadness but not happiness following bilateral amygdala damage. *Journal of Cognitive Neuroscience, 16*(3), 453–462.

Adolphs, R., Tranel, D., & Damasio, A. R. (1998). The human amygdala in social judgement. *Nature, 393*, 470–474.

Adolphs, R., Tranel, D., & Damasio, A. R. (2003). Dissociable neural systems for recognizing emotions. *Brain and Cognition, 52*(1), 61–69.

Alexander, M. P., Benson, D. F., & Stuss, D. T. (1989). Frontal lobes and language. *Brain and Language, 37*, 656–691.

Alexander, M. P., & Freedman, M. (1984). Amnesia after anterior communicating aneurysm rupture. *Neurology, 34*, 752–757.

Angrilli, A., Palomba, D., Cantagallo, A., Maietti, A., & Stegagno, L. (1999). Emotional impairment after right orbitofrontal lesion in a patient without cognitive deficits. *Neuroreport, 10*(8), 1741–1746.

Avis, J., & Harris, P. L. (1991). Belief-desire reasoning among Baka children: Evidence for a universal conception of mind. *Child Development, 62*(3), 460–467.

Bara, B. G., Tirassa, M., & Zettin, M. (1997). Neuropsychological constraints on formal theories of dialogue. *Brain and Language, 59*, 7–49.

Barber, R., Snowden, J. S., & Craufurd, D. (1995). Frontotemporal dementia and Alzheimer's disease: Retrospective differentiation using information from informants. *Journal of Neurology, Neurosurgery and Psychiatry, 59*(1), 61–70.

Baron-Cohen, S. (1989). Perceptual role taking and protodeclarative pointing in autism. *British Journal of Developmental Psychology, 7*(2), 113–127.

Baron-Cohen, S., Jolliffe, T., Mortimore, C., & Robertson, M. (1997). Another advanced test of theory of mind: Evidence from very high functioning adults with autism or Asperger syndrome. *Journal of Child Psychology and Psychiatry and Allied Disciplines, 38*(7), 813–822.

Baron-Cohen, S., O'Riordan, M., Stone, V., Jones, R., & Plaisted, K. (1999). Recognition of faux pas by normally developing children with Asperger syndrome or high-functioning autism. *Journal of Autism and Developmental Disorders, 29*(5), 407–418.

Baron-Cohen, S., Ring, H., Moriarty, J., Schmitz, B., Costa, D., & Ell, P. (1994). The brain basis of theory of mind: The role of the orbito-frontal region. *British Journal of Psychiatry, 165*, 640–649.

Baron-Cohen, S., Wheelright, S., Hill, J., Raste, Y., & Plumb, I. (2001). The "Reading the Mind in the Eyes" test revised version: A study with normal adults and adults with Aspergers syndrome or high functioning autism. *Journal of Child Psychology and Psychiatry, 42*, 241–251.

Baron-Cohen, S., Wheelwright, S., & Jolliffe, T. (1997). Is there a "language of the eyes"? Evidence from normal adults, and adults with autism or Asperger syndrome. *Visual Cognition, 4*(3), 311–331.

Baron-Cohen, S., Wheelwright, S., Stone, V., & Rutherford, M. (1999). A mathematician, a physicist and a computer scientist with Asperger syndrome: Performance on folk psychology and folk physics tests. *Neurocase, 5*(6), 475–483.

Bassili, J. N. (1978). Facial motion in the perception of faces and of emotional expression. *Journal of Experimental Psychology: Human Perception and Performance, 4*, 373–379.

Bauminger, N. (2002). The facilitation of social–emotional understanding and social interaction in high-functioning children with autism: Intervention outcomes. *Journal of Autism and Developmental Disorders, 32*, 283–298.

Beatty, W. W., Orbelo, D. M., Sorocco, K. H., & Ross, E. D. (2003). Comprehension of affective prosody in multiple sclerosis. *Multiple Sclerosis, 9*, 148–153.

Bechara, A. (2004). The role of emotion in decision-making: Evidence from neurological patients with orbitofrontal damage. *Brain and Cognition, 55*(1), 30–40.

Bechara, A., Damasio, A. R., Damasio, H., & Anderson, S. W. (1994). Insensitivity to future consequences following damage to human prefrontal cortex. *Cognition, 50*(1–3), 7–15.

Bechara, A., Damasio, H., & Damasio, A. R. (2000). Emotion, decision making and the orbitofrontal cortex. *Cerebral Cortex, 10*(3), 295–307.

Bechara, A., Damasio, H., Tranel, D., & Damasio, A. R. (1997). Deciding advantageously before knowing the advantageous strategy. *Science, 275*(5304), 1293–1294.

Berthoz, S., Armony, J. L., Blair, R. J. R., & Dolan, R. J. (2002). An fMRI study of intentional and unintentional (embarrassing) violations of social norms. *Brain, 125*(8), 1696–1708.

Bibby, H., & McDonald, S. (2004). Theory of Mind after traumatic brain injury. *Neuropsychologia, 43*, 99–104.

Blair, R. J. R., & Cipolotti, L. (2000). Impaired social response reversal: A case of "acquired sociopathy." *Brain*, *123*, 1122–1141.

Blair, R. J. R., Morris, J. S., Frith, C. C., Perrett, D. I., & Dolan, R. J. (1999). Dissociable neural responses to facial expressions of sadness and anger. *Brain*, *122*(5), 883–893.

Body, R., Perkins, M., & McDonald, S. (1999). Communication and cognition. In S. McDonald, L. Togher, & C. Code (Eds.), *Communication disorders following traumatic brain injury* (pp. 81–112). Hove, UK: Psychology Press.

Bornhofen, C., & McDonald, S. (in press, a). Treating deficits in emotion perception following traumatic brain injury. *Neuropsychological Rehabilitation*.

Bornhofen, C., & McDonald, S. (in press, b). Comparison of two approaches to remediating emotion perception after severe traumatic brain injury. *Journal of Head Trauma Rehabilitation*.

Borod, J. C. (1993). Cerebral mechanisms underlying facial, prosodic and lexical emotional expression: A review of neuropsychological studies and methodological issues. *Neuropsychology*, *7*(4), 445–463.

Borod, J. C., Koff, E., Lorch, M. P., & Nicholas, M. (1986). The expression and perception of facial emotion in brain-damaged patients. *Neuropsychologia*, *24*(2), 169–180.

Bowler, D. M. (1992). "Theory of mind" in Asperger's syndrome. *Journal of Child Psychology and Psychiatry*, *33*, 877–893.

Breen, N., Caine, D., & Coltheart, M. (2002). The role of affect and reasoning in a patient with a delusion of misidentification. *Cognitive Neuropsychiatry*, *7*, 113–137.

Broks, P., Young, A. W., Maratos, E., Coffey, P. J., Calder, A. J., Isaac, C. L., et al. (1998). Face processing impairments after encephalitis: Amygdala damage and recognition of fear. *Neuropsychologia*, *36*(1), 59–70.

Brown, P., & Levinson, S. (1978). Universals in language usage: Politeness phenomena. In E.N. Goody (Ed.), *Questions and politeness: Strategies in social interaction*. Melbourne: Cambridge University Press.

Buchanan, T. W., Tranel, D., & Adolphs, R. (2004). Anteromedial temporal lobe damage blocks startle modulation by fear and disgust. *Behavioral Neuroscience*, *118*(2), 429–437.

Calder, A. J., Lawrence, A. D., Keane, J., Scott, S. K., Owen, A. M., Christoffels, I., et al. (2002). Reading the mind from eye gaze. *Neuropsychologia*, *40*(8), 1129–1138.

Castelli, F., Frith, C., Happe, F., & Frith, U. (2002). Autism, Asperger syndrome and brain mechanisms for the attribution of mental states to animated shapes. *Brain*, *125*, 1839–1849.

Channon, S., & Crawford, S. (2000). The effects of anterior lesions on performance on a story comprehension test: Left anterior impairment on a theory of mind-type task. *Neuropsychologia*, *38*(7), 1006–1017.

Channon, S., & Watts, M. (2003). Pragmatic language interpretation after closed head injury: Relationship to executive functioning. *Cognitive Neuropsychiatry*, *8*(4), 243–260.

Chapman, S. B., Culhane, K. A., Levine, H. S., Harward, H., Mendelsohn, D., Ewing-Cobbs, L., et al. (1991). Narrative discourse after closed head injury in children and adolescents. *Brain and Language*, *43*, 42–65.

Chapman, S. B., Sparks, G., Levin, H. S., Dennis, M., Roncadin, C., Zhang, L., et al. (2004). Discourse macrolevel processing after severe pediatric traumatic brain injury. *Developmental Neuropsychology*, *25*(1–2), 37–60.

Charman, T., & Baron-Cohen, S. (1995). Understanding photos, models, and beliefs: A test of the modularity thesis of theory of mind. *Cognitive Development*, *10*(2), 287–298.

Cicerone, K. D., & Tanenbaum, L. N. (1997). Disturbance of social cognition after traumatic orbitofrontal brain injury. *Archives of Clinical Neuropsychology*, *12*, 173–188.

Cicone, M., Wapner, W., & Gardener, H. (1980). Sensitivity to emotional expressions and situations in organic patients. *Cortex, 16*, 145–158.

Clark, H. H., & Schunk, D. H. (1980). Polite responses to polite requests. *Cognition, 8*(2), 111–143.

Cornelissen, K., Laine, M., Tarkiainen, A., Jaervensivu, T., Martin, N., & Salmelin, R. (2003). Adult brain plasticity elicited by anomia treatment. *Journal of Cognitive Neuroscience, 15*(3), 444–461.

Cramon, D. Y. v., & Matthes-von Cramon, G. (1992). Reflections on the treatment of brain injured patients suffering from problem solving disorders. *Neuropsychological Rehabilitation, 2*, 207–230.

Cramon, D. Y. v., Matthes-von Cramon, G., & Mai, N. (1991). Problem solving deficits in brain-injured patients: A therapeutic approach. *Neuropsychological Rehabilitation, 1*, 45–64.

Critchley, H., Daly, E., Phillips, M., Brammer, M., Bullmore, E., Williams, S., et al. (2000). Explicit and implicit neural mechanisms for processing of social information from facial expressions: A functional magnetic resonance imaging study. *Human Brain Mapping, 9*(2), 93–105.

Croker, V., & McDonald, S. (2005). Recognition of emotion from facial expression following traumatic brain injury. *Brain Injury, 19*, 787–789.

Crosson, B. (1987). Treatment of interpersonal deficits for head-trauma patients in inpatient rehabilitation settings. *The Clinical Neuropsychologist, 1*(4), 335–352, 366.

Damasio, A. R. (1996). The somatic marker hypothesis and the possible function of the prefrontal cortex. *Philosophical Transactions of the Royal Society of London B Biological Science, 351*, 1413–1420.

Damasio, A. R., Tranel, D., & Damasio, H. (1990). Individuals with sociopathic behavior caused by frontal damage fail to respond autonomically to social stimuli. *Behavioral Brain Research, 41*(2), 81–94.

Damasio, A. R., & Van Hoesen, G. W. (1983). Emotional disorders associated with focal lesions of the limbic frontal lobe. In K. M. Heilman & P. Satz (Eds.), *Neuropsychology of human emotion*. New York: Guildford Press.

Davis, H. L., & Pratt, C. (1995). The development of children's Theory of Mind: The working memory explanation. *Australian Journal of Psychology, 47*, 25–31.

Delahunty, A., & Morice, R. (1994). *Frontal/executive training programs for cognitive deficits*. Paper presented at the Treatment Issues and Long term outcomes: The 18th Annual Brain Impairment Conference, Hobart, Australia.

Delahunty, A., Morice, R., & Frost, B. (1993). Specific cognitive flexibility rehabilitation in schizophrenia: Preliminary results. *Psychological Medicine, 243*, 221–227.

Delmolino, L. M. (2000). Teaching perspective taking skills to children with autism. *Dissertation Abstracts International: Section B: The Sciences and Engineering, 61*(5-B), 2752.

Dennis, M., & Barnes, M. A. (1990). Knowing the meaning, getting the point, bridging the gap, and carrying the message: Aspects of discourse following closed head injury in childhood and adolescence. *Brain & Language, 39*(3), 428–446.

Dennis, M., & Barnes, M. A. (2000). Speech acts after mild or severe childhood head injury. *Aphasiology, 14*(4), 391–405.

Dennis, M., Purvis, K., Barnes, M. A., Wilkinson, M., & Winner, E. (2001). Understanding of literal truth, ironic criticism, and deceptive praise following childhood head injury. *Brain and Language, 78*, 1–16.

Docking, K., Jordan, F. M., & Murdoch, B. E. (1999). Interpretation and comprehension of linguistic humour by adolescents with head injury: A case-by-case analysis. *Brain Injury, 13*(12), 953–972.

Docking, K., Murdoch, B. E., & Jordan, F. M. (2000). Interpretation and comprehension of linguistic humour by adolescents with head injury: A group analysis. *Brain Injury*, *14*(1), 89–108.

Donahoe, C. P., Carter, M. J., Bloem, W. D., Hirsch, G. L., Laasi, N., & Wallace, C. J. (1990). Assessment of interpersonal problem solving skills. *Psychiatry*, *53*, 329–339.

Dujardin, K., Blairy, S., Defebvre, L., Duhem, S., Noel, Y., Hess, U., et al. (2004). Deficits in decoding emotional facial expressions in Parkinson's disease. *Neuropsychologia*, *42*(2), 239–250.

Ekman, P., & Freisen, W. V. (1976). *Pictures of facial affect*. Palo Alto, CA: Consulting Psychological Press.

Esteves, F., Dimberg, U., & Ohman, A. (1994). Automatically elicited fear: Conditioned skin conductance responses to masked facial expressions. *Cognition and Emotion*, *8*(5), 393–413.

Ferstl, E. C., & Yves von Cramon, D. (2002). What does the frontomedian cortex contribute to language processing: Coherence or Theory of Mind? *Neuroimage*, *17*, 1599–1612.

Fine, C., Lumsden, J., & Blair, R. J. R. (2001). Dissociation between "theory of mind" and executive functions in a patient with early left amygdala damage. *Brain*, *124*(2), 287–298.

Flanagan, S., McDonald, S., & Togher, L. (1995). Evaluation of the BRISS as a measure of social skills in the traumatically brain injured. *Brain Injury*, *9*, 321–338.

Fletcher, P. C., Happe, F., Frith, U., Baker, S. C., Dolan, R. J., Frackowiak, R. S. J., et al. (1995). Other minds in the brain: A functional imaging study of "theory of mind" in story comprehension. *Cognition*, *57*, 109–128.

Frommann, N., Streit, M., & Wolwer, W. (2003). Remediation of facial affect recognition impairments in patients with schizophrenia: A new training program. *Psychiatry Research*, *117*, 281–284.

Gallagher, H. L., Happe, F., Brunswick, N., Fletcher, P. C., Frith, U., & Frith, C. D. (2000). Reading the mind in cartoons and stories: an fMRI study of "theory of mind" in verbal and non-verbal tasks. *Neuropsychologia*, *38*, 11–21.

Goel, V., Grafman, J., Sadato, N., & Hallett, M. (1995). Modelling other minds. *Neuroreport*, *6*, 1741–1746.

Gordon, A. C. L., & Olson, D. R. (1998). The relation between theory of mind and capacity to hold in mind. *Journal of Experimental Child Psychology*, *68*, 70–83.

Gorno-Tempini, M. L., Pradelli, S., Pagnoni, G., Baraldi, P., Porro, C., Nicoletti, R., et al. (2001). Explicit and incidental facial expression processing: An fMRI study. *Neuroimage*, *14*, 465–473.

Grafman, J. (1994). Alternative frameworks for the conceptualisation of prefrontal lobe functions. In F. Boller & J. Grafman (Eds.), *Handbook of neuropsychology* (Vol. 9, pp. 187–202). Amsterdam: Elsevier.

Green, R. E. A., Turner, G. R., & Thompson, W. F. (2004). Deficits in facial emotion perception in adults with recent traumatic brain injury. *Neuropsychologia*, *42*, 133–141.

Greene, J. D., Sommerville, R. B., Nystrom, L. E., Darley, J. M., & Cohen, J. D. (2001). An fMRI investigation of emotional engagement in moral judgement. *Science*, *293*, 2105–2107.

Gregory, C., Lough, S., Stone, V., Erzinclioglu, S., Martin, L., Baron-Cohen, S., et al. (2002). Theory of mind in patients with frontal variant frontotemporal dementia and Alzheimer's disease: Theoretical and practical implications. *Brain*, *125*(4), 752–764.

Gustafson, L. (1993). Clinical picture of frontal lobe degeneration of non-Alzheimer type. *Dementia*, *4*(3–4), 143–148.

Hadwin, J., Baron-Cohen, S., Howlin, P., & Hill, K. (1996). Can we teach children with autism to understand emotions, belief or pretence? *Development and Psychopathology*, *8*, 345–365.

Happe, F., & Frith, U. (1996). The neuropsychology of autism. *Brain, 119*(4), 1377–1400.

Happe, F., Malhi, G. S., & Checkley, S. (2001). Acquired mind-blindness following frontal lobe surgery? A single case study of impaired 'Theory of Mind' in a patient treated with stereotactic anterior capsulotomy. *Neuropsychologia, 39*(1), 83–90.

Happe, F. G. E. (1993). Communicative competence and theory of mind in autism: A test of relevance theory. *Cognition, 48,* 101–119.

Happe, F. G. E. (1994). An advanced test of theory of mind: Understanding of story characters' thoughts and feelings by able autistic, mentally handicapped, and normal children and adults. *Journal of Autism and Developmental Disorders, 24*(2), 129–154.

Hariri, A. R., Bookheimer, S. Y., & Mazziotta, J. C. (2000). Modulating emotional responses: Effects of a neocortical network on the limbic system. *Neuroreport: For Rapid Communication of Neuroscience Research, 11*(1), 43–48.

Harmer, C. J., Thilo, K. V., Rothwell, J. C., & Goodwin, G. M. (2001). Transcranial magnetic stimulation of medial-frontal cortex impairs the processing of angry facial expressions. *Nature Neuroscience, 4,* 17–18.

Heberlein, A. S., Adolphs, R., Tranel, D., & Damasio, H. (2004). Cortical regions for judgments of emotions and personality traits from point-light walkers. *Journal of Cognitive Neuroscience, 16,* 1143–1158.

Holland, A. L., & Sonderman, J. C. (1974). Effects of a program based on the token test for teaching comprehension skills to aphasics. *Journal of Speech and Hearing Research, 17,* 589–598.

Hopkins, M. J., Dywan, J., & Segalowitz, S. J. (2002). Altered electrodermal response to facial expression after closed head injury. *Brain Injury, 16,* 245–257.

Hornak, J., Bramham, J., Rolls, E. T., Morris, R. G., O'Doherty, J., Bullock, P. R., et al. (2003). Changes in emotion after circumscribed surgical lesions of the orbitofrontal and cingulate cortices. *Brain, 126,* 1691–1712.

Hornak, J., Rolls, E. T., & Wade, D. (1996). Face and voice expression identification in patients with emotional and behavioral changes following ventral frontal lobe damage. *Neuropsychologia, 34*(4), 247–261.

Hughes, C. (1998). Executive function in preschoolers: Links with theory of mind and verbal ability. *British Journal of Developmental Psychology, 16,* 233–253.

Hughes, C., & Cutting, A. L. (1999). Nature, nurture, and individual differences in early understanding of mind. *Psychological Science, 10*(5), 429–432.

Humphrey, G. W., Donnelly, N., & Riddoch, M. J. (1993). Expression is computed separately from facial identity and is computed separately for moving and static faces: Neuropsychological evidence. *Neuropsychologia, 31,* 173–181.

Jackson, H. F., & Moffat, N. J. (1987). Impaired emotional recognition following severe head injury. *Cortex, 23,* 293–300.

Kampe, K. K. W., Frith, C. D., Dolan, R. J., & Frith, U. (2001). Reward value of attractiveness and gaze. *Nature, 413,* 589.

Kan, Y., Kawamura, M., Hasegawa, Y., Mochizuki, S., & Nakamura, K. (2002). Recognition of emotion from facial, prosodic and written verbal stimuli in Parkinson's disease. *Cortex, 38*(4), 623–630.

Karafin, M. S., Tranel, D., & Adolphs, R. (2004). Dominance attributions following damage to the ventromedial prefrontal cortex. *Journal of Cognitive Neuroscience, 16,* 1796–1804.

Karmiloff-Smith, A., Klima, E., Bellugi, U., Grant, J., & Baron-Cohen, S. (1995). Is there a social module? Language, face processing, and theory of mind in individuals with Williams syndrome. *Journal of Cognitive Neuroscience, 7*(2), 196–208.

Kawashima, R., Sugiura, M., Kato, T., Nakamura, A., Hatano, K., Ito, K., et al. (1999). The human amygdala plays an important role in gaze monitoring. A PET study. *Brain, 122* (Pt. 4), 779–783.

Keane, J., Calder, A. J., Hodges, J. R., & Young, A. W. (2002). Face and emotion processing in frontal variant frontotemporal dementia. *Neuropsychologia, 40*(6), 655–665.

Keenan, T. (1998). Memory span as a predictor for false belief understanding. *New Zealand Journal of Psychology, 27*, 36–43.

Keightly, M. L., Winocur, G., Graham, S. J., Matyberg, H. S., Hevenor, S. J., & Grady, C. L. (2003). An fMRI study investigating cognitive modulation of brain regions associated with emotional processing of visual stimuli. *Neuropsychologia, 41*, 585–596.

Kendall, E., Shum, D., Halson, D., Bunning, S., & Teh, M. (1997). The assessment of social problem solving ability following traumatic brain injury. *Journal of Head Trauma Rehabilitation, 12*, 68–78.

Lavenu, I., Pasquier, F., Lebert, F., Petit, H., & Van der Linden, M. (1999). Perception of emotion in patients with frontotemporal dementia and Alzheimer's disease. *Alzheimers Disease and Associated Disorder, 13*, 96–101.

LeDoux, J. (1995). Emotions: Clues from the brain. *Annual Reviews: Psychology, 46*, 209–235.

LeDoux, J., Sakaguchi, A., & Reis, D. J. (1984). Subcortical afferent projections of the medulla geniculate nucleus mediate emotional responses conditioned to emotional stimuli. *Journal of Neurosciences, 4*, 683–698.

Leekam, S. R., & Perner, J. (1991). Does the autistic child have a metarepresentational deficit? *Cognition, 40*, 203–218.

Levin, H. S., Grossman, R. G., Rose, J. E., & Teasdale, G. (1979). Long term neuropsychological outcome of closed head injury. *Journal of Neurosurgery, 50*, 412–422.

Lough, S., Gregory, C., & Hodges, J. R. (2001). Dissociation of social cognition and executive function in frontal variant frontotemporal dementia. *Neurocase, 7*(2, Pt. 2), 123–130.

Lough, S., & Hodges, J. R. (2002). Measuring and modifying abnormal social cognition in frontal variant frontotemporal dementia. *Journal of Psychosomatic Research, 53*(2), 639–646.

Luria, A. R. (1976). *Basic problems in neurolinguistics*. The Hague: Mouton.

Martin, I., & McDonald, S. (2004). Weak coherence or theory of mind: What causes non-literal language to be misunderstood by high functioning individuals with autism? *Journal of Autism and Developmental Disorders, 34*, 311–328.

Martin, I., & McDonald, S. (2005). Exploring the causes of pragmatic language deficits following traumatic brain injury. *Aphasiology, 19*, 712–730.

McAlpine, C., Singh, N. N., Kendall, K. A., & Hampton, C. (1992). Enhancing the ability of adults with mental retardation to recognise facial expressions of emotion. *Behavior Modification, 16*, 559–573.

McDonald, S. (1992). Differential pragmatic language loss following closed head injury: Ability to comprehend conversational implicature. *Applied Psycholinguistics, 13*, 295–312.

McDonald, S. (1993). Pragmatic language loss following closed head injury: Inability to meet the informational needs of the listener. *Brain and Language, 44*, 28–46.

McDonald, S. (2005). Are you laughing or crying? Deficits in emotion perception following severe traumatic brain injury. *Brain Impairment, 6*, 56–67.

McDonald, S., & Flanagan, S. (2004). Social perception deficits after traumatic brain injury: The interaction between emotion recognition, mentalising ability and social communication. *Neuropsychology, 18*, 572–579.

McDonald, S., Flanagan, S., Martin, I., & Saunders, C. (2004). The ecological validity of TASIT: A test of social perception. *Neuropsychological Rehabilitation, 14*, 285–302.

McDonald, S., Flanagan, S., & Rollins, J. (2002). The awareness of Social Inference Test, *Harcourt Assessment/Psychological Corporation/Thames Valley Test Company*.

McDonald, S., Flanagan, S., Rollins, J., & Kinch, J. (2003). TASIT: A new clinical tool for assessing social perception after traumatic brain injury. *Journal of Head Trauma Rehabilitation, 18,* 219–238.

McDonald, S., & Pearce, S. (1996). Clinical insights into pragmatic language theory: The case of sarcasm. *Brain and Language, 53,* 81–104.

McDonald, S., & Pearce, S. (1998). Requests that overcome listener reluctance: Impairment associated with executive dysfunction in brain injury. *Brain and Language, 61,* 88–104.

McDonald, S., & Saunders, C. (2005). Differential impairment in recognition of emotion from still, dynamic and multi-modal displays in people with severe TBI. *Journal of the International Neuropsychological Society, 11,* 392–399.

McDonald, S., & van Sommers, P. (1992). Differential pragmatic language loss following closed head injury: Ability to negotiate requests. *Cognitive Neuropsychology, 10,* 297–315.

McFall, R. M. (1982). A review and formulation of the concept of social skills. *Behavior Assessment, 4,* 1–33.

McHugo, G. J., & Smith, C. A. (1996). The power of faces: A review of John Lanzetta's research on facial expression and emotion. *Motivation and Emotion, 20,* 85–120.

McKenzie, K., Matheson, E., McKaskie, K., Hamilton, L., & Murray, G. C. (2000). Impact of group training on emotion recognition in individuals with a learning disability. *British Journal of Learning Disabilities, 28,* 143–147.

Milders, M., Fuchs, S., & Crawford, J. R. (2003). Neuropsychological impairments and changes in emotional and social behavior following severe traumatic brain injury. *Journal of Clinical and Experimental Neuropsychology, 25*(2), 157–172.

Milne, E., & Grafman, J. (2001). Ventromedial prefrontal cortex lesions in humans eliminate implicit gender stereotyping. *Journal of Neuroscience, 21*(12), 1–6.

Milne, J., & Spence, S. H. (1988). Training social perception skills with primary school children: A cautionary note. *Behavioral Psychotherapy, 15,* 144–157.

Milton, S. B., Prutting, C. A., & Binder, G. M. (1984). Appraisal of communication competence in head injured adults. In R. W. Brookshire (Ed.), *Clinical aphasiology* (Vol. 14, pp. 114–123). Minneapolis: BRK.

Morris, J. S., Oehman, A., & Dolan, R. J. (1998). Conscious and unconscious emotional learning in the human amygdala. *Nature, 393*(6684), 467–470.

Murray, L. L., & Holland, A. L. (1995). The language recovery of acutely aphasic patients receiving different therapy regimens. *Aphasiology, 9,* 397–405.

Neary, D. (1990). Dementia of frontal lobe type. *Journal of the American Geriatrics Society, 38*(1), 71–72.

Nudo, R. J., & Milliken, G. W. (1996). Reorganization of movement representations in primary motor cortex following focal ischemic infarcts in adult squirrel monkeys. *Journal of Neurophysiology, 75*(5), 2144–2149.

O'Doherty, J., Winston, J., Critchley, H., Perrett, D., Burt, D. M., & Dolan, R. J. (2003). Beauty in a smile: The role of medial orbitofrontal cortex in facial attractiveness. *Neuropsychologia, 41,* 147–155.

Ohman, A., Flykt, A., & Lundqvist, D. (2000). Unconscious emotion: Evolutionary perspectives, psychophysiological data and neuropsychological mechanisms. In R. Lane & L. Nadel (Eds.), *Cognitve neuroscience of emotion* (pp. 296–327). New York: Oxford University Press.

Ohman, A., & Soares, J. J. F. (1994). "Unconscious anxiety": Phobic responses to masked stimuli. *Journal of Abnormal Psychology, 103*(2), 231–240.

Ozonoff, S., & Miller, G. A. (1996). An explanation of right hemisphere contributions to the pragmatic impairments of autism. *Brain and Language, 52*, 411–434.

Ozonoff, S., & Miller, J. N. (1995). Teaching theory of mind: A new approach to social skills training for individuals with autism. *Journal of Autism and Developmental Disorders, 25*, 415–437.

Park, N. W., Conrod, B., Rewilak, D., Kwon, C., Gao, F. -q., & Black, S. E. (2001). Automatic activation of positive but not negative attitudes after traumatic brain injury. *Neuropsychologia, 39*(1), 7–24.

Pearce, S., McDonald, S., & Coltheart, M. (1998). Ability to process ambiguous advertisements after frontal lobe damage. *Brain and Cognition, 38*, 150–164.

Penn, D. L., & Combs, D. (2000). Modification of affect perception deficits in schizophrenia. *Schizophrenia Research, 46*, 217–229.

Perner, J., & Wimmer, H. (1985). "John thinks that Mary thinks that...": Attribution of second-order beliefs by 5- to 10-year-old children. *Journal of Experimental Child Psychology, 39*(3), 437–471.

Phelps, E. A., Cannistraci, C. J., & Cunningham, W. A. (2003). Intact performance on an indirect measure of face bias following amygdala damage. *Neuropsychologia, 41*, 203–208.

Phelps, E. A., O'Connor, K. J., Cunningham, W. A., Funayama, E., Gatenby, J., Gore, J. C., et al. (2000). Performance on indirect measures of race evaluation predicts amygdala activation. *Journal of Cognitive Neuroscience, 12*, 729–738.

Phillips, M. L., Drevets, W. C., Rauch, S. L., & Lane, R. (2003). Neurobiology of emotion perception I: The neural basis of normal emotion perception. *Society of Biological Psychiatry, 54*, 504–514.

Pizzamiglio, L., Perani, D., Cappa, S. F., Vallar, G., Paolucci, S., Grassi, F., et al. (1998). Recovery of neglect after right hemisphere damage: H2150 positron emission tomographic study. *Archives of Neurology, 55*, 561–568.

Prigatano, G. P., & Pribram, K. H. (1982). Perception and memory of facial affect following brain injury. *Perceptual and Motor Skills, 54*, 859–869.

Prigatano, G. P., Roueche, J. R., & Fordyce, D. J. (1986). *Neuropsychological rehabilitation after brain injury.* Baltimore: John Hopkins University Press.

Pulvermuller, F., Neininger, B., Elbert, T., Mohr, B., Rockstroh, B., Koebbel, P., et al. (2001). Constraint-induced therapy of chronic aphasia after stroke. *Stroke, 32*, 1621–1626.

Robertson, I. H., & Murre, J. M. J. (1999). Rehabilitation of brain damage: Brain plasticity and principles of guided recovery. *Psychological Bulletin, 125*(5), 544–575.

Roncone, R., Mazza, M., Frangou, I., De Risio, A., Ussorio, D., Tozzini, C., et al. (2004). Rehabilitation of theory of mind deficit in schizophrenia: A pilot study of metacognitive strategies in group treatment. *Neuropsychological Rehabilitation, 14*(4), 421–435.

Rowe, A. D., Bullock, P. R., Polkey, C. E., & Morris, R. G. (2001). "Theory of mind" impairments and their relationship to executive functioning following frontal lobe excisions. *Brain, 124*(3), 600–616.

Santoro, J., & Spiers, M. (1994). Social cognitive factors in brain injury associated with personality change. *Brain Injury, 8*(3), 265–276.

Sarfati, Y., Passerieux, C., & Hardy-Bayle, M. -C. (2000). Can verbalization remedy the theory of mind deficit in schizophrenia? *Psychopathology, 33*(5), 246–251.

Snowden, J. S., Gibbons, Z. C., Blackshaw, A., Doubleday, E., Thompson, J., Craufurd, D., et al. (2003). Social cognition in frontotemporal dementia and Huntington's disease. *Neuropsychologia, 41*(6), 688–701.

Spell, L. A., & Frank, E. (2000). Recognition of nonverbal communication of affect following traumatic brain injury. *Journal of Nonverbal Behavior, 24*(4), 285–300.

Sperber, D., & Wilson, D. (1986). *Relevance: Communication and cognition.* Oxford: Basil Blackwell.

Spiers, M. V., Pouk, J. A., & Santoro, J. M. (1994). Examining perspective-taking in the severely head injured. *Brain Injury, 8,* 463–473.

Sprengelmeyer, R., Young, A. W., Calder, A. J., Karnat, A., Lange, H., Homber, G. V., et al. (1996). Loss of disgust: Perception of faces and emotion in Huntingdon's disease. *Brain, 119,* 1647–1665.

Stewart, C., & Singe, N. (1996). Enhancing the recognition and production of facial expressions of emotion by children with mental retardation. *Research in Developmental Disabilities, 16,* 365–382.

Stone, V., Cosmides, L., Toobey, J., Kroll, N., & Knight, R. T. (2002). Selective impairment of reasoning about social exchange in a patient with bilateral limbic system damage. *Proceedings of the National Academy of Science: USA, 99,* 11531–11536.

Stone, V. E., Baron-Cohen, S., Calder, A., Keane, J., & Young, A. (2003). Acquired theory of mind impairments in individuals with bilateral amygdala lesions. *Neuropsychologia, 41*(2), 209–220.

Stone, V. E., Baron-Cohen, S., & Knight, R. T. (1998). Frontal lobe contributions to theory of mind. *Journal of Cognitive Neuroscience, 10*(5), 640–656.

Stuss, D. T., Alexander, M. P., Leiberman, A., & Levine, H. (1978). An extraordinary form of confabulation. *Neurology, 28,* 1166–1172.

Stuss, D. T., Gallup, G. G., Jr., & Alexander, M. P. (2001). The frontal lobes are necessary for "theory of mind." *Brain, 124*(2), 279–286.

Surian, L., Baron-Cohen, S., & Van der Lely, H. (1996). Are children with autism deaf to Gricean maxims? *Cognitive Neuropsychiatry, 1*(1), 55–71.

Tager-Flusberg, H., Sullivan, K., & Boshart, J. (1997). Executive functions and performance on false belief tasks. *Developmental Neuropsychology, 13,* 487–493.

Taub, E., Crago, J. E., & Uswatte, G. (1998). Constraint-induced movement therapy. A new approach to treatment in physical rehabilitation. *Rehabilitation Psychology, 43,* 152–170.

Thomsen, I. V. (1984). Late outcome of very severe blunt head trauma: A 15 year second follow-up. *Journal of Neurology, Neurosurgery and Psychiatry, 47,* 260–268.

Togher, L., McDonald, S., Code, C., & Grant, S. (2004). Training the communication partners of people with traumatic brain injury: A randomised control study. *Aphasiology, 18,* 313–355.

Tranel, D., Bechara, A., & Denburg, N. L. (2002). Asymmetric functional roles of right and left ventromedial prefrontal cortices in social conduct, decision making and emotional processing. *Cortex, 38*(4), 589–612.

Turkstra, L., McDonald, S., & DePompei, R. (2001). Social information processing in adolescents: Data from normally-developing adolescents and preliminary data from their peers with traumatic brain injury. *Journal of Head Trauma Rehabilitation, 16,* 469–483.

Turkstra, L., McDonald, S., & Kaufman, P. (1996). A test of pragmatic language function in traumatically brain-injured adolescents. *Brain Injury, 10,* 329–345.

Turkstra, L. S., Dixon, T. M., & Baker, K. K. (2004). Theory of Mind and social beliefs in adolescents with traumatic brain injury. *Neurorehabilitation, 19*(3), 245–256.

van der Gaag, M., Kern, R. S., van den Bosch, R. J., & Liberman, R. P. (2002). A controlled trial of cognitive remediation in schizophrenia. *Schizophrenia Bulletin, 28,* 167–176.

Watson, R. I. (1978). *The great psychologists.* New York: J. B. Lippincott.

Weinstein, A., Patterson, K. M., & Rao, S. (1996). Hemispheric asymmetries and processing of affective stimuli: Contribution of callosal communication. *Brain and Cognition, 32,* 223–226.

Wellman, H. M., Baron-Cohen, S., Caswell, R., Gomez, J. C., Swettenham, J., Toye, E., et al. (2002). Thought-bubbles help children with autism acquire an alternative to a theory of mind. *Autism, 6*(4), 343–363.

Whalen, P. J., Rauch, S. L., Etcoff, N. L., McInerney, S. C., Lee, M. B., & Jenike, M. A. (1998). Masked presentations of emotional facial expressions modulate amygdala activity without explicit knowledge. *Journal of Neuroscience, 18*(1), 411–418.

Wimmer, H., & Perner, J. (1983). Beliefs about beliefs: Representation and constraining function of wrong beliefs in young children's understanding of deception. *Cognition, 13*(1), 103–128.

Winston, J. S., Strange, B. A., O'Doherty, J., & Dolan, R. J. (2002). Automatic and intentional brain responses during evaluation of trustworthiness of faces [see comment]. *Nature Neuroscience, 5*(3), 277–283.

Ylvisaker, M. (2000). Reflections on dobermanns, poodles, and social rehabilitation for difficult to serve individuals with traumatic brain injury. *Aphasiology, 14*(4), 407–431.

Young, A. W., Aggleton, J. P., Hellawell, D. J., Johnson, M., Broks, P., & Hanley, J. R. (1995). Face processing impairments after amygdalotomy. *Brain, 118*(Pt. 1), 15–24.

Zelazo, P. D., Burack, J. A., Benedetto, E., & Frye, D. (1996). Theory of Mind and rule use in individuals with Down's syndrome: A test of the uniqueness and specificity claims. *Journal of Child Psychology and Psychiatry and Allied Disciplines, 37*(4), 479–484.

Author Index

Subject Index